PHILOSOPHY IN RUSSIA

by the same author

A HISTORY OF PHILOSOPHY
VOL. I: GREECE AND ROME
VOL. II: AUGUSTINE TO SCOTUS
VOL. III: OCKHAM TO SUAREZ
VOL. IV: DESCARTES TO LEIBNIZ
VOL. V: HOBBES TO HUME
VOL. VI: WOLFF TO KANT
VOL. VII: FICHTE TO NIETZSCHE
VOL. VIII: BENTHAM TO RUSSELL
VOL. IX: MAINE DE BIRAN TO SARTRE

CONTEMPORARY PHILOSOPHY
FRIEDRICH NIETZSCHE: PHILOSOPHER OF CULTURE
ARTHUR SCHOPENHAUER: PHILOSOPHER OF PESSIMISM
THOMAS AQUINAS
ON THE HISTORY OF PHILOSOPHY
PHILOSOPHERS AND PHILOSOPHIES
RELIGION AND THE ONE

PHILOSOPHY IN RUSSIA

From Herzen to Lenin
and Berdyaev

BY

FREDERICK C. COPLESTON, S.J.

Professor Emeritus of the
University of London

SEARCH PRESS

UNIVERSITY OF NOTRE DAME

Search Press Ltd
Wellwood, North Farm Road,
Tunbridge Wells, Kent, TN2 3DR, England

University of Notre Dame Press
Notre Dame, Indiana 46556, USA

First published in Great Britain and USA 1986

ISBN (UK) 0 85532 577 1

ISBN (USA) 0 268 01558 9
Library of Congress No.: 85–40601

Typeset by Phoenix Photosetting, Chatham, Kent
Printed and bound in Great Britain by Thetford Press Ltd., Thetford, Norfolk

CONTENTS

129527

Author's Preface

My original intention was to write a number of essays on selected Russian thinkers who happened to interest me, with a view to their possible publication as a book. On reflection, however, I decided to transform the material into a connected account of the development of philosophical thought in Russia. There are already several histories of Russian philosophy available in English. It could therefore be objected that any additional account by myself would be superfluous, but, justifiably or not, I came to the conclusion that this objection was not a sufficient reason for abandoning my project.

The existence of the histories by V. V. Zenkovsky and N. O. Lossky did not bother me overmuch, as the authors, while treating at length of the more religiously oriented Russian thought and of the philosophers who emigrated or were expelled from the Soviet Union, devote relatively little space to the Russian radical thinkers and to the Marxists. The two works are certainly valuable, but they leave room for another. It can also be argued that any need for a further work is admirably met by A. Walicki's impressive *History of Russian Thought from the Enlightenment to Marxism*. But I wished to dwell at greater length than Walicki does on certain aspects of Russian thought and to continue the story beyond the 1917 Revolution by discussing both philosophical thought in the Soviet Union and the Russian philosophers in exile. To be sure, there are valuable monographs in various languages on a considerable number of individual Russian thinkers, and there are specialist works on particular phases of thought in Russia. But this is the sort of situation with which any author of a general work on the development of philosophical thought is faced. For example, one could not write a history of western philosophy since the Renaissance without discussing the thought of Immanuel Kant, even though the specialized literature on Kant is enormous. Unless one is prepared to reject the composition of general histories of philosophy, one simply has to accept this situation.

What, however, is one to count as philosophical thought? If one were to find place only for those lines of thought which would be regarded as properly philosophical according to the criteria commonly accepted in English and American university departments of philosophy, one's material would be very restricted. Moreover, it would be of interest only to a very limited number of specialist students. The plain fact of the matter is that, for historical reasons, philosophical ideas in Russia have tended to be given a social-political orientation or subordinated to the realization of some social ideal. If one intends to write a general account of the development of philosophical thought in Russia, one is well advised, in my opinion, to take a broad view of the relevant field and not to worry much about distinctions between the history of philosophy, the history of ideas, the history of social theory and religious thought. But as further reference is made to this theme in the first chapter of the book, there is no need to pursue the matter here.

When I had completed a draft of this volume, I thought that it would be desirable to shorten the work by cutting out much of what I had written about the general history of Russia. But a friend remarked that some readers would probably know very little about Russian history. The reply could be made, of course, that if anyone wants to learn about Russian history, he or she can turn to one of the available books on the subject. At the same time, the social-political orientation of so much of Russian thought constitutes a sound reason for providing an historical context. Some knowledge of this context is required in order to understand why the theories arose and took the forms which they did take. I therefore decided to abandon the idea of making substantial excisions in the extra-philosophical historical material, although the fact that the material would be inevitably sketchy still causes me some misgiving.

In view of the length of the volume I decided that the bibliography would have to be confined to books mentioned in the text and notes, with the addition of some works, available in English, which I have at some time read or consulted. With the exception of some titles mentioned in the text or notes no attempt has been made to give a bibliography of works in a language other than English. Omission of titles of works written in or translated into English should not be understood as implying any negative value-judgment, though an omission may, of course, indicate ignorance on my part. As for works in Russian, a lot of research into the development of social thought in Russia and into the ideas of individual thinkers and the relations between them has been done by Soviet historians. If no attempt has been made to list the relevant books in the bibliography included in this volume, no disrespect to Soviet scholarship is intended. Without increasing the size of an already large volume it was not possible to attempt to provide anything approaching a full bibliography.

The author has concentrated on telling a story. His own attitudes and beliefs doubtless find expression in a variety of ways, but relatively extensive treatment of a particular theme or movement of thought does not necessarily indicate the author's personal convictions. It is probably unnecessary to say that if several chapters are devoted to Marxism in

Russia, this expresses a judgment about the importance of the subject in the context of Russian history and should not be taken as indicating that the author is a Marxist, nor even that he believes that Lenin, for example, was an outstanding philosopher. It may, however, be as well to note that the lengthy treatment of the thought of Russian philosophers in exile does not express any desire on the author's part that this thought (heterogeneous in any case) should be imported into the Soviet Union and substituted for the reigning ideology. The author's hope is certainly that freedom in the expression of philosophical thought will come to be fully realized in the Soviet Union. But this is not at all the same thing as the substitution of one official ideology for another. More is said on this theme in the Epilogue.

Finally, the author wishes to express his thanks to the following publishers for permission to quote:

To the Oxford University Press for permission to make brief quotations from *Sons against Fathers* by E. Lampert (1965), *A History of Russia* by Nicholas V. Riasanovsky (3rd ed. 1977), *The Slavophile Controversy* by A. Walicki (1975) and *A History of Russian Thought from the Enlightenment to Marxism* by A. Walicki (1980).

To the Cambridge University Press for permission to quote from *Vladimir Akimov on the Dilemmas of Russian Marxism, 1895–1903*, edited by J. Frankel (1969).

To Messrs George Allen and Unwin for permission to make short quotations from *Historical Materialism: A System of Sociology* by N. Bukharin (translated from the third Russian edition, 1926) and from N. Bukharin's contribution to *Marxism and Modern Thought*, translated by R. Fox (1935).

To Messrs Sheed and Ward for permission to make brief quotations from Donald Attwater's English translations of Nicolas Berdyaev's *Dostoevsky: An Interpretation* (1934), *The End of Our Time* (1933) and *Christianity and Class War* (1933).

To Messrs Lawrence and Wishart for permission to quote from their English edition of *Selected Philosophical Works* by G. V. Plekhanov (1974–81); from the English translation of *V. I. Lenin's Materialism and Empirio-Criticism*; and from *Communism and Philosophy: Contemporary Dogmas and Revisions of Marxism* by Maurice Cornforth (1980).

In the case of some Russian writers, V. Solovyev for example, I have translated directly from the Russian text, adding references, for the convenience of readers, to available English translations, even when my own translation is slightly different.

In cases in which requests to publishers for permission to quote have met with no response, either positive or negative, I have assumed either that the request was judged superfluous (in view of the brevity of the quotation) or that copyright may have lapsed.

PHILOSOPHY IN RUSSIA

Chapter 1

Introduction

1. Any reader who studies the development of philosophical thought in Russia can hardly fail to notice two prominent general features. One is the very considerable extent to which philosophy in Russia was derivative, dependent, that is to say, on Western influences. The other is the way in which the derived philosophical ideas were given a social and political application, relating primarily to conditions in Russia itself, though often placed within a much wider perspective. In other words, the reader can hardly fail to notice the socially committed nature of much of Russian thought.

Both these features are explicable in terms of Russian history; and they will be exemplified in the course of this volume through particular movements, lines of thought and thinkers.

As for the derivative character of so much of Russian philosophical thought from the eighteenth century onwards, attention is customarily drawn to the fact that Russia lay outside the Roman empire and did not receive from the ancient world the legacy which was transmitted to western Europe. Russia received Christianity not from Rome but from Byzantium, and after the schism between the western and eastern Churches, which occurred in 1059, she was relatively isolated from western Christendom and cut off from the cultural influence of the Catholic Church. Taken simply by itself, however, this fact is not sufficient to explain Russia's later dependence on the West for the reception of philosophical ideas. The isolation of Kievan Russia (the first Russian state, formed at about the end of the ninth century) can be exaggerated; and if her development had proceeded smoothly, Russia might conceivably have given birth to her own philosophical tradition. While, however, western Europe was constructing the civilization of the Middle Ages with its educational and intellectual life, Russia was subjected to the Mongol, or Tartar, yoke and was in no position to develop the culture of early days. It is true that when the Mongols had once succeeded in establishing their overlordship, they hardly interfered at all with the cultural life of the Russian principalities and cities. But what with internal squabbles, incursions from the West and the need to meet Mongol demands for tribute, Russia's cultural life declined rather than developed. When she finally succeeded, under the leadership of Moscow, in throwing off the Mongol yoke and became a unified, independent and expanding state, she was far behind western Europe in the level of intellectual life.

Russia experienced nothing comparable either to the intense study and appropriation of ancient philosophy which was characteristic of the medieval universities in western Christendom, nor did she share in the subsequent ferment of the Renaissance. The vast bulk of the population consisted of illiterate peasants; Russia had no universities; and there was no philosophical thought apart from a meagre measure in ecclesiastical institutions. It was therefore only natural that, as the opening to the West developed, the opening to which Peter the Great (1672–1725) gave such a powerful impetus, it should come to include the reception of western philosophical ideas. Russia could not repeat in herself the history of western Europe, but she could learn from the West.

According to Peter Chaadaev, whose thought is discussed in the second chapter of this book, the Russia which Peter the Great set out to modernize was 'a blank sheet of paper', without any values or traditions of her own. This point of view was regarded as a gross exaggeration by the Slavophile thinkers in the first decades of the nineteenth century. They were convinced that Russia possessed a cultural tradition of her own, on which she could build, and they demanded the development of a philosophy in harmony with this tradition, especially with Orthodox faith, a philosophy which would be free of western 'rationalism'.[1] Russia's greatest religious philosopher, Vladimir Solovyev (1853–1900), can be seen as having made a large-scale attempt to meet this need, though his philosophy was certainly not uninfluenced by western thought. Although, however, he had his spiritual successors in the twentieth century, it was a philosophy of Western origin, namely Marxism, which was to become Russia's officially sponsored ideology after the revolution.

In regard to the orientation of philosophical ideas to the realization of social-political goals, it is true that pure philosophy, so to speak, philosophy, that is to say, considered as a purely theoretical discipline, has never flourished in Russia. Marxists, of course, lay emphasis on the unity

1 We shall have occasion later to examine what the religiously oriented thinkers understood by 'rationalism.'

of theory and practice, in accordance with Marx's famous assertion that, whereas philosophers had hitherto tried only to understand the world, the point was to change the world. But long before Marxism came to the fore in Russia there were socially committed thinkers, who were quick to apply philosophical ideas derived from the West to 'the problem of Russia' and to demand social and political reforms. If there was a clear tendency to move from philosophical discussion to revolutionary activism, this was largely because, under the autocracy, reform had to be effected from above, whereas the regime either resisted change, or when it did initiate reform, did so too late or in an insufficient way. There were, of course, some academic philosophers in Russia, at any rate from the closing decades of the nineteenth century, who tried to avoid political involvement, Neo-Kantians for example, but the radicals commonly regarded them as people who evaded the important issues of their time.

To recognize the fact of the prevalence of socially committed thought is not, however, the same thing as accounting for the fact. Some people have tended to claim that it was a strong sense of Russia's inferiority, of her social and political backwardness in comparison with the more advanced countries of western Europe, which was the root cause of the fact that so many of the leading Russian thinkers were socially committed thinkers, who either tended to abandon philosophy for social activism or to combine the two. But though a sense of Russia's backwardness was certainly an influential factor, it is possible to exaggerate the idea of catching up with the West. Russian radical thinkers such as Alexander Herzen (1812–70) were inspired by a genuine moral idealism, a desire for human emancipation, which led them to demand social reforms and to propose social-political goals. Sometimes, of course, they compared Russia with western countries to the disadvantage of the former. This was notably the case with demands for the abolition of serfdom. But the same moral idealism which expressed itself in denunciations of the glaring evils of Russian society could and did express itself too in criticism of western society and in the demand that Russia should follow a path of her own. In other words, the radical thinkers were not animated simply by a blind admiration of western Europe and a desire to catch up with it. The Populists, for example, had no wish to catch up with the development of capitalist society in the more highly industrialized countries of the West. On the contrary. It is true that the so-called 'Westernizers' of the first half of the nineteenth century began by maintaining that Russia's salvation could be found only in carrying on, intensifying and completing Peter the Great's opening to the West, but it was not long before they were sitting in judgment on western society as well as Russian. It must be remembered that Russia claimed to be a Christian society. The radicals generally abandoned religion and were hostile to the Church as a servant of the régime, but it is reasonable to see in their moral idealism a secularized form of the Christian ideals which they accused the Russian Orthodox Church of neglecting. In this connection it is worth noting that when religiously oriented philosophy revived with Solovyev and his successors, the religious thinkers too tended to be socially committed and to be deeply concerned with 'the problems of Russia,' though the sort of society which they desired was naturally different from that desired by atheistic revolutionaries.

There are, of course, other factors which are relevant to explaining why philosophical thought in Russia tended to fuse with social and political commitment. One such factor is the heavy hand laid by the régime on freedom of expression. To take an extreme example, Nicholas I (Tsar, 1825–55) closed the departments of philosophy in universities. The retort can obviously be made that it was the philosophers who aroused the suspicion and hostility of the authorities in the first instance. True enough, but one did not need to be a revolutionary in order to incur disapproval, and the attitude of the régime naturally contributed to the radicalization of thought.

However this may be, the question can be raised whether the socio-political orientation of so much of philosophical thought in Russia should not be regarded as depriving it of its philosophical character and transforming it into ideological thinking.[1] There is no need to deny the historical importance of socially committed thought in Russia. But one can perfectly well recognize its historical importance without classifying it as philosophy. If anyone wishes to write about the development of philosophical thought in Russia, should he not disentangle thought which is properly philosophical from thought which is best considered under the heading of the history of ideas or of social theory, focusing his attention simply on the former?

Some attempts have in fact been made to recount the history of philosophical thought in Russia in terms of what can be described as academic philosophy. But, as Andrzej Walicki notes, this is a thankless task, resulting in an impoverished picture of Russian thought and giving

---

1 The word 'ideology' is here understood as a system of ideas oriented to the realization of a social or political goal through concerted human action, the action of a group. In other words, the term is understood in a neutral sense. If desire to attain a certain goal through action leads to neglect of objective truth, to asserting the truth of statements solely because this seems useful from a pragmatic point of view, ideological thinking is clearly undesirable. But, in itself, ideological thinking, as I understand it, is a legitimate human activity.

the impression that Russian thinkers were lacking in any originality.[1] Whatever view an author holds of what philosophy ought to be, it seems far the best policy, if he is treating of Russian thought, not to impose on it a restricted concept of the nature of philosophy but to operate with a broad idea, one which allows for 'practical philosophy'. Pure philosophy, in the sense of exclusively theoretical inquiry, never flourished in Russia; and to confine one's attention to the academic philosophers who can be found from the closing decades of the nineteenth century would be to give a most inadequate picture of philosophical thought in Russia. As for the policy of disentangling, of excluding, for example, from an account of Herzen's thought all that some would assign to social theory rather to philosophy, this would result in a caricature of his thought. Indeed, it would give rise to the question whether Herzen was worth mentioning. Obviously, common sense has to be exercised in the selection of material. But one's criteria for selection should be broad enough to enable a writer to convey the spirit of thinkers such as Herzen and Lavrov, to illustrate their primary interests.

Reference has been made to 'the problem of Russia'. From Chaadaev onwards serious thinkers in Russia were naturally preoccupied with the problem of the destiny of their country. Peter the Great's opening to the West gave rise to the question whether Russia's future development should take the form of increasing assimilation to western Europe or whether she should follow a path of her own, appropriating the elements of western civilization which harmonized with this policy. But it was not simply a case of dispute between Westernizers and Slavophiles. There was the feeling that Russia had a mission to mankind, that she was called on to lead the nations, to show where progress lay. This Messianic sense of Russia's destiny manifests itself in, for example, the writings of Dostoevsky. But it could also manifest itself in writers of a very different kind. We can see it expressed, for instance, in the concept of 'Russian socialism', a socialist society to be achieved without the country having to pass through the horrors of capitalist exploitation. For the matter of that, the sense of Russia's mission to mankind has survived the 1917 revolution and has tended to prevail over Marxian universalism.

The problem of Russia, taken by itself, may seem to have little to do with philosophy. But among the philosophically inclined thinkers the

---

1 *A History of Russian Thought from the Enlightenment to Marxism*, by Andrzej Walicki, p. XIV (Oxford and Stanford, 1979). Walicki is referring, for example, to G. Shpet's *Outline of the Development of Philosophy in Russia* (Petrograd, 1922). Gustav Shpet (1879–1937) was a phenomenologist who argued in favour of Husserl's idea of philosophy as a vigorous science, and who was hostile to both religion and metaphysics. He perished in one of Stalin's labour camps.

tendency was to see the problem within the context of a general philosophy of history. In the Foreword to his book *The Meaning of History* Nikolai Berdyaev (1874–1948) asserts that Russian thought in the nineteenth century was mainly preoccupied with problems in the philosophy of history 'which, indeed, laid the foundations of our national consciousness'.[1] In Berdyaev's opinion the special task of Russian philosophical thought was that of developing a religious philosophy of history, as with Solovyev. Obviously, non-religious Russian thinkers would not agree with this judgment. Philosophy of history loomed large in the thought of Populist thinkers such as Lavrov, who were not religious believers. However, Berdyaev is doubtless justified in claiming that when philosophical thought had come to birth in Russia, 'its central theme was man, the fate of man in society and in history'.[2] This may not apply to the academic philosophers who were more interested in, for example, epistemological themes, but it certainly applies to the better known representatives of Russian thought, whether religious believers or not. As one writer has said, 'the most widely debated of all the "cursed questions" during Nicholas' reign was the meaning of history'.[3]

2. Russia of the Kievan period[4] enjoyed an economic (trading and agricultural) life even before the conversion of Vladimir I in about AD 988 and the adoption of Christianity as the official religion.[5] But acceptance of Christianity brought with it a stronger cultural influence from Byzantium, the centre of eastern Christendom. This culture was mainly of an ecclesiastical nature. Architecture and art developed under the inspiration of Orthodoxy, and Russia's first legal code, the *Russian Justice*, has traditionally been ascribed to Yaroslav the Wise, grand prince of Kiev from 1019 until 1054. Yaroslav was an active patron of cultural life and seems to have gathered together scholars and translators to form a

1 *The Meaning of History*, translated by George Reavey, p. vii (London, 1936). This work represents lectures given by Berdyaev at Moscow in 1919–20, before his expulsion from the Soviet Union in 1922.

2 *The Russian Idea*, translated by R. M. French, p. 86 (London, 1947).

3 *The Icon and the Axe. An Interpretive History of Russian Culture*, by James H. Billington, p. 314 (New York, 1966). The Nicholas in question is Nicholas I.

4 Kievan Russia was not, of course, coterminous with the Russia of Peter the Great and his successors. But it extended from Pereiaslav and Kiev in the South to Novgorod and the borders of Finland in the north and included centres such as Chernigov, Smolensk, Riazan, Vladimir, Suzdal, Polotsk and Pskov. In other words, it was by no means confined to the immediate neighbourhood of Kiev.

5 Christianity was not unknown before the time of Vladimir I. His grandmother, Olga, became a Christian. But it was Vladimir who substituted the Christian religion for the previous religion of Kievan Russia. From that time the Church in Russia had its own Metropolitan and an increasing number of dioceses, even if, with some exceptions, the bishops tended to come from Byzantium.

library, the relevant literature consisting of chronicles, sacred texts, sermons and lives of saints. The literary language of ancient Russia was Church Slavonic, which at the time was fairly close to East Slavonic or Slavic or Old Russian and could be understood by the people.[1] The writings translated from Greek into Church Slavonic were mainly of a religious nature and did not include the secular philosophical literature of the ancient world. It is true that translations of writings by the Greek Fathers of the Church, such as St John Damascene, introduced the more learned monks to some philosophical ideas,[2] but learning was predominantly ecclesiastical, within the framework of the Orthodox world-view. In addition to the written literature there were the orally preserved indigenous Kievan epics and songs.

Situated on important trade-routes, Kievan Russia was by no means an isolated country. In the first section of this chapter it was suggested that if early Russia or Rus had enjoyed a peaceful development, she might have given birth to a philosophical tradition of her own. At the same time it is obvious that sooner or later she would have received intellectual stimulus from the West, in spite of the religious difference. In actual fact, however, the natural development of early Russia was arrested in the thirteenth century. The decline of Kievan Russia is generally regarded as having begun after the death of Yaroslav the Wise in 1054. There is no complete agreement about the reasons for this decline, or at any rate about their respective importance; but it is clear that the Kievan state had difficulties in maintaining its trade relations in view of aggression by neighbouring peoples, and that the loose system of government, leading to the multiplication of principalities which tended to squabble among themselves, weakened the cohesion of the country. As different territories of Kievan Russia came increasingly under the immediate control of different members of the dynastic family, the country became more and more an aggregate of principalities, with the Prince of Kiev as its nominal overlord. Moreover, the centre of the state tended to shift from Kiev to the north-east, to Suzdal-Vladimir, and certain cities, in particular Novgorod, became, to all intents and purposes, autonomous. The country was thus not in a favourable position for offering effective resistance either to incursions from the west and north-west — from Poles, Lithuanians and Teutonic Knights — or to the

1 Spoken Russian, namely East Slavonic or Old Russian, came to be used for legal and administrative purposes and for private correspondence, when, that is to say, it had been made a written language by use of the Cyrillic alphabet. But Church Slavonic remained as the principal literary language for a considerable time. Now it is confined to the Liturgy.
2 The more or less philosophical introduction to St John Damascene's main theological treatise was not translated in its entirety until the fifteenth century.

Mongol, or Tartar, invasion from the east. The sack of Kiev by the Mongols occurred in 1240, and Mongol domination over Russia lasted until 1480, when Ivan III renounced allegiance to the Khan, but from 1380, the date of the battle of Kulikovo, Mongol control had become increasingly weaker.

In their movement westwards the Mongols sacked cities and monasteries, massacring citizens, as at Ryazan and Kiev, and enslaving survivors. But once they had established their overlordship their main interest was in receiving regular tribute from the princes and dukes and cities of Russian territories. They did not interfere with the Orthodox Church, not at any rate as far as religion was concerned, and, for the most part, they left internal affairs in the hands of the relevant Russian authorities. Indeed, Russian principalities were able to war with one another (or with invaders from the west), one side or the other, or both, sometimes invoking the assistance of the Khan. Apart, therefore, from the exaction of tribute, which had to be collected by the Russian authorities under Mongol supervision, the ordinary life of the population was not affected directly by the Mongol domination, provided, of course, that no attempt was made to throw off the yoke. There were even some trade relations with foreign merchants. At the same time conditions were not such that cultural life could flourish, and the Mongols had really nothing to offer in this respect. They certainly showed military genius, but they were not like the Arabs who developed a flourishing culture in, for example, southern Spain. The long period of Mongol domination was for Russia a period of cultural stagnation and, in some respects, decline. Historians have given different assessments of the effects on Russia of the country's subjection to Mongol overlordship. Some have seen the Mongols as cutting off Russia both from the West and from Byzantium and as giving the country a semi-Asiatic character, the Russian autocracy being a legacy of the rule of the khanate of the Golden Horde. Others have minimized the effects of Mongol overlordship on the grounds, for example, that the Mongols never really occupied Russia in a stable manner. Russian princes had to get their titles to rule ratified by the Khan and periodically went or were summoned to Sarai, whence they might or might not return. But the Mongols did not live on the spot and mix with Russians, and they increasingly left the exaction of taxes or tribute to Russians. In other words, the Mongols exercised remote control, and it is an exaggeration to depict them as having 'asiatized' the country.

During this period the Russian Orthodox Church played an important role in holding together the inhabitants of the Russian lands, maintaining the sense of nationhood and sustaining the people's spirit and morale.

Indeed, until the rise of Moscow to a position of pre-eminence in the political sphere the Church was the one unifying factor. The Mongol overlords had not interfered with religion, they had also exempted the Church from taxation, and during the period of their domination the Church amassed land and wealth. Whether this benefited the Church from a religious or spiritual point of view is another matter.

It hardly needs saying that no effective opposition to Mongol domination was possible as long as Russia was internally divided into more or less independent and often mutually hostile principalities and cities, which the khans of the Golden Horde could play off one against another. There was need for some central authority or leadership, capable of rallying the Russian people and of organizing armies. This need came to be met by the rise of Moscow from the position which it occupied in the twelfth century, namely that of an unimportant town on the borders of the territory of Vladimir-Suzdal, to being the centre of a progressively more unified Russian state. It may seem odd that the Mongols permitted this development, but there were several contributing factors. One was the cooperative and submissive attitude shown by Moscow to the Mongol overlords, an attitude which enabled it to increase its territory at the expense of other Russian principalities. Thus Ivan Kalita ('John the Moneybag'), who reigned as Grand Prince of Moscow from about 1328 until 1341, managed, while maintaining good relations with the Khan, to extend his domains to some extent. Further, it was during his reign that the Orthodox metropolitan settled in Moscow, thus making the city the religious capital of the country. Another factor which probably contributed to Mongol tolerance of the rise of Moscow was that the Khans came eventually to look on a strengthened Moscow as serving as a useful bulwark against expansionist tendencies on the part of Lithuania.[1]

The possibility of action against the Mongol overlords was obviously increased by the emergence of dissension and division within the ranks of the Mongols themselves. In 1380 Dmitry Donskoy, Grand Prince of Moscow, won a resounding victory over the Mongols at Kulikovo. It is true that the Mongols staged a comeback, sacked Moscow, carried off a large number of Russians as slaves, and reasserted their overlordship. But their power was on the decline. By the end of the reign of Ivan III (1462–1505) the republic of Novgorod and principalities such as those of Tver and Rostov had been subjected to the suzerainty of Moscow, and Ivan III added to his title of Grand Prince of Moscow the phrase 'and of

---

1 See, for example, *The Emergence of Moscow, 1304–1359*, by J. L. I. Fennell (Berkeley and Los Angeles, 1968).

all Russia'. In 1480 a Mongol attempt to restore rule over the rebellious Russians failed, and some historians regard this year as the date of Russia's final liberation from Mongol overlordship.

Consolidation of the Russian lands into a unified political entity centred around Moscow as the capital can be seen as symbolized by the coronation of Ivan IV in January 1547 with the title of Tsar. Russian seizure of Kazan in 1552 and of Astrakhan in 1556, which brought the course of the Volga under Russian control, were cases of extending Russian territory, not of liberating existing Russian cities from foreign domination. It is true that when Ivan IV involved Russia in the Livonian war, he left the country open to attack by the Crimean Tartars, who took and burned Moscow, apart from the Kremlin, in 1571. When, however, the Tartars attempted a fresh invasion in the following year, they were decisively defeated by the Russians.

Moscow had taken the place once occupied by Kiev as centre of Russian unity. But there were notable differences between Kievan and Muscovite Russia. For example, the princes of Kiev had enjoyed only a loose authority over the other principalities of Kievan Russia, and within their own domain they ruled with the council of nobles (boyars), while the citizens were free to express their desires in a popular assembly, the *Veche*. As for Novgorod, the city pretty well ruled itself. If the citizens were dissatisfied with their prince, whose powers were very limited, they were prepared to show him the door. In Muscovite Russia, however, there was a growing process of centralization. Ivan IV, first Tsar of Russia (1547–84) and better known as Ivan the Terrible[1], conducted what amounted to a campaign against the boyars, the old nobility, substituting for them new landowners whose position depended on their services to the monarch, the so-called service gentry or nobility. In the first part of his reign Ivan IV followed the practice of his predecessors, such as Ivan III, of asking the advice of the Boyar Council or Duma, but he later came to treat the hereditary nobility as his personal enemies, suspecting them of trying to limit his authority. In point of fact, the great hereditary landowners did constitute, in fact though not by law, a check on the development of autocracy. The Tsar therefore created a new class of gentry, holding land from the sovereign and entirely dependent on him. Early in his reign Ivan IV enacted a series of reforms, which were approved by an Assembly of the Land (*zemskii sobor*). But in 1565 he

---

1 The epithet *Groznyi* appears to have been first applied to Ivan IV in a spirit of admiration, and some writers insist that it should be translated as 'severe' or 'formidable'. However this may be, 'Ivan the Terrible' has doubtless come to stay. As customarily understood, it obviously refers to Ivan's behaviour in the second part of his reign.

divided the country into two parts, the so-called *Oprichnina*, treated by the Tsar as his own personal property and administered by his servants, the dreaded *Oprichniki*, and the *Zemschina*, with a baptized Tartar as its nominal ruler and administered in the old way. Most of the boyars of the *Zemschina*, however, came to a sticky end at the hands of the Tsar and his henchmen, and after some years Ivan abolished the division and ruled the whole country as an autocrat, not to say tyrant. A German visitor to Muscovy noted, in words which have often been quoted, that 'all in the land call themselves the prince's *kholopi* or slaves. The grand-duke exercises his favour over both clergy and laymen, both property and life. He holds one and all in the same subjection'.[1]

The process of centralization was accompanied by the rise and strengthening of serfdom. That is to say, the freedom of peasants to choose their location, to move from one part of the country to another, was progressively diminished. Peasants unable to repay loans from or debts to landowners became serfs, but even in the Muscovite period peasants who were not in debt to landlords were free to change their abode, and some peasants became wealthy. It is understandable, however, that landowners did not wish to lose their peasants, and the times at which peasants were free to move were gradually whittled down to St George's Day in the autumn. Ivan the Terrible suspended this freedom, in the interest of the small landowners, the new class which he had created. He thus contributed to the consolidation of serfdom, though it was under later monarchs that the process was completed.

The significance of Ivan the Terrible in Russian history has been, and is, a subject of controversy. Generally speaking, Soviet historians have seen his reign as 'historically progressive'. Under Stalin, a great admirer of the Tsar, this point of view was obligatory. But even apart from Stalin, Soviet historians have tended to see the centralization of power, the subjection of economic life to the control of the state, the campaign against the 'reactionary' boyars, the establishment of the service gentry dependent on the Tsar, and even, sometimes, the consolidation of serfdom (the tying of peasants to the land) as expressions of progress. Emigrés, such as Prince Kurbsky, were regarded as traitors.[2] This assessment of Ivan the Terrible may seem surprising in Marxist writers, but

---

1 *Description of Moscow and Muscovy, 1577*, by Sigmund von Herberstein, edited by B. Picard and translated by J. B. C Grundy, pp. 43–4 (London, 1969).
2 In 1564 the boyar and general Prince Andrey Mikhailovich Kurbsky left the service of the Tsar and took refuge in Lithuanian territory, whence he exchanged letters with Ivan IV. See *The Correspondence between Prince A. M. Kurbsky and Tsar Ivan IV of Russia, 1564–1579*, edited by J. L. I. Fennell (Cambridge, 1955, reprint 1963). The

there is a strong current of nationalist thought in the Soviet Union. In spite of all his cruelty Ivan IV has been seen as contributing powerfully to the transformation of Russia into a unified, centralized and authoritarian state, which combatted not only the Tartars but also its western neighbours and pursued its own path. Other historians, however, have represented Ivan IV as arresting the process of Russia's re-Europeanization after the period of Mongol domination,[1] as doing away with all *de facto* limitations on autocracy and treating Russia as the Tsar's personal patrimony. They have emphasized the fact that it was not only the boyars but also the peasants and the proto-bourgeoisie who suffered at his hands, and that people's lives depended not simply on what they had done or actually tried to do, as in a law-ordered state, but also on the sovereign's suspicions and his arbitrary will. This refers, of course, to those historians who regard these phenomena with disapproval, not simply on moral grounds but also on the basis of what they think would have been beneficial to Russia.

In view of the emphasis customarily laid on Peter the Great's opening to the West it should be mentioned that Muscovite Russia was by no means completely isolated from Western influences. For example, Ivan III invited Italian architects to Moscow to construct churches and palaces, and though Ivan the Terrible took a dim view of most other countries (he admired the authoritarianism of the Turkish Sultan), he granted trading privileges to English merchants. Again, Boris Godunov (Tsar, 1598–1605) sent some eighteen young Russians to the West in the hope (a vain one, as it turned out) that they would return and open schools in Russia.

Cultural development, however, was hindered by the outbreak of what is called the 'Time of Troubles'. Some historians date this period as beginning in 1598, the year of Boris Godunov's accession, inasmuch as the early years of his reign were marked by disastrous drought and famine and the consequent appearance of large bands of desperate and impoverished men who took to looting and pillage. In any case, in 1604 the first Pseudo-Dmitry, claiming to be Ivan IV's youngest son (who had died or was murdered in 1591) took up arms, with Polish backing, against the Tsar. In 1605 the pretender entered Moscow, soon after Boris

---

authenticity of the correspondence was challenged by Edward L. Kennan, Jr. in *The Kurbskii-Groznyi Apocrypha* (Cambridge, Mass., 1971), but his thesis has not been widely accepted. Kurbsky regarded himself as a refugee from tyranny, whereas Ivan IV (followed by most Soviet historians) looked on him as a traitor.

1 For a forthright and polemical statement of this point of view see *The Origins of Autocracy. Ivan the Terrible in Russian History*, by Alexander Yanov, translated by Stephen Dunn (Berkeley, Los Angeles and London, 1981).

Godunov's death, only to be overthrown and killed in 1606. The throne was then occupied by the boyar Prince Basil Shuisky, who promised not to put anyone to death without the consent of the Boyar Council and not to punish (as Ivan the Terrible had done and Stalin was to do) innocent relatives of condemned persons. The new Tsar, however, had to face fresh disorders, revolts, and a succession of pretenders, and though he called in the Swedes to aid him, he lost his throne in 1610. Government, such as it was, was exercised by a council of boyars until 1613, when Michael Romanov was elected Tsar by an Assembly of the Land. The new sovereign, then a boy of sixteen, expressed the wish that the Assembly would remain in session and assist him in governing the country, and it seems that for a number of years the assembly did in fact continue to meet.

Though the Time of Troubles ended in 1613 with the establishment of the Romanov dynasty, the reigns of Michael Romanov (1613–45) and his son Alexis (1645–76) were by no means free from disturbances. Thus in 1670–1 there occurred the serious peasant uprising led by the cossack Stenka Razin. However, centralized monarchical government had been restored. In 1649 a new legal code, the *Ulozhenie*, was introduced. Though it was doubtless an improvement, it contained clauses which further consolidated serfdom. All peasants working on private estates, together with their dependants, were reduced to the status of serfs. In 1652 Nikon was appointed Patriarch of the Russian Orthodox Church and proceeded to push through reforms which led to a split in the Church, with the Old Believers sticking to the old ways with great determination, even at the cost of their lives. Nikon was an able and energetic man, but he was also given to grandiose ideas, asserting the superiority of the Church to the State. In the end even the pious Tsar Alexis could not stand any more, and in 1667 the Patriarch was deposed by a church council and sent to a monastery. In 1654 the Ukranians swore allegiance to the Tsar, and Russia's expansion in Siberia was proceeding apace.[1]

Rather surprisingly perhaps, given his known Orthodox piety, the Tsar Alexis was interested in Western culture, including the theatre. Further, during his reign the number of foreign merchants and manufacturers operating in Russia increased considerably. Though, however, it is a mistake to think that before Peter the Great Russia had no contacts with Western Europe, the phrase 'the opening to the West' is rightly associated with his name.

1 Russian expansion into Siberia had begun during the reign of Ivan IV.

The successor of Alexis, Theodore III, died in 1682, leaving no heir. Peter, son of Alexis's second wife, was proclaimed joint-monarch with Ivan V, a son of Alexis's first wife. At the time Peter was a boy of ten. His effective rule dates from 1694.[1] A man of dynamic energy, determined to break through the lethargy and somnolence of his country and to enable it to compete with other and more advanced nations, he turned out to be a revolutionary on the throne.

The revolution in question did not, of course, come from below. It was imposed from above, not as the result of any popular movement. Peter could be, and often was, not only remarkably coarse but also extremely cruel, but he had an iron will, was not deterred by opposition and was certainly devoted to what he believed to be the interests of Russia. Obviously, he could not, single-handed, achieve all that he would like to do. But by the time of his death in 1725 he had created a centralized secular state, with a bureaucracy responsible to himself and with the Church subordinated to state control, the patriarchate being abolished.[2] Muscovy had yielded place to the empire.

Though Peter the Great was primarily impressed by Western technological achievements, of which he wished to make use in turning Russia into a great military and naval power, and though he devoted a large amount of time and energy to military exploits, he was by no means indifferent to his country's backwardness in the sphere of education. Not only did he send a good many young Russians to study abroad but he also founded a number of educational institutions, such as a school of mathematical and navigational sciences at Moscow and the Naval Academy at his new capital, St Petersburg. He also provided for the opening of schools in provincial cities and founded medical schools at Moscow and St Petersburg. In addition, he founded a library and a museum of natural history in his capital, and he was responsible for planning the Academy of Sciences which was opened by his wife, Catherine I, shortly after her husband's death. The Tsar also saw to the reform of the Russian alphabet and made provision for the publication of books, besides editing the first issue of a Russian newspaper. In view of his other multifarious occupations all this constituted an astonishing achievement.

1 Peter the Great reigned jointly with his half-brother, Ivan V, until the latter's death in 1696. The Regent Sophia was overthrown in 1689, and Peter's mother died in 1694. As Ivan was interested only in religious matters, Peter was then to all intents and purposes the sole Tsar.

2 In 1721 Peter the Great replaced the patriarchate by the Holy Synod, with a layman as its director. Though comprised mainly of clerics, the Holy Synod was in effect a state department. Subordination of the church to the state meant, of course, that when, in later years, opposition to the autocracy became a characteristic of the Russian intelligentsia, it was accompanied by hostility to the Church as the ally and instrument of the régime.

It is hardly necessary to say that Peter the Great's opening to the West did not affect the vast bulk of the population, except to the extent in which the peasants were caught up in his military machine, in working (and often dying) in the construction of his new capital in the northern marshes, or in his taxation arrangements. It was obviously the gentry and bureaucrats who were most affected by the impetus given by the Tsar to the process of westernization, as far as ways of living and thinking were concerned.

Peter the Great was certainly not a philosopher. He was primarily interested in promising young Russians acquiring scientific and technological knowledge and in the formation of properly educated bureaucrats for his civil service. But his opening to the West obviously meant that Western philosophical, social and political ideas would eventually come to influence the minds of the educated layer of society. What else could one expect if young Russians were sent to study abroad, and when foreign books were making their appearance in Russia? The Tsar thus paved the way for the entry of philosophical ideas into Russia, an entry which is associated with the reign of Catherine II. But first, the developments in theological and philosophical studies in the Russian ecclesiastical world should be considered.

3. In the seventeenth century the Orthodox theologians of Kiev, eager to combat Polish Catholicism, had to acquaint themselves with Catholic works, and they thus came not only to acquire some knowledge of scholastic thought but also to make use of it themselves. In 1631 Peter Moghila, Metropolitan of Kiev, founded a college, on the basis of an existing school, which was renamed 'Academy' in 1701. Peter Moghila had studied at Paris, and he was acquainted both with scholasticism and with Renaissance philosophy. The theological revival associated with Kiev spread from the Ukraine to Moscow, and in the second half of the seventeenth century a Moscow Theological Academy was founded, at which scholars in Greek and Latin could work and teach. Subsequently other theological academies were established, as at Kharkov and St Petersburg. Theologians in Great Russia, being less immediately concerned than those of the Ukraine with combatting the influence of Catholicism, laid more emphasis on the study of the Greek Fathers than on scholastic thought.

The Russian theological academies were to produce some noted scholars, and their standards were higher than those prevailing in ordinary seminaries. At the same time the theological academies were hardly a favourable milieu for the development of free philosophical speculation.

The ideas were derived largely from patristic literature, although the presence of teachers who had studied in or visited the West made it possible for students to obtain some knowledge of the development of Western philosophy. In general, western rationalism was mistrusted, as alien to the Orthodox spirit, but in the course of time the philosophy of Christian Wolff (1679–1754) became quite influential, as it seemed to be compatible with the Christian faith.

A notable representative of religious thought in the eighteenth century was Gregory Savvich Skovoroda, a layman. Born in 1722, the year before the death of Peter the Great, he studied for a while at the Kiev Academy and was later offered a post in the Moscow Theological Academy. He declined the offer, doubtless believing that teaching in an ecclesiastical institution would place restrictions on his thought. Besides, he wanted to be in touch with the people. In 1759 he did indeed accept an appointment at the Kharkov Academy, but opposition to his views led to his resignation in 1765. After this he led the life of a mendicant holy man until his death in 1794.

Skovoroda said that he wanted to be the Socrates of Russia, and he has sometimes been described as Russia's first philosopher, though many Western philosophers would doubtless prefer to describe him as a religious thinker or a moralist. Temperamentally opposed to the spirit of the Enlightenment and at the same time sitting very loosely to any definite ecclesiastical affiliation, he taught a kind of higher religion, centering around the idea of a God who has been symbolized in various ways by different peoples, a God with whom the human being can enter into contact in virtue of his or her possession of the 'spark' of the soul, the dwelling-place of God. Though he drew inspiration from the Bible and the Fathers, he interpreted the texts symbolically and as a religious poet. In the ethical sphere he emphasized a dualism between spirit and the body (or lower man), the latter being plagued by lust and ambition. He expressed his ideas in poems, letters and dialogues, but for a considerable period no collected edition of his writings was permitted by the authorities.[1] Though he was venerated by the ordinary inhabitants of his native Ukraine, his thought was out of harmony with official Orthodoxy.

4. The death of Peter the Great brought with it a slackening of the drive from above to develop and spread education on Western lines. Neither the Empress Anne (reigned 1730–40), who was much disliked and left affairs

1 In 1894 a one-volume edition of Skovoroda's writings was published at Kharkov. This was followed by another edition in 1912, edited by P. Bonch-Bruevich and published at St Petersburg. In 1961 a two-volume edition was published at Kiev by the Ukrainian Academy of Sciences.

of state to her hated German favourite Ernst-Johann Biren or Biron, nor the much more attractive Elizabeth (reigned 1741–62) possessed the driving energy of Peter the Great, though Elizabeth announced her intention of following her father's policy.[1] Western influence, however, continued to penetrate. During Elizabeth's reign sculpture, painting and architecture flourished, and French and German books appeared in Russian translation. Further, in 1755 the University of Moscow was founded, largely through the initiative of the scientist and poet Michael Lomonosov.[2] Elizabeth also made an attempt to get the legal code simplified and humanized, and she abolished capital punishment.[3]

It was during the reign of Catherine II (1762–96), commonly known as Catherine the Great, that the idea of the French Enlightenment became fashionable with those members of the gentry who liked to think of themselves as mentally emancipated. When Catherine ascended the throne, she set out to be an enlightened autocrat and represented herself as a disciple of Voltaire. A woman of ability and energy, she managed to combine a succession of love affairs with an untiring attention to public affairs. Further, she projected, and in some cases carried through, a series of reforms. In 1766 she set up a commission to revise and codify the laws, and she personally composed an *Instruction* for its members, an impressive document in which she made use of Montesquieu's political theory and of Beccaria's ideas on the penal code.[4] Unfortunately, the

1 Anne, daughter of Ivan V and widow of the Duke of Courland, was offered the throne by the Supreme Secret Council on conditions which severely limited the monarch's authority. She accepted, but when she saw that the humiliating conditions imposed by a small group were by no means popular, she tore up the document and abolished the Council. She then proceeded to leave public affairs largely in the hands of Germans, a policy which did not endear her to the Russians. Elizabeth, daughter of Peter the Great, who came to the throne with the support of the Guards, had the good sense to make use of Russian favourites.

2 Michael Lomonosov (1711–65) was the son of a fisherman. Imbued with a passion for learning, he studied metallurgy in Germany and became one of the leading figures in the intellectual life of Russia. He had very wide interests, and Pushkin described him as being, in himself, the first Russian university. He made a signal contribution to the development of spoken Russian as a literary language. In the Soviet Union he is held in great and deserved esteem.

3 The alternative punishments were hardly mild. Nor did Elizabeth's action mean a final end to all executions in Russia, certainly not for political offences. But her abolition of capital punishment put Russia, even if only temporarily, ahead of western Europe in this respect.

4 A translation of the *Instruction* is included in *Documents of Catherine the Great*, edited by W. F. Reddaway (Cambridge, 1931; re-issued 1971). The Empress envisages the Senate (established by Peter the Great in 1711) as being concerned with 'the care and execution of the laws'. She condemns the use of torture for extracting confessions or information (e.g. about accomplices), but what she says about capital punishment is ambiguous. In section 79 she asserts that murderers deserve death, but her general principle is that a punishment is justified only insofar as it can be shown to be necessary, and in section 210 she refers to the example of the Empress Elizabeth and states that in

commission was too large, and different groups of members started squabbling with one another, about serfdom for example. When war against Turkey broke out in 1768, the commission ceased functioning, though some sections or sub-commissions continued discussion until the Pugachev revolt in 1773–4. Catherine tried to increase the sense of law in Russia, and she interested herself in prison reform and in lessening the barbarities of penal practice. Again, she should be given credit for her efforts to promote the spread and the improvement of education. It is worth mentioning that she founded some schools for girls, and that in 1783 a college for training teachers was established at St Petersburg. Further, after the Pugachev revolt, which caused a breakdown of authority in large areas of the country, the system of local government was reformed, partly under the influence of English writers. The Empress had no intention of diminishing or restricting the power of the monarchy, but she aimed at improving the quality of administration and at increasing the number of people (not only nobles) who participated in it. Local government provided an obvious field.

As for serfdom, it is not uncommonly said that the situation of the serfs became worse during Catherine's reign. It is true that serfdom was extended to the Ukraine (at any rate in so-called Little Russia). It is also true that the Empress made generous grants of lands, with serfs, to her favourites and as rewards for service, state peasants being thus converted into serfs. At the same time she saw that serfdom was an abuse, and she urged that serfs were and should be treated as human beings. Apart, however, from the problems which would arise in connection with any general emancipation of the serfs, Catherine was hardly in a position to alienate the landowners. She was a German by birth, and she came to the throne in circumstances which inevitably provided ground for suspicion. She does not seem to have instigated the murder of her husband, Peter III[1], but she was certainly privy to his deposition, and she obviously profited by it. To alienate the nobility would have been to invite a palace revolution in favour of her son the Grand Duke Paul. It is unlikely that she would have done much about serfdom, even if it had not been for the

normal times, when the state is not threatened by external enemies or by internal disorder, capital punishment is not required. It should be added that the *Instruction* was intended to provide guiding-lines for the Commission, not as a law or as a series of mandatory decrees. Catherine, however, was more enlightened than most of her servants. Paul I forbad Russians to read his mother's *Instruction*.

1 Peter III, a grandson of Peter the Great and son of the Duke of Holstein-Gottorp and of Anne, the Empress Elizabeth's older sister, was a fanatical admirer of Frederick II of Prussia and had a low opinion of Russia and the Russians. He was deposed in a palace revolution and was killed shortly afterwards, perhaps by Alexis Orlov, brother of Catherine's lover Gregory Orlov, in a brawl.

Pugachev revolt which gave the government a rude shock.[1] But it does not follow that her plea that serfs should be treated as human beings was insincere.

During Catherine's reign the publication of books greatly increased, and so did that of periodicals, in which the Empress herself liked to write. The ideas of Voltaire, Diderot, Helvétius, Rousseau and other thinkers of the Enlightenment spread among the more rationalistically minded gentry, at first with Catherine's encouragement, and there arose the movement which has been described as Russian Voltaireanism. To a considerable extent it was a question of a vogue, of a dilettante playing with Western ideas and theories. But it is obvious that the philosophy of the French Enlightenment could not become diffused among educated Russians without giving rise to sceptical reflections about political and social conditions in their country. When in 1825, at the beginning of the reign of Nicholas I, the Decembrist revolt occurred, the leaders were educated members of the upper class, mostly aristocratic army officers, who wanted constitutional reforms in the spirit of the Enlightenment, people who had imbibed the ideas which had become fashionable during the first part of the reign of Catherine II but which had produced few, if any, tangible results in the political sphere.

Though it was French thought which exercised the most influence during Catherine's reign, British thought too came to penetrate the country. The Empress was an admirer of Jeremy Bentham, and, on her instructions, two Russians went to study under Adam Smith in Scotland. One of them, S. Y. Desnitsky, who became professor of jurisprudence in the University of Moscow, derived ideas from Hume and Adam Smith and preferred the British philosophers to those of France.[2]

Voltaire hoped for the advent of an enlightened monarch, able and willing to introduce reforms from above, rather than for violent revolution. But it is understandable that the French revolution, and, above all, the execution of King Louis XVI, changed Catherine's attitude to Voltaire and his colleagues.[3] It was not only the Empress, however, whose attitude was affected by events in France. For example, the historian Nikolai Karamzin (1766–1826) was led by the Jacobin Terror

1 Emelyan Pugachev was a Don Cossack who tried to pass himself off as Peter III. He gathered together an army of cossacks, peasants, serfs, mine workers and others and, for a time, enjoyed a series of successes, creating a serious threat to the government. Finally, defeated and handed over by his own followers, Pugachev was taken to Moscow and executed in 1775.

2 Desnitsky died in 1789.

3 Copies of Voltaire's writings were confiscated from bookshops, and Catherine turned against the liberal-minded intellectuals.

to abandon his admiration for Rousseau and his own vaguely liberal ideas, and to become a staunch supporter of the autocracy. This support, however, was motivated more by what Karamzin considered to be necessary for Russia than by abstract theory. Abstractly, a republic was, in Karamzin's opinion, preferable to monarchy, but republicanism was in accord neither with Russian tradition nor with Russian needs.

Catherine's change of attitude is well exemplified by the treatment meted out to A. N. Radischev (1749–1802), after publication of his rambling and repetitive work *A Journey from Petersburg to Moscow*, which appeared in 1790. Radischev, who had studied in Germany, was well acquainted with the radical thought of the Enlightenment. In his book he attacked both serfdom and despotism, though he himself was a member of the gentry class and an official in government service. He published the book under a pseudonym, but when the Empress had read and annotated the work and expressed her displeasure, the author was quickly discovered. Radischev was put on trial and condemned to death, but Catherine commuted the sentence to ten years exile in Siberia.[1] In 1796, however, her son and successor, Paul I, who hated his mother and was eager to reverse her decisions whenever possible, allowed Radischev to return home. The erring author's full civil rights were restored to him by Alexander I, who ascended the throne in 1801, a year before Radischev's death.

Though Radischev was a critic of political and social conditions in Russia and contributed to turning serfdom into a burning issue, he had scant sympathy with materialism and challenged the thesis that all knowledge is reducible to sense-experience. In a work on man and immortality he first expounded the arguments of the materialists against human immortality and then proceeded to criticize them. His conclusion was that the soul is a simple, non-extended entity, the existence of which must be postulated if the unity of consciousness is to be accounted for. Some historians have conjectured that he really accepted the arguments of the materialists. It seems, however, that he regarded belief in immortality as required for the maintenance of absolute moral standards. Anyway, he is best remembered for his *Journey* and as a forerunner of the later Russian radical intelligentsia.

5. Among the educated class in eighteenth-century Russia there were people who were detached from Orthodoxy but who none the less sought a religious vision of the world and of human life, combined with

1 As things turned out, the conditions of Radischev's sojourn in Siberia were relatively mild. He was able to live on his own with his family and books. Count A. R. Vorontsov interceded for Radischev with the Empress and paid the exile an allowance.

moral idealism. Some of them found what they were looking for in Freemasonry, which seemed to offer esoteric truth as distinct from the exoteric truth of the Orthodox Church suitable for uneducated peasants and for uncritical minds.

Introduced from Britain, Freemasonry had already established itself during the reign of the Empress Elizabeth. As time went on, it became less of an upper-class association or club in the capital, the members of which took pleasure in adhering to a rather exclusive secret society, and tended, under the influence of Scandinavian and German Freemasonry, to assume the character almost of a religious brotherhood, united by a belief in human perfectibility and an interest in mysticism and esoteric doctrines. During the reign of Catherine the Great there were a large number of lodges in St Petersburg, Moscow and some provincial towns, the members belonging almost entirely to the gentry. Among the mystical writings popular with the Russian Freemasons were those of the German Protestant mystic Jakob Boehme (1595–1624) and the Frenchman J. C. Saint-Martin (1743–1803).

In Russian Freemasonry there was also a current of social and political criticism. Some historians have made a sharp distinction between the mystical tendency on the one hand, and, on the other, the moral and social line of thought. Dr Walicki expresses the opinion that interest in mysticism usually leads to a progressive abandonment of interest in social-political reform.[1] Though there is doubtless some truth in this assertion, the two tendencies can be combined, up to a point. It is natural to assign N. T. Novikov (1744–1818) to socially and politically oriented Freemasonry, as he was an active publicist and critic of social conditions, besides doing much to intensify intellectual life in the University of Moscow. In his writings he emphasized the need for moral idealism to counteract the destructive spirit of an exclusively rationalist enlightenment. But I. G. Schwarz (1751–84), a professor at the University of Moscow, not only devoted his attention to religious mysticism and to penetrating the alleged secrets of nature (he became an adherent of Rosicrucianism) but also, like Novikov, denounced social abuses. We can say, in general, that though Freemasonry could provide a kind of pastime for bored nobles, as Novikov apparently thought was the case at St Petersburg, and though it catered to a taste for esotericism, it also contributed to developing a social conscience among the gentry.

Though Freemasonry flourished in the first part of the reign of Catherine II, the Empress herself became hostile to the movement. She

1 See *A History of Russian Thought from the Enlightenment to Marxism*, p. 21.

mistrusted mysticism and, above all, she disliked secret societies. She had the Masonic printing-presses shut down and in 1792, Novikov was arrested and imprisoned in the Schüsselburg fortress. The reason why Novikov was selected for such harsh treatment has been a subject of debate. Discovery of his correspondence with leaders of Prussian Rosicrucianism, who hoped that the Grand Duke Paul could be enlisted in the movement, probably had a good deal to do with the matter. Anyway, on Catherine's death Paul set Novikov free. In 1822, however, Freemasonry was banned under Alexander I.[1] A hundred years later, in 1922, it was again banned, this time by the Soviet government. A secret society, especially of an international nature, could not be tolerated.

6. The influence of French and British thought in Russia came to be eclipsed by that of German philosophy. By the end of the eighteenth century some knowledge of Kant had developed in Russia, and at the beginning of the nineteenth century translations of his writings started to appear. Although the thought of Kant, in the form of Neo-Kantianism, was to have some influence on Russian academic philosophy at a later date, in the first half of the nineteenth century, in the 1820s to the 1840s, it was Kant's idealist successors who captured the interest of Russian teachers and students of philosophy. A number of German professors took posts in Russia, and they had their Russian pupils and successors.

Of the German idealists it was Friedrich Wilhelm Joseph von Schelling (1775–1854) who first exercised a notable influence, the elements of his thought which aroused most interest being his philosophy of nature and his aesthetic theory. M. G. Pavlov (1793–1840), who had been a pupil of a German professor at the University of Kharkov, was an enthusiastic exponent of the philosophies of nature of Schelling and of Lorenz Oken. Pavlov occupied a chair of agronomy and physics at Moscow, but it seems that his pupils heard as much about speculative philosophy of nature as about agriculture and physics. Again, D. M. Vellansky (1774–1847), who had studied for a while in Germany, used his chair of botany at the Medical Academy of St Petersburg to expound philosophy of nature on Schellingian lines. This may seem odd, but the authorities kept a close eye on professors of philosophy, for it was regarded as a potentially subversive subject, which Nicholas confirmed in 1848, after the revolutionary movements in Western Europe, when he closed the

1 Michael Speransky (1772–1834), the statesman who, under Alexander I, prepared plans for constitutional reform but fell out of favour in 1812, was a Freemason for a time, combining a search for inner or esoteric Christianity and an interest in mysticism with an insistence that Christianity could and should be applied in the political and social spheres.

university departments of philosophy. It was not uncommon for philosophical ideas to be expounded by occupants of chairs, the titles of which had little, if anything, to do with philosophy. Literary criticism in periodicals also provided a medium for proposing philosophical ideas.

One of the groups interested in Schelling's philosophy of nature and aesthetic theory was the Society of Wisdom-Lovers, which functioned at Moscow from 1823 until 1825, when it thought it prudent to dissolve itself in view of the Decembrist rising and its aftermath. The members of the group were mainly gifted young men in governmental service, specifically in the Archives of the Ministry of Foreign Affairs at Moscow, a fact which led to their being known as 'the young men of the Archives'.[1] The society included Prince Vladimir Odoevsky (1803–69), who came to philosophy by way of natural science, the poet Dimitry Venevitinov (1805–27), Ivan Kireevsky (1806–56), the future Slavophile[2], and his friend Alexander Koshelev (1806–83). Supporters of the Decembrist movement regarded the Society of Wisdom-Lovers as romantically minded young men who turned away from important social and political issues to seeking an esoteric knowledge of reality through study of Schelling and of Oken's theory of correspondences in the world. But after the Decembrist rising, when members of the formally dissolved Society met informally, there was political discussion in which the need for changing the Russian system was emphasized. Thus Koshelev relates that during such discussion the influence of German philosophy, regarded by the Wisdom-Lovers as the antidote to Enlightenment rationalism, tended to yield ground to that of French socialist writers.

The Society of Wisdom-Lovers preceded the development of the Slavophile–Westernizer controversy. However Venevitinov called for the creation of an independent Russian philosophy, as Slavophile thinkers were to do, and in 1844 Odoevsky published *Russian Nights*, in which he criticized the capitalist society of Western Europe and affirmed his faith in Russia's youthful vigour and cultural mission, which would be a means of saving western Europe as well as Russia.

The influence of Hegel was felt at a rather later date than that of Schelling. Some of those who fell under Hegel's spell came to him by way

---

1 Pushkin refers to the 'archive youth' in *Evgeny Onegin* (vii, 49).

2 When Ivan Kireevsky was a boy, the poet Vasily Zhukovsky (1783–1852), who was a friend of the family, recommended that the youth should study British philosophers such as Locke and Hume, Thomas Reid and Dugald Stewart, in order to acquire simple, manly and practical moral convictions. Zhukovsky, baffled by philosophical 'profundity', heartily disliked the German thought which was by then penetrating Russia. A much greater poet, Alexander Pushkin (1799–1837), shared this dislike for German thought. Indeed, Pushkin had little use for academic philosophy in general.

of Schelling or of Fichte or of both. For example, Nikolai Stankevich (1813–40), the leader of a philosophical circle at Moscow, had first found in the philosophy of Schelling the religious and unified view of nature and history for which he was looking. He then made a somewhat cursory study of Fichte but soon came to the conclusion that Fichte had spun a phantom world out of pure thought. Searching for a philosophy which combined Schelling's concern with the totality and Fichte's conception of philosophy as a rigorous science, he found it in Hegelianism.

Stankevich's philosophical circle at Moscow included members who were to become famous, notably the literary critic Vissarion Belinsky (1811–48) and the future anarchist Michael Bakunin (1814–76). Other members were Konstantan Kavelin (1818–85), who was to become a well-known scholar, and Timofey Granovsky (1813–55), who occupied the chair of universal history at the University of Moscow from 1839 until 1855. Konstantin Aksakov (1817–60), the future Slavophile, was also a member and attempted, at that time, to interpret Hegel in an orthodox Christian sense.

Though Bakunin was to become an anarchist and Belinsky a strong opponent of the autocracy and a critic of the Orthodox Church, the Stankevich circle, while its members were engaged in discussions at Moscow, was far from being a nest of revolutionaries. Indeed, both Bakunin and Belinsky, fascinated by Hegel, proclaimed their 'reconciliation with reality', though they did not remain reconciled for long. We shall return later to this idea of 'reconciliation with reality'.

At the time political interests were more characteristic of a small group centreing around Alexander Ivanovich Herzen (1812–70) and his cousin and close friend Nicolai Ogarev (1813–77). Referring to the two groups Herzen later remarked that the members of the Stankevich circle 'disliked our almost exclusively political tendency, while we disliked their almost exclusively speculative interests'.[1] There was some tension between the two groups, Granovsky, as Herzen relates, being acceptable to both. 'In contrast with his affectionate, serene, indulgent spirit all awkward discord vanished . . . He was a link of union among us.'[2]

More will be said later about the Slavophile–Westernizer controversy, but whereas Schelling appealed to the Slavophiles, Hegel fascinated the Westernizers. Although this statement cannot be described as false, it

---

1 *Sobranie sochinenii* (Complete Works), IX, p. 17 (30 vols., Moscow, 1954–66). This edition will be referred to as *SS* here and in chapter 4. In *My Past and Thoughts*, translated by Constance Garnett, revised by Humphrey Higgens (4 vols., London, 1968), the quotation will be found on p. 397 of volume 2.
2 *SS*, IX, pp. 121–2. *My Past and Thoughts*, II, p. 499.

does stand in need of some qualifications. For example, Westernizers such as Belinsky, Bakunin, and Herzen came to Hegel by way of Schelling's philosophy of nature and aesthetic theory. Having fallen under Hegel's spell, they then moved away from him, in the first instance by way of left-wing Hegelianism, especially the philosophy of Feuerbach, and also under the influence of French socialist theory. As for the Slavophile thinkers, they certainly attacked Hegel as representing the culmination of western rationalism, but what they wanted was, not so much adoption of Schelling's philosophy as such, as the development of a specifically Russian line of philosophical thought. It was the late phase of Schelling's philosophizing which came to attract them, when Schelling was criticizing Hegelianism as a 'negative philosophy', as a logical deduction of abstract concepts allegedly divorced from concrete existing reality. In their view Schelling showed an awareness of historical reality in its varied organic development, an awareness which could serve as a point of departure for the emergence of a recognizably Russian philosophical tradition, in harmony with the Orthodox religious spirit. Schelling's philosophy of religion, as developed when he was combatting the influence of Hegelianism, may have had relatively little impact on the course of Western European thought, but it seemed to Slavophile thinkers to provide a basis or starting-point for the development of Russian philosophy. In other words, though Hegel and Schelling did indeed appeal to Westernizers and Slavophiles respectively, 'Hegel' has to be seen as leading on to left-wing Hegelianism and 'Schelling' as a point of departure for the emergence of a Russian philosophical tradition.

Obviously, the mere fact that German idealism exercised an influence in Russia during the first half of the nineteenth century is of very limited interest, especially as none of the Russian thinkers who felt this influence at the time were outstanding philosophers in the academic sense. What is of interest is the use made of philosophical ideas by those who earned names for themselves in the field of social theory and in radical or revolutionary activity. But this theme can best be treated when we come to discuss individual Russian thinkers, such as Herzen and Bakunin. Meanwhile it was Peter Chaadaev who gave clear expression to the problem of Russia, about which the Slavophiles and the Westernizers had different ideas.

Chapter 2

Chaadaev: Russia and the West

1. In 1836 the journal *Telescope* (*Telescop*) published an article which led the Tsar, Nicholas I, to declare the author insane, to place him under house arrest for a year and to subject him to visits by doctors. The Soviet authorities, not being much addicted to half measures, prefer consigning awkward dissidents to psychiatric hospitals until they see the light.

The author of the article was Peter Yakovlevich Chaadaev (1794–1856), who had composed a series of *Philosophical Letters* in French between 1828 and 1831, purporting to be a reply to a letter received from a Madam Panova. The first *Philosophical Letter*, the one which aroused the Emperor's indignation, was the only one published during Chaadaev's lifetime. After its appearance in 1836 the author was forbidden to publish any more writings. Other *Letters*, together with Chaadaev's *Apologia of a Madman*, written in 1837, were published at Paris in 1862 by a Russian Jesuit, Prince I. S. Gagarin, in his selections from the writings of Chaadaev.

The son of a landowner, who had died while he was a boy, Chaadaev was brought up by Prince and Princess Shcherbatov, who saw to his education and his studies at the University of Moscow. Entering the Army in 1812, he participated in the war against Napoleon during the reign of Alexander I. In 1821 he abandoned military service, for reasons which remain somewhat obscure, and in 1823 he went abroad to recover his health, which had been impaired, it appears, in connection with a religious crisis which he underwent. The victorious war against the French invaders had naturally increased not only national self-consciousness and pride but also hopes for a liberalization in Russia.[1] Chaadaev was associated with the liberal movement and he was a friend

---

1 After the second world war too, the Great Patriotic War as the Russians call it, there were hopes of liberalization, that life would be different from what it was before. Stalin had different ideas. The post-war years witnessed the 'Leningrad affair' (a monstrous treatment of that heroic city) and Zhdanov's repressive policy in the cultural sphere.

of some of the Decembrists, though it does not seem that he had been initiated into the conspiracy. In any case he was fortunate to have been abroad at the time of the actual rising in 1825 and, although he was arrested on his return to Russia in 1826, he was quickly released. After the storm aroused by his first *Philosophical Letter* he had to remain silent as far as publication was concerned, but he spoke pretty freely at gatherings of friends and visitors, at any rate until the 1848 revolutionary movements in Western Europe. At that time he expressed in a private paper his sympathy with anti-monarchical movements, but when Herzen wrote in praise of him, he hastened to cover himself by expressing to the authorities his loyalty to the throne. He even endorsed the action of Nicholas I, the so-called 'gendarme of Europe', in suppressing the Hungarian revolt. He was doubtless exercising prudence, as he explained to his nephew. At the same time he was not really a revolutionary, and he had come to believe in his country's historic mission.

2. Chaadaev's *Philosophical Letters* are remarkable for the comparison made by the author between Russia and the West, to the disadvantage of the former. In his view, Russia had given nothing of value to the world. On the contrary, if there was anything of value in Russia, it had been derived from the West. Russia lacked an historic past and was 'only a blank sheet of paper'[1] on which Peter the Great had been able to write. It was not simply a matter of the existence of serfdom, that 'terrible ulcer' and 'fatal stain',[2] a 'repulsive violence committed by one part of the nation against the other'.[3] The fact of the matter was that when Orthodox Russia became separated from western Christendom, she cut herself off from the life-giving principle of unity and social progress.[4] During the Middle Ages in Western Europe 'intellectual life

1 *The Major Works of Peter Chaadaev*, translation and commentary by R. T. McNally, with an introduction by R. T. Pipes, p. 205 (Notre Dame, Indiana, and London, 1969). This work will be referred to in notes as *MW*. The quotation, which comes from Chaadaev's *Apology*, can be found in *Sochinenia i Pis'ma*, edited by M. Gerschenzon, vol. 2, p. 32 (Moscow, 1914). This edition will be referred to as *G*. But Gerschenzon gives only the first, sixth and seventh *Philosophical Letters*, plus the *Apology*. There is another English translation of the *Letters* and *Apology* by Mary-Barbara Zeldin (Knoxville, Tennessee, 1969).

2 *MW*, p. 60 (Second letter).

3 *Ibid.*, p. 39. *G*. 1, p. 85 (First letter).

4 As part of Eastern Orthodoxy, the church in Russia, linked with Byzantium, was involved, though not by any formal statement, in the growing estrangement between Rome and Byzantium. But, as far as Russia was concerned, it was more a question of isolation and of lack of communication with Western Christendom than of any 'schism', until the Russian Orthodox Church formally repudiated the terms of the union between East and West which had been agreed at the Council of Florence (1438–9).

was directed solely towards the unification of human thought',[1] whereas in Russia 'we have absolutely no universal ideas'.[2] Western society has been integrated through the pervasive ideas of 'duty, justice, law and order',[3] whereas Russia lacks the unity which comes through the progressive absorption of such ideas through membership of society. Russians may indeed show indifference to the hazards of life, but they are also indifferent 'to good and evil, to truth and falsehood'.[4] To be sure, Western Europe has its disfiguring blemishes, but 'despite all that is incomplete, vicious, evil, in European society, as it stands today, it is none the less true that God's reign has been realized there in some way, because it contains the principle of indefinite progress. . . .'[5] Russia has not progressed, except to the extent in which it has been influenced by the West.

What Chaadaev emphasized was not so much the influence of Greek intellectual life and of Roman law on western Christendom as the role of the Catholic Church in unifying medieval Europe and in inspiring the West with the idea of social progress. He never actually became a Catholic, but he insisted that in Russia Christianity had failed to bear the fruits which it had produced in western Europe. For example, the slavery of the ancient world, which had been condoned or even defended by eminent philosophers, was abolished in Christian times, whereas in Russia serfdom was established and made progressively more rigid and oppressive only when Russia was Christian. 'Can the Orthodox Church explain this phenomenon?'.[6] In point of fact she had done nothing to remove the evil of serfdom. The Orthodox Church had a splendid liturgy and had provided examples of personal piety and holiness, but, in Chaadaev's judgment, she had failed lamentably to apply Christian principles to the organization and betterment of society. She looked inwards rather than outwards, and her contribution to social progress and to promoting a better perception of values and standards in the national life was negligible. Instead of exercising a dynamic activity, as the Catholic Church had in western Europe, the Russian Orthodox Church was static.

Chaadaev was perfectly well aware, of course, that in the West there had been a turning away from Christian belief, and that in the eighteenth century demands for social progress had been made independently of,

1 *MW*, p. 39.
2 *Ibid.*, p. 35. G. 1, p. 82.
3 *Ibid.*, p. 34. G. p. 81.
4 *Ibid.*, p. 36. G. p. 83.
5 *Ibid.*, p. 47. G., p. 91.
6 *Ibid.*, p. 61 (Second letter).

and often in a spirit of hostility to, the Christian religion. But he claimed that what had been recognized in the West as social progress had been, in large measure, an application of Christian principles. The impulse or drive to social progress came originally from Catholic Christianity, even when it had assumed a secularized form. But though Russians were Christians, most of them adherents of the Orthodox Church, Christianity in Russia had failed deplorably to influence social conditions. What is more, it had made no sustained effort to do so.

It is not surprising that such ideas were unacceptable to Nicholas I. Perhaps he really believed that Chaadaev had taken leave of his senses. Apart from official reaction, even some of those who agreed with the policy of Westernization thought that Chaadaev had been guilty of exaggeration in his picture of Russia as lacking any historic past and devoid of anything of value of her own. Others doubtless thought that Chaadaev was an unpatriotic denigrator of his country. But he was not an enemy of his country. As he was to say in his *Apologia*, 'I love my country in the way that Peter the Great taught me to love it'.[1] He was doubtless thinking of Peter as having tried to get people to see the truth about ancient Russia and its need for an awakening, but, although it may not be evident from the first *Philosophical Letter*, which caused all the trouble, Chaadaev's view of Russia and her relation to the West had another side to it than simply criticism.

Chaadaev had likened Russia to a blank sheet of paper. It may therefore seem strange that in 1835 he wrote to Alexander Ivanovich Turgenev, a friend and literary critic, that Providence had entrusted Russia with the interests of humanity, and that in his *Apologia* he asserted that, given a strong will, the future belonged to Russia. 'The future belongs to us'.[2] Such remarks, however, should not be understood as implying a recantation of what Chaadaev said in the first *Letter* about Russia's past. His point of view was this. It was obviously impossible for Russia in the nineteenth century to recapitulate in herself the past of western Europe, to go through the same process of development. She could not inherit the legacy of Greece and Rome in the way that the West had, nor could she repeat in her own life the culture of medieval Western Christendom or experience what we call the Renaissance. At the same time, precisely because she was pure potentiality, she could assimilate western scientific achievements, and she could follow a path of her own, unburdened by the weight of the rich and varied past of western Europe. Russia could

1 *Ibid.*, p. 213. G., 2, p. 38 (*Apology*).
2 *Ibid.*, p. 215. G., p. 39.

build on the foundations which Peter the Great had given her and, given the requisite will and energy, she could pass beyond and above the state of western Europe, developing a genuinely Christian society and thus acting as a guide and stimulus to a West which had tended to be unfaithful to its Christian tradition.

In other words, Russia had, or could have, a mission on behalf of other nations. Chaadaev did not see this mission in terms of conquest or of military glory. His hope was that Russia would rise above self-centred interests and serve those of mankind, not in the sense of claiming that her particular interests were those of humanity in general but of realizing more fully the ideals which had inspired other societies and by showing, through her example, how their own problems could be solved.

3. In his *History of Russian Philosophy*[1] N. O. Lossky includes his treatment of Chaadaev in a chapter entitled 'Westernizers'. In point of fact Chaadaev antedated the controversy between the two more or less definite groups who are described respectively as Westernizers and Slavophiles. It is, however, obvious that if we focus our attention on one particular aspect of his thought, it is perfectly natural to assign him, in anticipation at any rate, to the first of these groups. He had little use for what he described as 'our fanatical Slavists',[2] he extolled the achievements and policy of Peter the Great, and he emphasized Russia's need to learn from the West. In his opinion, the Russian people, left to itself, would remain where it was, in a fog. 'Our princes', he said in his *Apology*, 'were always ahead of the nation'.[3] He was obviously thinking chiefly of Peter the Great and of his opening of Russia to the West.

Though, however, Chaadaev's emphasis on Russia's backwardness and on the need for continuing Peter the Great's policy of Westernization constitutes an obvious link with the Westernizers, and though publication of his first *Philosophical Letter* was greeted enthusiastically by Herzen, his views about the cultural role of religion constitute a link with the Slavophiles rather than with Westernizers such as Herzen, Belinsky and Bakunin. True, Chaadaev emphasized the beneficial role of Catholicism and the Papacy at the expense of the Russian Orthodox Church, whereas the Slavophiles demanded adherence to the Orthodox tradition and were generally hostile to Catholicism, contrasting it unfavourably with Orthodoxy and seeing in it the major defects which they attributed to western European society. But this does not alter the fact that Chaadaev's ideal was

1 New York, 1951.
2 *MW*, p. 206. *G.*, 2, p. 33 (*Apology*).
3 *Ibid.*, p. 202. *G.*, 2, p. 31.

that of a Christian world, whereas the leading Westernizers tended, in varying degrees, to see religion as an obstacle to progress, intellectual and social, and to adopt an atheist position.

Further, Chaadaev's belief in a special future for Russia and in her mission to mankind puts us in mind much more of the Slavophiles than of the Westernizers. It is true that Herzen, for example, also came to believe in a special future for Russia, in the sense that he proclaimed the possibility of Russia by-passing the capitalism of the industrialized West and making the transition to agrarian socialism, 'Russian socialism', by building on the existing foundation of the village commune. But this was not, of course, quite the future which Chaadaev had in mind for Russia. His hope was for a religious society, not for the triumph of secular humanism.

In his illuminating study of the Slavophile controversy Andrzej Walicki entitles his chapter on Chaadaev 'The Paradox of Chaadaev'.[1] Looking back on him in the light of the Slavophile-Westernizer controversy, his thought may indeed tend to appear as paradoxical. But we can see the first *Philosophical Letter* as having two different effects. On the one hand the emphasis laid on Russia's shortcomings and on the need for continuing Peter the Great's policy of opening Russia to the West had a stimulating effect on Herzen and other Westernizers, even if they did not agree with his assessment of the cultural role of Catholic Christianity. On the other hand his picture of Russia as a blank sheet of paper and as lacking any cultural life of her own stimulated the Slavophiles to seek in Russia's past, in pre-Petrine Russia, evidences of the existence of a Russian spirit, of Russian values and of a specifically Russian tradition, which could be contrasted with the West, to the latter's disadvantage. This should not, of course, be understood as a claim that the different views of the Westernizers and the Slavophiles were simply responses to Chaadaev's bombshell. After all, a process of Westernization had been in existence for a very considerable time, even if it had not borne the fruits which its supporters hoped for. And we have noted that Chaadaev himself referred to 'our fanatical Slavists' who, in his opinion, spent time grubbing about in the soil of history without being able to dispel the fog afflicting Russian minds or to fill the void in their souls. But Chaadaev's first *Letter*, precisely because it depicted the situation in black and white, undoubtedly had a stimulating effect. And the stimulus was capable of working in two directions, on the one hand

1 *The Slavophile Controversy. History of a Conservative Utopia in Nineteenth-Century Russian Thought*, by Andrzej Walicki, translated by Hilda Andrews-Rusiecka (Oxford, 1975).

to confirm the Westernizers, on the other hand to push the Slavophiles
into finding a response to the charges brought against Russia. The fact
that the Westernizers became a more or less definite group for a time
in reaction against Slavophile conservative and antiquarian utopianism does not disprove the claim that Chaadaev's *Letter* had a
two-pronged stimulating effect. We can see Chaadaev, the Westernizers and the Slavophiles as representing different phases and positions in a movement of thought about 'the problem of Russia'.

4. Let us now widen the horizon, beyond, that is to say, the limits of
the relations between Russia and western Europe. Chaadaev had a
general view of human history, the goal of which he saw as the realization of the kingdom of God on earth. In the eighth *Philosophical
Letter* this is interpreted as 'the accomplished moral law'.[1] To meet the
objection that he is secularizing Christianity, in the sense of reducing it
to an ideal to be attained within history, he explains that he does not
intend to imply that the kingdom of God can be fully and perfectly
realized on earth. But emphasis is certainly laid on this world. After
all, one of Chaadaev's objects of attack was precisely a purely other-
worldly conception of religion. As we have seen, he praised Catholicism for its active cultural and social role, in contrast to what he
regarded as the failure of the Russian Orthodox Church to exercise an
effective influence in the social sphere. What he envisaged was the
creation of a unified Christian society, in which religion would form
the basis of moral and cultural life and of social structures. It is understandable that writers who have described him as a mystic have felt
themselves obliged to add that the mysticism in question was 'social
mysticism'.[2] In any case the fact that a person lays emphasis on religion as the basic unifying factor does not necessarily make him or
her a mystic. But some further remarks will be made later about
Chaadaev's concept of unity.

   The question arises whether it is possible for human beings to
realize God's kingdom, the unification of all men in one Christian
society, by their own efforts. For the human being, when looked at
from one point of view, is an isolated individual, the centre of his or
her own world. We are confronted with a plurality of free wills 'which

---

1 *MW*, p. 197.
2 In a work on the life and thought of Chaadaev (St Petersburg, 1908) Gerschenzon
described Chaadaev as a social mystic. His idea that Chaadaev was a mystic was
apparently due to a mistake about the authorship of a certain memoir or journal, the
Mémoire sur Geistkunde which Gerschenzon included in his edition of Chaadaev's
writings (Vol. 1, pp. 39–52).

do not recognize any rule except their whim'.[1] At this level freedom means freedom to satisfy one's own needs and desires, to pursue what contributes to one's own pleasure or advantage. To be sure, human beings are capable of joining together to pursue certain ends, but each pursues the common end as a means to his or her own good or profit. In other words, apparent altruism can be interpreted as egoism. This is not a promising basis on which to establish a unified society of the kind envisaged.

There is, however, another aspect of human beings which we have to bear in mind. 'We come into the world with a confused instinct for moral good',[2] and love or sympathy, whatever we call the capacity for union, is rooted in our nature. In spite of their natural tendency to follow their own whims, human beings are also capable of recognizing universal moral values and a moral law which units rather than divides.

It may seem, therefore, that the answer to the question whether human beings are capable of attaining the goal of history, of realizing the kingdom of God, by their own efforts, is that this, though difficult, is not impossible. But this answer would not properly represent Chaadaev's point of view. In his opinion, if human beings come into the world with what we might perhaps describe as inchoate moral ideas, waiting to be developed, these ideas must have come from outside the human being. They are, so Chaadaev claims, 'more or less obliterated traces of the original teaching given to man by the Creator himself on that day on which he made him with his own hands'.[3] These ideas, originally implanted by God at creation, are transmitted by society, by tradition, through successive generations. In the process of transmission, however, they become faint, and sometimes obliterated. They then need to be recovered and pro-claimed. This takes place primarily through the agency of privileged human beings such as Moses, Christ and Mohammed, through whom the original communication is renewed and extended. At the same time the transmission of the original divine communication by tradition means that the succession of human beings can be considered, from one point of view, as a unity, as one human being. A universal intelligence develops 'which corresponds to universal matter and in which moral phenomena occur'.[4] This universal intelligence is said to be 'nothing but the sum of all the ideas which live on in man's memory',[5] and which has become the

---

1 *MW*, p. 94 (Fourth Letter). Chaadaev is talking here about the difference between the law-ordered world of natural science and the world of free human choices and decision.
2 *Ibid.*, p. 56 (Second letter).
3 *Ibid.*, p. 69.
4 *Ibid.*, p. 113 (Fifth letter).
5 *Ibid.*

patrimony of mankind. The human being should submit himself or herself to this universal intelligence, and in the *Letters* Chaadaev claims that reason becomes reason only through submission, submission, that is to say, to the truth which comes ultimately from above.[1]

Chaadaev was not given to precise statement, explanation and development of his philosophical ideas. For example, to the present writer at any rate it is none too clear how his theory of 'universal intelligence' should be understood. Sometimes Chaadaev writes in such a way as to imply that it is only moral ideas, and ideas of spiritual reality, which were originally communicated by God and transmitted by tradition, and that he is not referring to the universal ideas of natural science. Other statements, however, seem to imply that the so-called 'universal intelligence' is the locus of all universal ideas. In this case the human being, considered purely as an isolated individual, would presumably be confined to sense-impressions and the pursuit of personal whims. Indeed, Chaadaev mentions, in a quite general way, universal ideas which precede 'all experimental knowledge',[2] and refers to the archetypes of Plato, the innate ideas of Descartes and Kant's theory of the *a priori* as seeds of reason 'without which man would be simply a two-legged and two-armed mammal – no more, no less'.[3] It is, however, clear that Chaadaev is emphasizing the dependence of the human being's intellectual life on society, on education and communication with others, though there is, of course, a theological component in his thought.

What is clear is the influence on Chaadaev's mind of French Traditionalism.[4] Joseph de Maistre represented the King of Sardinia at the Russian court from 1802 until 1817 and was well known in the capital, and Chaadaev was acquainted not only with his ideas but also with those of writers such as De Bonald and Ballanche. He had also read some of the writings of Lammenais. It is true that Chaadaev refers to Plato, Descartes and Kant, but the theory which he actually employs is neither Plato's idea of recollection nor the Cartesian theory of innate ideas nor the Kantian doctrine of the *a priori* element in knowledge but the French Traditionalist theory about the social communication of ideas. A major attraction of this theory for Chaadaev was its emphasis on the importance and role of society. Apart from social relations, the human being is little, if at all, superior to the higher animals. It is as a social being that man has access

1 See especially the third letter.
2 *Ibid.*, p. 122.
3 *Ibid.*
4 For a short account of Traditionalism in France see, for example, *A History of Philosophy; Vol. IX, Maine de Biran to Sartre*, by Frederick C. Copleston, pp. 1–18 (London, 1975).

to the higher world of the spirit. The original thrust, as Chaadaev puts it, comes from God, but man's openness to the influence of the divine action belongs to him as a social being, not simply as an individual.

Indeed, Berdyaev does not hesitate to assert that 'Chaadaev was particularly interested not in individual persons but in society'.[1] Berdyaev's statement seems to be true. Chaadaev was far from emphasizing individuality in the way that Belinsky and Bakunin (in some moods) subsequently did. To be sure, he stressed the importance of great religious figures, as has been already remarked; but it does not follow that he intended to assert the value of the individual apart from his or her membership of society. He maintained, indeed, that human beings cannot effectively grasp and act in accordance with moral and spiritual truth, unless their eyes are opened from on high. Though, however, the divine action took the form, in the first instance, of what can be described as a primitive revelation, human beings, left to themselves, tend to forget it or distort it. Religious leaders and prophets are therefore required. But leaders such as Moses give rise to the tradition of a society, and it is through the society, through tradition, that the message is communicated. It is true that Chaadaev contrasted the efficacy of religious leaders and prophets with what he believed to be the relative inefficacy of philosophers. For example, Moses was contrasted with Socrates and Mohammed with Aristotle, in both cases to the advantage of the first named member of the pair. But emphasis was laid on the fact that Moses promulgated a law which was transmitted socially, while Mohammed's message was transmitted in and through Islamic society. In both cases individuals were represented as having access to and as participating in religious and moral convictions through membership of a given society and adherence to a socially transmitted tradition.

While showing a genuine, even a perhaps somewhat surprising, respect for the prophet of Islam, whom he regarded as a far greater benefactor to mankind than Aristotle, Chaadaev's vision of the goal of history was, as already noted, the vision of a Christian society. It was not, for him, a question of any law of progress, of an inevitable historical advance. 'There is no proof of any permanent and continuous advancement of society in general.'[2] Indeed, man, left to himself, 'has never advanced except towards an infinite degradation.'[3] There have, it is true, been progressive epochs, flashes of reason, manifestations of

1 *The Russian Idea*, by N. Berdyaev, translated by R. M. French, p. 35 (London, 1947).
2 *MW*, p. 139. *G.*, 2, p. 104 (Sixth letter).
3 *Ibid.*

human initiative and energy, but mankind would not have reached the point of development which it has reached, had it not been for the coming of Christ, which was a unique phenomenon, without natural causes.[1] It was the coming of Christ and the founding of a Christian society, the Church, which made possible, though not inevitable, the future realization of one Christian society, God's kingdom on earth. For a 'genuine ascending movement and a real principle of progress'[2] can be found only in Christian society.

Chaadaev was not altogether blind to the achievements of non-Christian societies. He was prepared to allow that, at the time of the Renaissance, the Christian world, by turning its attention to Greek civilization and culture, 'rediscovered the forms of the beautiful which it still lacked',[3] and in his *Apology* he referred to the East (India) as pouring on to the earth 'waves of light from the womb of its silent meditation'[4] and as 'the fatherland of science and of vast thoughts'.[5] At the same time he maintained that the East had become immobile, stationary,[6] whereas the Christian West embodied activity and hopes of progress. Further, although the Greco-Roman world had had its splendours, its thinkers, such as Aristotle and the Stoics,[7] had contributed little to social advance. Referring to western Europe, Chaadaev asserted that 'it is Christianity which has produced everything over there.'[8] In spite of the squabbles between medieval monarchs and disputes between Church and State, religion formed the basis for a more or less united family of nations, a unity symbolized by the papacy and shattered by Protestantism. As for the period following the Middle Ages and the Reformation, anything of value in movements promoted by unbelievers was usually an attempt to realize what were originally Christian ideals.

If we look at Chaadaev in the light of the development of radical thought in Russia and recall his forthright condemnation of serfdom, we may be inclined to think of him as a revolutionary. Though, however, he lauded Peter the Great's revolution from above, he certainly did not desire a revolution from below. He was not the man to claim that the voice of the people is the voice either of God or of absolute reason. In his *Apology* he explicitly disclaimed any such view. True, he maintained that

1 *MW G.*, p. 105.
2 *Ibid. G.*, p. 104.
3 *Ibid.*, p. 40. *G.*, 2, p. 86 (First letter).
4 *Ibid.*, p. 208. *G.*, 1, p. 34.
5 *Ibid. G.*, p. 35.
6 Chaadaev did not include Islam under 'the East', as he regarded the spread of Islam as part of the spread of Christianity.
7 Rather surprisingly, the Epicureans receive praise.
8 *MW*, p. 44. *G.*, 1, p. 89 (First letter).

the populace needs to be led, but the leaders whom he had in mind (besides, of course, the great religious and moral reformers of mankind) were, at any rate as far as Russia was concerned, 'our princes'. The fact that he expressed the view that the rulers of Russia had always been in advance of the people both in his *Apology* and in a memoir addressed to Count Benckendorff, the Chief of Gendarmes,[1] inevitably suggests a desire to rehabilitate himself in the eyes of the authorities. But he had made clear in a letter to Alexander Ivanovich Turgenev his negative attitude to the revolution in France in July 1830,[2] an event which contributed to his disillusionment with western Europe. As for serfdom, Chaadaev doubtless hoped that it would be abolished from above and not as a result of popular revolution.

If Chaadaev was no revolutionary, it does not necessarily follow that he must be conceived as a diehard conservative, opposed to any change in the existing state of affairs. It was his conviction that a nation begins to have a history, as distinct from simply existing, when it is inspired by an 'idea'. This idea, however, manifests its fertility in development, in progressive self-unfolding, not in stagnation. Progress is not inevitable, but it is both possible and desirable. For example, in the case of Russia development in accordance with the 'idea' inspired by Peter the Great would involve the end of serfdom and the realization of ideals such as that of justice. Apart from the abolition of serfdom Chaadaev did not spell out in concrete terms what progress in Russia would mean. Partly, no doubt, in order to avoid statements which would be considered dangerous or subversive by the authorities, he emphasized intellectual development, progress in the realm of ideas. But he certainly did not conceive stagnation or immobility as an ideal. This was precisely what he wanted Russia to overcome. And he laid stress on the social implications of the Christian faith.

In arriving at his theory of national 'ideas' and of the several contributions which different nations could make to the realization of a common goal Chaadaev was undoubtedly influenced by German philosophy of the romantic period. When abroad he had become personally acquainted with the philosopher Schelling, and for a while he corresponded with him. Writing to Schelling in 1842, the year following Schelling's appointment to a chair at Berlin, Chaadaev expressed his hopes that the German thinker would be successful in combating the influence of Hegelianism. According to Chaadaev, the natural effect of Hegelianism

1 G., 1, p. 339.
2 *Ibid.*, p. 184. The July revolution, bringing Louis-Philippe to the throne, was a victory won by the French bourgeoisie.

was to turn away a nation from the course of development demanded by
its character, distorting 'this principle hidden at the bottom of the heart
of each people, the principle which produces its consciousness, the
manner in which it conceives itself and goes forward on the road which is
assigned to it in the general ordering of the universe.'[1] Anyone who is
aware of Slavophile criticism of Hegel is likely to be surprised at the way
in which, in the letter in question, Chaadaev ascribes what he calls 'a
retrospective utopianism'[2] to the nefarious influence of Hegelianism. His
thesis is, however, that the thought of Hegel possesses a 'prodigious
elasticity' and 'lends itself to all possible applications',[3] and that the
fanatics who depict pre-Petrine Russia as a lost paradise which needs to
be recovered are really revolutionaries who want to reverse the natural
and proper development of their country. It naturally strikes one as odd
that Hegel should be represented as responsible for Slavophile ways of
thought and that Schelling should be appealed to in support of continuation of the Petrine policy, when one is aware that during the Slavophile-
Westernizer controversy it was the Westernizers who were influenced by
Hegel, whereas the Slavophiles preferred Schelling's (later) thought. But
this does not alter the fact that Chaadaev regards each historic nation as
having its own mission or vocation, in accordance with its own spirit or
'idea'.[4] As for Russia, she cannot undo her history or make it otherwise
than it was. Nor should she allow herself to be weighed down by her past.
She should learn from Western Europe. 'Science is ours'.[5] That is to say,
Russia can appropriate modern western science and use it in following
the path marked out by Peter the Great. It is only in this way that she can
fulfil her destiny.[6]

Though Chaadaev emphasized the idea of distinct national missions or
vocations, he thought of them as converging, ideally at any rate, towards
an harmonious unity, ultimately to the common realization of the kingdom of God. We have seen that he laid emphasis on the unity of medieval
Christendom, before it was impaired at the Reformation. He desired a
return to unity on a higher level and on a wider scale. Material conditions
for a closer unity between peoples were developing. In a letter Chaadaev
referred, in this connection, to 'the epoch of railways'.[7] Science promoted

1 G., p. 245.
2 Ibid.
3 Ibid.
4 In point of fact this was maintained not only by Schelling but also by Hegel.
5 MW, p. 215. G., 2, p. 39 (From the Apology).
6 Obviously, apart from Chaadaev's insistence on the basic and lasting cultural
importance and role of religion, Soviet historians can find a good deal to approve of in
what he has to say about Russia.
7 G., 1, p. 278.

unification of thought. The soul of unity, however, could come only through religion, through the unification of human thought in one thought, which Chaadaev described as 'the thought of God himself' or, 'to put the matter in another way, as the accomplished moral law'.[1] This is the sort of remark which provides some ground for those critics who have regarded Chaadaev as a 'post-Christian', tending to reduce Christianity to morality and to its social implications. Though, however, he certainly emphasized the social implications of the Christian religion, it should be remembered that, for him, the universal moral law was not a human invention but came from above, from a divine source. In any case the moral and spiritual unification of mankind was regarded by him as the ideal goal of history.

5. Chaadaev's vision of unity was not confined to unity between human beings. In the third *Letter* he wrote that the goal of progress could be only 'a complete fusion of our nature with the nature of the whole world',[2] a 'great fusion of our being with universal being'.[3] This idea was doubtless inspired by German idealism, in particular by Schelling's philosophy of identity (the identity of the objective and subjective spheres), to which Chaadaev refers in a letter to Turgenev.[4] Entry into this 'great fusion' or all-encompassing unity is equated by Chaadaev with entry into heaven. Aware, however, that what he has said may be misunderstood, he adds a note to explain that he has been talking not about a 'material fusion in time and space'[5] but about a fusion in ideas. One might compare his notion of unity with Chuang Tzu's intuitive perception or awareness of oneness with the universe. As for heaven, Chaadaev explains that he did not intend to claim that heaven is wholly attainable in this life but only that it begins, or can begin, in this life.

The idea of total-unity was to play a prominent role in later Russian philosophy, in the thought of Solovyev and in that of twentieth-century metaphysicians such as Semyon Frank. The idea goes back to Neoplatonism, even if it was proximately suggested by Schelling. As, however, the idea did not play a prominent role in the thought of Chaadaev, who was more concerned with philosophy of history and the problem of Russia, there is no need to pursue the theme here. It is sufficient to note that

1 *MW*, p. 197 (Eighth letter).
2 *Ibid.*, p. 84.
3 *Ibid.*, p. 85.
4 *G.*, 1, p. 188. In the same letter to Turgenev Chaadaev asserts that 'there is really then a Universal Spirit which hovers over the earth, this *Welt-Geist* (World-Spirit), of which Schelling spoke to me' (p. 183).
5 *MW*, p. 85, note.

Chaadaev's emphasis on society and his claim that the human being is properly human only in virtue of membership of a social whole transcending the individual can be seen in the light of a wider idea of unity, even though he left this idea undeveloped.

6. Andrzej Walicki, who criticizes the emphasis laid by Zenkovsky on Chaadaev's metaphysical and theological ideas, is certainly justified in claiming that 'the problem of Russia is undoubtedly the starting-point and central issue of Chaadaev's philosophy'.[1] At the same time Chaadaev did propose some theories of a more general nature, theories, that is to say, which did not apply simply to Russia and her relationship to the West. The trouble is that his treatment of these theories is rather impressionistic, leaving much to be desired in regard to systematic development and clarity and precision of thought. To criticize Chaadaev on these grounds may seem tiresome, pedantic and carping. But unless we choose to disregard the theories and not bother our heads about their truth or falsity, it is obviously desirable to have a clear idea of what Chaadaev was actually asserting, and why. It is not, however, always a simple matter to decide what Chaadaev's position really was.

Consider what he has to say about human freedom. In the third *Letter* we are told that the highest level of human perfection would be attained if man could carry submission to the point of completely forfeiting his own freedom.[2] The context makes it clear that Chaadaev is not defending political totalitarianism, but that he is talking about submission to the moral law. A natural question to ask is whether submission to the moral law is not itself voluntary, an expression of freedom. Why does Chaadaev talk about forfeiting freedom or leaving it behind? The answer is, of course, that he understands freedom in a restricted sense. He thinks of the individual human being, considered apart from society, as following his or her 'whims', that is to say as pursuing what at the moment seems pleasurable or advantageous, without any general concept of values, as pursuing what commends itself here and now to the senses. This is the freedom which has to be transcended by submission to the socially mediated moral law. And it is in this sense that we should understand the statement in the seventh *Letter* that 'man has no other destiny (goal) in this world than the task of annihilating his own personality and substituting for it a perfectly social and impersonal being',[3] a statement which obviously supports Berdyaev's claim that Chaadaev was concerned with

1 *The Slavophile Controversy*, p. 87 (see note 16).
2 *MW*, p. 81.
3 *Ibid.*, p. 164. G., 1, p. 121.

society rather than with individuals. As Chaadaev sees things, the human being is a *human* being, distinct from animals, in so far as he or she is a member of society and participates in the universal ideas and moral values which are a social phenomenon and which together form the 'universal intelligence'.

This line of thought may seem to be clear enough, whether or not we are prepared to endorse it. After all, given Chaadaev's restricted idea of freedom and given his conviction that human beings should rise above the life of seeking simply one's own personal pleasure and advantage, it follows that the human being cannot be perfected unless he or she transcends 'freedom'. If anything is missing, it is a distinction between counterfeit freedom and real freedom. In point of fact Chaadaev tells us that it is the image of God in us, our likeness to him, which is our liberty or freedom.[1] He does not develop this idea, but he is surely claiming that obedience to God is true freedom, whereas the freedom which consists in acting as though one were the only pebble on the beach is something to be transcended.

The matter is not as simple as this. According to Chaadaev, when we act in a manner which is contrary to the moral law, 'it is our environment which determines us'.[2] 'Our freedom consists only in the fact that we are not aware of our dependency'.[3] It is doubtless tempting to apply this idea simply to the feeling of freedom which one may have when one follows the attractions of sense and not to obedience to the universal moral law. But when he says that our freedom consists only in the fact that we are unaware of our dependence on the influence of an external cause, he is talking precisely about submission to the divine will. As we do not see the divine action, we believe ourselves to be free. It is not surprising that Chaadaev prefaces his fourth *Letter* with a quotation from Spinoza, in which Spinoza says that the will is nothing but a mode of thinking and that it requires a cause which determines it to act.[4]

Chaadaev was obviously opposed to any attempt to set the human being in the place of God or to represent man's reason and will as autonomous and as sufficient in themselves to produce a better world. The human being participates in the moral life only as a member of society, but society consists of individuals. If society transmits moral values and knowledge of the moral law, this knowledge must be originally communicated from

1 *MW*, p. 104 (Fourth letter).
2 *Ibid.*, p. 102.
3 *Ibid.*
4 The quotation is actually from Spinoza's *Ethics*, Part 1, proposition 32. Chaadaev ascribes it to Spinoza's *De Anima*. For an explanation of this mistake see *MW*, p. 241, note 1.

without, by God that is to say. An original transmission, however, a communication at the creation of man is not sufficient, inasmuch as the truth can be distorted or forgotten by mankind. As we have seen, Chaadaev accordingly emphasizes the role of outstanding religious prophets and moral reformers. It seems to the present writer, however, that even within the framework of thought which he took over from French Traditionalism, there arise questions which Chaadaev leaves unanswered. For example, if moral knowledge is conserved and transmitted only by society, must not social pressure, the voice of society, be the voice of the moral conscience, indeed of God? It is quite true that Chaadaev allows for distortion and inadequacy of knowledge. But what are the criteria for judging distortion? Perhaps we should recall the fact that, according to Chaadaev, human beings come into the world with a confused instinct for moral good. Is this confused instinct sufficient to enable them to discern between true and false moral teaching? If so, is it not possible in principle for human beings to discern for themselves moral values and the moral law, without being dependent simply on a communication from on high? As Chaadaev had little confidence in the rationality and judgment of mankind in general and believed that it 'could advance only by following its élite',[1] he doubtless thought that distortion or forgetfulness of the moral law must be corrected by outstanding individuals who are the vehicles of divine action and illumination. But the question of criteria for assessing the claims of people who believe that they are the spokesmen of God might still be raised. And Chaadaev says little, if anything, about this matter.

In his philosophy of history Chaadaev assesses progress in terms of degrees of approximation to a religious ideal, the kingdom of God, a unified Christian society, in which the social implications of the Christian religion have been fully realized. As we have seen, however, he asserts that there is no proof of continuous and inevitable advance in human history. At the same time he believes in the operation of Providence in history, and in his first *Letter* he says that 'in the Christian world everything should converge necessarily to the establishment of a perfect order on earth and actually does so, otherwise the Lord's word would be given the lie by the facts'.[2] Similarly, he refers to Christ's 'omnipotent hand' as leading man to his destiny, without violating human liberty.[3] The picture is evidently that of Providence working in history and leading mankind to a certain goal, while not interfering with freedom in the sense mentioned above, namely absence of a sense of dependency.

1 *MW*, p. 201. *G.*, 2, p. 30 (From the *Apology*).
2 *Ibid.*, p. 41. *G.*, 1, p. 87.
3 *Ibid.*, p. 48. *G.*, p. 92.

Although, however, there may appear to be a contradiction between the denial of inevitable progress and assertion of the sure outcome of divine action in history, it seems that the two positions can be reconciled if we assume that what Chaadaev denies is that there is any law of progress operating in human society apart from the action of divine providence. The goal of history cannot be achieved by human effort alone. We have already quoted Chaadaev's statement that, left to itself, the human race tends to degradation rather than to advance. For him, it was Christ who set mankind on the road to the divinely appointed goal.

To represent Chaadaev as being interested exclusively in 'the problem of Russia' would be to misrepresent him. For he placed the problem in a wider setting, in the framework of general theories about the human being and human history. It can hardly be claimed that he developed and thought through these theories in a systematic and professionally philosophical manner. But at any rate it is clear that he had a religious vision of the world and of history. In this respect, as we have already noted, he differed from the leading Westernizers such as Herzen, in spite of their sympathy with his emphasis on the need for continuing the policy of Peter the Great. As far as a religious interpretation of history was concerned, his successors were writers such as Dostoevsky and philosophers such as Solovyev.

At the same time Chaadaev's emphasis on the social implications of Christianity and on the coming of the kingdom of God on earth constitutes a link with the radical movement in Russia, in the sense that it is possible to see the radical thinkers as striving after the realization of a secularized version of Chaadaev's ideal. With the early Slavophiles we find what Chaadaev described as a 'retrospective utopianism', a utopia in the past, an idealized pre-Petrine Russia. With Chaadaev and the radical thinkers we find what might be described as a 'prospective utopianism'. They looked forward to a utopia in the future, though for Chaadaev the utopia was a Christian society, whereas for the radicals it was a secular society. In this respect Chaadaev may seem more akin to the Slavophiles, though the latter exalted Orthodoxy at the expense of Catholicism, whereas Chaadaev emphasized the shortcomings of the Russian Orthodox Church and the benefits conferred on Europe by the Catholic Church. We should, however, also bear in mind the fact that the stress laid by Chaadaev on the importance of the cultural role of Catholicism was a feature of his Westernizing outlook, of his assessment of the superiority of western Europe in relation to Russia as it actually was. Both he and the Westernizers were convinced that Russia should learn from the West, but in this respect their views of what Russia should learn diverged.

In a letter which he wrote to Pushkin in 1831 Chaadaev expressed a feeling that soon there would arise a man who would communicate 'the truth of the time. Perhaps this will be at first something like the political religion now preached by Saint-Simon in Paris, or like the new-style Catholicism that some rash priests attempt to put in the place of the old Catholicism, sanctified by time'.[1] Obviously, this statement should not be understood as an endorsement of the social ideals either of Saint-Simon or of Catholic thinkers such as Lamennais.[2] Chaadaev was talking about a possible stage of development, not about the goal of history. But his reference to the possible advent of 'a man', a bearer of the truth for the time, is significant. As has already been noted, Chaadaev was convinced that people in general needed to be led by an élite, by those in whom human intelligence manifests itself most powerfully.[3]

On this point he was at one with most of the radicals, who came to see that while little could be expected from the autocracy, neither could much be expected from the mass of the population. A critically thinking and socially committed élite was required. Chaadaev, however, did expect the autocracy to initiate reform, and he had no desire for revolution. Further, he thought of the real élite, the truly beneficial leaders, as possessing not only scientific knowledge but what was ultimately divine illumination, in regard to moral values and social ideals.

1 G., 1, p. 165.
2 Chaadaev read Lamennais' Essay on Indifference in Matters of Religion (1817–23) and greatly respected the author. Later on, however, he found himself in disagreement with the French writer's acceptance of belief in the sovereignty of the people and in popular democracy.
3 M.W., p. 201. G., 2, p. 30 (The Apology).

Chapter 3

Ivan Kireevsky and Integral Knowledge

1. It was natural that the process of Westernization, to which Peter the Great had given such a powerful impetus, should give rise in some minds to a reaction. It was not so much a question of western science and technology as of the penetration of western beliefs, ways of thought, values and social ideals, a penetration which seemed to some to mean contamination of Russia by an alien spirit and to constitute a threat to the traditions and values of their country. Obviously, this point of view presupposed that Russia had something of her own which was worth preserving. For if she was totally lacking in any tradition or way of life or values or institutions of her own, she would clearly have to look outside herself. The natural place to look was to western Europe, which at any rate shared with Russia a Christian background and which was much less alien to the educated class in Russia than the eastern cultures. The East seemed to have become ossified, stagnant, whereas western Europe showed a dynamic creative spirit. In any case the educated class was already Europeanized or Westernized to a considerable extent, and it is natural that to reflective members of this class the problem should appear as one of Russia's relationship to the West rather than to the East. After all, it was western ways of thought which were penetrating Russia. There was therefore a choice between maintaining that Russia's salvation and future lay in an ever greater assimilation to the West and maintaining that she should pursue a path of her own. It was incumbent on those who adopted the second position to show that Russia had the potential to pursue a path of her own, that the idea of a specifically Russian cultural and social development was not meaningless. To put the matter in a different way, it had to be shown that Chaadaev's picture of Russia was unjustified, that she was not simply a blank sheet of paper on which Peter the Great had written 'the West'.

The task of showing this was undertaken by the early Slavophiles. In this context the term 'Slavophile' should not be understood as equivalent to 'Panslavist'. Later on Slavophilism did, indeed, tend to become transformed into Panslavism, into the claim that Russia should act as champion and protector of all the Slavic peoples, that she should rescue them from their respective overlords, particularly the Turks, and unite them under her leadership. At the beginning, however, the Slavophiles occupied themselves with delving into Russian history, distinguishing a Russian spirit and tradition from that of western Europe, and pointing out the Russian way to national self-development. The change can be illustrated by the story of the two Aksakov brothers, Konstantin and Ivan. Konstantin Aksakov (1817–60), one of the early Slavophiles, made himself notorious by carrying his idealization of the simple Russian people to the extent of going about in peasant dress.[1] Ivan Aksakov (1823–86), however, though also one of the group of early Slavophiles, was to become an ardent proponent of Panslavism.

One might be inclined to think that as the early Slavophiles devoted themselves to trying to show that Russia had a spirit and a tradition which were distinctive and embodied values which were, in certain respects, superior to those of the West, their activity would be highly acceptable to the established régime. In the reign of Nicholas I Count Uvarov, who was Minister of Education from 1833 until 1849, proclaimed the slogan 'Orthodoxy, Autocracy and Nationality'.[2] The Slavophiles emphasized the virtues of Orthodoxy, as distinct from the Catholicism and Protestantism of the West; they were not revolutionaries out to dethrone the Tsar; and they were given to idealizing the Russian people. It seems natural to conclude that Nicholas I must have recognized in them valuable allies in combating dangerous and subversive ideas.

This was not in fact the case. In their search for values exemplified in Russian life the early Slavophiles naturally looked back to pre-Petrine Russia, to a period before Peter the Great's opening to the West. In ancient Russia, before the development of a bureaucratic State, they saw the Tsar ruling with his council of boyars, the old nobility.[3] They saw a

1 The eccentricity of Konstantin Aksakov should not, of course, be taken as typical of the Slavophiles in general.

2 It is difficult to think of any one English word other than the customary 'nationality' which can be used to translate Narodnost. Narod means people or nation. When Slavophiles attributed special virtues to the Russian people, they were thinking mainly of the simple and supposedly deeply devout peasants.

3 As Ivan IV (the Terrible) conducted what amounted to a campaign against the boyars, his reign created a difficulty for those who emphasized the concept of Tsar and boyars in the Muscovite period. But they could contrast the first part of Ivan's reign with the second.

country in which serfdom was not as oppressive as it was later to become, and if they looked back far enough, they saw a country in which serfdom had not yet been established. What is more, they turned their attention to the 'democratic' organization of ancient cities such as Novgorod and Pskov. To be sure, they tended to idealize pre-Petrine Russia, but the point is that they found their utopia in the past, not in the present, and, as they were all aware, their picture of it implied criticism of the bureaucratic autocracy established or consolidated by Peter the Great. This was clear, of course, to the authorities. Later on propagation of Panslavism involved acceptance of the autocracy as the centre of unity for a Slav world, but thinkers such as Ivan Kireevsky were not concerned with Panslavism. They were concerned with extolling what they considered to be the good points of pre-Petrine Russia, and their attitude could hardly be acceptable to a monarch who regarded himself as a modern emperor, the successor of Peter the Great and Catherine II, rather than as a Tsar of Muscovy. Even Slavophile emphasis on the village commune could be considered offensive, inasmuch as it implied approval of a measure of local self-government and criticism of increasing control by the bureaucracy. As was remarked above, the Slavophiles were not revolutionaries. They had no wish to abolish the monarchy. But they tended to confine the exercise of political power to protection of the nation from external aggression and to maintenance of internal order, leaving all else to the private sphere. In particular, there should be freedom not only of thought but also of expression. In other words, the censorship and control by the State of intellectual life were abuses. This was obviously not an attitude likely to win favour in the eyes of Nicholas I and his bureaucrats. The emperor had no intention of confining his activities to defence of the country and maintenance of public order. Or, rather, maintenance of public order implied for him a great deal more than it did for the Slavophiles.

It has often been emphasized that the early Slavophiles, such as the Kireevsky brothers, Khomyakov, the two Aksakovs and Yury Samarin, came from landowning families of the gentry class, and it has been maintained that Slavophile idealization of pre-Petrine Russia and criticism of western civilization reflected an attachment to the patriarchal life of rural Russia. There is doubtless some truth in this contention. Ivan and Peter Kireevsky, for example, could look back on a happy and united family life on a country estate run by their highly educated and Anglophile father, while the Aksakovs were sons of the Sergei Aksakov who wrote the delightful family chronicles and personal memoirs which have given pleasure to many readers.[1] It would be a mistake, however, to think of the Slavophiles simply as noblemen from the backwoods who decried Western influences as a threat to the romantic vision of the peaceful and unsophisticated idyllic life of master and peasants on a country estate. They were highly educated men, well acquainted with western literature and thought, who in most cases came to embrace Slavophile ideas only after an initial attraction to a western thinker. For example, Alexsei Khomyakov (1804–60) studied mathematics at the University of Moscow and also made himself acquainted with natural science,[2] history, philosophy, comparative religion and theology. He travelled in Germany, France and England, where he met a number of writers and thinkers. As a young man he was an admirer of Hegel for a time. Indeed, he retained an admiration for Hegel's 'gigantic power'.[3] But he was to become the most learned of the Slavophiles, a lay theologian and a philosopher of history. Again, Konstantin Aksakov was an enthusiast for Hegel at the time when he was a member of the Stankevich circle, which included Belinsky and Bakunin among its members. In other words, Konstantin Aksakov can be regarded as having been a Westernizer before his conversion to Slavophilism and his break with the Stankevich circle. Ivan Kireevsky also came to form his Slavophile ideas only gradually, and his criticism of western thought was a reasoned criticism, not simply an instinctive reaction. As for Alexander Koshelev (1806–83) and Yury Samarin (1819–76), who were both to become active politicians,[4] they too were once admirers of Hegel. Indeed, Samarin tried for a time to combine Hegelian and Slavophile ideas.

This chapter will be devoted mainly to Ivan Kireevsky, in particular to his critique of Western rationalism and his idea of integral consciousness or integral knowledge, though references to other Slavophiles will not, of course, be precluded. Selection of Ivan Kireevsky for special treatment should not be understood as meaning that in the present writer's opinion there was one uniform Slavophile system of ideas or ideology which found its most adequate expression in Kireevsky's writings. It is a matter of Kireevsky having expounded some theories, the theory of integral

---

1 In the 'World's Classics Series' there are English translations by J. D. Duff; *Years of Childhood* (1916), *The Autobiography of a Russian Schoolboy* (1917) and *A Russian Gentleman* (1923).

2 Khomyakov made some technological inventions.

3 *Polnoe sobranie sochinenii* (Complete Works), 1, p. 297 (8 vols., Moscow, 1911). Khomyakov also remarked that as between Hegel and his left-wing successors, he preferred to 'err with Hegel' (*ibid.*).

4 They were both to be involved with the preparations for the emancipation decree of 1861, under Alexander II.

knowledge for example, which have some interest in themselves and which were adopted by later religious philosophers.

2. Ivan Vasilyevich Kireevsky was born in 1806, the eldest son of an Anglophile landowner who was well acquainted with Russian and western European literature, but whose mind turned increasingly to natural science. His father died in 1812, and his mother subsequently married A. A. Elagin, who was interested in philosophy, particularly in the thought of Schelling, one of whose writings he translated into Russian. Ivan Kireevsky's education was taken care of by tutors, though the poet Vasily Zukovsky (1783–1852), a relative, was also involved. It is related that by the age of ten Ivan was thoroughly acquainted with Russian and French literature, and that by the age of twelve he had a good knowledge of German. He also developed an interest in philosophy, while Zhukovsky directed his attention to English writers and thinkers. When the family moved from their country estate to Moscow in 1821, Ivan was well qualified to undertake studies in the University, where he attended courses on such subjects as Latin and Greek, law and political economy.

At Moscow Kireevsky[1] entered government service in the Archives of the Ministry of Foreign Affairs in 1824 and became a member of the Society of Wisdom-Lovers (see Chapter 1). While appreciating the clarity of Locke's writing and even forming a favourable impression of Helvétius, he was strongly attracted by Schelling's philosophy of nature and aesthetics. He had probably been introduced to Schelling's thought, even before he went to Moscow, by D. M. Vellansky (1779–1847), the St Petersburg professor who was a friend of the family. At Moscow, however, Kireevsky came under the influence of M. G. Pavlov, who had expounded Schelling's philosophy of nature by way of an introduction to the study of agriculture and physics. The enthusiasm of the philosophically inclined Russian university youth for German idealism, especially for Schelling, has been explained in terms of the socio-political situation. It has been argued, that is to say, that as the effecting of social and political change was out of the question at the time, during the reign of Nicholas I, a substitute was found in the sphere of abstract thought. After the failure of the Decembrist rising metaphysics, as represented by Fichte, Schelling and other German idealists, had to take the place of action. It seems to the present

1 When the name Kireevsky is used by itself in this chapter, it refers to Ivan Kireevsky. His relations with his brother Peter were very close, but Peter, a collector of Russian songs and folktales, does not concern us here.

writer that this theory, which belongs to the sociology of knowledge, is a sensible one.[1]

In 1828 Kireevsky published a perceptive article on Pushkin's poetry in the *Moscow Messenger*. In it he represented Pushkin as expressing the national soul, the soul or spirit of the Russian people. Nowadays Pushkin is pretty well universally recognized as the greatest Russian poet, but at the time Kireevsky's assessment of him was novel. Pushkin had little use for philosophy in general; he disliked German idealism; and he disapproved of the enthusiasm shown by 'the young men of the Archives' for Schelling. But he appreciated the qualities of the young men, and he was on friendly terms with members of the Society of Wisdom-Lovers, including Kireevsky.

Kireevsky followed up his essay on Pushkin with a 'Survey of Russian Literature in 1829'. In this essay he paid tribute to Karamzin, Novikov, Pushkin, Zhukovsky, Del'vig but found fault with the quality of Russian journals (they would be improved if the censorship were relaxed) and with the Russian theatre, apart from the productions of Fonzivin and Griboedov. More generally, Kireevsky saw a close relationship between poetry and philosophy, and his remarks about Europe are of interest. The nations of western Europe were represented as having already attained maturity, as having developed their 'ideas' and as having become fully formed individuals, each distinct from the others. For this reason neither England nor France nor Germany was capable of providing the focal point of the cultural unity which was required. Only a young nation could meet this need. There were two such, the United States and Russia. The former, however, was not only too far from Europe but also 'one-sided', because of its historical relationship with England. That left Russia. Precisely because of her backwardness, her potentiality for absorbing Western influences and embodying them in a creative development, Russia had the mission of being the leader of Europe. But in order to fulfil this role her cultural development was essential.[2]

This may sound as though Kireevsky were already a Slavophile. While, however, Kireevsky's idea of each nation having its own 'idea' or essence and his vision of a leading cultural mission for Russia can be seen as steps on the way to his later Slavophile ideology, he was not at this time the critic of western Europe which he was to become. He admitted that

1 See *European and Muscovite. Ivan Kireevsky and the Origins of Slavophilism* (Harvard University Press, Cambridge, Mass., 1972). The author, Abbott Gleason, treats the matter in his second chapter, pp. 33–4.

2 Zhukovsky did not like the essay, partly because it expressed the influence of German philosophy and partly on the ground that Russia really had nothing of her own to boast about.

Russian culture was an importation, and this admission implied endorsement of Peter the Great's opening to the West. In January of 1830 he set out for Berlin in the company of his brother Peter. In the Prussian capital he listened to Hegel lecturing and found the experience disappointing, though personal acquaintanceship led him to esteem Hegel as a great thinker. In Munich he met Schelling and took some interest in the new developments in Schelling's thought. But he was repelled by what he considered to be the bourgeois philistintism of the Germans, and he was not sorry when an outbreak of cholera drove him to cut short his European tour and return to Russia in November 1830.

Back in Russia, Kireevsky undertook the editorship of a new journal, to which he gave the name *European*. The first number, which appeared in 1831, included his essay on 'The Nineteenth Century', an essay which historians have been inclined to see as the high water mark of Westernizing tendencies in his thought. Comparing Russia with western Europe, Kireevsky maintained that the former did not differ from the latter by possessing cultural values which Europe lacked. It was a matter of western Europe possessing traditions and values which Russia lacked. Both western Europe and Russia had received the Christian religion, but Russia lacked the Greco-Roman heritage which had had such a profound influence on western Europe's intellectual life, on its legal systems, on its urban organization, and also on its religion, inasmuch as the Catholic Church, in virtue of what it received or inherited from Rome, was able effectively to unite Europe in the medieval period and enable it to withstand aggression from outside. There was a cultural unity, whereas in the case of Russia the unity required for casting off the Mongol yoke had been achieved by 'physical' means, by the rise of Moscow to a position of pre-eminent power and military leadership. Cultural advance had come only through an opening to Western influence, and this was still the case. True, Russia had its poets and writers, but the fact that it had them was due to stimulus from the West.

This line of thought naturally puts one in mind of Chaadaev. It is true that Chaadaev's first *Philosophical Letter* was not published until 1836, but the *Letters* were written between 1827 and 1831. It is thus quite possible that Kireevsky was acquainted with Chaadaev's ideas, but there does not seem to be sufficient evidence to enable us to assess what direct influence, if any, these ideas exercised on Kireevsky's thought. What we can say is that, irrespective of the question of direct influence, there are similarities and dissimilarities. For example, while Kireevsky's claim that Russia owed her cultural achievements to the influence of the West is obviously similar to Chaadaev's point of view, there is also a clear

difference between their respective pictures of western Europe. Chaadaev took a pretty dim view of Greece and Rome and laid emphasis on
the cultural and social roles of Catholicism and on what he considered to
be the unity of medieval Christendom. Kireevsky, however, emphasized
the role of the Greco-Roman heritage in the development of western
Europe and the lack of this heritage in Russia. He did not deny that the
Catholic Church played its part in the cultural and social development of
Europe, but he was inclined to lay stress on what Catholicism had itself
received from the ancient world. As for the purely religious aspect of the
matter, Kireevsky believed that the Orthodox Church had preserved
Christianity in a purer form. In general, Eberhard Müller is doubtless
justified in seeing Chaadaev as an adherent of the traditionalism 'of a de
Maistre or de Bonald'[1] and Kireevsky as standing under the influence of
German idealism. Thus for Chaadaev the Renaissance was an attempted
return to a past which the Christian world should have left behind and
the Reformation a lamentable shattering of the unity achieved in the
Middle Ages, whereas for Kireevsky the Renaissance, the Reformation
and even the French revolution were necessary steps in historical development, in the dialectic of history, in spite of any objectionable features.

When discussing the development of Europe, it was on intellectual life
that Kireevsky laid emphasis. He regarded the eighteenth-century
Enlightenment as destructive, as expressing a spirit of negation which
culminated in the French revolution. This process of negation, however,
prepared the way for a fresh attempt at synthesis, as exemplified in
German idealism. In Kireevsky's opinion, however, though an adequate
synthesis could not be attained by eighteenth-century rationalism,
neither could it be achieved through mysticism, by means of a fusion with
nature or with the Absolute. Both rationalism and mysticism were
removed from contact with real life. Real life is historical, developing.
Societies and cultures must be seen as having each its own mission, but
these missions must in turn be seen as contributing to and as interacting
on the culture of humanity in general. Each people has its part to play 'in
the culture of all humanity, in that place which it occupies in the general
march of human progress'.[2]

What is the part to be played by Russia in this process? Inasmuch as
Kireevsky emphasizes not only the importance of the Greco-Roman
heritage, especially the Roman, in the development of western Europe

1 *Russischer Intellekt in Europäischer Krise. Ivan V. Kireevskij (1806–1856)* by
Eberhard Müller, p. 129 (Böhlau Verlag, Köln, 1966).
2 *Polnoe sobranie sochinenii* (Complete Works), edited by M. Gerschenzon, (2 vols.,
Moscow, 1911), vol. 1, p. 104. This edition will be referred to in notes as *CW*.

but also Russia's lack of this heritage, it may seem to follow that Russia can never emerge from her state of backwardness in relation to the West. For she obviously cannot cancel her history, so to speak, and receive the heritage of Rome in the nineteenth century. Kireevsky argues, however, that at the time of the Enlightenment a break occurred in the development of European culture, in the sense, that is to say, that a new chapter began. Russia cannot recapitulate in herself the culture of the ancient world, nor that of western Christendom in the Middle Ages, but she can perfectly well appropriate what is of value in contemporary European culture. Indeed, that is what she has been doing. Witness the penetration first of the ideas of the Enlightenment, then of German philosophy, not to speak of western science. Russia is not, however, condemned simply to appropriation and imitation. What she appropriates must be used in such a way as to fit in with the Russian national spirit. And Russian culture can develop on this foundation. It may even be that western Europe will turn out to be for Russia what the ancient world was for western Europe.

In 1832, after only two issues, the *European* was suppressed. Count Benckendorff, head of the Third Section (police), wrote that the Emperor, having deigned to read Kireevsky's article, had also deigned to find that the essay was not really about literature, as it purported to be, but about political affairs. According to Nicholas I, the word 'enlightenment' meant 'freedom', while 'activity of the mind' meant 'revolution'. He therefore directed that further publication of the journal should be forbidden. Zhukovsky did his best to defend Kireevsky, whom the Emperor had described as disloyal and untrustworthy. Although Kireevsky was not subjected to arrest, but only to police supervision, the journal was finished.

Two years later, in 1834, Kireevsky married a very pious young lady, Natalya Petrovna Arbeneva. At this time Kireevsky, though not anti-religious, was certainly not an orthodox believer. When, however, he and his wife were reading Schelling, his wife told him that what attracted him in Schelling was all in the writings of the Greek Fathers of the Church. Her comment prompted him to study the Fathers, and he also became acquainted with his wife's confessor and adviser, a monk named Filaret. Kireevsky also became a close friend of Khomyakov, who was deeply attached to the Orthodox Church. To assess degrees of influence exercised by particular persons is obviously an impossible task when firm evidence is wanting, nevertheless the indisputable fact is that Kireevsky returned to the faith in which he had been brought up.

Kireevsky's reconversion to Orthodoxy provided one of the bases for the development of his Slavophile ideology. It seems probable that the suppression of the *European*, which was a great blow to him, also influenced the development of his views by stimulating him to look back beyond the establishment of the imperial system to the traditions and life of pre-Petrine Orthodox Russia. An important factor was doubtless discussion with Khomyakov and others at the salons or evening receptions held at the house of Kireevsky's mother. Indeed, Kireevsky's first statement of his Slavophile ideology took the form of a brief essay *In Answer to A. S. Khomyakov*, which was read to participants in the Elagin salon early in 1839. The Chaadaev affair must obviously have been a subject for discussion in these gatherings, and the views expressed by Chaadaev in the *Letter* which prompted the authorities to diagnose madness doubtless helped to crystalize Kireevsky's own views, if only by way of reaction. In any case it is clear that between the publication of his article on the nineteenth century in the *European* and composition of his reply to Khomyakov Kireevsky's outlook had developed in the direction of what is known as Slavophilism.

In view of the fact that Khomyakov was himself a leading Slavophile, it may seem strange that Kireevsky's first statement of Slavophile views should take the form of an 'answer to Khomyakov'. But Kireevsky was not attacking Khomyakov's claim that Russia should pursue a path of her own. His criticism was directed, for example, to the way in which Khomyakov had posed the problem of Russia in his essay *On the Old and New*. Khomyakov began by attacking those who idealized pre-Petrine Russia in an uncritical manner. Being an historian, he had no difficulty in showing that their romantic picture of Muscovy was far removed from the reality, and that their claim that pre-Petrine Russia was better than post-Petrine Russia was open to serious objection. He then proceeded to underline what seemed to him the valuable elements in Russian history, such as the division of powers in ancient Russia (before the rise of Moscow) between the Prince, responsible for foreign affairs and defence, and the popular assembly, responsible for the administration of justice and other internal affairs. Khomyakov did not condemn the consolidation of the State which had been stimulated by the need to throw off the Mongol yoke. But he evidently believed that Russia's future lay in developing according to its own 'principles'. Kireevsky objected that instead of asking whether pre-Petrine was better than post-Petrine Russia, it would be more useful to start with present-day Russia and to ask whether 'it is necessary for the improvement of our life to return to old Russia or to develop the opposed

Western element'.[1] His point was that to ask whether old Russia was better or worse than post-Petrine Russia was too academic an approach. The plain fact was that, for good or for ill, Russia as it actually was embodied both elements derived from the past and from western elements. The important question was which set of elements should be cultivated and developed. In other words, Kireevsky was suggesting that Khomyakov had taken an antiquarian approach, and that the important question was not so much the nature of the past as what should be done in the present. The issue between the two men was not, however, of basic importance.

In point of fact Kireevsky himself turned to reflection on the past, of western Europe as well as of Russia. The development of European culture, he maintained, had three foundations, the Greco-Roman civilization, the barbarian tribes which destroyed the Roman Empire, and Roman Christianity or Catholicism. In ancient Rome he saw the spirit of rationalism, a rationalism which had been inherited by the Catholic Church, later by Protestantism, and to which Russian Orthodoxy, with its pure Christianity, was opposed. In the West rationalism grew and 'is now the sole characteristic of the culture and way of life of Europe'.[2] Kireevsky could profitably have brought to bear on his interpretation of western European culture something of Khomyakov's more balanced approach to his assessment of pre-Petrine Russia. But his attack on rationalism and his claim that the spirit of Orthodox Russia was free from this evil and opposed to it were to be prominent features of his Slavophilism.[3] For the matter of that, Khomyakov too extolled Orthodoxy at the expense of both Catholicism and Protestantism.[4] Both men saw the future of Russia as depending to a great extent on the maintenance of the Orthodox tradition, which they tended to identify with pure or genuine Christianity.

Kireevsky also contrasted European individualism with the social organization of Russia in small communities, individual and community belonging to one another, inseparable. He was obviously looking back to the village commune, for example, but he failed to show how such

1 *CW*, 1, p. 110.
2 *Ibid.*, p. 113.
3 It should be added that, according to Kireevsky, rationalism was introduced into the Orthodox Church at a Church Council of 1551. He believed rationalism to be alien to the Orthodox spirit.
4 Khomyakov objected to Catholicism as authoritarian and Protestantism as individualistic. He contrasted both with the Orthodox conception of community. The individual was not the measure of faith, but participated in the faith of the community, and the community was not subject to an 'external' authority, to an authority, that is to say, which appeared as above the community, dictating to it.

communities could survive as a basis of society, unless Russia were to isolate herself and resist all industrialization. Kireevsky was no socialist, but this question was to become an acute one for the propagators of a specifically Russian agrarian socialism, based on the village commune. However, Kireevsky was more concerned with the clash between two conceptions of the human being, the one individualistic, attributed to western Europe, the other organic (in terms of membership of a limited community), attributed to Russia. As historians have noted, his preference doubtless reflected to some extent his experience of patriarchal country life.

In 1845 Kireevsky assumed editorship of the *Muscovite*, a journal which had been founded in 1839 under the editorship of M. P. Pogodin. He hoped that the journal, while serving as a Slavophile organ, would also receive contributions from friendly Westernizers such as Herzen and Granovsky. Instead, the two parties became polarized. In the initial issue of the journal after he had taken over the editorship Kireevsky published the first of three instalments of his 'Survey of the Contemporary State of Literature', the word 'literature' including a good deal more than the term would ordinarily suggest. We cannot follow Kireevsky on what Dr Gleason calls his 'whirlwind tour'[1] through European literature, philosophy and theology, but mention should be made of his general position in regard to the problem of Europe.

Despite the permeation of Europe by rationalism, Kireevsky argued, there was a discernible relation between the national histories of the Western nations and their literatures. In the case of Russia, however, there was a gap between her literary culture, which owed so much to western influence, and those elements in her cultural and social life which were derived from the past and preserved by the simple folk. In other words, the literary culture was something foreign to the mass of the population, lacking roots in the past of the nation. Russia was thus faced by a choice. On the one hand, she could strive after the most complete assimilation of foreign culture possible in the hope that eventually 'the whole complex of our culture will come to agree with the character of our literature'.[2] On the other hand, Russia might try to blot out all western elements 'from our intellectual life by the development of our special culture'.[3] In Kireevsky's opinion these two extreme courses should both be ruled out. Europe was exhausted, and a policy of complete assimilation to the West would be a disaster for Russia. At the

1 *European and Muscovite*, p. 203 (see note 1, p. 50).
2 CW, 1, p. 152.
3 *Ibid.*, p. 154.

same time an inward-turning policy of isolation would also be disastrous. It would mean cutting out what had already become part of Russian life, and it would involve isolation from the general culture of mankind. Russia needed the West. 'European culture, as the ripe fruit of the general development of mankind, torn from an old tree, ought to serve as nourishment for a new life, a new means of stimulating development of our intellectual life'.[1] Kireevsky was no fanatical anti-European. On the contrary, 'love of European culture, as well as love for our culture, come together finally in one love, in one striving after a living, full, universally human and genuinely Christian culture'.[2] At the same time Kireevsky, believing that western Europe had exhausted itself, hoped that Russia would develop its culture, enriched by its European heritage, to a new and higher level and that it would thus serve as a light and guide to other nations.

After editing three issues of the *Muscovite* Kireevsky retired to the family country estate (Pogodin resumed editorship of the journal). In the 1840s his interest in religion showed itself in his work of translating and editing writings by Greek Fathers and by theologians and spiritual writers of the Orthodox Church. His friend the monk Filaret died in 1842, and subsequently Kireevsky turned to Makary, an elder of the Optina monastery, with whom he collaborated in publishing Orthodox spiritual literature. This interest in religious thought had a close connection with his Slavophilism and with his previous reflections on the relations between Russia and western Europe, and in 1852 he published a long essay 'On the Character of the Culture of Europe and its Relationship to the Culture of Russia' in the *Moscow Miscellany*. His ideas about Europe and Russia were substantially the same as those which he had expressed in earlier essays, and the censorship discerned a lack of enthusiasm for the work of Peter the Great and his successors. But in the essay Kireevsky began to formulate his idea of integral knowledge, and this idea was discussed more fully in his essay 'On the Necessity and Possibility of New Principles for Philosophy', which appeared in 1856, in the journal *Russian Colloquy*, edited by Koshelev and Ivan Aksakov. As Kireevsky's concept of rationalism and his idea of integral knowledge will be discussed in the next section, there is no need to dwell here on the contents of the two articles just mentioned.

Kireevsky's later years were clouded by illness, by deaths in the family, including that of a daughter, and, apparently, by a sense of failure and

1 *Ibid.*, p. 162.
2 *Ibid.*

personal unworthiness. In 1856 he contracted cholera on a visit to St Petersburg and died. He was buried at the monastery of Optina, and his brother Peter, who died shortly afterwards, was laid to rest beside him. Kireevsky therefore had no opportunity to work out a philosophy on the lines indicated in his essay on the need for new principles in philosophy. But it is doubtful whether he would have done this, even if he had lived longer. For he does not seem to have been gifted with the energy and will to carry projects through to their completion.

Kireevsky often expressed his ideas in literary journals and in the form of discussion of European and Russian literature. Also the authorities saw politically subversive ideas presented under the disguise of his talk about literature and philosophy. N. O. Lossky was doubtless justified when he referred to Nicholas I's interpretation of Kireevsky's article in the *European* as sounding 'like the ravings of a madman suffering from persecution mania'.[1] But it must be remembered that at the time literary criticism was regularly used as a cover for the expression of ideas which were likely to seem dangerous to the authorities, and that lecturers who wanted to insinuate liberal or radical ideas were well advised to do so indirectly, in the form, for example, of criticism of other countries, perhaps in the past, leaving it to the audience to make the topical applications. Especially after 1848, when Nicholas's régime became even more illiberal than it had been, there developed what we might describe as an art of expressing liberal or radical ideas in disguised forms. The censorship was sometimes perceptive, at other times astonishingly blind or stupid. As for Kireevsky, he was indeed no revolutionary, but he certainly disliked the autocracy and the bureaucratic régime, which he regarded as a product of western rationalism.

As for serfdom, the Slavophiles regarded it as an abuse. Apart from the fact that it was objectionable from a Christian point of view, its introduction and strengthening had dealt a blow to the independent life of the village commune, the virtues of which the early Slavophiles liked to extol. But whereas most of the leading Slavophiles were convinced that serfdom should be abolished directly certain problems had been solved[2] and practical measures for effecting emancipation had been worked out, Kireevsky was more timid. He agreed with his fellow Slavophiles that serfdom was an abuse and would have eventually to be abolished, but he

---

1 *History of Russian Philosophy*, p. 17 (International Universities Press, New York, 1951).
2 For example, it was necessary to settle such questions as whether the serfs should be liberated with land or without land and whether and how the landowners should be compensated.

feared that emancipation would bring about disorders, that it would greatly increase immorality among the peasants, and that the freed peasants would receive worse treatment from the officials of the bureaucracy than they had, generally speaking, from the landowners.[1] He therefore hoped that emancipation of the serfs would be postponed until Russia had undergone a kind of conversion, which would lead people to treat others as human persons, as possessing value as human beings. In other words, Kireevsky envisaged emancipation by imperial decree (as distinct from acts of manumission by individual landowners) as being put off for an indefinite period. To be sure, what he thought did not make much practical difference. Though Nicholas I understood that serfdom would eventually have to go, he had no intention of effecting emancipation himself. It had, however, become one of the burning issues of Russian social life.

3. The fact that Kireevsky criticized western rationalism and its influence has already been mentioned. But what did he understand by rationalism? We can say that it meant, for Kireevsky, the exaltation of reason, in the sense of understanding, to the status of the sole organ for apprehending truth. The rationalist divides the human psyche into distinct faculties or powers, reason, will, feeling, imagination, and by reason he means the understanding as concerned with grasping the logical connections between abstract concepts. Reason in this sense is the sole judge of what is true. Other faculties or powers of the human being, such as Pascal's 'heart', are regarded as irrelevant in this respect. Further, reason recognizes no authority except its own. What reason cannot prove to be true the rationalist refuses to accept as true. In other words, reason is looked on as omnicompetent, as far as apprehension of truth is concerned. To be sure, the rationalist does not claim to know everything. He does not claim to be omniscient. But he does claim that the human understanding is the sole arbiter of truth.

Looking at the matter historically, Kireevsky saw Aristotle as the great embodiment of the spirit of rationalism in the ancient world. But it was not simply a question of the ancient world. The thought of Aristotle came to dominate that of western Christendom in the Middle Ages. Medieval thought was, of course, subject to the 'external authority' of the Catholic Church, in the sense that philosophers were not permitted to come to

---

1 When emancipation actually took place under Alexander II, there were, indeed, a good many cases of disorder. For when they discovered the terms of emancipation, the peasants believed that they had been cheated. This was also, of course, what thinkers such as Herzen believed, and not without justification.

conclusions incompatible with the doctrine of the Church. And there was also the influence of St Augustine, the most Latin and least Greek of the great Fathers. But medieval scholasticism was basically a continuation of Aristotelian rationalism, even if the medievals had a one-sided understanding of the Greek philosopher's thought. 'Aristotle, never fully understood, but endlessly studied in details, was, as is known, the soul of scholasticism, which, in its turn, represented the whole intellectual development of the Europe of the time and was its clearest expression'.[1]

After the Middle Ages there was a reaction against Aristotle, but this did not mean a repudiation of rationalism, apart from individuals such as Pascal. On the contrary, rationalism triumphed in the eighteenth-century Enlightenment. Further, Kireevsky ingeniously finds a connection between rationalism and Protestantism. Given the lack of a common understanding of Christian doctrine and the Scriptures in Protestantism, the factor uniting men's minds had to be reason, the common logical functioning of the understanding. According to Kireevsky, rationalism has tended to flourish especially in Protestant territories. (He is doubtless thinking largely of Hegel, who was a Lutheran.)

The inadequacy of the abstract reason to play the role of the sole arbiter of truth was, indeed, seen and expressed in several ways. On the one hand, it was seen by the empiricists, who emphasized the role of sense-experience. On the other hand, it was seen by the German philosophers who distinguished between a higher and lower reason, *Vernunft* and *Verstand*, or between higher and lower functions of reason. But the spirit of Aristotle was by no means dead. It reappeared with Hegel. In his 1856 essay on new principles in philosophy Kireevsky states that 'Aristotle's basic views – not those which his medieval commentators atrributed to him but those which emerge from his works – are completely identical with those of Hegel'.[2] True, 'Hegel constructed another system, but (it was) such as Aristotle himself would have constructed, if he had been born in our time'.[3] This last remark shows a remarkable perceptiveness on Kireevsky's part. Elsewhere in the same essay, however, he omits Aristotle and asserts that 'the scholastics were the first rationalists; their progeny are called Hegelians'.[4]

We can take it, therefore, that by rationalism Kireevsky means the claim that the human understanding is the sole arbiter of truth, and that the understanding is concerned with the logical connections between

---

1 CW, 1, p. 194. From the 1852 essay on the character of European culture.
2 CW, 1, p. 233.
3 *Ibid.*, p. 234.
4 *Ibid.*, p. 226.

concepts. The scope of reason in this sense was limited in the Middle Ages by belief in divine revelation, mediated by the Church; but the authority of the Church, according to Kireevsky, was 'external', imposed from outside. When this external authority was rejected, reason was left free to assert its independence and omnicompetence. Hegelianism represented the culmination of this process. Instead of reason being subordinated to an external authority, that of the Church claiming to mediate divine revelation, Hegelianism subordinated faith to reason.

To say, however, what Kireevsky understood by rationalism is not the same thing as to explain why he attacked it. For it would be possible to accept his concept of rationalism, in broad outline at any rate, and at the same time claim that the rationalists were right, that logical reasoning is indeed the sole criterion of truth.

Kireevsky does not, of course, deny that the human reason is capable of grasping the logical connections between ideas or concepts, what Hume called 'relations of ideas'. He is perfectly well aware that there can be valid syllogistic reasoning, and that there is such a thing as mathematical demonstration. What he objects to is the claim, whether made explicitly or implicitly, that the exercise of logical reasoning in the sense of apprehending the logical connections between abstract concepts is the sole way of attaining truth. And by truth, in this context, he obviously means truth by which one can live, a truth grasped by the powers or faculties of the human being working in unison. Referring to scholasticism (in his 1852 essay on the character of European culture) he asserts that this 'endless, wearisome game of concepts which was continued for seven hundred years, this useless kaleidoscope of abstract categories incessantly revolving before the mind's sight, inevitably produced a general blindness in regard to those living convictions which lie above the sphere of reason and logic, convictions at which the human being cannot arrive by way of syllogisms. On the contrary, by trying to ground them on syllogistic inference the human being only distorts them, when he does not destroy them completely'.[1] These living convictions can be attained only by a 'union of all spiritual forces',[2] by bringing together the distinct powers of the human psyche 'into one indivisible whole'.[3] For example, aesthetic experience or perception has a role to play in the apprehension of truth, not as an isolated activity of the psyche but in a state of organic union with reason and other mental powers. In other words, apprehension of the truth which can guide us in life is a function

1 *Ibid.*, p. 195.
2 *Ibid.*, p. 249. From the essay on new principles in philosophy.
3 *Ibid.*

not of any one isolated power or faculty, whether logical reasoning or imagination or any other, but of the whole human spirit, the human being considered as a unity. Pascal had a glimpse of this when he underlined the limitations of reason in its abstract analytic and deductive functions and made his famous statement that 'the heart has its reasons which the reason does not understand'.[1] According to Kireevsky, 'the thoughts of Pascal could have been a fruitful embryo for this new philosophy of the West',[2] the reference being to a philosophy on lines suggested by Port-Royal and by Fénelon. But this was not how things were to work out.

To clarify the matter, it is as well to explain that one of the main themes of which Kireevsky is thinking is the relation of philosophy to religious faith. Philosophy, he tells us in his essay on new principles in philosophy, 'is not one of the sciences, nor is it faith'.[3] But it is 'the common foundation of all the sciences and the guide of thought between them and faith'.[4] Kireevsky does not mean to imply that it is philosophy's business to prove the truths of faith. He means that if 'new principles' come to prevail in philosophy through an overcoming of rationalism and a recovery of 'mental wholeness',[5] an integration of psychical powers into a unity, philosophy could be a path to faith and to its living convictions, instead of leading away from faith, as rationalism does.

The concept, of philosophy as a path to faith does not express Kireevsky's ideal. What he desires is the development of philosophical thought within, so to speak, the area of faith. If a philosophical system is adopted which is alien to faith, conflict results. Philosophy will try to drive out faith, while faith will reject philosophy. What is required is a philosophy which issues from faith and remains in harmony with it. One might feel inclined to comment that the medieval thinkers whom Kireevsky criticizes had the ideal of philosophy being in harmony with religious faith. But Kireevsky would doubtless retort that though the scholastics did indeed try to harmonize philosophy with faith, the philosophy in question was basically an imported system of thought which was, in itself, rationalistic and alien to faith, and that this feature became evident when the 'external authority' of the Church could no longer be effectively imposed. What Kireevsky really wants is the development of a

1 *Pensées*, 4, 277 (p. 458 in Léon Brunschvicg's edition, 7th edition, Paris, 1914, re-edited 1934). The present writer discusses what Pascal meant by 'heart' in chapter vii of his *History of Philosophy, vol. 4, Descartes to Leibniz*.
2 CW, 1, p. 231.
3 *Ibid.*, p. 252.
4 *Ibid.*
5 *Ibid.*, p. 275.

Russian philosophy issuing from the Greek Fathers and remaining within Orthodoxy. At the same time he believes that if it is not to be a question of simply repeating what the Fathers have said, some point of departure for the development of Russian philosophical thought is required. 'I think that German philosophy, in the totality of those developments which it received in the last system of Schelling, can serve us as the most convenient stepping-stone of thought from borrowed systems to an independent love of wisdom.'[1] The word 'independent' is important. Kireevsky is not calling simply for the adoption of Schelling's later thought. He means that reflection on Schelling's intellectual odyssey can point the way to the development of Russian philosophizing within Orthodoxy. If it were objected that a purely national philosophy would not be genuine philosophy, he would presumably reply that it was Russia's vocation to show other nations the way to authentic wisdom, to integral knowledge, as opposed to rationalism. The task facing thought in Russia is 'to elevate reason itself above its accustomed level . . . to a sympathetic agreement with faith'.[2] But 'the first condition for such an elevation of reason is that man should strive to gather together into one indivisible whole all his separated powers which in man's ordinary condition are in a state of uncoordination and opposition'.[3] If this condition could be fulfilled in the Orthodox world and if reason could be elevated, this would serve as a stimulus and a beacon to Western thinkers who have departed from faith and put their trust in abstract reason alone.

This trust, however, has been seriously weakened. Rationalism, according to Kireevsky, deprived western man not only of religious faith but also of poetry, which had become an empty amusement. In other words, the hypertrophy of reason had led to the withering of other psychical powers, such as imagination. In fact rationalism has deprived western man of so much that in the end he is left with industry as his sole serious concern. Industry 'is the real deity in which people sincerely believe and which they obey',[4] it 'rules over a world without faith and poetry'.[5] We have seen only the beginning of the industrial era, but it is already evident that though industry can give rise to treaties and agreements and unite peoples, and though it stimulates scientific research, it can also give rise to wars, intensify class division and conflict,

1 *Ibid.*, p. 264.
2 *Ibid.*, p. 249.
3 *Ibid.*
4 *Ibid.*, p. 246.
5 *Ibid.*

and determine political structures. Kireevsky, like other Slavophiles (and, indeed, Westernizers such as Herzen) thoroughly disliked western bourgeois and industrialized civilization and hoped that Russia would not have to experience in herself the development of such a society. But his main line of thought in the present context is that industry is the characteristic activity of a world which has lost religious faith and recognition of values other than those relating to man in his 'physical nature'.[1] This is the fruit of rationalism, which has led in the end to belief that industrialization and progress are synonymous.

A natural comment is that Kireevsky does not do justice to the complexity of European history, and that his statements about scholasticism, Catholicism, Protestantism, the Enlightenment and industrialization are too sweeping. At the same time he certainly expresses views which are worth considering. As for his ideas about industry, he must be given credit for seeing through Saint-Simon's claim that industrial society would be a peaceful one and Comte's over-optimistic confidence that the development of industrial society would be accompanied by moral regeneration. What is obvious to us today was not so obvious at the time when Kireevsky was writing.

4. In his 1852 essay on the character of European culture Kireevsky contrasted eastern and western thinkers. 'Eastern thinkers,' he claimed, 'are concerned above all with the right inner condition of the thinking soul; western thinkers more with the external linking of concepts. For the attainment of the fullness of truth the eastern thinkers seek the inner wholeness of the mind, the middle point or focus, so to speak, of the mental powers, where all the separate activities of the soul are fused into one living and highest unity'.[2] This idea of the integration of all the powers of the soul was reaffirmed in the 1856 essay on the need for new principles in philosophy. Kireevsky explained that when he rejected the belief that reason in its activity of discerning relations between abstract ideas was the sole organ for attaining truth, he did not intend to imply that feeling, provided that it was strong enough, was an infallible guide to truth, nor that aesthetic experience, taken by itself, was a reliable criterion of the nature of reality, nor that love, considered in isolation, should be regarded as pointing unerringly to the supreme good. No one power or faculty of the soul, taken simply by itself, could justifiably claim to be the one sole means of attaining truth. What he was urging was that

1 CW.
2 Ibid., p. 201.

man should 'constantly seek in the depths of his soul that inner root of understanding where all the separate forces (of the soul) are fused into one living and total vision of the mind'.[1]

It is possible to object that Kireevsky presupposes there are such things as separate faculties of the soul or psyche, and that this is an obsolete theory. But in his talk about powers or faculties of the soul Kireevsky was influenced, to some extent at any rate, by writers such as Maximus the Confessor (seventh century) who belonged to the Platonic tradition. For present purposes, however, it is sufficient to recognize that there are conceptually distinguishable psychical or mental operations. For example, to see that one proposition implies another or that a certain conclusion follows logically from a given set of premises is clearly not the same thing as to experience a feeling of attraction to someone or something, and to reflect on the nature of the value-judgment is not the same thing as to give orders to a platoon of soldiers or to pray to God. If we are concerned primarily with the question whether there is any truth in Kireevsky's theory of integral knowledge, it is not necessary to discuss Plato's talk about 'parts' of the soul or the later theory of really distinct faculties. Recognition of conceptually distinguishable mutual operations will do.

If, with Kireevsky, we understand 'reason' as referring to the activity of discerning logical relations between abstract concepts, we can certainly say that it is not, by itself, sufficient to provide us with positive knowledge of the world, including human beings. Let us assume that it is true to say that all consciousness is intentional, consciousness *of* (an object). To say this is equivalent to saying that if there is consciousness, it is intentional. But this statement does not tell us that there is consciousness, that the concept is exemplified. That there are conscious beings in the world is known by experience. To put the matter in Humean terms, to attain positive knowledge of the world we require knowledge of 'matters of fact' and not only of 'relations of ideas'.

It would not be true to say that the point just made has no relevance to what Kireevsky had in mind, for he interpreted rationalism as claiming that the analytic and deductive reason is the sole organ for attaining truth, and he noted that the empiricists saw the untenability of this thesis, and emphasized the role of sense-experience. Kireevsky certainly did not believe that mere deduction from abstract concepts was able to give us positive knowledge of the world. It is true that in modern theoretical physics deductive reasoning plays a prominent role; but if we take a

1 *Ibid.*, p. 249.

realist view of science and regard astronomy, for example, as providing us with positive knowledge of the world, we cannot reasonably claim that it does so simply and solely by discerning the logical connections between abstract concepts or by proceeding in a purely *a priori* manner.

What this suggests, it may be said, is no more than that we need an enlarged concept of reason. Instead of confining reason to discerning logical relations between abstract ideas, we need to envisage it as concerned also with 'matters of fact'. After all, the historian is concerned with matters of fact,[1] but historiography is a rational activity. Does not Kireevsky claim, for example, that in addition to reason other powers or forces of the soul, such as feeling and aesthetic experience, can also guide us on the path to truth? If so, the claim seems to be highly questionable. How are feeling and aesthetic experience related to the attainment of truth?

If we look to Kireevsky for a clear answer to this question, we shall be disappointed. On the one hand, he speaks of the concurrence (or even 'fusion') of the powers of the soul in seeking for truth. Taken by itself, this way of speaking does not entail the claim that the actual perception of truth is enjoyed by a power other than the intellect. We might perhaps say that in regard to truth about maters of fact sensation concurs or has a role to play in its attainment, without claiming that sensation is an independent means of knowing what is true. On the other hand, however, Kireevsky's rejection of the claim that reason is the *only* organ for attaining truth suggests that other powers or activities of the psyche can be paths to truth, though no single one would be the only path.

Obviously, a good deal depends on how the word 'truth' is understood. If we mean by truth what has been described as propositional truth, it is natural to claim that it is reason which discerns the truth of propositions. As for other psychical operations or activities, they may or may not be of service in the attainment of truth. If we heartily dislike someone, if we have a feeling of hostility towards the person, this may get in the way of our seeing the person's good points. Similarly, though love may help us to discern a person's good qualities, it may blind us to the person's shortcomings or lead us to forming an unjustifiably rosy view of the person's character.

If, however, we interpret Kireevsky as claiming that psychical powers

---

1 We cannot discuss here the concept of 'historical facts'. Common sense takes it that historians are concerned with 'facts', even though this is not their only concern. And the verdict of common sense will have to do for present purposes.

other than reason can attain truth, we need a wide concept of truth which does not confine truth to propositional truth. Some writers have spoken, for example, of truth in art and of aesthetic experience as attaining truth.[1] That a work of art can be true (quite apart from the question whether it is a faithful representation of a scene or person or object) is a view which has been defended seriously. The present writer does not feel competent to discuss it. But it seems clear that the view requires something more than a concept of truth as a property of propositions. An 'ontological' theory of truth is required, which makes it possible to speak of something other than a proposition as true. In other words, we must regard 'truth' as an analogous term.

It would be understandable if the preceding reflections have made the reader impatient, on the ground that they are pedantic and have little to do with Kireevsky's main point. Kireevsky, it may be said, is surely thinking primarily of 'existential' truth, in the sense of truth by which a person can live and which can have a formative and beneficial effect on society. His objection to rationalism is that one cannot live by propositions expressing the logical relations between abstract ideas, and that if this is accepted as the only idea of truth, the relevant society is left without a truth or set of ideas which can inspire its development. Above all, he is thinking of religious truth, of a faith which cannot be reduced to, say, analytically true propositions, nor, of course, to those of empirical science. In the modern world, Kireevsky would obviously object to the tendency to reduce philosophy to logical studies, not on the ground that logical propositions are untrue, but on the ground that a philosophy which is confined to logical inquiries has become cut off from the important concerns of human life, personal and social. Further, when Kireevsky talks about the concurrence of the powers of the soul in the attainment of truth, his basic meaning is surely that response to religious truth and to values is a response of the whole person, not of some particular faculty within the person. For recognition of the logical connections between abstract concepts 'reason' is quite sufficient. This is to say, it is only the person in his or her analytic and deductive mental capacity who is engaged. But this is not the case when it is a question of responding effectively to truth as determining life, attitudes and conduct. For example, a merely 'rational' assent to propositions about a transcendent divine reality is inadequate from a religious point of view. More is

---

1 See, for example, *Truth and Art* by A. Hofstadter (Columbia University Press, New York, 1965) and *On Truth. An Ontological Theory* by Eliot Deutsch (University Press of Hawaii, Honolulu, 1979).

involved. There must be a response of the whole person, the thinking, willing, feeling, acting human being. Moreover, for such a response moral conditions are required. Finally, even if we prescind from the specifically religious theme and consider the psychological aspect of the matter, it is clear that Kireevsky's ideal was that of the harmonious integration of the human being's powers, the ideal of an integrated personality. The person can no more be reduced to the logical and deductive reason than he or she can be reduced to sensation or instinctive behaviour. The concept of mental wholeness is that of an integrated personality. And there is certainly nothing wrong with this ideal.

The foregoing reflections are doubtless substantially true. Their truth, however, does not alter the fact that while in his writings Kireevsky certainly indicated the lines on which he believed that philosophy should develop, he did not himself work out this philosophy. Nor did he state the basic ideas with the clarity and precision which most modern philosophers would consider desirable. It may be said that he was feeling his way. But this is just the point. Kireevsky called for 'new principles' in philosophy and for the development of a philosophy which would be faithful to the Orthodox spirit without being theology. Some would probably argue that this is not possible. However this may be, the most convincing proof of its possibility would be the actual development of such a philosophy. Kireevsky did not himself produce one. The sustained attempt to do so was left for later thinkers, such as Vladimir Solovyev.

5. Somewhat similar views of rationalism and of 'wholeness' were advanced by Aleksei Khomyakov (1804–60), the other leading Slavophile thinker. Among other things Khomyakov was an historian, and he worked for many years on a projected universal history. His 'Notes on Universal History' are a collection of draft material for the work rather than the work itself. In regard to Russia, though Khomyakov was more critical of pre-Petrine Russia than Kireevsky was, he was also more nationalist in outlook, approaching Pan-Slavist ideas, which were alien to Kireevsky's mind.

All his life Khomyakov was deeply attached to the Russian Orthodox Church, regarding it as an organic community with a collective consciousness, inspired by the indwelling Holy Spirit. In formulating his idea of *sobornost* he seems to have been influenced by the concept of unity in multiplicity as expounded by the Catholic theologian Johann Adam Moehler (1796–1838). This idea of the Church as an organic community was used by Khomyakov in his criticism of the papacy as exercising 'external authority' and of Protestantism as individualistic,[1] a line of criticism in which he was at one with Kireevsky. Khomyakov, however, made it clear that he was opposed not only to papal absolutism but also to authoritarian attitudes within the Orthodox Church. It was not until 1879 that publication of his complete works was permitted.

Khomyakov did not write any major philosophical work. His ideas are expressed in essays and letters, as in the two letters of Yury Samarin in which he discusses German thought. As a young man Khomyakov had been an admirer of Hegel. Though, however, he continued to think that the Hegelians manifested a profundity of thought which was conspicuously lacking in French philosophy, he came to accuse Hegel of having substituted for reality a realm of abstract possibility, identified with the concept, and to object that 'the transition from potentiality to actuality is impossible without a pre-existing actuality'.[2] In other words, for development to take place there must be something to develop, something which actually exists; reality cannot proceed from a concept.[3] To be sure, Hegel's left-wing successors supplied a substrate, matter. But if we try to conceive matter as such, matter as the ultimate and indeterminate substratum of all things, it turns out to be 'an immaterial abstraction with none of the characteristics of matter'.[4] Further, pure matter could not develop into spirit or consciousness, unless spirit were inherent in it. And in this case it would not be pure matter. In brief, materialism is unintelligible.

According to Khomyakov, both Hegel, the rationalist, and his materialist successors were heirs of Spinoza in denying human freedom. Both rationalism and materialism 'unconsciously embodied the idea of unfreedom' (necessitarianism).[5] Khomyakov represents the materialists as pouring scorn on the belief in freedom on the ground that at a primitive stage of human development man ascribed freedom to non-human objects too, with the implication that having ceased to attribute freedom to natural forces, for example, man should go on to cease ascribing

1 After a visit to England Khomyakov kept up a correspondence with William Palmer, an Oxford theologian. Palmer tried to persuade Khomyakov that the Roman, Orthodox and Anglican Churches were all branches of one Catholic Church, while Khomyakov tried to convert Palmer to Orthodoxy as interpreted by himself. Eventually Palmer became a Roman Catholic.

2 *Polnoe sobranie sochinenii* (Complete Works), Vol. 1, p. 292. (4th edition, 8 vols., Moscow, 1911).

3 The present writer does not believe that Hegel really maintained that the world proceeds from the Concept or Idea. He interprets Hegel's *Logic* as dealing with an abstraction, the intelligible structure of developing reality considered purely abstractly.

4 CW, 1, p. 304.

5 *Ibid.*, p. 310.

freedom to himself. Khomyakov retorts that at an early stage human beings ascribed to non-human objects not only freedom but also consciousness. The reason why they did this was because they themselves were conscious. They attributed to other things what they themselves possessed. So too in the case of freedom. Recognition of freedom means distinguishing between what, in oneself, comes from oneself and what does not. We cannot get rid of this recognition or awareness. It does not follow, however, that we have to postulate a distinct faculty of free will. Reason and will, for Khomyakov, are not two distinct faculties. Free will is the creative activity of reason; it is the 'active force'[1] of reason. But Khomyakov's account of will and freedom remained unfinished.

A point worth mentioning is that, for Khomyakov, faith precedes the logical activity of reason. But by 'faith' in this context he means immediate knowledge. It is faith in this sense which enables human beings to distinguish between what is real and its subjective representation, and between the actual and the possible.[2] In other words, we do not prove by logical reasoning that an idea of an object is not the object itself; we know it immediately without the need for argument. However, faith in this sense is not integral reason. For integral reason includes the reflective activity of the mind. And it is when all the powers of the mind are united in integral reason, in Kireevsky's mental 'wholeness', that faith, in the sense of a recognition of spiritual reality, appears. According to Khomyakov, however, faith in this religious sense belongs not to the individual as such but to the human being as a member of an organic community united by love. Faith in the first sense is common to all human beings; faith in the second sense is common to all genuine members of a religious community.

6. The critique of rationalism which was made by Kireevsky and Khomyakov was accompanied by a mistrust of constitutions and legal codes which claimed to be the product of reason but which seemed to them artificial and much inferior to custom and customary law, expressing the spirit and traditions of the community. Formal contract, for example, seemed to them a device for overcoming the centrifugal tendencies of a society consisting of isolated individuals. The cohesion of a society should be secured, ideally, by brotherly fellowship in an organic community rather than by external bonds such as penal law and formal contract. Among the

---

1 CW, p. 340. Khomyakov would interpret creation as the free activity of infinite reason.

2 We are justified in seeing some similarity between Khomyakov's idea of faith as immediate knowledge and Hume's idea of natural belief, though Hume would not be prepared to claim that we 'know', for example, that there are relatively permanent physical objects distinct from our ideas.

western nations Khomyakov singled out England for praise, as the country where, in his judgment, tradition, custom, the spirit of community, had been best preserved.[1]

This rather romantic attitude, with its devotion, especially with Khomyakov, to the concept of *sobornost*, the organic community, found an extreme expression in the thought of Konstantin Aksakov. Though Aksakov, when a student at the University of Moscow and a member of the Stankevich circle, passed through an Hegelian phase, trying to interpret Hegel's thought in such a way as to harmonize with Orthodox Christianity, he was not a philosopher.[2] His ideas about the people and its relation to political power are, however, of some interest in the context of Slavophilism.

According to Aksakov, Russia differed from all western nations in virtue of the fact that the Russian state had originated not through conquest, through the subjugation of the Russians to another people, but by the free act of inviting the Varangians to rule. Similarly, after the 'Time of Troubles' the Russian people had freely invited Michael Romanov to accept the throne. Obviously, the Mongol overlordship had been imposed, and Ivan IV had pretty well made war on his subjects. But the fact that the Russian state originated through a free vote of invitation to rule showed that the Russian people, described by Aksakov as 'the Land', had no wish to rule. They did not want to have anything to do with political power and its exercise, provided that they were left free to preserve their own traditions, customs, values, religion. In other words, between Land and State there was an understanding, based on mutual trust and goodwill rather than on any formal contract, that the state should exercise political power, defending the people against external aggression and seeing to foreign relations, but that it should not interfere with the ordinary life, beliefs, customs and practices of the Land, while the Land would not attempt to usurp political power.

Let us omit discussion of the historical basis of this theory. Considered in itself, the theory took the form of a distinction between State and Society. The former was regarded as possessing a monopoly of political power and action. It could, and, according to Aksakov, was actually accustomed to, listen to the opinions of the Land, but it was not bound by these opinions. The Russian people had no wish to seize power, as the French did at the revolution. At the same time, if the state interfered with

1 Khomyakov even tried to find Slavic influences in English history.
2 Aksakov's dissertation on *Lomonosov in the History of Russian Language and Literature* was published in 1846. He also wrote a work on *The Manners and Customs of Ancient Slavs in General and of Russian Slavs in Particular*, which appeared in 1852.

the traditions and customs of the Land, as Peter the Great did, it was overstepping the limits of the powers entrusted to it by implicit agreement.

From one point of view this theory can be regarded as supporting the autocracy, inasmuch as it restricted the possession and exercise of political power to the throne. Aksakov represented the Russian people as not wanting to demean itself by taking over or directly participating in political power. In his opinion, the Land wanted to steer clear of politics. From another point of view, however, the theory was clearly opposed to the autocracy as it had developed from the time of Peter the Great. That is to say, the theory was opposed to the bureaucratic state which interfered left and right with the 'private' domain. In practice the state had, of course, to punish criminals and consequently enact a legal code, but as far as possible life should be governed by custom, by the values and traditions of the organic community, rather than by some legal code which claimed to express the dictates of abstract reason. In particular, the state should not interfere with or curtail freedom of expression. The Censorship should be used simply to prevent libellous attacks on other people, not to stifle the expression of opinions which did not involve libelling or calumniating individuals. In a memorial addressed to Alexander II Aksakov maintained that if a Land Assembly were to come into being, it should enjoy complete freedom of speech, even though it would be a consultative and not a legislative body.

Aksakov's theory of Land and State was based on an anthropology, a theory about the human being. In his view, it was only as a member of society, not as an isolated individual, that the human being could develop, attain truth and live a properly human life. In this context society meant a community united by inner bonds, by a common sense of values, a common cultural and religious tradition; it was a brotherly fellowship of persons, a kind of extended family. This organic community, exemplifying the concept of *sobornost*, was what Aksakov meant by 'Land'. And he looked on the Russian people as at any rate approximating to this concept, more so at any rate than any western European nation. Human nature being what it is, however, it is not possible to dispense altogether with the external bonds of positive law, backed by a penal code, and other functions of the state. The Russian people therefore entrusted the distasteful business of politics to a sovereign, who sacrificed himself by taking on his shoulders the burden of political authority, defending the country against external enemies and punishing criminals. The practical need for the state did not, however, alter the fact that what is really worth while in human life is realized in an organic community of free human beings, united by the internal bonds of mutual trust and respect and by sincere participation in common traditions, economic, social, cultural, religious. If the Russian people left the exercise of political power to the autocracy, it did so in order to preserve its existence as an organic community, not to have this community broken up into a plurality of self-seeking individuals, united only by fear of a common master. Disintegration of the community in this way would mean the ruin of Russia. Perhaps we can say that Aksakov had a keen sense of what Hegel called the *Volksgeist*, the spirit of the people, though he, unlike Hegel, set the people, the Land, over against the state.

Obviously, one can criticize Aksakov's theory of Land and State on various grounds. The western mind is likely to find his idea of handing over all political power to the government, as though politics were simply a regrettable necessity which the people would do well to avoid, not only uncongenial but also dangerous, as asking for trouble. It can also be argued that the distinction between internal and external uniting bonds is something to be progressively transcended, not intensified. And the Hegelian would doubtless start talking about the need for achieving a synthesis of universality and particularity at a higher level. To understand Aksakov's point of view, however, we have to bear in mind such factors as the vast size of the Russian empire, the history of the country, and the people's lack of political education. It can, indeed, be objected that Aksakov succeeds in finding a peculiarly Russian spiritual heritage only by idealizing ancient Russia in a somewhat unhistorical manner. But at any rate he was not blind to the evils of contemporary Russia. The Slavophiles tended to look to the past, whereas the Westernizers looked to the future. But neither party was in love with the régime of Nicholas I.

At the University of Moscow Aksakov had been a close friend of Yury Samarin (1819–76), and at the time they shared an enthusiastic admiration for Hegel[1], from which both were to recover. In regard to Aksakov's distinction between Land and State, Samarin too distinguished between Society and State, but he used the distinction in a different way. He did not take as rosy a view as Aksakov did of Society or the Land. In his opinion, Society, left to itself, generates divisions and conflicts of interest. To overcome these divisions, to prevent social disintegration, the authority and action of a centralized State are required. Holding this

---

1 Samarin maintained for a time that Orthodoxy neither had nor ought to have a theological system. To be sure, Orthodoxy needed to attain the state of being not only 'in itself' but also 'for itself', but Hegelianism was the appropriate means for achieving this advance. In other words, Hegel's contention that speculative philosophy reveals the truth of religion was correct. It was Khomyakov who succeeded in disabusing Samarin of the notion that Orthodoxy, having no 'science' of its own, should rely on Hegelianism.

conviction, Samarin was later to oppose liberal proposals for even a mild form of constitutionalism. The idea that the autocracy should share power with the educated upper class seemed to him misguided. He believed that it was the bureaucracy, not the nobility, which represented concern with the common good.[1] Samarin was certainly not against reform as such. As has already been mentioned, he participated in the preparations for the emancipation of the serfs under Alexander II. But he was convinced that reforms should be imposed from above, by the autocracy. Moreover, Samarin manifested a chauvinism which was really foreign to Konstantin Aksakov's mind. In 1849 he was confined for some days in the Peter and Paul fortress at St Petersburg and then interviewed and sharply rebuked by Nicholas I for having criticized, at any rate by implication, the government's lack of zeal in the Russification of the Baltic provinces and its lack of concern with the plight of the peasants exploited by the German barons.[2] Later, at the time of the Polish uprising in 1863, Samarin published an article in which he argued that the Polish people was essentially Slavic, that the Catholic clergy and the nobility represented an alien 'Latinism' which produced division, and that Poland's future lay with the Slavic world, under the leadership of Russia of course. In other words, with Samarin, as with Ivan Aksakov, Konstantin's brother, Slavophilism came to assume the form of Panslavism. This involved a degree of support for the autocracy which was certainly not a feature of the thought of Kireevsky or of Konstantin Aksakov.

7. The Russian term *sobornost* has its primary use in a religious context.[3] Thus N. O. Lossky defines the concept of *sobornost* as that of 'a combination of unity and freedom of many persons on the basis of common love of God and for all absolute values'.[4] This idea of a synthesis of unity and freedom enabled writers such as Khomyakov to contrast the Russian

1 Hegel had emphasized the role of the bureaucracy as representing a 'universal' interest.

2 It may seem odd that Nicholas I of all people should reprimand Samarin for advocating Russification of the Germans in the Baltic provinces. But the implication of what Samarin said in his *Letters from Riga* in 1848 (not published at the time but read to friends and distributed to officials) was that since the time of Peter the Great the autocracy had become Germanized and that in the Baltic provinces its officials were favouring Germans at the expense of Russians. What Samarin said may well have been justified, but it did not please Nicholas I. After all, his own grandmother, Catherine II, was a German by origin. Moreover, the Emperor doubtless understood that any policy of Russification by coercion would cause trouble.

3 The Russian verb for to gather together or collect is *sobiratj*. The noun *sobor*, besides meaning 'cathedral', is also used for a council or synod (of bishops).

4 *History of Russian Philosophy*, p. 407.

Orthodox Church with Catholicism on the one hand and Protestantism on the other. According to such writers, the Catholic Church did indeed possess unity, but it was deficient in freedom. Its members were subjected to the 'external authority' of the papacy. Protestantism, however, while embodying a freedom which was not enjoyed in Catholicism, was deficient in unity, too individualistic. The synthesis of unity and freedom was realized in the Orthodox Church and manifested its superiority.

Khomyakov also found the concept of *sobornost* exemplified in the Russian village commune, the *obschina*, the members of which came together in the *mir*. The concept could, indeed, be extended to cover the nation. Ideally at any rate Konstantin Aksakov's 'Land' would exemplify the principal of *sobornost*, the State remaining outside, as the organ to which the community had tacitly agreed to leave political power. From the ideal point of view, Land and Church would be one, united in one community of free persons. Samarin, however, would not leave the State 'outside', as he saw in the autocracy and its bureaucrats a necessary principle of unity. In any case the alleged exemplification of *sobornost* in the village commune and, ideally, in Russian society in general enabled Slavophile writers to contrast Russia with western European nations to the disadvantage of the latter.

Emphasis on the concept of *sobornost* can, of course, be seen as expressing a reaction to awareness of Russia's backwardness in relation to the more advanced nations of western Europe. That is to say, the early Slavophiles, looking for Russian traditions of value and features of Russian life which were relatively absent in the West, idealized both the village commune and the Orthodox Church as exemplifying the Russian concept of *sobornost*, to which they attached great value. They could then exalt Orthodoxy as superior to both the Catholicism and the Protestantism of the West, and they could turn the absence in Russia of any large commercially-minded and individualistic bourgeoisie into a virtue. What Hegel called 'civil society' could be regarded as a second-rate kind of organization. They were able to represent the nations of western Europe as rapidly disintegrating into a plurality of self-seeking individuals and contrast this picture with at any rate what Russia could be if she developed her own traditions.

The emphasis on *sobornost* was not, however, simply a way of overcoming an inferiority complex in relation to western Europe. It represented a seriously held position in philosophical anthropology. Man is indeed free, a free person, and to treat him as a slave is morally unjustifiable. At the same time he cannot develop except in and through membership of society, of a greater whole. It is as a member of society that the human being attains truth, and recognizes common values and practises love, self-sacrifice and other virtues. It is as a member of the Church that he grasps Christian truth and shares a right relationship to God.[1] From this concept of a synthesis of unity and freedom conclusions can be drawn about the desirable organization of society. Thus in the first half of the twentieth century Berdyaev gave expression to the concept of *sobornost* in his idea of a personalistic socialism, distinct from bourgeois individualism on the one hand and Marxist collectivism on the other.

The idea of *sobornost*, therefore, is the idea of society as a whole, the unity of the members being secured not by coercion or by elimination of freedom but rather through brotherly fellowship and a free pursuit of goals in the light of shared values. Perhaps it is not altogether fanciful to see an expression of this idea in Kireevsky's concept of the concurrence of psychical or mental powers in the pursuit and attainment of truth and in his idea of mental wholeness. After all, if the good of society requires a unity in multiplicity and a harmony of interests in the light of shared values, it is reasonable to conclude that something analogous is required in the case of the members considered as distinct persons. Without properly integrated members we can hardly expect to have a properly integrated society. Kireevsky employed both concepts, that of *sobornost* and that of mental wholeness, and it does not seem unreasonable if one sees a link between them.

---

1 For Khomyakov, the bearer of religious truth was the Orthodox community as a whole, not Church officials, nor even a council, as councils could err.

Chapter 4

From Reconciliation with Reality to Revolution

1. Writing in 1860 Alexander Herzen remarked that Peter the Great had driven civilization into Russia 'with such a wedge that Russia could not stand it and split into two layers'.[1] This remark could be interpreted as meaning that as a result of Peter's opening to the West Russia was divided between a small educated élite, open to western ideas and culture, and the vast bulk of the population. But it can also be understood as meaning that Russia was divided into the autocrat and his or her bureaucrats on the one hand and the rest of the people on the other. In between the two layers, Herzen added, were the 'superfluous men' with their 'faith in western liberalism'.[2]

It is arguable that at first the autocracy was 'historically progressive'. By his driving force and energy Peter the Great contributed powerfully to changing Russia. But it was not long before the autocracy became a brake on further change. The liberal-minded gentry looked to the monarch to initiate and carry through the reforms which they desired. When the government, as under Nicholas I, gave no sign of following this policy, they became aware of their impotence, of their status as 'superfluous men'. When the new breed of revolutionary activists arose in the middle of the nineteenth century, it too regarded the liberal-minded gentry as ineffective, 'superfluous'.

In 1825 the liberal-minded gentry made an unsuccessful attempt to secure constitutional and social changes by revolt. The Decembrist rising, which occurred in December 1825, was basically an upper-class or gentry revolt. Although it was the death of Alexander I and the ensuing confusion in regard to the succession to the throne that provided the immediate occasion for the outbreak of the rising, the actual revolt was the culmination of some years of conspiracy, stimulated by the failure of

1 *My Past and Thoughts*, IV, p. 1576. *SS*, XIV, p. 318. From an article in *The Bell* for October, 1860.
2 *Ibid.*, p. 1577. *SS*, XIV, p. 320.

the well-intentioned but vacillating Alexander I to realize plans for reform proposed, for example, by Michael Speransky. The Emperor was not blind to the need for change, but he entirely lacked Peter the Great's determination to do what he believed desirable in spite of opposition. The Decembrist conspirators were spurred on by a sense of frustration, and the death of Alexander, coupled with the prospect of the accession of Nicholas to the throne, provided them with an opportunity. When the Grand Duke Constantine, Nicholas's brother, had married a Polish lady, he renounced his claim to succeed, but the renunciation was not made public. At Alexander's death there was a hope that Constantine would ascend the throne, as it was supposed that he was more liberally inclined than Nicholas. After a confusing interval of three weeks, Constantine at last confirmed in writing his renunciation of all claims to succeed, and the army, which had already taken an oath of loyalty to Constantine, was required to take another oath, this time to the unpopular Nicholas. This state of affairs provided the occasion for the outbreak of the revolt, with Decembrist officers at the head of soldiers who really knew nothing of the conspirators' ideals and plans.

The Decembrist revolt has sometimes been represented as a last attempt by the nobility to regain the position which it had lost with the establishment of the autocracy and the bureaucratic state. Indeed, Pushkin, who had friends among the conspirators, saw the revolt in this light, namely as a continuation and concluding phase of the struggle of the old nobility against the monarchy's concentration of all political favour in its own hands. Though, however, some of the Decembrists did in fact envisage a monarch whose favours would be limited by the rights of the aristocracy, it would be an injustice to the Decembrists as a whole to depict them as concerned simply with the interests of the class to which most of the leading figures belonged. They were by no means all of one mind in regard to the political and social structures which they considered desirable, but in general they were opposed to the autocracy and wanted a state ruled by law in accordance with the ideals of the Enlightenment. They also demanded the abolition of serfdom.

For various reasons the original loose association, the Union of Welfare, had split into two main groups of conspirators, the Northern and Southern Societies. The former was inclined to leave the drawing up of a constitution to an assembly which would be convened after a successful revolt, whereas the latter inclined to the view that the constitutional question should be settled in advance. Draft constitutions were, however, proposed by members of both groups. Nikita Muraviev of the Northern Society prepared a draft constitution which retained the monarch as a figurehead, legislative power being vested in a two-house assembly. Although serfdom was to be abolished, the draft clearly favoured the gentry and the richer citizens. In other words, the suffrage would be restricted. The draft prepared by Colonel Pavel Pestel of the Southern Society was more radical, envisaging the establishment of a republic and fairly drastic land reform. Pestel even envisaged the possibility of assassinating the whole imperial family, although after the revolt he claimed that he had not seriously intended to carry out this proposal. The actual Decembrist revolt represented both societies, and the five leaders who were hanged came from both groups.

The speedy crushing of this extremely badly prepared revolt, followed by the execution or exile to Siberia of the leaders and by inauguration of the repressive régime of Nicholas I (reigned 1825–55), naturally dampened hopes of any radical reform and discouraged subversive action. It is not surprising, therefore, that liberal-minded members of the gentry tended to take refuge in discussing theoretical and philosophical problems. In the first chapter attention was drawn to the interest shown in German philosophy and the fascination exercised on some minds by the thought of Hegel. It was Hegelianism which provided certain Russian thinkers with the means for making a virtue out of necessity.

2. In *The Philosophy of Right* Hegel asserts that 'I am at home in the world when I know it, still more so when I have understood it'.[1] Hegel did not in fact canonize any actual state. Just as no individual human being embodies in himself or herself all possible human perfections, so no actual political society completely exemplifies the concept of the rational state. To be sure, some states provide more grounds for criticism than others, but improvement is always possible. Activity directed to improving social and political conditions is not, however, the philosopher's job. The task of the philosopher is to show how the idea of the rational state is progressively exemplified in human history, and thus to illustrate the onward march of Reason. If a man understood the rational process at work in history, a process lying at the heart of all contingent events, he would be at home in his world, reconciled with it, instead of being in a state of revolt against reality.

Stankevich's philosophical circle at Moscow had included among its members Vissarion Belinsky, who in his short life (1811–48) became a very influential literary critic, and Michael Bakunin (1814–76), who was

1 *Werke* (Works), edited by H. G. Glockner, VII, parag. 142 (additions). In the preface to *The Philosophy of Right* Hegel speaks of recognizing reason as the rose in the cross of the present, a recognition which reconciles us with the actual.

to become an anarchist leader and an inspiration to revolutionaries. At the end of the 1830s both men, under the influence of Hegel, proclaimed their reconciliation with reality. In both cases the reconciliation was short-lived, but while it lasted, the thought of Hegel enabled them to make a virtue out of necessity in the sense that it provided them with a way of converting a sense of isolation (from the régime on the one hand and the people on the other) and of practical ineffectiveness into a positive acceptance of the self-manifestation of Reason in the actual, including Russian actuality. Indeed, as the march of Reason through history was represented by Hegel as the operation of divine Providence, acceptance of reality could be seen as a religious duty, as acceptance of the divine will.

Belinsky, unlike Bakunin and Herzen, did not belong to the nobility. He was the son of a provincial doctor. At the University of Moscow he was attracted by writers of the romantic movement, such as Schiller and Schelling, but his studies were interrupted as a consequence of his having written a play in which he attacked serfdom.[1] Belinsky then came under the influence of Fichte, in whose thought he found a justification for the idea of a moral vocation fulfilling itself in action. Heroic action in the service of a moral ideal seemed, however, to be impracticable in the circumstances of the time, and Hegel's identification of the real and the rational appeared to provide a solution for Belinsky's problem.

The most striking expression of Belinsky's reconciliation with reality is to be found in his essay (1839) about the Russian Nation and the Russian Tsar. It makes rather odd reading, especially if we remember that the monarch at the time was Nicholas I. The reader is told that the Tsar's authority (not simply that of Nicholas I, of course) has always been 'mysteriously fused with the will of Providence, with rational reality',[2] and that the Russian rulers had always divined and brought to the light of consciousness the needs of the state. Hence Russians should submit to the monarch's will 'as to the Will of Providence itself'.[3] The life of every nation is 'a rationally necessary form of the universal idea',[4] and the principle of Russia's life can be expressed in the one word 'Tsar'.[5] It is the sovereign who embodies in himself

1 The reasons actually given for the termination of his studies at the university were bad health and mediocre talent. But it is clear that the real reason was the disapproval shown by the university censors to the text of his play.
2 *Polnoe sobranie sochinenii* (Complete Works), III, p. 247 (Moscow, 1953).
3 *Ibid.*
4 *Ibid.*
5 *Ibid.*, p. 248.

'our freedom'.[1] In the same year Belinsky wrote about the individual and society that society is a higher reality than the individual, and that reality demands full reconciliation.[2]

Belinsky's enthusiasm for reconciliation soon waned. He was not the man to be satisfied for long with what he believed to be Hegel's exaltation of the universal at the expense of the particular. Nor was Russian reality of such a kind that he could remain reconciled with it.[3] As soon as 1841 he was writing to V. P. Botkin that it was better to die than to be reconciled with the conclusions derivable from Hegel's philosophy, and the attitude expressed in his famous *Letter to Gogol* (1847) is well known. In his *Selected Passages from a Correspondence with Friends* Nikolai Gogol had proclaimed his acceptance of the actual social order and of Orthodoxy. This astonished and infuriated Belinsky, who had thought of the novelist, not without reason of course, as a critic of Russian society, and he proceeded to attack not only Gogol himself but also the Russian régime and the Russian Orthodox Church.

Michael Bakunin was of aristocratic origin, a landowner's son. After studying as a military cadet at St Petersburg, he was commissioned as an officer. Abandoning the army for philosophy, he came to Hegel by way of Fichte and, like his friend Belinsky, embraced reconciliation with reality. Thus in his *Foreword to Hegel's School Addresses* (1838) he demanded total reconciliation with reality in the spirit, as he put it, of Hegel and Goethe. At the time Bakunin was a passionate adherent of philosophy, in which he clearly found a substitute for religion, and he considered becoming a professor of philosophy, though it is difficult to imagine him occupying such a position.

In 1840 Bakunin went abroad, consorted with left-wing Hegelians at Berlin and Dresden, and came to the conclusion that what was required was not simply understanding of reality, still less reconciliation with the actual, but action with a view to transforming reality, existing social structures that is to say. At first he continued to use Hegelian concepts, or at any rate Hegelian language. This was natural, as it was left-wing Hegelians, such as Arnold Ruge, who had convinced him that Hegelianism, properly understood, was a philosophy of revolution rather than of reaction or of conservatism. The feature of Hegelianism on which he came to lay emphasis was the concept of negation, the power of the

---

1 *Ibid.*, p. 247.
2 *Ibid.*, p. 341.
3 In Hegelian terms the 'reality' in Russia would be the rational element rather than what we would ordinarily regard as Russian 'actuality.' But reconciliation with reality, as understood by Belinsky, involved seeing the actual as the rational.

negative, though with Bakunin negation meant destruction of the thesis, Hegel's theory of preservation at a higher level tending to be overlooked.

In an essay on 'The Reaction in Germany', which appeared in Ruge's *Deutsche Jahrbücher für Wissenschaft und Kunst* in October 1842, Bakunin represented what he described as the reactionary or conservative party as the given positive moment (the thesis) in a dialectical movement, while the democratic party constituted the negative moment (the antithesis) which was destined to negate and destroy the thesis, only to be itself negated. From this process of destruction a qualitatively new world of real freedom would arise, inasmuch as the eternal Spirit, as Bakunin put it, annihilates only to create fresh life. In a frequently quoted statement he asserted that the passion for destruction is also a creative passion.

Bakunin came to focus his attention on the state as the chief object for destruction. As, however, the state, in his view, could not exist without religion, and as he saw church and state as united in preventing the development of freedom and equality, the church too needed to be negated. Only after the abolition of state and church could the desirable form of social organization be created.

Some observations will be made later about Bakunin's idea of the desirable form of social organization. For the present it is sufficient to note that he moved right away from the Hegelianism which had once cast a spell over his mind. But it was not simply a question of Hegelianism. Bakunin came to mistrust abstract thought in general. The man who had once wanted to become a professor of philosophy, turned instead to action and became an ardent revolutionary, leaving reconciliation with reality far behind.

3. In addition to Stankevich's philosophical circle at Moscow, there was also a small circle centering around Alexander Herzen and his cousin Nikolai Ogarev. Herzen, the illegitimate son of a rich landowner, Ivan Yakovlev, and a young German girl, was a boy of thirteen at the time of the Decembrist revolt, and after the hanging of five leaders he and Ogarev vowed vengeance for the victims. His opposition to the Russian régime thus began in boyhood. In 1829 he entered the University of Moscow to study in the faculty of Natural Science. At this time he and Ogarev were attracted, like Belinsky, by the romanticism of Schiller and the philosophy of Schelling, partly under the influence of M. G. Pavlov, the professor to whom reference was made in the first chapter. In 1834 Herzen's little discussion circle was dissolved as a result of the arrest, first of Ogarev and then of himself. He had written some letters which the

authorities found objectionable. After a period of exile in provincial towns Herzen returned to Moscow, to find Belinsky and Bakunin proclaiming reconciliation with reality. Setting himself to the serious study of Hegel's philosophy, Herzen interpreted it not as a philosophy of reconciliation with reality but, as he later put it, as an 'algebra of revolution'.[1] He was impressed by Hegel's theory of negation and saw the actual as something to be negated, not accepted. He was, of course, justified in seeing in Hegelianism implications other than those drawn by Belinsky and Bakunin at the end of the 1830s. Hegel's thought lends itself to more than one line of interpretation.

When Herzen returned from exile early in 1840, he was subject to the condition of entering government service. In this capacity he was transferred to St Petersburg. He was soon exiled for a second time, on this occasion to Novgorod, and it was there that he read with approval Feuerbach's just published work *The Essence of Christianity*. He also began writing a series of articles on the general theme 'Dilettantism in Science', which he continued on his return to Moscow in 1843. In this context 'science' really meant Hegelianism, and the 'dilettantes' were various groups of professed Hegelians. Those who reflected on the relation between thought and reality, expounded a formal system and preached reconciliation with reality were named 'the Buddhists.' According to Herzen, 'the Buddhists' tried to become universal thought, discarding their own individual personalities and playing the role of spectators of history instead of being actors, agents, within history.

Real reconciliation with reality, Herzen insisted, could be achieved only through action, that is to say, by changing reality to accord with one's ideals. If we succeed in changing the social world so that it embodies our ideals, we then become reconciled with reality, our own creation. Simply to accept the actual, on the ground that it represents the rational, even though it is clearly repugnant to our moral sense, is to adopt the attitude of a morally irresponsible spectator of history.

In his *Letters on the Study of Nature* (1845–6) Herzen rejected the idea of a philosophy which proceeded in a purely *a priori* manner, with scant regard for the empirical sciences and genuine positive knowledge of how things actually are. At the same time he insisted on the need for philosophy, by which he meant reflection on the human being as a free, morally responsible agent, striving to actualize what ought to be but does not yet exist. In other words, as science tells us how things are and not how things ought to be, its development has not rendered philosophy

1 *My Past and Thoughts*, II, p. 403. *SS*, IX, p. 23.

superfluous. It is not a question of philosophy providing us with knowledge of a higher level of existing reality than that accessible to any empirical science. It is a question of the philosopher treating the human being as a free moral agent in a social context.

We can say that Herzen moved from Schelling to Hegel, from Hegel to Feuerbach, and then nearer to a positivist position. But his belief in the importance of trying to realize social goals through concerted action never left him. Further, he saw that calls to realize social goals through action, in the name of ethical ideals, presupposed belief in freedom. On the theoretical level, therefore, he was faced with the problem of reconciling the belief in freedom, which he regarded as presupposed by activity directed to the realization of social ideals, with the positivist tendency to look on belief in human freedom as an illusion, incompatible with natural science. When he left Russia in 1847, never to return, a great deal of his time and energy was devoted to journalism and social and political propaganda. But though he moved further away from philosophy, he was conscious of and reflected on the problem mentioned. His line of thought will be indicated later in this chapter.

When Herzen returned to Moscow after his first exile and found Belinsky and Bakunin proclaiming their reconciliation with reality, he had rejected their attitude and interpreted Hegel in a different way. But Belinsky and Bakunin also very soon abandoned reconciliation with reality for themselves. Belinsky rejected Hegelianism in the name of the free individual and as attempting to justify what could not be justified. Bakunin, for a time, laid stress on Hegel's theory of negation, seeing as Herzen did, a revolutionary aspect in Hegel's thought. All three men, however, came to jettison the idea of an infinite divine Spirit which does the destroying and the creating. Partly under the influence of Feuerbach and partly driven on by their own desire for action, they soon came to regard the human being, and not the Absolute, as the agent in history. In their substitution of man for the Absolute, the divine Spirit, we can see them as moving from Hegel to Feuerbach. But in formulating their social ideas they were influenced by French Socialist theory. As some historians have put it, left-wing Hegelianism represented thought, while French Socialist theory represented action. The context, however, and the field of application were provided largely by Russian problems, though in various degrees. Bakunin was to become what might be described as an international anarchist, eager to participate in revolutionary movements wherever they might occur, whereas Herzen became a proponent of 'Russian socialism'.

4. It was stated above that Belinsky rejected the Hegelianism which he

once accepted. This is true if we understood Hegelianism as meaning Hegel's metaphysics of the Absolute and a view of the rationality of historical development which would justify, as Belinsky put it in a letter, the sacrifice of 'all the victims of life and history'.[1] At the same time Belinsky retained some Hegelian ideas and ways of thought. He was not prepared to jump from the Hegelian philosophy of history into the claim that history is an irrational and meaningless process, but maintained that a dialectical movement is discernible. In an essay on Peter the Great (1891) he maintained that both individuals and nations pass through three phases: the phase of immediacy; that of consciousness and reflection; and that of rational reality, the unity or reconciliation of the two previous phases.

Belinsky found this dialectical scheme exemplified in Russia. Thus Russia before Peter the Great was Russia in a state of immediacy. His description of this state, emphasizing the unity of faith and custom, of tradition, was akin to the Slavophile picture of ancient Russia. But whereas the Slavophiles tended to extol pre-Petrine Russia at the expense of Russia after Peter, Belinsky regarded the transition to Petrine Russia as an inevitable advance. To remain in the state of immediacy would be to stagnate. Growing up, so to speak, involves advance to the phase of reflective consciousness. Before Peter the Great, Belinsky agreed, Russia was simply a people (*narod*), whereas Peter changed her into a nation. In his evaluation of the role of the Emperor, Belinsky was clearly a Westernizer. In his view Russia, to avoid the living death of stagnation, had to enter the community of European nations, absorbing western values and culture.

It does not follow that Belinsky regarded Petrine Russia as the highest stage of growth, in the sense that all that was needed was the continuation and intensification of the opening to the West, as though reception of western values and culture was enough by itself. For one thing, the Slavophiles were right in claiming that the effect of Peter the Great's opening to the West was to divide Russia into a small Europeanized élite on the one hand and the vast bulk of the population on the other. But the Slavophiles failed to see that this was an inevitable phenomenon, if progress was to be maintained. The social division and the pangs of conscience this caused in liberal-minded gentry and 'superfluous men' were analogous to the torments of reflection in the individual when passing into adulthood. What was needed was the synthesis of immediacy and reflective consciousness. The universal values received

1 *Works* (see Note 5), XII, p. 22.

from the West had to become truly national possessions, not simply abstract ideas to be discussed but genuinely national values; and the gulf between 'society' and the people had to be overcome by raising the latter to the level of the former. In other words, a new explicit national consciousness had to take the place of the old instinctive feeling of *narodnost*, immediacy being recovered on a higher level, the level of 'rational reality.'

In the political sphere Belinsky saw the successful war against Napoleon as contributing powerfully to the creation of this new national consciousness. As a literary critic, he saw in Pushkin the first outstanding poet of Russia in whose work universal and national elements were fused. The universal elements came from western Europe, and Belinsky, to the disgust of the Slavophiles, continued to insist that great literature, though national, must also be of universal significance, thus uniting universality and particularity.

One of the factors which turned Belinsky away from Hegel was his aversion to what he regarded as the philosopher's emphasis on the universal at the expense of the individual human being. Belinsky protested in the name of the value of the individual and of his or her emancipation. His use of Hegelian language in the theory of Russian history just outlined should not be understood as implying that he had forgotten about the individual. In his *Letter to Gogol* he insisted that what Russia needed was not mysticism or asceticism, not sermons or prayers, but civilization, education, humanitarian values and an awakening of the sense of human dignity.[1] Nor should Belinsky's ardent praise of Peter the Great be understood as meaning that he desired the continuation of the autocracy. Peter's revolution from above was one thing, the régime of Nicholas I quite another. 'The gloom of autocracy' was a phase used in the *Letter to Gogol*.

Though 'Furious Vissarion,' as Belinsky was nicknamed, was given to exaggerated statements and highly coloured, impassioned language, he was more a champion of bourgeois democracy than of proletarian revolution. To be sure, a visit abroad in 1847 helped to bring home to him the sufferings of the proletariat at the hands of capitalists, but he refused to accept the view of those who condemned the middle class wholesale. Nor did he share Bakunin's hope that Russia would be preserved from industrialization and from the growth of a bourgeoisie. On the contrary, while admitting that capitalism had caused great suffering, he saw in the middle class, apart from oppressive capitalists, an organ of progress.

1 For the *Letter to Gogol* see vol. X of the *Works*.

What were Belinsky's criteria of progress? This is a question of some importance. For even if history passes through the phases mentioned by Belinsky, it does not necessarily follow that the dialectic exemplifies advance in an evaluative, as distinct from a purely temporal sense. The answer is, I suppose, that the criteria were settled by Belinsky's own values and moral ideals. We shall have to return to this theme later in connection, for example, with the thought of Peter Lavrov, who reflected explicitly on the subject.

5. Emphasis has often been laid on Bakunin's passion for destruction. This emphasis is understandable. Bakunin was an extremist. For example, he did not demand that existing states, Russian or otherwise, should be improved; he demanded the abolition of the state. It was his conviction that the state was an institution which should be negated, negation meaning destruction by revolutionary action, not merely a conceptual negation. The conceptual negation had to express itself in action. Again, his own active participation in revolutionary movements which had no immediate success gives the impression of a man who was primarily concerned with overthrowing the existing order than with positive construction.

At the same time we have to remember two things. The first is that Bakunin was passionately concerned with human freedom. He dreamed of the abolition of all authority exercised by man over man, not only the authority exercised by state or church but also, for example, that exercised by a revolutionary élite over the masses. It is doubtless true that the differences between himself and Karl Marx, which led to his expulsion from the First International in 1872, were partly personal, in the sense that it was largely a question of who was to be at the head of the revolutionary movement of the working class. But Bakunin also saw the dictatorial tendency in Communism and understood that in the event of a successful revolution a minority would be likely to capture the state apparatus and use state power to transform society from above. It was Bakunin's conviction that the transformation of society should develop from below, rather than be imposed from above. To be sure, there was certainly a Jacobin and authoritarian side to his character, but he was nonetheless opposed to dictatorship in any form.

The second point to be remembered is that Bakunin did not desire destruction simply for destruction's sake. He believed that only after the abolition of state and church could the desirable form of social organization be created, namely a free association of workers, first in separate associations, ultimately in one international federation. In arriving at this idea of the desirable form of society Bakunin was influenced by French radical thought, especially that of Proudhon. Whereas, however, Proudhon wanted peasants and artisans to own land and tools respectively, Bakunin envisaged common ownership of all the means of production. It is difficult to imagine workers and peasants freely organizing syndicates of this kind on a wide scale, even given the persuasive powers of anarchist leaders. What is much more likely is that the anarchist leaders, if they had the opportunity, would have to use coercion, recreating a version of the abolished state. But this was a problem to which Bakunin offered no satisfactory solution.

Another problem which Bakunin failed to solve was this. On the one hand he claimed not to condemn individuals or to want to make war on them. The attitude of a member of the bourgeoisie, for example, was determined by his upbringing and by class mentality; there was no point in denouncing him for possessing this mentality. On the other hand (apart from the fact that Bakunin himself came from a noble family) he did his best to promote violent revolution, and violent revolution would obviously be accompanied by shedding of the blood of individuals, not of institutions.

Bakunin was no armchair theorist of revolution. As was mentioned above, he left Russia for Berlin in 1840. In 1848–9 he participated in revolutionary movements in Paris, Prague and Dresden; in 1870 he took part in a revolt at Lyons; and in 1874 he acted in a similar manner at Bologna. Wherever revolution seemed imminent, Bakunin was there, ready to fight on the barricades. Moreover, he suffered for his activities. After the Dresden revolt he was captured by the authorities and condemned to death. Eventually he was handed over by the Austrians to the Russian government, which promptly consigned him to the Peter and Paul fortress at St Petersburg. After six years of imprisonment he was exiled to Siberia in 1857. Escaping in 1861, he journeyed by way of Japan and the United States to England and thence to the continent of Europe to resume his revolutionary activities.

It is understandable that, among Russian radicals, Bakunin became a heroic legendary figure. His emphasis on destruction, on clearing the ground, appealed to the Nihilists who regarded overthrow of the régime as the primary task and were content to leave plans for positive construction to their future successors. His theory of revolution from below, with its reference to such events as the popular revolts of Stenka Razin (1670–1) and of Pugachev (1773–4) appealed to those Populists who had the unrealistic idea that the peasants were ready to rise in rebellion for political ends. Although he was a dynamic personality and a tireless revolutionary activist, as a thinker he was greatly inferior to Karl Marx, whom he considered far too much of a theorist.[1] In the celebrated *Confession* which Bakunin addressed to the Emperor Nicholas I, a document which has constituted something of an embarrassment for his admirers, he referred to his need to be constantly active, constantly in movement, and to his hankering after an adventurous life.[2] This self-assessment was doubtless substantially correct. Bakunin's move from theory to practice, from philosophy to revolutionary action, manifested his character. So did the enthusiasm which he brought to each in turn.

Bakunin is numbered among the Westernizers. He certainly was a Westernizer at the time when he was studying philosophy at Moscow, and he remained a Westernizer in the sense that he was never a Slavophile. But he was no admirer of existing western society, and the adjective 'internationalist' seems to be more appropriate than 'Westernizer,' as far as his life outside Russia is concerned. One of his reasons for fulminating against the state was that it divides the citizens of one country from those of another. It is therefore anti-human, irreconcilable with a universalistic ideal. Socialism, of course, could be universalistic, as it was with Marx and Engels. But socialism, like the state, could be dictatorial and incompatible with human freedom. For Bakunin, socialism without freedom was equivalent to slavery. His ideal, however utopian, was that of a free federation of individuals, associations, nations, without the state in any form.

An attempt to combine anarchism with communism was made by Prince Peter Kropotkin (1842–1921). Kropotkin was more of a theorist than Bakunin was, even if some of his ideas seem rather fantastic. Although Kropotkin admitted that some violent action would be inevitable, if there was to be a revolution at all, he hoped that it would be kept to a minimum. He disliked the thought of bloodshed and was out of sympathy with terrorist methods. In 1917 he left England, where he had been living in exile and returned to Russia. The new authoritarianism, however, was not to his taste.

1 Bakunin admired Marx, especially as an economist. He translated the *Communist Manifesto* into Russian and proposed, though failed, to translate *Capital* too. But he came to regard Marx as doctrinaire and as having authoritarian ideas. We can add that by imprudently giving some assistance to Sergei Nechaev (1847–82), the author of the *Revolutionary Catechism* and a fanatic who turned out to be a murderer, Bakunin caused embarrassment not only to himself but also to the First International, which he had involved in the matter without authorization.

2 After the Decembrist revolt Nicholas I personally questioned the leaders about their motives and seemed to be genuinely interested, though this did not prevent the hanging of five of them. The Emperor was doubtless also genuinely interested in reading Bakunin's account of his ideas and his activities outside Russia, though this did not procure Bakunin's release. It was Alexander II who permitted him to go into exile in Siberia.

6. In 1846 Alexander Herzen came into the possession of a considerable sum of money on his father's death. In the following year he left Russia. When he refused to return to Russia at imperial command, the Russian government tried to hold on to the money. However, Herzen succeeded in obtaining a substantial amount of it through the mediation of Baron James Rothschild. He was thus able to help other exiles and to carry on journalistic and propagandistic publication.

Though abroad, Herzen none the less exercised a great influence in his own country through the journals which he edited, in particular *The Bell* (*Kolokol*), which he started in 1852 as a successor to *The Polar Star*. His writings, with their forthright denunciations of the Tsarist régime, were smuggled into Russia and eagerly read. When Alexander II ascended the throne on the death of Nicholas I in 1855, Herzen was prepared to give the new monarch a chance, so to speak, and welcomed the plans for reform. But after the emancipation of the serfs in 1861, the terms of which were certainly not favourable to the peasants, he resumed his attacks.[1] He was convinced that real freedom was not possible in Russia as long as the autocracy remained.[2]

It might be expected that Herzen, as a Westernizer, would be attracted either by western liberal democratic ideals or by some form of French socialist theory. Either position would be consistent with his opposition to the Russian autocracy and, in particular, to the repressive régime of Nicholas I. In exile, however, Herzen became disillusioned with western society, especially after the failure of the revolutionary movements of 1848, which profoundly affected his mind. He clearly had an aristocratic and aesthetic distaste for the 'petty bourgeoisie,' particularly of France, but, more importantly, he came to think of bourgeois democracy as marked by the proclamation of noble ideals which were not realized in concrete life. Exploitation of the workers manifested the hollowness of fine-sounding slogans. As for western socialist theories, they were only

1 The emancipation decree of 1861 was intended to be, and indeed was, a major reform. It was not designed to trick the peasants. But many serfs expected more than they got. The land which they received was in many cases insufficient or of poor quality, and they were involved in making redemption payments to landowners, which it was difficult, or impossible for them to do out of their incomes. The former serfs of landowners tended to be worse off, more burdened with debts, than the liberated state serfs. At the same time some landowners were badly hit by the emancipation. In other words, there was a compromise which did not fully satisfy any of the parties involved.

2 Alexander II, the 'Tsar-Liberator,' undoubtedly desired reforms, but he was cautious and conservative in outlook, and disturbance and terrorist acts, such as Karakozov's attempt on the Emperor's life in 1866, did not encourage an adventurous policy on the government's part. Ironically, when Alexander II was assassinated in 1881, he had just signed a plan, drawn up by Count Michael Loris-Melikov, to initiate some mild measures of political reform. The plan was at once abandoned by his successor, Alexander III.

too likely, if put into practice, to lead to a new form of despotism, the thought of which was abhorrent to Herzen as a lifelong champion of Liberty. If he did not desire for Russia capitalism as he observed it in England and France, neither did he desire for his country the socialism of Karl Marx or of other theorists who were sure that they knew the right path and were prepared to dragoon others into following that path. Besides, Marx envisaged socialism as presupposing capitalism.[1]

Herzen came, therefore, to look for something in Russia which could form the basis for a 'Russian socialism,' and he found it in the village commune (the *obschina*) and in the free associations, the 'artels', of the artisans. If the spirit of cooperation manifested in these institutions were to be extended and cover the whole nation, Russia could develop a socialism of her own, a predominantly agrarian socialism, thus escaping the evils of capitalist exploitation. Inspired by the spirit of community, she could then provide a light in the darkness for other nations.

This emphasis on the village commune brought Herzen closer to the Slavophiles, though he was far from sharing their idealization of pre-Petrine Russia. His disillusionment with the West even led him to speak on occasion in a manner which might be taken to suggest Panslavist ideas. For example, in a letter to J. Michelet, which was published in 1851, Herzen wrote that 'once grasped and bound together in a league of free, autonomous peoples the Slav world will at last be able to enter upon its genuine historical existence. Its past can be regarded only as a period of preparation, of growth, of purgation.'[2] But he was careful to add that 'the imperial Panslavism, as it has been extolled until today by men who have been suborned or who have lost their bearings has, of course, nothing in common with any union based on the principles of liberty'.[3] What Herzen had in mind was Russia's treatment of the Polish nation. What he wanted was not unification of and domination over the Slav peoples by Russia, not an extension of the Russian empire, but a free association of the Slav peoples, embodying what he described as 'the communism of the peasants'.[4]

It is understandable that in a desire to spare Russia a phase of capitalist exploitation Herzen should lay emphasis on associations such as the village commune and the artels of the artisans. In his post-1848 dis-illusionment he believed that the forces of reaction had triumphed in

1 Later on Marx showed himself prepared to consider the possibility of Russia following a path of her own. But we need not discuss this theme here.
2 *My Past and Thoughts*, IV, p. 1655. *SS*, VII, p. 280.
3 *Ibid.*, p. 1656. *Ibid.*, p. 281.
4 *Ibid.*, p. 1668. *Ibid.*, p. 294.

western Europe, that the West was finished, its vigour exhausted, and
that the British parliament was an instrument for defending the rights of
property-owners at the expense of the underprivileged. He had come to
the conclusion that the salvation of Russia could not be expected from
western Europe. It is all very well to suggest that Herzen, living abroad,
could have recognized the claims of western democracy to be a viable
alternative to the Russian régime. This is a natural point of view to adopt
by one who looks back with knowledge of the later effective pressure of
labour movements on governments, of the growth of social legislation
and of parliaments in which social democrats have been the predominant
party. In the earlier years of Herzen's sojourn in western Europe such
developments lay in the future. What he actually saw engendered in him
the hope that Russia could pursue a path different from that of the West.

In view, however, of the fact that Herzen was impatient with the
utopianism of French socialists, it is natural to accuse him too of proposing a romantic, utopian dream. It was none too clear how the village
commune and the artel of the artisans could form the basis for socialism
in the modern world, and it was unrealistic to suppose that the land-
hungry peasants of Russia would freely embrace any form of agrarian
socialism or 'communism'. Stalin had to use brute force to collectivize
the peasants, at a great cost to Russian agriculture, not to speak of the
ensuing famine. Herzen, of course, had no such methods in mind.

In some important respects, however, Herzen was notably realistic.
For example, he saw that the masses were interested not so much in
personal freedom as in keeping what they had earned by their labour.
'They are indifferent to individual freedom, to freedom of speech; the
masses love authority . . . the masses desire a social government which
will govern them, and not, like the existing one, against them. To govern
themselves – this does not enter their heads.'[1] In this case the transformation of society could never take place except through the agency of
an élite leadership. If goaded beyond a certain point, the masses might
revolt, but insurrection is not the same thing as positively changing social
structures for the better. This requires leaders. But any such élite or group
of leaders would be prone to treat the masses as so much passive material
for the realization of their own ideas. This was likely to happen, according to Herzen, if the élite, instead of being concerned with benefiting
people here and now, actual living men and women, thought in terms of
abstractions, in terms, that is to say, of humanity and the future human

1 *Sobranie sochinenii* (Collected Works), VI, p. 124 (30 vols., Moscow, 1954–65).
This edition is referred to here as *CW*.

being who does not yet exist. Herzen was certainly drawing attention to an important point.

The failure of the revolutionary movements of 1848 in western Europe dealt a final blow to any lingering belief Herzen may have had in inevitable progress. He was to write later that 'you know that I am not a fatalist and do not believe in any predetermination, not even in the famous "perfectability of humanity" ... when I talk of possible development, I am not talking of its unavoidable inevitability ...'[1] Herzen did not believe that the advent of 'Russian socialism' was inevitable. As far as possibility was concerned, the autocracy might continue, or it might be succeeded by capitalist bourgeois democracy, or Marxism might be triumphant. What he was doing was to present the ideal of a socialist society in which freedom would be respected.

In his later years Herzen came to lay emphasis on historical continuity, on the idea that history proceeds at its own pace, so to speak, and that it is foolish to think that society can be transformed simply at will. People's consciousness has first to be changed. That is to say, a radical transformation of society cannot be achieved by a sudden overthrow of the established order, if the mentality and outlook of the great mass of the population remain what they have previously been. Living until 1870, he witnessed the beginning of the working-class movement, and he came to think that western Europe might not be as played out and moribund as he had once imagined. In his campaign against the autocracy he had more sympathy with the radical activists than with the liberal-minded gentry, but he was not attracted by terrorist policies and methods.[2] After Karakozov's unsuccessful attempt on the life of Alexander II, Herzen remarked that in civilized nations politics was not conducted by assassination. In any case, in his later years he ceased to believe 'in the old revolutionary ways',[3] and this change in outlook was accompanied by a less pessimistic view of western Europe.

Herzen's voice, speaking through his writings, was feared by the Russian authorities. But he found himself out of sympathy with the new breed of revolutionaries who emerged in the middle of the nineteenth century, and they tended to look on him as out of touch with the situation in Russia and as belonging to a generation which had had its day. This was, of course, pretty well inevitable in the case of a

1 *My Past and Thoughts*, IV, p. 1569. *SS*, XII, p. 433.
2 Ogarev, Herzen's cousin and friend, tried to promote the turning of the first Land and Freedom movement in Russia into a conspiratorial organization.
3 *CW.*, XX (part 2), p. 586. From Herzen's second 'Letter to an Old Comrade' (1869).

man who had been living in western Europe from 1847.[1] There was, however, a particular factor which did much to diminish Herzen's popularity in Russia, namely his attitude in regard to the Polish uprising of 1863. He strongly supported the Poles in their desire for freedom and independence, whereas in Russia itself the reaction to events in Poland was strongly chauvinistic, even among some radicals, who forgot for a moment their hostility to the tsarist régime and endorsed the suppression of the revolt.

7. Natalia Alexandrovna, whom Herzen had married during his first internal exile, influenced her husband's mind in the direction of religion. It was not long, however, before he discarded religious belief, together with belief in the 'rationality' of history[2] and in absolute values. Human beings create their own morality, their own moral codes; ethical values are relative. Herzen also came to adopt a naturalistic point of view in philosophy, rejecting any dualistic theory of soul and body and emphasizing the part played by heredity, environment and education in determining a person's consciousness and reactions. From the point of view of natural science belief in freedom was, he thought, an illusion.

At the same time Herzen was indubitably a moral idealist. He had strong convictions about the value of the individual person and a hatred of oppression in any form, whether coming from the right or from the left. Further, in spite of his belief that science favoured determinism he was convinced that human beings could and should refashion their social environment and that, to the extent in which this was possible, human beings should take their destiny into their own hands. His constant call to fight against oppression and to work actively to create a better social world obviously presupposed a belief in man's ability to rise above his environment, to judge it, and to make deliberate choices directed to changing it.

Herzen was too occupied with his journalistic work and with a variety of interests to work out a developed theory which would bring together in one consistent whole the two aspects of his thought. But he did at any rate indicate lines on which a synthesis could, in his opinion, be constructed. Let us first consider the question of freedom.

1 Russian visitors abroad, including some who were by no means of a revolutionary disposition, frequently made a point of calling on Herzen and discussing problems with him. There was a kind of pilgrimage.

2 That is to say, Herzen did not believe that history was a teleological process, moving inevitably towards attainment of a predetermined goal or end. He did not, of course, regard history as 'irrational,' in a sense which would exclude historical explanation as practised by historians.

It can hardly be denied that there is a tendency in Herzen's thought to regard determinism as the objective truth and belief in freedom as simply a psychological need or, rather, necessity, as an unavoidable illusion that is to say. 'Moral freedom,' he asserts, 'is a psychological reality or, if you like, an anthropological reality.'[1] It is 'a phenomenological necessity of human intelligence'.[2] Herzen's respect for natural science, combined with his conviction that the approach of the natural scientist involves treating human actions as causally determined effects, inclined him to regard belief in freedom as an assumption made by the human agent, an assumption which could not be avoided but the truth of which could not be proved.

At the same time Herzen's moral and social idealism obviously inclined him to regard freedom of choice as a reality. Following this inclination, he tended to maintain that freedom belongs to the concept of the human being *as a whole*, whereas determinism is postulated by the natural scientist who looks at the human being from a limited or restricted point of view, as constituting the subject-matter of physiology. The human being is more than an object of scientific investigation by the physiologist. The human being is capable of consciousness and of reflection, and it is on the level of reflective awareness that moral independence appears. 'The moral independence of man is just as much an indisputable truth and reality as his dependence on his milieu, with this difference — that one is in inverse relation to the other.'[3] That is to say, the greater the awareness, the greater is the independence, whereas the weaker the awareness, the more does the influence of environment prevail. There has developed in the human being the capacity to weigh possibilities and to decide what action or actions are to be performed. It is the human being considered under this aspect who constitutes the subject-matter of sociology, as distinct from physiology. 'For sociology man is a moral being, that is to say a social being who is free to determine his acts within the limits of his consciousness and intelligence.'[4] And it is in this light that man's activity in history should be seen. 'Sociology will snatch man from the anatomical theatre and return him to history.'[5]

If we are prepared to allow, for the sake of argument at any rate, that sociology does treat the human being as free, Herzen seems to be faced with two alternatives. On the one hand he might claim that physical

1 CW., XX (part 1), p. 438.
2 *Ibid.*
3 *Ibid.*, VI, p. 120.
4 *Ibid.*, XX (part 1), p. 435.
5 *Ibid.*, p. 435.

science postulates determinism, and that this is the objective truth. He should then maintain that sociology adopts an 'as if' procedure, regarding human beings in the light of their subjective feeling of freedom but not asserting that determinism is false. On the other hand Herzen might claim that the human being is indeed free, that belief in freedom is not an illusion, and that in sociology human beings are conceived in this way. He should then modify what he says about physiology or natural science, by, for example, attributing to it a purely methodological, not a dogmatic, determinism. The trouble is that Herzen does not make his position sufficiently clear. His mind is drawn in two directions. In the opinion of the present writer, it was belief in freedom which tended to prevail. In his *Letter to My Son* Herzen wrote that, in his judgment, recognition of oneself as a conscious agent is not an hallucination, and that the sense of freedom is not an illusion. But though this may very well be what Herzen really believed and wanted to maintain, the theoretical basis remains insufficiently clarified and developed.

The distinction, mentioned above, between the respective points of view of the physiologist and the sociologist will be encountered again in the thought of Peter Lavrov. Lavrov considered the matter more at length, though it is questionable whether he really carried it much further than Herzen had done, in regard to solving the relevant problem that is to say.

As for ethics, although Herzen asserts that 'there is no eternally stable morality',[1] he none the less admits that there are some perenially valid moral principles. In making this admission, however, he is thinking of very general statements, insufficient to provide solutions for concrete moral issues. For example, it is doubtless always true that one should not act in a manner contrary to one's moral convictions, but this does not tell us what moral convictions one should have. Again, Herzen refers to Kant's claim that we can assess the moral quality of our action by asking whether we are able, without contradiction, to universalize as a law the subjective maxim implied by the action. Even if this is true, Herzen comments (and he is not the only person to have done so), Kant's principle is formal, devoid of concrete content. To be sure, Herzen is not altogether fair to Kant, who was perfectly well aware that he was giving a test for assessing maxims relating to conduct and that to state a test is not the same thing as to apply it. But it is clear that Herzen makes a distinction between very general principles which are always valid precisely because of their extreme generality and concrete judgments about

1 CW, VI, p. 131.

what actions are right and what are wrong. In his view, the former can be described as stable, whereas the latter are subject to change. It is hardly necessary to say that the matter needs more prolonged consideration than Herzen gave to it.

On the subject of the relation between egoism and altruism, Herzen very sensibly remarks that the concepts stand in need of careful analysis. Moralists are accustomed to 'talk of egoism as of a bad habit',[1] but how can a human being be himself or herself without egoism of any kind? 'The simple fact is that egoism and social consciousness are not virtues or vices. They are the basic elements of human life, without which there would be neither history nor development.'[2] If man lacked any social sense, he would be like a wild beast. If he lacked all egoism, any sense of his value, he would be like a slave or a tame monkey. The fight for independence, for recognition of human rights, presupposes both egoism and a social sense, and the moral task is to unite these basic elements in one harmonious whole, rather than to demand the extirpation of egoism or to exalt it to the exclusion of altruism.

Obviously, Herzen's reflections on themes such as freedom, morality, egoism and altruism, express his reactions to current philosophical lines of thought, such as positivism, ethical relativism and utilitarianism. Though, however, he did reflect to some extent on the presuppositions of his campaign against oppression and on behalf of freedom, he left prolonged philosophical discussion of the relevant issues to others. He was a man of great gifts as a writer, but he used these gifts in the service of a cause, that of human emancipation as he understood it, primarily, though by no means exclusively, in relation to his own country. He respected philosophy; he did not believe that it could ever be supplanted by empirical science;[3] but he had no desire to lose himself in mental abstractions. 'Action,' he said in an early essay, 'is the personality itself,'[4] and we can reasonably claim that he employed his writing as a species of action, at any rate as a stimulus to action. As we have seen, reconciliation with reality, in his opinion, could be achieved only through action, through transforming social reality in accordance with ideals.

Herzen was no saint; nor was he a great philosopher. For the matter of that, though his idea of 'Russian socialism' exercised a powerful influence, whether directly or indirectly, on the Populist movement in Russia,

1 *Ibid.*, p. 129.
2 *Ibid.*, p. 130.
3 According to Herzen, the conscious ego cannot act without assuming itself to be free. 'Without this belief, individuality is dissolved and lost' (*CW.*, XX, Part 1, p. 436). Philosophy conceives the human being as a free, moral agent.
4 *CW.*, III, p. 69.

this movement, having reached its zenith in the 1860s and 1870s, had to give way before the rise and eventual triumph of Russian Social Democracy, that is to say, Marxism. In this sense Herzen's campaigning was a failure, though he did, of course, contribute in a notable way to confirming, strengthening and making articulate the alienation of the Russian intellectuals from the tsarist régime. Although, however, when we look back on Herzen's activity in the light of our knowledge of subsequent history, we naturally tend to see him as propagating a utopian dream, he remains one of the most attractive figures among the Russian radical thinkers.

He was a cultured and humane man, neither a brilliant fanatic such as Bakunin nor a narrow, grim and embittered person such as Dobrolyubov. He genuinely sought his country's good, and if he became a resolute foe of the régime, this was largely because he had come to the conclusion that it was useless to expect radical and effective reform from above. His dislike of tsarist authoritarianism, however, was one manifestation (the more directly relevant one in the historical circumstances) of a dislike of authoritarianism in any form. The man who said of himself that, from his thirteenth year, he had been an enemy of every kind of oppression mistrusted those revolutionary activists in whom he discerned dictatorial inclinations. With Herzen it was not a question of overthrowing one repressive régime in order to impose another and different one. He fought oppression in the name of human freedom. And the freedom which he sought was the freedom of actual men and women, not freedom simply as an abstract ideal, something to be attained by Humanity at the expense of people living here and now. Obviously, he was aware, or became more reflectively aware, that real recognition of the value of the human person and of human rights is not something which can be attained simply by a stroke of the pen, nor even by the overthrow of a régime. To get rid of an obstacle to such recognition is not the same thing as to develop the required outlook and moral standards. Herzen saw, however, that this development would be arrested if a new obstacle, a new form of oppression, were created. His idea of 'Russian socialism' may be primarily a matter of historical interest, but his resolute opposition to all forms of oppression is of lasting significance. Being no believer in historical inevitability, he did not think that the overthrow of the autocracy would necessarily be followed by the imposition of a new dogmatism, with its own 'New Commandments'.[1] But he certainly feared this development, and, as things turned out, not without reason.

1 *Ibid.*, V, p. 216.

We cannot call Herzen a liberal, if we understand the term as referring to someone who looked for reform only from above, the sense given to the term by, for example, the novelist Turgenev. But he was certainly a liberal in the sense that, for him, genuine human freedom was incompatible with the imposition of any ideology by a self-constituted authority.

Chapter 5

The New Men

1. Nikolai Kirsanov, the kindly, highly educated, courteous and liberal-minded landowner in Ivan Turgenev's novel *Fathers and Sons* can be seen as a fictional example of the 'superfluous men', who were aware of their ineffectiveness, their inability to change the existing situation in Russia. According to Herzen, the place of these 'superfluous men' was taken first by 'the jaundiced and exasperated'[1] and then by 'men of quite a different stamp, with untried powers and stalwart muscles, appearing from remote universities, from the sturdy Ukraine, from the sturdy north-east'.[2]

However this may be, in the middle decades of the nineteenth century there arose a 'new breed', consisting, for the most part, of people who came not from aristocratic families, as Herzen and Bakunin (but not Belinsky) had come, but from those of priests, doctors, merchants, and petty officials in government service. These people formed the Russian intelligentsia. To be sure, a number of the leading thinkers of the intelligentsia continued to come from the gentry class, but some prominent radical theorists and the bulk of the intelligentsia represented the rising middle class. Having succeeded in entering universities, they then joined the ranks of the radicals. The intelligentsia was separated by its education from the great mass of the population, but it was also, generally speaking, separated by birth, as well as by sympathies, from the nobility. It is notable that some leading thinkers of the new generation came from the families of priests, abandoning the seminary for revolutionary activities.[3]

1 *My Past and Thoughts*, IV, p. 1579. *SS*, XIV, p. 322.
2 *Ibid.*
3 The sons of priests were expected to attend church schools and 'seminaries' (equivalent to secondary schools), which should not be confused with the Theological Academies. Some of the pupils who lost their faith in the process and abandoned the idea of entering the ranks of the clergy found a purpose or meaning for their lives in radical ideologies. For descriptions of life in church schools during the late forties and early

It is hardly necessary to say that many of the new generation of radicals were little concerned with what would ordinarily be regarded as philosophy. But their intellectual leaders were strongly influenced by the positivist, materialist and utilitarian ideas which entered Russia from western Europe. In their younger days thinkers such as Belinsky, Herzen and Bakunin had been powerfully attracted by German idealism. The fascination once exercised by German idealist philosophy was now succeeded, in the middle of the nineteenth century, by a rejection of speculative philosophy in favour of science and by a utilitarian line of thought in ethics. The new slogans, as it has been put, were 'realism', 'science' and 'utility'. A few Russian thinkers, such as the philosopher and historian Boris Chicherin (1828–1904) remained faithful to Hegel, but those who influenced the young intelligentsia of the 1860s manifested a positivist attitude and employed the criterion of utility in assessing the value of disciplines and of art.

One of the main features of Russian radical thought in the middle of the nineteenth century was a rather naive belief in science as capable of solving pretty well all problems which could be regarded as real or genuine problems. For those who shared this belief study of Schelling or Hegel or of any speculative philosophy was a waste of time. When, however, radical thinkers extolled science, what they had in mind was not so much the pursuit of, for example, theoretical science by a scientific élite, interested in advancing knowledge for the sake of knowledge, as the practical utility of science. Diffusion of scientific knowledge would have the useful effect of freeing people from traditional beliefs and prejudices, and it would be of obvious practical utility in such fields as medicine, hygiene and agriculture. Instead of being the prerogative of a few, scientific knowledge should be made accessible to the many, popularized.

Art too should be made accessible to the many; it should be socially useful. This is a theme on which something more will be said below. For the present it is sufficient to point out that underlying this emphasis on utility there lay a recognition of the great gap between the small cultured class in Russia and the great mass of the population. There was the laudable desire to diminish this gap by making appreciation of art and literature more widely accessible. Unfortunately, there was a marked tendency to take as a criterion of value

fifties, see *Seminary Sketches* by N. G. Pomyalovsky (1835–63), translated with an introduction and notes by Alfred Kuhn (Cornell University Press, Ithaca and London, 1973). The schools in which Pomyalovsky studied were attached to the Alexander Nevsky monastery at St Petersburg.

what was thought to be the general public's capacity for appreciation and understanding.

In the sphere of ethics the influence of Jeremy Bentham was pronounced. This was not due to ignorance of the ideas of J. S. Mill; it was a question of 'realism'. That is to say, it was regarded as realistic to maintain that the individual seeks his or her own good, that everybody is by nature egoistic. As the Russian thinkers in question wanted their followers to devote themselves to promoting the common good, the good of society, this 'realistic' view obviously gave rise to a problem. One way of coping with this problem was to claim that the individual's own good, properly understood, is identical with, or, rather, a part of and inseparable from, the common good.

2. The leading thinkers who inspired the young members of the Russian intelligentsia in the 1860s have sometimes been described as 'Nihilists'. This epithet is much more applicable to some than to others, to Pisarev more than to Chernyshevsky, but as ordinarily used, the word 'Nihilist' tends to conjure up images of bomb-throwing terrorists, such as those who assassinated Alexander II, or fanatics such as Nechaev, inspired by a passion for destruction. Originally, however, the term referred to those who claimed to accept nothing on authority or faith, neither religious beliefs nor moral ideas nor social and political theories, unless they could be proved by reason or verified in terms of social utility. In other words, Nihilism was a negative attitude to tradition, to authority, whether ecclesiastical or political, and to uncriticized custom, coupled with a belief in the power and utility of scientific knowledge. The Nihilists can be described as materialists, in the sense that they rejected as fable belief in spiritual realities such as God or an immortal soul in the human being. They tended to accept Feuerbach's celebrated statement that man is what he eats. But this did not prevent them from having social ideals and envisaging creation of a better world, even if what they emphasized was the clearing away of what they regarded as rubbish. Obviously, one could go on to use bombs to clear away obstacles to progress, when words seemed to be insufficient for the purpose. But a writer such as Pisarev was no bomb-thrower, nor even a revolutionary activist. His main contention was that no belief should be accepted unless it had a scientific basis or unless its social utility could be clearly shown. In fiction one of the best known representatives of the Nihilist attitude is the young frog-dissecting Bazarov in Turgenev's *Father and Sons*. It is true that the Nihilists were inclined to protest that Turgenev was guilty of caricaturing them, but Pisarev dissented, thinking that the portrait was an

excellent one. Perhaps he discerned that the novelist, though a liberal, had a measure of sympathy with 'the sons' in their revolt against 'the fathers'.

Writing in 1880 Turgenev asserted that 'I am and have always been, a "gradualist", an old-fashioned liberal in the English dogmatic sense, a man expecting reform *only from above*. I oppose revolution in principle'.[1] The Nihilists, in the original sense of the word thought the liberals ineffective and outmoded. But they were not wild revolutionaries. They sought the liberation of human beings from shackles imposed on them by social convention, the family and religion, but they believed that this goal would be attained through the spread of a scientific outlook. A writer such as Pisarev was not concerned with propagating terrorist methods, nor even with fomenting violent revolution. To be sure, the label 'Nihilist' will continue to be used for people such as Nechaev and for the terrorists belonging to one branch of *The People's Will* organization, men and women such as the assassins of Alexander II. But though the original Nihilist thinkers doubtless contributed to radicalizing the minds of the intelligentsia, they should not be confused with Nihilists in the popular sense.

Nihilism in the original sense can be described as a phenomenon of the 1860s. It was to give way before the rise and influence of the Populist ideology, an influence which, in its turn, was to be eclipsed by that of Marxism.

3. The chief radical hero of the sixties was Nikolai Gavrilovich Chernyshevsky (1828–89). The son of a devout and learned priest in the city of Saratov, he received an excellent education at home and then entered the local theological seminary. After graduation, however, he decided not to proceed any further with theological studies and, with his parents' permission, enrolled in the faculty of history and philosophy at the University of St Petersburg. At first attracted by Hegel, he soon came to the same conclusion, as had Belinsky and Bakunin, that the German philosopher justified the actual state of affairs. In 1849 he was deeply impressed by Feuerbach's *Essence of Christianity,* after which he came to find stimulus in the thought of French philosophers of the eighteenth century, such as Helvétius, and in French socialist theory, especially that of Fourier. In the course of his wide reading he gradually lost his Christian faith. Or perhaps we should say that it became secularized, the kingdom of man taking the place in his mind of the kingdom of God.

1 *Polnoe sobranie sochinenii i pisem* (*Collected Works and Letters*), XV, p. 185 (Moscow, 1960–8).

In 1851 Chernyshevsky, after completing his studies at the university, returned to Saratov as a literature teacher in a secondary school. In 1853, however, after marrying, he went back to St Petersburg to study for a higher degree. His dissertation *The Aesthetic Relations of Art to Reality* appeared in 1855. In this year he became a member of the editorial staff of the *Contemporary*, of which the poet Nekrasov was the chief editor. Finding that editing the literary section of the periodical took up time which he wished to devote to study and writing, he relinquished the post in 1857 to his friend Nikolai Dobrolyubov (1836–61), who, like Chernyshevsky, was the son of a priest and an ex-student of theology. Dobrolyubov, a resolute critic both of the liberals and of the older generation, was more uncompromising than his older colleague, and an article of his which appeared in 1860 led, in spite of Nekrasov's efforts to prevent a break, to a severance of their relations with the *Contemporary* by Turgenev, Tolstoy and Goncharov.

In 1858 Chernyshevsky published *A Criticism of Philosophical Prejudices against the Obschina*, in which he defended the idea of the village commune as the nucleus of socialism in Russia. In 1859 he was writing on capital and labour, and in 1860 he published an annotated translation of J. S. Mill's *Principles of Political Economy*. The same year saw the publication of his long philosophical essay *The Anthropological Principle in Philosophy*.

There was little solid evidence of Chernyshevsky's active involvement with any revolutionary organization,[1] but he was certainly an intellectual leader of the radicals, and the authorities were doubtless only too glad to avail themselves of any opportunity which offered itself to laying their hands on him. In 1862 he was arrested, on the ground that he had been in communication with emigré groups in London. A letter from Herzen had provided a pretext for the charge. After two years of imprisonment in the Peter and Paul fortress at St Petersburg, he was brought to trial. No real evidence against him was forthcoming, but nonetheless he was condemned to fourteen years hard labour and then to exile for life in Siberia. The Tsar reduced the sentence of imprisonment to seven years. In 1883 Chernyshevsky was allowed to return to European Russia and to reside, under police supervision, first at Astrakhian and then at Saratov, his home town. His long years of suffering, endured in an exemplary manner, won

---

1 In point of fact Chernyshevsky had connections with the first *Land and Freedom* group, which was established at the beginning of the sixties. It stood for land and freedom for the peasants. Further, Chernyshevsky wrote a proclamation addressed to the peasants, envisaging an eventual revolt as a result of disappointment over the terms of the emancipation decree. But the authorities were apparently unaware that he was the author.

for him a reputation as a martyr, or at any rate as a confessor, for the radical cause, and as a kind of godless saint of the radical movement. In other words, the heavy-handed behaviour of the authorities had the effect of turning Chernyshevsky's life into a powerful legend.

It was while he was incarcerated in the Peter and Paul fortress that Chernyshevsky wrote his novel *What Is To Be Done?* The novel which, until the authorities realized what was going on, was serialized in the *Contemporary*, made a great impression on the radicals of the sixties. From the literary point of view it was far from being a good novel, but his pictures of the lives (and loves) of the 'new men' exercised a profound influence. Indeed, his influence was not confined to the sixties. Lenin was to say that, as a young man, he had been deeply influenced by Chernyshevsky, the title of whose novel he adopted for one of his own writings. For the matter of that, Marx himself esteemed Chernyshevsky.

4. It is a mistake to think that Chernyshevsky aimed at the abolition of aesthetic theory. He had one of his own. What he attacked was not aesthetics as such but idealist aesthetics. For Hegel, beauty was the sensuous appearance of the Absolute, the Idea manifesting itself to aesthetic intuition through the veils of sense. Art, therefore, had a metaphysical significance, expressing the Absolute, spiritual reality, in a variety of media. In Chernyshevsky's opinion Feuerbach had shown that the Hegelian Absolute, like the concept of God, was a human projection, man's projection of his own essence outside himself. The Russian thinker concluded from this that the function of art could not be that of expressing the Absolute, the divine Idea; it was concerned with manifesting beauty where it is actually to be found, in human life and also in nature as related to the human being.

One of the functions of art, according to Chernyshevsky, is thus to reproduce beauty in life and nature. He at once links this idea with that of usefulness to the human being. For example, a painting of a scene of natural beauty in mountainous country reawakens in the mind of a person who once saw and appreciated the original the aesthetic experience he had enjoyed. The painting can also, of course, arouse a similar aesthetic experience in a person who has never seen the original and perhaps never will. The work of art then serves as a 'substitute'. Though, however, Chernyshevsky talks in this way in his essay on *The Aesthetic Relations of Art to Reality*, he also explains that he does not intend to imply that art is confined to reproducing objects in the external world. The poet, for instance, can 'reproduce' or express phenomena of the human being's inner life, the emotive life.

Though Chernyshevsky certainly emphasizes beauty as a content of
the work of art (he does not deny that form is required as well as content),
he goes on to maintain that a definition of the content of art solely in terms
of beauty is too narrow. The fine arts can concern themselves with
anything which is of interest to the human being, not to the human being
as a scholar, for example, but to the human being as such, the 'ordinary'
human being. Further, Chernyshevsky is anxious to distinguish between
his theory of art as 'reproduction' and the claim that art is simply
'imitation'. He does this by arguing that by reproducing what he believes
to be of interest, the artist comments on life, and judges phenomena. He
reproduces what he judges to be essential or significant features of
phenomena. Art possesses, therefore, a second function, a moral one.
This does not mean that the function of art is to make people moral in a
conventional sense. It means rather that a function of art is to make
people more fully human beings by drawing their attention to or revealing to them what is significant in human life and in nature. This moral
function of art is an additional reason – in addition, that is to say, to the
human need for 'substitutes' – why art should be widely accessible.

Chernyshevsky is, of course, aware that standards of beauty have
differed and do differ, and that there can be different assessments of what
is of interest to man. Referring to feminine beauty, he remarks that the
aristocratic ideal is different from that of the peasant, thus relating
different standards to class membership. The former ideal, however, is
artificial, the product of an artificial life, whereas the ideal of people
living a natural life, a life of work and one in touch with nature, is the
ideal which really corresponds to human nature. In other words, Chernyshevsky desires art which is accessible to the many instead of being
intelligible to and appreciated by a small class only.

The theory of art proposed by Chernyshevsky can be summarized in
his own words. 'The reproduction of life is the general, characteristic
direction of art, its constitutive essence; often works of art have a second
purpose too, the explanation of life; often they have too the purpose of
judging the phenomena of life.[1] What Chernyshevsky insists on,
however, is the claim that reality is superior to art. Art has its uses; it
provides substitutes. But these substitutes are substitutes for reality. It is
better to see a beautiful scene in nature than to see the reproduction of it
by an artist. One can obviously object that works of art have their own
intrinsic value, and that they should not be regarded as substitutes for

---

1 *Polnoe sobranie sochinenii* (Collected Works), II, p. 92 (15 vols., 1939–53). I have
translated *priznak* (sign, indication) as 'function.'

something better. But this is the point of view which Chernyshevsky attacks in the name both of 'realism' and of social utility. His aesthetic theory may well be considered banal and unsatisfactory, but it helped to form the outlook of the radicals of the sixties. With Pisarev, the criterion of social utility was pushed to an extreme point.

5. Chernyshevsky did not claim that art is superfluous, that it served no useful purpose or purposes in life. On the contrary, he maintains that it does serve useful purposes, meeting human needs. He rejects the idea of art for art's sake, but this does not mean that he rejects art. Its existence is justified by human nature and human needs.

What, however, is the human being? According to Chernyshevsky, the human being is one organism, one nature. That is to say, any dualistic theory of human nature is to be rejected. In his essay on *The Anthropological Principle of Philosophy* he asserts that there are two different kinds of phenomena in the life of the human being, physical phenomena, such as eating or walking, and psychical phenomena, such as thinking or feeling. The two kinds of phenomena are distinct, but it does not follow that they should be ascribed to two different substances or natures in man. They belong to one being, one organism, one nature, and their causes are to be found in this single organic whole. Chernyshevsky concedes that what are called the 'moral sciences' (such as psychology, ethics, sociology) have not yet been developed to the same extent as the natural or 'exact' sciences. But it does not follow that they cannot be so developed. In principle they are capable of becoming exact sciences, indeed, they are on their way to this goal. Physical and mental phenomena may be distinct, but both are caused; the causes can in principle be ascertained; and the greater our knowledge becomes of the causes of psychical phenomena, so much the more do the moral sciences become worthy of the label 'science'.

In regard to human conduct, this means that the different ways in which human beings behave are all causally explicable. Chernyshevsky does not claim that the words 'good' and 'bad', as applied to human beings or to their actions, are without meaning. A man is called good when 'in order to obtain pleasure for himself, he must give pleasure to others'.[1] Conversely, he is called bad when his nature is such that, to obtain pleasure for himself, he must cause displeasure or pain to others. Obviously, Chernyshevsky accepts as clearly true, as the only realistic thesis, the Benthamite claim that every human being seeks his or her own

1 *Ibid.*, VII, p. 264.

pleasure. Some people find pleasure in benefiting others, and these are called good. There is, therefore, a distinct line of conduct which can be described as altruistic, even though all feelings and actions 'are based on the thought of personal interest, personal gratification, personal benefit'.[1]

This is, for Chernyshevsky, the theoretical position. The practical problem is how to increase the number of the good, of those who see their own good as involving that of others, and how to diminish the number of the bad, of those who seek their own advantage at the expense of others, who are egoists in the pejorative sense of the term. One way of coping with the problem is obviously to convince people that the person who thinks that his or her interest is opposed to the interests of others, that his or her good can be attained only at the expense of that of others or by neglecting the promotion of the common good, is mistaken. People need to be shown that their real good is inseparable from the good of others. For Chernyshevsky, this is clearly true and can be confirmed by reference not only to individuals but also to classes and nations. In his view, it can be shown, for example, that if a nation sets out to further its own interests at the expense of the good of mankind in general, its calculations are wrong. 'Conquering nations have always ended by being exterminated or themselves enslaved.'[2] Hence the need for turning ethics into an exact science. It must be explained that 'only good actions are prudent; only he who is good is rational; and he is rational only to the degree that he is good.'[3]

It is obvious enough that Chernyshevsky wanted to encourage people to promote or contribute to the common good, not only of Russia but also of mankind in general, and that he regarded human beings who respect the interests of others as morally better than those who seek their own advantage without any regard for other people. Similarly, he sincerely disapproved of the exploitation of one class by another and of predatory and imperialistic conduct on the part of nations. In this sense he was an idealist, and there is no need to labour the point. His ethical theory, however, may well seem naïve. He was doubtless concerned with debunking not only what he regarded as lofty-sounding but hollow and unrealistic idealistic ethical theories but also pessimistic talk about human sinfulness and depravity. He wanted to put morality on a scientific basis, on a scientific or realistic view of human nature. Having adopted the utilitarian claim that the human being always seeks his or

1 *Ibid.*, p. 283.
2 *Ibid.*, p. 287.
3 *Ibid.*, p. 291.

her own advantage or pleasure, he then represented altruistic conduct as an expression of rational or enlightened egoism and argued that the great majority of people would abandon unenlightened egoism, egoism in the pejorative sense of the term, once they had become convinced that the pursuit of one's own interest is inseparable from respect for the interests of others. Herzen, as we have seen, claimed that both egoism and altruism are rooted in human nature, but Chernyshevsky wanted to bring everything under one formula, so to speak, and utilitarianism enabled him to do so. But his utilitarianism was of a primitive kind, of the Benthamite variety. There was in his thought a strong dose of the spirit of the Enlightenment, and he was blind to the problems which compelled J. S. Mill to move towards a more Aristotelian view of human nature. Besides, there is really no room in Chernyshevsky's ethical theory for the concept of moral obligation; theoretically there are only considerations of expediency, prudence, enlightened self-interest. At the same time his no-nonsense theory was certainly able to appeal to the minds of the young radicals of the sixties, who had rejected the edifying talk of the older generation in favour of realism and science but who nonetheless certainly wished to benefit mankind in general and the Russian people in particular.

6. Moral education, therefore, was seen by Chernyshevsky as one main way of securing a better society. He did not believe, however, that it was simply a question of increasing the number of good people and diminishing the number of the bad, while social structures remained unchanged. In his view, the autocracy, pursuing its own interests and favouring those of the gentry at the expense of the bulk of the population, had to go. To be sure, overthrow of the autocracy or conversion of it into a limited, constitutional monarchy would make little difference, if one class continued to exploit another, whether the exploiting class consisted of landowners, or of capitalists on the western model. Political freedom might be a condition for a transformation of society, but political freedom, if purely formal, could co-exist with a great deal of oppression and exploitation. The end of the autocracy would not be, in itself, sufficient to transform society, but it was a necessary condition for such transformation. Chernyshevsky did not think highly of the liberals with their demands for political freedoms and a constitutional monarchy, but if their demands were met (which he thought unlikely), this would at any rate be a step in the right direction.

As has already been mentioned, Chernyshevsky shared Herzen's dream of a 'Russian socialism', realization of which would bypass the phase of capitalist bourgeois democracy as found in the West. It must be understood, however, that Chernyshevsky was not an enemy of the West. Nor did he follow the early Slavophiles in idealizing the village commune, which he regarded as a primitive institution. It was not peculiar to Russia, but in western Europe it had been superseded by more advanced structures. Russia, Chernyshevsky was convinced, should learn from the West, discarding the 'Asiatic' elements in her life and society and appropriating all that was of value in western achievements, such as scientific advances. At the same time the village commune, though a primitive institution, embodied in itself a principle of communal ownership and of cooperation which could form the nucleus, when expressed in modernized forms, for a Russian socialism, realization of which could serve as an inspiration to other nations.

Through his presentation of the idea of Russian socialism Chernyshevsky exercised a powerful influence on the Populist movement, which will be discussed in the next chapter. But it was not simply a question of Populists. By his writings and by his own fate he gave a notable stimulus to radical thought in general. Further, the young members of the intelligentsia in the sixties found in his novel *What Is To Be Done?* (in the person of the fictional character Rakhmetov) the portrait of a youth who led an ascetic life in order to devote himself exclusively to the cause of social equality and of the demand that all should be able to enjoy life to the full. True, as Chernyshevsky wished to publish the novel which he wrote in prison, the revolutionary aspects of Rakhmetov's ideas had to be played down or slurred over, but readers were perfectly capable of seeing that they were being given a picture of a dedicated activist. Further, though the modern reader is likely to find some aspects of the portrait of this 'uncommon man' bordering on the ludicrous (such as Rakhmetov's practices of sleeping on nails and of eating large quantities of meat to keep up his strength for the chosen task), the young radicals of the sixties took these aspects in their stride. A good many of them regarded Rakhmetov as a model of the 'new man' or 'uncommon man', the revolutionary hero. Incidentally, Rakhmetov was, as one might expect, a good deal less sinister than Nechaev's description of the dedicated revolutionary activist, with his passion for destruction.[1]

Chernyshevsky was by no means a great philosopher, but he was a very

1 Sergei Nechaev (1847–82) founded an organization known as 'The People's Vengeance', the importance and extent of which he greatly exaggerated. He was the author, with some collaboration from Bakunin, of the *Revolutionary Catechism*, which described the dedicated and single-minded revolutionary and advocated total and merciless destruction. Bakunin came to regret his association with the young fanatic. In 1869 Nechaev was leader in the murder of Ivan Ivanov, a student member of his group, falsely accused of disloyalty. Escaping to Switzerland, Nechaev was eventually extradited to Russia and imprisoned in the Peter and Paul fortress, where he died. Dostoevsky had the Nechaev affair in mind when he wrote *The Possessed*.

influential writer. While some have described him as one of the fathers of
Populism, others have described him as a Nihilist. Though, however, he
did indeed insist on a scientific outlook and pursue a policy of debunking
in the name of realism and of social utility, the label 'Nihilist' can be
misleading. In any case it refers to only some aspects of his thought. He
criticized the liberals and advocated socialism, but he certainly did not
wish to see one repressive régime succeeded by another. To be sure, he
emphasized the role played by social structures in determining ideas,
outlooks, attitudes, desires, but he clearly wanted people to have the
opportunity of developing themselves and enjoying life fully. In some
respects he was a man of the eighteenth century, sharing the confidence in
reason and also the doctrinaire attitude of eighteenth-century philosophers. But he also shared their desire for human emancipation. One
might perhaps have expected him to embrace the ideals of liberal democracy. But he was faced not only with an intransigent autocracy in his
own country but with a capitalist society in the West which he did not
wish to see exemplified in Russia. He therefore pinned his hopes on
'Russian socialism' and represented common interests as higher than the
interests of individuals, trying to reconcile this position with his theory of
human beings as natural egoists by arguing that egoism properly understood, rational egoism, includes altruism.

7. Though Chernyshevsky was not a great philosopher, he was more of a
philosopher than Dmitry Pisarev (1840–68), who had little use for
philosophy and looked almost exclusively to science, or, rather, the
spread of scientific knowledge, as the instrument of progress. So far as
Pisarev had a philosophy, it was what Marxists describe as 'vulgar
materialism', the materialism which enjoyed a vogue in Germany after
the collapse of idealism and was represented by such writers as Karl Vogt
(1817–95), Jakob Moleschott (1822–93) and Ludwig Büchner
(1824–99). Pisarev believed that most philosophy was of little, if any,
social utility. Materialism, however, was, in his view as in that of its
proponents, based on science and in accordance with it.

   Whereas Chernyshevsky and Dobrolyubov were sons of priests,
Pisarev was the son of a landowner, though the family was in somewhat
straitened circumstances. In 1856 he entered the University of St Petersburg, but his studies were interrupted by a serious nervous breakdown,
leading to two suicide attempts and a period in a mental hospital. During
his time at the university Pisarev read widely in radical literature and
abandoned the Orthodox faith, in which he had been brought up. On
leaving the university in 1861 he started writing for the magazine

Russian Word (*Russkoye Slovo*). In the following year he was arrested. He had tried to get a reply to a government-sponsored attack on Herzen printed on an illegal printing-press, and the concluding sentences of the reply seemed to the authorities to constitute a clear incitement to revolution. While this does not seem to have been Pisarev's intention, one can understand how the authorities came to interpret his strong words against the Romanov dynasty and the bureaucracy as a summons to violence. The author of the reply was kept in the Peter and Paul fortress until 1866, though he was able to continue publishing articles in the *Russian Word*. He had only a brief period of life after his release. In 1868 he was drowned while swimming in the Baltic. It is not known whether this was an accident or a third, and this time successful, suicide attempt.

In 1861 Pisarev published an article on Plato's idealism. Plato, he argued, wanted to make people virtuous citizens by regimentation, by reducing them to cogs in a machine. If this project were realized, one of two things would happen. Either the citizens would rebel, in which case Plato's plan would be frustrated. Or they would submit, in which case, as cogs in a machine, they would lose the capacity for genuine virtue, and Plato's purpose would come to nothing. Obviously, Pisarev was not concerned only with delivering a broadside against idealist philosophy in general and Plato's thought in particular. He was arguing that for people to become genuinely virtuous members of society they must enjoy freedom, and that they should not be dragooned for their own good. He also maintained, with reference to Plato's suggestion about lying to the populace, that political authorities, no less than individual citizens, had moral obligations, and that if the former employed immoral means for an allegedly good end, this expressed a contempt for the people. Pisarev was following in the footsteps of thinkers such as Herzen in demanding human emancipation and individual freedom. He talked about Plato's *Republic* and *Laws*, but his readers did not, of course, need to be told that what he wrote had a more topical application. In the context the extent of Pisarev's knowledge and understanding of Plato is a matter of little importance.

This emphasis on the individual's free development is a conspicuous feature of Pisarev's article on 'Nineteenth-Century Scholasticism', also belonging to the year 1861. Having proclaimed his acceptance of materialism, he attacks idealism and all 'abstract' philosophy as useless rubbish, starting with some rather unfair criticism of Peter Lavrov's 'scholasticism'. Abstract philosophy is a luxury for the few, and it produces no tangible results. For that matter ethical idealism is also a luxury for the few. Indeed, the preaching of common moral ideals is one form of encroaching on the liberty of others. The human being needs to develop freely and naturally, uninhibited by tradition, prejudices, ethical systems, ascetic ideals which produce division and struggle within the self. It is in the light of ideas of this sort that we should understand Pisarev's often-quoted statement of the Nihilist attitude. What can be smashed, he tells his readers, ought to be smashed; what withstands the blows is fit to survive; what breaks into pieces is rubbish.[1] If we isolate such statements from the immediate context and consider them in the light of our knowledge of Russian history and the radical movement, they naturally give the impression of being a call to violent revolution. Though, however, Pisarev doubtless believed that the autocracy was an outmoded régime and should go, the smashing which he had in mind was more a smashing of what he regarded as useless beliefs, traditions and ideals which, in his view, prevented the individual from developing freely as an internal personality. He was speaking in the name of realism, utility and science rather than in the name of violent revolution. It was enlightenment which was required, not bloodshed.

Pisarev regarded abstract philosophy as useless, as producing, as he put it, no tangible results. Science, of course, he regarded as useful. But to make scientific knowledge genuinely useful, it had to be made accessible to the many, diffused as widely as possible. It would then contribute to setting people's minds free from the burden of obsolete traditions and beliefs, and, by its application in various fields, it would improve the material conditions and quality of their lives. To do Pisarev justice, he was not blind to the fact that, if popularized science was to be of any real use to people in general, genuine scientific research had to precede. He also saw that not all sciences lend themselves to popularization and diffusion. But 'utility' was his slogan.

A similar attitude was shown by Pisarev in regard to art, literature and history. As things stood, art, literature and history were the prerogative of a cultured and idle minority. Even so, their utility could be questioned. Thus Pisarev invited admirers of the English historian Macaulay to prove that Macaulay had made any contribution at all to public utility, with the clear implication that no such proof could be given. If history were transformed into a science – enabling us to know, for example, the causes of the rise and fall of civilization and societies – it would be useful, but not if it was simply a set of stories. Further, to satisfy the criterion of public utility, art and literature had to be made accessible to the many, and their utility shown. In his article *The Realists* (1864) Pisarev claimed

1 *Sochinenya* (Works), I, xi, p. 375 (6 vols., St Petersburg, 1894–7).

that a thoroughgoing realist despises everything which does not produce substantial utility. While he did not condemn poetry as such, he was prepared to write off Pushkin, and, in the field of music, he challenged his critics to show that Mozart was of the slightest use to the public. When reading Pisarev's more forthright statements, we obviously have to allow for his determination to debunk idols and for his desire to provoke and shock. When he chose he could write – of Pushkin, for instance – in more appreciative terms. The fact remains, however, that he judged art and literature in terms of accessibility to the many and of utility. In so far as utility includes the capacity to produce or strengthen desirable social convictions, Pisarev's position can be likened to what is described as 'social realism.'

We can say, therefore, that Pisarev wanted to extend the cultural heritage of the minority to the people at large. The trouble is, of course, that instead of demanding the progressive spread of education with a view to raising the cultural level of the majority upwards, he tended to speak in terms of bringing down art and literature to the level of the majority's capacity for understanding and appreciation. Pisarev, however, would presumably reply to this stock objection by maintaining that there was no point in trying to elevate the public to appreciate what was 'useless', what served as an amusement for a small minority. This would simply spoil the natures of ordinary people. What was needed was to give them something of real substantial benefit, and this was primarily scientific knowledge and a scientific outlook.

These remarks may have given the impression that Pisarev's tendency to emphasize individual freedom was complemented by a romantic idealization of 'the people'. This impression, however, would be incorrect. It is true that from a predominantly nihilistic attitude (forthright criticism and rejection of 'rubbish' and 'twaddle') Pisarev moved on to making some more constructive suggestions. In *The Realists* he insisted, for example, on the need to increase the property in the hands of the producers, and on the need for non-producing consumers to devote themselves to socially useful work, such as the popularization of scientific knowledge. But he had little faith in the utility of the great mass of producers to improve their lot or the quality of their lives. They had to be led and educated by 'thinking realists', in other words by the intelligentsia. In *The Realists* he referred explicitly to Bazarov in Turgenev's *Fathers and Sons* and to Rakhmetov in Chernyshevsky's *What Is To Be Done?*

Pisarev was, however, thinking primarily in terms of education. That is to say, the 'thinking realists' would be concerned with educating the people. He was not talking about a revolutionary élite seizing power and then dragooning and regimenting the people for their own good. He had not recanted his condemnation of Plato, even though he had come to see the need for leaders, if the division of society between a great mass of poverty-stricken producers and a small minority of idle non-producing consumers was to be overcome.

In Pisarev's short life as a writer we can discern a shift of emphasis from the individual to society, from the emancipation of the human being from old traditions and beliefs, from all that is not supported by science, to the positive promotion of the common good. In his essay on 'The Thinking Proletariat' (1865) Pisarev asserts that the 'new men', as he calls them, are imbued with a passion for working for the benefit of society. This task does not, of course, exclude the diffusion of scientific knowledge, but there is a clear emphasis on benefiting the great mass of exploited producers. It is not so much a question of seeking one's own free development as of serving the interests of the community.

Pisarev refused to admit that there was any incompatibility between seeking one's own good and seeking the common good. Thus the personal good of the 'new man' coincides with the good of society, and his 'selfishness' includes the broadest love for humanity.[1] The exploiter lives by exploiting; he displays a selfishness which runs counter to the interests of the exploited. But the 'new men' are not exploiters; they love work; they are thinking workers, producers; and with them there is no disharmony 'between inclination and moral duty, between selfishness, and love for mankind'.[2] In other words, the members of the intelligentsia should be concerned not simply with their own emancipation from the burden of the past but also with working positively for the common good. The two activities are two sides of the same coin; there is no incompatibility between them.

Both Chernyshevsky and Pisarev assumed that the individual seeks his or her own good or advantage. At the same time both men (especially Chernyshevsky) were concerned with promoting the common good of society, ultimately of mankind. To harmonize the alleged psychological fact, namely that every individual is an egoist, seeking his or her own good, with the moral demand that one should seek the common good, they maintained that one's own good, properly understood, is inseparable from the common good, that they go together. Neither writer, however, could deny, nor did he wish to deny, that there are people who

1 *Izbrannyye filosofskiye i obschestvenno – politicheskiye stati*, p. 663 (Moscow, 1949). From 'The Thinking Proletariat,' section IV.
2 *Ibid.*, p. 654, section III.

seek their own advantage at the expense of others. It was thus necessary
to argue that these people do not understand where their own good lies;
that they are unenlightened, in need of proper instruction, though
Pisarev held out little hope of converting all 'old men' into 'new men'. (In
fact, he declared it impossible.) It is difficult, however, to read Chernyshevsky and Pisarev without forming the impression that they disapprove of egoism, in the pejorative sense of the word, in a way which it is
difficult to accommodate within the framework of their ethical theory. It
seems clear enough that basic value-judgments are presupposed, which
go beyond what can be established or proved by 'science'. If one starts
with the assumption that every human being is impelled by nature to seek
simply his or her own advantage, this is not a promising foundation on
which to base appeals to work for the common good. The reply that
seeking one's own advantage, if properly understood, is also to seek the
common good is apt to seem a verbal conjuring trick. We may well think
that a more adequate conception of the human being is required. Herzen's contention that the roots of both egoism and altruism are to be
found in human nature can form a point of departure for such a conception, even if Herzen himself did not develop the theme.

8. In so far as Pisarev can be described as a philosopher, his ideas are
impressionistic and not properly thought out. Chernyshevsky, though
more of a philosopher than Pisarev, is hardly conspicuous for rigorous
thought. That he lacked what the Germans would consider profundity
scarcely needs saying, and though his thought may give the impression of
clarity, it is deficient in conceptual analysis. However, as the philosophical shortcomings of the two writers are sufficiently obvious, it is unnecessary to dwell on them. In any case these shortcomings did not stand
in the way of their exercising a very considerable influence on the 'new
men' or 'new breed'. On the contrary, the no-nonsense, and *simpliste*,
nature of their ideas contributed to their effect on an intelligentsia, the
members of which were far from being all devoted to prolonged theoretical reflection or to patient conceptual analysis.

    As Chernyshevsky expounded the ideal of 'Russian socialism', some
writers represent him as one of the fathers of the Populist movement,
reserving the epithet 'Nihilist' for Pisarev. Though, however, this procedure may well be justified, both men were iconoclasts, in the sense that
they subjected to trenchant criticism the traditional beliefs and values
which, in their view, could be confirmed neither by science nor by the
criterion of social utility. This process of debunking extended to ethical
theories and ideals. In his novel Chernyshevsky put into the mouth of one

of his characters, Lopukhov, the claim that all actions can be explained in terms of self-interest and that what are called ideal aspirations are nothing but self-interest clearly understood. As for Pisarev, in his essay on 'nineteenth-century scholasticism' he asserted, with typical exaggeration, that he (as distinct from Lavrov) had eliminated ideals. Both men employed the criterion of utility.

To be sure, both Chernyshevsky and Pisarev wanted people to work for the common good. Apart, however, from the problem of determining what constituted the common good, what were the criteria for judging possible means for realizing it? If utility was the sole criterion, any means would presumably be justified, provided that they could be shown to be useful. In principle, therefore, not only violent revolution but also terrorist methods, such as individual assassinations, would be justified, if they were useful means to the attainment of the common good. One could, of course, object that terrorist methods are incompatible with recognition of the value of the individual person. But then one would be appealing to absolute values, recognition of which was hardly allowed for within the framework of the rather primitive utilitarianism espoused by the Nihilists. It was indeed possible to deny the utility of terrorist methods. Generally speaking, the orthodox Marxists were to regard the terrorist methods of the People's Will group as unproductive or counterproductive. But the terrorists obviously regarded their methods as useful, as the only means left to them of fighting against an intransigent régime in the cause of the common good.

To avoid misunderstanding, the present writer wishes to emphasize that he does not intend to depict either Chernyshevsky or Pisarev as would-be assassins of public personages. As for violent revolution, Chernyshevsky certainly envisaged its possibility, but Pisarev clearly preferred legal means of securing reform. Nor does the present writer intend to imply that there is a necessary connection between Nihilism in the sense of intellectual iconoclasm and Nihilism in the popular sense. A person can obviously reject religious beliefs and idealist philosophy in the name of realism and science, and assert a utilitarian ethical theory, without approving of either violent revolution or terrorist methods. The point, however, is that Nihilism in its original sense, the wholesale rejection of 'rubbish' and 'twaddle', contributed to creating a mentality which was open to the employment of drastic methods as a way of solving an urgent social-political problem. The methods could indeed be rejected on the ground that they were counterproductive, but to condemn them as inherently immoral one would have to go beyond the criterion of utility.

Obviously, to say this is not the same thing as to claim that the increasing extremism in the radical movement in Russia was due simply to the writings of Chernyshevsky, Dobrolyubov and Pisarev. This was certainly not the case. At the same time, though, it is true to say that in the original sense Nihilism referred to the sort of debunking and iconoclastic attitude manifested by Bazarov in Turgenev's *Fathers and Sons*, it would be going too far if one maintained that there was no historical connection at all between Nihilism in the original sense and Nihilism in the popular sense of the term. Given the nature and attitude of the bureaucratic autocracy, there is little difficulty in understanding how the clearing away of rubbish, or the smashing of what could be smashed, came to assume other forms than intellectual criticism of beliefs in the names of science and materialism.

Chapter 6

Peter Lavrov and the Subjective Method

1. What is known as the Populist movement in Russian radical thought flourished in the 1860s and, especially, in the 1870s. Populism was not a monolithic system of social theory, but the Populist thinkers shared a number of basic convictions. Like Herzen, and also like Chernyshevsky, whose thought exercised a considerable influence on the movement, the Populists were strongly opposed to the autocracy and desired its overthrow. This meant, of course, that the prospect of a series of reforms being initiated and carried through by the régime tended to be unacceptable in their eyes, as any such policy might well prolong the régime's life and postpone its overthrow indefinitely. Besides, they believed that the sort of reforms which the régime would be likely to effect would not be such as to meet the real basic needs of the vast mass of the population. For example, to emancipate the serfs, even perhaps to allow them voting powers in electing delegates to some consultative assembly, would neither feed them nor clothe them nor educate them nor give them real security. What was required was not tinkering about with the existing system but a transformation of society.

Again like Herzen and Chernyshevsky, the Populists believed that the basis or point of departure for this transformation was already present in Russian life, in the village commune, the *obschina*, and in its common meeting or assembly, the *mir*, as well as in the artels or free associations of artisans and small producers. In their view the village community and the workers' associations could form the nucleus from which what Herzen called 'Russian socialism' could develop.

The Populist ideal has been described as that of agrarian socialism. This description, however, should not be understood as implying that the Populists so romanticized the life of the Russian countryside that they rejected any idea of making use of western science and technology, or that they simply wanted to get rid of the autocracy and the domination of the landowners, leaving an idyllic pastoral life to develop spontaneously.

They were not anti-science, nor enemies of all scientific technology. What they hoped was that Russia would be able to make use of western science and technology while successfully avoiding the growth of capitalism.

This last point is of great importance for understanding the Populist ideology. The Populists' conception of capitalism was largely derived from Karl Marx, and they had no wish for the people of Russia to be subjected to the horrors of capitalism as described by Marx. Some of the Populist leaders were acutely conscious of their debt to the people, as Lavrov put it, of the fact that it was the labours of the people which had enabled a small minority to enjoy education, leisure and a cultural life. These 'conscious-stricken gentry' were certainly not going to do anything to promote new forms of exploitation. And when, in the later decades of the nineteenth century, Marxist theorists talked about laws of social development and insisted that Russia could not make the transition to socialism without having passed through the phases of capitalist development, they were opposed by the Populists in the name of ethical ideals.

Although the Populist leaders shared some common convictions, there were also differences between them. Some believed that members of the intelligentsia should go to the people and learn from them, as though the Russian peasantry embodied a wisdom and virtue which could not be found elsewhere. Others believed that the intelligentsia should go to the people not so much to learn from it as to teach it. Both lines of thought were represented by those young men and women who participated in the remarkable pilgrimage to the people of 1873–4, which reached its culmination in the summer of 1874. Again, while some believed, mistakenly, that the peasants were ready to revolt and needed only a little encouragement to do so, others insisted that it was necessary to form a revolutionary élite among the intelligentsia which could lead a revolution and, in the event of its success, use the power of the state to dismantle the old order and transform society. This idea naturally aroused in the minds of some Populists the spectre of a new tyranny, of the coercion of the many by the few, the latter transforming society according to their own blueprint without bothering about the actual desires of the masses.

At first the Populists tended to concentrate on preparing the people for socialism, leaving aside revolutionary activities directed immediately against the régime. But after the failure of the pilgrimage to the people there was a marked change, caused not so much by the failure itself as by the reaction of the authorities.

The students who participated in the 'go to the people' movement were idealists. Some, setting out to share the life of the peasants, took jobs of various kinds and tried to establish relations of friendship and mutual confidence with the peasants. While some of these taught in schools or provided medical assistance, many undertook physical labour of a sort which proved too much for a good many of them. Others tried to plant the thought of revolution in the minds of the peasants by telling them that the land belonged by right to all, that the landowners had appropriated what did not really belong to them, and that revolution was required if communal possession was to be established. But neither group was successful. The students found the peasants, generally speaking, suspicious, unreceptive, and not infrequently hostile. The first group discovered that the bulk of the peasants were far from being as idealistic as they were themselves. As for the second group, a peasant would, of course, prick up his ears on hearing talk about land and the expropriation of landowners, but what he wanted was land for himself. He had little interest in collectivism or in building up a socialist society. Further, there were cases in which peasants, so far from being fired with the idea of revolution, handed over their exhorters to the police authorities. The young men and women had tried to bridge a real gap, between the intelligentsia on the one hand and the bulk of the population on the other. But the attempt was not a success. And the failure of the venture naturally tended to convince the radicals that revolution could be brought about only by training an élite, a group of dedicated activists with a clear idea of ends and means, who could eventually seize power and bring to the people the benefits which it showed little sign of really wanting.

The pilgrimage to the people had not been organized and directed from above. It was mainly a spontaneous movement by young idealists who wished to bridge the gulf between intelligentsia and people and to 'pay the debt' of which they had been told, especially by Lavrov. The authorities' best policy would doubtless have been to do nothing and to let the largely disillusioned students return to their studies. Instead, they arrested hundreds of people, including a good many women, and of these a substantial number were detained in prison.[1] This behaviour naturally contributed to radicalization in the Populist movement.

In 1876 the second *Land and Freedom* secret society was founded by

1 According to the Minister of Justice, Count Pahlen, of 770 persons wanted by the authorities 265 were already in prison, 452 subjected to police surveillance, and 53 not yet caught. These figures are taken from *Roots of Revolution. A History of the Populist and Socialist Movements in Nineteenth Century Russia*, by F. Venturi, p. 506 (London, 1960).

Mark Natanson, Alexander Mikhailov and their collaborators. The society was a broadly based organization which included members or associates who would not ordinarily be described as Populists, such as Prince Peter Kropotkin and Lev Tikhomirov.[1] Originally, *Land and Freedom* was not a terrorist organization but was primarily concerned with conducting revolutionary propaganda among the peasants and workers, though it included both moderate elements (known as 'Lavroists', after Peter Lavrov) and others who were influenced by Bakunin.[2] In 1879, however, a split occurred in the society. A more moderate group, known as Black Repartition,[3] was led by Plekhanov, who was at that time a Populist. This group was very quickly dissolved through the actions of the police, and Plekhanov fled to Switzerland in 1880. The other group, known as *The People's Will*, was composed of conspirators who regarded themselves as the real representatives and agents of the people's will. It was this group which was responsible for the assassination of Alexander II in 1881. A number of the conspirators were hanged. Others addressed a letter, written by Tikhomirov, to the murdered Tsar's successor, Alexander III, in which they said that their party would accept the decisions of a National Assembly, if power were conferred on elected representatives of the people. Alexander III, however, had no intention of adopting any such policy.

The ideas and methods of *The People's Will* organization differed considerably from those of the original Populists. The latter were revolutionaries in the sense that they desired the eventual demise of the autocracy, but they were primarily concerned with preparing the Russian people for socialism and they were not terrorists. *The People's Will*, however, was largely inspired by the thought of Peter Tkachev (1844–86), who not only encouraged terrorism and had been a patron of Nechaev but also demanded a seizure of state power by a revolutionary élite, which would then carry out a radical transformation of society by dictatorial means. In other words, he represented what is described as the Jacobin current of thought in Populism. He shared some basic Populist beliefs, such as the conviction that it was possible to achieve socialism of

1 Tikhomirov, who became the main theorist of *The People's Will*, advocated the seizure of power by a revolutionary élite, but he was against the continued retention of power by the élite, once the social revolution had taken place. In 1888, however, he repudiated the revolutionary cause, returned to Russia from Switzerland, and wrote as a staunch upholder of the tsarist régime. He died in 1923.

2 The 'Bakuninites', or members of the 'Jacobin' wing, desired revolution as soon as possible, whereas the 'Lavroists' concentrated on the preparation of the masses for socialism.

3 The name 'Black Repartition' referred to dividing up the land among the peasants, the 'black' people.

an agrarian type in Russia without its being necessary for the country to pass through the phases of capitalist development first. But in his insistence on the need for a dictatorship run by a revolutionary élite, as in his rejection of Lavrov's individualism in favour of collectivism, he was more akin to the Marxists,[1] even though the latter took a dim view of the claim that the capitalist phase could be bypassed and that socialism could be established in Russia antecedently to its realization in economically more advanced countries.

Though the peak point of the Populist movement was reached in the pilgrimage to the people of 1873–4, Populist ideas lasted on through the 1880s and 1890s, in opposition to the growing influence of Marxist thought. But the more industrialization developed, with the help of the government, the less plausible became the Populist idea of bypassing capitalism. In the nineties the 'legal' Populists made their appearance, claiming that it was possible to secure the implementation of a socialist programme in the economic sphere without a political revolution. They believed that the autocrat, not being tied to any particular class but standing above them all, was in a position to promote the interests of the Russian people as a whole, interests which, in their view, would not be served by the further development of bourgeois capitalism. In other words, they hoped to enlist the autocracy itself in the task of furthering the realization of 'Russian socialism'. This optimistic attitude naturally elicited ridicule from some Marxist writers, such as George Plekhanov.

It is reasonable to regard 'legal Populism' as the heir to the more moderate line of thought in the earlier phases of the Populist movement. The heirs to the Bakuninite or Jacobin strain in Populism, to *The People's Will* organization, were the Socialist Revolutionaries, whose party was founded in 1901 and who were active during a great part of the reign of Nicholas II (1894–1917). After the revolution the Socialist Revolutionaries were the largest group in the Constituent Assembly which met in 1918, and their leader, Viktor Chernov, was elected chairman. Even when the Bolsheviks executed a *coup d'état* and dissolved the Assembly, the left-wing Socialist Revolutionaries cooperated with the triumphant majority for a while, three of their number accepting ministerial posts. It was not long, however, before the Socialist Revolutionaries were hunted down by the Bolsheviks as counter-revolutionaries. In point of fact

---

1 As early as 1865 Tkachev was describing himself as a follower of Marx. His emphasis on the role to be played by a revolutionary élite certainly influenced Russian Marxism, notably the thought of Lenin, even if Soviet historians have played down Tkachev's influence on Lenin, in their desire to represent Lenin as the direct heir of Marx and Engels.

Socialist Revolutionaries were involved in anti-Bolshevik activities during the Civil War.

The chief thinkers of what might be described as classical Populism were Peter Lavrov and Nikolai Mikhailovsky, on the more moderate side, and Peter Tkachev on the Jacobin side. In this chapter we are concerned with Lavrov and, in particular, with his attempt to bring together in one overall view the positivist elements in his thought and his ethical and social idealism.

2. Peter Lavrov (1823–1900) was the son of a landowner. Entering the Artillery School at St Petersburg at the age of fourteen, he was commissioned when he was nineteen. In 1844 he began to teach mathematics at the school and was soon appointed professor of mathematics. In his professional capacity he lectured on mathematics and the history of natural science, but he read widely in European philosophy and wrote on philosophical themes. In 1860 he delivered a series of public lectures 'On the Contemporary Significance of Philosophy', and in the following year he applied for the chair of philosophy in the University of St Petersburg. Though his application was strongly supported by the eminent scholar Konstantin Kavelin, it was rejected, as the authorities already suspected Lavrov, and not without reason, of radical sympathies and associations.

At first Lavrov sympathized with liberal progressive thought, but he came to draw closer to socialism, though he tried to keep aloof from any active participation in secret revolutionary societies and activities. In 1866 he was arrested, in the aftermath of Karakozov's unsuccessful attempt on the life of Alexander II. Lavrov had had nothing to do with the attempt at assassination, but the authorities used the opportunity to round up a number of people suspected of dangerous and subversive ideas. Anyway, in 1867 Lavrov was exiled to the province of Vologda. Conditions of life, however, were not onerous. Lavrov was able to continue writing and even to publish. His use of a pseudonym was of no great significance, as the authorities were aware of the author's identity.

During his period of exile Lavrov wrote his *Historical Letters*, which appeared in *Week* (*Nedelya*) in the years 1868–9 and were reissued as a book in 1870. In 1891 he published a new edition, with additional material and some alterations, often to make plain what prudence had led him to express in a more obscure or indirect way in the first edition.

The *Historical Letters* are usually described as dull and pedantic, the work of a scholarly, reserved and somewhat pedantic man, who was happiest when surrounded by his books and papers and who was very unlike what most people would expect a revolutionary leader to be. For example, Tibor Szamuely says that 'the book was as earnest and as dull as any of Chernyshevsky's writings'.[1] However, although Lavrov was by nature and temperament a scholar and well fitted in some ways to be the university professor which he never became, we must remember that writers in Russia itself (as distinct from those living abroad, such as Herzen and Bakunin) were given to expressing their ideas in a way which, they hoped, would enable their productions to get past the censorship and not arouse the repressive attentions of the authorities. In any case, dull or not the *Historical Letters* enjoyed a great success, just as Chernyshevsky's bad novel had done. In his work Lavrov criticized the naïve faith in natural science shown by Pisarev and others, though he did not mention them by name, and emphasized moral idealism. But what most impressed the minds of the young members of the intelligentsia was his insistence on the debt which they owed to the people. In spite of Lavrov's rather dull way of writing, the message was clear enough. 'Go to the people; learn from them; prepare their minds for the trans-formation of society on Populist lines, according to the ideals of Russian socialism'.

In point of fact Lavrov wanted the young people to prepare themselves first, by a process of self-education and discussion. And a good many set about doing just this. But the radically inclined youth, who were waiting for a message, were fired by the idea of 'going to the people', and the remarkable 'mad summer' of 1874 was the result. The young people were not manipulated by Lavrov. He provided the message; they did the rest. When the pilgrimage to the people failed and the students returned disillusioned, not to speak of being harassed by the authorities, there was a natural tendency to turn against Lavrov and to look for another leader.

Lavrov, however, was no longer in Russia. In 1870 he escaped from his place of exile to western Europe. After visits to Paris and London, where he entered into friendly relations with Marx and Engels, he settled in Zürich. He had hoped to be able to continue his learned work in peace, but in 1872 he accepted a pressing invitation to edit a radical periodical and lead the revolutionary movement. At first he edited *Forward* (*Vper-yod*) as an organ of Populist ideology. But reflection on the situation in Russia pushed him increasingly into sympathy with revolutionary activi-ties, and he came to the conclusion that his followers, the so-called 'Lavroists', were not sufficiently militant. Indeed, in his years outside Russia his thought was influenced by Marxism. In 1876 he abandoned the editorship of *Forward*, and from 1883–6 he edited *Herald of the*

1 *The Russian Tradition*, p. 273 (London, 1974).

People's Will (*Vestnik Narodnoy Voli*), an organ of the People's Will party. In spite, however, of his move to the left, he did not turn his back on scholarly activity. In 1894 he was able to publish two volumes of an *Essay in the History of Modern Thought*, a work which he left unfinished at his death in 1900. He also wrote *Problems in the Interpretation of History*, which appeared in 1898, while *Important Stages in the History of Thought* was published posthumously in 1903.[1] His work on the Paris Commune had appeared in 1880.

Ivan Turgenev, the novelist, said of Lavrov that he was 'a dove trying hard to pass himself off as a hawk. You must hear him cooing about the need for Pugachevs and Razins. The words are terrible, but the glance is gentle, the smile is most kind, and even the enormous and unkempt beard has a tender and peaceful character'.[2] Herzen was, in several ways, an attractive character. And Lavrov was widely respected and liked. He was not a genius, but he was a man of solid intellectual ability, and it is not unreasonable, even if useless, to regret that after he had left Russia he did not confine himself to scholarly work instead of undertaking revolutionary propaganda which was really out of accord with his character. However, he had a genuine love of his country and was doing what he thought the times demanded. It was only abroad that a radical periodical could be openly produced.

3. Nicholas Riasanovsky describes Lavrov as an 'erudite adherent of positivism, utilitarianism, and populism'.[3] Zenkovsky describes him as a semi-positivist.[4] Walicki asserts that to call Lavrov a positivist is 'absolutely unwarranted'.[5] Evidently, a lot depends on the way in which one understands the term 'positivism'. It can hardly be denied, however, that there are positivist elements in Lavrov's thought. For example, he denied the cognitive value of metaphysics, at any rate in so far as metaphysics claims to be capable of attaining knowledge of a metaphenomenal reality. He did not deny that the human mind experiences the impulse or inclination to pursue metaphysical speculation. On this subject his thought had some resemblance to that of Kant. But as far as positive knowledge of reality or of the world was concerned, he believed that in its development science had taken the place of metaphysics. To this

1 These two works appeared in Russia under pseudonyms.
2 I. S. Turgenev. *Polnoe sobranie sochinenii i pisem*, edited by M. P. Alekseev, vol. XII, p. 411 (28 vols., Moscow, 1966).
3 *A History of Russia*, by Nicholas V. Riasanovsky, p. 498 (New York, 1977), 3rd edition).
4 See Zenkovsky's *A History of Russian Philosophy*.
5 *A History of Russian Thought from the Enlightenment to Marxism*, p. 350.

extent at any rate he shared in the positivist line of thought which tended to prevail in Russia when the influence of German idealism declined. In the modern world, according to Lavrov, physical science had become the ABC of literacy. Nobody who lacked any acquaintance with science, and who had failed to grasp and appropriate the idea of a law-ordered world, could justifiably regard himself or herself as literate. Belief in a supernatural reality and in the action of supernatural agents in the world may have served a useful purpose in its time, but it could no longer lay claim to the status of knowledge.

It would be a mistake, however, to suppose that Lavrov subscribed to materialism. In his view, materialism was as much a species of metaphysics as idealism. That is to say, there was no good reason for postulating the existence of a 'matter' which was believed to underlie phenomena and to constitute the ultimate reality. Knowledge, according to Lavrov, is confined to phenomena and the relations between them. Metaphysicians have often postulated an immaterial or spiritual metaphenomenal reality, but rejection of this postulate does not entitle us to assert the existence of a material metaphenomenal reality instead. As far as positive knowledge of what actually exists is concerned, it does not extend beyond phenomena.

Though, however, knowledge is confined to phenomenal reality, there are various kinds of phenomena, and thus a variety of sciences. There are, for example, sensory phenomena, possible objects of sense-experience, but there are also the phenomena of consciousness, accessible to introspection, reflection on which gives rise to the phenomenology of consciousness and to psychology. In addition, there are historical phenomena, which include the human being's pursuit of moral ideals and social goals. In history as a discipline we consider human actions as directed to the attainment of ends.

Lavrov's position can be expressed in this way. Though there are various distinct sciences, there would be no science at all without the human being as an active subject. Man can, of course, objectify himself as an object of scientific study, in physiology, for example, or anthropology or psychology. But it is man who performs the objectifying of himself and who constructs science. In spite, therefore, of their heterogeneity the sciences have a common integrating factor, namely the human being. Obviously, in astronomy the human being is not the object of study, but there would be no astronomy without the human being. The modern world-view should therefore be 'anthropological', in the sense that the human being should be recognized as the creator of and common integrating factor in all the sciences. Passing reference has already been made to the three public lectures which Lavrov gave in 1860 'On the Contemporary Significance of Philosophy'. In them he presented his anthropological standpoint to a receptive audience. In 1862 he published in the *Encyclopaedic Dictionary* an article entitled 'The Anthropological Point of View in Philosophy'.

In the three public lectures Lavrov had made it clear that, in his view, philosophy was required for understanding the human being. 'We must either philosophize or renounce understanding ourselves'.[1] To philosophize, therefore, is to find oneself 'in the area of anthropology, the science of man'.[2] In the article mentioned at the end of the last paragraph Lavrov stated that 'the anthropological point of view in philosophy is distinguished from other philosophical points of view by the fact that as basis for the construction of a system it takes the *whole* human personality or the physical-psychological individual, as an indisputable datum'.[3] The reason why the existence of the human person as a physical-psychological whole is indisputable, not subject to doubt, is that it is presupposed 'by all the facts of our activity, and of the inner world of consciousness and personal thought'.[4] According to Lavrov, the phenomenon of consciousness must be the starting-point for any contemporary metaphysics.

The term 'metaphysics' should not, of course, be understood in the sense of study and knowledge of a reality transcending the phenomenal world. It refers to a transcending of the area of physical or natural science. That is to say, there are phenomena, those of consciousness and those which presuppose consciousness, with which the physiologist, for example, is not concerned, but which are as real as any other phenomena. Thus the human being's pursuit of ends, his or her striving to realize ideal goals, constitutes a central theme for any philosopher who adopts the 'anthropological' point of view, reflecting on the human being as a totality.

Perhaps we might put the matter in this way. Physical science is concerned with what exists. But the human being strives to realize what does not yet exist. And this aspect of the human being must be taken into account by anyone who wishes to develop a conception of the human being as a totality. In one sense Lavrov does not wish to go beyond science. For there are sciences which treat of the human mind and of human activities which presuppose consciousness. For example, history,

1 *Sobranie sochinenii*, I, 112 (Petrograd, 1918).
2 *Ibid.*, I, 152.
3 *Ibid.*, I, 197.
4 *Ibid.*, I, 199.

according to Lavrov, is a science which treats of human beings pursuing ends or goals. At the same time, if the mind is to obtain a general view of the sciences and the relations between them, and of the human personality as a whole, it must in a sense go beyond science and practise philosophy. Artistic production is a human activity, but there can be a philosophy of art. Historiography as such is not philosophy, but there can be a philosophy of history.

In so far as Lavrov denies, or at any rate regards as unproved and unprovable the claims of religion and metaphysics to provide us with knowledge of metaphenomenal reality (while admitting that religion and metaphysics played a significant role in the development of human thinking), it seems perfectly reasonable to speak of positivist elements in his thought. His contention that human knowledge is confined to phenomena and the relations between them represents a positivist point of view. But if we understand positivism as involving a faith in the ability of science to solve all genuine problems, Lavrov cannot be described as a positivist. Rather, however, than embark on a tiresome discussion of the range of meaning which can or should be given to the word 'positivism', it seems preferable to admit that there are in fact positivist elements in Lavrov's thought and turn to consideration of his 'subjective method'.

4. The basis for Lavrov's theory of 'subjective method' is the idea of the human being as an active subject. As active subject, man conceives goals and consciously pursues them. In doing so, he cannot help seeing himself as free, as choosing and acting freely. Even if from the 'objective' point of view, in physical science, he considers himself as subject to determining laws, from the 'subjective' point of view, the point of view of the acting subject, he cannot avoid conceiving himself as freely choosing to develop scientific knowledge and as freely choosing to strive after the realization of consciously envisaged moral and social ideals. 'Man cannot in any way rid himself of the subjective conviction that he voluntarily sets goals for himself and chooses means of achieving them'.[1] As this conviction is ineradicable, we have to accept it, recognize it as a phenomenological datum.

Lavrov had studied European philosophy, and he was certainly influenced by the thought of Immanuel Kant. It would, however, be a mistake to suppose that his emphasis on freedom was simply due to reading Kant.

---

1 *Historical Letters*, translated with an introduction and notes by James P. Scanlon, p. 196 (University of California Press, Berkeley and Los Angeles, 1967). As this translation is fairly easily available, it will be referred to (as *HL*) even when the present writer has given a translation of his own.

Lavrov, as we have seen, was a social reformer. He did not believe in the inevitability of progress. Social advance depended on human choice and human action, and the human being, Lavrov was convinced, could not choose and pursue social goals except with the idea of freedom. Social activism and belief in freedom were inseparable.

Belief in freedom, according to Lavrov, lies at the basis of 'practical philosophy'. 'At the basis of practical philosophy there lies a practical principle . . . The personality is conscious of itself as free . . . It is this personal principle of freedom which distinguishes the sphere of practical philosophy from that of theoretical philosophy'.[1] If we regard theoretical philosophy as concerned with answering the question 'What is the case?', we can look on practical philosophy, moral philosophy for example, as concerned with answering the question 'what ought to be the case?', 'what ought to exist?'[2] As far as Lavrov's writings are concerned, we can regard theoretical philosophy as having been treated in *The Mechanistic Conception of the World* (1859), in which he dissociated science from materialism, whereas his *Outlines of Problems of Practical Philosophy*, and his *Historical Letters* can be regarded as belonging to practical philosophy. The uniting factor is the anthropological point of view. Man is subject in both, in the sense that he is the creator of both theoretical and practical philosophy. But whereas in the former he takes the objective point of view and considers himself simply as an item in the world as studied in the empirical sciences and as subject to laws, in the latter he adopts the subjective point of view and considers himself as a free subject.

A natural question to ask is the following. 'Does Lavrov claim that the human being *is* a free agent, or is he simply asserting that the human being as active subject cannot help *believing* that he or she is free, even if the belief is objectively false?' To the present writer it seems evident that as an ardent social reformer Lavrov certainly believed in the reality of human freedom. It is, however, undeniable that he referred to belief in freedom as 'a constant, inescapable illusion'.[3] This statement puts him in an awkward position. It is true that, as Lavrov remarks, in another context, there can be faith in an illusion.[4] The fact that I believe something does not make it true. The question arises, however, whether faith in an illusion can persist, if the illusion is known or believed to be an

1 *Sobranie sochinenii*, I, 69. From an 1860 article on 'What is Anthropology?'
2 *Outline of the Theory of Individuality* (1859) in *Notes of the Fatherland (Otechest-vennie Zapiski)*.
3 *HL*, p. 196.
4 *Ibid.*, p. 276.

illusion. If scientific knowledge really does tell us that belief in freedom of the will is an illusion, any claim that we should act on the supposition that we are free is at any rate open to criticism. It can, indeed, be objected that Lavrov is talking about an inescapable and ineradicable conviction and not about an 'as if' attitude. But if belief in freedom is really ineradicable and inescapable, how can Lavrov be justified in describing it as an illusion? One might perhaps interpret him as referring to a belief accepted by the active subject precisely as such, while choosing and acting that is to say. One can interpret him as claiming that one cannot deliberately choose and act except with the idea of freedom. But we are then confronted with two opposed points of view, the theoretical and the practical, which are left unreconciled.

It is true that the two points of view can be found in the thought of Kant. But this august patronage does not necessarily make the idea satisfactory. Lavrov might perhaps have made a distinction between scientific methodology (always looking for natural causes of events) and the dogma of determinism. In any case he would have done well to analyse the concept of freedom more carefully.

However this may be, it is clear that Lavrov distances himself from the 'scientism' of the so-called Nihilist thinkers, such as Dmitry Pisarev.[1] The Nihilists, rejecting all beliefs, religious, metaphysical and ethical, which could not be proved by rational argument, tended to put their faith in the advance of scientific knowledge as a panacea for the ills of humanity. As has been mentioned, the frog-dissecting Bazarov in Turgenev's *Fathers and Sons* expresses the sort of attitude in question. Lavrov, however, was no believer in the salvific properties of natural science. Physical science, as he remarked, has little to say about morality or social goals. As a social reformer, Lavrov laid emphasis on the subjective point of view as manifested in thought oriented to the pursuit and attainment of moral and social ideals. Presumably this is one reason why Walicki asserts that Lavrov should not be described as a positivist. It can, of course, be objected that there is no reason why a positivist should not have moral ideals, inasmuch as positivism, while not admitting the concept of moral knowledge (as distinct from knowledge about morals), does not claim either that people should not have moral ideals or that it is unimportant

1 In his 1861 article on 'Nineteenth-Century Scholasticism', Pisarev criticized Lavrov's account of the significance of contemporary philosophy. According to Pisarev, Lavrov, in his lectures on this topic, had failed to come to grips with the real issues of the day, though he had indeed shown a genuine historical knowledge. In other words, Pisarev represented Lavrov as a 'scholastic' who tried to maintain an objective attitude and was not sufficiently committed. Later on, of course, Lavrov became more obviously committed (*engagé*), but he continued to be attracted by learned 'objectivity'.

whether one has them or not. At the same time Lavrov advocated the use of the 'subjective method' in sociology and also in history and emphasized the practical orientation of thought in these disciplines, as distinct from the purely theoretical sciences. This is hardly a positivist position.

The 'subjective method' involves treating human beings as free agents, as freely choosing and pursuing goals. It also involves evaluating goals and thus providing a concept of progress. 'Until sociology establishes the idea of progress, it does not exist as one integral science'.[1] For Lavrov, the genuine sociologist should not confine his or her attention to the study of social facts and actual relations but should also present the realization of socialism as a goal. Let us, however, turn to his thoughts about history.

5. According to Lavrov, the subjective point of view is the point of view of the historian. That is to say, Lavrov conceives the historian as treating primarily of man's pursuit of goals with the subjective consciousness of freedom. Further, he argues that 'we inevitably see *progress* in the course of history'.[2] A good many people would doubtless object that this is simply not true of all historians and readers of history. But before one objects, one should try to understand what Lavrov means by the statement in question.

When he says that we inevitably see progress in history, Lavrov is not reinstating Hegel's metaphysics, with its teleological interpretation of history. He means that anyone who seriously reflects on history cannot help seeing historical events or phenomena in terms of their approximation to or divergence from his or her own values and ideals, and thus as better or worse, as the case may be. It can doubtless be objected that even if the historian as a human being does see historical events in this way, he should not introduce his personal evaluations into his account of what happened. Lavrov, however, clearly rejects the concept of history as value-free. The historian necessarily distinguishes between the important and the unimportant, between the more and the less important, and it can also be argued that he cannot help seeing the French revolution, for example, as exemplifying progress or as standing in its way.

A point to notice is that, for Lavrov, the historian's values and ideals are, like anyone else's, subjective. 'Distinctions between the important and the unimportant, the beneficial and the harmful, the good and the bad are distinctions which exist only *for man*; they are quite alien to nature and to things in themselves'.[3] Indeed, to say that the historian

1 *Sobranie sochinenii*, III, p. 54.
2 *HL*, p. 102.
3 *Ibid.*, p. 103.

writes from the subjective point of view is to imply that his value-judgments are subjective. This applies, of course, to judgments about progress. If, like Lavrov, we attach great value to the development of the individual, we shall assess progress differently than we would if, like Tkachev, we regarded egalitarian uniformity as the desirable goal.

Tkachev objected that by representing all ideals as subjective and by asserting that moral distinctions exist only for man Lavrov effectively barred the way to finding any objective criteria of social progress. In point of fact Lavrov tried to dispel the impression that he regarded value-judgments, and thus assessments of progress, simply as matters of individual taste.

In the first place Lavrov argues that to say that values are subjective does not necessarily imply that value-judgments are arbitrary. For example, it is the historian who determines the criteria of importance in regard to historical data, and in this sense his judgments relating to importance and unimportance (or relevance and irrelevance) are subjective. But it does not follow that his judgments are arbitrary or that they cannot be defended by argument. Suppose that the historian is concerned with economic history. His judgments about what is relevant and what is irrelevant, what is important and what is unimportant, are obviously guided by his choice of subject-matter. In the second place Lavrov argues that, as mankind develops, there is an ever-widening circle of persons who recognize a certain ideal as the only rational one. In one passage this ideal is formulated as 'the physical, intellectual and moral development of the individual [and] the incorporation of truth and justice in social institutions'.[1] In Lavrov's judgment, this idea was present, with varying degrees of clarity, in the minds of all thinkers of recent centuries and was becoming a truism. Obviously, it remained to determine what was implied by this ideal in a given set of historical circumstances, especially, of course, in contemporary society. This was the job of 'critically thinking individuals', members of the intelligentsia, representing the conscience of society.

It is doubtless arguable that Lavrov lays himself open to the charge of arguing in a circle, by maintaining that there is a moral and social ideal which is accepted by all rational persons and at the same time defining a rational person as one who accepts this ideal. However this may be, it is clear that when he asserts the subjectivity of value-judgments, he does not intend this to be understood as implying that no rational argument is possible in this area. He tells us, for example, that critical thought can

1 *Ibid.*, p. 322.

examine hierarchies of values, using as a criterion the satisfaction of human needs, beginning with basic economic needs. The critical thinker can ask whether a given social institution or practice really satisfies the needs which it is established to satisfy, or whether it no longer does so and has become a hindrance or obstacle to progress, when progress is assessed in terms of the satisfaction of needs. Further, in Lavrov's opinion, while originally every human being pursued his or her own good (pleasure), in the course of human development human beings have come to conceive moral ideals, and reflective minds have come to see that the individual's good is inseparable from the common good.[1]

As has been indicated, Lavrov refused to admit that there is any law of progress which operates independently of human choice or uses human beings as instruments. But he went further than this, denying that there are any historical laws at all, a matter which he discusses in the second of his *Historical Letters*. It is true that when living outside Russia he came increasingly under the influence of Marx, a fact which is clear from the added sixteenth Letter.[2] But in *Problems of Understanding History* (1898) Lavrov reasserted his claim that the historian should employ the subjective method, regarding historical phenomena, that is to say, as not subject to causal determinism.

This denial of historical laws requires some explanation. Lavrov did not deny that if historical phenomena are looked at from the objective point of view, they provide a basis for the formulation of empirically based laws or generalizations or exemplifications of already formulated laws. But he assigned concern with such laws to disciplines other than history, such as sociology. He conceived the historian as interested in historical phenomena considered as being unique, unrepeatable and non-recurrent, and so as not providing material for laws stating relations between repeatable and recurrent phenomena, which enable us to predict. The historian of France, for example, is interested in the French revolution as such, in its special or particular characteristics, that is to say, rather than in comparing the French revolution with, say, the American revolution and trying to formulate a general law which enables us to predict that, given certain conditions, revolution will occur. It is not a question of its being impossible to formulate some generalizations. It is

---

1 Lavrov's ethical thought was influenced by utilitarian hedonism. In *An Outline of the Theory of Individuality* he tried to show, even if not very convincingly, how out of primitive egoism there develops a sense of personal dignity and the concept of an ideal self, how the concept of one's own value develops into the concept of the value of the human being as such, and how reason comes to see that the individual's good is inseparable from the common good.

2 See, for example, pp. 314–17.

a question of the point of view of the historian. According to Lavrov the historian is concerned with telling a particular story as particular. In this sense there are no historical laws. Human history is, of course, affected by physical events. But the formulation of physical laws is not the job of the historian. He presupposes them as established in another discipline.

This sharp distinction between the repeatable phenomena of, say, physical science and non-repeatable historical phenomena is doubtless open to challenge. In a literal sense physical phenomena do not recur. That is to say, the identical events do not recur, even though there is obviously a sense in which we regard a phenomenon such as the rising of the sun as repeatable. Lavrov could, however, reply that, in his view, the physical scientist is interested in what phenomena have in common (in, for example, 'the atom', rather than in individual atoms), whereas the historian is interested in differentiating factors (in, for instance, the particular characteristics of the American revolution), and that this distinction between approaches or points of view is sufficient for his purpose.

At the same time it seems clear that Lavrov thinks of laws as curtailing human freedom, and that this is one main reason why he is intent on denying the existence of historical laws. As he attaches great value to the human being's ethical life and agrees with Kant that this presupposes freedom, he insists on the use of the 'subjective method' in history, on the historian seeing human beings as free agents. As we have noted, he puts himself in an awkward position by describing belief in freedom of the will as being, from the objective point of view, an inescapable illusion. But there can be no doubt that he envisages the historian as being concerned with human beings as freely choosing and pursuing ideal goals.

Moreover, Lavrov, as a Populist thinker, had a particular axe to grind. That is to say, he believed that it was possible for Russia to bypass the phase of capitalist exploitation as described by Marx, and that overthrow of the tsarist régime could be succeeded by the establishment of the sort of socialism which Populist theory demanded. He therefore thoroughly disliked the idea of an iron law, according to which socialism could not be established until capitalism had fully developed and run its course. It may be said that the idea of 'iron laws' determining the course of history was characteristic more of Plekhanov than of Marx himself;[1]

1 Plekhanov ridiculed the 'subjective method', arguing that if history was governed by laws from an objective point of view, it was silly to pretend otherwise. In his view, Lavrov and Mikhailovsky wanted to bypass the operation of law and therefore invented a point of view for which there were no historical laws, thus flying in the face of reality.

however we are concerned here not with exegesis of Marx but with Lavrov's attitude to the concept of historical laws.

It should be added that Lavrov did not think of human beings as being free, in a practical sense, to do anything which took their fancy. He thought of their activity as being limited by, for example, physical laws. Referring to the activities of what he described as 'progressive parties', he remarked that 'historical conditions determine what is *possible* for every activity'.[1] In other words, he saw freedom as exercised within a given objective framework or order, not as existing in a vacuum. It was this conception of an objective order which Mikhailovsky had in mind, when he wrote of human beings influencing the 'objective course of things'. When Lenin ridiculed Mikhailovsky's statement, on the ground that the so-called objective course of things was nothing but human activities, he was not being fair to the Populist writer.

6. We have been considering some of Lavrov's theories. As a social reformer, however, he obviously desired action, not simply discussion. 'The theory of progress', as he put it, 'merges with practice'.[2] The thought of the 'critically thinking individual' should be oriented to practice, to action. But the isolated individual can achieve little. Individuals, therefore, have to come together to form a closely united and resolute band, each member being prepared to subordinate himself or herself to the group, when a question of principle is not involved. At the time of the accession of Alexander II Lavrov hoped that reforms could be carried through without revolution. But as time went on, he came to believe that the overthrow of the régime was required if his socialist ideal was to be attained, and his critically thinking individuals thus tended to become identified with the revolutionary leaders who, as Lavrov admitted, would have to seize the power of the state to effect the needed transformation of society. On the one hand, he wanted to see the power of the state diminished, partly on the Marxist ground that it tended to represent class interest.[3] On the other hand, he came to look on State power as an

---

Plekhanov, who considered himself the expounder of authentic Marxism, can hardly have been pleased when Marx intervened to assert that he had had no intention of postulating universal iron laws which necessarily applied in all countries irrespective of their histories and conditions.

1 *HL*, p. 267.

2 *Ibid.*, p. 322.

3 Tkachev claimed that Lavrov's emphasis on critically thinking individuals was the expression of bourgeois individualism. It is true that Lavrov desired the maximum development and flowering of the individual personality, whereas Tkachev desired an egalitarian uniformity. At the same time Tkachev himself saw the future of Russia as dependent on the concerted action of a revolutionary group, even if he disliked Lavrov's talk about critical inquiry as encouraging intellectual élitism.

unavoidable instrument for realizing the desired social goal. In other words, Lavrov's thought, as we have already noted, was influenced both by the realities of the situation (the intransigence of the régime, for example) and, during his years outside Russia, by the thought of Marx, though he never became a Marxist.

The phrase 'critically thinking individual' obviously suggests the idea of critical inquiry. However, although critical inquiry may cover not only criticism of existing institutions but also thought aimed at determining rational goals, there is a gap between it and what would ordinarily be understood by action. To be sure, thought is itself an activity, but this does not alter the fact that criticism of institutions is not the same thing as changing them, even if the former is pursued with a view to the latter. If we wish to act, in the ordinary sense of action, must we not suspend critical inquiry by adopting one of our options as the basis for action and disregarding other possibilities? A person in a restaurant may be attracted by several alternative dishes offered on the menu and be able to give reasons for choosing them, but he or she will never actually eat anything if discussion of the merits of different possibilities is indefinitely prolonged.

Lavrov was perfectly well aware of the gap between critical inquiry and action, and he postulated 'faith' as a bridge and as the springboard for action. 'Critical inquiry paves the way for activity and faith generates the action'.[1] It is hardly necessary to say that the word 'faith', in this context, has no specifically religious connotation. Lavrov describes it as 'a physical or overt activity in which consciousness is present but critical inquiry is absent'.[2] It means definite adhesion to one out of two or more possibilities of action, an adhesion which has the effect of suspending further critical inquiry and discussion. 'That in which a man has faith he *no longer* subjects to critical inquiry'.[3] But Lavrov hastens to add that 'this in no way rules out the case in which the object of today's faith was *yesterday* examined critically'.[4]

What Lavrov has in mind is clear enough. The young men and women who participated in the pilgrimage to the people during the 'mad summer' of 1874, can quite fairly be said to have been inspired by 'faith' and to have suspended critical inquiry. If they had continued to discuss whether or not it was a good thing to go among the people, they would obviously not have acted in the way that they did. Moreover, it does not

1 *HL*, 273.
2 *Ibid.*
3 *Ibid.*
4 *Ibid.*

follow that their faith was blind or impervious to doubt. When they had
become disillusioned by the reception which they received from the
peasants, some turned to other ways of effecting social change, while
some simply resumed their studies.

At the same time it is reasonable to maintain that when critical inquiry
is suspended and 'faith' takes its place, we are confronted with an
ideology. And if a group of revolutionary leaders who put their faith in
an ideology succeed in obtaining political power, there is the very real
possibility that they will silence adverse criticism. Revolutionaries, intent
on action, are only too apt to believe that they know what is best for
everybody, irrespective of what other people may believe to be best for
them. Lavrov saw this possibility and disliked it. He was no Tkachev. But
it is difficult to see how one could guard against the occurrence of a
dictatorship of this kind except by means of a constitution with inbuilt
machinery for dislodging governments from power when the people are
tired of their policies and want a change. As we are all aware, this device
is not an infallible guarantee against dictatorship, whether of an individual or of a party. Short, however, of counter-revolution, it is not easy to
think of any other safeguard. In other words, there is more to be said in
favour of a liberal democratic constitution than the Russian radicals
were prepared to recognize. We can, of course, understand their mistrust
and even contempt for liberal attitudes. But, looking back, the folly of the
established régime in not granting a constitution before it was too late is
evident.

Lavrov himself had no wish to see revolution resulting in a dictatorship exercised by those who were convinced that they were in the
possession of the saving truth. His 'critically thinking individuals' represented, for him, the conscience of society, and his emphasis on the
orientation of critical inquiry to practice, to action, was an expression of
his conviction that human reason and will could influence history and
determine its course. He thought in evolutionary terms. That is to say, in
the course of their development and of the growth of reflection human
beings had become aware of their power to reform society in accordance
with ideals. In his view, as we have noted, certain basic ideals had
become, or were becoming, common coin among those capable of
critical reflection. It does not follow, however, that Lavrov envisaged a
minority as coercing the majority. It is true that when living in exile and
editing a journal for *The People's Will* he came to assert the need for an
élite group and for the subordination of the individual member to the
group as a whole. But his characteristic idea, the one which bore fruit in
the pilgrimage to the people, was that the critically thinking individuals,

members of the intelligentsia, should go to the people not to coerce them but to prepare their minds by persuasion and argument for popular action. Lavrov wished to bridge the gulf between the intelligentsia and the people. The government, however, regarded such attempts as subversive. And this contributed to pushing the Populists into a more active revolutionary policy. Hence Lavrov's endeavour to pass himself off as a hawk, as Turgenev had put it.

Originally, Populism involved an idealization of the people and of the village commune. The failure of the pilgrimage to the people dealt a severe blow to this idealization. Even Mikhailovsky came to admit that the voice of the village was often in conflict with its 'real' interests.[1] The natural conclusion to draw was, of course, that the real interests of the people were discerned by the radical intelligentsia. Unless the Populist thinkers were to remain content with an archaic utopianism, it is hard to see how they could avoid laying increasing emphasis on the leading role of the intelligentsia.

7. Though nobody would describe Lavrov as one of the world's outstanding philosophers, he was certainly a scholar and a serious thinker. He has, indeed, been accused of a lack of originality. For example, Tibor Szamuely describes Lavrov's *Historical Letters* as 'based largely on the ideas of Comte, Spencer and Buckle'.[2] This is certainly true in regard to his ideas about the development of the human mind and of society. Again, Walicki describes Lavrov's philosophy of history as drawing its inspiration from Kant (progress as a 'regulative idea'), Bruno Bauer's notion of 'critical thought' (as giving the impulse to progress) and Feuerbach's emphasis on anthropology.[3] In regard to general influences on Lavrov's thought, Walicki is probably correct. Attention has also been drawn to the fact that Comte had proposed the idea of a 'subjective method'. Comte did indeed distinguish between objective and subjective methods, the latter consisting in viewing the sciences in their relations to the needs of man as a social being, the idea of humanity and its needs, thus providing an organizing principle for the unification of scientific knowledge. Though, however, Lavrov may well have been influenced by Comte in this matter, the present writer would prefer to emphasize the link between Herzen and Lavrov. Similarly, though Lavrov was doubtless influenced by Kant in his treatment of human freedom, he had a predecessor in Herzen. As for Lavrov's later views, reference has

1 *Polnoe sobranie sochinenii*, III, p. 707 (St Petersburg, 1896).
2 *The Russian Tradition*, p. 273.
3 *A History of Russian Thought from the Enlightenment to Marxism*, p. 240.

already been made to the influence of Marx's thought on his mind, an influence which is manifested in the increasing attention paid by Lavrov to the economic factor in history.[1]

Every philosopher is indebted to others in some degree or other, and if Lavrov drew inspiration or derived ideas from a number of sources, there is no need to make a song or dance about the matter or to dismiss him as being of no account. It is arguable, however, not only that he did not provide satisfactory solutions of the philosophical problems which he discussed (philosophers are not much given to finding their colleagues' solutions completely satisfactory) but also that he did not carry matters much further than his predecessors, such as Herzen, had already done. At the same time he discussed some real problems. Consider the following quotation from a work on Russian radical thought. 'History abounds in apparently irreducible conflicts between freedom and necessity; it is the realm of man's actions and responsibilities, and yet it pursues no recognizable human end'.[2] Lavrov would have agreed that history has no predetermined 'human end', which will be inevitably attained. As for the conflict between necessity and freedom, he tried to find a synthesis, and he had a real problem to cope with, even if he did not solve it in a way which is universally acceptable. Again, the problem of harmonizing subordination of the individual's good to the common good of society and belief that society should be so organized as to facilitate the individual's attainment of his own good, his own development, can hardly be described as a pseudo-problem, even if it is objected, and not without reason, that it cannot be solved in a purely theoretical and abstract way but has to be made more specific and treated in terms of a concrete situation.

When Lavrov called for the introduction of the subjective method into sociology, he did not mean that the sociologist should abandon the objective method altogether. He meant, in part, that the sociologist should see human beings as freely choosing and pursuing social ends. But it was also his claim that the sociologist should establish goals. In other words, he conceived sociology as being not only descriptive but also normative. In a sense he envisaged a fusion of sociology as objective knowledge with ethics. Inasmuch, therefore, as Lavrov, like Herzen before him, rejected belief in absolute and eternal values, the question arises whether his idea of sociology as a normative discipline would not imply a fracturing of sociology into a number of personal points of view.

1 This is clear from the added sixteenth Historical Letter. See, for example, pp. 314–17.
2 Sons against Fathers, by E. Lampert, p. 10.

To answer this question we must recall his conviction that, in the course of history, human beings, or at any rate the thinkers among them, had progressively moved towards the acceptance of commonly shared ideals. To put the matter in another way, Lavrov believed that rational reflection tends to produce agreement rather than disagreement, harmony rather than discord. A community of ethically inspired sociologists could thus make a powerful contribution to the reform of society. The conception of sociology as a normative discipline is certainly not commonly accepted nowadays.[1] But Lavrov's view is of some interest as illustrating the importance which he attached to rational reflection and to 'critically thinking individuals'. He was much more inclined to the life of the mind than to revolutionary activity.

It has been said of Lavrov that 'apart from Herzen, he was probably the only important Russian radical ideologist whose ideas have even a limited resemblance to Western concepts of liberalism and democracy'.[2] The nature of the Russian régime naturally tended to drive would-be social reformers into the revolutionary fold. In this sense the régime was its own worst enemy. But among the radical thinkers, as distinct from the gentry liberals, it is Herzen and Lavrov who usually strike the western student of Russian social theory as being conspicuous among the more moderate. Tkachev certainly thought of Lavrov as a gradualist who was busy obstructing the advent of violent revolution. The fact of the matter is that Lavrov was a moral idealist, stressing the primacy of the ethical. The profoundest impression which he made on radical youth was his doctrine of the intelligentsia's (and, indeed, of the whole cultured class's) moral debt to the people and of their obligation to repay it.

1 It would be generally held that though value-judgments constitute part of the sociologist's data, it is not the sociologist's business (as a sociologist) to propose or preach values.
2 *The Russian Tradition*, p. 272.

Chapter 7

Dostoevsky and Philosophy

1. The great novelist Fyodor Mikhailovich Dostoevsky (1821–81) neither was nor claimed to be a philosopher in an academic sense. Herzen wrote at any rate one philosophical work, his *Letters on the Study of Nature*, and he often touched on philosophical topics, even though he is best known for his writings on social and political themes. But Dostoevsky published no philosophical treatise. It would thus be unfair to blame N. O. Lossky for not having included any section on Dostoevsky in his *History of Russian Philosophy*. It is true that Dostoevsky was far from being simply a story-teller. He presented ideas. But, as V. V. Zenkovsky notes, the novelist 'thought as an artist; the dialectic of his ideas was embodied in the collisions and encounters of his "heroes". The utterances of those heroes, although they often have an independent value as ideas, cannot be isolated from their personalities'.[1] This, it can be argued, is an excellent reason for omitting Dostoevsky from any historical account of philosophy in Russia. Besides, was it not in psychological penetration that Dostoevsky's genius showed itself, and not in what would normally be regarded as philosophical thought?

The fact remains, however, that the dialectic of ideas presented in Dostoevsky's writings has influenced philosophical thought, at any rate of the existential variety. Among Russians, Nikolai Berdyaev and Leo Shestov provide examples of such influence. This is presumably why Zenkovsky, who devoted some twenty-five pages of his work on Russian philosophy to Dostoevsky, felt himself justified in claiming that the novelist 'belongs as much to philosophy as to literature'.[2] Even if we understandably demur at describing the novelist as a philosopher, it by no means follows that he did not present ideas which are relevant to philosophy. Presumably, this is why an article on Dostoevsky is included

---

1 *A History of Russian Philosophy*, I, p. 410.
2 *Ibid.*

in *The Encyclopaedia of Philosophy* edited by Paul Edwards.[1] It is all very well to say that we ought to let Dostoevsky be what he really is, a great novelist gifted with psychological insight. His novels present problems and a dialectic of ideas which have influenced thinkers who would generally be described as philosophers.

Obviously, this can be admitted even by those who take a dim view of some of Dostoevsky's ideas. For example, the author of the article on Dostoevsky in the *Great Soviet Encyclopedia* not only pays tribute to the novelist's genius as an artist and to his psychological insight but also draws attention to the influence exercised by his 'philosophical, social and moral concerns'.[2] To be sure, the writer refers to Marxist critics as struggling against Dostoevsky's 'reactionary' ideas,[3] but this does not prevent him from recognizing the novelist's genius and his influence on the minds of a number of philosophers, especially Russian ones. Similarly, in a history of Russian thought published in the Soviet Union under the auspices of the Institute of Philosophy of the Academy of Sciences we find it stated in the chapter on Dostoevsky that the novelist exercised an 'enormous influence on the development of philosophy, accomplishing a great deal to stimulate, deepen and sharpen philosophical thought'.[4] In his evaluation of Dostoevsky's ideas the author speaks, of course, as a Marxist, but this does not mean that he denies the philosophical relevance of the novelist's ideas.

It is not possible here to make a thorough and complete study of Dostoevsky's philosophically relevant ideas; what follows, therefore, is centred around two claims made by Nikolai Berdyaev, namely that Dostoevsky was not only 'a dialectician of genius'[5] but also 'Russia's greatest metaphysician'.[6] Berdyaev may have been an impressionistic thinker, lacking in precision of statement and not much given to formal

1 Vol. 2. The author, Professor Edward Wasiolek of the University of Chicago, refers to Dostoevsky's 'mature philosophical views' (p. 411, column 2).

2 *Great Soviet Encyclopedia*, translated from the third Russian edition, vol. 8, p. 391 (New York, Macmillan; London, Macmillan-Collier, 1973–81).

3 The writer refers to Dostoevsky's Christian ideas and claims that historical experience has shown that Christianity is incapable of producing heaven on earth. Presumably the implication is that Communism is capable of performing this feat, an idea with which Dostoevsky would obviously not agree.

4 *Istoria filosofii v CCCR*, vol. 3, p. 392 (Moscow, 'Nauka', 1968). It is sometimes said that Dostoevsky is a proscribed writer in the Soviet Union. This is not true. He is obviously an awkward customer to deal with, and for a period (1947–55) he was pretty well passed over in silence. But a good deal has been published on him in the USSR. An edition of his *Collected Works* in ten volumes (an incomplete edition) appeared in 1956–8. In 1965 the Academy of Sciences adopted a resolution to publish a complete critical edition of Dostoevsky's writings. The first volume appeared in 1972.

5 *Dostoevsky*, translated by Donald Attwater, p. 11 (London, 1934).

6 *Ibid*. See also p. 218.

argumentation, but he certainly intended his remarks about Dostoevsky to be taken seriously.

2. The description of Dostoevsky as a dialectician of genius may seem highly eccentric. What resemblance is there, one feels inclined to ask, between Dostoevsky on the one hand and logicians, whether dialectical logicians or not, on the other? But Berdyaev was not, of course, trying to make out that Dostoevsky was a logician. He was obviously referring to the interplay of ideas in Dostoevsky's novels, to the clashes between them and to the way in which one or other idea might in a sense emerge victorious. Berdyaev disliked 'static' ideas, as he called them, and in Dostoevsky he saw a thinker whose ideas were 'never frozen categories'.[1] In a philosophical system we may be presented with a set of categories which are supposed to be fixed, determinate, eternally applicable to reality or, as with Kant, to human thought in its thinking of reality. With Dostoevsky the ideas are involved in a dialectic. There is a continuing presentation of different ideas, sometimes antithetical. It is not a question of an 'unearthly ballet of bloodless categories',[2] but of ideas as forms or expressions of life in its variety and movement.

To talk about 'Dostoevsky's ideas' is, however, misleading, if, that is to say, we are thinking of his novels. For they are ideas expressed by his characters, manifesting their attitudes, reactions, hopes, fears, ambitions, emotions. From one point of view, it is not so much a question of Dostoevsky's ideas as of Raskolnikov's ideas, Prince Muishkin's ideas, Stavrogin's ideas, Ivan Karamazov's ideas, or the ideas of Alyosha. The characters are not simply pegs on which Dostoevsky hangs his own ideas. The ideas are expressions of the personalities of the characters, expressions of their experiences and of their reactions to these experiences. At the same time there is obviously a sense in which the ideas are Dostoevsky's, namely in the sense that he was the creator of the characters. To be sure, some of the characters were suggested by real people. For example, in *The Possessed* (or *The Devils*) Stepan Verkhovensky is said to have been suggested by Timofey Granovsky, Peter Verkhovensky by Nechaev and Stavrogin by Nikolai Speshnev (the dominating personality in the Petrashevsky circle), while Alyosha Karamazov in *The Brothers Karamazov* is said to have been suggested by Vladimir Solovyev. But

---

1 *Dostoevsky*, p. 12.
2 *The Principles of Logic* by F. H. Bradley, II, p. 591 (2nd edition, 2 vols., London, 1922). Bradley's phrase comes in an attack on the Hegelian claim that logical categories reveal the essence of reality. For Bradley, the work of discursive thought belonged to the sphere of appearance.

such associations do not alter the fact that it was Dostoevsky who created the characters and their ideas. These ideas, however, were not conceived by the novelist in a purely cerebral manner and then put into the mouths of fictitious characters. Dostoevsky had either experienced or lived through them himself or had at least entered into them imaginatively. They were obviously not all Dostoevsky's in the sense that he agreed with them all. This would be difficult to do in any case, as they were sometimes clearly antithetical. Nonetheless, we cannot identify the novelist with any one of his characters to the exclusion of others, with Alyosha Karamazov, for example, to the exclusion of his brother Ivan. There is a sense in which the novelist is all of his characters, all the leading ones at any rate, even if some of them were suggested by real people other than the author. Dostoevsky understood from within himself the revolt of the man from underground, the ideals of Father Zosima and Alyosha Karamazov, the rebellion against God, or at any rate against God's world, of Ivan Karamazov, the nihilism of some characters, the sensuality of others. He understood clearly the force of the line of thought presented by the Grand Inquisitor, and he wondered whether he could succeed in counterbalancing it, as he wished to do.[1] On the religious level he recognized in himself both belief and unbelief. His statement that 'I am a child of my century, a child of unbelief and doubt'[2] has often been quoted. His inner life was a dialectic, and this is reflected in the diversity of his characters and their ideas.

When, however, Berdyaev described Dostoevsky as a great dialectician, he obviously saw the novelist's ideas as possessing a significance which transcended the limits of his personality. He saw the dialectic of ideas as an expression of human nature in general. Thus he refers to an 'anthropology in motion',[3] as distinct from an abstract, static theory of human nature. The struggle between good and evil, between, as Mitya Karamazov puts it, the ideal of Our Lady and the ideal of Sodom, the struggle between faith and its opposite, the clash between the ideal of the God-man and that of the Man-god, all these struggles and conflicts – this dialectic – proceed not in some abstract sphere of categories and concepts but in the minds, hearts and wills of human beings, manifesting the polarities of human nature. The dialectic has a universal significance, not, of course, in the sense that the attitudes of Raskolnikov or of any

1 Konstantin Pobedonostsev (1827–1907), with whom Dostoevsky was friendly in his later years, also wondered whether Dostoevsky had not given such a forceful presentation of an atheist position in the utterances of Ivan Karamazov and the Grand Inquisitor that he would find it difficult to present the opposite standpoint in a convincing manner.
2 Letters (Pisma), I, p. 142 (Moscow, 1928).
3 Dostoevsky, p. 45.

other particular Dostoevskian character are exemplified in all human beings, but in the sense that the various attitudes and ideas express potentialities of human nature and not simply the peculiarities or idiosyncracies of individuals.

If Berdyaev's description of Dostoevsky as a dialectician of genius is interpreted in this sort of way, it seems to be reasonable. It is not a question of trying to turn the novelist into a philosopher in the traditional sense. The clash of ideas is presented dramatically, in terms of the lives and ideas of individual human beings. In so far, however, as the ideas have a wider significance, they, or some of them, can be seen as being philosophically relevant, provided, of course, that one does not insist on a concept of philosophy which excludes the kind of problems raised by the novelist from the area of philosophical reflection. An obvious example of a problem of philosophical relevance is the existence or otherwise of a God who can be described as good, a problem which has been discussed by a good many philosophers, Leibniz for instance. Dostoevsky, it is true, presents such problems in the course of narrative, not in an abstract manner. But this does not prevent his presentation from being philosophically relevant. Precisely because of the concrete manner in which a problem is presented, it can stimulate philosophical reflection. What stimulates or arouses philosophical thought is relevant to philosophy. Gabriel Marcel sometimes presented a problem or theme in dramatic form, in a play, before discussing the problem or theme in an abstract manner. For example, in 1933 he published *The Broken World* (*Le Monde cassé*), the essay on 'the ontological mystery' appearing as a philosophical postscript.[1] The case of Dostoevsky is not, of course, the same. He did not follow any of his novels with a philosophical, abstract discussion of problems raised in the novel. But if Marcel's plays can be regarded as philosophically relevant, so can Dostoevsky's novels.

Even if it is granted that the novels of Dostoevsky can be philosophically relevant in the sense mentioned, exception might nonetheless be taken to the description of him as a dialectician. The word 'dialectic', it can be argued, suggests a movement of concepts through a conflict or antithesis to a synthesis. This synthesis may give rise to a further antithesis, but it provides at any rate a temporary or provisional 'solution'. And if the possibility of a final synthesis is envisaged, such as Hegel's truth as a whole, there could be a final solution, at any rate as the ideal term of the dialectical movement of concepts. But Dostoevsky, it may be said, pro-

---

1 The reference is to *Positions et approches concrètes du mystère ontologique*. An English translation is included in *Philosophy of Existence* (London, 1948).

vides no theoretical solutions to his problems, at any rate within his novels. There are plenty of antitheses, conflicts, clashes, but there are no syntheses.

The accuracy of this contention might perhaps be challenged. But let us assume that the novelist does not in fact provide any syntheses, any solutions, whether provisional or final. In the opinion of the present writer, the dialectic of ideas in Dostoevsky's novels faces people not with theoretical solutions to problems but with options. For example, the novelist does not undertake to tell his readers whether there is a God or not, or whether human beings are free agents or simply creatures of their environment. He faces his readers with options, for or against God, for or against freedom. He does not provide proofs that these theses are true, those false; he presents contrasting positions between which human beings have to choose. In this sense his dialectic is an 'existential' dialectic, and it is no matter for surprise that his writings have exercised an influence on thinkers who can reasonably be described as 'existentialist' thinkers.

3. Let us turn now to Berdyaev's description of Dostoevsky as a metaphysician, indeed as 'Russia's greatest metaphysician'. At first hearing this description may seem even more eccentric than the description of the novelist as a 'dialectician of genius'. What resemblance is there between Dostoevsky's novels on the one hand and the writings of Spinoza and Hegel on the other? Even if we happen to have little belief in the cognitive value of metaphysics and regard it as akin to poetry, the fact remains that the great metaphysicians have given to their thought a theoretical framework of argument which is lacking (rightly so, of course) in works such as *Crime and Punishment*, *The Idiot*, *The Possessed* and *The Brothers Karamazov*. It is quite true that characters in the novels propose and discuss ideas about the meaning of life, freedom, God and evil. But does this make Dostoevsky a metaphysician? If so, then all those people whom the novelist calls 'our Russian boys' or 'our Russian lads', people who meet for a drink and endlessly discuss problems of life and social problems, would count as metaphysicians. And what about poets such as T. S. Eliot and novelists such as Iris Murdoch or William Golding? Are they to be described as metaphysicians on the ground that ideas of a philosophical nature can be found in some of their poems or novels, as the case may be?[1]

1 I am aware, of course, that Iris Murdoch is a philosopher and was actively engaged in philosophical teaching and writing. But I am talking here about her novels.

It hardly needs saying that Dostoevsky does not present us with a metaphysical system. Nor had Berdyaev any intention of claiming that he does. We have to remember, however, that what Berdyaev valued in metaphysical systems was not the argumentation but the element of vision. In his autobiography Berdyaev says of himself that 'my vocation is to proclaim not a doctrine but a vision'.[1] Berdyaev disliked philosophical thought which had hardened into a system, and he saw in Dostoevsky a kindred spirit, whose perception of truth was intuitive.

This, it may be said, is all very well but if Dostoevsky had a vision, what was it a vision of? When we think of metaphysics, we probably think of a picture of reality as a whole, an account, for example, of the world in terms of basic categories, as with Aristotle or Whitehead, or in terms of the relationship of phenomenal reality to some ultimate reality, the One or Absolute, as with Plotinus or Śaṁkara. Human nature is doubtless discussed, but within the context of a conception or vision of reality as a whole and of man's place in the cosmos. With Dostoevsky, however, it is human beings who are in the centre of the picture. He shows little interest in our physical environment. And in so far as he raises metaphysical problems, his approach is anthropological. For example, he does not try either to prove or to disprove the existence of God. What he does is to try to show what belief and unbelief mean in terms of human life. Again, Dostoevsky does not try to prove that human beings are free. The question is whether human beings are capable of bearing the burden of freedom. Dostoevsky is much more interested in psychological problems than in metaphysics. In any case his approach to metaphysical problems is psychological rather than ontological. Further, in so far as a world-view is presented in the novels, it is a question not of one world-view which can be described as Dostoevsky's but of a plurality of world-views, those of certain of his characters. Obviously, the novelist regards these world-views as possible ways of seeing the world and human life, psychologically possible at any rate. But he does not present any one world-view of his own, not as far as the novels are concerned. All in all, is he not a most unsuitable person to describe as a metaphysician?

When Berdyaev described Dostoevsky as a metaphysician, he was perfectly well aware of the novelist's anthropological approach to problems. Thus he says of the novelist that he was 'the greatest Russian metaphysician or rather anthropologist'.[2] Berdyaev is obviously not

1 *Dream and Reality. An Essay in Autobiography*, translated by Katherine Lampert, p. 289 (London, 1950).
2 *The Russian Idea*, translated by R. M. French, p. 179 (London, 1947).

referring to anthropology as pursued in the relevant university departments. He presumably means that problems as raised by Dostoevsky
arise not out of reflection on the physical world as such, on our physical
environment (as in the case of St Thomas Aquinas's Five Ways) but out of
human life, as human or existential problems. Indeed, it seems true to say
that it is only in an indirect way that Dostoevsky raises problems in his
novels, namely through the interplay of his characters in their experiences, reactions and words. Raskolnikov's problems are *his* problems,
though they can, of course, be seen as having a wider significance. In a
sense Dostoevsky lets his characters raise their own problems, the problems which are real for them. He does not impose problems on them, and
still less does he propound ready-made answers.

Rather than describe Dostoevsky as a metaphysician, as Berdyaev
does, the present writer would prefer to say that some of the problems
raised in the novels are metaphysically relevant, in the sense that they
can form a point of departure for philosophical reflection on metaphysical themes. The fact that the novelist's approach is 'anthropological',
that the problems are presented as arising in the lives of human beings,
out of their experiences, serves to make the problems more real. It is
not a question of a philosopher proposing a problem or theme for discussion because it belongs to the problems or themes traditionally discussed by philosophers. It is a question of problems arising, so to speak,
out of life. It does not necessarily follow, of course, that because a
problem appears to one person as real and urgent, it appears in the same
light to everyone else. But it is more likely to win attention, if its
existential significance or relevance has been shown and grasped. There
is much to be said for the anthropological or 'subjective' approach to
metaphysical problems.

As for the contention that Dostoevsky presents no world-view of his
own, it seems to be open to question. Nobody would deny that different
attitudes to life and different interpretations of reality are portrayed or
suggested in Dostoevsky's novels. The attitude of the man from underground is certainly not that of Prince Muishkin in *The Idiot*. Nor does the
novelist either identify himself with the outlook of any particular character or present any world-view in his own name. At the same time it is
reasonable to claim that, in and through the ideas expressed by the
characters, there emerges dialectically a general view of human life and,
by implication at any rate, of reality, which is that of Dostoevsky or at
least that which he strove to embrace. The novelist was capable of
entering into the mind of the man from underground. After all, he
created it. But it by no means follows that he regarded it as accept-

able.[1] For the matter of that, the man from underground himself does not find it really acceptable. He admits to knowing that there is 'something different, something for which I hunger but which I shall never find. To hell with the underground'.[2]

This 'something different', something better, shows itself progressively in Raskolnikov's eventual change of heart, in the person of Prince Muishkin, in Alyosha Karamazov.[3] If one hesitates to speak of Dostoevsky's 'theistic' conception of the universe, this need not be because one regards him as an atheist or even as an agnostic, in spite of his own admission of the difficulty which he found in believing in God. The point is that Dostoevsky's vision of what human life might be and should be and of human history is markedly Christocentric. This becomes clear if we take into account not only the novels, in which the characters speak rather than Dostoevsky in his own person, but also *The Diary of a Writer*, where Dostoevsky does speak in his own person. It is doubtless true that a character such as the man from underground represents something in the author, but the present writer finds it hard to understand how anyone, given Dostoevsky's writings as a whole, can seriously suppose that he came down in the end on the side of the man from underground or, for the matter of that, of Ivan Karamazov or of the Grand Inquisitor.

4. Anyone who is acquainted with Dostoevsky's life is aware that he was once a member of the Petrashevsky circle, which held its meetings at the home of Michael Butashevich-Petrashevsky in St Petersburg from the early 1840s until the authorities took drastic action in 1849. Dostoevsky began to attend meetings of the circle early in 1847. The followers of Petrashevsky were Fourierists. Petrashevsky himself set up a 'phalanstery' on his estate on the lines laid down by the French socialist François Fourier (1772–1837), but the peasants soon burned it down. Life

---

1 In *Notes from Underground* Dostoevsky attacked the sort of idea expressed by Chernyshevsky, that all human beings seek their own pleasure or advantage, and that all would act in a social manner if they once understood that the welfare of society is their welfare too. According to the novelist, people who expound such ideas forget freedom. The human being does not want to be reduced to a member of the ant-heap or beehive or chickencoop. Man can rebel, even if he perceives that his rebellion is useless.

2 *Notes from Underground*, XI.

3 Dostoevsky planned to write a sequel to *The Brothers Karamazov*. It seems that Alyosha might have become a revolutionary or a sinner, or both, though presumably he would eventually return to Christ. The sequel, however, was never written and it appears that, by the time of his death in 1881, the novelist had not made up his mind about the line which he would take in it.

according to Fourier was by no means to their taste. The members of the circle were also strongly influenced by left-wing Hegelianism, especially the thought of Feuerbach. In other words, they thought that socialism and Christianity were incompatible.

Dostoevsky's acquaintance with socialism antedated his introduction to the Petrashevsky circle. He had already heard plenty about it from Belinsky, with whom he had enjoyed a short-lived friendship. His first novel, *Poor Folk* (1846), had been enthusiastically received by Belinsky, though in 1848 the critic described Dostoevsky's story *The Landlady* as 'rubbish'. As for Fourierism, Dostoevsky had learned something about it through his relations with a group centring round Alexey Beketov. But the novelist seems to have had little interest in the plans for any form of utopian socialism. They seemed to him fantastic. What drew him to socialism was a hatred of injustice. As for religion, some writers have represented him as being at the time an atheist, an idea to which Dostoevsky was later to lend support, but others have denied the accuracy of this account of the novelist's attitude. In any case it seems certain that Dostoevsky disliked Petrashevsky's contemptuous attitude towards the Christian religion.[1]

The members of the Petrashevsky circle were great talkers, and an informer in their midst supplied the authorities with records of what was said at their gatherings. The circle as a whole, however, was not a band of dangerous conspirators, even though the minds of its members moved further to the radical left after the events of 1848. At the same time Nikolai Speshnev, the most formidable figure in the circle, formed an inner circle of his own, into which Dostoevsky was to some extent drawn. Speshnev's group was intended to be a closely-knit political organization, and Speshnev himself later provided Dostoevsky with the prototype of a revolutionary radical.

In 1849 the authorities struck, arresting a considerable number of members of the Petrashevsky circle, including Dostoevsky. One of the charges against the novelist was that he had read aloud to the circle Belinsky's reply to Gogol, a document which contained an outspoken attack on serfdom. This particular charge was true, as Dostoevsky freely admitted. Indeed, he read the letter three times. But, more importantly, he was charged with conspiracy to assassinate the Tsar, an accusation

---

1 On the subject of Dostoevsky's relations with Belinsky, Beketov and the Petrashevsky circle see the relevant chapters of *Dostoevsky. The Seeds of Revolt*, 1821–49, by Joseph Frank (Princeton and London, 1977).

which was false.[1] Dostoevsky, with Petrashevsky and other members of the circle, was condemned to death by firing squad. As they had not actually committed any crime, Nicholas I commuted the sentence, but the condemned were not informed of the reprieve until the last moment, when they were already standing in the square awaiting imminent death. This experience provided the novelist with material which he was to use in his description in *The Idiot* of a man awaiting execution.

In view of Dostoevsky's later polemics against socialism, it may be appropriate to note two points. In the first place his conception of socialism was not derived simply from hearsay or from reading. He had himself been involved in close contacts with socialists, as a member of the Petrashevsky circle. In the second place his later picture of socialism as substituting man for God was not simply a piece of eccentricity, as it may well appear to Westerners accustomed to forms of socialist thought which maintain a neutral attitude to religion or, in some cases, have consciously drawn inspiration from Christian ideals. From the beginning socialism in Russia was generally hostile to religion and bitterly critical of the Orthodox Church. Dostoevsky had had experience of the attitudes of Petrashevsky and Speshnev, and the thought of Feuerbach, with its substitution of anthropology for theology, had made a lasting impression on his mind.

Dostoevsky was sentenced to penal servitude in Siberia, to be followed by compulsory service as a private in the army. After four years as a convict at Omsk he was sent as a private to Semipalatinsk. After a short while he was allowed to live outside the barracks. In 1859 he was permitted to return to European Russia, first to Tver and then to the capital.

In Siberia Dostoevsky had undergone a spiritual crisis, and he returned as a champion of Russia and of Orthodoxy (at any rate as he understood it). In 1861 he published *The Insulted and Injured* and his famous *Notes from the House of the Dead*, the latter work being the fruit of his experience and reflections as a convict.[2] In the same year he and his

1 The court proceeded on the assumption that if someone declared that the autocracy should be done away with, he thereby intended to take active means to overthrow it, in particular by assassinating the autocrat. The authorities were also aware of the plans of the Speshnev group to establish a clandestine printing press. To their own satisfaction at any rate they succeeded in presenting the group as dangerous conspirators. However, there was no question of extorting confessions in the way that confessions were extorted under Stalin. The tsarist régime did not deprive political prisoners of all human dignity at their trials.

2 *The House of the Dead* was naturally acceptable to Lenin, as distinct from Dostoevsky's other works, which the Bolshevik leader is recorded as having described as 'trash'. Such remarks by Lenin were quoted at the time when Dostoevsky was out of

brother Mikhail undertook the editorship of *Time* (*Vremya*)[1] a journal
meant to serve as the organ of the so-called *Pochvenniki* group, which
included Apollon Grigoryev (1822–64) and Nikolai Strakhov
(1828–96).[2] In 1863 *Time* was suspended, in consequence of an article
by Strakhov on the Polish insurrection. Subsequently Dostoevsky
succeeded in reviving the journal under a new name, *Epoch*, but financial difficulties soon made it impossible for the editors to carry on.

The word 'Pochvenniki' was derived from the Russian word
pochva, meaning 'soil'. What was called for was a 'return to the soil'.
In this context 'soil' had various shades of meaning. It referred to the
traditions and spirit of Russia, and it also referred to the common
people as the bearer of this tradition and spirit. We can say, therefore,
that the Pochvenniki were akin to the Slavophiles. However, although
they were critics of Western rationalism, they tried to avoid the idealization of ancient Russia which was characteristic of the early Slavophiles. They preached reconciliation, in the sense that they aimed at
transcending the opposition between Westernizers and Slavophiles by
advocating the development of a Russian culture enriched with what
was believed to be of value in Western life and civilization. For
example, though Dostoevsky asserted that 'our salvation lies in the
soil and the common people',[3] he maintained that the concept of community, represented by the village commune, could be united with that
recognition of the value and freedom of the individual which was
characteristic of the West.

The Pochvenniki as such were not of any great importance. For one
thing, their programme of reconciliation or synthesis was rather out of
date; in the 1860s there were more immediate and pressing issues than
trying to reconcile the attitudes of the Westernizers and the Slavophiles. We can note, however, that the programme of a 'return to the
soil' anticipated Populism, which was to reach its culminating point in

---

favour in the Soviet Union. When, however, the time came for the novelist to be
recognized as one of the great and lasting glories of Russian literature, it was conveniently
revealed that, on the whole, Lenin had had a high regard for the novelist's talents.

1 Mikhail was officially the editor, but most of the work devolved on Fyodor, the
novelist.

2 Grigoryev saw in Orthodoxy the manifestation of the Russian spirit and in Pushkin
the embodiment of a synthesis between national tradition and Western individualism,
between the Russian spirit and cultural life. Dostoevsky shared these views of Orthodoxy
and of the significance of Pushkin. Strakhov tried to combine admiration for Hegel (seen
as a mystic rather than as a rationalist) with opposition to the secularizing rationalism of
the West. A deeply religious man but also a firm believer in freedom of thought, he was to
fall more and more under the spell of Tolstoy's ideas.

3 *Dostoevsky's Occasional Writings*, selected, translated and introduced by David
Magarshack, p. 212 (New York, 1963).

the next decade and which was of much greater importance in Russian history than the Pochvenniki group. We can also note that the assertion that Dostoevsky had come to repudiate socialism is open to challenge. To be sure, he had repudiated socialism as he understood the term, namely atheistic socialism, socialism which substituted Humanity for God. But it is arguable that what he wanted was a de-secularized form of 'Russian socialism', provided that it did not involve a failure to recognize the value and freedom of the individual and did not sacrifice the interests of actual human beings on the altar of an abstraction, Humanity. In other words, it is arguable that what Dostoevsky really wanted was a Christian and personalistic socialism.

If this line of thought is accepted, we must add that Dostoevsky had a strong sense of the special mission of Russia, a mission, that is to say, on behalf of mankind. He thought of Russia as peculiarly qualified to represent universal humanity and as destined to bring about a union of nations. This sense of his country's mission to mankind remained a permanent feature of his thought, though it came to be associated with unpleasant chauvinistic elements. A Polish revolutionary, who had been a fellow prisoner with Dostoevsky in Siberia, later referred to the chauvinistic attitude manifested by the novelist in the convict prison, to his exaltation of Russia at the expense of other nations. We shall have occasion to refer again later to the unpleasant features of Dostoevsky's thought, but his exaltation of Russia was, at its best, an expression of an idealistic or romantic idea of his country's capacity to lead the way in establishing universal human brotherhood.

The programme of reconciliation expounded by the Pochvenniki included reconciliation between the educated class and the people, an idea which became a prominent feature of Populist thought. Dostoevsky warmly welcomed Alexander II's emancipation of the serfs in 1861, seeing it as laying the foundation for a reconciliation between the intelligentsia and the people. As we have noted, he regarded Russia as specially qualified to promote universal brotherhood. He sympathized with the ideal of 'fraternity' as proclaimed by the leaders of the French Revolution, but his visits abroad in 1862–3 had led him to the conclusion that the French were incapable of realizing this ideal. To his eyes the bourgeoisie seemed unscrupulous, the workers capitalists at heart, and the peasants simply out for themselves. Apart from a visit to Florence in Strakhov's company, Dostoevsky was not happy abroad. He saw everything through jaundiced eyes, and what he saw confirmed him in his belief in the superiority of Russia and the Russians.[1]

1 Dostoevsky found London impressive but sinister. His sharpest barbs were reserved for the French.

5. Though Dostoevsky was not the man to maintain that literature and art should be opposed to the world of reality and confine themselves to a world of romantic dreams, neither was he the man to accept the claim that the value of literary or artistic production should be measured simply by its social utility. More concretely, he did not accept the line of thought expounded by Chernyshevsky and, in an even more provocative way, by Pisarev, and he wrote an article on the subject, directed principally against Chernyshevsky's disciple and friend Nikolai Dobrolyubov (1836–61). In it Dostoevsky makes clear that if the slogan 'art for art's sake' is understood as meaning that art should be divorced from reality and from human needs, he rejects it. In his opinion, however, there never has been, and cannot be, art of this kind. 'Art which is not contemporary and which is not in line with modern requirements cannot even exist. If it does exist, it is not art'.[1] Art is an expression of human creativity, and the artist, the creator, is a man or woman living here and now. As artistic creation is part of life, an expression of it, it cannot be divorced from life. As for the utility of art, its relation to human needs, 'beauty is useful because it is beauty, because a constant need for beauty and its highest ideal resides in mankind'.[2] It is true that art 'has an independent, inseparable, organic life of its own',[3] but by living this life it is useful, in the sense that it fulfils the human being's need for beauty.

In other words, Dostoevsky does not assert that art is, or should be, useless. What he claims, in effect, is that writers such as Chernyshevsky, Pisarev and Dobrolyubov have a too narrow conception of utility. Art is useful, when it is permitted to be itself. If people prescribe non-aesthetic ends to the artist, artistic creativity is hampered. 'The more freely it (art) develops, the more normal the development of its true and *useful* path will be'.[4] The 'utilitarians' fail to see this.

There is nothing startling in this point of view. To most people it probably reads like an expression of common sense. But we have to bear the context in mind, the spread of 'utilitarianism' in Russia in the middle of the nineteenth century, a utilitarianism which was supposed to be required by radical social thought, and by concern with the welfare of the people. Dostoevsky's claim was that people would be benefited by allowing art to be itself rather than trying to force it into a mould of 'social realism'. He was not against the introduction of social themes into literature. He introduced them himself. But he was strongly opposed to

1 *Dostoevsky's Occasional Writings*, p. 134.
2 *Ibid.*, p. 136.
3 *Ibid.*, p. 124.
4 *Ibid.*, p. 135.

any attempt to curtail the freedom of the artist or writer by demanding that art and literature should serve non-aesthetic ends. This position may seem obviously valid to most of us. It did not, of course, seem obvious to such people as Andrey Zhdanov (d. 1948), who did their best to subject Soviet writers, artists and composers to the stifling grip of a Party ideology.[1]

6. *Notes from Underground* (1864) is generally said to be a reply or retort to Chernyshevsky's novel *What is To Be Done?* This is partly true, but it does not follow that Dostoevsky can simply be identified with the fictitious author of the *Notes*. 'Both the author of the notes and the "Notes" themselves are, of course, fictitious'.[2] It would obviously be a great mistake to suppose that Dostoevsky's answer to secular socialism and 'scientific' materialism was to extol irrationalism and moral weakness. The man from underground expresses aspects of human nature and a spirit of revolt which, in Dostoevsky's opinion, are bound to shatter the facile optimism and deterministic assumptions of the Nihilists. It hardly needs saying that Dostoevsky himself, and not simply the fictitious man from underground, is convinced (or at any rate strongly hopes) that human beings would not be satisfied with the ant-heap or hen-coop or Crystal Palace, as the socialist paradise is variously called, and that the dissatisfaction would express itself in revolt, even if only interior revolt. But it certainly does not follow that the man from underground, who describes himself as 'a sick man . . . a nasty man . . . a truly unattractive man',[3] represents Dostoevsky's ideal of a human being. When the man from underground says that the human enterprise 'really consists only in man's proving to himself every minute that he is a man and not a cog, proving it even if it costs him his own skin, proving it even if he has to become a cannibal',[4] Dostoevsky doubtless agrees up to a point. But we are not justified in concluding that the novelist intends to endorse all the choices which the man from underground envisaged or made. It pertains to the human being to choose between good and evil, and the capacity for choosing evil is an essential feature of the human being. But it does not follow that it is a matter of indifference which one chooses. What Dostoevsky does is to present his readers with a dialectic, a dialectic rooted in the nature of the human being. And though he

1 I do not mean to imply, of course, that Chernyshevsky wanted artists to be coerced into following the line which he considered desirable.
2 *Notes from Underground*, edited by Robert R. Durgy, translated by Serge Shiskoff, p. 3 (New York, 1969).
3 *Ibid.*, p. 3.
4 *Ibid.*, p. 30.

clearly indicates that reduction of human beings to the status of ants in the ant-heap is 'unnatural', his own solution of the way out not only from the path to atheistic socialism but also from the underground is not presented in this work.

Writing to his brother Mikhail in March 1864 Dostoevsky complained that 'those pigs of censors', while letting through passages in which he railed at everything and pretended to blaspheme, had deleted the passages (from Part I, Chapter 10) in which he had asserted the necessity of faith and of adherence to Christ. Quite apart, however, from the question of what the censors may have had in mind, commentators have reasonably remarked that a profession of religious faith by the man from underground would have seemed very odd. Moreover, as the novelist did not restore the deletion when the work was later reprinted, he presumably had seen for himself that the negative attitude of the man from underground would be best left intact. After all, he had made his point, namely that the fashionable radical theories or dogmas of the time failed to understand human nature and take it into account.

Dostoevsky was on the threshold of fame. His first great novel, *Crime and Punishment*, appeared in 1866, and the others followed up to the publication of *The Brothers Karamazov* (1879–80). In the succession of his novels the novelist's own world-view (or, perhaps better, his view of the human being and human history) progressively emerges; but this view is not, of course, stated by the novelist in his own person. And it would be difficult to justify a picking and choosing, so to speak, among the conflicting attitudes and points of view presented, if we had no evidence of Dostoevsky's ideas apart from the novels themselves. This is not, however, the case. For example, *The Diary of a Writer* is an important source of knowledge of Dostoevsky's social and political opinions during the relevant period. The first part of the Diary contains articles which the novelist contributed to *The Citizen* (*Grazhdanin*), a conservative journal of which he was the assistant editor from 1872 until 1874, when he resigned. The other parts of the Diary contain later material, the final items being written shortly before Dostoevsky's death. The famous speech on Pushkin, which Dostoevsky delivered at Moscow in June 1880, and which was received enthusiastically by the audience, is printed in the Diary.

It is as well to say at once that the reader of the Diary cannot help noticing expressions of prejudices which leave an unpleasant taste for many people. Referring to Dostoevsky's career as a right-wing journalist after his return from Siberia, Professor Riasanovsky remarks that 'his targets included the Jews, the Poles, the Germans, Catholicism, socialism, and the entire West'.[1] Perhaps this statement is a little too sweeping. Dostoevsky professed to have a love for western Europe, in spite of his sharp criticism of it. As for the Jews, he certainly made anti-Jewish remarks of a repugnant nature. For example, 'Jewry is thriving precisely there where people are still ignorant, or not free, or economically backward. It is there that Jewry has a *champ libre*'.[2] But he had at any rate the grace to add 'despite . . . everything I have written above (about Jews), I favour full and complete equalization of rights because such is Christ's law, such is the Christian principle'.[3] Again, while Dostoevsky could express decidedly chauvinistic views in regard to Russia and her relations to other nations, his ideal was that of brotherly communion among nations. Basically, however, what Riasanovsky says is true. There is no point in trying to conceal the fact that the great novelist was a man of prejudices, to which on occasion he gave intemperate expression, and which do him no credit. This having been admitted, we can proceed to consider his distinction between the Man-god and the God-man.

Dostoevsky associated socialism with atheism. Consider what he says about Belinsky, 'the most ardent person of all those whom I have met through my life'.[4] Dostoevsky admits that Belinsky was aware that socialism without moral foundations can produce nothing but an anthill, without any genuine social harmony. But he adds that Belinsky 'as a socialist, had to destroy Christianity in the first place. He knew that the revolution must necessarily begin with atheism'.[5] 'As a socialist, he (Belinsky) was in duty bound to destroy the teaching of Christ'.[6] According to Dostoevsky (and he was right) the *intelligentsia* as a whole had become alienated from the Orthodox Russian people and its faith. But it was not simply a question of an historical fact about the Russian intelligentsia. For socialism, in Dostoevsky's eyes, was by its very nature atheistic, substituting the kingdom of Man for the kingdom of God and the Man-god for the God-man, namely Christ.

Obviously, it can be objected that the link between socialism and atheism becomes, for Dostoevsky, a matter of definition. That is to say, he understands by 'socialism' atheistic socialism. There is, however, an historical aspect of the matter. The novelist sees what he sometimes calls

1 *A History of Russia*, p. 490.
2 *The Diary of a Writer*, translated and annotated by Boris Brasol, I, p. 648 (2 vols., New York, 1949). This edition will be referred to as *D*.
3 *Ibid.*, p. 651. Dostoevsky is referring to Jews in Russia.
4 *Ibid.*, p. 5.
5 *Ibid.*, pp. 6–7.
6 *Ibid.*, p. 7.

'French socialism' as the result of a movement away from Christ, a movement which he regards as exemplified in Catholicism, of which he believes socialism to be the child and heir.

Though Dostoevsky was prepared to admit that there had been and were individual Catholics who were genuine Christians, he saw the Catholic Church, especially as represented by the papacy and its Jesuit cohorts,[1] as having abandoned Christ for the pursuit of worldly power, thus succumbing to the third of the temptations suggested to Christ by the devil. And in socialism he saw the offspring of Catholicism, an offspring in which the movement away from Christ had taken the form of an open and explicit rejection of Christianity. The novelist awarded high marks to Prince Bismarck as being the only European statesman who had understood the real nature of Catholicism and of 'the monster begotten by it – socialism'.[2]

An important point is that Dostoevsky saw the Catholic Church as trying to impose its beliefs on mankind, to reduce its members to members of its own kind of ant-heap. This policy was inherited by socialism, the offspring of Catholicism. As we have noted, Russian radical thinkers of the time saw that a transformation of society would never be achieved except through the activity of leaders, an élite minority. While some, Tkachev for example, were quite prepared for a dictatorship of the minority over the majority, others feared this development and rejected the idea of one repressive régime being succeeded by another. The second group naturally believed that the reduction of the majority to plastic material to be moulded by the few was not a necessary feature of socialism. Dostoevsky, however, was convinced that it was. A triumphant socialism, in its endeavour to establish the kingdom of Man, would inevitably destroy human freedom and would also neglect the needs of actual men and women in the name of the needs and welfare of an abstraction, Humanity, or of future man.

It is easy to write off Dostoevsky's line of thought as the expression of strong and uncriticized prejudices against both Catholicism and socialism, as the point of view of a man who had become a reactionary in politics, a friend of the arch-conservative Pobedonostsev, and of one who had carried to extremes the hostility to Catholicism shown by early Slavophiles, with their insistence on the superiority of Orthodoxy. Besides, the Poles, another of Dostoevsky's targets, were mostly Catholics. It is

1 Joseph Frank speaks of Dostoevsky's 'horrified fascination with the Jesuits' as becoming one of his 'persistent obsessions'. *Dostoevsky, the Seeds of Revolt*, 1821–49, pp. 8 and 218.
2 *D.*, II, p. 909.

hardly surprising if a Russian upholder of the monarchy and of the virtues of Orthodoxy, a man who described the Jews as 'reigning in Europe', as rushing to exploit the emancipated serfs in Russia, and as exploiting liberated blacks in America, should also succumb to anti-Catholic and anti-socialist prejudice, representing both Catholicism and socialism in the worst possible light. If it were taken simply by itself, we might justifiably hesitate to attribute to Dostoevsky himself the view expressed by Prince Muishkin in his wild outburst against Catholicism in *The Idiot*. Given, however, what we know of Dostoevsky's views from the *Diary of a Writer*, we can reasonably see Prince Muishkin's outburst as representing substantially the novelist's own prejudiced outlook.

There is a good deal more to his treatment of socialism, however, than uncriticized prejudice. Naturally, living in the last decades of the twentieth century and looking back, we see Dostoevsky's utterances as prophetic. We see his view that revolution and the triumph of socialism would result in a dictatorship exercised by the few over the many as confirmed by the course of history in his own country. But this is not the point to which I wish to draw attention.

When Dostoevsky said that socialism would result in a dictatorship of the few over the many, he did not mean that the few would necessarily tyrannize over the many in the sense of maltreating them. He conceived of human beings in general as tending to find freedom or liberty a burden too heavy to bear, as wanting to be taken care of and to be told what to believe and what to do. This idea is clearly expressed in the Legend of the Grand Inquisitor in *The Brothers Karamazov*. From one point of view the Grand Inquisitor represents the Catholic Church, but he also represents socialism. After all, the Grand Inquisitor is represented as being himself an unbeliever. His argument is that human beings do not want to be free, and that they can be happy only in what the man from underground called the ant-heap or hen-coop or Crystal Palace. He reproaches Christ for calling men to freedom, and for trying to lay on their backs a burden which they cannot bear, and as thus trying to destroy their happiness and peace of mind. Dostoevsky regards freedom as a precious gift, and in his view belief in freedom is essential to Christianity: 'Making man responsible, Christianity *eo ipso* also recognizes his freedom'.[1]

But freedom involves the power to choose evil and the ability to revolt even against what reason dictates, in the spirit of the man from underground. Freedom involves the ability to destroy oneself and others. Dostoevsky can therefore feel the seductiveness of the Grand Inquisitor's

---

1 *D.*, I, p. 13.

line of thought, which the novelist states in such a masterly manner. Socialism may mean social engineering, the manipulation of human beings, their indoctrination, but it may make the majority of human beings content, satisfied from a material point of view – at a cost, the loss of freedom. Is what is gained worth what is lost? As far as the novels are concerned, the question has no clear answer given by Dostoevsky himself. In spite of all his diatribes against socialism, he knew that it had a case. Further, he saw that socialism could have a quasi-religious nature. Thus he said of atheists such as Belinsky and Herzen that 'having lost faith in one thing, they would promptly start passionately believing something else'.[1] For Dostoevsky at any rate, the atheistic socialists believed in the Man-god.

As the converse to socialism's ideal of the kingdom of Man, to the exclusion of God. Dostoevsky put forward his own view of the goal of history. In the *Diary of a Writer* this is presented as the union of 'nations abiding by the law of Christ's Gospel'[2] or 'the brotherhood of men'[3] in the spirit of Christ. Brotherhood, for Dostoevsky, involves respect for the value and freedom of the human person, as opposed to the reduction of human beings to cells in the social organism. Socialism, according to Dostoevsky, taught that what we call moral evil is simply the effect of a bad social environment and upbringing, and that society rather than the individual is responsible. Christianity teaches that in spite of influences from the social environment the individual is morally responsible and hence, by implication free. Evil therefore remains a possibility. But the ideal is that of universal Christian brotherhood, which should be conceived as the goal of history.

The thought of this ideal goal is linked with a grandiose conception of Russia's mission to mankind. Belonging both to the West and to the East, Russia was specially qualified to represent universal humanity. In his speech on Pushkin Dostoevsky asks, 'what else is the strength of the Russian national spirit than the aspiration . . . for universality and all-embracing humanitarianism?'[4] To be a genuine Russian means 'to become brother to all men, a universal man',[5] and Russia's mission is to unite mankind 'not by the sword but by the force of brotherhood'.[6] Further, in Dostoevsky's opinion genuine Christianity had been preserved best by the Russian Orthodox people, at any rate by the

1 *Ibid.*, p. 158.
2 *Ibid.*, II, p. 980.
3 *Ibid.*
4 *Ibid.*, pp. 978–9.
5 *Ibid.*, p. 979.
6 *Ibid.*

peasants,[1] and the union which he has in mind is a union in Christ. 'Not in communism, not in mechanical forms is the socialism of the Russian people expressed; they believe that they shall be finally saved *through the universal communion in the name of Christ*. This is our Russian socialism!'[2]

There has been some discussion about the extent to which Dostoevsky's Christ, as portrayed, for example, in the story of the Grand Inquisitor, resembles the Christ of the gospel narratives. But let us pass over this theme and raise another question. How, it may be asked, could a writer who was acutely aware of the dark aspects and abysses of human nature, who gave us the portraits of the man from underground, of Stavrogin, of Peter Verkhovensky, of Fyodor Karamazov, possibly imagine that the whole human race would be united in brotherhood and that 'the former beast in man would be vanquished'?[3] Dostoevsky was by no means always consistent, but could he possibly have been blind to the fact that he had himself provided good reasons for thinking that 'socialism', in the rather ill-defined sense in which he approved of socialism, was impractical, and that the only form of it which had any real chance of success was the very form which he abominated? Moreover, it is obvious that the path which Russia actually came to follow was different from the path which Dostoevsky prophesied that she would follow. To be sure, the ideal of universality remained, but it was to assume a form which would have been anathema to the novelist.

The reference to 'the goal of history' is not intended to imply that Dostoevsky looked on history as a process moving inevitably towards a certain predetermined end. In his utterances about universal brotherhood and about the spiritual mission of Russia he may indeed give the impression that this is precisely what he has in mind. The present writer, however, while recognizing that Dostoevsky ardently desired the realization of a certain goal, and that he did in fact make prophesies, does not believe that the novelist seriously thought that the course of history was determined. Christ, as portrayed by Dostoevsky, was a Christ who invites freely given allegiance, who has no intention of using coercion or power either to save himself or to win followers, and who inspires human

1 'It is said that the Russian people know the Gospel poorly, that they are ignorant of the basic principles of faith. Of course, this is true; but they do have Christ . . . Perhaps, Christ is the only love of the Russian people'. *D*, I, pp. 38–9. In his reply to Gogol Belinsky had made a different kind of assertion, namely that by nature the Russians were a profoundly atheistic people. Others maintained that the peasants' religion was skin deep. Dostoevsky, however, liked to contrast the faith of the common people with the Russian intelligentsia's lack of it and with western 'enlightenment'.

2 *D*., II, p. 1029.

3 *Ibid*., p. 999.

beings to unite together through mutual love rather than by means of a uniformity imposed from above. As far as this world is concerned, the reign of Antichrist remains a possibility. The choice rests with the human being. Leontyev regarded Dostoevsky (not to speak of Tolstoy) as having a 'rosy-coloured' view of Christianity, as looking forward to the advent of the kingdom of God on earth, whereas the New Testament provided no ground for any such expectation. In other words, Leontyev thought of Dostoevsky as forgetting about human evil, the fear of God and the prophecies relating to Antichrist. But though the novelist did indeed speak as though the kingdom of God could be realized on earth, it seems most unlikely that he believed its advent to be inevitable. He laid too much emphasis on human freedom for this.

Dostoevsky of course made a sharp contrast between the ideal of the Man-god and that of the God-man, between, one might say, the sort of ideas expounded by Feuerbach (supplemented by French socialism) on the one hand and Christian faith and ideals on the other. What would he say, it may be asked, about the contention of Max Stirner that, after God had been killed, it was then necessary to kill Man, in the sense that it was necessary to get rid of the abstraction 'Man' in the name of actual men and women, to reject the universal in the name of the concrete particulars? Presumably the answer is that Dostoevsky would agree only up to a point, to the point, that is to say, of sharing the view that the substitution of Man for God would end in slavery for actual human beings. Having, however, given us in the person of Raskolnikov in *Crime and Punishment* his conception of an isolated individual without God, Dostoevsky would certainly not regard Max Stirner's philosophy of egoism as acceptable.

It may be objected that, in this section, Dostoevsky has been represented as a firm believer in God, whereas in a letter he said plainly that the existence of God was the principal question or problem which had tormented him throughout his life.[1] However, although the novelist certainly experienced in himself the dialectic between belief and unbelief, a dialectic which is reflected in his writings, this does not alter the fact that he opposed the idea of the God-man, the ideal of Christ, to the apotheosis of Man. Besides, though Dostoevsky saw faith as best preserved in the Russian peasantry and advocated submission to 'the people's truth',[2] he was not himself a peasant. It is a great mistake to suppose that, if religious faith exists at all, it must always be untroubled,

---

1 *Letters (Pisma)*, II, p. 263.
2 *D.*, I, p. 204.

calm and serene. This was certainly not the case with Dostoevsky, except perhaps at the end.

From one point of view Dostoevsky's position during the later period of his life was that of an upholder of the monarchy, the Orthodox Church and Panslavism, and a resolute opponent not only of revolution and terrorism but also of the radical movement in general. When the novelist died on 28 January 1881, Alexander II (soon to be assassinated) granted his widow a substantial pension, and Pobedonostsev wrote to the future Alexander III, who was personally acquainted with Dostoevsky, that there was no one to take the place of the fiery champion of religion, nationalism and patriotism. It does not follow, however, that Dostoevsky had been satisfied with the actual state of affairs. We should not attach great weight to his admission to a friend that if he knew of a plot, he would probably not inform the authorities. But in some ways his social ideal resembled that of the Populists, except, of course, that it was a religious, and not a secular ideal. It may be said, and not without reason, that Dostoevsky's idea of 'Russian socialism' was extremely vague, and that he simply offered an ill-defined concept of universal brotherhood in Christ to secular radical ideals. This is substantially true, but it must be remembered that the secular radical ideals were also apt to be pretty vague. To conceive particular measures of reform was more a characteristic of liberal 'gradualists'. Utopian socialism, which despised gradualism, looked to the overthrow of the régime and a subsequent transformation of society, the precise nature of which could be determined when the break with the past had occurred. Dostoevsky, apart from the chauvinist elements in his thought, looked for a transformation in the minds and hearts of human beings as a condition for the development of a better society. He certainly had a point. But we cannot claim that he had a definite social programme. In the area of social theory he is remembered not for any social-political programme but for his critique of atheistic socialism and for prophecies about its development, if it were to triumph, prophecies which, as far as his own country is concerned, have been by and large fulfilled.

7. If we reflect on Dostoevsky's positive views as expressed in articles, in correspondence, and in the *Diary of a Writer*, and as suggested in his novels, we can hardly fail to note the conspicuous role which judgments of value played in his thought. One would not expect a novelist to pepper his novels with formal arguments presented in his own name. But it would be an exaggeration to say that Dostoevsky only asserts and never argues. The argumentation, however, which tends to be implicit, often takes the form of drawing inferences from judgments of value.

An example is provided by his attack on atheistic socialism. Dostoevsky does not offer metaphysical arguments to refute atheism and support belief in God. He argues that atheistic socialism, which seems to give human beings the freedom to create a society simply according to their own judgment of what society should be, inevitably ends in a new form of slavery. As Shigalev says in *The Possessed*, 'I began with unrestricted freedom and I ended with unrestricted despotism'.[1] Shigalev adds that this is the only solution to the social problem. Dostoevsky, however, offers an alternative, brotherhood in the spirit of Christ, a brotherhood in which the value of the human person as more than a cell in the social organism would be respected. He presupposes a positive evaluation of human freedom, argues that atheistic socialism negates or leads to the negation of freedom, and rejects it. This sort of argument will not work with anyone who does not value individual freedom. Nor will it work with someone who does value freedom but who is not prepared to admit that atheistic socialism involves the negation of freedom. For he can then consistently accept Dostoevsky's premise and deny his conclusion, that atheistic socialism should be rejected. But if someone agrees both with the relevant judgment of value and with the contention that atheistic socialism involves the negation of freedom, he will accept Dostoevsky's conclusion.

The present writer does not intend to imply that no theoretical support for the value-judgment in question can be offered. Support could take the form of working out a philosophical anthropology, for which the development of the human being requires the exercise of individual freedom. This is obviously what Dostoevsky thinks. Any such philosophical anthropology would doubtless itself include value-judgments, but they would form part of a justification of the positive evaluation of human freedom. The point being made here, however, is that in his attack on atheistic socialism Dostoevsky appeals to a basic judgment of value instead of giving metaphysical arguments to refute atheism. Of course, an atheistic socialist who was prepared to endorse Dostoevsky's thesis about the end-product of 'French socialism' and who also shared the novelist's evaluation of this end-product, might well be prompted to reconsider his or her world-view. But it seems safe to say that when this occurs, it is more as a result of seeing what atheistic socialism has actually produced, in historical fact, than as a result of accepting a not yet empirically verified hypothesis.

Another example. After his return from Siberia Dostoevsky wrote to a

1 *The Possessed*, Part 2, 7, 2.

lady who had befriended him that, even if it were ever proved to him that Christ was 'outside the truth', he would prefer to remain with Christ rather than with the truth.[1] This statement is likely to seem shocking to some (on the ground that it shows an indifference to truth), to others edifying. I suggest, however, that the novelist is identifying himself with Christ's assertion of love as the supreme value, with his respect for human freedom, his rejection of earthly power, and his refusal to unite human beings by coercion. In other words, even if it could be shown that there is no God and that reality is indifferent to human values, Dostoevsky would nonetheless desire that human beings should become what Christ wanted them to be and that human brotherhood should be realized. To put the matter in another way, even if there were no God and Christ had no divinely given mission, Dostoevsky would nonetheless stick to certain judgments of value. There is nothing shocking in this attitude. It does not involve an indifference to truth in a pejorative sense. It is the expression of a distinction between what is and what ought to be.

It is not a matter of Dostoevsky trying to deduce truths about the nature of reality from judgments of value about desirable social goals. It would be odd to represent the novelist as trying to deduce metaphysical or religious truths. It seems to me more a matter of his inviting those radical thinkers who may share his judgments of value, at any rate in regard to freedom and the value of the individual person, to reconsider their view of reality in the light of the probable consequences of substituting Man for God, of following Feuerbach and Saint-Simon[2] rather than Christ.

To conclude. Although Bertrand Russell could speak like a positivist when he chose, he nonetheless claimed, on occasion, that one of the jobs of philosophy was to keep alive awareness of problems such as that of the end or ends of life, even if it could not answer them. 'It is one of the functions of philosophy to keep alive interest in such questions'.[3] Dostoevsky's writings are relevant to philosophy primarily in virtue of their capacity to stimulate awareness of and personal reflection on such problems. And they have this capacity largely because the novelist himself was passionately interested in them and by no means indifferent. For

1 *Letters* (*Pisma*), I, p. 142. *Polnoe sobranie sochinenii*, vol. X, p. 311 (Leningrad, 1974). This the edition sponsored by the Academy of Sciences.

2 Saint-Simon, like Dostoevsky after him, regarded socialism as the offspring of Catholicism. But whereas Saint-Simon was a socialist and therefore emphasized the historical value of Catholicism, Dostoevsky disapproved strongly of the offspring, and so of the parent.

3 *Unpopular Essays*, p. 41 (London and New York, 1950). Russell adds, however, that philosophy, in the sense implied, is 'not compatible with mental maturity'. *Ibid.*, p. 77. Russell's attitude to philosophy was complex.

example, whatever we may think about Dostoevsky's personal belief in God, as distinct from adherence to the Christ-ideal as he conceived it, he was certainly not indifferent to the problem of God.[1] Nor, for the matter of that, were the atheistic radicals whom he attacked. It has been said that a passionate interest in such problems is a characteristic of Russians, and that Dostoevsky thereby shows himself to be a peculiarly Russian writer. He was, of course, a Russian writer, one of the greatest, and it is natural to think of him as such. At the same time he was concerned with human beings and human problems, not simply with Russians and Russian problems. In spite of some marked prejudices and a tendency to chauvinism, at any rate in his later years, he can speak significantly not only to people of later generations but also to members of nations other than his own, not by offering them any ready-made philosophical system, which he neither had nor claimed to have, but by stimulating them to personal thought about important issues, important, that is to say, to reflective human beings in general. Dostoevsky was not a 'nice' man. He could be spiteful and malicious. Granovsky and Turgenev, whom he caricatured, were much 'nicer'. But this does not diminish his relevance to philosophy. To be sure, if the problems raised in his great novels are formulated in a manner which makes them amenable to treatment in one of our departments of philosophy, the magic tends to evaporate. And it is no matter for surprise that, among philosophers, he has appealed mainly to those whom we tend to label as existentialists. It has been said of Dostoevsky that his 'views' are of importance mainly for understanding the novelist himself, rather than for understanding the real world, as distinct from the one which he created in his novels. The present writer, however, would wish to emphasize not so much Dostoevsky's 'views' as the stimulative value of the dialectic of ideas which he presents through his characters.

1 Dostoevsky makes one of his characters (Shatov in *The Possessed*) profess belief in the Orthodox Church and in Christ, while hesitating to claim that he believes in God and saying that he *will* believe in God. The novelist himself admitted that he was tormented by the problem of God. He obviously could not have suffered this 'torment', if he had been indifferent.

Chapter 8

Meaning in Life and History

1. It hardly needs saying that a person can give a meaning to his or her life by choosing an end or goal which serves to unify or bring together in a common pattern a multitude of successive particular choices and actions. Thus we might say of a devoted revolutionary that the meaning of his or her life was to work for the transformation of society or the realization of social justice. Again, the man who sincerely believes that he has a religious mission to mankind and strives, throughout his active life, to fulfil this mission can be seen as giving meaning, direction, purpose to his life, in the sense indicated. For the matter of that, the man who seeks consistently to maximize pleasure can be said to have given meaning or purpose to his life. So, of course, can the man who strives constantly to do the best (as it appears to him) for himself and his family. It is simply an empirical fact that people can and do give meanings or purpose to their lives.

If, however, someone asks 'what is the meaning of life?' or 'what is the goal of history?', he or she is probably thinking of a meaning or purpose which is determined independently of human choice and which it remains for human beings to discover, if they can. And if someone denies that life has any meaning, he or she is probably denying not that individuals are capable of choosing different goals or ideals or assigning meaning to their lives but that there is any common given meaning, purpose or goal which human beings do not determine themselves but have only to discover.

If someone asks 'what is the meaning of life?' or 'what is the goal of history?' in this sense, it can, of course, be objected that the question presupposes an assumption or assumptions (such as that life *has* a meaning) which stands in need of justification and cannot be taken for granted. It is possible, however, to ask not 'what is the meaning of life?' but whether there is any good reason for believing that human life has a meaning or purpose, or that history has a goal, independently of the meanings or goals which individuals choose to assign to life or history. Or, if an assumption is made, it can be stated, with a view to examining its implications, if any, in regard to human life and history. It is also possible to ask whether there is any ideal or goal of such preeminent intrinsic value that we are justified in claiming that human beings ought to accept it as the goal of history, a goal to be realized through concerted human effort.

In other words, even if questions such as 'what is the meaning of life?' are open to criticism, and even if it is difficult to find satisfactory formulations for such questions, this is not a sufficient reason for dismissing problems relating to the meaning or purpose of human life and history as pseudo-problems. Questions about values, ideals, goals, arise out of reflection on life as experienced and history as known, not simply out of muddle-headedness.

To say this is not to deny that distinctions are required. A person might ask 'what meaning have I given to my life?' In other words, 'what is my truly operative ideal (which may be different from my professed ideal)?' Or a person might ask 'what meaning ought I to give to my life?', 'what is really worth striving after?' In raising such questions a person may be primarily concerned with his or her own individual life. But if a person asks, in a general way, 'what is the meaning of life?' or 'what is the ultimate goal or purpose of human life, if there is one?', the person is probably thinking not simply of his or her individual life but of human life in general, or of his or her life as the life of a social being, a member of society. In this case questions about what meaning I should attach to my life merge with questions about the goal of history.

For a good many Russian thinkers problems relative to the meaning of life and of human history have been real problems, urgent and important problems. This was the case with Dostoevsky. It was also the case with another great Russian writer, namely Tolstoy. Although the questions may have arisen in a personal context, in the form of asking, for example, 'has *my* life any meaning or value or worthwhile goal?', they tended to become general questions about human beings in their historical and social development. This is clear in the case of Tolstoy.

2. Count Leo Nikolayevich Tolstoy (1828–1910) was brought up in the Orthodox faith. In his *Confession* he tells us that he began to read philosophical works at the age of fifteen, and that in the following year he abandoned prayer and attendance at church. All that remained

to him of his religious faith was a 'belief in perfection. But in what perfection consisted and what its aim was, I would not have been able to say'.[1] With most educated members of his social class, he remarks, it was impossible to tell from their actions in ordinary life whether they were believers or not. In other words, the profession of Orthodoxy made little practical difference in life, and it was easy to shed the beliefs inculcated in childhood.

Despite an initial vague desire for self-perfection, the passions soon took over, and, according to his own account, Tolstoy led a dissolute life, accompanied by a desire for literary fame[2] and by the fashionable belief in 'progress'. Perhaps we can say that he tried to find the meaning of life in life itself, in zest for the varied experiences which it offered. The word 'tried' is required, as Tolstoy admits that in his heart he was far from being satisfied with his manner of life while, as the saying goes, he was sowing his wild oats.

After a period of service in the army (1852–6) Tolstoy travelled in western Europe, visiting, for example, Germany, France, Italy and England, and developed an interest in educational theory and method. On his return to his estate of Yasnaya Polyana after the second of his visits to the West (1860–1) he founded a school for peasant children, published an educational magazine and wrote textbooks. At this time he still shared more or less in the belief in progress which was characteristic of the literary circle with which he had become acquainted at St Petersburg, though the sight of an execution in Paris (Tolstoy was convinced of the wrongness of capital punishment) and the death of his brother Nikolai in 1860 had raised doubts in his mind about the sufficiency of belief in progress as a faith and guide for life. Of the early and agonizing death of his brother he says that Nikolai died 'not understanding for what purpose he had lived and still less for what purpose he was dying'.[3] In his educational work for the peasant children on his estate Tolstoy found an occupation which was useful and also interesting, as he had to consider what they really needed to learn and how to teach it. At the same

1 *Polnoe sobranie sochinenii*, XXIII, p. 4, p. 97 (91 vols., Moscow, 1928–64). This edition of Tolstoy's writings will be referred to as *SS*. In the reprint (AMS Press, New York) of L. Wiener's English translation of Tolstoy's *Complete Works* 'My Confession' is included in Vol. XIII.

2 While on military service in the Caucasus, Tolstoy wrote sections of a largely autobiographical novel. *Childhood* was published in 1852 in Nekrasov's journal *The Contemporary*. *Boyhood* and *Youth* followed in 1854 and 1857 respectively. Other early writing included *A Landlord's Morning* (1856), *The Cossacks* (1863) and *Family Happiness* (1859). In *The Cossacks* Olenin seeks a natural and spontaneous life among the Cossacks, illustrating the influence of Rousseau on Tolstoy's thought.

3 *SS*, XXIII, p. 8.

time he felt, so he tells us, that he could not teach others what was necessary, as he himself did not know what was necessary.

In 1862 Tolstoy married Sophie Andreyevna Bers and lived a happy family life for some fifteen years, managing his estate and writing his two most famous works, *War and Peace* (1863–9) and *Anna Karenina* (1873–7). Although, however, he tells us that in his writings he advocated what was for him the one truth, that one should live so as to win the greatest possible good for oneself and one's family, questions about the meaning of life became more insistent. There are expressions of this even in the great novels. For example, in *War and Peace* Pierre Bezukhov raises the problem of the meaning of life, and in *Anna Karenina* Levin asserts that it is not possible for him to live without knowing why he is here. 'But I cannot know that, and therefore I cannot live'.[1] It is not simply a question of how he should live. Death ends all, and in the light of death the question arises why he should live. The novelist's official conclusion, so to speak, in both novels may be that love and family life constitute the answer to the problem, but when he was engaged in writing the later parts of *Anna Karenina* Tolstoy had already started to undergo the spiritual crisis which reached its culminating point in 1879, and of which he writes in his *Confession*.

Tolstoy likens himself to a man who has lost his way in a forest, who searches for a way out, and who cannot find one. The point is that he wants to escape. If Tolstoy were thoroughly convinced that life is meaningless, he could accept the situation. But he is seeking an answer to the problem of life, and it is the conflict between the desire for light and the inability to find it which prompts thoughts of suicide. Previous answers, such as satisfaction in family life, no longer satisfy him. Science, he realizes at last, cannot answer his problem, for it has no place for consideration of final causality. As for philosophy, 'however I may twist the speculative answers of philosophy, I receive nothing which resembles an answer – not because, as in the clear, experimental sphere [i.e. empirical science], the answer is unrelated my question, but because here, although the whole mental labour is directed precisely to my question, there is no answer. Instead of an answer one receives the same question, only in a complicated form'.[2] The question 'why live?' arises because life, ending in death, seems to be nothing, a vanity, an evil. The answer given by Schopenhauer, for example, that life is indeed a vanity, an emptiness, is or implies a repetition of the question. At any rate it restates the ground for the question.

1 *SS*, XIX, p. 370 (Part 8, section 9).
2 *Ibid.*, XXIII, p. 20.

Finally Tolstoy came to the conclusion that it was not life as such which was meaningless or evil but rather *his* life, his manner of living. 'Real life'[1] was to be found not among the upper classes or the sophisticated and sceptical but among the Russian peasantry. The peasants might have, and did have, all sorts of superstitions and irrational beliefs, but they were sustained by a faith in the meaningfulness of life, in the context of belief in God and of acceptance of God's will as providing a rule of life. Real life, in other words, was a life sustained by religious faith. It was not, for Tolstoy, a question of proving God's existence. He did indeed make an attempt to refute Kant's claim that it was impossible to prove the existence of God[2], but any proof, it seemed to him, provided only a concept of God, the concept being different from the reality. What he was searching for was God himself. He was seeking 'the shore'. 'The shore – this was God'.[3] As participating in this movement towards God, towards closer union with him, Tolstoy believed that he had grasped the meaning of life. He had found the truth among the simple and illiterate.

Except for those who adhered to breakaway sects, the religion of the peasants was, of course, that of the Russian Orthodox Church. And it is not surprising that Tolstoy tried at first to live the life of an Orthodox Christian. In spite, however, of his confidence that 'real life' was to be found among the peasants, he was not one of them; he was an aristocrat, a landowner, a highly educated man and a great writer. He did indeed lay emphasis on the intuitive grasp of truth. In *Anna Karenina* Levin had been depicted as knowing infallibly what was right and what was wrong when he left off thinking about such problems and seeking rationally proved answers and trusted instead to his innate moral knowledge, to the immediate voice of conscience, to an intuitive apprehension of the moral quality of an action. At the same time Tolstoy had his rationalist side, and he could not remain content for long with the official Orthodox religion. In his view, Orthodoxy, as adhered to by the mass of believers, was a mixture of truth and falsity, of luminous truth and of doctrines which exceeded the bounds of credibility. He therefore set himself to sort out the elements of truth and falsity. He studied theology, and the result was his *Critique of Dogmatic Theology* (1881–2), which followed on his *Confession*.

The *Critique of Dogmatic Theology* amounted to a wholesale rejection of the official doctrines of the Church, of the Church's exclusiveness (in regard to other Christian bodies and to non-Christian religions), of

1 *SS*, p. 43. *Confession*, section 12.
2 *Ibid.*, p. 44.
3 *Ibid.*, p. 47.

the hierarchy's qualifications for teaching the faithful, and of the sacramental system. Although, however, the *Critique*, as its title implies, was predominantly critical, Tolstoy's rejection of Orthodoxy was not the expression of an anti-Christian attitude. He was concerned with getting rid of all that he believed to be false, superstitious, misleading, in order to present the genuine message of Christ, of the Gospels, as he conceived it. This he did in such writings as *What I Believe* (1884), *The Kingdom of God is Within You* (1892) and *What is Religion?* (1902). Tolstoy had by no means attained unruffled peace and serenity within himself. And his struggles to implement his ideals of poverty and sexual abstinence led to tensions and conflicts within the family, especially in relation to his wife. But he had assumed the mantle of a preacher or prophet, and he expounded the meaning of human life in general. As a great and famous writer, with an international reputation, the sage of Yasnaya Polyana could not be ignored. In 1901 he was excommunicated by the authorities of the Russian Orthodox Church, but this did not prevent him from continuing to proclaim what he regarded as the genuine Christian message to mankind.

Tolstoy's conversion to Christianity as he understood it is generally regarded as having had a deleterious effect on his literary work. It is, of course, true that his novel *Resurrection* (1899) does not measure up to the standards of *War and Peace* and *Anna Karenina*, and that, apart from the story *Hadji Murat*[1], his later fictional pieces show the influence, in one way or another, of his new ideas. For example *The Kreutzer Sonata*, *The Devil* and *Father Sergius* bear witness to the author's preoccupation with sexual temptation[2], while *The Death of Ivan Ilyich* (1886) recalls Tolstoy's own sense of the meaninglessness of life in the face of death and his conversion to the gospel of love. But though in his later fictional writing, apart from *Hadji Murat*, we can see Tolstoy as moralizing, he had by no means lost his ability as an artist. And if we had not got his two masterpieces as standards of comparison, the stories which he wrote subsequently to his conversion would probably seem more notable than they do when we inevitably see them in relation to *War and Peace* and *Anna Karenina*.

As Tolstoy was sincere in his beliefs about the way in which life should be lived, he was not only well aware of but also deeply troubled by the contrast between his ethical ideals and his position as an aristocratic

---

1 *Hadji Murat* was finished in 1904 but it was not published until after Tolstoy's death.
2 The *Kreutzer Sonata* was banned in 1890, but the Tsar gave Tolstoy's wife permission to include it in a collection of his writings. *The Devil*, written in 1889, was published posthumously. *Father Sergius* appeared in 1898.

landowner. But it was also trouble within the family[1] which led to his abandoning wife and home at the age of eighty-two and setting out to find a refuge elsewhere. Contracting pneumonia on the journey, Tolstoy died in the railway station of Astapovo, in the Province of Ryazan, on 20 November 1910.

3. From an early age Tolstoy was attracted by Rousseau, and he continued to respect the French philosopher. Rousseau's claim that human beings were originally good, that they have been corrupted in the process of developing civilization with its division of labour, its multiplication of needs, its class and national enmities, its hypocrisies and artificiality, and that everywhere people are in chains, lacking true freedom, was congenial to Tolstoy. It harmonized with the conclusions which he himself drew from reflection on Russian society and on his own life. Further, Tolstoy naturally sympathized with Rousseau's claim that the principles of morality are graven on every heart and with the simple, intuitive and non-dogmatic religious faith of Rousseau's Savoyard priest. At the same time Rousseau's justification of the state through his doctrine of the General Will was obviously unacceptable to a man who came to reject the state as being essentially an organ of coercion and violence.

Another philosopher who exercised some influence on Tolstoy's mind was Schopenhauer. During the period when he was dominated by the apparent meaninglessness of life, Tolstoy was attracted by what seemed to him Schopenhauer's honest portrayal of human life, a portrayal which distinguished him from most other philosophers. Tolstoy had come to think that, whereas Schopenhauer had a clear grasp of the problem – that is to say the problem of the meaning of life – the solution of the problem must be sought elsewhere than in the German philosopher's theory of the Will. At the same time Schopenhauer's phenomenalism seems to have made an impression on Tolstoy's mind. In his Diary he wrote of man's consciousness of individuality, of separateness, as being an illusion, dependent on corporeality or matter as the principle of individuation. And he came to think of the real self as a manifestation not of Schopenhauer's Will but of the life of God as love. Thus in *The Law of Violence and the Law of Love* (1908), which forms part of his last testament, Tolstoy asserts that what we call our self is 'a divine principle, limited in

1 Tolstoy's wife understandably wished to maintain a comfortable family life and resisted her husband's attempts to give away his possessions. She also had to cope with Tolstoy's attitude to sexual relations. The wife had managed to obtain the copyright of works published before 1880. But relations between the two became increasingly strained.

us by the body, which reveals itself in us as love'.[1] He does not undertake to explain the precise relationship between the real self and God, but at any rate he makes it clear that, in his view, the human being without love is simply the 'animal personality', living an illusory life, whereas the true or real self is the self inspired by the love which constitutes the divine life.

Though, however, Tolstoy's thought was influenced to some degree by Rousseau and Schopenhauer, the source of his inspiration after his conversion was first and foremost the New Testament, in particular the gospels and the epistles of St John. This statement needs, however, some elucidation. Tolstoy did not accept the doctrine of the Incarnation, and what he found in the gospels, after he had eliminated miraculous events and the bodily resurrection of Christ, was a moral message, the message of love. This is, of course, why he laid stress on St John's epistles. He recognized that love appeared in the hierarchy of values of other religions, such as Buddhism, but, in his view, Christianity alone had conceived the law of love as 'the supreme law of life, admitting no exceptions'.[2]

It would not be accurate to say that Tolstoy reduced Christianity simply to the law of love. The principles which he enunciated in *What I Believe* include the prohibition of lust, a matter which caused Tolstoy a lot of difficulty in his personal life. But, apart from a perhaps rather vague belief in God, he certainly reduced Christianity to its ethical content, and he laid special emphasis on the law of love, which he regarded as the key to the meaning of life. If a human being were inspired by universal love, the meaning of life would be clear, even if the person could not state it.

The idea of loving without making any exceptions implied, of course, that one should love the members of all nations, all races, all classes. It also meant that one should never practise coercion or violence, not even to resist aggression or evil. For Tolstoy, coercion and violence were incompatible with love. And he was prepared to draw the logical conclusions of this belief, however unrealistic or even outrageous they might seem to many minds.

One of these conclusions relates to the state. As has already been noted, Tolstoy regarded the state as being, by its very essence, an organ of coercion. He therefore condemned it and desired its disappearance. He can thus be described as an anarchist. At the same time this descriptive epithet can be misleading. For it suggests the idea of someone who works

1 *SS*, XXXVII, p. 168. (Chapter 7).
2 *Ibid*. (and elsewhere).

for or plans or at any rate desires the overthrow of the state by revolution. If, however, all coercion and violence are wrong, political revolution is also wrong. Given his view of the state, Tolstoy obviously could not approve of those who supported the existing régime. But neither could he approve of the Russian revolutionaries. What he wanted was a change of heart, a moral conversion. If everyone pursued moral perfection and tried to realize ever more fully the ideal of a love which knows no exceptions, the state would wither away. Further, mankind would come to enjoy all the blessings promised by socialists, communists and other would-be transformers of society, without the employment of the means which they advocated. Tolstoy obviously could not endorse the idea of a minority capturing political power and then using this power to mould society. While he recognized and deplored existing social evils and cannot be described as a conservative (conservatives do not condemn the state as such), he cannot be described as a revolutionary either. If we call him an anarchist, as indeed he was, we have to add the adjective 'Christian'.

For Tolstoy capital punishment was a glaring example of violence exercised by the state. After the assassination of Alexander II in 1881, he appealed to the new Tsar to act in a Christian spirit and show clemency to the assassins. Needless to say, Alexander III disregarded this appeal. In *I cannot be Silent* (1908) Tolstoy, indignant at recent executions, expressed his horror of capital punishment. 'Human love – it is the love of man for man, for every man, as a son of God and therefore a brother. Whom do you love in this way? Nobody. And who loves you? Nobody'.[1]

War also was condemned, war as such, not only aggressive but also defensive war. Tolstoy took literally Christ's injunctions to love one's enemies and not to offer resistance. As far as he was concerned, the principle of non-resistance, of not returning evil for evil, violence for violence, was not simply a lofty ideal which only a few people could be expected to realize. It bound all. Compromise was anathema to Tolstoy, and he was contemptuous of the way in which, in his opinion, the Church betrayed her Master by justifying capital punishment and the military exploits of the state. Zenkovsky not inaptly remarks that, although Tolstoy denied that Christ was divine in a unique sense, he nonetheless accepted Christ's words (those of them, that is to say, which he was prepared to recognize as Christ's) as though they were the words of God himself.[2] At the same time Tolstoy believed that the validity of the law of

1 *SS*, XXXVII, p. 96.
2 *A History of Russian Philosophy*, I, p. 396.

love should be clear to all unspoiled minds, and that to meet violence with violence was incompatible with obedience to this law.

Even those who have a profound respect for Tolstoy's uncompromising moral idealism may well feel doubts about his sweeping condemnation of the state and his conviction that its disappearance is desirable. It is arguable that even if everyone sincerely loved everyone else and never did anything wrong, political society and government would still be required to exercise certain functions. How, it may be asked, could there be a stable society without government in some form? Moreover, as it is most unlikely that all members of a given society will live as Tolstoy thinks they should live, how can coercion be entirely avoided, even if it is made as mild and humane as possible?

Tolstoy was, of course, aware that he would be accused of being unrealistic and of making impractical demands. One of his answers to such criticism is that when people try to imagine human society without governmental authority, they immediately think of what Hobbes described as the war of all against all, and that this amounts to conceiving human beings as possessing by nature or essence the characteristics which have been produced and fostered in them by the institution of the state. In other words, the state's example of coercion and violence stimulates human beings to act, when they can, in the same sort of way. It is the state which has corrupted human beings. If the state were abolished, natural goodness would manifest itself. Another line of answer proposed by Tolstoy is that we cannot know in advance what life without government would be like. Those who claim that life without the state would be a war of all against all do not speak from experience.

From the historical point of view, we can see Tolstoy as re-echoing Rousseau's view of the corrupting effects of civilization as it has developed. Abstractly, we can see Tolstoy as emphasizing the role of organized society in determining individuals' attitudes, reactions and values. But we have to balance the element of social determinism in his thought by adding that, in his judgment, a change in political and social structures is no guarantee that a truly human society will result. Nothing can take the place of an interior moral conversion, a change of heart. One cannot make people love one another by legislation or by coercion. We are thus faced with the old problem. A bad régime is likely to corrupt the citizens. But if the citizens are bad, even a well-planned social edifice will soon become riddled with corruption. Perhaps one might draw the conclusion that political, educational and moral reform should accompany one another. But this policy would smack of a liberalism or gradualism which was not to Tolstoy's taste, even if he himself sometimes followed it, as in his educational work among the peasants before his marriage.

As for Tolstoy's principle of non-resistance, his most famous heir was Mahatma Gandhi, with his condemnation of violence and his policy of passive resistance, a policy which was not unsuccessful. In regard to war, a good many people would obviously argue that it is clearly the duty of a government to see to the defence of a nation from attack, if defence is possible and unless the citizens as a whole voluntarily choose surrender rather than resistance. In the contemporary world, however, Tolstoy's condemnation of war is likely to meet with more sympathy than it did in the nineteenth century. The reasons for this are obvious.

4. Tolstoy's belief in the primacy of the ethical, or moral goodness, naturally affected what he had to say about art in the years after his conversion. Thus in *What is Art?* (1897–8) he is particularly concerned with refuting any theory which represents art as being independent of morality. Art, he tells us, is a subject which has interested him for fifteen years, and in the work he refers to a large number of writers on aesthetics, German, French and English.

Let us suppose, for the sake of argument, that art is devoted to the portrayal of beauty, whereas morality is directed to the attainment of goodness, beauty, goodness and truth forming a triad of distinct basic concepts. What is beauty? If we prescind from the empty statements of metaphysicians, it is 'nothing but what pleases us'.[1] But the pursuit of pleasure should be subordinated to the pursuit of moral goodness, which is 'the eternal, highest goal of our life'[2], our life being 'nothing but a striving towards the good, that is towards God'.[3]

In point of fact Tolstoy is not prepared to define art in terms of the portrayal of beauty. For if beauty is simply what pleases us, and if art aims solely at giving pleasure, art is 'an empty amusement for idle people'.[4] Artistic creation, according to Tolstoy, is 'an activity, by means of which one man, having experienced a feeling, consciously conveys it to another'.[5] Whereas speech is a means of uniting human beings in knowledge, art unites them in feeling. Genuine art, therefore, can be known by its capacity to unite human beings on the level of feeling, blending them, as it were, with the artist.

1 *SS*, XXX, p. 79, section VII.
2 *Ibid.*, p. 78.
3 *Ibid.*
4 *Ibid.*, p. 80.
5 *Ibid.*, p. 141. Section XIV.

It is natural to ask whether Tolstoy is referring to any sort of feeling, or to a particular kind or type. True art, he replies, is that which conveys the feelings which result from the religious consciousness of the time (not of an earlier time or age). The religious consciousness of 'our time' is Christian, and Christian art is that which unites all human beings, evoking the feelings of their oneness with God and with their fellows. Obviously, Christianity has to be understood here in terms of Tolstoy's own concept of Christianity, as being essentially the law of love without exception. Tolstoy is not thinking of Christian dogmas. In his view, these are alien to the religious consciousness of 'our time'. He is referring to universal love, and his contention is that the true art of 'our time' tends to unite or is capable of uniting all human beings on the level of feeling.

In this case, of course, art must be accessible to all. The art which is accessible only to a sophisticated, highly educated class is not, for Tolstoy, true art. Not being a man who is afraid to draw the conclusions which follow from his premises, Tolstoy is prepared, for example, to assign Beethoven's ninth symphony to the category of bad art, on the ground that it can be appreciated only by the few. It is no good telling him that instead of bringing down art to the level of the tastes of peasants, people should be educated in such a way as to facilitate appreciation of good art and music. For what he emphasizes is communication of universal love on the level of feeling, and, in his view, love is more likely to be found among the simple than among the sophisticated.

Tolstoy's rejection of the belief in art for art's sake and the emphasis which he lays on accessibility as a mark of good art can obviously be seen as forming part of that critique of culture, considered as the prerogative of the few, which found expression in the aesthetic theories of Chernyshevsky and Pisarev and in Lavrov's emphasis on the debt which the educated owed to the uneducated workers and peasants. Whereas, however, a Nihilist such as Pisarev was given to proclaiming the social utility of science at the expense of art, Tolstoy subordinated both science and art to the interests of morality. Science, as Tolstoy sees it, introduces into people's consciousness the truths 'which are considered the most important by the men of a certain time and society'[1], whereas art 'transfers these truths from the sphere of knowledge into the sphere of feeling'.[2] Both are required for progress, inasmuch as both contribute to unity among human beings, science on the level of knowledge, art on the level of feeling. But the final end, to which both science and art should be

1 *Ibid.*, p. 186. Section XX.
2 *Ibid.*

subordinated, is determined by the religious consciousness of the time and its conception of the goal of life. In 'our time' this is the Christian consciousness. It is in the light of this consciousness that we can see that the meaning of life is to be found not in knowledge as an end in itself, nor in art for art's sake, but in the universal love which constitutes genuine religion.

It is hardly necessary to say that in the Soviet Union Tolstoy is respected as one of the greatest Russian writers. As the author of *War and Peace* he is definitely *persona grata*. The Jubilee edition of his writings consists of ninety-one volumes (Moscow, 1928–64), and there is an extensive literature on individual works, various aspects of his thought, and his relations to other writers. As for his post-conversion ideas, his criticism of the régime and its ways, of contemporary society and of the Orthodox Church is obviously acceptable to Marxists. His positive ideals, however, and his preaching of non-resistance naturally appear unrealistic and 'reactionary' to adherents of 'scientific socialism'. Tolstoy was not, of course, a reactionary in the sense that he supported and wished to maintain the autocracy. He did nothing of the kind. Dostoevsky's ideas about loyalty to the Tsar and about the virtues of Orthodoxy were foreign to his mind. But from the Marxist point of view Tolstoy did not discern the movement of history. Though he was no friend of the régime, neither was he a supporter of the revolutionary movement. While condemning the reaction of the authorities to the revolution of 1905, his criticism was also levelled against the revolutionaries. As we have said, he insisted on the need for a change of heart and a rejection of violence by all parties. At the same time it is obvious that Tolstoy reduced Christianity, apart from a rather vague concept of God, to what he regarded as the content of intuitive moral knowledge. In a sense, both Dostoevsky and Tolstoy created their own pictures of Christ. But whereas with Dostoevsky the person of Christ, the 'Russian Christ', stands in the centre of the picture, with Tolstoy Christ tends to be little more than an eniment preacher of Tolstoyan morality, the law of universal love. Perhaps it is not altogether absurd if one suggests that for the Marxist Tolstoy is easier to digest than Dostoevsky. The latter, once a socialist, became a friend of Pobedonostsev, whereas the former, an aristocrat, became a 'Christian anarchist'.

5. As any persevering reader of *War and Peace* is aware, Tolstoy not only includes some reflections on history in the course of the novel but also devotes the whole of the second part of the Epilogue to a discussion of historiography and philosophy of history. Whatever one may think of

the appositeness or otherwise, from a literary point of view, of adding what amounts to a philosophical dissertation to one of the world's greatest novels, Tolstoy himself attached importance to his general conclusions about history and regarded them as exhibiting the point, so to speak, of the work. As for the validity and value of these reflections, opinions have differed.

The subject of history, according to Tolstoy, is the life of nations and of humanity in general. What, he asks, determines the movements of nations? What are the causes of historical events? Modern historians, we are told, assume that the causes of the movements of nations are a few men in their exercise of power. These men obviously include people such as Napoleon I, people described by Hegel as 'world-historical individuals', but they may also include thinkers such as the philosophers of the French Enlightenment, whose ideas are regarded as bringing about events such as the Revolution in France. Tolstoy then proceeds to argue that the role of 'great men' in history is really insignificant, that the movements of nations, as in the Napoleonic wars, are due to a multitude of causes and cannot be ascribed simply to the wills and decisions of individuals such as Napoleon and Alexander I of Russia, and that these causes are so numerous that we cannot know them all. Historians obviously find it easier to explain the course of history in terms of the lives, choices and decisions of certain individuals. And the 'great men' of history would doubtless endorse their point of view. In point of fact, however, historians, by concentrating their attention on a few individuals, fail to explain the course of history. Having discarded the ancient theological belief that God determines the cause of history, using human instruments, in view of a predetermined end or goal, historians have failed lamentably to produce a sound non-theological causal explanation. The 'great men' on whom they focus their attention are really the froth on the crest of the wave, not the causes of the wave's movement.

Let us leave aside the question whether Tolstoy was fair to the 'modern historians', even of his own time. His contention that the cause of history cannot be explained simply in terms of the wills of 'great men', such as Julius Caesar, Genghis Khan and Napoleon I, is obviously justified. The Reformation, for example, cannot be adequately accounted for simply in terms of the choices of a few prominent figures, and it is hardly necessary to say that Napoleon would have got nowhere without his armies. Tolstoy, however, goes to the opposite extreme. To take an example from the later history of his own country, Lenin was certainly not the sole cause of the Russian revolution, but neither was he simply the froth on the crest of a wave. Lenin took advantage of an opportunity which, for the most part, was not of his making, but the point is that he took advantage of it. The Bolshevik seizure of power in the autumn of 1917 was largely due to the determination of one man, namely Lenin. Similarly, though Napoleon's commands would have been inoperative if nobody had obeyed them, it would be absurd to claim that his commands were ineffective, and still more absurd to claim that he really did not command at all and exercised no effective power.

To make these points may be to labour the obvious, but Tolstoy's debunking of the role of 'world-historical' figures is probably the best known feature of his reflections on history. It is therefore appropriate to observe that, while he is quite right in maintaining that the course of history cannot be explained simply in terms of the lives and activities of a few prominent individuals, it is an exaggeration to depict people such as Genghis Khan or Napoleon as impotent pawns in mass movements. Stalin was certainly not the sole cause of the development of Russia during a period of some twenty-five years, but he was by no means impotent.

There is another aspect to the matter. Reason, according to Tolstoy, demands an infinite chain of causes. Let us assume that Napoleon's decisions did have historical effects. The decisions themselves were caused, and their causes had other causes, and so on. But we do not know, and cannot know, the whole chain of causes. Great men and small men alike are caught, as it were, in a web of causal relations which the human mind cannot grasp. As long as we remain content with a superficial point of view, we can ascribe historical events to the choices of a few individuals; but once we start to penetrate below the surface, we come up against our ignorance.

The natural conclusion to draw is that a causal explanation of the movements of nations cannot be given. In this case there is obviously no point in blaming historians for not providing us with one, even if we blame them for offering a bogus substitute. But the conclusion just mentioned seems to imply an identification of 'cause' with 'sufficient cause.' True, we cannot know all the causal factors involved in the movements of nations or the life of humanity in general, but it by no means follows that one cannot discern any contributing causal factor or any necessary condition for the occurrence of an historical event. The situation in Russia in the autumn of 1917 was due to a multitude of causes. There was what can be described as a revolutionary situation. The Provisional government was unstable. But for the small group of Bolshevik leaders to seize power a decision was required. Lenin made it. To be sure, nothing would have happened, if his colleagues had refused to listen, judging an attempt to seize power premature and too foolhardy. The fact remains that a decision was required, and that it was taken by Lenin. We can, of course, sympathize with Tolstoy's evident conviction that in history there are causal factors lying below the surface, but it is clearly wrong to suppose that, because no complete causal explanation of an event can be given, partial causal explanations are unenlightening. Nobody supposes this in ordinary life. Why should we do so in regard to history, except because one has settled on a standard of causal explanation which cannot be attained?

What Tolstoy actually says, however, is that the idea of causation can be laid aside in favour of a search for laws. Natural scientists, knowing that they cannot grasp the infinite chain of causal relations, seek for laws, and if there is to be a science of history, the example of the natural scientists should be followed by seeking to discover the laws of the movements of people and nations. 'To discover and define these laws constitutes the task of history.'[1] Tolstoy does not undertake to state such laws himself, but this is the task which he assigns to historians.

It seems that by laws Tolstoy understands laws which determine the cause of history in such a way that no exception is possible. For he proceeds to discuss the subject of human freedom. To the present writer at any rate the conclusion which he intends his readers to draw from the discussion is not altogether clear. On the one hand he asserts that there is an unwavering consciousness of freedom, which is felt by everyone without exception, and that to imagine a human being without any freedom at all is to imagine a human being destitute of life. On the other hand he asserts that if human freedom is admitted, there can be no historical laws, and that, for the historian, any appeal to human free choice simply expresses a gap in our knowledge of the operation of law, of necessity.

As Tolstoy makes a distinction between consciousness and reason and maintains that while consciousness gives us awareness of freedom, reason demands recognition of law and necessity, we might perhaps interpret him on these lines. History as a science, which looks at the human being from 'outside,' as an object, does not allow for freedom, but we have an inner and unavoidable awareness of our freedom, which is a reality. After all, Tolstoy says that consciousness expresses the reality of freedom. At the end of the Epilogue, however, Tolstoy draws an analogy between astronomy and history. To accommodate their minds to the Copernican hypothesis human beings had to surmount the

---

1 SS, XII, p. 338. Section XI.

immediate 'feeling' that the earth is stationary, immobile, and recognize a motion of which they were not conscious. Analogously, in regard to history we have to renounce the feeling of freedom and recognize a necessity of which we are not conscious. This analogy seems to imply that belief in freedom is an illusion, an expression of our ignorance of necessity.

Tolstoy's apparent desire to assimilate history to the natural sciences is likely to seem surprising to anyone who knows him only as a great novelist who became a preacher of love and non-resistance. In his brilliant and stimulating monograph *The Hedgehog and the Fox*[1] Sir Isaiah Berlin asserts that Tolstoy had a hatred of scientism and positivism, and that he wanted to emphasize the limitations of our knowledge and the superficiality of the explanations of historical events offered by historians. If we were to press this line of thought we might perhaps interpret Tolstoy as claiming that if history were a science, it should be able to discover and state the laws governing the movements of nations and the life of humanity in general; that historians have not formulated and cannot formulate such laws; and that history cannot therefore be a science. At the same time Berlin admits that it is 'Tolstoy's explicit doctrine in *War and Peace* that all truth is in science,'[2] and that the novelist sometimes speaks 'as if science could in principle, if not in practice, penetrate and conquer everything'.[3]

Tolstoy always attached importance to the views expressed in the Epilogue to *War and Peace*. In the final section of the Epilogue, however, he asserts that though some philosophers have used the 'law of necessity' as a weapon against religion, the idea of necessity in history 'far from destroying, even strengthens the ground on which the institutions of state and church are erected'.[4] As Tolstoy was to take the position of a resolute opponent of these institutions, his statement provides us with food for thought. It suggests at any rate that in the Epilogue to *War and Peace* he pursued a line of thought which was really alien to his mind, though he was doubtless convinced, and remained convinced, that the cause of history cannot be explained simply in terms of the ideas, projects and decisions of selected prominent individuals. After all, there is a sense in which all human beings make history by the very fact of living and acting in the world. But, as Marx pointed out, though man makes history, he does not make it just as he pleases.

1 London and New York, 1953. Reprinted in *Russian Thinkers*, London, 1979.
2 *Russian Thinkers*, p. 69.
3 *Ibid.*, p. 72.
4 *SS*, XII, p. 341. Section XII.

It is doubtless tempting for a Marxist to claim that Marx and Engels actually did what Tolstoy did not do but said that historians ought to do, namely discover and state the laws of historical development. But if we bear in mind the attitude adopted by Tolstoy as a religious and ethical thinker, it is reasonable to interpret him as saying in the Epilogue to *War and Peace* that if we are determined to formulate an overall cosmic philosophy which claims to understand everything, we must assimilate history to natural science, state its laws, and reduce the element of free will to what he calls 'the infinitesimal'.[1] Instead, however, of trying to develop any such cosmic philosophy, Tolstoy came to focus his attention on the human being's religious and moral life.

6. It would hardly occur to anyone to detect a similarity between the sage of Yasnaya Polyana with his idea of universal love and his preaching of humility and non-resistance, and the ideas of Friedrich Nietzsche. When Tolstoy talked about love, he was not referring simply to love of an abstraction, future humanity, human beings who did not yet exist; he was referring to love of all human beings, including those existing here and now. And his Christian anarchism certainly did not lend itself to being used in support of a policy of social differentiation. There was, however, a contemporary of Tolstoy, namely Konstantin Nikolayevich Leontyev (1831–91), who had been described by Berdyaev as 'the Russian precursor of Nietzsche'.[2] Berdyaev did not intend to imply that either man was actually influenced by the other. He was drawing attention to certain similarities. Such phrases as 'the medieval Hume' (used of Nicholas of Autrecourt) and 'the Russian Nietzsche' are obviously open to objection on one ground or another. But provided that they are understood simply as drawing attention to certain similarities and not as asserting parallelism in all respects, they can doubtless have a use.

The son of a landowner, Leontyev entered the Faculty of Medicine at the University of Moscow, served as an army doctor during the Crimean War, and then devoted himself to writing and journalism at St Petersburg. After marrying in 1861, he entered the diplomatic service in 1863, spending some years as a consular official in Crete, Greece and Turkey. In Turkey he became fascinated by 'the East', which he extolled in contrast with the West. After experiencing a religious conversion, he resigned from government service and passed a year (1870–1) with the monks on Mount Athos. On his return to Russia he resumed writing,

1 *Ibid.*, p. 338–9. Section XI.
2 *Leontiev*, by Nicolas Berdyaev, translated by George Reavey, p. vii (London, 1940).

winning for himself a good many enemies on all sides by his forthright
and sharp criticism of ideas of which he disapproved, not only liberal and
socialist ideas but also Panslavism and what he regarded as 'tribal'
nationalism. For a while he served as an official censor at Moscow, but in
1887 he obtained a divorce from his wife and retreated to the monastery
of Optina Pustin. At the end of his life he became a monk, taking the
name of Clement.

What has been described above as a religious conversion was basically
a change from a predominantly aesthetic outlook on the world and
human life to preoccupation with the thought of personal salvation.
Both attitudes represented elements in Leontyev's personality. It was a
question not so much of the religious supplanting the aesthetic attitude to the exclusion of the latter as of which predominated or had
the upper hand. From the time of Leontyev's conversion the religious
attitude predominated, but to say this is not to claim that the aesthetic
attitude was completely eradicated. If Leontyev ever attained real
peace within himself, it was during his last days. Obviously, the
complex nature of his personality makes him more interesting than he
would otherwise be.

In the first part of his life Leontyev's mind was dominated by the ideal
of beauty and the search for it. 'The aesthetic criterion', he wrote, 'is the
most trustworthy and general, for it is the only one applicable in
common to all societies, to all religions, and to all epochs'.[1] As with
Nietzsche, the concepts of the beautiful and the ugly, the aesthetically
pleasing and the aesthetically repugnant, took the place of the concepts
of right and wrong, good and bad. Or, rather, the moral concepts were
interpreted in terms of the aesthetic concepts. It was not a question of
choosing what was immoral because it was immoral. It was a question of
what was conventionally regarded as immoral being sometimes beautiful
or aesthetically pleasant and, as such, justified. Inasmuch as the aesthetic
consciousness prevailed over the moral consciousness, it is preferable to
speak of an amoral, rather than of an immoral, attitude. In regard to
religion, Leontyev had been brought up by his pious mother as a member
of the Russian Orthodox Church, but from his student days his attachment to the Church was aesthetic. That is to say, it was the beauty of the
Orthodox liturgy which attracted him, not the Church's doctrines, in
which he had little belief, espousing, as a medical student, what he
described as a vague deism.

1 *Sobranie sochinenii* (Moscow, 1912–14), VI, p. 63. From an essay on the average
European. This edition of Leontyev's Collected Works will be referred to as *W*.

Beauty, for Leontyev, was the expression of unity in complexity or variety. There must be differentiation, diversification, but there must also be a comprehensive unity which prevents disintegration of the diverse elements. Translated into social-political terms, this meant that, from the negative point of view, Leontyev was an enemy of any process of levelling-out, of equalization, a process which he saw at work in democracy, liberalism and socialism, and which, in his opinion, as in that of Nietzsche, would be productive of universal mediocrity and destructive of cultural excellence[1]. To put the matter in another way, Leontyev saw only ugliness in western bourgeois and capitalist civilization. On this matter at any rate he was in agreement with Herzen, whose attitude he explicitly endorsed. To Leontyev's eyes the bourgeois, whether western European or Russian, represented an ideal of 'universal utility, shallow, commonplace work, and inglorious prosiness'[2], an ideal which he detested.

From the positive point of view Leontyev's ideal of beauty and right order, as applied in the social-political sphere, involved defending the idea of a hierarchical society, exemplifications of which he found in Catholic Europe of the Middle Ages, in the France of Louis XIV, in the England of Elizabeth I and in the Russia of Catherine II. Leontyev had no sympathy with any claim that it was desirable for the state to wither away or disappear. In his opinion, the state should be 'despotic' (with a strong monarchy to secure unity) and 'feudal' (in the sense of preserving an aristocracy and social differentiation). Only in such a state, he believed, could cultural excellence flourish. The struggle against despotism, which was labelled progress, was nothing but 'a process of disintegration'[3]. As for Russia, Nicholas I was commended for having done his best to preserve despotism, the autocracy that is to say, and Leontyev naturally looked on the policy of Alexander III as a salutary attempt to arrest the process of disintegration. He had a particular dislike of the liberals and their desires for a constitution which would limit the powers of the monarchy, if it did not do away with it altogether. To be sure, he also disliked socialism and communism, as aiming at equalization, at levelling out. But in his later years, when he had come to the conclusion that socialism would triumph, he foresaw that the victorious socialists would have recourse to the principle of despotism, using 'conservative'

---

1 Leontyev found one expression of this process of levelling-out in the growing tendency for members of different nations and social classes to dress alike.
2 W., V, p. 426.
3 Ibid., p. 199.

positions for their own ends. And he asserted that the socialists were right in despising the liberals[1].

Given Leontyev's view of the state, it may seem to follow that if he had been acquainted with Nietzsche's writings, he would have been unable to endorse the German philosopher's description of the state as the 'Cold Monster' and as destructive of cultural excellence. He could, however, have pointed out that Nietzsche was referring to the bourgeois state, not to the Greek *polis*, nor to the states of the Renaissance or of the eighteenth century. Leontyev was not an enemy of the West as such. He did not share the hostility of Slavophiles (and of Dostoevsky) to Catholicism and the papacy, and he believed that, in the period from the Renaissance to the eighteenth century inclusive, European culture had reached its zenith. But he also believed that western bourgeois civilization represented the decay of Europe, and he both expected and feared the extension of the process of disintegration in his own country. If it could be arrested, it could only be done by preserving the autocracy, representing the principle of despotism. In his last years Leontyev was inclined to think that the process could not be arrested.

Leontyev's dislike of democracy, liberalism, socialism and communism, together with his romantic fascination with past epochs and with the East, may justify us in describing him as a reactionary, but it does not follow that he had any sympathy with the Panslavism which had invaded the Slavophil outlook. For him, Byzantinism provided the ideal. Byzantium belonged to past history, but Russia was its heir. And if Russia had a mission, it was as the heir to Byzantium, not as a Slav people. In point of fact the population of the Russian empire was mixed, which, for Leontyev, was a good thing, not something to be deplored. The mission of Russia was to develop a Byzantine culture, not a peculiarly Slav culture. As for the so-called Slav peoples, such as the Bulgarians, they too were mixed. Further, if they had value, it was as bearers of original cultures, and, in Leontyev's view, they would maintain their several cultural traditions only if they were left as they were, under various overlords. Russia would confer no benefit on them by liberating them, from the Turkish yoke for example. Once free, they would tend to forget about their own distinctive culture and set about assimilating themselves to the rest of Europe. Leontyev did indeed desire conquest of Constantinople by Russia. But this was because he hoped that the conquest would increase Russia's consciousness of her Byzantine heritage and of her distinctive cultural mission, which was rooted in her relationship to

1 W., VII, p. 217.

Byzantium, not in any specifically Russian virtues. Leontyev had no great esteem of the Slavs as such, and he agreed with Nicholas I's reserved attitude to those who advocated Panslavist adventures and a policy of Russification.

Leontyev also took a dim view of German and Italian unification. The establishment of the German empire would be likely to lead to the loss of the rich cultural diversification of the multitudinous states and principalities, and to the growth of one uniform bourgeois and capitalist society. Much the same could be said of Italy. Leontyev had nothing against patriotism when it was invoked to defend a cultural tradition, but nationalism as such, divorced from a distinctive culture, left him cold. In his opinion, it contributed to the process of levelling-out, of equalization, which he so much disliked. While, therefore, Leontyev was obviously *persona non grata* with liberals and socialists, he was also *persona non grata* with Panslavists and chauvinists.

The Christianity to which Leontyev was converted was very different from Tolstoy's. The God of Leontyev was a fear-inspiring God, the transcendent creator and judge, not a vaguely conceived immanent Spirit, expressing itself in universal love. As has already been indicated, he regarded the religious ideas of Dostoevsky and Tolstoy as amounting to a 'rosy-coloured' Christianity, to Christianity reduced to moralism and a humanitarian religiosity[1]. In his view, not only the secular socialists but also the two great novelists looked for the attainment of the kingdom of God or of universal happiness where it could never be found, namely on earth. Leontyev even broke off relations with Vladimir Solovyev, when he came to the conclusion that Solovyev too was showing signs of confusing Christianity with humanitarian principles. In other words, his religious conversion did not involve any real change in his evaluation of democracy and of socialist aspirations. It simply added religious reasons for rejecting them. For example, the autocracy was justified not only as being the maintainer of unity but also because the Tsar was a representative of God.

These remarks may suggest that Leontyev became a religious bigot. In point of fact, however, he sympathized with Solovyev's admiration for Catholicism and with his desire for the reunion of the Catholic and Orthodox Churches, even though he refrained from publicly supporting such a policy without the official approval of the Orthodox Church. Moreover, Leontyev's sympathy with Islam and his liking for the poetic

---

1 In regard to literary or artistic talent, Leontyev recognized the genius of Tolstoy, but he failed lamentably to appreciate that of Dostoevsky, whose novels seemed to him sordid and aesthetically repugnant.

qualities of the Koran were not eradicated by his conversion. At the same time Byzantine Christianity was for him Christianity in its most authentic form, and the purest embodiment of Orthodoxy was to be found in monasticism, in renunciation of the world and of the aesthetic attitude. But if he himself ever succeeded in thoroughly renouncing the aesthetic attitude, it was only at the end of his life.

7. As he freely admitted, Leontyev was not at home with abstract ideas. Though he commended Solovyev for having stirred up a storm of religious ideas on the surface of the somnolent sea of ecclesiastical thought, he claimed not to be able to understand Solovyev's speculative theories. He is not alone, of course, in making such a claim. But in any case Leontyev was not attracted by metaphysical speculation. His interest lay in a more concrete area, that of philosophy of history. In forming his ideas on this subject he was influenced, as he explicitly stated, by Nikolai Danilevsky (1822–85), author of *Russia and Europe* (1869), though, according to Zenkovsky, this influence was felt only after Leontyev had formed his basic ideas[1]. In any case Leontyev thought for himself, expressing his ideas in a series of studies, which include *Byzantinism and Slavdom* (1895). Between them, Danilevsky and Leontyev anticipated the theories of Oswald Spengler.

Apollon Grigoryev (1822–64), who had been a member of the *pochvenniki* group to which Dostoevsky belonged, attacked the Hegelian view of history as one total process of dialectical advance, in which different societies and nations played their successive roles as instruments of the *Weltgeist*, the World-spirit or spirit of Humanity. In his view, each nation was analogous to a biological organism, which evolved according to its own laws. Danilevsky developed this theory, dividing civilization into distinct historico-cultural types, such as the Chinese, Hindu, Iranian, Hebrew, ancient Greek, Roman and Germano-Romanic or European types. There were ten types of civilization, according to Danilevsky, though Russia was destined to create an eleventh type, a Slav civilization. Each type developed according to its own immanent principles, not according to any alleged laws of universal history, but not all types were completely self-contained and exclusive in the sense of being unable to assimilate material derived from another culture. For example, whereas the Hebrew civilization was an exclusively religious type, ancient Greece

1 *A History of Russian Philosophy*, I, p. 481.

was able to assimilate a variety of elements within itself[1]. European civilization, according to Danilevsky, had entered a phase of decay, analogous to senility and the approach of death in a biological organism, whereas Russia, because of the Slav capacity for assimilating a great variety of elements, would, when it had conquered Constantinople and united all Slav peoples under its hegemony, come nearest to realizing the ideal of universal humanity. In other words, Danilevsky tried to combine the theory of distinct cultures, each developing according to its own set of principles or laws, with Panslavism and an exalted view of the historical mission of his own country. Understandably, he emphasized the need for Russia actively to resist contamination by a decaying western Europe. If, however, we focus our attention simply on Danilevsky's theory of distinct historico-cultural types, it is obvious that he was committed to holding that there was no common yardstick by which one culture could be judged superior to another, and that there could no more be a universal culture than there could be a universal biological organism. Thus he insisted that it was a mistake on the part of the Slavophiles to regard the values of Slav culture as absolute. At the same time, though he maintained that the principles or laws of distinct cultures were incommensurable, he allowed, as we have seen, that a culture was not necessarily cut off, as by a hatchet, from all other cultures, as far as content was concerned. A given culture might assimilate material derived from another culture. This line of thought left the door open for making some special claims, in regard to richness of content, in the case of his eleventh historico-cultural type, even if the Slav culture could not have a universal mission in any strict sense, inasmuch as the principles of Slav culture would be *its* principles and not those of humanity in general.

Leontyev too regarded a society as analogous to a biological organism, and as passing through successive stages of growth, maturity, decay and death. In his view, the normal development of a society or civilization takes the form of a movement from the simple to the complex in such a way that the society's inner content is enriched while its unity is not impaired. The high peak of maturity is reached when complexity, internal differentiation, reaches the maximum point compatible with unity, with an inner 'despotic' unity. It is this movement towards maturity which should be conceived as progress. Leontyev was perfectly ready to

1 Danilevsky regarded culture as developing in four main areas, religion, culture in a narrow sense (science and art), political life, and social-economic life. One culture could not assimilate the 'principles' of another culture, but it was no more necessarily debarred from assimilating derived material than a biological organism was necessarily debarred from assimilating material derived from other organisms.

draw the conclusion which followed from this thesis. For example, in pre-Petrine Russia there was more homogeneity than in the Russia of Peter the Great and Catherine II. Differentiation between the monarch and the aristocracy and between the aristocracy and the peasant population was intensified; the institution of serfdom was strengthened. The reigns of Peter and Catherine were thus progressive. Indeed, Leontyev does not hesitate to assert that Catherine the Great's chief contribution was to have 'increased inequality'[1] by extending serfdom and by strengthening the position of the nobility as a distinct class or estate. This increase in complexity, in differentiation, was, of course, accompanied by the consolidation of the autocracy, representing despotic unity, by Peter the Great and his successors.

On this matter Leontyev's attitude was obviously different from that of the early Slavophiles, who looked back to and tended to idealize pre-Petrine Russia. What they conceived as unfortunate divisions within Russian society, Leontyev regarded as healthy differentiation. And whereas the early Slavophiles were unhappy with the development of the autocracy, Leontyev looked on it as an expression of progress. In his opinion, Nicholas I was rightly suspicious of the Slavophiles, who, without being aware of the fact, expressed the attitude of 'a vulgar European bourgeois'.[2]

The disintegration of a society sets in when the number of distinct parts or members of the social organism is diminished, when the unity is weakened, and when the parts, instead of being clearly differentiated, become confused. In plain language, the process of growing equalization, of levelling out, accompanied by a weakening of the central government, of despotic unity, is a sure sign of a society's decay. Here Leontyev takes the opposite point of view to that of liberals and socialists. What they regard as progress, in an evaluative sense, he regards as a process of disintegration, leading to cultural death. In relation to this process of disintegration it is the reactionaries who are the true progressives, inasmuch as they attempt to arrest the process and to conserve the life of the society or civilization. For Leontyev, of course, western Europe was well on its way to disintegration, and he hoped that Russia would be able to resist the contaminating influence of Europe. On this matter he was in agreement with the Slavophiles up to a point, but only up to a point. As we have seen, he did not attach any particular value to Slavdom. What he wanted was a neo-Byzantine culture, characterized

1 W., V, p. 133.
2 W., VII, p. 432.

by autocracy and Orthodoxy. It was the prospect of a renewed Byzantine culture, not of a Panslav society, which made Russia worth saving.

Although Leontyev wrote about the need for Russia to resist the forces of disintegration, it is obvious that if a society really is analogous to a biological organism, the process of decay cannot be indefinitely arrested. Leontyev was not, of course, blind to this aspect of the matter, and at the end of his life he came to the conclusion that socialism was bound to triumph. Perhaps a Tsar would place himself at the head of the movement; perhaps Russia would become secularized and dominated by the spirit of Antichrist. In any case triumphant socialism would establish its own form of despotism, and if there were to be a revolution in Russia, the result would be a régime, the despotic nature of which would surpass that of the Tsars[1].

It may seem very odd that a man who had undergone a religious conversion and who was to die as a monk should expound such a naturalistic view of history as the one outlined above. But although Leontyev believed in God as creator and sustainer of the world, he also believed that just as there are physical laws, relating to nature, so there are laws relating to the development of societies or civilizations. In other words, he tried to treat history as though it were a branch of natural science. Further, he had little sympathy with the use of the 'subjective method' as recommended, for example, by Peter Lavrov. In Leontyev's view, the concept of final causality, of moral ends, was no more appropriate in the study of social development than it was in physics. Human beings as individuals act for ends; their actions can properly be described in moral terms. But social organisms do not act for moral ends; their development conforms to statable laws; and moral epithets are as inapplicable in their case as in that of stars or physical phenomena such as earthquakes. To put the matter in another way, God judges individuals, not social organisms. Leontyev would doubtless agree with Henri Bergson's statement that it is Frenchmen, and not France, who go to heaven.

Obviously, the question can be raised whether there are in fact social organisms, which are irreducible to their members, individual human beings that is to say. It is indeed reasonable to argue that a living organism, functioning as a totality, is more than the sum total of its parts, but it does not necessarily follow that a civilization, say that of ancient China, can properly be described as a living organism. Let us suppose, however, that it can. It may seem that on this assumption Leontyev is right in restricting moral epithets to individual human beings and main-

1 *Ibid.*, p. 205.

taining, for example, that while a ruler such as Peter the Great or Nicholas I can be more or less humane, the state cannot properly be described in this way, when the word 'humane' is being used in an evaluative sense. But if the state is an organism, does this necessarily follow? After all, the individual human being is an organism. Leontyev might perhaps reply that though the state is analogous to an organism, it is not a person, and that it is only persons who are morally responsible. But even so we may still wish to be able to talk about the state acting immorally, though we would doubtless be prepared to add that we are then talking about individuals acting in their public capacity. Is Leontyev ready to admit that this way of talking is legitimate? Or does he imply that it is only as private individuals, and not in their public capacity, that rulers, politicians and state functionaries are subject to moral judgment? It is all very well to assert that morality 'has its own sphere and its own limits'[1], namely the sphere of individual consciousness and life. Individuals do not cease to be individuals when they are acting in a public capacity.

These remarks do not answer the question whether or not there are laws of social development. As far, however, as morality is concerned, it seems to the present writer that the course of social-political development can be placed outside the ethical sphere only at the cost of representing societies as entities on their own, distinct from individuals. But even if a society is more than the sum total of its members, it cannot be set over against individuals. For without individuals it is nothing; it depends on them for their existence. And individuals acting in a public capacity are still moral agents. If to promote a certain policy is to promote social injustice, it is unsatisfactory, from the moral point of view, to justify the social injustice by describing it as apparent and claiming that it conduces to 'social health'[2]. The trouble is that Leontyev is preoccupied with the thought of personal salvation in a Christian sense and tries to make a sharp distinction between the lives of individuals in their relationship to God and the lives of historico-cultural types without paying sufficient attention to the implications of his theory.

8. We can say that Leontyev was concerned, both in regard to himself and on a wider scale, with the problem of the relation between human culture, in all its richness and variety, and orthodox Christianity, with its demands. A younger writer who was also concerned with this problem

1 W., VI, p. 98.
2 Ibid.

(which can be seen as the problem of the meaning of life) was Vasily Vasilyevich Rozanov (1856–1919). But whereas Leontyev opted, even if not with complete success, for Christian asceticism or, as he put it, for heavenly beauty in preference to earthly beauty, Rozanov opted for the world of 'the flesh' as against Christian asceticism. In point of fact Rozanov died as a Christian, with the sacraments of the Orthodox Church, but, as a writer, he is best known for his vehement critique of Christianity. It is this aspect of his thought which has led people to compare him with Nietzsche.

Rozanov was brought up in poverty. After his school education, he was able to enter the University of Moscow in the Faculty of History and Philology, where he had a low opinion of his teachers. After graduating, he spent some thirteen years teaching history and geography in provincial secondary schools. He seems to have been as bored with this occupation as he had been with his university studies. In 1886 he published a large volume *On Understanding*, the only one of his writings which was concerned with academic philosophy[1]. He maintained that there are seven basic categories of reason; existence, essence, property, cause, purpose, similarity and difference, and number. It is, he argued, through combining speculation, governed by these categories, with experience that we arrive at understanding, considered as integral knowledge. Reason belongs to the human spirit which is creative, in the sense that it creates ideas and imposes them on 'matter', as in art and in the development of social structures.

This book was a dismal failure, being ignored rather than attacked, and it is generally regarded as dull and as altogether lacking the colour of Rozanov's later writings. In 1893, however, through the good offices of his friend Nikolai Strakhov, Rozanov obtained a post in the Department of Inspection and State Control at St Petersburg, where he gave himself to journalistic work and in the course of time became a regular contributor to the conservative periodical, the *New Times*.

In 1894 Rozanov published a study of Dostoevsky, *The Legend of the Grand Inquisitor*, which set him on the road to literary fame. Unlike Leontyev, Rozanov was a great admirer of Dostoevsky, so much so that in 1880 he had married the novelist's former mistress, Apollinaria Suslova, to establish some sort of connection with the object of his admiration. Unfortunately, after a few years the good lady repeated her performance with Dostoevsky and left Rozanov, though she refused to agree to a divorce.[2] For Rozanov, Dostoevsky was 'the most profound analyst of the

1 Rozanov included in his volume an attack on the teaching in the University of Moscow.
2 When he found that he could not obtain a divorce, Rozanov took a common-law wife, with whom he lived happily and by whom he had children.

human soul'[1], a man who included in himself 'both abysses, the abyss above and the abyss below'[2], a man whose problems were those of human beings in general. One of the conflicts which Rozanov found portrayed by the novelist was 'the struggle between the denial of life and its affirmation'.[3] It was precisely this struggle which was to find expression in Rozanov's critique of Christianity. He had never met Dostoevsky, but he felt a temperamental affinity with the novelist. And it has been said of him that he might have been a character in one of Dostoevsky's novels.

A good many of Rozanov's works, such as *Religion and Culture* (1901) are collections of articles. The articles, however, which he wrote after settling down in the capital, present us with a problem. On the one hand he wrote in defence of the régime and its policy, attacking leftist and radical writers, supporting Tolstoy's excommunication by the Holy Synod in 1901, and even publishing some inflammatory anti-Jewish articles[4]. As we have noted, he contributed to the very conservative *New Times*. On the other hand he also wrote essays, under a pseudonym, for *The Russian Word*, in which he sharply criticized the régime and the Church. In his later years he developed a destructive critique of Christianity, culminating in *The Apocalypse of Our Times*. These later productions were written in an aphoristic style.

Besides being a critic of Christianity, Rozanov was also an enemy of the Bolsheviks. The revolution reduced him to poverty, and he took refuge with the theologian Father Paul Florensky near Moscow. After repudiating his anti-Christian and anti-Jewish utterances, he asked for and received the Orthodox sacraments and died early in 1919. He was buried in a grave next to Leontyev.

Various explanations of Rozanov's behaviour as a writer have been offered, such as cynicism and lack of principle, psychological instability, and a desire to express different points of view. Rozanov himself once remarked that he had no fixed convictions, while later he spoke of his having lived his life behind an impenetrable veil, behind which he was truthful with himself. The present writer is not in a position to throw fresh light on the matter and is content to leave discussion to psychologists. We can note, however, that in spite of his critique of Christianity Rozanov was far from being an irreligious man. His attack on Christianity was made in the name of religious ideas of his own rather

1 *Dostoevsky and the Legend of the Grand Inquisitor*, translated by Spencer Roberts, p. 51 (Ithaca, Cornell University Press. 1972).
   2 *Ibid.*, p. 16.
   3 *Ibid.*
   4 Rozanov's anti-Jewish diatribes led to his expulsion from the Religious-Philosophical Society of St Petersburg in 1913.

than in that of atheism. Moreover, it seems that the attraction to Christ which appeared in his study of Dostoevsky reasserted itself at the end. It is true that in the closing years of his life (1918–19) he was attacking Christianity (as well as the revolution) in *The Apocalypse of Our Times*. But there does not seem to be any good reason for doubting the sincerity of his profession of the Christian faith during his final illness.

9. In his work on Dostoevsky Rozanov expressed views about Christianity which recall to mind, to some extent at any rate, the ideas of the leading early Slavophiles. In Catholicism he saw an emphasis on universality at the expense of individuality, while in Protestantism he saw the opposite, an emphasis on the individual at the expense of the universal. In each case, however, he ascribed such characteristics not to the Christian religion as such but to the characters of the relevant groups of peoples, Latin and Germanic. In other words, Catholicism was the Latin way of understanding and appropriating Christianity, whereas Protestant Christianity derived its special features from the nature of the Germanic peoples. According to Rozanov, 'contempt for the human personality, only a feeble interest in the conscience of another, force used against man, against the race, against the world – all this is a fundamental and indestructible characteristic of the Latin races'[1], a characteristic which has manifested itself in a variety of phenomena, such as the Roman Empire, Catholicism and the socialism of writers such as Fourier, Saint-Simon and Louis Blanc. Again, 'the spirit of the Germanic race, on the contrary, everywhere and always, no matter what it is engaged in, is directed towards the particular, the specific, the individual'[2], a spirit manifested, for example, by Martin Luther and in Kant's idea of the kingdom of ends.

As one would expect, Orthodoxy is associated with the Slav peoples. The Slavs, in Rozanov's view, manifest 'a spirit of compassion and endless patience and simultaneously an aversion to all that is chaotic and gloomy'[3], a spirit which leads the Slavic race to create harmony. It is in the Orthodox Church, in its life of simple faith and hope and love, that we find the life which exemplifies most nearly the spirit of the Christian religion.

Obviously, what Rozanov has to say about the Latin, Germanic and Slav peoples is open to a good deal of criticism. But it is interesting to see the way in which he sees the differences between Catholicism, Protestantism and Orthodoxy as due not so much to doctrinal issues, the issues about which theologians write, as to the characteristics of ethnic groups which

1 *Dostoevsky*, p. 194 (see note 2, p. 185).
2 *Ibid.*, p. 196.
3 *Ibid.*, p. 201.

have, as it were, moulded Christianity in their own image and likeness. When discussing the legend of the Grand Inquisitor, Rozanov insisted, and rightly, that Dostoevsky was not thinking only of the Catholic Church and the historic Inquisition, and that the Inquisitor was referring to a lasting pervasive desire in human beings, to be freed from the burden of freedom and responsibility. Rozanov himself relates the differences between the three main streams of Christian belief and life to ethnic characteristics.

Since, according to Rozanov, the Slavs feel an aversion for all that is gloomy. Rozanov believed that religion should be animated by a spirit of joy, expressing an affirmation of life, of human life in this world. And it was not long before he was representing western Christianity in general as world-fleeing, as 'anti-world'[1], whereas Orthodoxy was depicted as being full of gaiety and joy, expressing the spirit of the New Testament, in contrast with the Old Testament spirit of western Christendom.

This line of thought may have been edifying from the Orthodox point of view, but it could hardly last, even if we assume that Rozanov was fully sincere in his exaltation of Orthodoxy as against the Christianity of western Europe. His criticism was extended to historic Christianity in general. That is to say, the Church (or Churches) became the villain of the piece, being accused of having transformed the religion of Bethlehem, as Rozanov put it, into a religion of ascetism and suffering, the religion of Golgotha and 'the worship of death'.[2] True Christianity had never had the opportunity of realizing itself; the gospel message had been perverted by the Church, which preferred the spirit of the Old Testament to that of the New. In other words, the Church, preaching suffering and death rather than the affirmation of life, was an anti-cultural force.

The thought of Bethlehem suggests the idea of the family. Rozanov conceived nature as a totality pulsating with life and love, and in the human sphere he saw this life as expressed, above all, in sexual love (not simply in its physical aspects) and in the family. Indeed, he came to develop a kind of mystique of sexual love, representing it as the chief way of entering into communion with God[3]. As it could hardly be claimed that Christianity was characterized by an exaltation of sexuality, of sexual love in a literal sense, it is understandable that Rozanov came to identify the religion of Golgotha not simply with what the Church had

---

1 *Religiya i kutura*, p. 64 (St Petersburg, 1901).

2 *By the Walls of the Church* (*Okolo tserkovnykh sten*, St Petersburg, 1906), I, p. 15.

3 'The connection of sex with God – greater than the connection of the mind with God, greater even than the connection of conscience with God – is gathered from this that all a-sexualists reveal themselves also as a-theists'. *Solitaria*, translated by S. S. Koteliansky, p. 103 (London, 1927). *Solitaria*, published in 1912, was suppressed by the censorship.

made of Christianity but with the Christian religion itself. 'It is not the human heart which has corrupted Christianity; it is Christianity which has corrupted the human heart.'[1] Given this point of view, one would not expect the founder of Christianity to remain unscathed. Christ, as Rozanov came to see him, declared that the works of the flesh were sinful, whereas the works of the spirit were holy. 'I believe that the "works of the flesh" are the essential thing, whereas the "works of the spirit" are, one can say, only talk'.[2] Like Leontyev, Rozanov saw in monasticism the purest embodiment of the Christian spirit, but their respective evaluations of monasticism were sharply opposed.

It may seem odd to assert that Rozanov saw the meaning of life in religion. But the assertion is nonetheless justified, for he did not attack Christianity in the name of irreligion or atheism. He had a horror of positivists and atheists. Religion, he stated, was the most important, essential and needed thing in life, and there could be no discussion with those who were unaware of the fact[3]. The question was, what sort of religion? In opposition to Christianity Rozanov proclaimed life-affirming religion, which he found exemplified not only in the ancient fertility cults but also in the Old Testament (somewhat surprisingly perhaps in view of some of his other assertions). This was what he called the religion of the Father, as opposed to the religion of the Son. At the same time he explicitly admitted that in attacking Christianity he was attacking what he loved, that to which he was deeply attached. In 1911 he said, 'God, what madness it was that for eleven years I made every possible effort to destroy the Church. And how fortunate that I failed. What would the *earth* be like without the Church? It would suddenly lose its meaning and get cold'.[4] To be sure, this did not prevent him from returning to vehement criticism of Christianity. But it is perfectly clear that on one side of himself he was deeply attached to the Christian religion and the Orthodox Church, and it is not at all surprising that on his deathbed he expressed his faith, seeing in Christianity a religion of resurrection, of hope and joy. Nietzsche too, in his diatribes against Christianity, did violence to himself, but in his case negation, also in the name of the affirmation of life, was triumphant.

To imagine that Rozanov's critique of Christianity in *The Apocalypse of Our Times* was prompted in any way by the desire to curry favour

---

1 *Izbrannoye*, edited by George Ivask, p. 382 (New York, 1956). The quotation is from the section 'The Last Days' in *The Apocalypse of Our Times*.
2 *Ibid.*, p. 389. From the section 'Truth and Falsehood'.
3 *Solitaria*, p. 103 (see note 54).
4 *Ibid.*, p. 139.

with the successors of the Tsars would obviously be a great mistake. He had begun his critique well before the Revolution, and it did not proceed from any liking for atheistic socialism. The man who could say that it was superfluous to write 'about our stinking revolution and our thoroughly rotten empire – each is as bad as the other'[1] was hardly currying favour with the new masters of Russia. What Rozanov would have said about the new régime if he had lived longer and been able to see it consolidate itself and develop, is obviously a question which cannot be answered with certainty. But it is most unlikely that he would have adapted himself to the social conformity which was demanded after the turbulent days of the revolution and the civil war. He would have been lucky if he had been expelled from the country or allowed to emigrate.

Rozanov could write in an illuminating way about Russian literature, notably in his fine work on Dostoevsky. In articles he also discussed writers such as Pushkin, Gogol and Leontyev. As far as the present writer is aware, no edition of his writings has appeared in the Soviet Union. Perhaps this state of affairs will be eventually remedied.

1 *Izbrannoye*, p. 381 (see note 1 on previous page).

Chapter 9

Religion and Philosophy: Vladimir Solovyev

1. The active members of the radical intelligentsia in nineteenth-century Russia were dedicated persons, devoted to the cause of overthrowing the autocracy with a view to transforming society. This is true, of course, of the terrorists as well as of the more moderate members who disliked violence. If the revolutionaries were ready to sacrifice others in the struggle, they were also ready to sacrifice themselves. It was this devotion to a cause and the spirit of self-sacrifice which won for the revolutionaries a sympathy and reluctant admiration on the part of a good many educated Russians who had no intention of becoming involved in subversive activities, and still less in assassination. Though the means adopted by the revolutionaries were often open to objection on moral grounds, as well as on grounds of expediency, they can nonetheless be regarded as having sought the realization on earth of a secularized form of the kingdom of God.

At the same time the radical intelligentsia, generally speaking, showed a contempt for the theory of absolute values and a marked hostility to religion as ordinarily understood. Obviously, dislike of the autocracy did not entail an anti-religious attitude. The early Slavophiles, such as Kireevsky, Khomyakov and Konstantin Aksakov, were certainly not enamoured of the autocratic régime as it had developed from the time of Peter the Great, but they were sincerely religious men. They saw in Orthodoxy the basic principle of the Russian tradition which seemed to them to be endangered by the policy of Westernization. For the matter of that, even active opposition to the autocracy, motivated by the desire for liberal reforms, was by no means necessarily accompanied by an anti-religious attitude. Several members of the Decembrist conspiracy were devout Christians. When, however, we turn to the radical intelligentsia, we find a different situation. If we use the term to cover not simply the 'new men', the successors of the early Westernizers, but all radical thinkers, whether of noble or humble birth, who devoted themselves to the cause of transforming society in accordance with socialist ideas borrowed, for the most part, from the West[1], we can say that the nineteenth-century Russian intelligentsia – from Herzen, Belinsky and Bakunin through Chernyshevsky, Dobrolyubov and Pisarev to Lavrov, Mikhailovsky and Tkachev – was increasingly and strongly opposed to traditional religion and that it rejected traditional religious belief. Generally speaking, the members of the radical intelligentsia saw the Orthodox Church as a lackey of the régime and as a hindrance to social progress. Further, as positivism, materialism and utilitarianism spread in the middle of the century, so did contempt for Christian belief and doctrine increase. In other words, the radical intelligentsia stood on one side, the Church on another. Any real dialogue was excluded by both parties.

In regard to the subordination of the Church to the State, the intelligentsia clearly had a very strong case. Peter the Great had deprived the Orthodox Church of any degree of independence and autonomy which it possessed and had established a strict control over it, which his successors maintained. Though the Holy Synod consisted mainly of bishops (with the addition of a few selected priests), it could not move hand or foot without the approval of the lay Procurator, representing the Emperor. Parish priests, for a time at least, were supposed to submit any sermons which they might wish to deliver for previous censorship, a state of affairs which did not encourage the ministry of the word. Only persons acceptable to the régime were appointed bishops[2]; bishops and parish clergy could be removed or transferred at the will of the political authorities; and utterances on social and political issues were taboo, except when it was a question of supporting decisions and regulations of the State. Obviously, the lamentable situation of the Church had been forced on it, rather than chosen by it, but this does not alter the fact that the intelligentsia was justified in regarding the Orthodox Church as pretty well an organ of the régime.[3]

It does not follow that the Church was spiritually lifeless. Though it obviously stood for certain beliefs, to be a member meant participating in

1 Obviously, the concept of 'Russian socialism', as expounded by Herzen and then the Populists, was not derived simply from the West. But it presupposed western socialist theory, which was then adapted to Russian conditions.

2 The bishops were appointed from among the celibate clergy, the monks that is to say. If anyone aspired to become a bishop, he had to take monastic vows, instead of marrying. A parish priest could not become a bishop, unless his wife had died and he was thus free to take monastic vows.

3 This does not apply, of course, to the 'Old Believers' (the *Raskolniki*) or to the sometimes very eccentric religious sects. But these bodies were not favoured by the régime, to put it mildly.

the liturgical life of the Church more than knowing and adhering to a certain set of precisely formulated doctrines, and it was the primary duty of the parish clergy to maintain the liturgical functions. As the parish priest generally had to keep himself and his family by working on his land, like any peasant[1], and by demanding payment from his parishioners for services rendered, a practice which hardly contributed to good relations, it was really only when presiding over the celebration of the liturgy that he appeared to the faithful as a man apart, a sacerdotal figure. The average parochial clergy were neither highly educated nor saints, but neither were they quite so ignorant, lazy, greedy and superstitious as the intelligentsia was inclined to depict them. Chernyshevsky's father, for example, was a genuinely devout priest, who was able, moreover, to give his son an excellent education at home. In any case the Russian Orthodox Church was capable of producing outstanding examples of holiness, such as St Seraphim of Sarov (1759–1833) and later, even if he was not to everyone's taste, Father John of Kronstadt (1828–1908). Further, those 'Elders' of monasteries who had a reputation for holiness were approached by people of all classes for advice and spiritual direction. Again, in the Theological Academies there were teachers of genuine learning and scholarship.

Piety and holiness of life, however, were not likely to impress members of the radical intelligentsia, whose concern was not with coming closer to God or with participation in the spiritual communion of the Church but with social change and with taking means to secure it. Further, though there were professors of real ability and scholarship in the ecclesiastical institutions for advanced theological studies, they spoke a language which was alien to the intelligentsia. That is to say, their interests were different, and their ways of thought were different. As has already been remarked, to all intents and purposes there was no dialogue, no mutual understanding.

At the beginning of the twentieth century a great change took place. In the cultural life of Russia there was a turning away from materialism and positivism and a revival of interest in religion, mysticism and even the occult. For the first time joint discussions were started between some members of the intelligentsia and representative, lay and clerical, of the Orthodox Church. At St Petersburg dialogue took the form of the Religio-Philosophical Assemblies which were held from 1901 until 1903, when Pobedonostsev, the procurator of the Holy Synod, became alarmed by the outspokenness of the participants and asked that the

1 A large number of the clergy received no fixed income.

discussions should cease, in spite of the fact that he had originally consented to and supported the venture. Similar meetings were held, sometimes of a quite informal nature, at Moscow and Kiev. Those participating in such meetings and discussions were not all members of the intelligentsia in a narrow sense on the one hand and theologians, lay or clerical, on the other. Meetings were sometimes attended by philosophers, artists, poets and writers such as Rozanov. The proceedings of the sessions of the Assemblies at St Petersburg appeared in the magazine *The New Way* (*Novy Put*), the first contribution, by V. Ternavtsev, having as its title 'The Intelligentsia and the Church'.

It is hardly necessary to say that not all members of the intelligentsia who participated in such meetings became reconciled to the Orthodox Church. Some found the theologians unbending and unable really to appreciate points of view and attitudes different from their own. Others developed religious ideas independently of the Church and without committing themselves to Christianity. But in the early years of the twentieth century, before the Revolution, an impressive number of the intelligentsia turned to the Church, while insisting that it should be committed to the cause of social justice. For example Peter Struve (1870–1944), an economist, had become a Marxist at the University of St Petersburg but subsequently turned to Christianity. In 1907 he was elected a deputy in the second Duma, and in the same year he undertook the task of editing the journal *Russian Thought* (*Russkaya Misl*). Sergey Bulgakov (1871–1944), a political economist, who also abandoned Marxism for Orthodoxy, accepted a chair at the Moscow Institute of Commerce in 1906, and in 1907 was elected a deputy to the Duma. Nikolai Berdyaev (1874–1948), the philosopher, was another ex-Marxist. So was Semyon Frank (1877–1950), a philosopher, who was of Jewish origin but became an Orthodox Christian.

These men, together with some others, contributed articles to the symposium *Vekhi* (*Signposts*), which appeared in 1909 and caused a stir in intellectual circles. Some of the writers had already opted for Christianity, others were on their way, while one at any rate, M. Gershenzon (1869–1925), never actually joined the Orthodox Church.[1] But all were united in believing that a religious world-view was of basic cultural importance, and, from various angles, they criticized not only the atheism and materialism of the radical intelligentsia but also its political irresponsibility in calling for revolution without having any

---

1 Gershenzon was a Jew but well disposed towards Christianity. A noted historian of ideas, he wrote, for example, on Chaadaev and Kireevsky and edited their works.

clear idea of what was to take the place of the existing régime and of how the promised terrestrial paradise would be attained. Berdyaev, for example, while recognizing the moral idealism of the intelligentsia, maintained that its zeal for social justice had practically extinguished any real concern with objective truth.

Given the intellectual stature of the contributors to the symposium, the publication could not be ignored. It was vehemently attacked by marxists and Social Revolutionaries, and it encountered criticism, though expressed in a more polite manner, from the liberals with a positivist outlook. Although the work obviously did not bring about a mass conversion on the part of the intelligentsia, it was of considerable significance, inasmuch as it was largely the production of ex-Marxists who knew the intelligentsia from within. It showed that the atheist socialists no longer had the field to themselves.

Meanwhile the Church itself was, so to speak, on the move. A movement to secure its greater autonomy and freedom to act as a spiritual and social force had shown itself. Thus in 1905–6 proposals for the convocation of a Church Council, for the abolition of the Holy Synod and the election of a Patriarch, for reforms relating to the election of bishops and parish priests, the ecclesiastical courts and the training of the clergy, were discussed, the bishops' replies to a questionnaire being published in 1906. The proposals naturally came under attack, not only from conservatives who wished to maintain the *status quo* but also from radicals who feared that an autonomous Church would gain in social influence and would prove a more formidable rival. In point of fact a Preconciliar Commission was set up and started its work in 1906, but the vacillating monarch, Nicholas II, had failed to convoke the Council, before it became too late to do so.[1]

After the initial revolution there was a brief period of freedom, which continued during the very early days of the Communist régime. Berdyaev was for a short time a professor of philosophy in the University of Moscow, while Bulgakov, ordained a priest in 1918, occupied a chair in the University of Simferopol for two or three years. But it was not long before the Communist authorities expelled from Russia or imprisoned those teachers and writers whose ideas were not in conformity with their own. This applied not only to religious thinkers but to all who were, from

1 In 1917, under the Provisional Government, the Holy Synod, presided over by Prince V. N. Lvov, announced its intention of convoking a Council. The Council began its sessions in August of that year, and in November Tikhon, Metropolitan of Moscow, was enthroned as Patriarch. But in December the Communist authorities started their campaign against the Church, and in 1918 Tikhon was imprisoned. In 1922 the Metropolitan of Petrograd, Venyamin, was executed, along with some other prominent Christians.

the Party's point of view, dissidents. In other words, the Soviet government brought the intelligentsia to heel much more effectively and drastically than the Tsarist régime had ever done, even under Nicholas I. And though art and drama and poetry flourished for a while, the dead hand of 'social realism' eventually clamped down on cultural life. As for the Church, when the government came to abandon obvious persecution, it was once more subordinated to State control, this time to control by an atheistic Party. Its activities were confined to the walls of the remaining churches, and it was effectively prevented from exercising an influence on education or on the intellectual life of the nation.

That religious metaphysics could have revived in the face of widespread positivism and materialism and that it could even attract to itself thinkers who had thrown in their lot with Marxism was due in part to the work of Vladimir Solovyev in the second half of the nineteenth century. His influence in this respect should not, of course, be exaggerated. After all, it was natural that the ideas of the radical intelligentsia should lead to a reaction, to the emergence of a different intellectual atmosphere. But there can be little doubt that Solovyev's sustained attempt to present a religious view of the world, to present Christianity in the form of philosophical reflection, made a powerful contribution to conferring intellectual respectability on a line of thought which was sharply opposed to materialism, positivism and utilitarianism. There were, of course, other outstanding writers with a religious outlook, such as Dostoevsky and Tolstoy. But neither was a professional philosopher. And while Dostoevsky, in his later years, tended to appear as firmly on the side of conservatism, or even 'reaction', Tolstoy stood apart from all groups, conservative, liberal and socialist, and expounded ideas which to many seemed both eccentric and impractical. Solovyev, however, was a professional philosopher, who tried to bring together in one coherent worldview religious faith, philosophy and social thought. Not all of those who contributed to the revival of religious thought in the early years of the twentieth century had been directly influenced by Solovyev. But in an indirect way at any rate they all owed him a debt as to one who had prepared the way for a change in the intellectual climate.

2. Vladimir Sergeyevich Solovyev (1853–1900) was the son of a noted historian, Sergey M. Solovyev, a professor at the University of Moscow. His grandfather was a priest. The young Solovyev was brought up in the Orthodox faith, but at the age of fourteen he embraced atheism, materialism and socialism. In other words, he was carried away for a time by the spirit which prevailed in the radical intelligentsia. The atheist phase

did not last long. By the time that he was eighteen, Solovyev had regained his Christian faith, which he was to retain to the end of his life. Although he abandoned atheistic socialism and the cult of the Man-god, as Dostoevsky would put it, he by no means abandoned his interest in the transformation of society and the regeneration of mankind. Solovyev was indeed mystically inclined, but recovery of Christian faith did not involve a focusing of attention on personal salvation and interior union with God to the exclusion of concern with social and political problems. His social ideals changed their form, but they did not disappear. And, as we shall see, in the closing decade of his life he was to speak appreciatively, from a Christian point of view, of the moral and social idealism of the intelligentsia.

When a boy of sixteen, Solovyev read Spinoza, whose thought influenced his mind in a religious direction. The concept of total-unity, of a unity embracing God, the human race and the world, was to be a leading idea in his thought, and the philosophy of Spinoza provided material for reflection. Solovyev was also influenced by his reading of Kant and Schopenhauer, followed by study of Fichte, Hegel and Schelling. The later philosophy of Schelling was to provide stimulus for his theological ideas.

During the years 1869–73 Solovyev studied in the University of Moscow, first in the Faculty of Natural Science and then in that of History and Philology. After graduating in 1873 he spent a year at the Theological Academy at Zagorsk, not far from Moscow, where he deepened his knowledge of theological and mystical literature. His university thesis for the Mastership, *The Crisis in Western Philosophy – Against Positivism*, was published in 1874.

Having completed his year at Zagorsk, Solovyev began teaching in the University of Moscow. But in the summer of 1875 he went to London to pursue research in the library of the British Museum. Cutting short his stay in London, he visited Egypt, in obedience, so he was later to relate, to a mystical call. In the autumn of 1876 he resumed his teaching at Moscow, but in the following year dissensions in the University led him to move to St Petersburg, where he successfully defended his doctorate thesis, *A Critique of Abstract Principles*, in 1880. His work *The Philosophical Foundations of Integral Knowledge* had appeared in 1877. The title of this work shows the influence on his mind of Ivan Kireevsky's concept of integral knowledge.

For a while Solovyev lectured in the University of St Petersburg. His public *Lectures on Godmanhood*, in which he expounded his religious metaphysics and which attracted a distinguished audience, including

Dostoevsky and Tolstoy[1], appeared in 1878. It seemed that he had a brilliant career before him in the university of the capital. But in 1881 he blotted his copybook in the eyes of the authorities by publicly exhorting the Tsar Alexander III to pardon the assassins of his father, Alexander II. At the time he adhered to the theocratic ideal of a political society governed by Christian principles, and he believed that Orthodox Russia should set an example of Christian love. Alexander III and his government were not prepared to accept Solovyev's demand that the late Tsar's assassins should be spared the death penalty, and, being in disfavour, he retired from the University and devoted himself to writing.[2]

Like the Slavophiles, Solovyev believed in the spiritual mission of Russia, but it did not take him long to see the incompatibility between the Christian ideal of universal love on the one hand and, on the other, the nationalistic spirit and the hostility to the West, not only to Western rationalism but also to Catholicism, which disfigured Slavophile thought. And in the 1880s his attention focused on the thought of the universal Church and on reunion between the Eastern and Western Churches. It was his conviction that the basic requisite for reunion was mutual understanding in the spirit of brotherly love. And in 1882–4 he wrote *The Spiritual Foundations of Life*, a work which was designed to be meaningful even for those who were not members of the Church. It is important to understand that, for Solovyev, the Christian Church was already spiritually or mystically one. That is to say, he rejected the spirit of exclusiveness; he did not believe that either the Orthodox Church or the Catholic Church was 'the one true Church'. He accepted the need for a symbol and organ of unity, the papacy, but he did not envisage reunion as taking the form of submission of one Church to the other. Basic unity on a spiritual level was, for him, already there; formal reunion would be a visible expression of an already existing spiritual union. In *The Great Dispute and Christian Politics* (1883), which consisted of a series of articles published during the years 1881–3 in *Russia* (*Rus*), a journal edited by the Slavophile Ivan Aksakov, Solovyev emphasized the part which Russia should play in working towards Christian reunion. But his

1 Solovyev seems to have met Dostoevsky for the first time in 1874. His friendship with the novelist dates from 1877. Dostoevsky is said to have taken Solovyev as a model for Alyosha in *The Brothers Karamazov*. After the novelist's death in 1881 Solovyev gave three addresses in his memory. In them he endorsed Dostoevsky's idea of the God-man (as opposed to that of the Man-god) and his theory of the reconciling mission of Russia. Solovyev's attraction to Catholicism and his plans for reunion were, of course, foreign to Dostoevsky's mind.

2 Solovyev was reprimanded and told not to give public lectures for a while, but abandonment of his post in the University was not demanded of him. This was his own decision.

criticism of the spirit of exclusiveness in Orthodoxy and of nationalism led to a break with the Slavophiles, and Solovyev started publishing articles in the Westernizing and liberal periodical *European Messenger* (*Vestnik Evropi*), which formed the basis for his work *The National Problem in Russia* (1891), in which he conceived his country as rising above nationalism and serving the cause of mankind's spiritual unification. The first volume of his *History and Future of Theocracy* had appeared in 1884.

In 1886–8 Solovyev was in Croatia, where he had discussions with Josip Juraj Strossmayer (1815–1903), Catholic bishop of Djakovo, who was keenly interested in the subject of reunion between the Catholic and Orthodox Churches.[1] Solovyev entertained the rather eccentric vision of Pope and Tsar working together to achieve reunion. Pope Leo XIII is said to have commented that, though the philosopher's idea was a beautiful one, without a miracle it was quite impractical. As for Alexander III, he was not the man to show enthusiasm for the idea of uniting Orthodoxy and Catholicism. Anyway, in 1887 Solovyev lectured at Paris on the Russian Orthodox Church, and in 1889 he published in French *Russia and the Universal Church* (*La Russie et l'église universelle*), a work which was not well received in his native land.

Solovyev's interest in and friendly attitude towards Catholicism not unnaturally gave rise to rumours or reports that he had become a Catholic, reports which seemed to be confirmed by the fact that in 1896 he received communion in a Catholic church. Though, however, in the early 1880s Solovyev became convinced that the denunciations of Catholicism by Orthodox zealots were exaggerated and in the main unjustified, and though he himself accepted some Catholic doctrines to which the Orthodox took exception, he denied reports of his conversion and he certainly died as a member of the Russian Orthodox Church, after making his confession to and receiving the sacraments from an Orthodox priest. To the present writer it seems a mistake to make heavy weather about the question whether Solovyev did or did not become a Catholic. From his point of view, he was a member of the universal Church, which was immanent in both Orthodoxy and Catholicism. It is doubtless true to say that, whereas in the 1880s Solovyev came close to Catholicism, in the 1890s his enthusiasm diminished and he felt more strongly his bond with the Orthodox Church. Though, however, he

1 Strossmayer was opposed to the project of defining papal infallibility at the First Vatican Council, though he accepted the Council's decree. He considered the definition 'inexpedient', as serving no useful purpose but as creating a fresh hindrance to Christian reunion.

rejected Rome's claims to unconditional submission, neither did he accept exclusive claims made by the Eastern Church. Besides, in the last decade of his life he became notably critical of the Church, any Church, as an institution.[1]

In 1891 Solovyev read a paper to the Moscow Psychological Society on the collapse of the medieval world conception. What he had in mind was this. When Christianity had triumphed and become the official religion, the majority of professing Christians were quite content to accept Christian principles in theory, provided that social and political structures and life remained as before. In other words, by the medieval world-conception, whether in western Christendom or in the Byzantine East, he understood a compromise between Christianity and 'paganism', between, as we can express it, Christian principles on the one hand and worldly values on the other. Christianity teaches active love for all men. This demands, for example, a concern with social justice and opposition to nationalism and war. The Church, however, in both the West and the East, had failed lamentably in fulfilling its task of furthering realization of the kingdom of God. To be sure, devout Christians had not ceased to exist, but they had limited themselves to concern with personal salvation and had not given external expression to their faith by promoting the regeneration of human society, including political life, in accordance with Christian principles and values. It was mainly unbelievers who, in both West and East, were showing active concern with social justice and the transformation of society. In acting in this way they were, unwittingly and in spite of their unbelief, instruments of the divine Spirit. They were carrying out a task which the Chistian Church had neglected. And they were contributing to breaking down the 'medieval world-view', with its dogmatism and its inward-turning spirituality.

Solovyev's paper startled his hearers. For he was obviously putting in a good word on behalf of the Russian radical intelligentsia, though he did not, of course, endorse their atheist and positivist attitudes. His paper also led to his being denounced by Leontyev as an instrument of Antichrist. Previously, Leontyev had admired Solovyev and had sympathized with his promotion of the cause of reunion. But his indignation was aroused when the famous religious thinker maintained that the

---

1 In his *Answer to N. Y. Danilevsky* (1885), who had accused him of partiality and of being on the side of Roman Catholicism, Solovyev said that in Russian literature, when the subject of Catholicism was treated, he found 'almost nothing but hostile polemics, prejudices and misunderstandings', but that he saw Orthodoxy and Catholicism as complementary and that it was not a question of being on *one* side. See *Sobranie sochinenii* (photographic edition, Brussels, 1966), IV, p. 193. This edition is referred to here as *SS*.

Christianity of the desert was not what was needed and that unbelieving radicals were, unknown to themselves, performing a task which the Church should have been doing. In Solovyev's paper Leontyev detected a surrender to the idea of progress and to the dream of a terrestial paradise.

In point of fact, though Solovyev certainly believed that the Church had missed its opportunities and had failed to realize the human brotherhood and solidarity at which the radicals aimed, he had no intention of claiming that the kingdom of God would be fully realized on earth. On the contrary, he lost faith in the realization of the theocratic ideal which he had proclaimed in the eighties and expected instead an increasing religious apostasy. This point of view found expression in the publication of *Three Conversations on War, Progress and the End of Universal History* (1889), to which he added *A Short Story of Antichrist*. Solovyev had become acutely aware of the power of evil. While he was confident in the ultimate triumph of the good, he foresaw, as far as this world was concerned, the reduction of the followers of Christ to a small and persecuted minority, without any power to coerce others. All external power would belong to the forces of Antichrist. It was then, in the last days, that the reunion of Christians, Orthodox, Catholic and Protestant, would take place, with the pope as the symbol of unity. Christianity would enjoy no outward triumph; there would be no theocratic society. But in the midst of the kingdom of Man, the reign of Antichrist, the union of the Christian remnant would take place at the end of history. Perhaps even Leontyev might have revised his harsh judgment of Solovyev, had he lived long enough to be aware of the philosopher's apocalyptic vision of the future.

The foregoing paragraphs may have given the impression that Solovyev, having published some philosophical writings in the 1870s, then abandoned philosophy and concerned himself with the reunion of the Churches and, finally, with speculation about the future. This impression would be incorrect. In 1892–4 Solovyev published a series of articles in the journal *Problems of Philosophy and Psychology*, which constituted his book *The Meaning of Love*, in which he reflected on the implications of his metaphysics in regard to human love. In 1897 he published a large work on ethics, *The Justification of the Good*.[1] He tried to develop ethics independently of metaphysics, but the link between them was clear. Finally, at the end of his life he was working on his (unfinished) *Foundations of Theoretical Philosophy* (1897–9), a work which, by itself, is quite sufficient to show that the author was perfectly able to discuss philosophical themes in a professional manner.

1 Second edition, 1898.

Although Solovyev was a professional philosopher, he was also a poet. In this area he exercised a considerable influence on Alexander Blok (1880–1921), the most eminent of the Russian symbolists. Solovyev also had several visionary experiences, which he described in his poem *Three Meetings* (or *Encounters*). When, as a boy of nine, he was attending a service in the Moscow University church, he 'saw' a beautiful woman, whom he was later to identify with Sophia, the divine wisdom personified. A similar vision was experienced in 1875, when Solovyev was in the British Museum, and it appears that he had the impression of being told to visit Egypt. Having done so, he had another similar vision in the desert. His last vision occurred during a further visit to Egypt in 1899, but this time he seems to have seen something evil and menacing. Presumably it was connected with his idea of the growing influence of the forces of evil, of Antichrist. Solovyev's own attitude to such experiences is best expressed by his remark that even an hallucination can have meaning for the person who experiences it. The vision of Sophia, for example, was connected, as Solovyev indicates in his poem, with his idea of total-unity, and he also saw it as a call or summons to work for the regeneration of mankind. Obviously, an experience could have meaning for Solovyev, even if it was explicable in naturalistic terms. The fact that a dream can be explained in psychological terms does not necessarily prevent a person from seeing meaning or significance in the dream.

Solovyev has been accused by some theological critics of a marked inclination to rationalism. The meaning of this accusation will be discussed presently. In any case, he was also a poet, a man of imagination, and a mystic. Mention of his visionary experiences helps to illustrate this aspect of his personality. The different aspects were doubtless interconnected in a variety of ways. At the same time his philosophical thought can be outlined without reference to visions.[1] And it is to this subject that we must now turn.

3. Solovyev not only possessed a wide knowledge of the development of western philosophy[2] but also reflected deeply on the kinds of philosophizing which he found in Western thought and on the relations between them. This is evident from his philosophical writings, in which his approach to a theme tends to be historical. One aspect of his treatment is,

1 As remarked above, Solovyev's first vision of a beautiful lady was later interpreted by him as a vision of Sophia. This interpretation was inspired by the idea of divine wisdom as found in Scriptural and Patristic literature. Solovyev's theory of Sophia was not simply the result of mystical experience.
2 He had also some acquaintance with oriental philosophy.

as one would expect, critical. He argues, for example, that the empiricists, in their reductive analysis into impressions, failed to grasp what actually exists, and that pure empiricism, relying simply on sense-experience, would fail to understand anything. At the same time he sees the development of rationalism as culminating in the reduction of being to pure thought. In their different ways both empiricism and rationalism fail to grasp what *is*, real being. Yet both express truths and correspond to real aspects of the human being. We cannot understand reality without sense-experience, and we cannot understand it without ideas or concepts and the rational discernment of relations. What is needed is a synthesis of complementary truths, of distinct principles. Thus when Solovyev says in his first published work *The Crisis of Western Philosophy* that 'philosophy in the sense of abstract, *exclusively* theoretical knowledge has completed its development and passed irrevocably into the world of the past'[1], the operative word is 'exclusively'. Solovyev does not mean that philosophy should not be concerned with theoretical knowledge. Indeed, in the work on which he was still engaged at the time of his death he insisted that 'philosophy strives from the start after unconditional or absolute truth'[2]. He saw philosophy as also having a practical function, as being concerned with the good and its attainment. Moreover, 'exclusively' theoretical philosophy was for him equivalent to rationalism, in the sense of knowledge of the forms of thought as exemplified in the critical philosophy of Kant, with its denial of the possibility of knowing the 'thing in itself'.

In general, Solovyev saw the intellectual life of western man as having undergone a process of fragmentation. Not only had science, philosophy and religion become distinct spheres but they were often regarded as opposed to one another. The positivists, for example, looked on science as the only way of acquiring knowledge of reality and rejected metaphysics. Science and religion were frequently thought of as antithetical. Within philosophy, ethics, as knowledge of what ought to be, was conceived as having no intrinsic relation with metaphysics or with knowledge of what is. Philosophy had become separated from religion, and it was fairly widely believed that adherence to one excluded adherence to the other. The creative activity of man as manifested in art was regarded as having no real relation to the pursuit either of truth or of the good. In brief, the unity of the truth, the good and the beautiful as different aspects of being had been lost sight of.

---

1 SS, I, p. 27. *The Crisis*, introduction.
2 *Ibid.*, IX, p. 94. *Theoretical Philosophy*, I, 4. This work will be referred to as *TP*.

It would be a mistake to suppose that Solovyev was concerned simply with deploring this state of affairs, and that he desired a return to a point at which distinctions had not yet emerged. He desired a *universal synthesis* of science, philosophy and religion', which would mean 'the restoration of the inner *unity of the intellectual world*'.[1] As he also expressed the matter, he sought a synthesis between the good (as object of the will), the true (as object of the reason) and the beautiful (as the object of artistic creation). This emphasis on synthesis had as its presupposition that 'truth is the whole'.[2]

This last statement recalls to mind Hegel's statement to the same effect in the preface to *The Phenomenology of Spirit*. Solovyev, however, while admiring Hegel, regarded absolute idealism as a one-sided rationalist system. He saw a precursor, so to speak, of the desired synthesis in the thought of Eduard Von Hartmann (1842–1906). Solovyev was not, of course, satisfied with Hartmann's philosophy as it stood. What he maintained, at any rate in his earlier writings, was that 'this newest philosophy, with its logical perfection of *western form*, strives to unite with the full content of the spiritual insights of the East. Resting on the one hand on the data of *positive science*, this *philosophy*, on the other hand, holds out its hand to *religion*'[3]. In other words, Solovyev saw in contemporary thought, as exemplified in Hartmann's 'philosophy of the unconscious', signs of a movement towards the synthesis of science, philosophy and religion. We can add that, according to Solovyev, 'the first question which any philosophy that has a claim to be of general interest must answer is the question about the goal of life'.[4] This question was certainly treated by Schopenhauer and Hartmann, even if neither of them gave an answer which Solovyev could consider satisfactory.

Solovyev's ideal of synthesis can hardly be understood without reference to his concept of total-unity. Metaphysics, as he conceives it, aims at understanding reality, and reality is a unity which diversifies itself both internally, in the divine life, and externally, in the sense of the creation of actual individuals. The emergence of individuals can be conceived as a loss of original unity, as what Schelling represented as a 'Fall'. The task is to restore unity. Religion is concerned with this task, with 'the reunion of man and the world with the unconditional and all-one principle'.[5] But religious faith needs to come to exist 'for itself'[6], in the form of rational

1 *SS*, I, p. 151. *The Crisis*, 5.
2 *Ibid.*, II, p. 296. *Critique of Abstract Principles*, 42. This work will be referred to as *Critique*.
3 *Ibid.*, I, p. 151. *The Crisis*, 5.
4 *Ibid.*, I, p. 250. *Philosophical Principles*, I. This work will be referred to as *PP*.
5 *Ibid.*, III, p. 12. *Lectures*, III. (This work will be referred to as *L*.).
6 Solovyev often used Hegelian terms.

thought. Metaphysics tries to understand reality as a unity, while moral philosophy and social thought show how the egoism of individuals can be overcome and unity restored. Theoretical knowledge, therefore, knowledge of the structure of reality, is oriented to practical knowledge and, finally, to actual restoration of unity between human beings and between them and the divine Absolute. Thus the synthesis which Solovyev aims at goes far beyond some intellectual reconciliation between science, philosophy and religion. An intellectual reconciliation or harmonization is indeed envisaged, but the ultimate aim is to establish a unity in life, including social and political life. In the unfinished work on theoretical philosophy which he was writing in his last years Solovyev insisted that the philosopher must examine his presuppositions and not take them for granted, but philosophy was far from being for him simply an intellectual exercise, without any practical relevance to human life and history.

This emphasis on the practical relevance of philosophy, of its value for life, should not be understood as implying a pragmatist conception of truth. Referring to rationalism, Solovyev asserts that it regards philosophical knowledge as an end in itself and as 'the highest form of spiritual activity'.[1] He recognizes that 'in so far as philosophy is the fulfilment of the theoretical need for knowledge, it is its own end'.[2] But he objects against rationalism that 'this theoretical need is only a particular need, one among many, and that man's universal and highest need is for complete and absolute life, to the attainment of which all the rest, and consequently philosophy too, can be only a means'.[3] The sphere of philosophy is indeed that of knowledge, but the purpose or function of this knowledge is to change 'the centre of man's life from his nature as given to the absolute transcendent world'.[4] It is not, of course, every kind of philosophy which does this. Rationalism does not do so, nor does positivism. But 'true philosophy' does, striving to be the 'educative and directive force in life'.[5]

What therefore, we may ask, is the relation of philosophy to religion, as envisaged by Solovyev? If 'the task of religion is to set right our distorted life'[6], must not religion, rather than philosophy, be the directing force in life? If, however, philosophy shares this task with religion, what is the relation between them?

1 *Ibid.*, I, p. 310. *PP.*, 3.
2 *Ibid.*
3 *Ibid.*
4 *Ibid.*, p. 311.
5 *Ibid.*, p. 291. *PP*, 2.
6 *Ibid.*, III, p. 301. *Spiritual Foundations of Life.*

Obviously, the more we insist that philosophy should leave no stone unturned, no presupposition unexamined, and that it should be a rigorous intellectual search for absolute truth, the more are we inclined to regard philosophy as an autonomous discipline. If we also adhere to a definite set of religious beliefs, we shall doubtless hope, or even be confident, that the conclusions of 'true philosophy' will harmonize with these beliefs and not be incompatible with them, but, even then, if we have followed a rigorous method in philosophy, its conclusions will be arrived at independently. Philosophy will be, so to speak, alongside religion, harmonizing with it but autonomous. It is not surprising therefore that in *Theoretical Philosophy*, after insisting on the nature of theoretical philosophy as a rigorous search for absolute truth, Solovyev should remark that the only thing which a zealous representative of a positive religion can derive or hope for is that the philosopher 'by the free investigation of truth should arrive at a full inner accord of his convictions with the dogmas of the given revelation – a result which would be equally satisfactory for both sides'.[1]

It would be a mistake, however, to think that, for Solovyev, the relation between 'true philosophy' and religion was purely external. We can say that he wanted to bring philosophy and religion closer together or, rather, to exhibit a harmony between them. But the relation which he envisaged was not simply external. Some remarks suggest that he regarded the function of philosophy as being that of Christian apologetics. Thus in the preface to *The History and Future of Theocracy* he spoke of his task as being 'to justify the faith of our fathers'[2], to 'show how this ancient faith, freed from the fetters of local isolation and national pride, coincides with eternal and universal truth'.[3] But this task of justification should not be understood as supplying external buttresses, in the form of arguments, to support the 'ancient faith' just as it stood. Solovyev's approach was much more akin to that of the German idealists than to that of the eighteenth-century Christian apologists. In his *Critique of Abstract Principles* he asserted the need to put religious truth into the form of freely-rational thought[4], and in his work on theocracy he explained that by justifying the faith of our fathers he meant 'raising it to a new stage of rational consciousness'.[5] In a real sense the content of religion and of true philosophy is the same. Both are concerned with the

1 *SS*, IX, p. 95. *TP*, I, 4.
2 *Ibid.*, IV, p. 243.
3 *Ibid.*
4 *Ibid.*, II, p. 349. *Critique*, 46.
5 *Ibid.*, IV, p. 243.

total-unity, with reality as a whole. But the content of religion needs to be thought, to be demonstrated and expressed in universal form. In his *Lectures on Godmanhood* Solovyev says that 'besides religious faith and religious experience religious thought is also required, the result of which is philosophy of religion'.[1] This philosophy of religion is not so much thought *about* religion as a thinking and demonstration of religious truth, Christian truth in particular. We are obviously put in mind of Hegel's view of philosophy of religion, though Solovyev was more indebted to Schelling and his concept of 'positive philosophy' as developed in his later years.

In Solovyev's judgment contemporary religion was 'not what it ought to be'.[2] 'Instead of being all in all, it hides itself away in a very small and very remote corner of an inner world; it is one of the many different interests which divide our attention.'[3] Reduced to this condition, religion is unable to fulfil its mission, the spiritual regeneration of mankind. Socialism and positivism aspire 'to occupy the empty place left by religion in the life and knowledge of contemporary civilized humanity'.[4] We can see Solovyev as endeavouring to use western philosophical thought (what he believes to be its valuable features and the results of reflection on its development) as an instrument for raising the religious vision of total unity, of God in all and all in God, to a level of reflective consciousness at which it can be an effective power for the transformation not only of the human being's intellectual view of reality but also of society and political life.

Obviously, in so far as Solovyev presupposes Christian faith and belief and tries to give to the content of faith a more adequate intellectual expression, the question arises whether it is not more appropriate to speak of theology than of philosophy. This is not, however, how he sees the matter. Referring to 'traditional theology', he remarks that it lacks two features which are necessary for the full knowledge of truth. 'In the first place it excludes the free relation of reason to the content of religion, the free mastering and development of the content by reason. In the second place it does not develop this content in relation to the empirical material of knowledge.'[5] In other words, freedom of thought is lacking, and also an adequate knowledge of nature, a cosmology. Again, in *Theoretical Philosophy* Solovyev says that though Christianity affirms the unconditional or absolute truth of its beliefs, it is 'not interested in the intellectual verification of its content'.[6] Further, Christianity is not the only religion

1 *Ibid.*, III, p. 35. *L*, III.
2 *Ibid.*, p. 3. *L*, I.
3 *Ibid.*, p. 4.
4 *Ibid.*, p. 5.
5 *Ibid.*, II, p. 349. *Critique*, 46.
6 *Ibid.*, IX, p. 94. *TP*, I, 4.

which affirms the absolute truth of its beliefs. The implication is that the truth of Christian belief needs to be demonstrated in a discipline which does not leave presuppositions unexamined. This process seems to involve, in effect, the transmutation of theology into philosophy or, if preferred, the subordination of faith to reason, even if Solovyev intended to bring religious faith and philosophy closer together, rather than to subordinate the one to the other.

Solovyev was a convinced and devout Christian believer. He wanted what might be described as a Christian philosophy, a philosophy developed within the area of faith. There is no ground for questioning his sincerity. At the same time we cannot simply dismiss the claim made by some writers[1] that, in spite of Solovyev's criticism of rationalism and of 'abstract' philosophy, he himself proceeded along this path. It was certainly not a case of a covert attack on Christianity. Solovyev sincerely believed that he had exhibited the truth of the Christian religion. It seems evident, however, there was a marked gnostic element in his thought, which shows itself in his metaphysics. He envisaged a higher truth or, better, a higher and more adequate expression of truth than could be found in theology. His instrument was philosophy, 'true philosophy' that is to say. It has frequently been asserted that Solovyev was the first really systematic Russian philosopher. This assertion is doubtless true. He treated extensively topics which would generally be described as theological. But his approach was that of a philosopher, of a metaphysician, who was also a devout Christian.

4. Solovyev always maintained that experience, conceived as immediate awareness of a phenomenal object or as a relation between a subject and a phenomenon or phenomena, is one of the basic sources of knowledge. But experience by itself is not knowledge. A phenomenon, according to Solovyev, cannot be known except in terms of its relations to other phenomena, and for this reason is required. It is reason which apprehends relations and grasps ideas or concepts. Experience provides material for knowledge, but without reason there would be no knowledge. Given Solovyev's idea of total-unity, of reality as a unity, and of truth as the whole, it is obvious that there could not be full or adequate knowledge of anything unless its relation to the Absolute were understood, but we can pass over this matter for the moment. It is sufficient to note that experience and reason are both basic sources of knowledge for Solovyev.

These two sources are not, however, sufficient for a knowledge of

1 See, for example, Zenkovsky's *A History of Russian Philosophy*, II, pp. 491–2.

reality. 'I can experience and think what is not true.'[1] If experience is conceived as a relation between a subject and a phenomenal object, when 'phenomenal' means 'appearing to a subject', one can say that the traveller in the desert who sees the mirage of an oasis, experiences an oasis; but there is no real oasis there, existing apart from the object within the traveller's consciousness. Similarly, one can have a concept which is not exemplified in extramental reality. Indeed, one could construct a system of thought which would fail to represent reality. For true knowledge of reality a third source is required. In *Philosophical Principles* Solovyev calls it 'intellectual intuition, which constitutes the true primary form of integral knowledge'[2] and is 'immediate experience of absolute reality'[3]. In the *Critique of Abstract Principles*, however, this source of knowledge is called 'faith'[4], though 'intellectual intuition' reappears in the *Lectures on Godmanhood*. In any case a third source of knowledge is required to put us in contact with or to assure us of the existence of metaphenomenal reality.

The close connection between Solovyev's ideas about knowledge and his metaphysics of total-unity is clear. For the metaphenomenal reality which he has in mind is the Absolute in its self-manifestation or self-unfolding, the One. This reality is not given to us as a phenomenon, and it is therefore not the object of 'experience' in the sense in which Solovyev uses this term. But the human being belongs, in his view, to the total-unity and can be aware of its reality from within, by a kind of connatural immediate perception, intuition or faith. Solovyev recognizes two ways of knowing, 'externally, from the side of our phenomenal separateness – relative knowledge, in its two aspects, as empirical and as rational – and interiorly, from the side of our absolute being, internally linked with the being of what is known – unconditional, mystical knowledge'.[5] 'Thus mystical knowledge is necessary for philosophy'[6], if the real object of philosophical knowledge is to be known. The word 'mystical' is used here to mark off the kind of knowledge in question, direct or immediate perception of the real, from 'experience' and reasoning, rather than to indicate any exceptional supernatural experience.

It is in the context of these ideas that Solovyev criticizes empiricism, rationalism and positivism. Empiricism reduces reality to subjective impressions or sense-data, while rationalism arrives in the end at identifying

1 SS, II, p. 289. *Critique*, 40.
2 *Ibid.*, I, p. 316. *PP*, 3. The idea of 'intellectual intuition' comes from Schelling.
3 *Ibid.*, p. 347. *PP*, 4.
4 *Ibid.*, III, p. 326. *Critique*, 45.
5 *Ibid.*, II, p. 331, *Ibid.*
6 *Ibid.*, I, p. 305. *PP*, 2.

being with thought, leaving itself without a thinker and without anything to think about, any object of thought. Neither apprehends existent reality, absolute being. As for positivism, by excluding metaphysics it too cuts itself off from reality. Yet there is truth in each of these lines of thought, though the truth which each expresses is only partial. An experimental basis for knowledge is certainly required. As for positivism, it is quite right in maintaining that natural science is confined to the phenomenal world, though by excluding metaphysics it renders itself incapable of grasping metaphenomenal reality.

In his unfinished *Theoretical Philosophy* Solovyev insisted that 'the unconditional validity of immediate consciousness is the basic truth of philosophy'.[1] That is to say, at the basis of knowledge there lies the subject-object relation of consciousness, the sphere of psychic immediacy. At the level of pure consciousness, however, 'there is no distinction between appearance and reality'[2]. The traveller in the desert who 'sees' an oasis cannot doubt that he is having this experience, but the occurrence of the experience does not tell him whether what he is seeing, the object of consciousness, is appearance or reality. '*Knowledge of psychic immediacy* pays for its absolute validity by the extreme narrowness of its limits.'[3] As far as pure consciousness is concerned, if I am conscious of a sound, I am conscious of a sound; I have an auditory experience. But this indubitable fact does not tell me what caused the sound nor even whether the sound was imagined, caused by an external object or the result of some physiological condition in myself.

Let us assume with Solovyev that pure consciousness, though absolutely valid within its limits, cannot answer the question whether what I am experiencing is experienced in a dream or in reality, inasmuch as 'the subjective validity, which alone is guaranteed by consciousness, is *equally valid* in both cases'.[4] It follows that it makes sense to ask whether there is any extramental world of things. Solovyev is quite prepared to accept this conclusion. Indeed, he insists on it. 'We *believe* in the reality of the external world, and it is the task of philosophy to give a rational justification for this belief, an explanation or proof.'[5]

If, however, it is possible to follow Descartes in applying methodic doubt to the existence of the external world, it is also possible to apply it to the 'reality of a *conscious subject*, as a particular independent being or

1 *SS*, IX, p. 102. *TP*, I, 8.
2 *Ibid.*, p. 105. *Ibid.*
3 *Ibid.*, p. 103. *Ibid.*
4 *Ibid.*
5 *Ibid.*, p. 106. *TP*, I, 9.

thinking substance'.[1] The phenomenological subject certainly exists within consciousness, just as the phenomenological object does, but it does not follow that the existence of a thinking substance is given in pure consciousness. Descartes thought that it was, and Solovyev remarks that while he once agreed with Descartes, he no longer does so. In his view, belief in a thinking substance, no less than belief in an external world, needs to be philosophically validated, if it can be.

It would be a mistake to suppose that Solovyev is suggesting that there is no external world and that there is no abiding self. He emphasizes the fact that he is concerned with delimiting the indisputable from the disputable, the unquestionable from the questionable, in the interests of rigorously pursued philosophical thought, which leaves no presuppositions and no natural beliefs (such as belief in an external world) unexamined. In regard to his own view of the self, he does not wish to deny that there is any such thing as an individual self, but at the same time he does not wish to represent the self as a self-enclosed separate substance. In *Theoretical Philosophy* he considers the maxim 'know thyself' as a maxim for the philosopher and distinguishes three senses in which the self can be understood. First, there is the empirical self. To know one's empirical self is not the task of the philosopher. Secondly, there is the self as logical subject, as the abstract subject of thought, irrespective of content. Knowledge of the self in this sense is not the aim of philosophy. Thirdly, there is the self as grasping absolute truth and as one with its content. Philosophy aims at knowing the self in this sense. 'Consequently, "know thyself" means – know truth.'[2] Solovyev is here hinting that the self is more than the individual self. And in *The Concept of God* he says that what is called the soul or the ego 'is not a complete circle of life enclosed in itself, possessing its own content, essence or life-significance, but only the bearer or support (*hypostasis*) of something other than itself and higher'.[3] This idea, however, carries us into metaphysics.

5. Let us turn to Solovyev's metaphysics. In works on Solovyev written by religious thinkers, especially those who adhere to the Orthodox tradition, emphasis is naturally laid on his metaphysical and theosophical speculation. It must be admitted, however, that to western philosophers who are representatives of the analytic current of philosophical thought this speculation is apt to seem fantastic. When Solovyev is

1 *Ibid.*, p. 107. *TP*, I, 10.
2 *Ibid.*, p. 166. *TP*, III, 7.
3 *Ibid.*, p. 20. *Concept of God*, 8.

discussing empiricism or rationalism or criticizing Descartes, they see him as a philosopher, whether or not they agree with all that he says. But when he starts talking about the Absolute and Sophia and Godmanhood, they probably feel that his thought belongs to another world. Although this is understandable, it would be absurd to treat of Solovyev without saying something about his metaphysical speculation. One might as well try to outline the thought of St Thomas Aquinas without mentioning God or to present Hegel's absolute idealism while omitting any reference to his idea of the Absolute.

The central idea of Solovyev's metaphysics is the concept of total-unity, of reality as one. In religious language it is the idea of God in all and all in God. This unity is not, however, something static, lifeless. Reality is life, the life, we can say, of God or the Absolute. 'Life is the most general and comprehensive name for the plenitude of reality every-where and in everything. We speak with equal right of divine life, of human life, and of the life of nature'.[1] The idea of reality recalls to mind the philosophy of Spinoza – which, as we noted, influenced Solovyev when he was a youth – while the idea of reality as creative life, as manifesting its essence creatively, reminds us of German idealism, of Fichte, Hegel and Schelling. But though Solovyev was certainly influ-enced by his reflection on the thought of Spinoza and of the German idealists, his mind was also powerfully influenced by meditation on the Scriptures, on the writings of the Greek Fathers, and on mystical litera-ture. He can, indeed, be seen as trying to express Christian truth in the framework of ideas derived from reflection on western philosophy, or at any rate as endeavouring to bring the two together; but the Christian inspiration is nonetheless basic. To be sure, we may sometimes be left wondering whether he is talking about the Biblical God or about the Absolute of German idealism. But such ambiguity is largely the result of the effort to raise religious truth to a new level of consciousness with the aid of western metaphysics. To put the matter in another way, Solovyev tried to conceive the mystical intuition of the One in terms of metaphysics.

The existence of God, the ultimate reality, could obviously not be given in 'experience', in the sense in which experience was conceived as a relation between a subject and a phenomenal object, which might or might not represent an objectively existing reality. Nor could it be given in what, in *Theoretical Philosophy*, Solovyev described as pure con-sciousness, for the same reason. But neither could the existence of God be

1 SS, III, p. 290. *On the Way to True Philosophy* (1883).

proved. Solovyev does indeed claim that what exists unconditionally (the Absolute) is *'what is known in all knowledge'*[1], that it is the presupposition of all knowing. But he also insists that the objective existence of the Absolute or God 'cannot be *deduced* by pure reason or demonstrated by purely logical means'.[2] It is given in religious experience, in 'mystical knowledge'. Further, the reality of God is 'not a *deduction* from religious experience but its *content – that which is experienced'*.[3] Obviously, Solovyev's third source of knowledge, mystical knowledge, is essential for his metaphysics, if this is to express knowledge of reality and not be simply an intellectual construction, which might or might not apply to reality.

Given the existence of God, the ultimate and unconditional reality, as grasped in religious experience, Solovyev proceeds to deduce the nature of God, the phases, so to speak, of the divine life. 'God is real, that is, being belongs to him. He possesses being. But it is impossible simply *to be*. The statement "I am" or "it is" necessarily gives rise to the question "what am I?" or "what is?".'[4] If, therefore, 'the verb "to be" is only a link between its subject and its predicate, then, in conformity with this, being is logically thinkable only as the relationship of a being to its objective essence or content – a relationship in which it in one way or another affirms, posits or manifests its essence'.[5] In other words, God manifests himself, positing his own essence. This means that God, as the unconditional reality, posits himself as the Logos. We must thus distinguish between the 'first Absolute', God in himself, and the 'second Absolute', the essence or content of the first as posited. The first Absolute, however, God as the ultimate and 'supra-existent'[6] principle, knows this posited essence as *his*, thus coming to exist 'for himself'. This relationship between the first and second Absolute constitutes the third moment in the divine life and can be described as Spirit.

Solovyev thus deduces the doctrine of the Trinity by reason, to his own satisfaction at any rate. The actual deduction is a temporal process, but each phase or moment in the divine life is conceived as eternal. The Father eternally begets the Son, the Logos, and the Holy Spirit proceeds eternally. There is no temporal succession in God himself. Further, although Solovyev distinguishes three 'subjects' in God and talks about

1 *Ibid.*, II, p. 306. *Critique*, 43.
2 *Ibid.*, III, p. 32. *L*, III.
3 *Ibid.*, X, p. 193. *D.*, p. 164. *D.* signifies the English translation of *The Justification of the Good* by Nathalie A. Duddington (New York, 1918).
4 *Ibid.*, III, p. 83. *L*, VI.
5 *Ibid.*, p. 84.
6 *Ibid.*, II, p. 306. *Critique*, 43.

the first and second Absolutes, he insists that the moments of the divine
life are moments within the life of the one God. In Christian language,
God is three Persons in one Nature. There are not three Gods, but one
only. If we ask why the life of God takes the form described, the answer is
that otherwise God would not be God. To be God, God must be not only
'in himself' but also 'with himself' and 'for himself'. We can add that
Solovyev correlates the three 'subjects' with goodness, truth and beauty,
the three forms under which the Absolute appears to itself.

The influence of European philosophy is clear enough. The idea of the
'second Absolute' comes from Schelling, while the idea of the Absolute
coming to exist 'for itself' was a prominent feature of the philosophy of
Hegel. The idea of the second Absolute or Logos also recalls to mind the
Neoplatonist *Nous* or divine mind, the seat of the eternal ideas of Plato.
One might therefore expect Solovyev to identify Sophia, the divine
wisdom, with the second Absolute or Logos. But this is not the case. And
something further must be said about the concept of Sophia.

In the *Lectures on Godmanhood* we are told that the Logos is God as
active force. It is productive unity. Sophia is the first produced unity,
'ideal or perfect humanity'[1], eternal Godmanhood. The Logos is the
direct expression of the first Absolute, whereas Sophia is the expression
of the divine essence as idea. When Solovyev talks about ideal humanity
as eternal, he is obviously not referring to individual human beings as
phenomenal realities which are born and die. He is referring to the ideal
and eternal realm, to archetypal humanity we might say. Christ, according to Solovyev, unites in himself the Logos and Sophia. He is both God
and Man. Individual human beings, in their inner essence, also partake in
ideal humanity. The human being is thus a member of both the eternal or
absolute and the phenomenal spheres, and he or she can establish contact
with the former through 'intellectual intuition'.[2]

We have said that in the *Lectures on Godmanhood* Sophia is identified
with ideal or perfect humanity, humanity as one perfect organism but as
archetypal idea, a unity produced by the Logos. But Solovyev does not
wish to represent Sophia as a 'mere idea', and in the *Lectures* it also
appears as the world-soul, as an active principle, and also as the body or
matter (in an analogical sense) of the Deity. We shall return presently to
the concept of the world-soul. Meanwhile we can note that in later
writings, such as *Russia and the Universal Church*, the idea of Sophia as
the world-soul is dropped, and that Sophia is variously represented as the

1 *SS*, III, p. 121. *L*, VIII.
2 *Ibid.*, p. 65. *L*, V.

substance of God, of the Trinity, as the archetype of creation, as the substance of the Holy Spirit. In addition, Sophia appears as the 'eternal Feminine' and is also associated with the Theotokos, Mary the Mother of God.

This multiplicity of descriptions certainly does not make for clarity. Successors of Solovyev have made much of the idea of Sophia and have tried to give it one definite meaning. Father Sergius Bulgakov, for example, understood by Sophia the unity of the world in the Logos, in the world of eternal ideas. With Solovyev, however, we find a plurality of somewhat different conceptions. At the same time we can say, in general, that, for him, Sophia is the mediator between God and the world, an expression of the Logos but at the same time a creative principle. As ideal humanity Sophia is eternal, but the ideal is creatively expressed in actual humanity, in human beings who progressively form the created expression of ideal humanity. As united with God through Christ, human beings are members of the Church, the body of Christ, of the Logos incarnate that is to say. And this body, when grown to its fullness and encompassing all mankind, is 'one universal divine-human organism'.[1] This full expression of Godmanhood can also be described as Sophia. In other words, Sophia can be conceived as both the principle of the creative process and its end, the kingdom of God. One may well ask why Solovyev was not content with Father, Son and Holy Spirit. But he doubtless thought that the Wisdom literature in the Bible and the reflections of Greek Fathers and theologians required a place for Sophia, a conviction which was reinforced by his 'visions', some of which he interpreted as visions of Sophia.

However this may be, the central idea of Solovyev's thought was not so much that of Sophia as of total-unity. If this idea is taken seriously, it demands that the world should be somehow included within the divine life, that it should be conceived as the self-manifestation of the Absolute. Further, if the existence of the world is required for the full expression of the divine life, creation must be necessary. It cannot indeed be necessary in the sense of God being compelled by any external influence to create. For there can be no influence external to the Absolute. But if the existence of individual beings is required for the full expression of the divine life, it follows that creation is necessary in the sense that it is the result of the nature of the Absolute.

Solovyev sees this, of course, and raises the question how the existence of the phenomenal world of plurality can be deduced. The problem is

1 *Ibid.*, p. 171. *L*, XI–XII (in one).

that of 'deducing the conditional from the unconditional, deducing what in 'itself is not necessary from the unconditionally necessary, deducing contingent reality from the absolute idea, the natural world of phenomena from the world of divine essence'.[1] This deduction, we are told, is not possible without a middle term. And the middle term is man, the human being who unites the absolute and the relative, the unconditional and the conditional. But even if we grant the presence in God of an idea of humanity, it by no means follows that the idea must be exemplified. It is, of course, a fact that there are individual human beings. But recognition of a fact is not equivalent to a philosophical deduction. Solovyev sees that it is necessary to introduce the concept of divine activity, and he has recourse to the idea of God as love. Without individuals 'the energy of the divine unity or love would have nothing in which it could manifest or reveal itself in all its fullness'.[2] Thus the existence of individual human beings is required for the self-unfolding of the Absolute. (Perhaps we can see here an example of what Fichte called a 'practical deduction'.)

The creation of distinct individuals has the effect that each human being is for his or her fellows an Other, an alien entity. Thus egoism, self-centredness and enmity arise. And Solovyev, following Schelling, represents creation as a Fall. 'The natural world, having fallen away from the divine unity, appears as a chaos of separate elements'[3]. This statement refers immediately to nature, but it also applies to the human race. Human beings, however, though distinct phenomena, are nonetheless united in essence, in the sense that each is an expression of ideal humanity and is comprised in the total-unity. The task of Sophia in the world is to restore unity, to unite human beings in one divine human organism. In other words, 'the gradual realization of the ideal total-unity is the meaning or goal of the world process'.[4] It is true that the 'organizer and orderer of the total-unity'[5] is the human being, operating in history, but human beings cannot fulfil this vocation unless enlightened and inspired by Sophia, the divine wisdom.

The emphasis laid by Solovyev on humanity and on the realization of Godmanhood obviously implies that nature is the presupposition of and the setting for human history. Human beings, embodied, belong to the world of nature, and if they are comprised within the total-unity, so too is nature. The existence, however, of actual nature is the result of a 'fall'

1 SS, p. 120. L, VIII.
2 Ibid., p. 137. L, IX.
3 Ibid., p. 143. L, X.
4 Ibid., p. 144. L, X.
5 Ibid., p. 150. L, X.

from the eternal ideal world, and the fall is reflected in the breaking up of unity into the plurality of atoms and in the 'chaotic' element in nature. At the same time unity is not entirely destroyed. The world of nature forms one body, as it were, a cosmos, animated by the world-soul.[1] As fallen away from the Logos, the world-soul asserts itself as an individual being; but it still participates in the divine life, and, as participating in the divine life, it strives to restore unity. As fulfilling this task on the level of consciousness, in and through human beings, it is called Sophia. We have already noted, however, that Solovyev came to drop this identification of Sophia with the world-soul and to conceive it more as the divine life in the Church. Anyway, the general picture is that of the actual world of nature and of human beings as a Fall, a falling away from ideal unity, and of a progressive recovery of unity, moving towards the realization of the kingdom of God. The ancient cosmological idea of plurality as a falling away from unity and of a return to unity in God or the Absolute is thus reaffirmed by Solovyev, though he places the idea in a Christian setting. Christ, both God and man, is the perfect expression of Godmanhood, and membership in the universal Church, the body of Christ, is the means whereby human beings realize Godmanhood in themselves.

6. It is noticeable how Solovyev insists on the unity of the human race. Ideal humanity, the eternal archetype, is one, and though the emergence of individual human beings is described as a fall from unity, human history is a process in which unity is restored in and through Christ, the incarnate Logos. This recovery of unity is possible, because human beings, though phenomenally distinct, participate in the one divine life. This participation makes possible the reconstitution of humanity as one universal organism. In other words, every human individual is part of a greater whole, namely humanity.

This idea explains Solovyev's appreciation of the thought of Auguste Comte. From one point of view this appreciation is unexpected and surprising. For Comte was the high priest of classical positivism, whereas Solovyev's first philosophical work, *The Crisis in Western Philosophy*, had as its subtitle *Against the Positivists*. Though, however, Solovyev was a determined critic of the positivist rejection of metaphysics, he greatly valued Comte's conception of humanity as one being, one organic whole. Thus in a paper on 'the idea of Humanity in Auguste Comte', which he read in 1898 to the Philosophical Society in the

1 The immediate source of Solovyev's idea of a world-soul was doubtless Schelling. But the idea went back, of course, to ancient times, to Platonism.

University of St Petersburg, Solovyev said that, while he was not a disciple
of Comte and did not share his idea of positivist religion, Comte nonetheless earned for himself a place in the memory of Christians inasmuch as
Wisdom 'found a place in the soul of this man and made him, though
half-consciously, a proclaimer of sublime truths about the Great Being
and about the resurrection from the dead'.[1]

The remarks in this essay about the resurrection are not simply an
expression of Christian belief. They show the influence on Solovyev's
mind of the thought of Nikolai Fyodorovich Fyodorov (1828–1903),
author of The Question of Brotherhood or Relatedness, and other articles.
This somewhat eccentric thinker regarded progress (in an evaluative
sense, of course) as consisting in the spread of brotherhood, of brotherly
relatedness, among human beings. The spirit of brotherhood, however,
should not be confined to relations between human beings living here and
now. Humanity forms a whole, and the spirit of brotherhood should be
extended to the dead, to 'our fathers'. But what is demanded is not simply
remembrance of the dead or sentimental feelings about them, but action.
And action in this context means concerted human action devoted to
raising the dead. Fyodorov was not prepared to set limits to the powers of
science, and he regarded it as a task for the scientific community to develop
the means of bringing 'our fathers', who had been lamentably forgotten,
back to life. This idea, which probably seems fantastic to most of us, was
coupled with Christian belief in the kingdom of God. Fyodorov did not,
for example, envisage the raising of cannibals from the dead precisely as
cannibals.[2] He thought of the raised as being transfigured and as taking
their places in the community of brethren and children of the heavenly
Father. In other words, he saw the kingdom of God as a goal to be achieved
on earth through concerted human effort.

Solovyev sympathized with Fyodorov's ideas and even spoke of him as
his spiritual teacher. When, in his paper on Comte, Solovyev asserted that
of all the famous philosophers it was Auguste Comte who came nearest to
'the task of the resurrection of the dead'[3], this phrase was obviously an
echo of Fyodorov's thought. It does not follow that Solovyev believed that
science would ever be in a position to raise all past members of the human

1 SS, IX, p. 193. The Idea of Humanity, 12.
2 Against Fyodorov's ideas Solovyev objected that the mere physical resurrection of
the dead could not be an end in itself. For example, to raise cannibals from the dead
would be undesirable, even if it were possible. Though, however, Fyodorov's emphasis
on the power and task of science provided a ground for Solovyev's interpretation,
Fyodorov made it clear that he had in mind not only physical resurrection but also moral
and spiritual transfiguration. This does not make his ideas more practical, but it at any
rate shows that Solovyev had not understood him properly.
3 SS, IX, p. 191. Idea of Humanity, II.

race. But Fyodorov's insistence on not forgetting 'our fathers' certainly fitted in with his own idea of the human race as an organic whole. Ideal humanity included the ideas of all individual members, and its objective exemplification, when complete, would include the dead, in accordance with the Christian doctrine of resurrection (which, in itself, has nothing to do with what scientists can accomplish).

7. Given the conception of the 'Great Being', of humanity as an organism, one would naturally expect Solovyev to emphasize the social aspect of morality. As an individual centre of consciousness and desire, the human being is, of course, capable of surrendering to egoism and self-centredness. The human being can set himself or herself against society and against God.[1] In this case man impairs or prevents the realization of the 'wholeness' of his being. Solovyev's ethical thought centres around the idea of the good and its realization. And the good, in the fullest sense of the term, is 'the true moral order, expressing the absolutely right and the absolutely desirable relation of each to all and of all to each. It is called the kingdom of God'.[2] Realization of the moral order is the true end of life and the supreme good. It is not a question of the goal being a common good which excludes the good of the individual or is attained at the expense of the individual's good. The question whether the individual is a means to attaining the good of society or whether society is a means to the attainment of the individual's good is, for Solovyev, a pseudo-problem, the expression of an unreal dichotomy. For the individual is by nature a social being, a member of a greater whole, and the supreme good is at once the good of society and the good of its members.

Obviously, the egoistic, self-centred individual is seeking his or her own good, what appears to him or her as good. There can certainly be different concepts of the good, different ideas of the goal of human life. There is therefore need for reflection, for moral philosophy, to determine the nature of the good for man. The actual content of the idea of the good is 'determined and developed only through the complex work of thought'.[3] True morality is 'the right interaction between the individual person and his environment, when the term "environment" is taken in the widest sense, to embrace all spheres of reality, the higher as well as the

1 Solovyev refers to what he describes as 'natural atheism', a practical atheism which consists not in denying the existence of God for theoretical reasons but in setting onself over against God, asserting one's own independence of him.
2 SS, X, p. 227. D., p. 199.
3 Ibid., p. 65. D., p. 40.

lower, with which man stands in a practical relation'.[1] But thought is required to determine what the right relations are. True, light can be derived from religion. There are, however, different religions, with somewhat different ideas of the goal of life and of how life should be lived. Moral philosophy is thus indispensable.

Writers on Solovyev have drawn attention to the fact that in *The Justification of the Good* he asserts, contrary to what he had said in earlier works, the autonomy of ethics. Moral philosophy, according to Solovyev, 'must not be conceived as a one-sided *dependence* of ethics on positive religion or on speculative philosophy'.[2] What he is attacking is the view that moral philosophy is *wholly* dependent on the theoretical principles of either positive religion or philosophy. At one time, he says, he came very near to holding this view himself, but he has seen that it is erroneous. In other words, Solovyev admits that he has changed his mind. Why not, we may ask? The answer is, of course, that there is nothing objectionable in this procedure as such. One might change one's mind for better or for worse. The critics are not, however, denying Solovyev the right to change his views. What they claim is that though in *The Justification of the Good* Solovyev asserts the autonomy of ethics, the moral philosophy which he actually develops in this work is certainly not independent of religious and metaphysical beliefs. This criticism is certainly not groundless. It is true that what Solovyev actually denies is that moral philosophy is *totally* dependent on the theoretical principles of religion or philosophy, as though it were simply a deduction from them. But he asserts that 'in working out a moral philosophy reason simply unfolds, on the soil of experience, the implications of the idea of the good which is inherent in it (or, what is the same thing, of the ultimate fact of moral consciousness)'.[3] And at the close of the work he talks about making the transition to theoretical philosophy. The trouble is that in the course of the work religious and metaphysical beliefs seem clearly to be supposed, for example when Solovyev comes to talk about Christianity and the role of the Church in realizing the kingdom of God.

However this may be, it is clear that in Solovyev's moral philosophy the concept of the good is primary, that of obligation secondary. In his view, what he calls 'the wholeness of man' is present in human nature as an ideal norm. This wholeness, however, has to be realized in human life and history by moral activity, by means of a 'struggle with the

1 *SS*, p. 233. *D.*, p. 204.
2 *Ibid.*, p. 26. *D.*, p. 3.
3 *Ibid.*, p. 32. *D.*, p. 9.

centrifugal and divisive forces of existence'.[1] There thus arises the concept of duty, of the obligation to promote the wholeness of one's being, to do what is required to attain this end and not to do what would impair wholeness or is incompatible with its attainment. Although there is only one basic moral law, it manifests itself in a variety of ways or takes various forms, according to the variety of relations in which the human being stands to his or her environment. The three main kinds of relation are those 'to the world below us, to the world of beings like ourselves, and to the higher world'[2]. There are many subdivisions, of course, in these three main classes. But all particular moral precepts are regarded by Solovyev as applications of one basic moral law, to promote 'wholeness', total-unity, and to do nothing which would impair it or be incompatible with its attainment[3].

The Justification of the Good is an impressive work. It is likely to impress even readers who find Solovyev's theosophical speculation more than they can stomach. But we cannot discuss here his ideas about the primary data of morality, values and virtues, or his critical reflections on hedonism, Kantianism and other moral theories. Some further comment, however, about the social aspects of his ethics may be appropriate.

8. Society in its essential significance, Solovyev insists, is not 'the external limit of the personality but its inner fulfilment'[4]. There can, of course, be clashes between what the individual considers to be his or her interests and what a given society, or its leaders, take to be its interests. Ultimately, however, there is no dichotomy between the good of society and the good of its members. In an ideal or perfect society the two would coincide. But the ideal society is a goal, something to be realized through moral action, through the development of a universal moral order. In history social or communal life undergoes changes. There was a time when social organization was based on kinship. This organization belongs to the past, but it is still preserved, according to Solovyev, in the family, though in a changed form. In the contemporary world the prevailing form of social organization is that of the national state. The third main form of social organization, a universal human

1 *Ibid.*, p. 175. *D.*, p. 147.
2 *Ibid.*
3 The idea of 'wholeness' is closely connected with Solovyev's metaphysics, and the claim that human beings are related to a higher world, in particular to God, obviously casts doubt on any claim that his ethics does not presuppose religious or metaphysical beliefs.
4 *SS*, X, p. 230. *D.*, p. 202.

community, is anticipated 'in the form of a social *ideal*'.[1] At each stage
the individual is fulfilled in society, in so far as the society in question
embodies the good or approximates to the ideal. But at each stage the
social environment to which the individual is related differs. In the first
stage the social environment is the tribe, in the second it is a wider whole,
the national state, while in the third it is, or rather will be, humanity as a
whole. This widening of the social environment corresponds with the
progressive realization of 'wholeness' in the individual.

Progress, in an evaluative sense of the term, demands the increasing
moral organization of society. Just as Solovyev rejects the idea of any
necessary and ultimate dichotomy between the good of society and the
good of its individual members, so does he reject any claim that morality
has as its sphere only private life, and that moral standards cannot be
applied in economic life or in political life. For him, the choice lies not
between personal morality on the one hand and social or political
morality on the other but, quite simply, 'between realized and unrealized
morality'.[2] There can be different degrees of insight into what is
demanded by the moral ideal. Slavery, once considered acceptable as an
institution by most people, is now considered morally unacceptable by
most people. The conviction is spreading that institutions such as
recourse to war and capital punishment ought to be transcended. Many
see that economic life should be regulated in such a way as to facilitate
the leading of a decent human life by all men and women. And some at
any rate understand that the idea that politicians are exempt in their
public capacity from the moral standards which they accept in their
private lives is a morally untenable idea. It is not the job of the moral
philosopher to propose concrete schemes for improving, for example,
economic relations. But it is his job to insist that morality should govern
not only so-called private life but also social, political and economic life,
legal and penal systems, international relations and the human being's
relationship to his non-human environment. In brief, morality should be
realized, in the fullest sense, and not confined to certain sections of life,
still less to the mere profession of certain ideals. It is only through this
increasing moral organization of society that the kingdom of God can be
attained.

In the section on Solovyev's life mention was made of the fact that on
one occasion he startled his hearers by maintaining that the radical
intelligentsia, in its pursuit of social justice, was carrying on a work

1 *SS*, p. 231.
2 *Ibid.*, p. 289. *D.*, p. 258.

which had been neglected by the Church. It does not follow, however, that he was ever a socialist, at any rate as he understood the term, apart from a short period in his youth. His objection to the socialists was not, of course, that they sought social justice, but that 'even in its most idealistic forms socialism has from the first regarded the moral perfection of society as directly and wholly depending upon its economic structure, and has sought to attain moral reformation or regeneration exclusively by means of an economic revolution'.[1] In Solovyev's judgment, 'consistent socialism is certainly not an antithesis to, but the extreme expression, the final stage of one-sided bourgeois civilization'[2], in which too material interests predominated. It may be possible to quarrel with Solovyev's idea of socialism as being too narrow, but it is clear that his critical attitude to both bourgeois capitalist society and to socialist theory is an expression of his anthropology, of his view of the human being as more than 'economic man'. Socialism, he insists, is more consistent than capitalist society. For whereas the latter, though in fact dominated by economic interests, recognized the existence of societies such as the Church and paid lip service to their teaching, the former, socialism, will have nothing to do with beliefs about God and the human being's divine vocation. But this greater consistency on the part of socialism simply makes the issue clearer, as far as Solovyev is concerned; it does not show that the socialists' views of the human being and of the goal of society are correct.

In his work on moral philosophy Solovyev makes the statement that *'just as the Church is collectively organized piety, so the State is collectively organized pity'.*[3] This may seem a very odd thing to say, especially as far as the state is concerned. We associate the Church with piety, but many people would associate the state with coercion rathei than with pity. Solovyev, however, is obviously talking about what Hegel would call the essence or 'idea' of each institution. The Church, he explains, is the collective recipient of divine grace, in spite of disfiguring features such as encouragement of religious persecution. As for the state, the word 'pity' refers to its essential duty to improve the conditions of human existence 'apart from which the kingdom of God could not be realized in humanity'.[4] It is not the business of the state to impose or teach theological or philosophical beliefs, but it is its business to care for the destitute and the hungry and the exploited, to overcome illiteracy and

1 *Ibid.*, p. 370. *D.*, p. 334.
2 *Ibid.*, p. 371. *D.*, p. 335.
3 *Ibid.*, p. 488. *D.*, p. 448.
4 *Ibid.*, p. 496. *D.*, p. 456.

provide for education.[1] In other words, the state's task is not simply to preserve law and order; it should develop the framework in which the kingdom of God can be fully realized. In so far as it consciously and genuinely tries to fulfil this task, in union with the Church but also as distinct from the Church[2], it can be described as a Christian state. We have mentioned that in the closing years of Solovyev's life the idea of 'theocracy' dropped into the background. But this was not because he had abandoned his ideal but because he had come to believe that the number of Christians would decrease and that the power of 'Antichrist' would predominate, though it would not have the last word.

9. If we conceive the moral life as involving conformity to certain laws or precepts and awareness of obligation as a feature of the moral conscious-ness, the question arises whether belief in freedom is not presupposed or implied. As Kant said, 'if I ought, I can'. What is the point of telling a man that he ought to do this or ought not to do that, if all his choices and actions are determined? If the truth of determinism is assumed, can we consistently ascribe moral responsibility to the human agent?

Solovyev admits that it is a common enough opinion that determinism is incompatible with morality and must be rejected by the moral philos-opher. But he denies that the opinion is true. More precisely, he maintains that it rests on a confusion between what he calls 'mechanical deter-minism' and other forms of determinism, on a confusion between distinct kinds of necessity. By 'mechanical determinism' he understands the claim that the human being is simply a cog in a machine, all choices and actions being determined by causes external to the agent, by the movements of other parts of the machine. This claim, he allows, makes hay of morality. But there are other forms of determinism, such as psychological deter-minism, which maintains that the causes or 'sufficient reasons' for choices lie in the human being, in his or her motives for example.

According to Solovyev, psychological determinism allows for some elements of morality, inasmuch as it is possible to appraise motives from a moral point of view and to judge that one person is better than another. At the same time Solovyev thinks of the motives in question as being determined largely by considerations of pleasure and pain and as

1 Though Solovyev was not a socialist as he understood the term, one might perhaps call him a Christian socialist without being guilty of absurdity.

2 Ideally, for Solovyev, the State should show moral solidarity with the cause of promoting the realization of the kingdom of God. But the State should no more be ruled by the clergy than the Church should be governed by the State. 'The Church must have no coercive power, and the coercive power exercised by the State must have nothing to do with the domain of religion' (SS, X, p. 499. D., p. 459).

excluding acting simply for duty's sake or out of respect for the moral law. Presumably he regards hedonism as permitting a moral appraisal of human beings in terms of the quality of the kinds of pleasure which they pursue. But in so far as psychological determinism excludes acting simply for the sake of duty, even if this is contrary to considerations of self-interest, it cannot be reconciled with the moral consciousness.

In point of fact human beings are capable of acting 'for the sake of the good itself, solely from reverence for duty or the moral law'[1], apart from, and even contrary to, self-interested motives. But this capacity does not imply freedom. 'This is the culminating point of morality, which is, however, fully compatible with determinism and in no way requires the so-called freedom of the will'.[2] Necessity in general is the dependence of an effect on a cause or ground which is described as 'sufficient' because it determines the effect. And the idea of the true good, imposing itself in the form of what Kant called the categorical imperative, is the sufficient, and thus determining, cause or ground of moral choice and action. We have here what Solovyev describes as rational or moral necessity, but it is nonetheless necessity.

Rather unexpectedly perhaps, Solovyev recognizes freedom to choose evil as such. People often choose an evil course of action, because they mistakenly think it good, in some sense or other. But it is possible to choose evil precisely because it is evil. This is irrational. There is no sufficient ground for such a choice. Hence the choice is arbitrary and exemplifies freedom of the will.

As writers on Solovyev are accustomed to remark, we are thus faced with the strange conclusion that moral choices, choices in accordance with the moral law that is to say, are determined, and that freedom of the will is exemplified only in what might be described as 'demonic' choice, choice of evil precisely because it is evil.

It is clear that Solovyev equates free choice with arbitrary choice, choice without any sufficient ground or cause. Insight into what is one's moral duty is a sufficient ground for choice and action, and it therefore determines the choice. In other words, Solovyev can be seen as subscribing to the common enough thesis that a free act would be an arbitrary and causeless act. But though a vision of the true good or insight into what one's moral duty is would doubtless be a sufficient *reason* for acting, it does not necessarily follow that it would be a determining *cause*, necessitating a certain choice. Solovyev seems to see this himself,

1 *SS*, X, p. 42. *D.*, p. 18.
2 *Ibid. Ibid.*

up to a point. 'For the idea of the good in the form of duty to assume the force of a sufficient reason or motive for action, a union of two factors is necessary: sufficient clearness and fullness in the idea itself in consciousness and sufficient moral receptivity in the subject'.[1] When the vision of the good as duty is sufficiently clear and full to move a morally sensitive agent to choice and action, the sufficient reason, we may say, becomes a determining or necessitating cause. But does the morally sensitive subject need necessity to move him or her to action? If this were the case, would we regard the subject as a genuinely morally sensitive subject? The problem of freedom is a complicated issue. The possible meanings of freedom and necessity have to be sorted out, if discussion is to be fruitful. Solovyev did indeed make an attempt to do this, but, in the opinion of the present writer, his analysis of the issue leaves a good deal to be desired.

10. Solovyev had a very strong sense of the reality of God. At the same time the idea of total-unity was, as we have seen, a central feature of his thought. This meant that he could not be content with, on the one hand, the concept of God in himself, eternal and unchangeable, and, on the other, the concept of the world as distinct from God. To be sure, any identification of the world of plurality with God was foreign to his mind. The coming into being of this world he represented as a Fall, a fall from unity. Total-unity then appeared as an ideal, as something to be attained. In other words, Solovyev thought in terms of the progressive transfiguration of the world, of its gradual divinization. This applied first and foremost to the human race, the crown, so to speak, of creation, of the evolutionary process. Mankind was called to become one divine-human organism, to attain God-manhood in and through Christ, the incarnate Logos, and as members of the universal Church, the body of Christ. In the end God would be all in all, though without the obliteration of human persons. This idea obviously implied development, becoming, on the part of God or the Absolute. Within God himself there was, according to Solovyev, an eternal becoming, in the sense that the generation of the Logos, for example, was not a temporal process. But the return of the human race to God was a temporal, historical process. And we can hardly avoid the conclusion that in the end the Absolute would be enriched, comprising not only the idea of the human race as a divine-human organism but also as an actual unity-in-distinction.

In working out a philosophy on these lines Solovyev reflected on a considerable number of distinguishable areas, such as theory of knowledge,

1 SS, p. 44. D., p. 19.

metaphysics, ethics, social and political theory, and aesthetics. Further, he tried to synthesize these reflections, to show their interconnections. For example, in an essay on beauty in nature (1889) he maintained that the ideal of total-unity or all-unity appears to desire as the good, to thought as truth, and to sense as beauty. This was one way of bringing together ethics or practical philosophy, theoretical philosophy and aesthetics. It would be an unjustified exaggeration to claim that Solovyev produced a perfect synthesis. There is, for example, no really clear explanation of the origin of the world of plurality. At the same time no profound study of Solovyev's writings is required in order to see that his reflections on various areas of thought are interrelated. We can quite properly speak of a synthesis, though admittedly not a perfect one, not one, that is to say, which measures up to an ideal of perfect coherence.

It would, however, be a mistake to represent Solovyev as concerned simply with constructing a coherent world-view, satisfying to the mind. He did indeed insist on the idea of objective truth, but knowledge of truth was conceived as necessary for life, for the attainment of the goal of life, realization of the idea of total-unity. The spiritualization of the world and the regeneration and divinization of mankind are key ideas. Solovyev thought, for example, of the artist as concerned with the expression and creation of beauty, but he also thought of the artist as having a task beyond that of giving aesthetic pleasure. Having asserted in *Philosophical Principles* that the aim of mysticism is contact with a higher world, he goes on to say that this aim is shared by 'genuine art'.[1] In *The Meaning of Art* (1890) Solovyev claims that the work of art, exhibiting the union of the spiritual and the material, the ideal and the real, the subjective and the objective, is the sensuous realization or expression of the absolute idea, that of total-unity. And he defines art as 'every sensuous expression of any object or event from the point of view of its final state or in the light of the world to come'.[2] Art, in its own way, serves the cause of the enlightenment and regeneration of mankind.

The ideas about art to which we have just referred obviously reflect the aesthetic theories of Schelling and Hegel. It would, of course, be possible to go through Solovyev's writings and attempt to assess the various influences on his thought, the influences, for example, of Plato, Neoplatonism, Nicholas of Cusa, Jakob Boehme, Kant, Fichte, Schelling and Hegel, Franz Baader, Schopenhauer and Eduard von Hartmann, Ivan Kireevsky and Khomyakov, Indian thought, the Greek Fathers, theo-

1 *Ibid.*, I, p. 286. *PP.*, 1.
2 *Ibid.*

logians and spiritual writers. Solovyev was a learned man, widely read in philosophical, theological and mystical literature, and he undoubtedly derived many ideas from earlier writers or under their inspiration. But wherever his ideas came from, he combined them in a synthesis, which, though containing some inconsistencies and lack of clarity, was clearly oriented to an ideal goal, the regeneration of mankind, the realization of the kingdom of God, a goal to be attained through effort, through action in the light of the truth. The goal can be described as that of the realization in a transfigured world of the ultimate unity of truth, goodness and beauty.

It is understandable if to some minds it seems that a sharp dichotomy should be made between Solovyev on the one hand and the Russian radical intelligentsia on the other, that is to say, on the one hand we have a philosopher who pursues airy and fanciful theosophical speculation, while on the other we have thinkers whose gaze is fixed on concrete social and political life, who turn their backs on metaphysical speculation, and who seek a practical goal in this world, to be attained by concerted human effort, under the leadership of an enlightened élite. Solovyev, it may seem, looks backward, whereas the Russian radical intelligentsia looks forward. Solovyev tries to preserve the past, for example, by giving a more rational expression to Christian faith, whereas the radicals are set on creating a new society.

This is one way of looking at the matter. But there is another. Solovyev was just as intent as the radicals on the transformation of human society. Having, however, a different view of the nature and vocation of the human being, he sought a society which differed in important respects from that sought by, for example, the Marxists. It was not a question of Solovyev being blind to the demands of social justice. This was far from being the case. It was a question of differences in belief about the nature of reality and about the human being. Both Solovyev and the radicals desired transformation of the human being. But whereas the radicals tended to believe that a revolutionary change in social structures would bring about the desired transformation of the human being, Solovyev, while allowing for the influence of society on the individual, was convinced that the spiritual and moral regeneration of mankind which he desired could not be realized by a post-revolutionary establishment of socialism under the leadership of a minority, whose minds were pervaded by materialist and positivist assumptions. In his view, a society of this kind would simply accentuate some of the worst features of bourgeois capitalist society and would effectively hinder mankind's attainment of its true end.

The point can be illustrated in this way. Solovyev found himself in agreement with Chernyshevsky's claim that art should serve life and not be regarded as an end in itself. At the same time his conception of the meaning of life or of the goal of life obviously differed from Chernyshevsky's. In general, Solovyev could sympathize, up to a point, with the ideals and aims of the Russian socialists. He could claim, as indeed he did, that in seeking to promote social justice they were performing a task which had been neglected by the Church, and to a great extent by the State, and that they were thus filling a gap. At the same time he did not turn his back on Christian faith, as the Russian radicals did, but desired the effective realization in human life of the implications of Christian faith as he saw them.

Solovyev can thus be said to have offered an alternative to the path of atheistic socialism. His successors in Russia during the first two decades of the twentieth century saw this. When thinkers such as Berdyaev and Bulgakov abandoned Marxism for lines of thought which were to a considerable extent inspired by the thought of Solovyev, they were not abandoning all social concern and retreating into metaphysical speculation. They presented visions of reality and social ideals which might have provided a powerful alternative to atheistic socialism. But they came too late. And though under Nicholas II there was room for different philosophies and the presentation of different social ideals and goals, under the régime which eventually took the place of the Tsarist autocracy there was room for only one philosophy.

While there is no dispute about Solovyev's sincere personal adherence to Christianity and his profound faith, there has been a good deal of controversy about the relation between his philosophical theories and Christian beliefs. It has been maintained, for example, that his philosophy of total-unity, if consistently developed, amounted to pantheism (while others have preferred the term 'panentheism'). Again, objections have been raised to his marked tendency to substitute philosophy for theology as the instrument for developing the content of faith. Solovyev, like Hegel before him, could, of course, retort that he was simply carrying on the traditional policy of faith seeking understanding. Some critics, however, object that in the process of 'understanding' faith tended to be transformed into a highly questionable metaphysics, and that some of Solovyev's theories are hardly reconcilable with Christian belief.

The fact of the matter is that Solovyev was opposed to what he regarded as the narrow ecclesiastic mind, with its fear of what he called 'freely rational thought'. Further, though he certainly did not reject the concept of revelation, appeals to authority, whether of the Bible or of the

Church, as a means of excluding further reflection did not impress him favourably. In addition, he did not think in terms of the sharp distinction between theology and philosophy such as we find in the writings of St Thomas Aquinas. We can say perhaps that he thought of himself as following in the footsteps of the boldly speculative minds among the early Greek Christian writers and of western thinkers such as Nicholas of Cusa, but within, of course, the intellectual content created by the development of philosophical thought in subsequent centuries. In any case, even if some of his theories express what we might describe as a 'gnostic' attitude, his thought embodies an obviously Christian inspiration. The idea of Christ as the God-man, as the meeting place of the divine and the human, the eternal and the temporal, the uncreated and the created, stands in the centre of the picture. Further, any Christian can admire the way in which Solovyev rises above nationalistic and ecclesiastical narrowness and prejudice. Today, of course, we are accustomed to 'ecumenical' ideas. But in the nineteenth century the situation was different.

Solovyev can properly be described as a religious thinker. But, as we have seen, he conceived religion as covering the whole of life, not simply as a department of life, and still less as an optional addition to what was basic in human life. Religion was, for him, 'the reunion of man and the world with the unconditional and all-one principle'[1], a reunion which consisted 'in bringing all elements of human life, all particular principles and powers of humanity into the right relationship to the unconditional, central principle, and through him and in him to their right relation of agreement between themselves'.[2] To say that Solovyev was a religious thinker is to say that he had a religious vision of reality, but it was not a question simply of seeing the world in a certain way. The vision was oriented to the attainment of a goal, in particular the regeneration or transformation of mankind. In this sense it was a socially oriented vision.

1 SS, III, p. 12. L, III.
2 Ibid.

Chapter 10

Marxism in Imperial Russia (1). Plekhanov

1. The presence in western Europe of Bakunin and Herzen and other Russian exiles was doubtless a contributing factor in the spread of knowledge of Marxism in Russia. To be sure, neither Bakunin nor Herzen was a follower of Marx. But both men had to take up attitudes to Marxism and, as their publications were smuggled into Russia and each was visited by Russian travellers, they contributed to arousing interest in Marxism, even though neither accepted it.

Russian intellectuals were not, however, confined for their knowledge of Marx's thought to critical discussion by exiles. Already in the middle of the nineteenth century there was some knowledge in Russia of the economic theory of Marx and Engels. In 1869 Bakunin, in spite of his rivalry with Marx, translated the Communist Manifesto into Russian, the translation being published at Geneva.[1] In 1872 N. F. Danielson, a Populist, published his Russian translation of the first volume of *Capital*, which had appeared in 1867.[2] Marx, who had not been well disposed to Russia and the Russians and expected little from them, was surprised that the first foreign translation of his volume was a Russian one.

Danielson was a Populist. Mikhailovsky, also a Populist (more or less), was already in 1869 using Marx's ideas in support of his own opposition to the division of labour. Even earlier than this, Tkachev, the leader of the 'Jacobin' wing of the Populist movement, had declared his adherence to Marx's theory of the dependence of all other spheres of life on the economic substructure. And in the relevant chapter we noted that Lavrov, under the influence of Marx, came in his later writings to emphasize the basic role played by economic life. In other words, the thought of

1 According to the *Great Soviet Encyclopaedia* (third edition, English version, New York and London, vol. 15, col. 166, 1977) Bakunin 'distorted the major theses'.
2 Danielson completed the translation begun by Herman Lopatin. Lopatin, a Populist and a friend of Marx, had tried unsuccessfully to organize Chernyshevsky's escape from Siberia. Later he helped to organize Lavrov's escape from Russia to the West.

Marx and Engels exercised a considerable influence on Populist intellectuals. The reason for this is clear. The Populists were weak on theory, while Marxism claimed to represent 'scientific socialism', to provide the theoretical basis for the socialist movement. Populist thinkers were thus inclined to adopt from Marxism those ideas which they considered compatible with Populist convictions and aims.

The Populists, however, were not prepared to accept the thesis that the development of a bourgeois class and of capitalism was a necessary prelude to the advent of socialism, that socialism was not possible unless the forces of production had been developed under capitalism and unless a proletariat, the truly revolutionary class, had been created. As with Lavrov, the picture of capitalist exploitation and proletarian misery presented by Marx horrified the Populists, and they hoped that Russia would escape such a fate. But it was not only a question of a clash between capitalist society as depicted by Marx and Engels and the ethical ideals of the Populists. The latter saw clearly enough that, in comparison with the West, Russia was an industrially undeveloped country, and that if it had to repeat for itself the history of the western capitalist societies, there would be no hope of realizing socialism until many years had elapsed. While recognizing the eminence of Marx as an analyst of western bourgeois society and accepting his critique of capitalist economics, the Populists clung to their idea that Russia could pursue a separate path and that socialism could be achieved on the basis of the village commune, without the need to pass through a capitalist phase of development. Further, the Populists tended to disapprove strongly of the idea that socialists should join with liberals in a political struggle, campaigning for the extension of political rights. From the Marxist point of view such cooperation would obviously be tactical, designed to create conditions of political liberty in which Communists could prepare the workers for a further revolution, when the proletariat would take the place of the bourgeoisie. But the Populists were not prepared to pursue a policy which might prolong the life of the monarchy, in a liberalized form and thus create a bourgeois state. What they were interested in was the complete overthrow of the state and the realization of a socialism suited to what they believed to be the peculiar conditions of Russia. And when the peasants as a whole showed little sign of being ready for revolution, the left-wing activists of the Populist movement turned to terrorism, their most eminent victim being the 'Tsar-Liberator'.

The attitude of the Populists naturally evoked criticism from the Marxists. According to Engels, anyone who failed to recognize that the development of a bourgeois class was a necessary precondition of socialism, had still to learn the ABC of socialism. It is true that in a letter written to the editor of *Notes of the Fatherland* in 1877 Marx said that in *Capital* he had been concerned with western Europe and was not laying down laws for the whole of history1, and that in 1881 he wrote to Vera Zasulich that he did not exclude the possibility of socialism being achieved in Russia without the country having first to pass through the capitalist phase as described by himself. Such remarks obviously provided material for Populists to use against their Marxist critics. The fact of the matter was, however, that as the nineteenth century drew towards its close, the question whether Russia could bypass the phase of capitalist development was becoming increasingly unrealistic. The reforms of the 1860s had opened the way for the gradual emergence of a middle class, and in the 1880s and 1890s industrialization expanded, with the assistance of the government and an influx of foreign investment. To be sure, industrialization was on a very small scale in comparison with that of England, but it was indubitably growing. The mass of the Russian population was still composed of peasants, but an urban proletariat was developing. What is more, the village commune, in which the Populists placed their trust, was showing signs of threatening disintegration. In 1893 Mikhailovsky, who never became a Marxist, attacked naïve belief in the virtues of the people and drew attention to the indignities suffered by individuals within the commune. Besides, the end of serfdom had meant the emergence of a tension between poverty-stricken peasants on the one hand and richer peasants on the other, who might employ hired labour on their land. In addition, while some peasants divided their time between working in a city or town and working in the village, others were being drawn into and absorbed by the urban proletariat.

The Marxists were thus able to accuse the Populists of being unable or unwilling to read the signs of the times and to analyse actual conditions as they really were. To the Marxists it was clear that capitalism had taken a hold on Russia and that it would develop, whatever the Populists might say. Lenin, who had a genuine regard for the Populists and maintained that Populism had been a progressive movement, nonetheless spoke of their 'economic romanticism', which was, for him, a polite description of their outlook. The young Lenin of the 1890s was too much of an activist to lay emphasis on 'iron laws' and historical

1 Marx did not actually send this letter. It was given by Engels to Plekhanov's 'Liberation of Labour' group in 1884, but it was not published until 1886, when it appeared in a Populist periodical at Geneva. In 1888 it was published in Russia, in the *Juridical Messenger*.

determinism, but, as far as he was concerned, Populism, though on the right side so to speak, was certainly not 'scientific socialism'.

Another point on which the Marxists criticized the Populists was the stress laid on terrorist tactics by the extreme left wing of the Populist movement. It was not a question of moral inhibitions against physical attacks on representatives of state power. It was a question of terrorist tactics being unproductive and of their diverting attention from more important and fruitful tasks. After all, the assassination of Alexander II brought the reactionary Alexander III to the throne, and if one chief of police was murdered, another was appointed in his place.[1] It was more important to secure, by legal means, the transition to a bourgeois, liberal State, in which socialist leaders would be free to develop their own organization and prepare the workers (primarily the urban proletariat, but also the peasants) for a socialist revolution.

While therefore convinced Populists tended to look on the Marxists as playing into the hands of the enemy, or even as betraying the cause of the revolution, the Marxists looked on the Populists as romantic utopians and on terrorist leaders as short-sighted hotheads, who sacrificed a well planned course of action to the desire for dramatic effect. Eventually, of course, it was the policy of a Populist, namely Tkachev, which was to prevail, in the sense that in 1917 it was a tiny minority, led by Lenin, which seized power and prevented 'bourgeois' democracy from developing in Russia. But it was the special conditions of the time which gave Lenin the opportunity for acting in a way of which Plekhanov, the 'Father of Russian Marxism', highly disapproved.

Populists and Marxists were, of course, at one in the general sense that both groups looked forward to the advent of socialism. Both groups can be described as revolutionaries, aiming at the radical transformation of society. However, although Populist thinkers, such as Lavrov, Mikhailovsky and Tkachev, had been influenced by Marxist thought, it became increasingly clear that one could not belong to both groups at once. A choice had to be made. Thus when Plekhanov (see below, page 254), who endeavoured to lead the more moderate Populist group from Geneva, came to believe that the Populists were on the wrong track, he abandoned Populism and opted for Marxism.

The claim of Marxism to be scientific socialism, and the fact that in any

---

1 In point of fact Marx praised the assassins of Alexander II. The general Marxist position, however, was to emphasize the role of classes in social development and to regard assassination of prominent individuals as an unpromising means of securing real change. Plekhanov, who disapproved of the way in which the People's Will group concentrated on terrorist tactics, had been opposed to the assassination.

case it embodied an impressive theoretical foundation, made possible the emergence in the last decade of the nineteenth century of what is known as 'Legal Marxism'. This term is often used to refer to Marxist publications which appeared with the approval of or without objection by the Censorship during the 1890s (or up to 1905), as distinct from underground literature. For example, the Russian translation of the first volume of *Capital* was passed by the Censorship on the ground that it was too dull and obscure to be of any real danger. In the nineties, at any rate, works devoted to the analysis of western capitalism, which were clearly intended for intellectual circles and which did not preach subversion or revolutionary activity in Russia, tended to appear more or less harmless to the Censorship, especially if they attacked the Populist ideology. It has been argued, however, that originally the term 'Legal Marxism' referred not so much to literature as to status.[1] That is to say, Marxist writers who lived 'above ground', with legal papers, and who were known to the police by their real names, were the 'legals', while those Marxists who lived 'underground' or with false papers and who would be liable to arrest if their real identities were known, were the 'illegals'.[2] Thus Lenin would count as an 'illegal', even though some of his writings appeared in legally published papers or periodicals. As far as the origin of the term is concerned, this may well be the case, but it came to be used to refer to literature.

Whatever the original meaning of the phrase may be, the Legal Marxists played down the revolutionary aspect of Marxism and emphasized the historical necessity of capitalist development. In their view, the village commune was destined to wither away, and they criticized Populism as unrealistic and unscientific romanticism. In point of fact there were Populist thinkers who were interested in social reform rather than in revolution, and who have sometimes been described as 'Legal Populists'.[3] As, however, it was with left-wing Populism that the policy of terrorism was especially associated, Marxist attacks on the Populists tended to commend the Marxists in the eyes of the authorities, at any rate for a time. After all, the Legal Marxists endorsed, so to speak, the rise of

1 For discussion of the original meaning of the term 'Legal Marxism' and also of the different ways in which the concept has been understood, see the first two Appendices to *The First Russian Revisionists. A Study of 'Legal Marxism' in Russia*, by Richard Kindersley (Oxford, Clarendon Press, 1962).

2 It has been suggested that we can see an analogy to the relation between legal and illegal Marxism in the relation between 'legal' and 'illegal' representatives of the KGB in foreign countries.

3 There is a section on 'Legal Populism' in Walicki's *A History of Russian Thought*, pp. 427–35. A leading figure was V. P. Vorontsov (1847–1918), who wrote under the initials 'V.V.' and was the author of *The Fate of Capitalism in Russia* (1882).

capitalism and industrialization in Russia, a rise patronized by the government, and adopted a gradualist attitude to social change.

The Legal Marxists had tended to focus their attention on theoretical issues. Needless to say, economic issues formed a prominent theme. A forerunner of the Legal Marxists of the 1890s was N. Ziber, a professor at the University of Kiev, who published in the 1870s a series of articles which formed the basis for his *David Ricardo and Karl Marx* (1885), a work which met with a favourable reception from Marx himself. According to Ziber, though social legislation could certainly do something to mitigate the worst aspects of capitalism, it was foolish to think that the capitalist phase could be bypassed on the way to socialism. As for the transition from a developed capitalist economy to socialism, this could be a peaceful event, the result of people coming to see what the logic of the situation demanded. Ziber's book did a lot to arouse interest in Marx's economic theories in Russian intellectual circles.

A leading figure among the Legal Marxists was the economist Peter Struve[1], who in his *Critical Remarks on the Economic Development of Russia* (1894) attacked Populism and asserted the progressive nature of capitalism. Believing that socialism would be the inevitable outcome of capitalism, he naturally thought that revolutionary activism designed to speed up the movement of history was inappropriate.

Though the so-called Legal Marxists contributed powerfully to disseminating knowledge of Marxist ideas, their interest in theoretical issues was accompanied by a readiness to revise Marxist theory, to 'improve' it or develop it, and to supplement it with elements taken from other systems of thought. In the economic sphere, for example, Marx's theory of value came in for criticism from Legal Marxists such as S. Bulgakov, the future theologian, and M. I. Tugan-Baranovsky (1865–1919). By 1900 the latter was prepared to assert that Marx's strength lay in sociology rather than in economics. In the second field Marx, in Tugan-Baranovsky's opinion, not only lacked any notable originality but was often wrong.

The Legal Marxists, however, did not confine their criticism to Marx's economic theory. They tended to be interested also in philosophical topics. With Struve and some others we find ideas from Neo-Kantian epistemology being introduced into Marxism, to 'improve' the orthodox realism. In the course of time it came to be thought that Marxism, as 'scientific socialism', was unable to offer any ethical guidance, and that it needed a dose of Kantian ethics. Further, in 1899 Struve advanced the

1 See above, p. 204.

claim that the dialectical movement was a feature of thought only, not of things. In extramental reality there was, indeed, development, evolution, but this meant that what evolved was recognizably continuous with that out of which it evolved. The concept of a social revolution as a negation of what went before should be jettisoned in favour of the concept of evolution.

Inasmuch as the Legal Marxists welcomed the development of capitalism in Russia while playing down the idea of revolution, it is understandable that Populist critics were not slow to depict them as defenders of capitalism and as indifferent to the sufferings and distress of workers and peasants. Moreover, as the Legal Marxists tended to accept the idea of cooperation with the liberals with a view to obtaining political reforms, they seemed to the left-wing Populists at any rate to be liberals masquerading as socialists. Indeed, Struve was more interested in securing political liberties than in revolution.

A rift tended to develop between the Legal Marxists and those who claimed to represent orthodoxy. At first the Legal Marxists and the revolutionary Marxists were able to cooperate. For example, Struve and Lenin could and did collaborate in various projects. The more, however, the Legal Marxists indulged in revisionism, the more did a division in the ranks make its appearance. Rather surprisingly perhaps Lenin, who wanted to preserve unity, was at first much more tactful than Plekhanov in his attitude to and in what he said about the revisionists. But in 1900 he criticized the leading representatives of Legal Marxism as becoming more and more 'bourgeois apologists'.[1] From his point of view Lenin was justified in his criticism of Struve and his colleagues. It was clear that the Legal Marxists had renounced the idea of revolution in favour of that of evolution, and in 1903 their leading representatives, including Struve, joined the liberal Union of Liberation. Indeed, most of them were later to be associated with the Cadets, the liberal party in the Duma.

The Legal Marxists were, of course, perfectly sincere in their original acceptance of Marx's ideas. They saw in Marx's analysis of contemporary society and in his theory of historical development a system of thought greatly superior to Populist ideology, and they tried to apply Marxian theories to Russia. But they were not prepared to regard the ideas of Marx and Engels as analogous to divine revelation, and they did not hesitate to criticize when reflection convinced them that criticism was demanded. In the end their revisionist tendencies led most of them out of

---

1 *Collected Works*, IV, p. 40 (New York, International Publishers, 1929). From Lenin's 'Declaration of the *Iskra*' (1900).

the Marxist fold. In the area of academic philosophy any introduction of Kantian or Neo-Kantian epistemology was hardly compatible with the Marxist dogma that being determines consciousness, when being is understood as knowable and as matter. And when Struve became convinced that bourgeois values, as expounded, for instance, by Kant were not simply bourgeois but independently valid, this conviction was incompatible with the orthodox Marxist view of morals. Obviously, the markedly theoretical interests of the Legal Marxists did not encourage revolutionary activism, and it is reasonable to say that they thought themselves out of Marxism. But it is also true that a thinker such as Struve came to the conclusion that revolutionary Marxism was 'utopian', and that what was needed, from a practical point of view, was political reform. It is hardly surprising that many of the Legal Marxists eventually came to side with the reformist liberals.

So far I have been discussing the so-called Legal Marxists in Russia. Now it is time to refer to the Russian Marxists in exile and 'illegal' Marxism in Russia. The first Russian Marxist organization was founded in 1883 at Geneva by George Plekhanov in conjunction with his fellow exiles Pavel Borisovich Akselrod (1850–1946) and Vera Zasulich (1849–1919).[1] This organization was known as the group 'For the Liberation (or Emancipation) of Labour'. During the 1880s, however, the group, centred in Switzerland and lacking financial resources, found it very difficult to make any real impression on revolutionary circles in Russia, in spite of its efforts to smuggle Marxist literature into the country. The government of Alexander III was pursuing a vigorous policy of suppressing subversive activity and revolutionary agitation, including the dissemination of radical literature. A good many radicals had lost heart and were not disposed to listen to the Marxists, especially as the latter devoted a good deal of attention to attacking the Populists, who, despite their failures, were regarded as the bearers of the revolutionary spirit. In 1884 Lev Deutsch, on whom Plekhanov relied heavily for practical organization and for winning adherents to Marxism in Russia, was arrested in Germany, extradited to Russia and consigned to Siberia. Further, several efforts to establish links with radical groups in Russia came to nothing.

In the early 1890s the situation changed. Plekhanov's early Marxist publications, in particular *Socialism and Political Struggle* (1883) and

---

1 Akselrod had been first a Populist and then a follower of Bakunin. Vera Zasulich had been a Populist, and it was she who had attempted to assassinate General F. Trepov in 1878. Having been acquitted by a sympathetic jury, she left Russia with the help of friends and became a devoted collaborator of Plekhanov.

Our Differences (1885) came to make a deep impression on a number of radicals such as A. N. Potresov and Iurii Martov, who was to become the Menshevik leader. Lenin too was much impressed by Plekhanov's writings. The growth of 'Legal Marxism' in Russia, from about 1894, had contributed powerfully to spreading knowledge of Marx's ideas; and after the famine of 1891–2 circles of people who accepted or sympathized with these ideas began to multiply. The government had caused widespread disgust by its failure to use available resources to relieve the distress of the starving and by the way in which, during the famine, it continued to export or permit exportation of grain which was needed at home. Further, when Nicholas II succeeded to the throne in 1894, he proceeded to make it clear, at the beginning of the following year, that he was determined to preserve the autocracy intact, and that it was useless to hope for even modest liberal political reform. The intransigence of the Tsar, coupled with the failure of the liberals to take a firm stand, naturally encouraged the dissatisfied to look to the radical left, while the growth of industrialization, which was proceeding apace with the active support of Sergei Witte, the able minister of finance, played into the hands of the Marxists rather than into those of the Populists. Marxism began to seem more relevant to Russia.

The result of the growth of Marxist influence in the nineties was the founding of the Russian Social Democratic Labour Party in 1898. The Russian Social Democrats were, of course, Marxists. It was not until after the 1917 revolution that the victorious faction of the Social Democrats adopted the label 'Communist Party'. In 1901 the Socialist Revolutionaries came into existence under the leadership of Victor Chernov (1876–1952). The members of this group, though influenced by Marxism, stood closer to the Populist tradition, of which they considered themselves the heir. As a loose generalization we can say that whereas the Social Democrats concentrated primarily on agitation among the growing number of urban workers, the Socialist Revolutionaries tended to concentrate on fomenting disturbance among the peasant population. We must add, however, that it was the left-wing Socialist Revolutionaries who continued the terrorist policy of the People's Will group, and who were responsible, for example, for the murder of the Tsar's minister V. Plehve in 1904 and that of the Grand Duke Sergei in the following year. In 1918 the left-wing faction of the Socialist Revolutionaries directed their terrorist activities against the Bolsheviks. They thus came to suffer the same fate as aristocrats, liberals and other 'counter-revolutionaries'.

The first convention of the Russian Social Democrats was held at

Minsk in 1898. The number of participants was small. Plekhanov and his colleagues in Switzerland were too prudent to risk a journey to Russia, and Lenin was in Siberia. Struve wrote a mild manifesto for the convention, in which emphasis was placed on the task of winning political liberty. As most of the delegates were arrested directly after the close of the convention, the gathering can hardly be described as a remarkable success.

The second convention, which took place in 1903, was wisely held outside Russia, at Brussels and then at London. It was at this time that the party became divided into two groups or factions. The group which eventually won the majority of votes and thus acquired the name of 'the Bolsheviks'[1] was led by Lenin, who thereby succeeded in obtaining control over the party's paper *The Spark* (*Iskra*). The Bolsheviks favoured the idea of a tightly knit organization, dominated by an exclusive élite, whereas the other group, known as the Mensheviks, supported the idea of a larger and less dragooned association. Both groups were, of course, Marxists.

It has often been said that Lenin and the Bolsheviks inherited the doctrine of Tkachev, the 'Jacobin' Populist, that a revolution, to be successful, must be carried out by a small band of disciplined revolutionary leaders, who would then transform society in accordance with their ideas. This is true, and in this sense we can say that Tkachev triumphed in 1917. It is important to remember, however, that the grounds for adopting different attitudes were present in Marxism itself, independently of anything which Tkachev may have said. It was Marxist doctrine that the proletariat was the naturally revolutionary class in a capitalist situation, and that it was this class which would eventually assume power. It was therefore reasonable to draw the conclusion that the revolutionary party should be a broad organization, representing the class as a whole. Further, assumption of power by the working class presupposed conditions in which the class could become self-conscious, aware of its aims and of the way to attain them. This meant that the potentially revolutionary proletariat should cooperate with liberal members of the bourgeoisie to secure political reforms and a state of affairs in which the proletariat could eventually bring about the change from bourgeois democracy to socialist democracy. At the same time it was obvious that the proletariat would not become a politically self-conscious united class except through the agency of leaders, the representatives of scientific socialism. Marx and Engels were perfectly well

1 The Russian word for 'majority' is *Bolshinstvo*.

aware of the need for leaders, activists, well versed in the true doctrine. It was possible therefore to lay more emphasis either on the working class itself and on its assumption of power for the benefit of the whole of society or on the role of a revolutionary élite. If one chose the first course, one would conceive the Party as ideally including the whole working class, and also those who were sufficiently in sympathy with its aims. If one chose the second course, one would be likely to conceive the Party as an exclusive and highly disciplined group, acting on behalf of the proletariat. As we have noted, grounds for both lines of thought existed in Marxism itself. Matters came to a head at the 1903 convention, and the split between Mensheviks and Bolsheviks resulted. Lenin, however, managed to obtain a majority of votes in support of his proposals in regard to conditions for membership of the Party only because a number of delegates who disagreed with some earlier proposals (for which Lenin had won majority acceptance) had left the convention. On behalf of Lenin, appeal can be made to considerations of efficient organization and the need for streamlining. But his policy pointed in the direction of dictatorship, dictatorship over the proletariat, as his opponents saw.

The opening years of the twentieth century were marked by strikes, peasant disturbances, and demands for reform not only from radicals but also from liberals. And Russia's humiliating defeat in the war with Japan (1904–05) obviously did nothing to increase respect for the government. The situation came to a head in the fateful year 1905, which started with 'Bloody Sunday' (January 22) when fire was opened on a mass of peaceful demonstrators (or, rather, petitioners) gathered outside the Winter Palace in the hope of being able to present a petition to the Tsar.[1] In October a general strike occurred, and Nicholas II at last capitulated, agreeing to the convocation of a legislative assembly, the Duma. The Tsar retained not only the title of Autocrat but also extensive powers.[2] Nonetheless, it looked as though a major step had been taken on the road to democracy.

The first Duma met in May 1906. The elections had been largely boycotted by the Social Democrats and Socialist Revolutionaries, and the former held only six seats. The Cadets (the Constitutional Democratic Party) formed the numerically strongest group. Of nearly five

1 The Tsar was not actually present in the palace at the time and did not give the order to open fire. But the event contributed powerfully to destroying the myth of the 'Little Father' who would come to the aid of the distressed, if he only knew of their plight.
2 The Duma was entitled to initiate legislation, but projected laws had to be approved by the State Council and could be vetoed by the Tsar. The Duma had no control over the finances of the Imperial family, nor over those of the armed forces (apart from supplementary estimates). Ministers were appointed by and responsible to the Tsar.

hundred members in all 184 were Cadets, while some 124 represented various groups to the Left. In the sessions the Left pursued what amounted to a policy of obstruction, while the Cadets made demands which the government was not prepared even to consider, such as distribution of the landowners' estates, including those of the imperial family, to the peasants (with compensation being paid to the owners). Relations between the Duma and the government were far from harmonious, and the former was dissolved by the Tsar on 21 July 1906.

In the second Duma, which met in March 1907, the number of Cadet deputies had declined[1], whereas the number representing groups more to the Left had risen. The Social Democrats held sixteen seats. From the government's point of view the second Duma was even less acceptable than the first. And it too was soon dissolved, in June 1907.

To secure a more cooperative assembly Nicholas II and his minister P. Stolypin adopted the high-handed procedure of altering the electoral law. More seats went to deputies elected by the landowners, and the third Duma lasted out its full term, 1907–12. The Social Democrats held nineteen seats. The fourth Duma, in which the Social Democrats held fourteen seats, lasted from 1912 until 1917, when the abdication of the Tsar deprived it of its mandate.[2]

Meanwhile, of course, the Social Democrats, both Bolsheviks and Mensheviks, were engaged not only in fomenting strikes but also in organizing workers in 'Soviets'. If Russia had kept out of the first world war, or if the war had been a short and victorious one, the government would probably have retained control of the situation. And if the Emperor had respected the constitution and made further political concessions, the country might have remained, perhaps for a considerable time, a constitutional monarchy. In actual fact the course of events sealed the fate of the monarchy. On 12 March 1917, the Duma, in spite of an imperial decree of dissolution, set up a Provisional Government[3], and on 15 March the Tsar abdicated.

The autocracy had at last ended. Plekhanov, and those Social Demo-

---

1 The swing to the Left was partly the consequence of the Viborg Manifesto. Among the signatories of the manifesto, which denounced the government and urged the people to adopt a policy of passive resistance until a new Duma was elected, was a large number of Cadet deputies. The signatories, besides receiving short jail sentences, were deprived of eligibility for election to the second Duma.

2 Both the third and the fourth Dumas were boycotted by the Socialist Revolutionaries.

3 The Tsar had foolishly taken over supreme command of the army and gone to the front. The Empress, left to hold the fort at home, was incensed at the suggestion, made by the leader of the Cadets, that there was treason in high places, and urged that the Duma should be dissolved.

crats who thought that Russia was not yet ripe for socialism and that Marxist theory demanded a period of bourgeois democracy before the proletariat could come into its own, were quite prepared for, and advocated, cooperation with the Provisional Government. Lenin thought otherwise. The Provisional Government tried to keep faith with Russia's allies by continuing the war, but Russia was in no position to do this. Conditions were chaotic. The government had to share power with the Soviets, especially the Petrograd Soviet, and it lacked either the authority or the power, even if it had the will, to withstand the forces aiming at its overthrow. Further, it made the mistake of postponing the convocation of the projected Constituent Assembly until arrangements for elections had been perfected.[1] Though it started well, it ended by being little more than a talking shop. On 7 November 1917 (25 October, Old Style) the Bolshevik faction seized power under the leadership of Lenin.

Needless to say, the Bolshevik seizure of power has been represented as a victory for Marxism-Leninism. History, however, is made by people. Lenin knew what he wanted, and he was prepared to risk failure in order to get it, despite the fact that the Bolsheviks formed a small minority even among the parties on the Left. His gamble succeeded. And after the horrors of the Civil War, when the Communist Party was firmly in the saddle, Marxism reigned triumphant, in the sense that its adversaries were silenced.

2. Reference has already been made several times to George Valentinovich Plekhanov (1857–1918), who is known as the 'father of Russian Marxism'. Born into a family of the minor landed gentry, one of those which had suffered financial loss as a result of the emancipation of the serfs in 1861, Plekhanov studied at the Military Academy at Voronezh. In 1874 he entered the Institute of Mines at St Petersburg. Becoming involved in the activities of the Populists, he helped to organize the Land and Freedom movement. As his part in a demonstration in 1876 placed him in imminent danger of arrest[2], he travelled to western Europe, returning to Russia in 1877. At this time he was an active revolutionary agitator. When the Land and Freedom movement split into two groups, he headed the more moderate group, known as Black Repartition[3], the other group being the People's Will. In 1880 Plekhanov had again to

1 It can, of course, be objected that in the circumstances of 1917 elections to a constituent Assembly were quite impracticable.
2 Plekhanov addressed the demonstrators in front of the Kazan Cathedral in the Nevski Prospekt at St Petersburg.
3 See p. 122.

leave Russia for the West and settled in Geneva. There he studied the writings of Marx and Engels and came to the conclusion that the future lay not with Populism but with Marxism. Whereas the Populists emphasized the differences between Russia and the West and demanded that Russia should take a path of her own, Plekhanov came to look on his country as becoming increasingly Westernized and as subject to the laws of historical development as discovered by western thought, in the person of Karl Marx.

Reference has also been made earlier to the foundation in 1883 of Plekhanov's Liberation of Labour group, and to the subsequent emergence of the Russian Social Democratic Labour Party. When Marxism began to win Russian adherents, tensions started to develop between Plekhanov's group in Geneva and the younger Marxists. Plekhanov believed that the Russian Social Democratic movement was, or should be regarded as, a development of his own Liberation of Labour group, and that the younger Marxists, whether in Russia or abroad, should follow the leadership of their elders, such as Akselrod and himself, who claimed to be able to see the whole picture from their vantage-point in Switzerland and to be the custodians of orthodox Marxism. The younger Marxists, however, especially those operating in Russia, naturally tended to think that the Geneva group was out of touch with the situation in Russia, and that though Plekhanov was indeed an eminent theorist, he and his group of exiles were unable to produce the sort of literature which would be meaningful to the Russian working class. Besides, as the Marxist movement grew, the younger Marxists understandably came to believe that the various Marxist circles needed to be united in a more clear-cut and disciplined organization than could be provided by the Geneva group. Plakhanov was inclined to take offence at such ideas and to see the younger generation of Marxists as ungrateful sons.

It was not, however, simply a case of wounded pride. From his place of exile the self-appointed guardian of Marxist orthodoxy fulminated against revisionists such as Eduard Bernstein, the German Social Democrat. And in the Social Democrat movement in Russia he detected a tendency to cater to the workers' desire for tangible improvements in the material and economic conditions of their life at the expense of political struggle and the revolutionary aims of Marxism. In other words, Plekhanov believed that Russian Social Democracy was in danger of becoming assimilated to Social Democracy in Germany and to the trade-union movement in England, losing sight of the class-struggle. He is best known for his insistence on orderly development according to the laws formulated in Marxist theory, but he had to try to combine the implied gradualism with the Marxist theory of class-struggle. And he was afraid that activists in the field, so to speak, might succumb to 'opportunism', adopting a pragmatic approach and losing sight of long-term goals. In 1900 he published *Vademecum*, designed to confound those of whom he disapproved. When aroused, Plekhanov could write in forthright and scathing terms, with little regard for tact. His zeal for orthodoxy, or for what he believed to be orthodoxy, took first place. If revisionists were offended by what he said, so much the worse for them. Concern for truth took precedence.

Plekhanov's zeal for orthodoxy had, of course, the sympathy of Lenin, who greatly admired the older man as a theorist. At the time, however, Lenin wished to conserve and increase Social Democratic unity. With this purpose in mind he was prepared, for the time being, to adopt a conciliatory attitude to those Marxists who showed revisionist tendencies, and he feared that Plekhanov's intransigence and caustic language would promote division in the ranks. In August 1900 he expounded his views to Plekhanov in person. Their conversations were hardly a success. Lenin found the older man's manner cold and condescending, and he was deeply offended.[1] Nonetheless, Lenin soon came to the conclusion that Marxist orthodoxy would be endangered if Social Democrats were free to expound any views they liked, including those which amounted to bourgeois liberalism in the eyes of a right-thinking Marxist. In other words, preservation of doctrinal orthodoxy demanded Party discipline, a measure of authoritarianism.

Having come to this conclusion, Lenin proceeded to go beyond what Plekhanov had envisaged. Plekhanov was, of course, well aware that the intelligentsia had an important role to play in developing the self-consciousness of the working class. This is obviously a main reason why he fulminated against revisionists, whom he regarded as false shepherds. But he paid insufficient attention to the fact that the workers themselves wanted tangible benefits, and that, provided they obtained real improvements in the conditions of life, many of them cared little about revolution or the realization of socialism. Lenin, however, saw that the opportunistic or pragmatic approach to which Plekhanov objected was not simply due to misguided members of the intelligentsia but that it also had roots in the mentality of the working class itself. Up to a point Plekhanov too saw this. For he emphasized the need for

1 Professor Samuel H. Baron suggests that, among other reasons for disgruntlement, Plekhanov may have divined in Lenin a serious rival for the leadership of the Russian Social Democrat movement. See his *Plekhanov: The Father of Russian Marxism*, p. 213.

heightening the political self-consciousness of the class. But it was Lenin who drew the practical conclusion that the Party, led and governed by a small group of professional revolutionaries, should restrict its membership, admitting to membership only those members of the working class who were properly instructed in Marxist ideology. He gave expression to his views in *What Is To Be Done?* (1902).

At the 1903 Russian Social Democrat convention Plekhanov gave a short opening speech and presided formally over the general meetings. But the moving spirit was Lenin, who had come to the congress with carefully prepared plans and with a determination to get what he wanted. As far as the principle of centralization and of the controlling power of the Central Committee was concerned, Lenin successfully routed his opponents. When, however, it was a question of determining conditions of membership of the Party in such a way that the bulk of the workers would be excluded, he faced strong criticism and opposition even from those who had accepted the idea of a centralized and authoritarian leadership. Nonetheless, as some of the delegates who had opposed the first proposals had left the congress, Lenin had succeeded in obtaining a majority of votes. The result was the division between Bolsheviks and Mensheviks.

During the convention Plekhanov supported and voted with Lenin, and he was elected president of the Council and co-editor with Lenin of *The Spark*. It was not long, however, before Plekhanov began to have second thoughts. Lenin's position, he thought, implied that the class-consciousness of the workers depended not on their objective situation but solely on the activity of the intelligentsia. In other words, Lenin's attitude implied that consciousness determines being, rather than the other way round, as Marxist orthodoxy required one to hold. He also believed that Lenin's policy, if it prevailed, would lead to a dictatorship *over* the proletariat rather than to the dictatorship *of* the proletariat. It is true that Plekhanov made some efforts to heal the schism in the Party, which had developed to such an extent that in 1905 the Bolsheviks and the Mensheviks held separate congresses. But his efforts were unsuccessful. And even if at the 1903 convention he had been, or at any rate had voted as a Bolshevik, the result of his reflections was that he found himself on the Menshevik side. Not that this prevented him from criticizing the Mensheviks, especially those who followed Trotsky. In the end he was at odds with both factions.

When Plekhanov returned to Russia and arrived at Petrograd in March 1917, he received an enthusiastic reception. After all, he was still the father of Russian Marxism and a respected theorist, even if, in his exile in the West, he had become, as one writer aptly puts it, 'a kind of historic monument'.[1] But this did not prevent him from expressing unpopular views. For one thing he supported the war against Germany, desired its continuation to a finish and highly disapproved of attempts to sabotage the war effort. For another thing, being convinced that Russia was not ready for socialism and that a period of liberal, bourgeois rule was required by the laws of historical development, he advocated co-operation with the Provisional Government and warned against any premature attempt by the Bolsheviks to seize power. By this time he regarded Lenin as an adventurer and as pretty well a follower of Bakunin. The actual seizure of power by the Bolshevik faction in the autumn of 1917 met with his condemnation. It seems that he was on one or two occasions in personal danger, even though the Bolshevik leaders decreed that he and his property should be respected. At the beginning of 1918 his wife took him to a sanatorium in Finland, where he died on May 30. His body was taken to Petrograd and buried in a grave next to that of Belinsky, to whom his mother had been distantly related and of whom Plekhanov himself had been an admirer.

Lenin had been impressed and influenced by Plekhanov's early Marxist writings, and the later serious differences between the two men did not prevent Lenin from paying generous tribute to Plekhanov's merits as a theorist. For example, in January 1921, while setting Bukharin right on the subject of dialectics, Lenin took the opportunity to praise Plekhanov as a philosopher, asserting that nobody could become a genuine Communist without having studied, and really studied, all that Plekhanov wrote on philosophy, as his writings were the best of all international literature on Marxism.[2]

3. A prominent characteristic of Plekhanov's thought is his historical approach. That is to say, Marxism is presented as the culmination of a dialectical process of development. Following in the footsteps of Marx and Engels Plekhanov sees the basic distinction in philosophical thought as that between materialism, which asserts the priority of matter to spirit, and idealism, which asserts the priority of spirit or mind to matter. All consistent philosophy, according to Plekhanov, is monistic, in the sense that it derives all phenomena from one ultimate principle or source. Dualism is not consistent philosophy in this sense, and it is unable to explain the interaction between mind and matter, which it itself asserts.

1 *Ibid.*, p. 277.
2 Lenin addressed these remarks to young Communists in his talk 'Once again on the trade unions'. See *Collected Works* (English), XXXIII, p. 94.

If therefore we are seeking a consistent philosophy, we have to choose between materialism and idealism. But though we can form minimal general concepts of materialism and idealism, in the history of thought they have assumed successive forms.

Consider materialism. The eighteenth-century materialists, such as Holbach, saw man as a material being and interpreted his ideas, beliefs, convictions, outlook, as products of his social environment. When, however, it was a question of determining the cause of the social environment, they ascribed forms of social organization to the causality of ideas, 'opinion'. In other words, consciousness was determined by social organization and social organization by consciousness. Helvétius had an inkling of the fact that this circularity could be overcome only in terms of the operation of causes underlying both forms of social organization and outlooks, but he did not pursue the matter. Even he, like other thinkers of the French Enlightenment, looked to a benevolent despot, 'a sage on the throne'[1] to improve the social environment, thus implying the idealist thesis that consciousness determines being. To progress further than eighteenth-century materialism, it was necessary to discover the 'factor which determines both *the development of the social environment* and *the development of opinions*'.[2] This was the problem for social science in the nineteenth century.

In the first instance, the advance to a dialectical interpretation of the historical process was made not by materialists but by idealists, especially by Hegel, who saw that 'dialectics is *the principle of all life*'.[3] Hegel understood that both in nature and in human society there are 'leaps', quantitative changes resulting in the emergence of new qualities, and that it was not simply a matter of gradual quantitative change. Again, Hegel understood how phenomena change into their opposites. For example, something which has once met a human need changes eventually into an obstacle to the satisfaction of human needs, which are themselves subject to change or development. In general, it was the great merit of Hegel to have regarded all phenomena from the point of view of their development, a way of thinking which, according to Plekhanov, 'excluded *all Utopias*'.[4] Further, Hegel grasped the need for studying the relations, the

1 *Selected Philosophical Works* (English translation), II (1976), p. 118. This work will be referred to as *SPW*. The quotation is from *Essays in the History of Materialism*, which appeared in 1896 but was written before the publication (1895) of *The Development of the Monist View of History*. In the separate English translation by R. Fox (London, 1934; New York, 1967), see p. 159.

2 *SPW*, I (1977, 3rd edition), p. 500. *The Development of the Monist View of History* (Moscow and London, 1956), p. 20. This work will be referred to as *D*.

3 *Ibid.*, p. 545. *D.*, p. 74.

4 *Ibid.*, p. 568. *D.*, p. 101.

interconnections, between, for example, social organization, art, religion and philosophy. He was a 'monist', though an idealist monist.

According to Plekhanov, however, Hegel and other dialectical idealists absolutized what was really one aspect of human nature, namely the process of logical reason, and thus rendered themselves incapable of understanding the true nature of social relations.[1] Idealism was bankrupt, and perception of this fact forced thinking people to return to materialism, not to the old materialism of the eighteenth century but to a materialism enriched by the insights of the idealists. 'The genius who represented the new direction of thought was Karl Marx.'[2] Marx was not, of course, the first thinker to revolt against absolute idealism. There was Feuerbach, for example. But it was Marx who laid the foundations of genuine social science. 'Before Marx, social science was not and could not be exact.'[3] 'Marx saw that in any age it is the productive forces which determine the qualities of the social environment. Once the state of the productive forces is determined, the qualities of the social environment are also determined, and so is the psychology corresponding to it, and the interaction between the environment on the one side and minds and manners on the other'.[4] For the most part, Marx confined his attention to solving problems relating to a particular historical period, but the basic principles of his thought apply to other periods too. The way in which they apply is a matter for empirical research.

It would be out of place to discuss here basic Marxian concepts such as those of productive forces and productive relations. It should, however, be remarked that, though Plekhanov insisted on orthodoxy, he did not claim that Marxism was a completed system of thought, admitting of no development. Though Marx himself focused his attention on the capitalist epoch, he did not cover his own selected field exhaustively, 'even approximately'.[5] Further, Plekhanov was careful to explain that if it was asserted that the philosophy of a given period reflected the social life of the period, and ultimately its economic life, this assertion should not be understood as implying that we can deduce the philosophy of a certain period simply from knowledge of the contemporary state of the productive forces and the corresponding economic relations. For there are other factors to consider, such as intra-philosophical connections, the connections between the philosophy of a given period and that of the preceding

1 *Ibid.*, p. 577. *D.*, p. 113.
2 *Ibid.*, p. 580. *D.*, p. 116.
3 *Ibid.*, p. 613. *D.*, p. 156.
4 *Ibid.*, pp. 631–32. *D.*, p. 178.
5 *Ibid.*, p. 653. *D.*, p. 204.

period or of another society. For example, Holbach was 'a theorist of the bourgeoisie'[1], but though this was the case, there were nonetheless connections between his ideas and the ideas of preceding and contemporary philosophers. Once an element in the ideological superstructure, such as religion or philosophy, comes into being, it takes on a life of its own, although its successive phases also reflect changes in social relations and ultimately in economic life. The particular relations between a philosophy and the economic substructure, and between it and other factors, are matters for empirical investigation, not simply for *a priori* deduction.[2]

A causal influence on which Plekhanov laid marked emphasis was geography. He asserted, for example, that it is the geographical environment which determines the development of the productive forces. 'In this way nature itself gives man the means for its own subjection.'[3] Intent, as he was, on maintaining the thesis that being determines consciousness, Plekhanov showed an odd desire to locate the ultimate cause of historical development outside man. His emphasis on the influence of geography helped him to do this. But Marxist thinkers, while recognizing, of course, that geographical factors influence economic and social life, have been accustomed to regard Plekhanov as guilty of having exaggerated this influence.

Though Plekhanov laid stress on correct theory, on orthodoxy, he did not, of course, forget the doctrine of the unity of theory and practice. Theory is oriented to practice. '*Dialectical materialism is the philosophy of action*'.[4] But action in this context means 'the activity of men in conformity to law'[5], the laws formulated, that is to say, in Marx's theory of historical development, which correspond, in the sphere of human history, to the laws of nature discovered and formulated by physical scientists.

It will be noticed that Plekhanov used the phrase 'dialectical materialism'. Some writers seem to think that this phrase should be reserved for philosophy in the Soviet Union, for the official ideology, and that it should not be used to refer to the thought of Marx himself. This contention is understandable if one assumes, for example, that Marx did not

1 *SPW*, II (1976), p. 58. See also p. 61. *Essays*, p. 43.
2 After Marx's death Engels explained that Marx and himself, while maintaining that the economic substructure was *ultimately* decisive, had never intended to claim that it was the *only* determining factor. There could be interaction between different elements of the ideological superstructure, between religion and philosophy for example. This superstructure was not conceived as a purely *ineffective* reflection of economic life.
3 *SPW*, I (1977), pp. 663–4. D., p. 217.
4 *Ibid.*, p. 667. D., p. 220.
5 *Ibid.*

accept Engels's extension of dialectical movement to nature. But though it was certainly Engels, and not Marx, who treated explicitly of the dialectical movement in nature, there is no cogent evidence, as far as the present writer is aware, that Marx ever expressed disapproval of Engels's line of thought. Anyway, Plekhanov explained that he used the phase 'dialectical materialism', 'because it alone can give an accurate description of the philosophy of Marx'.[1] His contention was that eighteenth-century materialism was not dialectical, whereas Marx enriched materialism by using the concept of dialectical movement which had been employed by Hegel in an idealist framework of thought.

Plekhanov thought of Marx as the man who made it possible for social science to become an 'exact science'. In his view, Marx laid the foundations of the science of social dynamics. Did he also regard Marxism as philosophy? He certainly used phrases such as 'the philosophy of Marx' and called dialectical materialism 'the philosophy of action'. But what did he understand by the term 'philosophy'? Was the word used simply as a conventional or as an honorific title for what in itself was supposed to be not philosophy but science? Or did Plekhanov use the word because he thought that some feature of Marxism justified or required its use? If so, what was the feature?

Some of Plekhanov's statements certainly give the impression that, in his view, philosophy had turned into or become science, in Marxism that is to say. For example, whereas in the first half of the nineteenth century philosophical thought was dominated by *idealistic* monism, 'in its second half there triumphed *in science* – with which meanwhile *philosophy* has been completely fused – *materialistic* monism . . .'.[2] Again, Plekhanov describes the view of Antonio Labriola as being that philosophy, in so far as it is distinct from theology, occupies itself with the same problems as scientific investigation, either anticipating science by offering conjectural solutions or by summarizing and submitting to further logical development solutions already found by science. Plekhanov's comment is 'this is true, of course',[3] though he qualifies the statement in order to accommodate thinkers such as Descartes, who were influenced by other factors, such as religious belief. He thus subscribes to a positivist conception of philosophy. We can also quote his statement that 'no fate is now strong enough to take from us the discovery of Copernicus, or the discovery of the transformation of

1 *Ibid.*, p. 666, note. *D.*, p. 220, note.
2 *Ibid.*, p. 489. *D.*, p. 12.
3 *SPW*, II (1976), p. 247. *The Materialist Conception of History*, p. 44 (New York, 1964).

energy, or the discovery of the mutability of species, or the discoveries of the genius Marx'.[1] This statement clearly implies that Marx did for social science what others had done in the fields of physics and biology.

At the same time it does not seem an adequate account of the matter if we say simply that, though Plekhanov certainly made use of the word philosophy, he meant by it, when applied to Marxism, simply Marx's theory of historical development. By 1900 Struve and Berdyaev had carried their revisionism to the point of asserting that there was no essential connection between Marx's sociological doctrine and materialism in a philosophical sense. Even if, however, we were prepared to grant that this is the case, Plekhanov was obviously convinced that one could not justifiably describe oneself as a Marxist unless one subscribed to the thesis that matter is prior to spirit. He may not have given any adequate explanation of the sense, or senses, in which he used the word 'philosophy', but he obviously saw Marxism as a comprehensive world-view, one which was based on scientific investigation and was in full accord with the findings of the sciences, but one which went beyond the area of any particular science and could reasonably be described as a philosophy.

4. By materialism in general Plekhanov understood, as he said explicitly, the thesis that matter is prior to spirit or mind or consciousness. But what did he mean by 'matter'? The Austrian philosopher Ernst Mach (1838–1916), in an endeavour to exclude the dichotomies which had given rise to opposed metaphysical theories (such as idealism and materialism) reduced phenomena to 'experience', to sensations which are neither purely physical, nor purely mental, but neutral. The revisionist Marxist Alexander Bogdanov (1873–1928), believing that Marxist epistemology needed updating and seeing in Mach's theories an instrument for accomplishing this task, also reduced reality to experience. At the same time he wished to allow for the Marxist thesis that matter is prior to mind, and he thought that he could do this by making a distinction between physical experience, which is collectivized or social experience, and mental experience, the experience of an individual or of a few individuals. Physical objects, according to his theory, belonged to collective experience and were the same for all, whereas psychical objects belonged, so to speak, to the private sphere and presupposed physical experience. Plekhanov, however, believed that the 'Empiriomonism' of Bogdanov and his associates was heterodox, and he insisted that there

1 *SPW*, I (1977), p. 645. *D.*, p. 194.

are real objects which cause experience. He thus defined matter as that which acts on our organs of sense, evoking or causing sensations in us.[1]

Adoption of this position threatened to put Plekhanov in the Kantian camp. Indeed, in answer to the question what is it, precisely, which acts upon our sense-organs? 'I answer with Kant: *things-in-themselves*'.[2] Matter, Plekhanov informs his readers, is nothing but the aggregate of things in themselves, in so far as they cause sensations in us.[3] He had, however, already attacked Marxist revisionists who thought that Marxism needed an infusion of Kantian or Neo-Kantian epistemology, and he had no wish to be left with Kant's unknowable thing in itself. For this would hardly fit in with the thesis that being determines consciousness, as understood by Marxists. One would have to say that consciousness is determined by a I-know-not-what. Plekhanov therefore proposed a theory of 'hieroglyphics', which would enable him to claim that things in themselves, things existing independently of human consciousness that is to say, are knowable. Briefly, the theory was that ideas, though not photographs of objects, correspond to them in a manner analogous to that in which a hieroglyphic corresponds to or represents the object to which it refers. There are, as it were, two languages, permitting translation from the one into the other. There is a language of sense-data, one might say, which is distinct from the language of objects but has the same meaning, in a manner analogous to that in which a statement in French and a statement in Russian can have the same meaning. As our sensations are caused by objects, they reveal something about the objects.

Plekhanov gets himself into an awkward position. In his *Notes to Engels' Book Ludwig Feuerbach* he maintains that things in themselves 'have no "appearance" at all'.[4] They have 'appearances' only in the consciousness of the subjects on which they act. In 'Once more Materialism' he admits that these appearances do not resemble things in themselves. For how could a sensation or the representation arising from it be said to resemble what is neither sensation nor representation? The forms and relations of things in themselves are not as they seem to us to be. 'Our representations of the forms and relations of things are only hieroglyphics'[5]. At the same time Plekhanov maintains

1 This view was stated by Plekhanov in his essays 'Materialism or Kantianism' and 'Once more Materialism'.
2 *SPW*, II (1976), p. 418. From 'Once more Materialism' or 'Materialism Yet Again'.
3 *Ibid.*
4 *SPW*, I (1977), p. 461. From 'Notes to Engels' Book Ludwig Feuerbach'. This work will be referred to as *Notes*.
5 *SPW*, II (1976), p. 419. From 'Materialism Yet Again'.

that these hieroglyphics 'designate the forms and relations of things 'with precision'[1], that there is correspondence between objective relations and their subjective reflections (or translations) in our heads. How does he know that this is the case? What warrant has he for making this claim? Plekhanov's argument is that if there were no correspondence between ideas and things existing independently of human consciousness, life would be impossible. That is to say, human life rests on action and reaction between nature and man. The physical environment acts on us by way of the senses. Human beings stand in active relations to the environment, producing food, for example, and using material things as instruments for attaining specific ends. This active relationship to the environment shows that we know at any rate some properties of things in themselves. Otherwise we could not successfully force them to serve our purposes.

Although in his Notes to Engels's *Feuerbach* Plekhanov denounced eclecticism and maintained that any attempt to combine Kantian epistemology with Marxism must appear monstrous to anyone who thinks logically, it may seem that his own theory of hieroglyphics constituted just such an attempt. This is what Bogdanov thought. Plekhanov, however, could reply that he agreed with Kant only to the extent of claiming that there are in fact things in themselves, in the sense of things existing independently of human consciousness and irreducible to subjective 'experience'. He did not accept the doctrine that the thing in itself is unknowable. Nor did he claim that the laws of nature are not expressions of objective relations but imposed by the subject, by mind. He was not therefore guilty of trying to combine the Kantian theory of knowledge with Marxism. The assertion that there are things in themselves, in the sense intended, could be made by any realist who rejected Empiriomonism. Bogdanov, it is true, demanded that one should choose between Kantianism on the one hand and Empiriomonism on the other. But there was a middle position, his own theory of hieroglyphics.

However this may be, Marxist philosophers, generally speaking, have not been satisfied with Plekhanov's theory. Lenin, for example, who was no friend of Empiriomonism, thought that the theory of hieroglyphics was incompatible with Marxist realism and led to agnosticism. As for Bogdanov, he argued that though Plekhanov's theory might be orthodox according to the letter, it was heterodox in spirit. Bogdanov's own theory was criticized at length by Lenin, but he may have been right in seeing in Plekhanov's theory of hieroglyphics an unadmitted expression of revisionism by the great critic of revisionists.

1 *SPW*.

Let us turn to an ethical theme. It is hardly necessary to say that Plekhanov, as an orthodox Marxist, regarded moral codes as class-related. He asserted, for example, that 'Kant's morality is bourgeois morality, translated into the language of his philosophy'.[1] Obviously, Kant was not aware of this fact. He believed that he had formulated absolute and universally valid moral imperatives of practical reason. But Marxism reveals the social conditioning of moral codes. Like Hegel, but in the context of materialism instead of idealism, the Marxist looks at morality from the point of view of development, a point of view which Kant was incapable of taking. The implication is, of course, that there can be a proletarian morality, with its own ideals. Indeed, the ideal of Engels was precisely 'the emancipation of the proletariat'[2], an ideal to the attainment of which he devoted his life.

It may be asked, Plekhanov remarks, why one should talk about Engels having ideals. The word 'ideal' suggests the thought of something which it is worth striving after or which one ought to strive to attain, but which would not be realized without human effort and which may possibly never be realized in fact. It would be very odd to talk about the rising of the sun tomorrow morning as an ideal. Short of a cosmic cataclysm, the sun is bound to rise tomorrow. In any case, human striving is irrelevant. Does not Marxism teach that there are also historical laws, that eventually the proletariat will certainly be emancipated, is bound to be emancipated, according to the laws of historical development? In this case why talk about a moral ideal?

Plekhanov's reply to this sort of objection is substantially as follows. It is true that Marxism maintains that there are laws of historical development, and that Engels's ideal was in accordance with historical reality. The Populists can be said to have had lofty ideals, but these ideals were divorced from reality, whereas Engels's ideal of the emancipation of the proletariat represented 'the reality of tomorrow'.[3] But it does not follow that human effort is irrelevant. For 'the laws of social development can no more be realized without the mediation of people than the laws of nature without the mediation of matter'.[4] The law of gravitation cannot operate unless there are bodies, but it does not follow that any body can flout the law of gravitation. The laws of history cannot operate unless there are people. And it is true that people, unlike inanimate things, can try to fly in the face of law, to flout laws. In this case they condemn

1 SPW, I (1977), p. 472. From Notes.
2 Ibid., p. 469. From Notes.
3 Ibid., pp. 469–70.
4 Ibid., p. 470.

themselves to impotence and are analogous to Don Quixote. They can also, however, identify themselves with the march of history. From the subjective point of view they can take it as their privilege and duty to strive after the goal revealed by a correct view of human history. This is what Engels did, and we can thus justifiably speak of him as having an ideal and as striving after its realization. In the case of human beings there is subjectivity; there is a subjective point of view; and the word 'ideal' belongs to the language of subjectivity. We can justifiably speak of a 'moral' ideal, as morality is based on the striving 'for the *happiness of the whole*: the clan, the people, the class, humanity'[1], a striving which '*always presupposes* a greater or lesser degree of *self-sacrifice*'.[2]

It may seem that by adopting this point of view Plekhanov is endorsing the 'subjective sociology' of the Populist thinkers, which Marxist theorists were accustomed to ridicule. He would presumably reply that what was objectionable in the Populist conception of 'subjective sociology' was not that it allowed for human beings having aims and ideals, which they certainly do have, but that its aims and ideals were not grounded in a correct analysis of historical reality and its development. All ideals are subjective in the sense that they are conceived and striven after by human subjects. But some ideals are products of subjectivity in the sense that they are out of accordance with any real understanding of social development. The trouble with the Populists was not that they had ideals, but that their ideals were unrealistic. They did not understand the direction in which social development in Russia was moving. This understanding was provided by Marxism.

Although Plekhanov, however, had dismissed Kantian morality as an expression of the bourgeois mentality, combining this judgment with an endorsement of Hegel's claim that Kant's formulations of the categorical imperative were empty statements, it was precisely to Kant that he turned in his later years by adopting the Kantian thesis that human beings should never be used merely as means. It is true that he found the idea useful for practical purposes. He was obviously able to use the Kantian principle in attacking exploitation of the working class, and in his pamphlet *On the War* (1914) he applied it to nations, denouncing the German violation of Belgian neutrality. At the same time, in view of the fact that he had previously asserted that Kant's ideal of the kingdom of ends was '*an abstract ideal of bourgeois society*'[3] his use of one of Kant's formulations of the categorical imperative was something of a *volte-face*.

1 *SPW*, p. 473. From *Notes*.
2 *Ibid.*
3 *Ibid.*, p. 472.

We can also note that his wartime summons to Russian workers to rally to the defence of the fatherland, even though this meant cooperating with the régime, was somewhat out of harmony with the statement in the *Communist Manifesto* that the proletariat has no fatherland.

One of the factors contributing to Peter Struve's progressive alienation from Marxism was his coming to the conclusion that while Marxism provided a theory about morality, it could not itself offer any positive moral guidance. Plekhanov did not come to this conclusion. He remained to the end the self-appointed custodian of Marxist orthodoxy. But one can reasonably see in the way in which he appealed, in his last years, to a Kantian moral principle the expression of a felt dissatisfaction with Marxism as an adequate source of moral guidance.

5. Plekhanov had asserted that there are laws of history, laws relating to the development of human society. One would not, of course, expect anything else from the high priest of Marxist orthodoxy. At the same time Plekhanov had no intention of denying the explicit statement of Marx and Engels that it is human beings who make history.[1] Nor did he wish to claim that talk about human freedom is completely meaningless. He was therefore faced with the problem of determining the relation between, as he put it, necessity and freedom. And he tried to solve it in terms of a dialectical movement.

If it is a question of discussing the relation between historical laws and human freedom, discussion would obviously be facilitated if we had a clear idea of the sense in which the concept of an historical law is to be understood in the context. If historical laws are conceived as entities which govern the course of history, it is then possible to hold that the historical process moves towards the realization of a certain state of affairs, which will inevitably be attained. But in this case it seems to follow that human beings make history only in the sense that historical laws operate through them as instruments. The laws take the place of what Hegel called 'the cunning of Reason'. If, however, laws of history are conceived simply as empirical generalizations, formulated by the human mind on the basis of observed regularities and enabling us to predict with some degree of probability, the claim that there are laws in this sense may well be compatible with admission of human freedom, but the concept of inevitability is sacrificed. There would be no justification for claiming that the realization of a certain state of affairs in the future is inevitable.

---

1 To say that it is human beings who make history may seem to be a truism, hardly worth stating. But Marx and Engels intended, of course, to exclude something, namely that history is made by God or by the Absolute of Hegel.

Marxist philosophers do not, of course, wish to claim that historical laws are metaphysical entities which, so to speak, push history in a certain direction, using human beings as instruments. At the same time, unless they are prepared to pursue a revisionist path, they do not wish to jettison the concept of inevitability. Mr Maurice Cornforth, the English Marxist philosopher, informs his readers that 'Marxism is not telling us what is historically inevitable, or making encouraging prophecies. It is indicating what we can practically attain, not a millenial vision of utopia'.[1] Although Mr Cornforth may be willing, however, to sacrifice the idea of historical inevitability, Plekhanov was not. He evidently believed, whether rightly or wrongly, that this idea, in some form at least, was part of orthodox Marxism. If therefore he wished to retain the concept of human freedom, he had to reconcile it with the idea of historical inevitability. The obvious way of doing this was to interpret the concept of freedom in such a way that the desired reconciliation could be effected.

Plekhanov, like Engels before him, saw an analogy between the relation of human beings to physical laws, laws of nature that is to say, and their relation to laws of history. If, for example, human beings wish to journey to the moon or to a planet, they have to respect and take into account laws of nature. They have, as one might say, to use the laws of nature, if they want to attain their aim. In this sense they are subject to necessity. It does not follow, however, that they are determined either to make or not to make such journeys. Analogously, it can be argued, if human beings wish to realize a certain social goal, intelligent and successful action demands knowledge of and respect for the relevant laws of social development. But it does not follow that human beings are mere automata, determined to act in certain ways.

This may seem to be evidently true. Marx very sensibly asserted that, though it is human beings who make history, they do not make it just as they please; what they are practically free to do is limited to situations which are not of their choosing.[2] Marx was thinking of the fact that all human beings are born in definite historical situations and that they are confronted with states of affairs inherited from the past or created by members of other societies or groups. People belonging to a nomadic tribe are obviously not free, from the practical point of view, to effect the transition from capitalism to socialism. For there is no capitalism from

---

1 *Communism and Philosophy. Contemporary Dogmas and Revisions of Marxism*, p. 253 (London, 1980).
2 The statement referred to is made by Marx in *The Eighteenth Brumaire of Louis Bonaparte* (1852).

which the transition can be made. We can extend this idea of the given which limits what can practically be done to include the laws of nature. To 'overcome' a physical law demands knowledge of other laws, and without this knowledge successful action is not possible. It may seem that we can apply this sort of idea to laws of history as well.

A lot depends on how we conceive the relevant historical laws. Let us suppose that it is true to say that the state of the productive forces in a given society determines the economic and social relations in that society. Members of that society would not be practically free to create social relations which presupposed productive forces that had not yet been developed. But there would presumably be room for the exercise of free choice within a certain given framework. Let us suppose, however, that when we talk about laws of history, we have in mind a law of successive stages, which states or implies that there is an inevitable pattern of development, culminating in a certain kind of society. If the process is inevitable, human beings would not be able to alter it. But would they have any freedom of action at all, within the framework of this 'iron' law? It might perhaps be argued that though the process would work itself out inevitably, human initiative would be able either to accelerate or to slow down the transition from one stage to the next. Marxist thinkers who believe in iron laws of history have, of course, to say something of this kind. For they obviously do not want to maintain that the action of revolutionary activists is useless and to advocate a policy of what has been described as 'tailism', passively letting the historical process work itself out and following in the rear or at the tail.

Plekhanov, who certainly inclined to the idea of 'iron laws', obviously wanted to leave room for the activity of revolutionary leaders. He wanted to leave room for the idea of increasing human control, control guided by knowledge of law. And he presented a theory of passage from the realm of necessity into that of freedom, or, more precisely, of a dialectical development from necessity to freedom, freedom to a new form of necessity, and from this new form of necessity to a higher level of freedom. Our primitive ancestors were members of 'the dark kingdom of *physical necessity*'[1], struggling with a physical environment which they did not understand. As the human being became a tool-making animal, necessity was subjected to consciousness, though at first only to a small extent. While, however, human domination over nature increased in proportion to the development of the productive forces, in the course of time this process of development and its results became so complex that

---

1 *SPW*, I (1977), p. 663. D., p. 216.

it slipped out of human control and the producer became the slave of his own creation. Plekhanov was thinking, of course, of the capitalist economy, in which he saw man as the slave of the machine and unable to control the structures which he had created. But this slavery is not a lasting state of affairs. When human beings come to understand their slavery and its causes, consciousness triumphs over necessity. Man subjects the process of production to his own will, thereby becoming master. Then begins the reign of freedom. Human beings can make economic and social life more reasonable, though they have to act in accordance with their knowledge of laws.

Being a Marxist, Plekhanov naturally lays emphasis on such general factors as the development of the productive forces and the relations between members of a society in the productive process, when he is talking about causes which determine the course of history. But he admits that 'the personal qualities of leading people determine the individual features of historical events'.[1] Though he stresses the activity of classes, he does not claim that individuals have no influence whatsoever on the course of events. For example, though he would explain the Reformation in the light of Marx's theory of history, he would not deny that Martin Luther gave a particular stamp to the movement in the relevant region, and that other 'individual features' were due to Calvin.

Plekhanov recognizes, therefore, that in the course of history human beings obtain an increasing degree of conscious control over their environment, both physical and social, and that in this sense there is a movement from the sphere of necessity into that of freedom. But this is not his only line of thought. For example, having asserted that capitalism necessarily produces its own negation and thus the transition to socialism, he remarks that the Marxist 'serves as an instrument of this necessity and cannot help doing so, owing to his social status and to his mentality and temperament, which were created by his status'.[2] Every person of talent who becomes a social force 'is the product of social relations'.[3] It may be rather difficult to see how Plekhanov can give a satisfactory explanation of the fact that Marx and Engels came from the bourgeois class and that neither he himself nor Lenin came either from the urban proletariat or from peasant families. But at any rate he makes it

---

1 SPW, II (1976), p. 308 (and 311). On the Role of the Individual in History, p. 55 (London, 1940). This essay will be referred to as Role.
2 Ibid., p. 290. Role, p. 17.
3 Ibid., p. 310. Role, p. 52.

clear that, in his opinion, one's activities constitute 'an essential link in a chain of inevitable events'.[1]

It should not be necessary to explain that Plekhanov does not intend to deny that human beings pursue consciously conceived goals or ends. For it is obvious that they do. Indeed, Engels asserted that history is '*nothing* but the activity of man pursuing his ends'.[2] Plekhanov's contention is that people pursue certain ends because they are socially determined to do so. Referring to a class which brings about a revolution, he states that its activities, together with the aspirations which are responsible for these activities, 'are themselves determined by *necessity*'.[3] Similarly, we read that 'sociology becomes a science only in the measure in which it succeeds in understanding the appearances of aims in social man . . . as a necessary consequence of a social process ultimately determined by the course of economic development'.[4]

This theory of determinism, Plekhanov insists, does not imply that human activity makes no difference, produces no effects. Religious leaders who believed that God was speaking and acting through them were not thereby rendered inactive or ineffective. On the contrary, they were all the more active because they believed that they were God's instruments. And if we claim that Napoleon I's aspirations and the activities which expressed these aspirations were determined, this claim does not imply denial of Napoleon's energy and achievements.

Plekhanov is doubtless justified in claiming that a theory of determinism is not incompatible with recognition of the fact that some human beings have displayed astonishing energy and have influenced the course of history in some way or other, even if it was only by affecting what Plekhanov called the 'individual features' of historical events. If one can be determined to be lethargic, one can also be determined to be energetic, a dynamic personality. At the same time the question obviously arises, how does Plekhanov reconcile this determinist theory with his claim that the realm of necessity passes into the realm of freedom? What room is left for freedom?

The obvious way of effecting a reconciliation is to find a suitable definition of freedom. Thus we are told that 'freedom means being conscious of necessity'.[5] Again, a person's '*free* actions become the

1 *Ibid.*, p. 285. *Role*, p. 12.
2 See Engels' contribution to *The Holy Family* (1845).
3 *SPW*, III (1976), p. 180. *Fundamental Problems of Marxism*, p. 85 (Moscow and London, 1974).
4 *Ibid*.
5 *SPW*, II (1976), p. 289. *Role*, p. 16.

conscious and free expression of necessity'.[1] The fact that a person's aspirations are causally determined represents necessity, but in so far as the person desires, perhaps passionately desires, to realize some goal, this represents freedom. Freedom and necessity are different aspects of the same coin. 'It is freedom which is identical with necessity – it is necessity transformed into freedom'[2], through the operation of consciousness and desire.

It has sometimes been said that Plekhanov's idea of freedom was derived from Spinoza. Though, however, Plekhanov was influenced to some extent by Spinoza, the latter ascribed belief in freedom to ignorance of the determining causes, whereas the former defined freedom as consciousness of necessity. In actual fact Plekhanov referred to Hegel's *Science of Logic* in support of his view of freedom.[3] Whether this support is to be considered a recommendation of Plekhanov's thesis is another question. I suppose, however, that the dialectical method demands that necessity should pass into its opposite. By defining freedom as consciousness of necessity Plekhanov is presumably partly thinking of consciousness of law as a prerequisite for successful control of the environment, including the social environment. Perhaps, however, we can also see him as identifying freedom with spontaneity. I may be determined to desire the realization of a certain ideal goal, but in so far as I desire it I experience this necessity as freedom. Here we have a link with Spinoza, but experiencing freedom from the subjective point of view or acting with the idea of freedom is not quite the same thing as consciousness of necessity. (Plekhanov refers to Martin Luther's 'I can do no other'.)

To the present writer it seems that, though Plekhanov can find room for freedom from ignorance (of law) and also for the feeling of being free, it is necessity which has the last word. Indeed, if we take literally some of the things which he says, we can arrive at the conclusion that, given the existence of human beings, the whole history of mankind is ultimately determined by extra-human factors, the productive forces and geography. To be sure, there is another aspect to Plekhanov's thought. As he was himself aware, he had a 'Jacobin' side to his character. He had been a revolutionary agitator, and he remained convinced of the important role to be played by a revolutionary élite. But he also believed in laws of history, and he interpreted this belief in a less flexible way than Marx had done. As we have noted, Plekhanov opposed the Bolshevik seizure of power as an attempt to flout the laws of history, the inevitable dialectical

1 *SPW*, p. 291. *Role*, p. 18.
2 *Ibid.*, p. 290. *Role*, p. 17.
3 *Ibid.*, note.

process of history. Lenin, however, did not bother about laws, when this was not to his purpose. It was not, of course, a question of Lenin denying the Marxist theory of history. Like Plekhanov, he accepted it. But when there was the opportunity for revolutionary action, he took it. Laws could be interpreted in accordance with achievement. Plekhanov was not a quietist, but Lenin was much more of an activist. It is not surprising if Soviet writers have been inclined to see in Plekhanov a tendency to adopt a 'mechanist' view of history.

6. Living abroad, unable to do much to influence the course of events in Russia, increasingly out of harmony with the various factions in the Russian socialist movement, though respected as an eminent theorist, and in ill health, Plekhanov not unnaturally turned his attention to scholarly pursuits. In 1909 he started work on a *History of Social Thought in Russia*. It appears that he had originally intended to write only one volume, ending with the 1905 revolution. In point of fact, by the time of his death he had almost completed three volumes, covering the ground up to the end of the eighteenth century. His approach was, of course, that of a Marxist, in the sense that he aimed at showing how the development of social life in Russia had been determined by 'objective' factors, including not only basic economic factors but also Russia's geographical situation. This approach did not, however, prevent him from making use of ideas from non-Marxist scholars. He was perfectly capable of appreciating contributions to knowledge made by bourgeois scholars, though he made use of them within a Marxist framework of thought.

Another subject to which Plekhanov devoted attention was art. His approach was explicitly stated. In the first of his *Unaddressed Letters* (1889) he said plainly, 'I shall say at once and without any circumlocution that I look upon art, as upon all social phenomena, from the standpoint of the materialist conception of history'.[1] This means, of course, that he looked upon art as reflecting the social system of the time, the social system itself being ultimately determined by the state of the productive forces (and geography). One can say with Hippolyte Taine, whom Plekhanov admired, that the art of a people is determined by the people's mentality, and that its mentality is determined by its situation, but one should not then relapse into 'idealism' by claiming that the situation is determined by the mentality, being by consciousness. In explaining the art of a people the Marxist looks for economic causes.

---

1 *SPW*, V (1981), p. 264. *Unaddressed Letters. Art and Social Life*, translated by A. Fineberg, p. 9 (Moscow, 1957). This work will be referred to as *UL*.

It does not follow, however, that the nature of a people's art can be deduced simply from the results of analysis of its economic life. This may be possible in the case of primitive peoples, inasmuch as a direct relationship tends to be discernible between the state of the productive forces and primitive art. But when it is a question of civilized peoples, the direct dependence of art on technology and the mode of production tends to disappear. Once the division of labour has taken place and classes have arisen, we find art reflecting the mentality not of society as a whole but of a particular class. This reflection, however, is subject to the influence of a variety of factors, which have to be discovered by empirical investigation. Marxism does not deny the complexity of the factors and relations involved. All that it insists on is that economic life is the *ultimately* determining factor.

This point of view is obviously that of orthodox Marxism. A phenomenon such as art is said to be *ultimately* determined by economic factors. This is, one may say, a basic act of faith; it is what has to be believed, if the Marxist framework of thought is accepted. Once this basic thesis has been asserted, it has, of course, to be supported by finding ways in which art has been conditioned by economic life. But by restricting his claim to the *ultimately* determining function of economic factors the Marxist leaves himself free to discern the influence of a variety of other factors, provided at any rate that he can fit them into the Marxist framework of thought without shattering it. And it is largely what a Marxist philosopher has to say about these 'other factors' that is really of interest. So it is in the case of Plekhanov.

In the first place Plekhanov claims that art, as a distinct kind of phenomenon, is characterized by having a language of its own. It begins, we are told, when a man reawakens in himself emotions and thoughts which he has previously experienced under the influence of his environment and *'expresses them in definite images'*.[1] Generally, the artist does this with a view to communication, to communicating to other human beings what he has re-thought and re-felt. The 'language' by which this is done is the language of images, and this language, we can say, has both expressive and evocative functions. It will be noticed that Plekhanov does not refer simply to emotions or emotive attitudes but also to thoughts. In his view 'there is no such thing as a work of art which is entirely devoid of ideas'.[2] This insistence that the function of art is not simply to express feelings, as Tolstoy maintained, but also ideas doubtless owed something

---

1 *Ibid.*, p. 264. *UL*, p. 3.
2 *Ibid.*, p. 658. *UL*, p. 187.

to the aesthetic theories of the idealists, such as Hegel. But, as we shall presently see, the belief that art expresses ideas in the language of images was important for Plekhanov in his treatment of the social function of art.

In the second place Plekhanov appeals to Darwin in support of the claim that there is in human beings a capacity for 'aesthetic taste', something which might be described as an aesthetic sense, which is not confined to human beings. To be sure, ideas of what is beautiful vary from society to society, and in order to ascertain the causes of the ideas with which certain sensations are connected, we have to turn to sociology. But this does not alter the fact that the capacity for aesthetic experience is rooted in human nature, or, more generally, in sensitive nature.

In the third place, when reflecting on the existence of common aesthetic tastes and ideas in a given society, Plekhanov draws attention to the role of imitation, a theme to which other writers had already referred. Imitation is a social phenomenon. As a social being, man has a natural impulse to imitate. In a society in which there is class-division one class may be impelled to imitate another. Thus in seventeenth-century France 'the bourgeoisie readily, though not very successfully, imitated the nobility'[1], as portrayed in Molière's *Le Bourgeois Gentilhomme*. It also happens that imitation within a given class is the expression of opposition to another class. Thus in England the literature of the Restoration can be seen as expressing a reaction to the bourgeois Puritan morality.

What we may describe as a play instinct is also recognized by Plekhanov. In his discussion of the art of primitive peoples he refers to the activity of play, as expressed, for example, in dancing. He then claims that work, activity directed to a utilitarian end, is prior to play and determines its nature.[2] Play is the offspring of work, even though the two can be combined.

Plekhanov does not deny that there is such a thing as a distinctive aesthetic standpoint. On the contrary, he asserts that there is. And he introduces a number of psychological factors, which he believes to be relevant to art and its development. At the same time he insists that '*beneath all this complex dialectic of mental phenomena lay facts of a social character*'[3], facts, that is to say, which can themselves be explained in terms of economic life. Obviously, one would expect him, as a good Marxist, to maintain this thesis. One difficulty, however, is to obtain a

1 *Ibid.*, p. 275. *UL*, p. 22.
2 *Ibid.*, p. 312. *UL*, p. 78.
3 *Ibid.*, pp. 275–76. *UL*, pp. 22–3.

clear idea of what the thesis is supposed to imply. Plekhanov asserts, for example, that at first human beings looked on objects and phenomena from a utilitarian point of view and only later came to regard them from an aesthetic point of view.[1] It may be that a Marxist is committed to accepting this statement, but, even if the statement is true, it is obviously insufficient to show that the sphere of art is determined by economic life. That art presupposes economic life, in the sense that human beings have to 'work', to enter into an active relationship to their environment with a view to sustaining life before they can paint pictures or compose music or create literature, is a truism, which the non-Marxist can accept. The Marxist position requires acceptance of the belief not simply that one has to eat and drink, to sustain life, in order to create works of art, but also that economic factors, via social relations, determine at any rate the content of art. At the same time the Marxist wishes to allow for the influence of other than economic factors, the influence, for example, of the art of one society on that of another, and the influence of religion. He therefore maintains that economic life is the 'ultimately' determining factor, though not the only causal influence. What precisely is meant by 'ultimately determining', if it does not mean simply that without productive activity of some sort human beings would be unable to create social institutions or practise art or religion or construct philosophies? In practice it seems to mean that the Marxist tries to show by specific examples how economic factors have influenced art directly or indirectly, how art has reflected, directly or indirectly, economic life. In so far, however, as he is successful, we may well think that what he has illustrated is an influence exercised by economic life on art rather than a relationship which can be properly described as that of determining causality. In any case, if one finds roots of aesthetic experience and artistic creation in human nature itself, as Plekhanov does, the case for the Marxist position seems to be considerably weakened. It is not suggested that Plekhanov ought not to have introduced psychological themes into his theory of art. The suggestion is simply that by doing so he weakens the force of his own attempt to attribute ultimate determining causal influence to economic factors.

To return from comment to exposition. In the course of his essay *Art and Social Life*[2] Plekhanov discusses the idea of 'art for art's sake'. He

1 *Ibid.*, p. 326. *UL*, p. 99.
2 This essay, which represents a lecture delivered in 1912, originally appeared in the journal *Sovremennik* (The Contemporary) in instalments, in November and December 1912 and January 1913.

quotes Pushkin for an expression of this idea[1] and refers to Chernyshevsky, Dobrolyubov and Pisarev as defenders of a utilitarian attitude, as defenders, that is to say, of the claim that art should be socially useful. The question whether or not he gives accurate accounts of the positions of the writers to whom he refers need not detain us. It does not really affect the main issue.

As one might expect, Plekhanov concerns himself with explaining, in terms of social conditions, the attitudes which poets and painters, artists and writers have actually adopted. Why, for example, did Pushkin, as Plekhanov sees the matter, adopt one point of view in the period of Alexander I and a radically different attitude, emphasis on art for art's sake, in the reign of Nicholas I? Plekhanov's general answer is that '*the belief in art for art's sake arises wherever the artist is out of harmony with his social environment*'[2], whereas the utilitarian view of art arises '*wherever there is mutual sympathy between a considerable section of society and people who have a more or less active interest in creative art*'[3]. For example, after the 1848 revolution Baudelaire, who had defended the theory of art for art's sake, abandoned it 'and declared that art must have a social purpose'.[4]

The utilitarian view of art, Plekhanov remarks, is not necessarily accompanied by a revolutionary attitude. Nicholas I, who was no revolutionary, wished to harness literature in the service of the imperial régime and its conception of morality. He would have liked to use Pushkin in this way, if the latter had been willing to become a court poet. At the same time all art worthy of the name expresses ideas of some sort, though in its own language; and when an artist is in sympathy with the new society which has been conceived and is maturing in the womb of the old and expresses the great emancipatory ideas of his time, we can speak of his art as 'progressive'.

What we have been outlining has been more an analysis of different attitudes to art, an analysis which relates these attitudes to social conditions, than a doctrine of what art ought or ought not to be. It is a matter of understanding rather than of making recommendations. It is natural, however, to ask, what was Plekhanov's own view? Did he not, as a Marxist, adhere to a utilitarian view of art, utility meaning, of course, social utility, measured in terms of what a Marxist would regard as progress?

1 Plekhanov quotes from Pushkin's *The Poet and the Crowd*.
2 *SPW*, V, p. 638. *UL*, p. 156.
3 *Ibid*., p. 643. *UL*, p. 163.
4 *Ibid*.

It seems obvious that, other things being equal, Plekhanov would prefer art which expressed what he describes as the great emancipatory ideas of the time to art which expressed what, to a Marxist, would be an obsolete mentality. Indeed, in the modern art of his day he saw examples of a blindness to social change and of 'the extreme individualism of the era of bourgeois decay (which) cuts off artists from all sources of true inspiration'[1] and leads them to adopt the theory of art for art's sake. Cubism he described as 'nonsense cubed'[2]. At the same time Plekhanov had no intention of committing himself to the view that artistic excellence can be assessed simply in terms of social utility, of subordination to what the Marxist would regard as social progress. He insists that there are objective criteria other than 'utility' for judging the merits of artistic productions. 'The more closely the form of an artistic production corresponds to its idea, the more successful it is. There you have an objective criterion'.[3] This enables him to say that the drawings of Leonardo da Vinci are objectively better than the drawings of 'some wretched Themistocles who spoils good paper for his own distraction'.[4] Plekhanov was certainly not the man to accept the claim that a poem or a picture or a symphony is a good work of art simply because the Party leaders find it socially useful.

This insistence on objective criteria for assessing the merits of works of art may have put Plekhanov in a somewhat awkward position. A. V. Lunacharsky (1875–1933), who was later to become Soviet Commissar for Education, expressed surprise at finding that Plekhanov recognized an absolute criterion of beauty. Plekhanov replied that this was not the case. He did not recognize an absolute criterion of beauty. He refused, however, to admit that he was thereby driven to reject the existence of objective criteria for assessing good and bad art. If one did reject all such criteria, one would relapse into an extreme subjectivism which was unfitting for anyone who called himself a Marxist[5].

Perhaps we should add that, when Plekhanov associated true art with beauty, he did not mean, for example, that in a picture comprising human beings the human beings must be what would ordinarily be described as 'beautiful'. As he remarks, to portray an old man beautifully is not the same thing as to portray a beautiful old man. 'The realm of art is much wider than the realm of the "beautiful".'[6] The old man may be

1 *SPW*, p. 679. *UL*, p. 216.
2 *Ibid.*, p. 677. *UL*, p. 214.
3 *Ibid.*, p. 685. *UL*, p. 225.
4 *Ibid. UL*, p. 226. The reference is to a character in Gogol's *Dead Souls*.
5 *Ibid.*
6 *Ibid.*, p. 686. *UL*, p. 226.

ugly according to the standards prevalent in a given society. There is no absolute standard of beauty in this sense. But the ugly old man is portrayed 'beautifully', if the form of the picture corresponds to its idea. This is, according to Plekhanov, an objective criterion. As we have already said, he was doubtless influenced by idealist aesthetics, though he would not, of course, regard art as an expression of Hegel's Absolute Idea.

We can say, in general, that Plekhanov tried to give an account of aesthetic experience and artistic creation which would preserve the distinct specific characteristics of the sphere of art but which at the same time would fit into a Marxist framework of thought. One of the main ways in which he sought to accomplish the first task was by claiming that art has its own 'language'. To fulfil the second task, however, he felt bound to maintain that the language of art could be translated into the language of sociology. Indeed, he thought of the Marxist art critic as being largely concerned with this job of translation, explaining art by relating it to its social basis. In other words the art critic, at any rate in the performance of this task, would be a sociologist of art. The question obviously arises whether it would not be simply a case of noting social influences on art and not what could properly be described as a translation.

7. Reference has already been made several times to Marxist orthodoxy. But what are the criteria of orthodoxy? Obviously, there are a number of basic ideas or theories, without acceptance of which it would be misleading, and in some cases patently absurd, to call oneself a Marxist. But there can be rather different interpretations of some of the statements made by Marx and Engels, and it is possible to emphasize one feature rather than another of their thought. Plekhanov attached little weight to statements which seemed designed to give comfort and encouragement to the Populists. Further, any Marxist would allow that Marxist thought is capable of development and ought to be developed. If we prescind from the varying pronouncements by official representatives of Communist Parties, such as those of the Soviet Union and of the People's Republic of China, what are the criteria for judging whether an alleged development is really a development or a perversion? There can obviously be alleged developments, acceptance of which would turn or contribute to turning Marxism into something else. But if Marxism is not to become a fossilized system of thought, there must be room for differences of opinion and for intellectual experimentation.

However this may be, Plekhanov regarded himself not only as an orthodox Marxist but also as a custodian of orthodoxy, part of whose vocation it was to attack manifestations of dangerous revisionist tendencies. As we have seen, he could be extremely doctrinaire. A signal example of this tendency is the persistence with which he clung to his conviction that the laws of social development, as discovered by Marx, demanded that the overthrow of the autocracy in Russia should be succeeded by a period of capitalist, bourgeois democracy. He would, of course, have liked to see unity preserved in the Russian Social Democratic Party, but not at the cost of sacrificing what he believed to be the orthodox point of view. Rather than compromising he preferred to break with the Bolsheviks, and he was quite prepared to criticize Mensheviks as well.

To describe Plekhanov as a doctrinaire thinker is to mention only one aspect of his thought. He was also capable of writing almost as a scientist trying out an hypothesis, to assess its capacity for covering and explaining the relevant phenomena or data. True, it is possible to see him as trying to fit the facts to a preconceived theory. At the same time he was a scholar, and he was capable of making a genuine effort to investigate the relevant phenomena in various fields, such as the history of philosophy and the sphere of art. In reading his writings we are aware all the time that the author was a Marxist. Or at any rate we are frequently reminded of the fact. But Plekhanov was able, within limits, to appreciate the value of lines of thought advanced by bourgeois writers and to make use of them. He was capable of conducting sharp polemics, not hesitating to use sarcasm and even sometimes abusive language, but he was also capable of patient theoretical work which has a certain impressiveness. He was a serious thinker, not simply a propagandist. And it is significant that Lenin, with whom he had broken and whom he had attacked as an adventurer and 'Bakuninist', was later to urge young Communists to study seriously the philosophical writings of Plekhanov, and that he expressed the desire that Plekhanov's papers should be collected and preserved for posterity, as was indeed eventually done.

Though, however, Plekhanov is best known as a theorist, he was certainly not like one of those Marxists who reduced Marxism to social science or sociology, to theory, playing down or passing over its revolutionary aspects. He regarded theory as oriented to practice. In youth he had himself been a revolutionary activist, and his small Liberation of Labour group was the first Russian Marxist organization. As time went on, as the Russian Social Democrat movement grew, and as Plekhanov found himself more and more in the position of a respected but rather isolated figure, he naturally tended to appear more and more as a theorist and less and less as a revolutionary, especially, of course, when he was recommending cooperation with the liberals and even becoming the presumably somewhat embarrassed recipient of compliments from the leader of the Cadets. But he never lost sight of the practical goal of Marxist thought. Indeed, his opposition to the Bolsheviks was largely motivated by his conviction that the goal of socialism, socialist democracy, could not be attained by following the policy advocated by Lenin.

It has been noted by writers on Marxism in Russia and on Plekhanov's position in the movement that his social thought contains in itself the points of departure for two divergent policies. On the one hand, Plekhanov insists that if the proletariat is to be emancipated, it must emancipate itself. According to Marxist theory, social revolution is achieved by a class, and in relation to capitalism it is the proletariat which is the naturally and truly revolutionary class. To be sure, other classes too may be adversely affected by the evils or shortcomings of the capitalist economy, but it is the proletariat whose interest it is to abolish capitalism and establish socialism. It is therefore the proletariat which will eventually assume power, not simply for its own benefit but for the good of all. On the other hand, Plekhanov saw that for the proletariat to become a class 'for itself', conscious of its interests and of its unity, it had to be educated, and that this task could be performed only by an élite well grounded in scientific socialism. Marxist leaders had to make the proletariat reflectively aware of its interests.

This may sound sensible enough, pretty well a matter of common sense. But what is meant by the interests of the proletariat? Does it mean what proletarians believe to be their interests? Or does it mean what the Marxist élite claims to be the 'real' interests of the proletariat, irrespective of what proletarians happen to consider their interests? Plekhanov was, of course, well aware that many workers wanted primarily improvements in their working and living conditions, tangible benefits, caring little about socialism. But he thought that, providing the workers were not led astray by people like Eduard Bernstein, the Marxist élite could educate the working class to a consciousness of its real mission. The first main step was the overthrow of the autocracy and the establishment of political democracy, the freedoms and rights of citizens being guaranteed by the constitution. In bringing about this change socialists could and should cooperate with liberals. Once political democracy was established, the proletariat could be educated to see the opposition between its interests and those of the bourgeoisie. When the proletariat had grown in numbers and constituted the bulk or a great part of the population, it, as the new and vigorous and self-confident class, would assume power, bringing about the transition from bourgeois to socialist democracy. In so far as one could speak of a 'dictatorship', it would be a dictatorship *of* the proletariat, but for the benefit of society as a whole. The freedoms of political democracy would not be simply negated but preserved, in a more advanced form of social organization.

According to this scheme, however, there might be a prolonged period of bourgeois, political democracy.[1] If during this period the workers were to make successive demands and succeed in obtaining what they wanted, was it not possible, or even probable, that they would progressively adopt a bourgeois mentality, a pragmatic attitude, paying little attention to what Marxist theorists said about their 'real' interests? The transition to socialism might be postponed for a long time. It might even never occur. Though Lenin naturally paid lip service to the doctrine that the proletariat was a revolutionary class, he was under no illusion in regard to the attitude of most workers, when left to themselves. As for the peasants, he thought of them as people who wanted only land. They would doubtless be prepared to destroy the landowners in order to obtain their land. But, as a body, they had no interest at all in socialism. In practice the revolution must be carried through by a revolutionary élite, able to see and make use of circumstances, which gave the revolutionaries a real chance of success.

This, of course, would mean not the dictatorship *of* the proletariat (except in words) but a dictatorship *over* the proletariat, and everyone else as well. The leaders, as the Populist Tkachev had envisaged, would mould society in the name of the interests of the people, whatever members of the people believed to be their interests. This is what Plekhanov feared would happen, if Bolshevik policy prevailed and was successful. Though he opposed this policy, he himself had provided a point of departure for it by emphasizing the role of the Marxist élite. To be sure, he thought of the élite as educating the proletariat, not as tyrannizing over it, and of the assumption of power by the proletariat as a class, exercising the power through elected representatives. As one writer has put it, 'Plekhanov believed that he had overcome the dichotomy between economic determinism and socialist impatience'.[2] The laws of history must be respected, but the period of bourgeois democracy in Russia could be short. The representatives of the proletariat should cooperate

1 Plekhanov held out hopes, at one time at any rate, that a socialist revolution in Russia might follow very shortly after a political revolution against the autocracy. This did not prevent him from later condemning Lenin's telescoping of the two revolutions as premature.
2 *Vladimir Akimov on the Dilemmas of Russian Marxism, 1895–1903*, edited and introduced by Jonathan Frankel, p. 11 (Cambridge University Press, 1969).

with the bourgeois liberals in obtaining political freedom, but they should also make clear to the proletariat the basic antagonism between its interests and those of the bourgeois. Plekhanov believed that he had effected a dialectical reconciliation of such different ideas, determinism and activism, cooperation with and opposition to. But it is not surprising if elements which he had joined together became separated and took the form of opposed policies, his own on the one hand and that of Lenin and the Bolsheviks on the other.

Plekhanov died at the end of May 1918. In January the Constituent Assembly had been summoned and then dissolved by Lenin, when it was clear that the majority of votes were not for the Bolsheviks but for the programme of the Socialist Revolutionaries. Russia was subjected to a dictatorship. The Bolsheviks triumphed, as far as power was concerned. But Plekhanov triumphed in the sense that his worst forebodings proved to be justified. If he had lived longer, he would have been faced with a choice. He could have retired into exile and denounced the régime in Russia as a perversion of Marxism. Or, conceivably, he might have abandoned Marxism, as he had once abandoned Populism. To the present writer it seems difficult to suppose that Plekhanov would have given his blessing to the Bolshevik dictatorship, as it actually developed.

Chapter 11

Marxism in Imperial Russia (2). Lenin

1. In the conclusion to the second edition (1905) of his work *A Short History of the Social Democratic Movement in Russia* Vladimir Akimov[1], a leading representative of the so-called 'Economist' group in the Russian Social Democratic Party[2], wrote as follows: 'The orthodox regards all attempts at critical thinking, from Bernstein to Bogdanov, as mere varieties of revisionism. That is why every thinking member of the Party suffocates in the atmosphere of the orthodox Social Democratic church'.[3] One may well sympathize with Akimov's protest against the 'scholastic, doctrinaire vulgarization of Marxism which is served up to us under the title of orthodoxy'[4] and with the policy of trying to stifle critical thought. At the same time it is certainly not unreasonable to describe Bogdanov as a revisionist, as far as philosophy is concerned, and we can do this without using the adjective as a term of opprobrium.

Alexander Bogdanov (1873–1928), whose real name was Malinovsky, studied at the University of Kharkov and graduated from the medical department. An adherent of Populism for a time, he joined the Social Democrats in 1896. In 1903 he sided with Lenin and the Bolsheviks.

---

1 Akimov's real name was Makhnovets. A Social Democrat, he took seriously the idea of democracy. That is to say, he believed that the Marxist élite should be at the service of the proletariat, helping the working class to obtain desired benefits, such as reduction of working hours and higher wages, and also political freedoms, besides assisting the workers to form their own democratically run organizations. He had no sympathy with dictatorial ambitions on the part of the leaders of the Social Democratic Party. From 1907 he collaborated, apart from a period when he was in exile, with the workers' cooperative movement. He died in obscurity in Russia in 1921.

2 The so-called 'Economists' were accused by their critics of seeking only economic benefits for the workers, neglecting political struggle and class war. Akimov denied the charge of being indifferent to political struggle. He believed that socialists should cooperate with liberals in securing political reform. As an opponent of Lenin's policy at the 1903 congress, he naturally incurred the hostility of the Bolshevik leader.

3 *Vladimir Akimov*, edited by J. Frankel, p. 361. (See Note 89 to Chapter 9.) The first version of Akimov's *Short History* appeared at Geneva in 1904, the second edition at St Petersburg in 1905.

4 *Ibid.*

Indeed, he stood very much to the left. When the Third Duma was convened in 1907, he advocated that it should be boycotted by the Social Democrats, and in the following year he joined in a protest against Bolsheviks collaborating in the work of any legal body. In 1909 he was expelled from the Party for 'factional activity', as the Great Soviet Encyclopedia puts it.[1] After the revolution he lectured at the University of Moscow on economics, a subject on which he had written several works, but from 1921 he devoted himself to medical studies and research, especially in the field of haematology. He founded and directed the Moscow Institute of Blood Transfusion.

Bogdanov's general thesis was that the philosophy of the proletariat, as he called Marxism, needed further elaboration and development, partly because Marx and Engels had not developed it fully, partly because philosophical thought ought to take into account recent scientific discoveries and theories. In 1899 he published *The Fundamental Elements of the Historical Outlook on Nature* and in 1901 *Cognition from the Historical Viewpoint*. Starting from a position more or less in accordance with 'orthodox' Marxist materialism, he came to be attracted and influenced by the 'energeticism' of Wilhelm Ostwald (1853–1932). For Ostwald, energy was the one basic reality which, in a process of transformations, assumed various forms, including psychic energy, both unconscious and conscious. This was a monistic philosophy, but from Ostwald's form of monism Bogdanov moved towards the empiriomonism or empiriocriticism of Avenarius and Mach, according to which the sole adequate basis or source of knowledge, both prescientific and scientific, is constituted by 'pure experience', which Mach conceived as reducible to sensations. The three books of his *Empirio-Monism* appeared in 1904–06.

In the light of empiriomonism Bogdanov launched an attack on Plekhanov's conception of matter as a metaphenomenal reality, lying beyond the sphere of experience but causing our sensations. This idea, Bogdanov argued, was philosophically indefensible in itself, and it did not represent what Marx and Engels understood when they talked about the priority of matter. To explain sensation as the effect of the activity of a metaphenomenal reality, equivalent to the Kantian thing in itself (*Ding an sich*), was to commit the cardinal sin of 'metaphysicians', explaining the known in terms of the unknown, the experienced in terms of the non-experienced. Again, if Plekhanov wished to re-introduce the Kantian thing in itself, he should not have described it as a cause of our sensations. For the idea of causality is derived from experience and cannot be applied to what is supposed to be beyond experience. Conversely, if Plekhanov conceived matter as the cause of our sensations, he should not have represented matter as lying beyond experience. The idea of matter as a metaphenomenal reality was incompatible with describing it as a cause. As for Marx and Engels, when they spoke about matter, they had in mind not a metaphenomenal reality, a Kantian thing in itself, but matter as known in ordinary experience and by scientific investigation. In other words, Plekhanov had no justification for representing his theory of matter as orthodox Marxism.

Short of denying the existence of matter altogether, the alternative to Plekhanov's theory of a metaphenomenal reality was obviously to conceive matter as phenomenal, as lying within the sphere of experience. As, for the Marxist, matter is the basic reality, this means that all reality falls within the sphere of experience, actual or possible. In fact, we can say that reality is experience. If, therefore, we accept the empiriomonism of Avenarius and Mach, it follows that reality is reducible to sensations, inasmuch as, according to empiriomonism, sensations are the ultimate data or elements of experience.

If, however, we assume that the ultimate elements of experience are sensations, it is obvious that what we ordinarily think of as the world of experience would not have arisen without a process of organization. According to Bogdanov, what we regard as the material world, nature, the common world, is the product of collectively organized experience, having a social basis. That is to say, the common world as experienced has been progressively formed in the course of human history out of the raw material of sensation. In addition, however, to the world which is basically the same for all, there are, so to speak, private worlds. That is to say, in addition to collectively organized experience there is organization in the form of ideas or concepts which differ from person to person or from group to group. There are different points of view, different theories, different ideologies. By emphasizing the priority of collectively organized experience Bogdanov thought that he had allowed for the Marxist claim that matter is prior to mind and that he had made room for the distinction between the economic substructure and the ideological superstructure. In other words, he believed that empiriomonism and the materialist conception of history were compatible.

We have been speaking of organization resulting in the world of physical objects, the common world, and, secondarily, the world of ideas. As a Marxist, however, Bogdanov did not forget the practical orientation of the activity of organization. Having tried to adapt the empiriomonism of Mach for use within Marxism, presenting it as a development of Marxist theory, he went on to outline a science of organization as such, which he called 'Tectology', emphasizing its practical aspect, its function of changing the world. Just as the scientific organization of experience develops, so does the social organization of experience; and social consciousness, that of the working class for example, is oriented to practice, to action.

Bogdanov's adoption of empiriomonism naturally affects his view of truth. Truth becomes a feature of the process of organizing experience. If it is claimed, for example, that a scientific hypothesis is true, this should be understood as meaning that the hypothesis in question is the most coherent and economical way of organizing the relevant phenomena, which has been found up-to-date. But a more intellectually satisfactory hypothesis may be found in the future. For Bogdanov, however, matter was not a Kantian thing in itself but that which scientific investigation reveals it to be. The scientific view of matter, however, is not something fixed once and for all. It undergoes development. In other words, there is no absolute truth. But it does not follow that there is no criterion of truth, simply because truth is relative. Coherence, for example, is a criterion.

It hardly needs saying that empiriomonism laid itself open to the accusation by Marxist critics that, so far from being a development of Marxist materialism, it was clearly an idealist philosophy, inasmuch as reality was reduced to sensations. Lenin himself expressed objections to empiriomonism in his book on the subject. In general, he regarded the philosophy of Avenarius and Mach and their followers as a regression to the thought of Hume, the 'sensations' of Avenarius and Mach being equivalent to Hume's impressions. For the Marxist, Lenin insisted, there is an objective order of things, presupposed by and independent of human consciousness. In the philosophy of Bogdanov, according to Lenin, there was no such objective order. And he made fun, for example, of Bogdanov's assertion that 'society is inseparable from consciousness. Social being and social consciousness are, in the exact meaning of these terms, identical'.[1] Social consciousness, Lenin insisted, presupposes objective conditions, and it is not identical with them. The objective conditions can be understood or misunderstood, but being, for the Marxist, is prior to consciousness, the objective to the subjective, whereas Bogdanov, following Mach, reduced reality to the subjective, namely to sensations. Plekhanov at any rate did not do this, however much one may object to his idea of matter as metaphenomenal.

1 From the Psychology of Society, p. 51 (St Petersburg, 1904).

Marxist criticism of other philosophies, it may be said, tends to take the form of pointing out where they differ from orthodox Marxism and concluding that they must be wrong in so far as they are different. But one does not have to be a Marxist, of course, in order to recognize that empiriocriticism gives rise to a number of problems. For example, if we assume that the world existed before human beings, and indeed before any sensing beings, how can we maintain that reality is reducible to sensations? We can introduce the idea of potential sense-data, sensibilia, but it is arguable that this concept is really fatal to the reduction of reality to experience and of experience to sensations. Again, the question arises, who or what performs the activity of organizing sensations? Can the active subject be itself reduced to sensations? If so, we seem to be left with the very odd idea of sensations organizing themselves. If not, we can hardly be justified in claiming that reality is reducible to sensations. Such objections are not, of course, new. But this does not show that they can be satisfactorily met within the framework of empiriomonism.

Marxist critics have accused Bogdanov not only of idealism but also of what is called 'mechanism'. This second accusation refers to his concept of dialectical development. He conceived organization as proceeding until a state of equilibrium is attained between the various factors involved. This equilibrium can be, and is, disturbed by external factors. The process of organization then begins again, until a new equilibrium is attained, which is disturbed in its turn. The conflict of opposites thus occurs *between* entities (an entity being a product of organization), not *in* entities. The Marxist objection is that the true concept of dialectic, as conceived by Hegel and then interpreted by Marx in a materialist context, is that of an immanent dialectic, of a conflict of opposites within a given entity. In a given society, for example, there is an internal conflict of opposites, the class struggle. It is not simply a case of conflict between different societies. The dialectical movement as conceived by Bogdanov and those who adopted the same point of view was analogous to the idea of the transmission of motion or energy from body to body in the mechanistic theory of the world, whereas for the Marxist the dialectic expresses the autodynamism of matter. It is the Marxist concept which is in accordance with modern science.

The question whether the dialectic should be conceived as occurring *between* or *among* things or whether it should be conceived as immanent in things themselves, constituting, so to speak, the inner life of an entity, may seem to be a matter of purely academic interest, and then only for those who are prepared to postulate a dialectical movement apart from the movement of thought. But for the orthodox Marxist this is not the case. For the materialist conception of history is bound up with the idea of a dialectical movement which operates not only between organized wholes but also within them. Capitalist society, for example, generates its opposite, the proletariat; it gives rise to what is destined to negate it. For an orthodox Marxist, an understanding of the dialectic is essential for understanding the movement of history and is a condition for intelligent and successful revolutionary action.

Bogdanov can be described as the leading Russian adherent of empiriomonism, but he was not the only one. There were also, for example, V. Bazarov, A. V. Lunacharsky, and P. Yushkevich. They were all attacked by Lenin on the ground that, while claiming to be Marxists, they were really idealists, who had abandoned materialism and reopened the way to religion. Criticism of Bogdanov's theory of the dialectic as adopted by Nikolai Bukharin came rather later, 'Mechanism' being finally condemned by the Party in 1931.

2. Vladimir Ilyich Ulyanov, commonly known as Lenin[1], was born at Simbirsk on 10 April 1870. His father was an inspector of schools, a conscientious and highly competent civil servant, who had attained the grade in government service which made him an 'hereditary nobleman'. On his father's side Lenin was, partly at any rate, of Kalmuck origin, while through his mother he had Germanic ancestry. Obviously, there is nothing in the least discreditable in this. But it means that those who wish to represent the founder of the Soviet Union as a pure Russian have to pass over some awkward facts in silence.

Family life in the Ulyanov household was a happy one. Lenin ('Volodya' to the family) attended school in Simbirsk and was an industrious and bright pupil, though inclined to be unruly and impertinent on occasion. None of the family were revolutionaries before the death of Lenin's father in 1886. It was very shortly after this event that Lenin embraced atheism and that his elder brother Alexander, who had had a considerable influence on Vladimir and who was then a student at the University of St Petersburg, became associated with a group of young revolutionaries. Alexander had read Marx's *Capital*, and it is related that he agreed with the programme of Plekhanov's Liberation of Labour group. Although he was attracted by Marxism, however, the group with which he became associated belonged to the People's Will, the terrorist offspring of the Populist movement. The group planned the assassination

---

1 Vladimir Ulyanov wrote under a number of pseudonyms. V. Lenin was one of them and became the name by which he is universally known.

of Tsar Alexander III, but the members were arrested before they could carry out their project. At his trial Alexander Ulyanov, so far from denying guilt or even trying to diminish his responsibility, calmly defended the policy of terrorism with reasoned arguments. Condemned to death, he was hanged on 8 May 1887, soon after his twenty-first birthday.

It is not clear precisely what effect Alexander's death had on his young brother Vladimir. As he graduated with distinction from his school at Simbirsk and entered the University of Kazan in December 1887, some biographers are unwilling to assert any causal connection between Alexander's execution and Vladimir's turning to the life of a revolutionary activist. But his brother's death can hardly have failed to make a deep impression on his mind. In any case Lenin had not been long at Kazan before participation in a student demonstration led to his expulsion from the university. While living with his mother and family in the province of Samara, Lenin studied law, and in 1892 he was admitted to the bar as a lawyer, after having passed the necessary examinations.

Lenin apparently felt some initial attraction towards the People's Will group, but by the time that he moved to St Petersburg in August 1893 he was a convinced Marxist. There then began his life as a revolutionary activist, punctuated by periods abroad and by spells of imprisonment or Siberian exile, a life which culminated in the Bolshevik seizure of power in 1917. It was a life of unremitting activity of various kinds. When arrested at the end of 1895 and sent to prison for his illegal political activities, he at once started work on his book *The Development of Capitalism in Russia*.[1] After a year in prison he was exiled to Siberia, where he continued work on his book. It was in Siberia that he formally married Nadezhda K. Krupskaya, and together they translated into Russian *The History of Trade Unionism* by Sidney and Beatrice Webb. During his exile Lenin was able to receive letters, periodicals and books and to correspond with fellow Marxists, both in Russia and abroad. He pursued his studies of foreign languages and, at the appropriate seasons, swam, skated and hunted.[2]

Released from Siberian exile early in 1900, Lenin soon afterwards

1 The work appeared at St Petersburg in 1899.
2 It is worth noticing the remarkable difference between the treatment of political offenders during the last decades of the autocracy and their treatment under the Tsar's successors, especially, of course, under Joseph Stalin. The Tsarist authorities could indeed be ruthless, as in the case of Alexander Ulyanov. But Alexander was able to speak in defence of terrorism in open court. He was not forced to 'confess'. In any case the facilities granted to political prisoners and exiles in the last period of the autocracy were far from being granted to political prisoners in the prisons and labour camps run by the Soviet régime.

went abroad, and, together with Plekhanov and others, began publication of *Iskra* (*The Spark*), which was mainly intended for clandestine importation into Russia. Besides being an indefatigable writer, Lenin was busy trying to guide the Russian Social Democratic Party along the path which he believed to be the right one; and the victory of his policy at the 1903 Congress produced the split between Bolsheviks and Mensheviks. The Menshevik members of the editorial board of Iskra, with the exception of Martov, were discarded. When Plekhanov insisted on bringing them back, Lenin resigned and edited *Vperyod* (*Forward*) from Geneva. Later he started a new Party organ, *Proletarii* (*The Proletarian*).

One day in 1902 a young man named Lev Davidovich Bronstein, commonly known as Trotsky, presented himself at Lenin's door in London. Having embraced Marxism, Trotsky sent contributions to *Iskra* from his Siberian exile. Escaping from Russia, he made his way to England and joined Lenin. At the 1903 Congress Trotsky opposed Lenin and supported the Mensheviks. Early in 1905 he returned to Russia and became head of the St Petersburg Soviet. He was destined to play an important role in the civil war, on the Bolshevik side.

Needless to say, Lenin's hopes and expectations were aroused by the revolutionary movements in Russia in 1905. He called for the formation of revolutionary squads, peasant uprisings, the overthrow of the autocracy, the establishment of a provisional government, and convocation of a Constituent Assembly. He did not envisage government simply by the Bolsheviks as an immediate prospect, but he got as far as imagining a revolutionary 'dictatorship' of the proletariat and the peasantry. It was characteristic of Lenin to think in terms of dictatorship, though what he promised was complete democratic freedom. As for the peasants, Lenin regarded them as a reactionary class, but he saw, of course, what they really wanted and he hoped that they could be roused to action by promises of support in seizing land from the landowners.

In November 1905 Lenin travelled from Switzerland to St Petersburg, but he saw at once that things had not worked out as he wished. In 1906–7 he flitted between Finland and Russia, while also attending Bolshevik congresses in Stockholm, London and Stuttgart. Towards the end of 1907 he left Russia and did not return until April 1917, when the Germans facilitated his journey from Switzerland to Stockholm, whence he travelled to Petrograd. In the intervening years Lenin had been busy trying to make his position prevail in the Russian Social Democratic Party. In 1910 the Central Committee met in Paris with the aim of restoring unity. As Lenin was not prepared to compromise, the meeting was not a success. In 1912 he convened a conference of Bolsheviks at

Prague. Its members declared that they alone represented the Party and elected a Central Committee. But though Lenin moved to Cracow, and was thus geographically nearer to Russia than he was in Switzerland, he could do little to determine the course of events in his own country. When he arrived in Petrograd, his Bolsheviks constituted a tiny minority among the revolutionary groups, and even they were divided in their opinions about the best policy to pursue. Within a few months, however, Lenin had become master of Russia and had won for himself a place in history.

3. Lenin was a highly educated man, and during his years as a revolutionary activist he poured out a stream of articles, pamphlets and books. But though he can be described as an intellectual of bourgeois origins, he was far too much of an activist to have much sympathy for 'intellectuals', looking on them as ineffective talkers. He even referred to them as 'swine' and 'petty-bourgeois filth', a way of speaking which did not commend itself to his friend Maxim Gorky, the famous novelist. In particular, Lenin was not by temperament a philosopher. When he made excursions into philosophy, it was to defend what he regarded as orthodox Marxism, orthodox theory being required for right practice. Thus it was that he regarded Bogdanov, Lunacharsky and other Russian 'Machists', as he described them, as misguided and dangerous thinkers who might destroy Russian Social Democracy, if their theories were left uncombatted. His own attack on empiriomonism was motivated not by any lively interest in philosophical problems for their own sake but by a determination to preserve Marxist materialism intact, to defend the 'faith', so to speak, of a true revolutionary as conceived by himself. He was not prepared to consider the possibility that the philosophical ideas of the Machists might be correct. If their ideas smacked of idealism, they must be wrong.

In order to refute the Machists Lenin had to study the relevant material, and with this purpose in mind he took refuge from interruption in the British Museum Library. The result of his study and reflection was *Materialism and Empirio-Criticism, Critical Comments on a Reactionary Philosophy*, a work which appeared in 1909 under the pseudonym of V. Ilin. In it Lenin refers not only to Avenarius and Mach and their Russian admirers, 'Bazarov, Bogdanov, Yushkevich, Valentinov, Chernov and other Machians'[1] but also to a considerable number of

---

1 *Materialism and Empirio-Criticism. Critical Comments on a Reactionary Philosophy*, p. 13, translated by A. Fineberg (London, 1948).

other philosophers, such as Berkeley, Hume and Kant, Wundt, Karl Pearson, T. H. Huxley, Henri Poincaré, Pierre Duhem, Abel Rey, Charles Renouvier, James Ward and William James. The author does, of course, argue against empiriomonism or empiriocriticism, as he calls it, but his thought would be easier to follow if he had been somewhat more sparing in his references to and quotations from a multiplicity of writers representing a wide variety of views. However, nobody can accuse Lenin of not being forthright in expressing his opinions.

One of Lenin's main theses is that empiriocriticism is simply a revival of the thought of Berkeley and Hume. Apart from the self and God, Berkeley reduced the world to 'ideas', while Hume reduced both selves and things to 'impressions'. Avenarius and Mach reduce reality to 'sensations'. They all belong to the same family, the idealist family. Obviously, this fact does not, by itself, prove that empiriocriticism is false. But this philosophy is at variance with the standpoint of modern science, whereas Marxism is in accordance with it. Bogdanov, for example, criticized Plekhanov's theory of matter as a metaphenomenal reality, a Kantian thing in itself. The criticism is justified. But then Mach and his followers go backwards in time to subjective idealism instead of going onwards with orthodox Marxism which, while agreeing with Kant that there is a reality existing independently of human consciousness, regard it as phenomenal, as revealing itself in scientific investigation. It is true that some modern physicists have strayed into idealism, but this is due to the fact that 'the physicists did not know dialectics'.[1] 'Dialectical materialism insists on the approximate relative character of every scientific theory of the structure of matter and its properties; it insists on the absence of absolute boundaries in nature, on the transformation of moving matter from one state into another, which is to us apparently irreconcilable with it, and so forth'[2]. The Marxist is not surprised by, for example, the theory of electrons. He does not regard it as incompatible with materialism. On the contrary, he sees in modern scientific theories 'another *corroboration* of dialectical materialism'.[3] The Machists, however, try to use modern physics in support of idealism. And if some physicists encourage them in this endeavour, this is because, while good physicists, they are bad philosophers.

Natural science, Lenin insists, tells us that the earth once existed in such a state that no human being, and indeed no organic life, could be present on it. We can take this as an established fact. But it is obviously

1 *Ibid.*, p. 268.
2 *Ibid.*
3 *Ibid.*

incompatible with the reduction of reality to human experience, in particular to sensations. To be sure, the empirio-critics were aware of the difficulty and tried to cope with it. Thus Avenarius introduced the idea of potential sensations. Physical things existing before human beings were potential sensations (*sensibilia*, that is to say). Lenin dismisses this line of thought in a summary manner, as he dismisses the argument that man can conceive the world as existing before himself only by 'introjecting' himself into the picture as subject, as one term of a correlation. 'How can one seriously speak of a co-ordination, the indissolubility of which consists in one of its terms being potential?'[1] That is to say, it is absurd to speak of the world as being necessarily related to a subject which does not yet exist but is only potential. One might just as well speak of the world, when human beings have ceased to exist, as having reality only in relation to a subject who did exist but no longer exists. The arguments of the empirio-critics are nothing but vain attempts to cover up insoluble objections with 'erudite philosophical gibberish'.[2]

What Avenarius and Mach are really asserting is subjective idealism. The world is reducible to my sense-impressions. It is all very well to talk about 'our' sensations, the sensations of human beings in general. The logical conclusion to be drawn from empiriocriticism is solipsism, 'recognition of the existence of the philosophizing individual only'.[3] 'Solipsism is Mach's fundamental error'[4], and solipsism is absurd. Nobody really believes it. And a philosophy which leads inevitably to a solipsistic conclusion is untenable.

Belief in the existence of a material world independently of consciousness involves, for Lenin, belief in the objectivity of space and time. When Mach says that space and time are well-ordered systems of series of sensations, 'this is palpable idealist nonsense'.[5] It follows, indeed, from the theory that bodies are complexes of sensations, but this theory is itself idealist nonsense. It is true that man's ideas of space and time change and develop. But this fact does not prove the subjectivity of space and time, as the Machists claim. Our relative concepts of space and time, 'in their development, move towards absolute truth and approach nearer and nearer to it'.[6] The fact that scientists' concepts of the structure of matter undergo change does not show that there is no material world existing independently of consciousness. It shows simply that our knowledge of

1 *Ibid.*, p. 70.
2 *Ibid.*, p. 89.
3 *Ibid.*, p. 90.
4 *Ibid.*, p. 93.
5 *Ibid.*, p. 179.
6 *Ibid.*, p. 177.

this world can increase. Similarly, our developing concepts of space and time reflect objective space and time 'ever more correctly and profoundly'.[1]

Lenin certainly draws attention to some real problems which arise if reality is regarded as ultimately reducible to sensations or to sense-impressions. In order to avoid subjective idealism and ultimately solipsism, concepts have to be introduced (such as that of 'sensibles', *sensibilia*) which may well seem to demand a revision of the original theory of reducibility. In the more sophisticated recent theory of sense-data, recourse was had to the idea of distinct and alternative languages, that of physical objects and that of sense-data, two languages which should not be confused, which one should not try to use at the same time. As, however, all students of modern philosophy are aware, the sense-datum theory has been subjected to trenchant criticism by philosophers who certainly had no Marxist axe to grind.

Though, however, Lenin undoubtedly raises some real objections to empiriocriticism, he is not really much interested in philosophical discussion for its own sake. One main ground of his hostility to the Machians is his conviction that they are idealists, and that idealism opens the way to religion. He draws attention to the fact that Berkeley used idealism in support of theism. To be sure, the Russian Machians are not Christian apologists in the sense in which Bishop Berkeley was. 'Bogdanov emphatically repudiates all religion.'[2] But this does not alter the fact that, if Machism is to escape from the absurdity of solipsism, it must proceed along the road traversed by Berkeley. In any case Machism opens the way to 'fideism'. According to Bogdanov, nature is the product of the experience of living beings. But so is God. 'God is undoubtedly a product of the socially-organized experience of living beings.'[3] If, therefore, nature is recognized, why not God? The only philosophy which effectively bars the way to religious belief is dialectical materialism, a philosophy which the Russian Machians reject, in spite of the fact that they call themselves Marxists.

Another main reason for Lenin's hostility to the philosophy of the Machists is his conviction that it is destructive of historical materialism and Marxist sociology. Marx calls on us to understand the objective course of economic development so that we may adapt our social consciousness to the objective situation. For example, the proletariat is in an objective situation, existing independently of consciousness. The task of

1 *Ibid.*, p. 189.
2 *Ibid.*, p. 233.
3 *Ibid.*, p. 234.

the Marxist activist is to educate the proletariat to consciousness of this situation and of its real interests, as a condition of changing the situation. In other words, the doctrine of Marx is that 'social consciousness *reflects* social being'[1], thus presupposing it. According to Bogdanov, however, social consciousness and social being are the same. There is no social being apart from social consciousness. To maintain this view is to deprive revolutionary Marxism of an essential feature, the distinction between the objective state of affairs and its reflection in consciousness, a reflection which can be distorted or faithful. And it is impossible to eliminate an essential feature or part of Marxism without relapsing into 'bourgeois-reactionary falsehood'.[2] There can be no Marxist social science, unless there is an objective reality of which it is a science. Machian idealism does away with this objective reality, presupposed by and distinct from consciousness, and thus knocks the bottom out of social science. True, Bogdanov claims to be a Marxist. But the fact is that he is a Marxist only when his thought has been purified from Machism.[3]

Obviously, these 'main reasons' are the expression of Lenin's firm conviction that Marxism, considered as theory oriented to practice, is the true philosophy. Indeed, in the conclusion to his work he says that to form a judgment about empiriocriticism the Marxist must first and foremost compare its theoretical foundations with those of dialectical materialism. This comparison will reveal 'the thoroughly reactionary character of empiriocriticism'.[4] 'The objective, class role played by empiriocriticism consists entirely in rendering faithful service to the fideists in their struggle against materialism in general and historical materialism in particular'.[5] The book as a whole reads much more like an impassioned assertion of the truth of Marxism than an open-minded examination of empiriocriticism.

There is an amusing review of Lenin's work by the Marxist writer Lyuba Isaakovna Akselrod (1868–1946), a lady who used the pen-name Ortodoks.[6] The review appeared in 1909, the year of the book's publication. While agreeing with Lenin's general theses, the reviewer maintained that the Bolshevik leader showed no flexibility of philosophical thought, no preciseness in definition, and no deep understanding of

1 *Ibid.*, p. 335.
2 *Ibid.*, p. 338.
3 *Ibid.*, p. 336.
4 *Ibid.*, p. 370.
5 *Ibid.*, p. 371.
6 L. Akselrod was opposed to the Machian revisionists. In 1903 she sided with the Menshevik faction. The review in question appeared in *The Contemporary World*. A translation is printed in *Russian Philosophy*, vol. 3, pp. 457–63.

philosophical problems. Lenin had misunderstood and misrepresented Plekhanov, while the chapters devoted to analysis of the causal relation and to the relation between freedom and necessity could not stand up under criticism. Further, Lenin's polemical style was marred by a coarseness and abuse which were intolerable in a philosophical work. However, the book was lively and fresh and had the merit of being a passionate defence of truth.

Akselrod-Ortodoks[1] supported Plekhanov's epistemology against Lenin's, which she considered an expression of naïve realism. A good deal of the criticism which she made of Lenin's book was doubtless justified, but it must be remembered that Lenin was an extremely busy activist, and that his main concern in writing the book was to preserve what he regarded as Marxist orthodoxy, not to discuss philosophical issues as open questions. In his opinion, while the professors of economics were, in general, simply 'learned salesmen of the capitalist class', the professors of philosophy (also 'taken as a whole') were the 'learned salesmen of the theologians'.[2] And he doubtless thought that phrases such as 'philosophical blockheads' were appropriate descriptive epithets, even if Lyubov Akselrod thought otherwise.

It should be added that Lenin's polemical and abusive way of writing was directed primarily against ideas of which he disapproved. Though he ridiculed, for example, Bazarov and Lunacharsky, this did not prevent Bazarov from being given a post in the Soviet Gosplan or Planning Commission, while Lunacharsky was appointed Soviet Commissar for Education. As for Bogdanov, though he retired from politics after the Revolution, he pursued medical researches, as has already been mentioned, until he eventually died as a result of one of his own experiments. Lenin could be ruthless, subordinating friendship and personal relations to the revolutionary cause. When he was in power, he could, and did, encourage the use of terror, when he thought it expedient. He was determined to preserve an effective monopoly of power in the hands of the Bolshevik leadership, and he was strongly opposed to 'factionalism' in the Party, to the emergence, that is to say, of organized opposition groups, as distinct from the expression of different points of view by individuals. But he was certainly not the man to liquidate Marxist colleagues simply because they had ventured to express philosophical ideas different from his own.

---

1 This is one way of distinguishing L. Akselrod from the P. B. Akselrod who was an associate of Plekhanov at Geneva.
2 *Materialism and Empirio-Criticism*, p. 356.

4. When Lenin attacked empiriocriticism not only as an idealist deviation from Marxist materialism but also as reactionary, what he had in mind was, of course, dialectical materialism rather than materialism in general. As a revolutionary activist, interested in the class struggle and in intensifying it, he laid particular emphasis on the dialectical aspect of Marxism, inasmuch as the class struggle and revolution were, for him, expressions of the dialectical movement of self-developing matter in the social sphere. This emphasis on the idea of dialectical movement shows itself clearly in his *Philosophical Notebooks*, especially in his notes on the logic of Hegel.

The *Notebooks* were not composed as a book. Nor were they published by Lenin. They appeared first in 1929–30, in a collection of his writings, and in 1933 they were printed as a separate volume. In his *Works (Sochineniya)* they form volume 38.[1] They consist of a variety of notes, jottings, remarks made by Lenin in connection with his philosophical reading from 1895 onwards, the bulk of the matter belonging to the years 1914–16, when he was living in Switzerland. While hoping for the outbreak of revolution in Russia and elsewhere, he read widely, paying special attention to Hegel's work *The Science of Logic*.

In the nineties Lenin had tried to dissociate Marxism from Hegelianism as much as possible. By the time he came to write his notes on Hegel's logic his attitude had changed to such an extent that he was able to say, in his often-quoted 'aphorism', that 'it is impossible fully to understand Marx's *Capital*, and especially its first chapter, without having studied and understood *the whole* of Hegel's *Logic*. Consequently, half a century later none of the Marxists understood Marx'.[2] The reason why Hegel's logical theory is so important is that 'the last word and essence of the logic of Hegel is the *dialectical method*'.[3] An understanding of this method is the chief feature which marks off dialectical from non-dialectical materialism[4]. And as the method was taken over by Marx from Hegel, we can say that 'intelligent idealism is closer to intelligent materialism than is stupid materialism'.[5]

Dialectics is described by Lenin as 'the doctrine which shows how *opposites* can be and are (how they become) *identical* – under what conditions they are identical, becoming changed into one another – why the human mind should conceive these opposites not as dead, frozen, but

1 Fourth Russian edition, Moscow, 1958; English translation, Moscow, 1961.
2 *Works*, XXXVIII, p. 171.
3 *Ibid.*, p. 227.
4 This was, as we have seen, a thesis maintained by Plekhanov.
5 *Works*, XXXVIII, 271.

rather as living, conditional, active, transforming themselves into one another. *En lisant Hegel'* (*sic*)[1]. The last phrase ('in reading Hegel') reminds us that Lenin's description of dialectics, in terms of the movement of concepts, is given in the context of a study of Hegel's logic. Lenin refers to Hegel's well-known argument that the concept of Being passes into that of Not-Being and *vice-versa*, this process generating the concept of Becoming.[2] The process of negation is a movement of creative life; something new is born, preserving and at the same time transcending the opposites. The transformation of quantity into quality is an example of this process. The dialectical movement does not, of course, stop with the generation of a given concept through the process of negation. For the generated concept discloses to thought opposition within itself. Further, within the continuous movement of concepts already negated concepts apparently recur, but they 'recur' at a higher level, to be negated in their turn. We thus have a process of negation and of negation of negation.

Lenin was far from denying that there is a dialectical movement of thought, in the sphere of concepts that is to say. On the contrary, he affirmed it and gave Hegel full marks for developing this idea. Further, he was impressed, as he might well be, by the way in which Hegel explored the dialectical movement in a variety of concrete spheres, such as human history. At the same time he believed that Hegel needed to be set firmly on his feet, instead of standing on his head, and that Marx and Engels had achieved this. That is to say, Hegel believed that the dialectical movement in, say, social development reflected the movement of pure thought as depicted in *The Science of Logic*, whereas it was really a matter of the dialectic in things, in concrete reality, being reflected in thought, in the movement of concepts. 'In the proper sense dialectics is the study of contradiction *in the very essence of objects*.'[3] It is this dialectical movement in things which is reflected in the dialectic of concepts, of thought, not the other way round. In other words, to set Hegel on his feet idealism has to be transformed into materialism. 'I am in general trying to read Hegel in a materialistic sense.'[4] Hegel, according to Lenin, was perfectly justified in eliminating the Kantian thing in itself. 'Kant belittles knowledge in order to make room for faith: Hegel exalts knowledge, asserting that knowledge is knowledge of God. The

1 *Ibid.*, pp. 97–8.
2 With Lenin, as with Hegel, opposition can sometimes mean contradiction (as in the case of Being and Not-Being), while at other times it is a question of contraries.
3 *Works*, XXXVIII, p. 249. Lenin accepted the thesis of Engels on this matter.
4 *Ibid.*, p. 92.

materialist exalts the knowledge of matter, nature, consigning God and the riff-raff which defends God to the rubbish pit'[1].

We are told by Lenin that 'the supporter of dialectic, Hegel, was unable to understand the *dialectical* transition *from* matter *to* motion, *from* matter *to* consciousness – especially the second. Marx corrected the mystic's mistake (or weakness?). It is not only the transition from matter to consciousness which is dialectical but also that from sensation to thought, etc.'.[2] Obviously, Lenin is not accusing Hegel of failing to understand dialectical movement as such. It is Hegel's idealism to which he objects, Hegel's failure to understand the primacy of matter. When Lenin notes that according to the German philosopher the idea gives birth to nature, he writes 'Ha-ha!' as an appropriate marginal comment[3].

What, however, is a dialectical transition as distinct from a non-dialectical transition? Lenin's answer is that the former is characterized by 'a leap. By a contradiction. By an interruption of gradualness. By the unity (identity) of being and not-being'.[4] A purely quantitative change, for example, is a non-dialectical transition, whereas in a dialectical transition there is a qualitative change, a transformation of quantity into quality, the emergence of something new. This change involves a leap, and it is the result of 'contradiction', opposition, antithesis, within a concept or phenomenon, as the case may be.

It is at any rate not unreasonable to describe the emergence of novelty as a leap, and a leap can reasonably be conceived as an interruption of gradualness. But what about use of the word 'contradiction'? 'Contradiction' is a logical term, applying to propositions of the type *p* and *not-p*. For Lenin, however, the dialectic is not confined to thought; it exists also in things. In fact, the dialectic of thought is a reflection of the dialectic in things. Can we properly speak about contradiction in things? It might be maintained, I suppose, that matter in itself is non-conscious, that the emergence of consciousness negates the previous state of non-consciousness, and that this negation is a contradiction. But in the quotation given above Lenin writes as though the transition from matter to consciousness is similar to the transition from matter to motion. If, therefore, we take it that matter in itself is non-conscious, it seems that we should also conceive matter in itself as inert, without motion. But this

---

1 *Works*, XXXVIII, p. 161. Lenin spells 'God' (*Bog*) with a small initial letter, a practice which is standard in the Soviet Union.
2 *Ibid.*, p. 279.
3 *Ibid.*, p. 164.
4 *Ibid.*, p. 279.

would not be compatible with the Marxist concept of self-developing or autodynamic matter, which was certainly Lenin's concept of matter.[1]

The reply can doubtless be made that while matter is never without motion, it can be conceived in this way, and that the transition to the concept of autodynamic matter reveals the essential nature of matter, negating or contradicting the inadequate concept. Just as the antithesis between Being and Not-Being is resolved in the concept of Becoming, which reveals the true nature of Being, so is the antithesis between the concept of inert matter and motion resolved in the concept of autodynamic matter, which reveals the true nature of matter.

In this case, however, what happens to the idea of the emergence of novelty? If matter is essentially and always autodynamic, motion can hardly emerge as a novelty, in a sense analogous to that in which consciousness emerges as a novelty. There may be the emergence of a new concept in the dialectic of thought, but motion cannot be an emergent novelty in the dialectic in things, if matter is essentially autodynamic, never inert. Motion does not really emerge from matter as a novelty. It is there already, as far as objective reality is concerned. Are we to say, therefore, that matter is never non-conscious, even though it may be conceived as such, and that the transition to the concept of consciousness reveals the true nature of matter? Evidently, what is really intended is the claim that consciousness is a novelty, and that matter is only potentially conscious, the potentiality being actualized by a leap. In this case matter should be potentially in motion, rather than autodynamic, whereas Lenin's contention is that matter and motion are inseparable.

The foregoing remarks doubtless tend to appear as captious and carping criticism, based on a pedantic interpretation of a jotting made by Lenin in his notebooks. Lenin, it may be said, was not an analytic philosopher, intent only on attaining the highest possible standard of clarity and precision in his statements. He was primarily a revolutionary activist. He was interested in dialectics not so much for its own sake as because of what he believed to be its revolutionary relevance.

This is certainly true. Lenin had no use for a programme of gradual social evolution, without sharp breaks. He thought in terms of the class war, and so in terms of the conflict of opposites. In his opinion, the interests of the bourgeoisie and those of the proletariat were sharply opposed, the latter contradicting the former. The capitalist economy generated the proletariat, and the proletariat class was destined to 'negate' the bourgeoisie. Out

1 According to Lenin, 'to divorce motion from matter is equivalent to divorcing thought from objective reality . . . in a word, it is to go over to idealism'. *Materialism and Empirio-Criticism*, p. 274.

of this negation something new would arise, a new form of society. The autocracy would be negated by the bourgeoisie, and bourgeois democracy would be negated by the proletarian revolution. Lenin wanted to intensify opposition and conflict, not to eliminate them. In the Hegelian dialectic he saw an instrument for expressing his view of history in a generalized, theoretical manner. The theory was, indeed, important, but it was important as required for intelligent and successful practice. To understand the world was, as Marx taught, a prerequisite for changing it; but it was changing the world in which Lenin was primarily interested. If he philosophized, as he did, he did so with a view to practice, to action, not in order to concentrate on the meticulous examination of philosophical themes for their own sake.

Plekhanov, as we have seen, came to insist more and more on the need for respecting what he believed to be the laws of social development. In the social sphere negation was the work of a class, the rising class turning against the previously dominant class. Negation by a class, however, presupposed the existence of a politically self-conscious class, one, moreover, which had grown and become a majority in the population of the relevant country. To stage a seizure of power by a tiny minority, acting in the name of a class which was by no means politically educated, would be premature. If the seizure of power was successful, it would mean the dictatorship of a few over the many. Between the overthrow of the autocracy and seizure of power by the proletariat, there must intervene a period of bourgeois, capitalist democracy, during which the working class could progressively become a class 'for itself', capable of establishing socialist democracy.

Lenin, however, was far from being disposed to let the dialectical movement proceed at its own pace, not if an opportunity for revolutionary action occurred. Provided that the term is not understood as casting doubt on the sincerity of Lenin's adherence to Marxism, we can call him a great 'opportunist', though 'realist' might perhaps be preferable. When circumstances occurred which made possible a Bolshevik assumption of power, he seized the opportunity, despite the risks of failure and the misgivings of a number of his colleagues, including Trotsky. After all, justification of successful action in terms of dialectical materialism could always be found, if not beforehand, then afterwards. Thus Lenin pointed out, not unreasonably of course, that knowledge of the existence of a dialectical movement in history, of the struggle of classes, does not, by itself, enable one to deduce that this or that particular revolutionary action should or should not be performed. (In point of fact, Lenin was counting, over-optimistically, on the working class in western industrialized countries following Russia's example.)

The fact that Lenin's gamble in the autumn of 1917 came off, and that the Bolsheviks succeeded in retaining power, in spite of opposition and major difficulties, has seemed to Soviet writers a proof of the truth of Marxism. It is hardly necessary to say that a successful seizure of power does not prove the truth of materialism in general, nor of dialectical materialism in particular. It may seem, however, that even if the Bolshevik success did not prove the truth of materialism and the falsity of idealism, it nonetheless showed that Lenin's interpretation of the implications of the dialectic was superior to that of Plekhanov, that, of the two men, Lenin had a better grasp of Marxism as a guide to practice. To the Marxist-Leninist this may well seem to be obviously true.

Although the Bolshevik seizure of power clearly bears witness to Lenin's determination and ability as a revolutionary leader, it is arguable that the results of the seizure of power were such as to justify Plekhanov's position. The Russian proletariat constituted a very small part of the population, and it was by no means all united behind Lenin. The peasants, who constituted the bulk of the population, tended to give their allegiance to the Social Revolutionaries rather than to the Bolsheviks. In order to retain power not only against monarchists, liberals and bourgeoisie but also against Social Revolutionaries, Mensheviks and anarchists, the Bolshevik minority substituted for the authoritarian government of the Tsar an authoritarian government by themselves. Although Lenin convened a Constituent Assembly, he soon got rid of it when he saw that the Bolsheviks were in a minority. He and his colleagues had no intention of sharing real power with other groups, much less of relinquishing power.[1] It is doubtless the case that the proletariat was incapable of governing, that the peasantry, apart from joyfully seizing land, was really counter-revolutionary, and that the leaders of the proletariat had therefore no choice but to establish centralized, authoritarian

1 For a time some Social Revolutionaries were included in the Soviet government, but this state of affairs did not last long. At the fifth All-Russian Congress of Soviets, in July 1918, the Left Social Revolutionaries were excluded from all soviets, including local ones. It should be added, however, that after the signing of the treaty of Brest-Litovsk at the beginning of March 1918, the Left Social Revolutionaries, who were strongly opposed to ratification of a treaty which made such wide-sweeping and humiliating concessions to the Germans, assassinated Count Mirbach, the German minister in Moscow, and did their best to unseat the Bolshevik government. Looking on themselves as heirs to the Populists, they also opposed the policy of requisitioning grain from the peasants. They could hardly expect to be welcome partners in administration. This, however, does not alter the fact that the Bolsheviks aimed at a monopoly of power, even if they were willing for a time to include in the government some representatives of other parties of the Left (not, of course, of the Right).

government; but if this is true, does it not justify Plekhanov's view that a premature second revolution would result in dictatorship *over* the proletariat?

Plekhanov had never really faced up to the possibility that under bourgeois or liberal democracy the working class, so far from becoming a revolutionary class 'for itself', might well be content with increasing concessions extracted by trade-union pressure and strikes and, under a reforming government, become increasingly imbued with a bourgeois mentality. Lenin saw and feared this possibility and telescoped, so to speak, the negation and the negation of the negation. But this does not alter the fact that he established the dictatorship of a small Party. When he was in power, he resisted proposals to decentralize, for example to grant a greater measure of autonomy to trade-unions, and the Soviets became no more than organs for carrying out the decisions of the dictatorship. It is true that by the end of his life Lenin had become aware of the threat to the spirit of the revolution from the growing bureaucratization of the State. But he had created the machinery which Stalin was able to manipulate for his own purposes, to serve the ends of personal power, a goal which, to do him justice, had not been Lenin's.

From 1918 Russia was wracked by invasion and civil war[1], and in 1921 there was a terrible famine. It is reasonable to argue that if the Bolsheviks, who were ultimately victorious in the war, wanted to create a unified Soviet state, they had to centralize government in their own hands and prevent further uprisings. To encourage the withering away of the state of which Engels had spoken[2] and which, before the revolution,

---

1 In the Civil War the Bolsheviks were not opposed simply by reactionaries who wished to restore the autocracy. They were also opposed by liberals and intellectuals who had no desire to restore the monarchy and by the Left Social Revolutionaries. Even some former terrorists fought against the Bolsheviks. Further, there were uprisings by ethnic and national groups who wanted autonomy. In addition, several foreign powers intervened against the Bolsheviks, but their activities, except for those of the Japanese, were not pursued with any great determination or on any considerable scale. At the same time, given the forces opposed to them, it may well seem surprising that the Bolsheviks were eventually victorious. They profited, however, from the lack of coordination between the anti-Bolshevik leaders and armies. And the peasants, of course, were hardly likely to give voluntary and enthusiastic support to those who wished to restore land to the landowners. For success in military operations the Bolsheviks owed a lot to Trotsky, though Stalin subsequently attempted to conceal the fact by silence and calumny.

2 In his work *State and Revolution* Lenin maintained, quite rightly, that Engels envisaged the state as withering away only after the socialist revolution and the seizure of the means of production by the proletarian state. Lenin added that as 'democracy' is itself a state form, it too must disappear when the state disappears. Every kind of state, including the democratic-republican state, will eventually disappear. Until then the dictatorship of the proletariat, using the power of the state, will persist. (This means, in effect, that the state will not begin to wither away until the proletarian revolution has triumphed everywhere.) Later, Lenin did not hesitate to claim that the Bolshevik state was truly 'democratic'.

Lenin had foretold as a future event, would have been to invite further chaos. But a good many years have passed since the revolution and the civil war, and it seems obvious that instead of the state being relegated to the museum of antiquities – which, according to Engels, would one day happen – it is the idea of the withering away of the state which has found a place in the museum of antiquities. It is still, of course, the theory that when there are no more classes, the state, as a class-instrument, will wither away and disappear. Meanwhile, however, the Soviet state has become a Great Power, and the dictatorship of the proletariat, the stage preceding the withering away of the state, has shown itself to be a phrase with little content. Something seems to have gone wrong with the operation of the dialectic, even though Soviet philosophers are skilful at interpreting facts to fit a theory.

5. Lenin never tried to conceal the fact that he was a partisan in philosophy. After all, if 'Marx and Engels were partisans in philosophy from start to finish'[1], one would not expect Lenin to disclaim a like attitude. But how should partisanship in philosophy be understood? Lenin was obviously not referring simply to holding certain views or adhering to a certain philosophical position. For every philosopher, even the sceptic, adheres to some position or argues in favour of some view or views. In point of fact, when Lenin said that Marx and Engels were partisans from start to finish, he added that they evaluated T. H. Huxley, for example, exclusively in terms of his consistency (or lack of it) as a materialist, and that they found fault with Feuerbach for not pursuing materialism to the end. What Lenin meant by partisanship was clearly, in part at any rate, a thorough-going and uniformly consistent adherence by a philosopher to his basic principles. Lenin much disliked eclecticism, and he described Marxist revisionism as a 'presentation of anti-materialist doctrines under the guise of Marxism'.[2] He had no use for the 'God-seeking' of Lunarcharsky and Maxim Gorky, for their hankering after a 'religious atheism' or an atheistic religion. The consistent Marxist, as a consistent materialist, should throw religion in all its forms out of the window. Marx and Engels were partisans in philosophy inasmuch as they pursued materialism to the end and judged all other philosophies in terms of their approximation to or divergence from their own. Lenin followed in their footsteps. He rejected every contamination of dialectical materialism by elements

1 *Materialism and Empirio-Criticism*, p. 352.
2 *Ibid.*, pp. 342–3.

derived from idealism[1]. And in judging other philosophies he used Marxism as his criterion or standard.

In her review of Lenin's book on empiriocriticism Akselrod-Ortodoks mentioned, as a positive feature of the book, the fact that the author defended the truth warmly and passionately. There can, of course, be no doubt that Lenin believed in the truth of Marxism and that he defended what he believed to be the truth warmly and passionately. If this is regarded as sufficient to warrant our describing a thinker as a partisan, then Lenin was obviously a partisan. But if we describe a philosopher as a partisan, we may mean something more than that he tried to adhere consistently to the basic principles or tenets of a given philosophy. We may mean that he was not prepared to question or re-examine seriously these principles or tenets, and that any reasons advanced by other philosophers for his doing so were simply dismissed or subjected to ridicule, that the philosophy in question was treated as analogous to a religious faith, the truth of which is taken as a premise which an adherent will defend as best he can but which he is not prepared to submit to serious doubt. It has been said of Lenin that 'he never questions his premises, never studies a philosophy for itself but always in relation to dialectical materialism and his interpretation of it . . . Whatever supports dialectical materialism is acceptable, whatever weakens it is to be opposed'.[2] Is this a fair judgment?

Consider materialism. For Lenin, materialism is essentially the doctrine that 'matter, nature, being, the physical – is primary, and [that] spirit, consciousness, sensation, the psychical – is secondary'.[3] He ridicules the Russian followers of Mach for demanding a definition of matter, which does not amount to a repetition of this basic distinction.[4] His reason for ridiculing them is presumably that the nature of matter is progressively discovered by scientists, and that the philosophical doctrine is precisely that matter, however described by scientists at a given time, is prior to mind. Lenin is not, however, simply claiming that in the empirical world matter existed before mind or consciousness. He understands the priority of matter to mind in a sense which excludes metaphysical idealism, such as Hegel's philosophy, and theism. And the truth of

---

1 It is true, of course, that the idea of the dialectic came from idealist philosophy, especially that of Hegel. But Lenin's thesis (and that of Plekhanov) was that Marxism, dialectical materialism that is to say, was the synthesis at a higher level of the truths contained in the non-dialectical materialism of the eighteenth century and in nineteenth-century German idealism.
2 *Russian Philosophy*, III, p. 408.
3 *Materialism and Empirio-Criticism*, p. 146.
4 *Ibid.*

materialism in this sense is assumed rather than proved. To be sure, Lenin believes and asserts that materialism is in accordance with science. But when critics refer to modern scientists who have questioned materialism, he replies that the scientists in question, while good physicists, are bad philosophers. When faced with the assertion that in modern physics 'matter is disappearing', Lenin retorts that what is called the disappearance of matter has nothing to do with the basic materialist doctrine that matter is prior to mind. It simply means that what were once taken to be absolute properties of matter are now known to be properties of matter only in certain states, that they are relative and not absolute properties. 'The *sole* "property" of matter, with whose recognition philosophical materialism is bound up, is the property of *being an objective reality*, of existing outside our mind.'[1] But however reasonable this may be as a reply to the claim that matter is disappearing, the assertion that matter is an objective reality, existing outside the mind, is hardly sufficient to dispose of metaphysical idealism, if this is understood as claiming that spirit is the ultimate reality. The idealist (in the Marxist sense of the term) is not necessarily committed to denying that there are material things, existing outside the human mind. He may claim simply that the ultimate reality is spiritual. True, it can be argued that there is no good evidence to support the idealist's claim, and that the thesis that there is an ultimate spiritual reality is a superfluous hypothesis. But Lenin makes little effort to show that this is the case. Nor is he inclined to treat the materialist thesis that matter is prior to spirit or mind as an hypothesis which might conceivably be false. It is treated as though it were an obvious truth, much as though it were self-evidently true, or as something already proven by Feuerbach and Marx. He is not really interested in re-examining the thesis. It constitutes his starting-point.

Lenin's statement that the only property of matter which the philosophical materialist is committed to recognizing is its extramental existence is obviously connected with his realism. This realism, according to Lenin, is 'naïve realism'. 'Materialism *deliberately* makes the "naïve" belief of mankind the foundation of its theory of knowledge'[2]. So-called 'naïve-realism' is the conviction that the world exists independently of human consciousness, a conviction which is shared by anyone who has been neither an inmate of a lunatic asylum nor a pupil of the idealist-philosophers.[3] This conviction is the product of experience, not in

1 *Ibid.*, p. 267.
2 *Ibid.*, p. 64.
3 *Ibid.*, p. 63.

Mach's sense of the term but in 'the human sense'.[1] Our sensations are images of the external world, and, according to Lenin 'an image cannot exist without the things imaged'.[2]

Most of us, of course, would have no inclination to challenge Lenin's assertion that there are realities which exist independently of human consciousness. At the same time his discussion of realism and idealism leaves a lot to be desired from the philosophical point of view. Consider the sentence quoted at the end of the last paragraph. It is doubtless possible to define 'image' in such a way that what Lenin says is true by definition. But if we do not do this, it is by no means clear that one cannot have an image without its being the reflection of something existing extramentally. It may be said that Lenin is not talking about the products of our imagination but about our sensations. He is asserting that our sensations are caused by things other than themselves. This is true. But in what sense is a sensation an image? Even if it is, can we prove that it is? Further, a sensation need not be caused by something which is existing here and now. Is it not possible to 'perceive' a star which no longer exists?

It is not a question of claiming that realism is false and subjective idealism true. The suggestion is that Lenin makes precious little effort to discuss in an open-minded manner the reasons which can be given for maintaining that what he calls 'naïve realism' – which is, in his view, the Marxist theory – must be transformed into critical realism, if it is to be philosophically acceptable. Still less does he give a serious hearing to the subjective idealist's case. He does, of course, make some perceptive remarks. For example, after telling us, characteristically, that the distinction between the phenomenon and the thing in itself is 'sheer philosophical balderdash'[3], he goes on to say that we have all often witnessed the transformation of the 'thing in itself' into a phenomenon, a thing-for-us, an object of knowledge. In other words, we must make a distinction between the hitherto unknown and the known, but it does not follow that the hitherto unknown is unknowable. This is surely true. But Lenin does not take the trouble to make explicit the distinction between the concept of the thing in itself, in the sense in which a realist like himself accepts the concept, and the Kantian concept of the thing in itself, which he rejects. The distinction is implied by what he says, but it is not clearly stated.

Let us turn for a moment to the subject of ethics. In a speech to a Congress of the Young Communist League in 1920 Lenin told his

1 *Materialism and Empirio-Criticism.*
2 *Ibid.*, pp. 63–4.
3 *Ibid.*, p. 117.

hearers that Communists did not reject all morality but had their own ethics. What they rejected was the moral code proclaimed by the bourgeoisie, deduced from alleged divine commandments or from idealist statements similar to divine commandments. What they accepted was proletarian ethics. 'Our morality is wholly subordinated to the interests of the class-struggle of the proletariat'.[1] That moral codes are class-based, related to the interests of a social class, is, of course, standard Marxist doctrine, and there is nothing surprising in Lenin's repetition of this doctrine. Any real discussion of philosophical issues is, however, conspicuous by its absence. To be sure, one could hardly expect Lenin to discuss philosophical problems in a rousing speech to Young Communists in the middle of a civil war. But, as far as the present writer is aware, nowhere does he accord a serious treatment to problems arising in connection with his view of ethics. To take a simple example, Lenin tells the Young Communists that a Communist should shun the mentality expressed in the statement, 'I seek my own advantage and don't care a rap for anybody else'.[2] This is doubtless the attitude which Lenin ascribes to the bourgeoisie. But it apparently does not occur to him to ask whether the attitude which he urges the Young Communists to adopt is simply an expression of 'proletarian ethics' or whether it expresses a principle of universal morality. Does 'proletarian ethics' mean the set of standards actually adopted by members of the proletariat and realized in conduct, or does it mean the moral code by which members of the proletariat *ought* to live? If the latter, are ought-statements, normative ethical statements, of universal application, or can they be confined to a particular group of human beings without depriving them of a specifically moral character? Whatever the answers to such questions may be (and it may well be that further distinctions are required for profitable discussion), they do not seem to bother Lenin. Again, he is interested in advancing the class struggle, in the victory of the proletariat, not in philosophical discussion as such.

The last sentence underlines an important point. The basic reason why Lenin adopted such a partisan attitude in philosophy is that he regarded dialectical materialism as the philosophy of revolution. Because of its connection with practice, with action, the theory had to be maintained in its purity. Any attempt to revise the theory by introducing alien elements constituted a danger in the social-political sphere. Even when they did not realize the fact, the revisionists were 'objective' reactionaries, serving

1 *Collected Works*, XXXI, p. 291 (Moscow, 1966).
2 *Ibid.*, pp. 293–4.

the cause of the bourgeoisie[1]. Lenin read a good deal of philosophical literature, an astonishing amount, indeed, in the case of a man so busy with practical affairs. But he did so primarily in order to defend a certain philosophy, dialectical materialism, which he believed to be of great importance for guiding mankind along the right historical path.

However, although Lenin regarded Marxism as an indispensable instrument in the revolutionary struggle, he also believed that it expressed objective truth. The question therefore arises how this belief fits in with his conviction that objective, absolute truth is something to which human knowledge progressively approximates, travelling, as it were, through successive stages of relative truth towards an ideal goal.

It seems to the present writer that one answer, or a part of the answer, can be given in terms of Lenin's concept of 'practice' as a test or criterion of truth. It is clear that Lenin conceives objective truth in terms of correspondence. If my idea of the world corresponds to the world as it is in itself, independently, that is to say, of my consciousness or thought, my idea is objectively true. It accurately mirrors or reflects the object. But practice, practical verification, is a test or criterion of truth. To be sure, it cannot 'either confirm or refute any human idea *completely*'.[2] But practice can nonetheless confirm a belief or theory so regularly and constantly that its rivals can be dismissed as false. For example, science, according to Lenin, constantly confirms the truth of materialism. Indeed, dialectical materialism is constantly confirmed, whereas agnosticism and all varieties of idealism are never confirmed by practice. We can thus conclude that if we follow the *path* of Marxian theory, we shall draw closer and closer to objective truth, whereas 'by following *any other path* we shall arrive at nothing but confusion and lies'.[3]

According to this account, Marxism provides the path for arriving at objective truth. But this can hardly be the case unless the basic principles or doctrines of Marxism are objectively true. Referring to ideologies, Lenin states that 'every ideology is historically conditioned, but it is unconditionally true that to every scientific ideology (as distinct, for instance, from religious ideology), there corresponds an objective truth, absolute nature'.[4] Passing over the objection that nature cannot properly be described as a truth, we can say that, for Lenin, it is objectively and absolutely true that there is objective truth. It is presumably also unconditionally true that consciousness reflects being and not the other way

1 *Materialism and Empirio-Criticism*, pp. 370–1.
2 *Ibid.*, p. 142.
3 *Ibid.*
4 *Ibid.*, p. 135.

round, and that there is a dialectical movement 'in things' and not only in thought. The actual movement of the dialectic is something which has to be ascertained by empirical, historical investigation, but that there is such a movement is objectively true. If it is asked how we know this, the answer seems to be that practice confirms it and never disconfirms it. Theory and practice go together and must not be sundered.

There is obviously nothing odd or eccentric in maintaining that the human mind can attain objective knowledge, or that the validity of truth-claims can often be tested empirically. It is perfectly reasonable to hold that we know that there are realities, people and things, the existence of which does not depend on human consciousness or knowledge, and that daily experience confirms this belief. It is true that philosophers can raise difficulties and problems in regard to these beliefs, but the beliefs are clearly held by most people. Indeed, as Hume noted, everyone, including the sceptical philosopher, acts in ordinary life on the assumption that they are true. At the same time, if a philosopher claims that practice is a reliable test of truth-claims, one can justifiably expect him to make it clear how he understands 'practice', what counts as practice in this context and what does not. Moreover, if a philosopher claims that the basic doctrines of a given philosophy are in fact always confirmed by practice and never disconfirmed, we can hardly remain content with his assertion that this is the case. If Lenin can successfully bring about a revolution, this certainly bears witness to Lenin's ability as a revolutionary activist, his ability to see and grasp an opportunity. But does it confirm the belief that there is a dialectical movement 'in things'? Can it not be explained without presupposing any such belief? Again, in what sense does science confirm materialism, when materialism is understood in a sense which excludes theism or the idealist theory of a spiritual ultimate reality? Something more needs to be said than a dogmatic assertion that science 'holds the materialist point of view'.[1]

The book from which I have been quoting, it may be said, is of course a polemical work. It was written by a Marxist activist against contemporary deviationists, who believed that they were improving Marxism, bringing it up to date, without realizing how they were playing into the hands of bourgeois theorists and without understanding the implications of their ideas in the social-political sphere. It was natural that Lenin, writing mainly against people who themselves claimed to be Marxists, should presuppose Marxism and concentrate on showing how the views of the Russian Machists deviated from it. If his attitude was that of a

1 *Ibid.*, p. 142.

partisan, and if he did not write in the way that a professional philosopher might be expected to write, this is a matter of little importance. He was a revolutionary leader, and it is absurd to complain that he did not measure up to the standards of an academic philosopher. He never claimed to be one.

This is, of course, precisely the point, namely that Lenin was a partisan in philosophy, an 'apologist', ardently defending the true 'faith', though not, indeed, a religious one. And the reason why it is a matter of some importance to emphasize this aspect of his activity is that, after his death, he was to be turned into an authority even in the sphere of philosophical thought, thus joining the founding fathers, Marx and Engels. Nobody disputes Lenin's historical importance. Because of his historical importance it is appropriate to say something about his philosophical ideas in any account of philosophical thought in Russia. If he had not been turned into an authority, even in the philosophical area, it would be unnecessary to dwell on his shortcomings as a philosopher. After all, they are sufficiently obvious. But as he was elevated to the rank of an authority, a measure of iconoclasm is desirable. He was the real founder of the Soviet Union and one of what Hegel called the world-historical individuals. But he was not a great philosopher. And the official belief that he was has been of no benefit to the development of philosophy in the Soviet Union.

Chapter 12

Marxism in the Soviet Union

1. During the period immediately following the Bolshevik seizure of power the new government, unsure whether it would be able to retain power and confronted by a variety of foes, was hardly in a position to force the cultural life of the country into an intellectual straightjacket. There were more urgent tasks and needs. Besides, as long as the Bolsheviks welcomed the cooperation of other groups on the Left, provided that these groups occupied a subordinate position, the government could hardly insist on a choice being made between orthodox Marxism on the one hand and silence on the other.

In the fields of art, poetry and the drama freedom of expression and experimentation lasted for a considerable time. Though Lenin certainly did not conceal his dislike for movements such as impressionism, cubism and futurism, he did not subject artists and poets to the punitive measures adopted by Stalin.[1] Lenin barked, but his bite was mild in comparison with that of his successor. Like Chernyshevsky, whom he greatly admired, Lenin maintained that art and poetry should be meaningful to the people and serve the revolutionary cause, but he was prepared to allow that works which he found distasteful, even unintelligible, and of questionable social utility might have positive qualities which were not apparent to him. After all, he came from a cultured family and was an educated man.

In 1918 a group of writers, poets, painters and sculptors founded the

---

1 Lenin's personal taste in literature was formed to a considerable extent by his upbringing. He liked the classics, especially Pushkin, also Lermontov, and in Siberian exile he read Turgenev with pleasure. Social considerations, however, played a part. Pushkin fell foul of Nicholas I, and Nekrasov, of whose poetry Lenin thought highly, wrote of the sufferings of the peasants and serfs. Again, while Lenin appreciated Tolstoy's great novels, he had little use for Dostoevsky, apart, of course, from *The House of the Dead*. Nor did he care for the poet Afanasy Fet, thinking him a 'feudalist'. As for contemporary poetry, Lenin found that much of it had little meaning for him. This applied even to the revolutionary poet Mayakovsky. Nor was he favourably impressed by Alexander Blok. The fact of the matter is that Lenin was not really interested in art or poetry or drama as such, though he liked Chekhov's plays and stories. Trotsky had a considerably higher opinion of the cultural value of art.

Proletkult organization, which concerned itself with the spread of 'prole-tarian culture', really culture for the proletariat, among workers students, soldiers and sailors. Lenin adopted a critical attitude and issued directions, and in 1923 the life of the organization was terminated. Lenin mistrusted any organization which was autonomous and not run by the state (under the direction of the Party, that is to say), and his mistrust was doubtless increased by the fact that Proletkult had among its patrons such people as Bogdanov, Lunacharsky and Bukharin. He doubtless feared that the organization would be deficient in genuine party-spirit. It must be added, however, that the Proletkult movement upheld the idea of proletarian, as distinct from bourgeois science, and that Lenin, being convinced that the new régime could not dispense with its bourgeois scientists, was not prepared to endorse the movement's attitude.[1]

Although Lenin's handling of individual thinkers, artists and poets was relatively mild, he laid down principles to which his successor could appeal, and he also indicated ways of controlling recalcitrants, which were later to be applied in a more vigorous manner. For example, he urged the Commissar for Education, Lunacharsky, to see that the printed and published works of 'futurist' poets and writers should be limited in number, so as to discourage the authors and restrict the extent of their influence. Obviously, this policy could be used, and later was used, to deprive of their means of livelihood writers, poets and artists of whom the régime disapproved. From one point of view it is an admirable thing that the state should act as patron of literature and the arts. But there are obvious dangers. In the old days, if an artist displeased one patron, he could look for another. In a totalitarian state, there is only one patron.

If a state is governed, to all intents and purposes, by a Party intent on transforming society in accordance with a comprehensive official ideol-ogy, it is difficult to see how the authorities can regard literature and the arts as belonging to a purely private sphere of life, with which they are in no way concerned. But there can be different degrees of interference. And though Lenin, if he had lived longer, might well have curtailed the freedom which poets, artists and dramatists believed the revolution had brought them, it was not he but Stalin who eventually stifled the upsurge of experimentation and free expression. It is doubtless true that Stalin applied in a much more ruthless manner principles which had been laid down by Lenin. But it is also true that they were different kinds of men. Apart from the fact that Lenin had enjoyed an education which his

1 Prolekult aimed at creating a proletarian culture, distinct from bourgeois culture. Lenin maintained that the working class should inherit the valuable elements in existing culture instead of attempting to start from scratch.

successor had not received, the former acted simply in accordance with what he believed to be required for the success of the revolutionary cause (this applied even to his use of terror), whereas in Stalin's case personal megalomania played a conspicuous role. In general, Stalin mistrusted and feared anyone whom he believed to be, or to be thought to be, more gifted and able than himself and anyone who had an independent following. He himself had to be the one sun in the Soviet sky. Lenin, however, though he was single-minded in the revolutionary cause and could be extremely ruthless, was personally unassuming and disliked manifestations of a 'personality cult' in regard to himself. He was not the man to claim to know poetry and art and drama better than the poets, artists and dramatists, even though he was convinced that they ought to serve the cause of the revolution and not form an esoteric circle.

It is understandable that freedom was curtailed in the philosophical area earlier than in that of art, music, poetry and drama. The Bolshevik leadership claimed to represent the dictatorship of the proletariat. Marxism was regarded as the philosophy, the creed one might say, of the proletariat. It was believed to be the one scientific philosophy and the one true guide to practice, to the realization of a new social order. No rival could be tolerated, whether the Church[1] or non-Marxist philosophies. After the revolution non-Marxist philosophers were able to continue teaching and publishing for a time. When, however, the civil war and the Polish war were over and the Bolshevik government, securely in power, was able to turn its attention to the organization of Soviet society, the time had come to take effective measures to muzzle philosophers whose thought was not in accordance with the official ideology. In 1922 more than a hundred philosophers and scholars, including Berdyaev and N. O. Lossky, were expelled from the Soviet Union.

2. Obviously, if a state ensures that only one particular philosophical system is presented as the truth, that it is taught, as far as possible, to all students, and that rival philosophies are mentioned only to be criticized and refuted in terms of the officially sponsored system of thought, a situation is created which is not conducive to original thought. To be sure, though the writings of Marx and Engels were assumed to be authoritative expositions of truth, there remained room for somewhat divergent interpretations and for development of the ideas of the two German sages. But when in the course of time Lenin too became an

1 Apologists for the Soviet Union tried to maintain that there was no religious persecution. Persecution, however, is not restricted to a policy of liquidating all believers, a policy which the Soviet government had, of course, no intention of pursuing.

authority (an elevation which did not take place during his lifetime) and the phrase 'Marxism-Leninism' took the place of the one word 'Marxism', the area for possible divergent interpretations became somewhat narrowed. There were then three authorities instead of only two. Further, when Joseph Stalin was temporarily raised to the rank of an authority in Marxist thought, the area was still more restricted. However, in the twenties a lively debate was pursued among those who are commonly described as the mechanists and those who are described as idealists. The leading thinker of the first group was Nikolai Ivanovich Bukharin (1888–1937), while the leading figure of the second group was Abram Moiseyevich Deborin (1881–1964), whose real name was Yoffe. The members of the second group are sometimes referred to as Deborinites.

Dialectical materialism claims, of course, to be a unity, distinct from non-dialectical materialism (or 'vulgar' materialism) on the one hand and idealism on the other. But it is possible to emphasize materialism, while playing down the concept of the dialectic or trying to strip it of all idealist elements, or to lay such stress on the concept of dialectical movement that one seems to be sliding into idealism. After all, the concept of dialectical movement was derived primarily from the absolute idealism of Hegel, and its compatibility with materialism is open to question. The Marxist is, indeed, committed to asserting the compatibility of the two elements and to regarding this as a great discovery made by Marx and Engels. But it is hardly surprising if one Marxist subordinates the theory of the dialectic to what he believes to be the implications of materialism, while another stresses the concept of dialectic to such an extent as to lay himself open to the charge that he is moving towards idealism.

In the years immediately following the revolution there were some writers who maintained that philosophy no longer had any field of its own, and that Marxism should therefore not be described as a philosophy. In 1922 O. Minin published an article entitled 'Overboard with Philosophy' in which he claimed that not only religion but also philosophy should be thrown overboard. It was true that Plekhanov and Lenin had referred to Marxism as a philosophy, but such references were nothing but slips of the pen. In reality, Marxism is science, not philosophy. Thus, according to I. I. Stepanov, who published *Historical Materialism and Modern Natural Science* in 1927, Marxism is nothing but the latest and most general findings of modern science. In other words, not only religion but also philosophy are obsolete elements of the superstructure. Science is the only way of increasing our positive knowledge of reality. There is no separate philosophical science, with its own subject-matter, distinct from that of the natural and social sciences. But it is possible to reflect on, coordinate and synthesize the most general findings of the positive sciences. This is what Marxism does. As for the dialectic, it is, indeed, a method, but it is not a distinct science which can be equated with philosophy.

With the more extreme representatives of this positivist attitude, dialectical materialism as a philosophy virtually disappeared. The dialectic was simply a way of arranging, so to speak, scientific data. The so-called mechanists, however, were not simply positivists; they claimed to be dialectical materialists, though their opponents, the Deborinites, questioned the validity of this claim. Mechanism was not a fixed doctrine or set of tenets. That is to say, the mechanists did not all hold precisely the same ideas. But they manifested a common tendency to a positivist conception of philosophy, and also a reductionist tendency, in the sense that they tended to reduce all phenomena ultimately to mechanical phenomena. In his fine work on dialectical materialism Gustav Wetter draws attention to the fact that to support their reductionism the mechanists appealed to the work of the famous Russian physiologist I. P. Pavlov (1849–1936)[1].

Among the mechanists the leading philosophical figure was Bukharin. Joining the Russian Social Democratic Party in 1906, he supported the Bolsheviks. In 1917 he became editor of *Pravda*, but his opposition to plans for signing the treaty with Germany led to his resignation. In 1918, however, he was reappointed editor. A friend of Lenin, in spite of his having opposed the leader on the matter of the treaty, he came to occupy a prominent position as a member of the Central Committee and of the Politburo, also in the Comintern organization. In the controversy about the role of trade-unions in the management of industry, he sided with Trotsky in advocating that the trade-union leaders should play a genuine role in management. In his 'last testament' Lenin described Bukharin not only as the most valuable and the most distinguished theoretician of the Party, even though he had never fully understood dialectics, but also as 'the darling of the Party'. After Lenin's death, Bukharin continued to occupy important posts and to edit *Pravda*, but in 1928 he opposed Stalin's policy of forced collectivization of the peasants, liquidation of the kulaks as a class[2], and concentration on the development of heavy industry

---

1 *Dialectical Materialism. A Historical and Systematic Survey of Philosophy in the Soviet Union*, by Gustav A. Wetter, translated by Peter Heath, pp. 141–2, (revised edition, London and New York, 1958). Pavlov tried to avoid dogmatism by claiming to be a methodological materialist.

2 The kulaks were richer peasants who employed labour and lent money to other peasants, thus being regarded as exploiters. But at the time of forced collectivization any recalcitrant peasant and any peasant who was better off than his fellows and excited envy was liable to be labelled and treated as a kulak. Stalin was putting an end to Lenin's 'New Economic Policy'. Bukharin favoured the idea of voluntary cooperatives, an idea which was evidently beginning to attract Lenin in his last years.

at the expense of agriculture. Thereupon Stalin discovered an opposition group centreing round Bukharin, Rykov and Tomsky, and in 1929 Bukharin was expelled from the Central Committee and Politburo and replaced as editor of *Pravda*. But he still enjoyed wide personal popularity in the Party, and Stalin bided his time. In 1930 Bukharin was appointed head of research planning in the Council of National Economy, and at the sixteenth Party Congress he was re-elected to the Central Committee. He was a prominent and active member of the Academy of Sciences, and he contributed to newspapers and journals. In 1934 he was entrusted with the editorship of *Izvestiya*. In the same year his speech at the newly founded Union of Writers won him an ovation from his audience. The murder of Sergei M. Kirov, the Party boss of Leningrad in December, 1934, provided Stalin with an excuse for the arrests of Zinoviev and Kamenev, which heralded the coming of the notorious public trials of prominent Bolsheviks. In 1936 Zinoviev and Kamenev were shot. Bukharin, it appears, realized that Stalin was engaged in eliminating potential rivals and those who had opposed him,[1] but nonetheless he returned to Russia from a visit to Paris. Arrested in 1937, he was shot in 1938, together with Rykov, the former prime minister. Tomsky had preferred to commit suicide.

As a philosopher, Bukharin was influenced by Bogdanov, and so by the empiriomonism of Avenarius and Mach. While, however, he accepted the claim that human knowledge is constructed out of ultimate elements, sensations, and while he agreed with Bogdanov that the task of science was that of systematizing, coordinating and organizing phenomena, discovering (not inventing) regular sequences and so formulating causal laws,[2] he objected against Avenarius and Mach that they did not properly understand the qualitative differences between the raw material of knowledge and the products of knowledge, such as general concepts and laws. Bukharin certainly asserted the objectivity of knowledge, in regard to both the physical and the social sciences. Regular sequences are discovered, not imposed by the mind, and this makes prediction possible. At the same time he accepted the view of human knowing as a process of construction out of ultimate elements, primitive phenomena.

1 Bukharin could hardly fail to notice what Stalin had in mind. His (Bukharin's) name was mentioned at the time of the first trial as that of a person whose activities were being investigated. He was doubtless relieved when it was announced that no grounds for prosecution of himself or Rykov had been found. But Stalin was simply waiting, and when he had replaced Yagoda by Yezhov as head of the 'secret' police, he was ready to catch Bukharin and Rykov in his net.

2 See, for example, *Historical Materialism. A system of Sociology*, translated from the third Russian edition, p. 20 (London, 1926). This work will be referred to as *HM*.

In spite of being influenced by the thought of Bogdanov, Bukharin did not, of course, describe himself as a Machian; he claimed to be a Marxist, a dialectical materialist, and he asserted the existence of a dialectical movement, in both nature and history. To interpret phenomena dialectically or from the dialectical point of view is to interpret any phenomenon in terms of its relations to other phenomena, not in isolation, and also to see all phenomena as being in motion.[1] 'There is nothing immutable and rigid in the universe . . . Matter in motion: such is the stuff of the world . . . This dynamic point of view is also called the *dialectic* point of view'.[2]

Where does the idea of contradiction, so beloved by Marxist philosophers, come in? According to Bukharin, Heraclitus in ancient times and Hegel in the modern world saw not only that there is in the world constant motion, constant change, but also that 'changes are produced by constant internal contradictions, internal struggle'.[3] Obviously this is the language of dialectical materialism. Contradiction, however, is interpreted by Bukharin as the disturbance of a state of equilibrium. Any system (any entity, physical or social) can be said to be in a state of equilibrium, when the system cannot, of itself, emerge from this state but can do so only when disturbed by an external force. As the world consists of opposed forces, moving, so to speak, in different directions, there is constant disturbance; it is only in exceptional cases that there is a state of rest, a state in which the conflict is concealed. Motion is produced by the conflict or antagonism of forces. A state of equilibrium is disturbed, and it is then reestablished in a new form. 'Taken all together, we are dealing with a process of motion based on the development of internal contradictions'.[4] Some contradictions are external, such as a contradiction between a society and its physical environment, as in the case when the population is increasing but the supply of food available decreases or does not increase in proportion to the rate of growth of the population. Other contradictions are internal, as in the case in which there is a conflict of interests between groups or classes in a given society. According to Bukharin, however, it is the relation between a system, such as a society, and its environment – an external contradiction, that is to say – which is the decisive and basic factor.

Bukharin thus used the language of dialectical materialism, speaking, for example, of 'internal contradictions'. He also asserted the law of the transformation of quantity into quality. A process of gradual development or evolution is the preparation for a leap, a sudden change, which in

---

1 *H.M.*, p. 67.
2 *Ibid.*, p. 64.
3 *Ibid.*, p. 72.
4 *Ibid.*, p. 74.

human society takes the form of a revolution. At the same time Bukharin, like Bogdanov, laid himself open to the accusation of having given a mechanistic interpretation of Marxism, which failed to do justice to the correct ideas of matter and of the dialectic. According to his Deborinite critics, he did not understand that matter is in itself, by its own nature, autodynamic, self-moving. He conceived the motion of an entity as resulting from an impulse coming from outside it. This view of motion, his critics maintained (or Mitin at any rate did) required the theory of a First Mover, or ultimate source of motion, and was thus incompatible with materialism. Again, although Bukharin talked about internal contradictions, he regarded external contradiction, the contradiction between a system and its environment, as primary and basic. This theory was equivalent to ascribing historical development to conflict or tension between a society and its physical environment, rather than to internal contradictions or oppositions within societies themselves. Besides, Bukharin did not really understand the nature of internal contradiction. He thought in terms of negation only, on the model of two conflicting forces, neglecting the fact that what is negated generates that which negates it and is thus presupposed by the latter. For example, the capitalist bourgeoisie generates the proletariat and is presupposed by the latter. Bukharin had no real grasp of dialectical movement.

As against the mechanist tendency to take a positivist view of philosophy, denying that philosophy has any field or subject-matter of its own, A. M. Deborin and his followers maintained that philosophy is an independent source, and that so far from being confined to synthesizing the most general findings of the positive sciences, it can give guidance to the empirical sciences and is presupposed by them. The concept of dialectical movement lies at the heart of philosophy, and as the dialectic operates in things, in nature and in human history, it is important that both physical and social scientists should have an understanding of dialectical movement, the general nature of which is revealed in philosophy.

Whereas the mechanists were inclined to appeal to Engels' *Anti-Dühring*, which contained some positivist-sounding statements, the Deborinites found support in Engels' *The Dialectics of Nature*, which was published in 1925. They were also much heartened, of course, when Lenin's *Philosophical Notebooks* appeared, with their tribute to Hegel as the discoverer of the dialectic and their emphasis on the importance of Marxists studying the logic of Hegel and grasping the nature of dialectical movement. In view of Lenin's book *Materialism and Empirio-Criticism*, and in view of his posthumously published *Notebooks*, the Deborinites were able to claim that the founder of the Soviet Union was on their side in the fight against mechanism. It is not surprising that for a time the Deborinites won the upper hand, in spite of charges by the mechanists that they were too Hegelian and were slipping into idealism, forgetting the unity of theory and practice. By 1929 it doubtless seemed to many interested persons that Deborinism had triumphed. Deborin himself was Director of the Institute of Philosophy and editor of the journal *Under the Banner of Marxism*. He was also in a position to control the selection of writers of philosophical articles in the Soviet Encyclopaedia, while control of the philosophy section of the State Publishing House was in the hands of his followers. Further, after Stalin had spoken against the Bukharinites, mechanism was condemned as a deviation at the 1929 Conference of Marxist-Leninist Institutes.

If, however, the Deborinites thought that they had won a final victory, they soon discovered their mistake. In the summer of 1930 the Deborinites were accused in *Pravda* of laying too much emphasis on the ideas of Hegel and Plekhanov, of failing to appreciate the importance of Lenin and his role in the development of Marxism, and of emphasizing theory to the detriment of practice. In December of the same year Stalin described Deborinism as 'Menshevizing idealism', and in January 1931 it was officially condemned by the Central Committee of the Party. *Under the Banner of Marxism* acquired a new editorial board, including the Party ideologists M. Mitin, V. V. Adoratsky and P. F. Yudin.[1]

Condemnation of Deborinism, however, was far from bringing with it a rehabilitation of mechanism. Both were condemned. The main significance of the joint condemnation was that a Party line in philosophy was being imposed, an officially approved version of Marxism-Leninism, which philosophers were expected to defend. In point of fact the official line of thought stood much closer to Deborinism than to mechanism. Besides being accused of divorcing theory from practice, the Deborinites were also accused of showing insufficient interest in the struggle against religion. They promised to correct these failings. Given such correction, their line of thought was not substantially different from the official version of Marxism-Leninism. And after having recognized his errors, Deborin was able to occupy important positions in the Academy of Sciences, in spite of the fact that he had been a Menshevik from 1907 until 1917.[2]

1 Mitin and Yudin were two of the three signatories of the original attack on Deborinism in *Pravda*.

2 Deborin did not become an actual member of the Bolshevik Party until 1928. Before the revolution he published an *Introduction to the Philosophy of Dialectical Materialism* (1916). After the revolution he published, among other writings, *Marx and Hegel* (1924), *Lenin the Thinker* (1929) and *Dialectics and Natural Science* (1930).

The reader may wonder why such an august body as the Central Committee of the Communist Party of the Soviet Union should bother its head about theoretical questions, of apparently no practical importance, in regard to the correct interpretation of Marxism. It is necessary, however, to bear in mind the doctrine of the unity of theory and practice. If theoretical positions are assumed to reflect social being and to have implications in regard to practice, they obviously cannot be simply dismissed as being of no concern except to thinkers who happen to be interested in purely theoretical issues. Both mechanism and 'Mensheviz- ing idealism' (Deborinism) were conceived as closely linked with deviations in social theory and as having important implications in regard to practice. At any rate this was what was maintained. Mechan- ism was regarded as the philosophical basis of 'Rightist' deviationism, and, of course, as expressing this form of deviation, whereas Deborinism was regarded as a 'Leftist' deviation. The mechanists were accused of failing to understand the law of the transformation of quantity into quality and of conceiving historical development as a process of gradual evolution, ignoring the theory of leaps. This was why Bukharin, in spite of his verbal acceptance of the occurence of leaps, of sudden changes, opposed Stalin's policy of bringing the New Economic Policy to an end and forcing the peasants to accept collectivization. He thought in terms of the gradual development of capitalism into socialism[1] and not in terms of the elimination of capitalism, of a sudden leap forward. Mechanism, in other words, led to opposition to the policy of the Party (i.e. of Stalin). The Deborinites, however, thought only in terms of sudden changes, of leaps, ignoring the fact that there is also gradual evolution. They could be associated, for example, with opposition to the concessions made to 'capitalism' by Lenin in the interests of practice.

In other words, to any deviation in the political-social sphere the Party ideologists felt compelled to assign a philosophical basis, a theoretical foundation. The Deborinites were accused of being left-wing deviationists. As Trotsky was seen as the principal figure on the Left, the accusation of being guilty of leftist deviationism was obviously, in Stalin's time, a potentially very dangerous charge, one that could be fatal to the accused. However, Trotsky was also seen as a proponent of mechanist positions, which were supposed to lie at the basis of rightist

---

1 After the civil war and famine, Lenin, seeing the crying need for the production of more food if the régime was to survive, allowed the peasants freedom in producing and in the sale of their products. This he regarded as a step backward in the direction of capitalism, designed to facilitate two steps forward when the new policy had done its work.

deviationism, a deviation of which Bukharin was alleged to be guilty in opposing Stalin's policy in regard to the peasantry. It is understandable, therefore, that the Deborinites got off lightly, being accused mainly of concentrating on theory to the neglect of practice, rather than of positively opposing the all-wise Leader, the successor of Lenin. Obviously, the attempts to link philosophical positions with forms of political deviationism involved tortuous reasoning. Given sufficient ingenuity, any thinker could be found guilty of deviationism, in the name of the unity of theory and practice. Underneath all the tortuous argumentation there lay the belief that the Party is always in the right, and the Party, from the late 1920s, meant Stalin. The dictator intended, sooner or later, to liquidate Bukharin, the 'darling of the Party' as Lenin had described him, but he had no real interest in eliminating Professor Deborin. It was sufficient that he should recognize his errors. Bukharin too was prepared to admit his errors. In his contribution to the Academy of Sciences' volume to commemorate the fiftieth anniversary of Marx's death he referred to Stalin as Lenin's heir in the role of 'theoretical and practical leader',[1] and lauded the dictator's accomplishments in the spheres of industrialization and agriculture. But this sort of thing did not help him. Together with most of the Old Bolsheviks he was doomed to destruction. This had really nothing to do with mechanism in a philosophical sense.

3. The 1931 condemnations of mechanism and Deborinism naturally put a damper on any original philosophical thought. Philosophers were expected to think with the Party, to adopt, expound and defend the Party line; and to think with Joseph Stalin. It was not, of course, a case of Stalin devoting himself to philosophical studies and writing as a daily occupation. The dictator had no real training in philosophy, and nobody would regard him as a professional philosopher. But he was the ultimate arbiter in regard to both theory and practice, and it would have been a bold man who was prepared to challenge his claim to be the authoritative interpreter of Marxism-Leninism. When he chose to intervene by some pronouncement or other, the matter was settled. Philosophers, therefore had to take the Party line as a criterion of truth and, if possible, to anticipate what it would turn out to be, if it was not already clear. At the same time philosophers who were well in with the régime could help to form the Party line. In other words, the Party ideologists had considerable influence, and it was unwise for other thinkers to become at loggerheads with

---

1 *Marxism and Modern Thought*, by N. I. Bukharin and Others, translated by Ralph Fox, p. 89 (New York and London, 1935). This work, which includes an essay by Deborin, contains a selection of material from the Russian volume mentioned in the text.

them, especially as theoretical 'errors' could be seen as linked with deviations in the social-political sphere, if the authorities chose to do so.

Among the philosophers in good standing with the régime were the three already mentioned, Adoratsky, Mitin and Yudin. In 1936, when the Philosophical Institute (along with the Communist Academy, of which it was a part) was incorporated into the Academy of Sciences, direction of the Institute was entrusted to Adoratsky and Mitin. In 1939 Yudin became its director. It is interesting to note that Deborin was a member of the Council of the Institute, along with Mitin who had attacked Deborinism as well as mechanism. The Institute undertook the publication of a multi-volume history of philosophy[1] and of a philosophical dictionary, Mitin being one of the editors of each of these projects. The Institute was also responsible for the publication of a few monographs and for the preparation of Russian translations of selected western philosophers. The authorities of the Academy of Sciences, however, evidently thought that the Philosophical Institute was in danger of becoming too remote from the ideological struggle. They urged the Institute to take a greater part in combating religion on an intellectual level.

In 1938 there appeared the *History of the Communist Party (Bolshevik) of the Soviet Union, Short Course*. This volume was published as edited by a commission of the Central Committee. And, though it was subsequently ascribed to Stalin, it was in fact the work of a number of authors, though Stalin doubtless had the final judgment about the contents. However, the section *On Dialectical and Historical Materialism* seems to have been written by the dictator himself. He had already written about dialectical materialism in his essays on *Anarchism or Socialism* (1906–7), but it was his treatment of the subject in the *Short Course* which was acclaimed as a masterpiece by Party ideologists such as M. Mitin and which no Soviet philosopher would have dared to criticize adversely during the dictator's lifetime.

The reader of Stalin's contribution to the *Short Course* finds that the author treats first of the dialectical method and applies it to social life, and then outlines the main features of philosophical materialism. During Stalin's lifetime Soviet philosophers understandably followed the dictator's example, but after his death they returned to Engels' policy of treating first of materialism, then of the laws of dialectics, and afterwards of dialectics as a method. Anyway, Stalin asserts that dialectics is the opposite of metaphysics. It treats phenomena as 'organically connected

---

1 The first two volumes appeared in 1939 and 1940 respectively.

with, dependent on, and determined by, each other'.[1] It maintains that nature is in a state of continuous movement, change, development. It allows for gradual evolution but regards it as a process of quantitative change which prepares the way for a sudden change or leap, whereby a new quality arises. Dialectics also maintains that 'internal contradictions are inherent in all phenomena',[2] and that the process of development takes place through a struggle between opposite tendencies.

We are told that these four tenets of dialectics are all contrary to what metaphysics holds. Evidently, the word 'metaphysics' is being used in a very restricted sense. There have been plenty of metaphysicians who have conceived all phenomena as organically interconnected, and who have certainly not conceived nature as being inert, motionless, at rest.[3] Besides, the theory that there are internal contradictions in all phenomena might itself be regarded as a piece of metaphysics. As for Stalin's assertion that the process of development should be conceived as 'an outward and upward movement . . . from the lower to the higher',[4] this is not simply a statement of what is the case but rather the expression of an evaluation of the process of development.

However this may be, the dialectical method, Stalin assures us, is of immense importance not only for studying the history of society but also as a guide to the Party's practical activity. For instance, as socialism is qualitatively different from capitalism, the transition from the latter to the former can be effected only by a leap, that is to say by revolution. 'Hence, in order not to err in policy, one must be a revolutionary, not a reformist'.[5] Again, if development proceeds by way of a conflict between opposites, 'we must not try to check the class struggle but carry it to its conclusion'.[6]

There is no need to dwell on Stalin's account of materialism, which is a summary of familiar Marxist doctrine; matter is primary, mind is a derivative, thought being a reflection of matter, and the world and its laws are fully knowable. It is, however, worth drawing attention to the emphasis laid by Stalin on the power of ideas. To be sure, he insists that the Party's activity should be guided not by the desires of outstanding

---

1 *Dialectical and Historical Materialism*, by Joseph Stalin, p. 7 (New York, International Publishers, 1940). This is a separate translation of the relevant section of the Short Course. It will be referred to as *DHM*.

2 *Ibid.*, p. 11.

3 Stalin can hardly be thinking of Parmenides. Perhaps he has in mind the philosophers who did not conceive matter as autodynamic but who regarded an entity's motion as due to an impulse coming from outside it.

4 *DHM*, p. 9.

5 *Ibid.*, p. 14.

6 *Ibid.*

individuals nor by any alleged universal moral standards but by knowledge of the laws governing social development. It is this knowledge
which converts socialism from being a dream into a science.[1] Stalin also
outlines the orthodox theory of the superstructure and its dependence on
the economic infrastructure. Having said all this, he then goes on to
assert that historical materialism stresses the role and importance of
'social ideas, theories, views and political institutions . . . in the life of
society, in its history'.[2] The development of the material life of society
sets new tasks before human beings, and it is impossible to fulfil these
tasks without new social ideas and theories. The 'Economists' and
Mensheviks, we are told, did not understand the role of advanced ideas,
of advanced theory, and sank into vulgar materialism. On the one hand,
Stalin emphasizes the dependence of social consciousness on social
being, 'Whatever is man's manner of life, such is his manner of thought',[3]
On the other hand, he emphasizes 'the *tremendous role* of new social
ideas, of new political institutions, of a new political power, whose
mission it is to abolish by force the old relations of production'.[4] On the
one hand, Stalin speaks of the operation of laws of social development in
a manner reminiscent of Plekhanov; on the other hand, he speaks as a
revolutionary activist, emphasizing the power of ideas as oriented to
action, or as incipient action.

Whether the two points of view fit together is a question which need
not detain us.[5] The point to notice is that Stalin was very well aware that
the revolution in Russia had given rise to tasks which required fresh
ideas, a development of Marxism to suit the new situation. The anti-
capitalist revolution had taken place in one country, a backward one.
There were no real signs of more advanced countries following Russia's
example. The task therefore was that of building socialism in one
country. As this country was a backward one, with a relatively small
proletariat and a peasantry which was capitalist-minded (in the sense
that the peasants wanted land for themselves), the task of building
socialism could be accomplished only by the leaders of the nation, by the
Party. Development had to be planned at the top and realized through
action emanating from the top. Planning, ideas, theory, were essential,
and they had to be put into practice in spite of opposition, forcibly that is

1 *DHM*, p. 20.
2 *Ibid.*, p. 22.
3 *Ibid.*, p. 29.
4 *Ibid.*, p. 43.
5 Some writers seem to regard them as incompatible. It must be remembered, however,
that Engels himself allowed that elements in the superstructure could, once formed,
exercise an influence.

to say, as with the collectivization programme. If for no other reason than to justify his own policies, Stalin had, therefore, to emphasize the 'tremendous role' of ideas. What else could the author of Five-Year Plans be expected to do? One could not find in the writings of Marx and Engels clear directives for the development of socialism and communism in a situation which they had not envisaged. Marxist theory had to be developed. And Stalin developed it through his idea of socialism in one country and the implications which he drew from it. As far as he was concerned, it was not a question of abandoning orthodox Marxist doctrine about the origin of ideas. It was a question of emphasizing the role of ideas, once conceived, the correct ideas, of course, the ideas reflecting the interests of the proletariat, as represented by the Party, as represented, ultimately, by himself, the mouthpiece of the Party.

In a quotation given above Stalin spoke about 'a new political power, whose mission it is to abolish by force the old relations of production'. What, it may be asked, did Stalin make of Engels's theory of the withering away of the state? The answer is simple. Stalin did not, of course, reject the theory. One did not reject the theoretical doctrines of Marx and Engels, not even if one was Stalin. What the dictator maintained was that the state could not wither away until the proletariat had triumphed on an international scale. This was a prerequisite for the withering away of the state. Meanwhile the power of the state had to be increased, not diminished. State power, in fact, had to be increased in order that the state might eventually wither away. If this seemed to be a paradoxical or contradictory point of view, it should be remembered that contradiction is the lifeblood of the dialectic.

In Stalin's time, of course, the law of the negation of the negation was passed over in silence. The notion that the Soviet régime would itself have to be negated by a further revolution was obviously not acceptable to the dictator. This is understandable. But did it follow that in Soviet society there were no classes, no oppositions, that the dialectic had somehow come to an end?

Stalin, needless to say, felt able to cope with this problem. He did so by maintaining that while there were in fact two classes in the Soviet Union, namely the working class (factory workers mainly) and the peasants, they were not antagonistic to one another. Why not? Because exploitation had been overcome and no longer existed, and because the interests of workers and peasants were not in conflict. Thus in his report on the draft constitution for the USSR, a report made in late November 1936, Stalin did not hesitate to assert that 'in the USSR there are only two classes, workers and peasants, whose interests – far from being mutually hostile – are, on the contrary, friendly'.[1] In other words, differences still exist, but not antagonisms. In the Soviet Union 'there are no longer any antagonistic classes in society; that society consists of two friendly classes'.[2] The goal is, indeed, a classless society. There are still differences to be overcome dialectically, but as exploitation and antagonism have disappeared, the transition to a higher level will not take the form of revolution. Other societies will experience revolutions, but as Soviet society 'no longer contains antagonistic, hostile classes'[3] and is free from class-contradiction, one can look forward to peaceful advance towards the classless, communist society. This does not mean, however, that the power of the state can be diminished. The Soviet Union is encircled by enemies, and these hostile forces do their best to penetrate into the USSR itself. After all, 'as the evidence shows', Trotskyites and Bukharinites 'were in the service of foreign espionage organizations and carried on conspiratorial activities from the very first days of the October Revolution'.[4] The organs of state power should therefore be strengthened rather than weakened.

It is difficult to avoid a sneaking admiration for the brazen way in which Stalin was able to take a downright lie as the basis for an argument leading to the conclusion at which he wished to arrive.[5] But it is unnecessary to dwell on this aspect of his activity. In the present context it is more relevant to note that in his report to the eighteenth Party Congress in 1939 he urged Marxist-Leninists not to confine themselves to learning and repeating some general tenets of Marxism, but that they should study it deeply, and state its general theses more precisely, even improve them, and apply them to situations which Marx and Engels could not possibly have foreseen. It was only natural that, under Stalin, Soviet philosophers should play for safety by repeating what they knew to be approved doctrine, avoiding speculations or developments which might get them into trouble. If any philosopher had set himself up as a successor of Plekhanov and custodian of Marxist orthodoxy, as, that is to say, a rival to Stalin, he would soon have experienced the dictator's displeasure. It does not follow, however, that Stalin respected those who, as he put it, 'calmly doze at the fireside and munch ready-made solutions'.[6] He would not, of course, tolerate denial of

1 *Joseph Stalin, Selected Writings*, p. 395 (Westport, Connecticut, 1970). The intelligentsia, though a social group, was not regarded as a class.
2 *Ibid.*, p. 388.
3 *Ibid.*, p. 458. From Stalin's report on the work of the Central Committee to the eighteenth Party Congress (March, 1939).
4 *Ibid.*, p. 469.
5 Stalin must obviously have known that the Old Bolsheviks who confessed to having been spies or agents of foreign powers were saying what was not true. But the confessions served his purpose.
6 *Selected Writings*, p. 472.

the truth of basic Marxist doctrines, doctrines which he himself reassert-ed without offering any proof. But he did at any rate expect something more than parrot-like repetition.

One would hardly expect very much attention to be given to phil-osophy during the second world war, when the Soviet Union was fighting for its existence. At the end of 1946, however, the Central Committee stuck its nose into the philosophical sphere by directing that logic and psychology should be taken seriously, that textbooks should be written on these subjects and teachers properly trained.[1] The Central Committee evidently took a dim view if not of the intellectual level of contemporary philosophical thought in the Soviet Union, at any rate of the philoso-phers' productivity and zeal for the cause.

This became clear in the summer of 1947, when a conference of philosophers was held at the direction of the Central Committee. The announced purpose of the conference was discussion of *The History of Western Philosophy* by Professor G. F. Alexandrov.[2] At first sight this seems very odd. For the work had earned a Stalin Prize for the author, and the book had been highly praised by the organ of the Central Committee. Further, though the book was indeed subjected to criticism at the conference by A. A. Zhdanov, speaking on behalf of the Central Committee of the Party, this did not prevent the appointment of Alexan-drov as head of the Institute of Philosophy not long after the meeting. The explanation seems to be that discussion of Alexandrov's work was used by Zhdanov as a point of departure for criticism of the Soviet philosophers in general. Thus in his speech Zhadanov, after having drawn attention to Alexandrov's failings, broadened the attack and embarked on criticism of the shortcomings of Soviet philosophers in general. There does not seem to have been any intention on the part of the authorities to eliminate Alexandrov from the philosophical scene. The aim was to teach philosophers a lesson.

Alexandrov was criticized by Zhdanov for what in the West would be described as 'objectivity'. In his *History of Western European Phil-osophy* he had treated Western philosophers simply as thinkers, not as class enemies. He had failed to make clear the social bases of philosophi-

---

1 The lack of work in logic had already been noted by Mitin.

2 Born in 1908, Alexandrov had already won a reputation for himself by his publica-tions, which included books on Aristotle. He had also received a number of decorations, including the Order of Lenin. And his scholarship had been highly praised by the Academy of Sciences in 1946 on the occasion of his election as an ordinary member. Possibly it was because he was a genuine scholar and not a hack writer that he was singled out for criticism at the 1947 conference. This procedure was likely to make more impression than if Alexandrov had been a nobody.

cal systems, and he had presented the history of western thought as a process of continuous development, instead of recognizing that Marxism was qualitatively different from all preceding systems and had raised philosophical thought to a new level. Further, he had neglected to treat of philosophy in Russia and of its advances. To put the matter briefly, Alexandrov was deficient in partisanship, in party-spirit. Features of his work which would probably be regarded in the West as matter for commendation were presented by Zhdanov as serious shortcomings.

The general lesson was clear, and Zhdanov drove it home. Soviet philosophers should be partisans; they should ruthlessly expose the errors of bourgeois thinkers; they should be less abstract and apply philosophy to concrete problems; they should be an instrument of the revolutionary proletariat – of the Party, that is to say, and particularly of its enlightened leader, Comrade Stalin. The Institute of Philosophy was too shut in on itself; it should be in contact not only with philosophers in remote republics of the Soviet Union but also with workers in other fields. It was the business of philosophers to aid the Party in its struggle, not simply to discuss theoretical problems among themselves. And they should act as a team instead of as a number of individual thinkers. In other words, they should regard themselves as an organ of the Party, not as an intellectual élite living in an ivory tower.

Intervention by the Central Committee, ultimately by Stalin, in intellectual matters was, of course, understandable, given the Party's determination to mould practically the entire life of the Soviet Union. But it could do great harm. A notorious case is the support given by Stalin to the biological theories of Trofim Denisovich Lysenko. Whatever the merits or demerits of Lysenko's ideas, problems in biology cannot be settled by the decrees of a political leader who finds a certain theory convenient for his purposes. As for philosophy, the level of philosophical thought was obviously unlikely to be improved by exhortations to partisanship and avoidance of objectivity. Philosophy cannot flourish if it is subordinated to what the Party which controls the State believes to be its interests. Productivity may be increased, but certainly not quality. It is true that one of the results of the 1947 conference was the foundation of *Voprosy Filosofii* (*Problems of Philosophy*), a leading philosophical periodical of the USSR, which listed among its aims not only the maintenance of a partisan attitude but also the development of Marxism-Leninism. Though, however, this development was conceived as a response to the directives of the Central Committee, the chief editor, B. M. Kedrov, was presumably judged to have too generous views about what constituted development, as he was soon replaced[1].

It would be unfair to depict the Soviet régime as having done nothing but harm to philosophy. When (in 1946), as already mentioned, the Central Committee directed that more attention should be paid to logic and psychology, this opened the way for developing the study not only of these particular subjects but of others too, such as aesthetics. As for the 1947 conference, it at any rate stimulated an increase in philosophical activity. As philosophers were expected to refute bourgeois thinkers, they had to study what the latter had written. Further, in 1950 Stalin himself indirectly conferred a benefit on philosophy and opened up the way to fruitful developments by his intervention in the controversy about linguistics.

Nikolai Yakovlevich Marr (1867–1934) had maintained that as language expresses thought and as thought is the reflection of social being, language belongs to the ideological superstructure and is therefore class-bound. In the future classless society there will be one universal language. Though this theory was taken to be standard Marxist doctrine for a time, it was subjected to criticism in *Pravda*, and the matter was referred to Stalin. The dictator was not, of course, a specialist in linguistics, but, apart from his megalomania and pathological suspicion, he had a good deal of common sense. His reply was that language did not belong either to the superstructure or to the infrastructure and that it was not class-bound. It was indeed a social phenomenon, but it was related to society as a whole, not to any particular class. There could be words and phrases characteristic of this or that class, but they constituted a very small part of language as a whole. Further, Stalin not only rejected Marr's thesis, he also asserted that no science could flourish unless people were free to criticize opinions maintained by those who claimed to be authorities on the subject. There should be free discussion. This attitude may have been inconsistent with Stalin's own conduct in regard to Lysenko's biological theories, but in itself it was admirable.

Stalin's letters to *Pravda* were published together in the same year, 1950, as *Marxism and Problems of Linguistics*. His thesis that language, though a social phenomenon, belonged neither to the superstructure nor to the infrastructure obviously gave rise to the question whether there were not other neutral areas of study. If there was no special proletarian language and no science of linguistics peculiar to the proletarian class,

---

1 Certain articles expressed points of view which were new for Marxists and which gave rise to lively discussion. To develop Marxism while at the same time remaining within the traditional framework of thought was a ticklish task.

could not the same be said, for example, of formal logic? And what about theoretical physics? Did not this too transcend any essential class-link? Logicians were quick to avail themselves of Stalin's pronouncements on linguistics. The dictator had opened the way for further 'declassification', as the procedure of declaring a subject neutral has been described.

Further, in his letter to *Pravda* Stalin, while reiterating the general Marxist theory of the superstructure, laid emphasis on the fact that ideological elements do not reflect economic production directly but only indirectly. He thus opened the way for the claim that provided one does not deny that a branch of philosophy such as ethics or aesthetics ultimately reflects the economic infrastructure through the mediation of social being and social consciousness, it can nonetheless be studied as a relatively independent discipline. In other words, Stalin's pronouncements in the pages of *Pravda* had much wider implications.

It is worth noting that in his letters Stalin took the opportunity of correcting the error of any Marxist theoretician who might think or be tempted to think that the theory of the dialectic required that the Soviet régime should itself be negated by an 'explosion', a revolution that is to say. According to Stalin, the law of the transformation of quantity into quality by a leap (in social life a revolution) applied necessarily to societies in which there were hostile, antagonistic classes but not to a society (such as the Soviet Union) in which there were no mutually hostile classes.

Stalin also explained to his readers how Marxism was free from fixed dogmas. Marx and Engels believed that a socialist revolution in one country only could not be successful. Lenin and Stalin had shown that it could. It did not follow, however, that the belief of Marx and Engels was false. It was true at the time, and if it is seen as relatively true, true in relation to the social conditions at the time when Marx and Engels were writing, it is not contradicted by Stalin's claim that socialism in one country is possible. It would be contradicted only if it were interpreted as a fixed dogma, valid for all time. Though Stalin was concerned with providing a reply to the possible objection that his project of building socialism in one country was incompatible with the teaching of Marx and Engels, his denial of fixed dogmas can be seen as opening up far-reaching possibilities of revisionism, even though this was not intended.

4. The death of Stalin in 1953 naturally resulted in some easing of the situation in regard to philosophical discussion. For there was no longer an infallible personal dictator, whose decisions about ideological issues might be unexpected. After the ritual panegyrics of the departed were safely over, Marxism-Leninism-Stalinism quietly reverted to being

Marxism-Leninism. Obviously, it was not a case of rejecting all Stalin's ideas. But critical discussion of them became possible when the 'personality cult' had been denounced.

It by no means follows, however, that Soviet philosophers became free to say what they liked. They had to remain within the framework of Marxism-Leninism, and they were still expected to be at the service of the Party and to maintain partisanship in philosophy. At the same time philosophers were exhorted, for example in editorial articles in intellectual periodicals, not to write as though all problems were already solved, not to be afraid to tackle fresh issues, not to caricature the thought of bourgeois philosophers but to make a serious study of their writings, not to try to assimilate the ideas of pre-1917 Russian revolutionary theorists to Marxism when they were not Marxists, and so on. In other words, philosophers were expected to be not only faithful Marxists but also militant ones, combating bourgeois ideas, including religious beliefs[1], and at the same time to be serious thinkers, developing Marxism-Leninism in a creative manner and basing their criticism of non-Marxist thought on a genuine understanding of the relevant philosophical literature.

It was, of course, an excellent thing that Soviet philosophers should be encouraged to avoid simply repeating what had been said by Marx, Engels and Lenin, to develop Marxism-Leninism by treating fresh problems or issues which had not yet been resolved, and to conduct a serious analysis of non-Marxist philosophies, based on first-hand knowledge of the literature. But to combine this attitude with a quasi-religious faith in what were reckoned to be the basic doctrines of Marxism and with militant partisanship was no easy task. It was like demanding that someone should be both dogmatic and non-dogmatic at the same time. And it is understandable if a number of Soviet philosophers have concentrated on what, after Stalin's pronouncements on linguistics, has come to be a 'safe' subject, such as formal logic. If formal logic is not essentially class-linked but transcends class-divisions, there is no need to bother about criteria other than those appropriate to this particular discipline. And provided that one does not deny Marxism-Leninism or reject the concept of dialectical logic, one can pursue one's studies in formal logic in the same sort of way in which any bourgeois logician would pursue them.

The present writer is certainly not in a position to hazard an opinion

---

1 In 1955 the Central Committee, while insisting on the need for continuing 'scientific' atheistic propaganda, explained that this should not involve interference with the legally permitted activity of religious bodies or insults to priests and believers, most of whom were loyal citizens of the Soviet Union.

about the extent to which such motives have actually influenced Soviet logicians. The desire to pursue logical studies can be 'disinterested', in the sense of expressing an interest in the subject-matter for its own sake. But this interest may, of course, be combined with the desire to escape from the demands of partisanship and 'apologetics'. And as Soviet philosophers are human beings, not machines, it would be odd if some at least did not look on professional logical studies as a kind of refuge.

As Lenin identified logic, dialectics and theory of knowledge, it is understandable that during the 1930s formal logic was neglected. It was commonly regarded as 'metaphysical', in the sense that it was seen as divorced from reality as it really is, namely moving, developing. The laws of logic should reflect the laws of nature, of reality, and this demand is fulfilled only in dialectical logic. Though, however, formal logic or traditional logic might be neglected, it nonetheless remained as a possible subject for study. Besides, in *The Dialectics of Nature* Engels had stated that formal logic is not nonsense, even if fixed categories are valid only for everyday use, within the context of brief periods of time.

The Central Committee's directive in 1946 that the study of logic should be introduced into schools and that suitable textbooks should be prepared naturally gave rise to discussion about the nature of logic. Had dialectical logic supplanted formal logic? If this was not the case, was formal logic a separate discipline or was it in some way a part of dialectical logic? If so, in what way? In the years following the intervention of the Central Committee different opinions were proposed in discussions and in philosophical periodicals, especially, of course, in *Problems of Philosophy*. In 1951, following Stalin's pronouncements in regard to linguistics, the editors of this periodical ruled that logic does not belong to the superstructure and is not class-bound. Further, though dialectical logic is a higher development, formal logic, as studying laws and forms of correct thinking, not only has a right to exist but is needed by all.

The formal logicians, however, were not content with being tolerated or with being allotted a subordinate place in relation to the upholders of dialectical logic. It was not long before the view was being defended that there is only formal logic. Thus in 1951 K. S. Bakradze published a *Logic* in which he maintained that the basic propositions of dialectical logic were simply applications of the principles of formal logic, and that it was a mistake to suppose that recognition of reality as dynamic, moving, developing, required the invention of a special logic in addition to formal logic. Similarly, in 1954 N. I. Kondakov argued in his *Logic* that when philosophers referred to 'dialectical logic', they were really thinking not of a special kind of logic but of Marxism as a whole, of dialectical materialism that is to say.

It is hardly necessary to say that views such as those expressed by Bakradze and Kondakov were subjected to violent attack by supporters of dialectical logic. But the offenders stuck to their guns. The final result seems to have been a kind of truce. That is to say, recognition was accorded to both formal and dialectical logic, the precise relation between them being left as matter for discussion. It has been formal logic, however, which has flourished and, by doing so, successfully vindicated its claim to independence. If one looks, for example at *Philosophical Problems of Many-Valued Logic* by A. A. Zinoviev[1], one sees that, apart from a passing acknowledgement of the existence of dialectical logic, the book might have been written by a 'bourgeois' logician, and in the same author's *Foundations of the Logical Theory of Scientific Knowledge* dialectical logic is not mentioned.[2] In both books appeals to the authorities, Marx, Engels and Lenin, are conspicuous by their absence. But, of course, these worthies had nothing to say on the subject of mathematical logic.

In 1959 a collection of essays by various authors, entitled *Logical Investigations*, was published at Moscow, and since then a large number of such works and also of monographs by individual logicians have appeared. The principal centres of logical study have been the departments of philosophy at the universities of Moscow and Leningrad, but logicians at other universities and academic institutions have also contributed to the relevant literature. Obviously, a good deal of the work has been devoted to the development of pure logic, but there has been a conspicuous tendency to emphasize the application of logical techniques to problems relating to the methodology of the sciences. On the question whether formal logic is to be regarded as part of philosophy or as a separate discipline, different opinions have been expressed. In any case there is agreement that modern logic can be of real use in solving philosophical problems, though it is not claimed that philosophy is reducible to logic or that the theory of scientific knowledge as a whole can be developed simply by mathematical logic.

As for dialectical logic, its supporters represent it as studying the laws governing the development of a reality (the only reality) which is essentially dynamic, changing. The laws are not simply laws of thought; they reflect the movement of things. And though there is a dialectic of

1 A revised edition edited and translated by Guido Küng and David Dinsmore Comey (Dordrecht, Holland, 1963).
2 Moscow, 1967. Revised and enlarged English edition (Dordrecht, 1973).

concepts or categories, these categories are exemplified in extramental reality, not indeed in the sense that thought imposes them on reality but in the sense that thought reflects reality. Dialectical logic thus tends to coincide with theory of knowledge and to have, for its supporters, ontological significance. The category of causality, for example, should not be conceived as a purely subjective category or concept. Causality reigns throughout the world, not simply in nature but also in the development of human society.

After the death of Stalin the law of the negation of the negation was quietly reasserted. Obviously, however, the dialecticians had to avoid the implication that the social organization of the Soviet Union was destined to be swept away in a manner analogous to that in which the Tsarist autocracy was swept away. Room had, indeed, to be found for real change in the future. For state socialism, ownership of the means of production by an all-powerful state, was certainly not the same thing as communism, as a classless society in which the state had withered away. But room had also to be found for Stalin's distinction between a society in which there were exploitation and antagonistic classes and a society in which there were allegedly no antagonistic classes (but only friendly ones) and no exploitation. So the law of the negation of the negation was interpreted in such a way as to allow for a transition from the old to the new of such a kind that the old was at the same time preserved and raised to a higher level, no violent repudiation and destruction of the old being involved.

As far as the present writer is aware, no additional laws of dialectics have been discovered since the time of Engels. Discussion has centred more around the interpretation and application of the laws, the nature of categories from the epistemological and ontological points of view, and the relation between categories and the laws. For example, are categories more fundamental than laws and presupposed by the latter? Or do they exemplify the laws, the laws being the basic factor? The more forthright or bold formal logicians have claimed that such issues, in so far as they are logical issues, can be perfectly well treated in formal logic, and that what is described as dialectical logic is really theory of knowledge or part of dialectical materialism. But at any rate recognition of the existence of dialectical logic does not preclude all critical discussion. After all, questions can be asked to which Marx and Engels gave no answer.

5. As dialectical materialism is said to be not only the philosophy of the proletariat but also the only philosophy which is fully in harmony with modern science, it is only to be expected that Soviet thinkers should show

a lively interest in philosophy of science. Indeed, the claim has been made that dialectics is the methodology of science, that scientific advances have been made by following (not necessarily consciously, of course) the laws of the dialectical method. Thus scientific advances have been regarded as confirming the truth of dialectical materialism, as exemplifying the fact that correct theory is verified by practice.

To make such claims is easy enough. To substantiate them in a way which is sufficient to convince doubters is more difficult. Soviet writers may make much of the Galileo episode, when it suits them. But the fact of the matter is that, in the case of several important scientific theories, the theories have been rejected because they clashed or seemed to clash with Marxist dogma. For example, physics as presented by N. Bohr, W. Heisenberg and others was initially attacked by Soviet philosophers, as it appeared to clash with the Marxist claims that all reality is knowable and that causal determinism operates universally. In other words, quantum physics, so far from confirming dialectical materialism, seemed to disconfirm it. It had therefore to be rejected. It is understandable that Soviet philosophers were pleased when western scientists such as Louis de Broglie questioned Heisenberg's principle of indeterminacy. In the end, of course, quantum physics had to be substantially accepted. Acceptance meant that the pronouncements of the founding fathers had to be reinterpreted. Once this had been done, the philosophers were in a position to claim that quantum physics, properly understood, confirmed dialectical materialism.

Another notorious example is that of relativity theory. Marxism maintained that space and time are objective. Einstein's relativization of space and time seemed at first to be incompatible with Marxist doctrine, and the special theory of relativity was attacked. Some of the critical articles were reprinted in the collection *Philosophical Problems of Modern Physics* (Moscow, 1952). This was by no means the only attitude adopted. For example, in 1953 Academician V. A. Fok published an article entitled 'Against ignorant criticism of modern physical theories', and A. D. Alexandrov, who, like Fok, was a mathematician, replied to critics of the relativity theory in an article entitled 'On certain conceptions of relativity theory' (1951). Both these articles appeared in the periodical *Problems of Philosophy*, in the pages of which there was a lively discussion in the early 1950s. In the end relativity won the battle, as far as the special theory of relativity was concerned. It was conceded that space and time, taken separately, are relative, though space-time is absolute, whatever this may mean. The general theory of relativity, however, was another matter. For the idea of a finite (though unbounded) universe seemed to the Marxist philosophers to imply a beginning in time and so to open the way for belief in a creator.

Attacks by dogmatic philosophers on scientific theories as being contaminated by idealism and out of accord with Marxist-Leninist materialism could sometimes be strengthened by pragmatic considerations, by the desire to obtain quick and tangible results. This is sufficiently obvious in the case of Lysenko (see page 330). His attack on modern genetics, as represented, for example, by N. I. Vavilov, was supported by such stalwarts of the official ideology as Academician M. B. Mitin. But Lysenko's claims that varieties of plants and animals could be improved by effecting appropriate changes in their environments and that characteristics acquired in this way could be inherited opened up before the Party leaders, especially Stalin, rosy prospects for Soviet agriculture. Never mind the fact that the empirical evidence offered by Lysenko on behalf of his theories would not stand up to serious critical scrutiny. Modern genetics was largely proscribed (N. I. Vavilov was arrested in 1940), and Lysenko was hailed as a genius in agrobiology not only during the reign of Stalin but also under Khrushchev. True, the situation was considerably easier once Stalin had departed from the world, but it was not until the Brezhnev era that Lysenko was finally discredited and modern genetics restored to life.[1]

Science in the Soviet Union, however, had to be relatively free in theorizing, if it was to advance and fulfil the expectations of the Party. The Party obviously could not at the same time look to scientists to carry out important tasks and force theoretical physicists to accept the dogmatic utterances of philosophers who felt themselves bound by what Marx, Engels and Lenin said or implied. Writing in 1962, the eminent scientist and Academician Kapitsa said that if in 1954 Russian scientists had paid attention to the philosophers, the conquest of space, of which the Soviet Union is justly proud, could never have been realized. Physicists, Kapitsa claimed, would not have been worth their salt if they had accepted the condemnation of the relativity theory by certain philosophers and failed to apply the theory in nuclear physics[2].

The scientists, of course, won the battle. If we look at the article 'Theory of Relativity' by I. U. Kobzarev in the third Russian edition of the

1 The sorry story of the Lysenko affair is related by D. Joravsky in *The Lysenko Affair* and by Z. A. Medvedev in *The Rise and Fall of T. D. Lysenko.* For the conflict between the ideology and science in the Academy of Sciences of the USSR see A. Vucinich's *Empire of Knowledge.* (See Bibliography.)

2 The article appeared in *The Economic Gazette.* The passages referred to are quoted by Richard T. De George in his book *Patterns of Soviet Thought*, p. 208 (Ann Arbor, 1966).

Great Soviet Encyclopaedia, we find a perfectly straightforward treatment of the subject without any reference to the founding fathers of Marxism. We are told, for example, that 'by revolutionizing the thinking of physicists, it (Einstein's theory) paved the way for the more-reaching rejection of "directly apparent" concepts that was required for the creation of quantum mechanics'.[1] Again, in the article 'Quantum Mechanics' by V. B. Berestetskii we read that 'the laws of quantum mechanics form the foundation of the study of the structure of matter'.[2]

What has happened is that dialectical materialism has had to be revised, or developed, in the light of modern science. Thus in an article on 'indeterminism' (understood as rejection, whether ontological or methodological, of the objectivity of causal relations) the author, A. P. Ogurtsov, asserts that 'dialectical materialism, while rejecting indeterminism, at the same time points out the insufficiency of earlier mechanistic concepts of determinism and presents a new generalized concept of determinism based on the achievements of modern natural and social science'.[3] We can note, however, that another writer describes the uncertainty principle as 'a fundamental proposition of quantum theory'.[4]

There is obviously no reason why Marxist theory should not be revised in the light of modern science. It is a perfectly sensible procedure. But any consequent claim that modern science verifies Marxist theory can hardly produce conviction. To be sure, such claims have sometimes been expressed in such a general form that they may seem plausible to some. For example, it has been claimed that the relativity theory confirms the Marxist teaching that all phenomena are interrelated. Perhaps it does confirm the teaching, but the teaching is not specifically Marxist. As for such specific claims as that the successful launching of sputniks confirms the truth of Marxism-Leninism, it is difficult to see how anyone can believe them. To be sure, it was the Soviet state which made the launchings possible by providing the facilities and the financial requirements. But, apart from the official backing, the credit is due to Soviet scientists and technologists, not to dialectical materialism.

6. As for psychology, the Central Committee had directed in 1946 that suitable textbooks should be prepared and teachers properly trained not only in logic but also in the field of psychology. This directive naturally gave rise to discussion about the nature of psychology and its relations to

1 Volume 18 (Moscow, 1974).
2 Volume 11 (Moscow, 1973).
3 Volume 10 (Moscow, 1970).
4 Volume 17 (Moscow, 1974).

philosophy on the one hand and to physiology on the other. After all, if studies in psychology were to be seriously pursued, it was desirable to have a reasonably clear idea of the subject-matter. But there was a problem in regard to this issue. On the one hand, I. P. Pavlov was held in great, and doubtless justified, esteem for his researches into conditioning and neural behaviour. Further, his determinism and his at any rate methodological materialism seemed to fit in admirably with Marxist theory. There was no mention of such objectionable concepts as those of a soul or of a vital principle. In addition, Pavlov's theories about the relation between a living organism and its environment and about the processes of conditioning doubtless seemed to be promising instruments for use in the education of the new Soviet human being. On the other hand, Pavlov did not recognize a science of psychology distinct from physiology. He did not regard a distinct psychology as a science at all. But if psychology was reducible to physiology, how could psychologists fulfil the directive of the Central Committee? Should not the task be left to the physiologists?

However highly Pavlov's researches might be esteemed, and however attractive the line of thought represented by him and his forerunner I. M. Sechenov (1829–1905) might be, a reduction of psychology to physiology could hardly be altogether satisfactory for Marxist thinkers. For they had to allow for the power and influence of ideas on human activity, and they were naturally inclined to lay emphasis on social psychology. As a basis for rejecting any simple reduction of psychology to physiology they could appeal to the idea of emergent evolution or, if preferred, to the law of the transformation of quantity into quality. That is to say, they could maintain that though consciousness and mental life have a material basis, they constitute a new level, a sphere of their own, once they have arisen. There is room, therefore, for psychology as a distinct discipline.

This was more or less the line taken by N. P. Antonov in an essay which appeared in *Problems of Philosophy* in 1953. Consciousness has a material foundation, and mental life is inseparable from its physical basis. But it is not the same thing. The task of psychology is not only to investigate the physiological basis of mental life but also to ascertain the laws of the formation and development of mental life, with a view to influencing this development in the process of education. There is only one reality, autodynamic matter, but it does not follow that all phenomena are of the same kind. Consciousness exists only in the human being, and mental life, though it cannot exist apart from its physical basis, is not identifiable with physical processes. Human consciousness is a product of highly-organized matter; it is a property of matter, dependent on the brain and neural system; but there are nonetheless laws of the development of consciousness, of mental life, of the formation of the psyche, which it is the business of psychology to ascertain.

To remain faithful to materialism and at the same time to recognize a specific difference between mental and physical phenomena is not an easy task, even if it is held that dialectical materialism, as distinct from 'vulgar' materialism, is capable of combining the two positions. It is not surprising that the views of Antonov and those who agreed with him should have been criticized by writers who insisted that thought was a material process. If the language of psychology was not translatable into the language of physiology, how was materialism to be preserved? One answer was that Pavlov's point of view smacked of 'mechanism', and that mechanism was an incorrect interpretation of dialectical materialism. But the retort could be made that the more the relative independence of mental life was stressed, so much the more was dialectical materialism given an 'idealist' slant.

In the end, of course, psychology was recognized as a science, having a distinct field of its own. In the *Great Soviet Encyclopaedia* it is defined as 'the science of the laws of the genesis and functioning of the mental reflection of objective reality by the individual, in human activity and animal behaviour'.[1] This general definition, which obviously incorporates Lenin's copy-theory (ideas conceived as copies or reflections of extramental reality) may seem too narrow. But at any rate it serves to show that the defenders of psychology as a distinct science have won the battle. In point of fact Soviet psychologists accept all the ordinary branches of psychology, such as physiological, medical, child, social and industrial psychology. For the matter of that, psychoanalysis, which was once rejected, is now accepted, though, as in the case of other branches of psychology, it is interpreted in the light of Marxist theory. Further, it has been claimed that more attention is now being paid to research in parapsychology in the Soviet Union than in most other countries.

The periodical *Problems of Psychology* (*Voprosy psikhologii*) has appeared since 1955, and the Institute of Psychology of the Academy of Sciences of the USSR was founded in 1971. Soviet psychologists have, of course, to keep within the framework of Marxist theory. They would hardly find a publisher if they set about reinstating the idea of a spiritual soul; or, if they did find a publisher, they would soon be subjected to adverse criticism. But the fact that they are expected to keep within the limits of a certain philosophical framework does not mean that no serious psychological research is done. We can also note that though

1 Volume 21 (Moscow, 1975). Article 'Psychology'.

Marxist convictions naturally incline the mind to stress social psychology, it is obvious to Soviet psychologists that consciousness and mental life do not exist apart from individuals. Individuals may be more or less integrated into society, and the importance of individual psychology (also of psychiatry) is recognized, even if emphasis is laid on social consciousness. Nor should it be assumed that all Soviet psychologists are at one either in their placing of emphasis or in their interpretation of the data. Even within the common framework there is room for a variety of opinions.

7. There are doubtless Soviet psychologists who are primarily interested in acquiring and extending knowledge in their own particular fields of study. From the point of view of officialdom, however, emphasis has been laid on the educational value of psychology, on its value as contributing to the development of the human being as a member of society. But for this purpose psychology is not enough. Norms, moral standards, are required. Marx and Engels assigned systems of morality to the class-linked superstructure and rejected the concepts of absolute values and of a universal, perennially valid moral law. Beyond implying the existence of a proletarian morality, they paid little attention to developing its content. They were concerned with other matters. Lenin, admittedly, spoke to Young Communists about proletarian morality and the need for unselfish service to the cause and for comradely solidarity, but it can hardly be claimed that he contributed to the development of moral philosophy. He made it clear that actions which served the Communist cause were right, whereas actions which hindered it were wrong; but his attack on empirio-criticism and his reflections on dialectics were not accompanied by any serious development of ethical thought. As for Stalin, though he naturally paid lip service to the ideals of proletarian morality, his rule was characterized by the use of coercion and terror and, during the second world war, by appeals to patriotism. But in the years following the death of the formidable dictator it became obvious that relaxation in the policy of coercion and terror had to be accompanied by education in moral standards which could serve as internalized principles of action, if the desired new society were to be realized. Law by itself was not sufficient. If genuine communism were ever to become a reality, people would have to act out of sincere conviction. Besides, even if obedience to law were regarded as a moral obligation, the field of human conduct was wider than the field which could be covered by positive law.

According to orthodox Marxism, changes in the economic infrastructure cause changes in 'social being', and changes in social conditions cause changes in social consciousness, and so in moral ideas. But it became obvious that even under the so-called dictatorship of the proletariat a change in social consciousness and in moral attitudes could lag behind changes in the substructure. The overthrow of bourgeois democracy at the Bolshevik seizure of power did not automatically entail the disappearance of what was regarded as the bourgeois mentality, with its self-seeking acquisitiveness and absence of comradely solidarity.[1] Hence the need for the Party to promote moral education. This was required to take the place of Stalin's terror and to supplement law. 'Socialist loyalty' was to be commended, but so was socialist morality. If rule by coercion and terror were to be relaxed and progressively diminish, Soviet citizens had to be morally motivated.

These considerations help to explain why, in 1961, the Twenty-Second Congress of the Communist Party of the Soviet Union included in its Party programme a code of morality. The context was the optimistic expectation that the development of a genuinely communist, classless society, would be realized in the not too far distant future, a society in which the state as a coercive power would be replaced by 'public self-government'. The code was promulgated as a moral code for the builders of Communism. But it was obviously meant to apply not only to Party members but to all Soviet citizens. For a communist society would not be possible without moral solidarity among the citizens in general. The first part of the Party programme dealt with creation of the material basis for the transition to Communism. The code of morality was included in the second part and was intended to be a guide for educators and propagandists in particular, though it was relevant to all citizens. It had to be communicated, propagated, inculcated.

The first thing mentioned in the code is devotion to the communist cause. In other words realization of a communist society is conceived as the highest goal or ideal. As one would expect, the social aspects of morality are emphasized. Conscientious labour for the good of society, a high sense of public duty, comradely solidarity ('one for all and all for one'), intolerance towards national or racial hatred among the peoples of the USSR, a love of peace, are all stressed. But the code also prescribes humane relations and mutual respect among individuals, honesty, truthfulness, moral purity, unpretentiousness in private and social life, mutual respect between members of families and care in the upbringing of children, while injustice, dishonesty, careerism, money-grubbing,

---

1 Plekhanov might have commented, 'I told you so. I warned against premature revolution, before the working class had been fully prepared to play its proper role'.

laziness are condemned. In other words, while some precepts of the code, such as devotion to the communist cause and an uncompromising attitude to 'the enemies of communism', would not be acceptable to non-Marxists a good many of the ideals expressed could perfectly well be accepted by people who do not subscribe to Marxism-Leninism. The code has, indeed, features which are relevant simply to Soviet citizens, such as proclamation of the ideals of loving the socialist motherland and of cultivating friendship and brotherhood among the various peoples of the USSR, but most people would think that a good many of the ideals expressed are of universal application.

Promulgation of the 1961 code of morality for the builders of communism can, of course, be seen as an expression of that recognition of the active influence of the superstructure which had been emphasized by Stalin. But though the Twenty-Second Congress of the Communist Party took upon itself the role of moral teacher, it was concerned with action, with promoting moral education, not with raising, discussing and solving philosophical problems in ethics. At the same time just as, at an earlier date, the Central Committee had given an impetus to logical and psychological studies, so did the 1961 Congress help to turn the attention of philosophers to ethical problems. Obviously, the philosophers were expected to work within a Marxist framework of thought. They were not free, for example, to question the belief that a genuinely communist society is the highest good for the human being. But it does not follow that no discussion was possible, or that there was no room at all for different opinions within the limits of the common framework of thought.

As one would expect, Marxist philosophers give a naturalistic account of the origins of morality. In general, it is held to have developed out of custom.[1] That is to say, human beings could not live in society without adopting certain customary ways of acting, and morality, one of the forms of social consciousness, has developed out of customs. Various theories are proposed about the precise characteristics of morality as distinct from custom and about the way in which the emergence of morality took place, but that morality is a social phenomenon, arising out of custom, and neither something of divine origin nor something created purely by reason, is universally held.

Customs, however, can differ from society to society, whether the societies are contemporaneous or successive. And so can moral codes. In

1 See, for example, A. F. Shiskin's *Foundations of Marxist Ethics* (*Osnovy Marksistskoi etiki*, Moscow, 1961). Among other topics, Shiskin discusses the relation between the person and society.

a society in which there are distinct and opposed classes, the content of morality is influenced by the interests of the dominant class. There is thus plenty of material for research into and writing about the history of moral ideas, convictions and ideals. Does it follow, however, that all morality is relative, that we can only say what content different societies and classes have given and give to morality, and that there is no criterion for judging the moral standards of different societies and classes? If so, ethics, considered as the science of morals, is purely descriptive. Or, if an ethical theory does include normative judgments, are not they simply the expression of the social consciousness of a particular society or class, there being no 'neutral' criterion by which we can judge between conflicting normative statements?

Pure ethical relativism is in fact rejected by Soviet moral philosophers. Social consciousness does indeed follow social being, with a greater or lesser time-lag, but morality has been developed in response to human needs, and human beings have objective needs. Some needs are common to human beings in all societies, while some are objective needs in relation to a particular social structure. In either case there are objective needs. A person belonging to a given society can therefore judge the commonly accepted moral standards and imperatives of this society in terms of this relation to objective needs. And, looking back, we can make similar judgments about the moral codes of past societies. Human nature changes, according to the Marxist, but it is nonetheless true that there are objective needs.

Further, whereas in a class-divided society it is the needs and interests of the dominant class which are primarily satisfied, in a society which had transcended class-division the needs of all would be satisfied, if not at once then progressively, and the morality of such a society would be a universal morality, a truly human morality. The classless, communist society, thus constitutes an ideal, in the light of which the moralities of other societies can be judged. But while communism is indeed an ideal, it is also, according to Marxism, the end towards which historical development is moving. Marxist ethics is thus a teleological ethics. Communist society constitutes the highest human good. Actions which contribute to the realization of this society are good, whereas actions which hinder its realization or are incompatible with it are bad.

It can be objected that though Marxist ethics is, indeed, teleological in form, with some resemblance to utilitarianism, in the long run it is an authoritarian ethics. Belief that a universal communist society is the goal of history and the highest good for man rests on certain texts, accepted as authoritative, and on the authority of the Party. The Soviet philosopher is not free to deny that communism is the highest good for man. He can, of course, try to prove that it is; but the conclusion at which he is expected to arrive is predetermined. He can discuss the meaning of 'good', and Soviet philosophers have in fact discussed this question in an historical context, examining various meanings which have been attached to the term, whether explicitly or implicitly. But when it is a question of deciding what is the highest good, what is the good which human beings ought to strive after as an ideal to be realized, the Soviet philosopher is not free to claim that it is something other than communism. It is, after all, a question of Marxist ethics.

Development within the limits of this framework is nonetheless possible. For example, Soviet philosophers have paid attention to the task of identifying ethical categories. One contribution to the subject is L. M. Arkhangelsky's *Categories of Marxist Ethics*[1] in which the author argues that the category of good is the basic and all-embracing ethical category. Again, Soviet philosophers have attempted to develop a theory of values. Among writings on the theme can be mentioned *On the Values of Life and Culture*[2] and *The Theory of Values in Marxism*[3], both by V. P. Tugarinov. Philosophers have discussed the nature of values, their hierarchical structure and their relation to action. Obviously, the Marxist does not believe that there are values 'out there', subsisting in some world of their own, but this does not commit him to regarding talk about values as meaningless or evaluation as unimportant or as being devoid of any objective basis.

In his *Theses on Feuerbach* Marx asserted that in its reality the human essence is 'the *ensemble* of the social relations'. Obviously if this statement is taken by itself, it can be understood as meaning that the so-called essence of the human being is nothing but a set of social relations. As so understood, the statement reduces the human being to a member of the collective, the social organism. Although, however, there has certainly been a tendency in the social-political movement stemming from Marx and Engels to treat human beings simply as cells in the social organism, as instruments for the realization of a social end, it is a mistake to think that all Soviet philosophers have been and are satisfied with this collectivist view. After all, Marx did not desire the crushing or obliteration of individuality. His ideal society was one in which each human being would be genuinely free to develop his or her talents. It has been

1 *Kategorii marksistskoi etiki* (Moscow, 1963). As one would expect, Arkhangelsky emphasizes the historical development of ethical categories.
2 *O cennostyax zizni i kulturi* (Leningrad, 1960).
3 *Teoriya cennostey v marksizme* (Leningrad, 1968).

argued, therefore, that if Marx's statement is interpreted in the light of its context, it can be understood in the following way. Feuerbach, according to Marx, abstracted from historical human beings and thought in terms of the human essence as 'genus', an essence which is exemplified in individuals. But Marx maintained that there is no more an abstract human essence, which happens to be exemplified in individuals, than there is a genuine essence of fruit, which happens to be exemplified in individual fruits of various kinds. There are only actual individual human beings, existing in different societies and realizing themselves through their social relations in a variety of ways.

Further, as Soviet philosophers have noted, it is not immediately apparent how the term 'relations' should be understood. Some writers have maintained that a distinction must be made between 'connections' and 'relations'. Non-human things are interrelated in the sense that there are connections between them. But Marx was thinking of social relations as conscious relations and as peculiar to human beings. In a 'relation', as so understood, man both distinguishes himself from and relates himself to others. What Marx meant was that unless a human being relates himself or herself in this way, he or she is not functioning as a human being. The human person is the subject of social relations, and if we abstract from all social relations, we are left with the biological organism. It is only in and through social relations that the human being is a person, something more than simply a biological organism. But this does not alter the fact that it is the individual who is the real subject of social relations. Inasmuch as Marx insisted that history is made by concrete, living human beings, he cannot have intended to claim that they are nothing but moments in the life of an abstract entity, named society.

Understood literally, Marx certainly described the human essence as being an *ensemble* of social relations, and some philosophers in the Soviet Union have defended a relationist theory, according to which a thing is reducible to relations, a theory which, as applied to human beings, would support collectivism. Other philosophers, however, for example, V. P. Tugarinov, have argued that things are presupposed by relations and cannot be reduced to them. The concept of social relations, that is to say, makes no sense, unless the relations are conceived as presupposing individual human beings. There have been other writers, such as A. I. Uemov, who have maintained that though relations are relations between things, a thing is not, as Tugarinov thought, a substance possessing properties or qualities but a system of qualities, one system differing from another1.

Theories about things, qualities and relations belong to ontology rather than to ethics. But they can have implications in the field of moral philosophy. For example, if emphasis is laid, as by Tugarinov, on the individual's irreducibility to social relations, it is easier to depict the human being as a relatively autonomous moral agent and to stress the idea of personal self-realization. In a well known article entitled 'Communism and the Person'2 Tugarinov made a distinction between individuality and personality, conceiving the latter as a property of the former, in the sense that personality is something which the individual possesses. A person is an individual entity which possesses, for instance, rationality and freedom and has certain rights and obligations. Further, though Tugarinov allowed that in one sense of personality every human being is a person, he tended to conceive personality as a moral category, as a normative ideal, as something which the individual does or does not attain. Other Soviet philosophers, however, have objected that though one can reasonably speak of a fully developed personality, as distinct from a less developed one, the distinction between individual and person could be used, even though this was not intended by Tugarinov, in an anti-humanistic sense, as a means of excluding groups of human beings from the class of persons. As for the positive content of the concept of person, we can find a variety of views, some writers emphasizing the idea of man as a social being, others laying stress on consciousness.

In view of the emphasis laid by Marxism on society and on the human being's formation by his or her social environment, one might expect that if a Soviet philosopher speaks of personality as a value, he is likely to be thinking of relative value. Marxism allows, of course, not only for society's influence on the individual but also for the human being's power to change (within limits) the social environment. But this would be compatible with the claim that the person is of value in so far as he or she contributes to a social end, ultimately the building of communism.

Somewhat surprisingly, however, certain Soviet philosophers have recognized truth in the Kantian claim that a human being should

1 Uemov is the author of *Things, Properties and Relations* (*Vesci, svoystva i otnosheniya*, Moscow, 1963).
2 In *Problems of Philosophy*, 1962 (VI, pp. 14–23). Tugarinov has also published *The Person and Society* (Moscow, 1965).

always be treated as an end and never as a mere means.[1] Thus in 'Communism and the Person' Tugarinov maintained that the human person as such possesses value, and in 1965 Shiskhin published an article entitled 'Man as the Highest Value' in *Problems of Philosophy*.[2] Both writers referred to Kant's doctrine. But they would not, of course, regard their thesis as an abandonment of Marx in favour of Kant. The thesis can be supported by appeal to Marx's concept of the ideal society, in which all would be able to develop themselves freely. In other words, some Soviet philosophers have emphasized what they believe to be the humanist elements in Marxism.

This line of thought is doubtless facilitated if appeal is made to the early writings of Marx, the manuscripts which remained unpublished either by Marx himself or by Engels. As these writings constituted a source of inspiration for non-Soviet revisionists, notably in Jugoslavia, it is understandable that some orthodox Marxists claimed that it was foolish to base theories on manuscripts which neither of the founding fathers thought worth publishing, and which represent a stage of thought which Marx abandoned or transcended. But there was another possible way of coping with the revisionists. One could appropriate, so to speak, Marx's early writings and interpret them in a sense more in harmony with his later writings. Thus, when writing about the subject of alienation, Soviet philosophers have argued that there is continuity between the earlier and later thought of Marx. The fact that he came to focus his attention on a particular form of alienation does not prove that he repudiated his more general ideas about human alienation. Even Academician M. B. Mitin, whom nobody could accuse of adventurous revisionism, has seen a unity in Marx's thought from the early writings up to *Capital*, a unity which, according to Mitin, was reproduced in the thought of Lenin.[3] It is therefore a mistake to think that it is only Polish and Jugoslav revisionists who have made use of Marx's early writings. It is true, however, that whereas the revisionists have used these writings to support a sometimes radically changed version of Marxism, Soviet philosophers have been much more conservative, being careful not to appeal to the early manuscripts against Marx's later writings and the ideas of Lenin.

1 Qualification such as 'never as a mere means' or 'never as being merely – or only – a means' are obviously important. We cannot help using other human beings as means. If one gets a haircut, the hairdresser functions as a means. But it does not follow that one has to regard the hairdresser, as a person, as being nothing more than a means to one's end.
2 Maintaining that true humanism is to be found in Communism, Shiskin argues that the individual, considered in abstraction from society, cannot be the 'highest end'.
3 See Mitin's article 'V. I. Lenin and the Problem of Man' in *Problems of Philosophy* for 1967 (VIII, pp. 19–30). Mitin criticizes any attempt to oppose Marx's early writings to his later ones.

In the Stalinist period, of course, the guardians of Marxist orthodoxy had attacked not only philosophers who flirted with ideas judged to be at variance with the ideology but also scientists who embraced or showed themselves favourably disposed towards theories of western origin which were believed, or at any rate said to be contaminated by 'idealism'. As the ideologists were able to rely on the Party to support their campaign against all forms of 'heresy', they were able to do considerable harm both to philosophical thought and to the free development of science. After Stalin's death, however, it became easier for scientists to resist unwelcome pressure from philosophers, and for philosophers to question interpretations of Marxism and its implications defended by their more narrow-minded and blinkered colleagues.

One of the issues discussed in the 1960s was the relation between science and ethics. Some scientists, such as the physicist E. Feinberg, distinguished sharply between moral judgments and scientific statements and denied that ethical conclusions could be derived from scientific premises, whereas the Marxist ideologists had been inclined to insist that in Soviet society morality had at last been given a solid scientific basis, and to view the ideas of Kant and of the neopositivists as infected by the poison of 'idealism'. There was obviously room for serious exploration of the relations between science and ethics, and philosophers were now able to express their convictions with a greater degree of freedom than they had been able to do during the reign of Stalin.

8. Soviet philosophers have been expected by the Party to study and understand non-Marxist philosophies and to refute them in so far as their theories are at variance with Marxism. But the Soviet philosopher is not required to caricature non-Marxist systems of thought. Some may have been guilty of this, but there is no obligation to pursue this path. It is doubtless true that the Marxist doctrine of the dependence of the superstructure on the infrastructure encourages philosophers to treat other systems of thought as expressions of class mentalities, without giving much serious attention to the arguments advanced by non-Marxist philosophers in support of their theories. At the same time recognition of the 'indirect' character of the influence of the infrastructure on the superstructure, and also of the fact that once an element in the ideological superstructure, such as philosophy, has come into existence, it takes on a life of its own, provides a ground for serious inquiry into the internal development of philosophical thought, for investigation into the relations between successive philosophical movements and systems. For example, even if a Marxist classifies Kant as a representative of the

bourgeoisie and tries to show in what particular ways the German thinker was the spokesman for a social class, this does not prevent him from dwelling on the connections between Kant's thought and previous philosophical movements, such as rationalist metaphysics on the one hand and British empiricism on the other. Nor, of course, does it exclude study of the relations between the critical philosophy of Kant and the science, religion and aesthetics of the time.

In other words, in spite of the fact that the Soviet philosopher is committed to maintaining that with Marx philosophy was raised to a higher level, he can nonetheless do serious work in the field of history of philosophy. A good deal has been published in this field. One example is G. Alexandrov's *History of Western Philosophy* (1946). Another is provided by I. S. Narskij's volumes on Western European philosophy in the seventeenth and nineteenth centuries.[1] Narskij is associated with publication of the learned journal *Filosofskie Nauki* (*Philosophical Sciences*).

As for the spirit of partisanship and the desire to refute, the activity of refuting need not, of course, obtrude itself when it is a question of theories which belong to the past and which can hardly be looked on as living rivals to Marxism. After all, one would hardly undertake to refute Thales' theory of water as the ultimate reality. Moreover, to emphasize the connections between, say, the political theories of Plato and Aristotle and contemporary social structures and economic life is not the same thing as setting out to 'refute' the theories. The Marxist would naturally see them as relative to an era which is past. When, however, it is a question of philosophies and movements, whether of contemporary or recent origin or coming from the past, which are capable of influencing minds today, the Soviet philosopher is expected to subject them to adverse criticism in so far as they are incompatible with Marxism. To be sure, standards both of understanding and of politeness have certainly improved, but however much the Soviet philosopher may claim to be following simply the voice of reason in his criticism, it is clear that Marxism-Leninism constitutes the basic criterion for judging other philosophies, though this does not prevent him from endorsing ideas which seem to him compatible with Marxism and of use in developing Marxist thought. Ideas derived from phenomenology, for example, can be used in this way.

---

1 *Zapadno-Evropjeskaya Filosofiya XVII Veka* (Moscow, 1974); *XVIII Veka* (Moscow, 1973); *XIX Veka* (Moscow, 1976).

Chapter 13

Philosophers in Exile (1)

1. It would be a mistake to suppose that all those thinkers who contributed to the renaissance of religiously oriented thought in the first two decades of the twentieth century were disciples of Solovyev, in the sense that they all derived their main ideas from his thought. The two brothers, Prince S. H. Trubetskoy and Prince E. N. Trubetskoy did indeed stand close to Solovyev, but the former, who was Rector of the University of Moscow, died in 1905 and the latter (of typhus) in 1920. Neither of them, therefore, was a member of the group expelled from the Soviet Union in 1922. Of this group Semyon Frank (1877–1950), L. P. Karsavin (1882–1952) and S. N. Bulgakov (1871–1944) adhered to Solovyev's idea of total-unity (cf page 222f.). N. A. Berdyaev (1874–1948), however, though influenced by Solovyev, took exception to the monist tendency in Solovyev's thought, while N. O. Lossky (1870–1965) tried to combine the concept of total-unity with ideas derived from the pluralist and spiritualist monadism of Aleksei Kozlov (1831–1901), a professor at Kiev who had been influenced by Leibniz. I. I. Lapshin (1870–1952) was a Neo-Kantian, while I. A. Ilyin (1882–1954), who had been a professor of law at the University of Moscow, specialized in the study of Fichte and Hegel, especially the latter. L. Shestov (1866–1938), who emigrated after the Revolution, had little use for systematic metaphysics and is commonly described as an 'irrationalist'. These were all religiously oriented thinkers, but it would be misleading to classify them as being all followers of Solovyev. Solovyev did a great deal to prepare the way for the revival of religious philosophy, but the extent to which the ideas of the relevant philosophers were actually inspired by him varied very much.

Some of the group were, or became, primarily theologians. This is true of Bulgakov, ex-professor of economics, who, in exile, occupied the chair of dogmatic theology in the Orthodox Theological Institute at Paris. Another prominent theologian was Father Pavel Florensky, who was also a scientist. Florensky, however, remained in the Soviet Union and in the middle of the 1930s was sent to a labour camp, where he apparently died. The authorities respected him as a scientist, but his rejection of their demands that he should renounce his priesthood led to a ten-year sentence. Other members of the group were primarily philosophers, for example Frank, Berdyaev[1], Karsavin, Lapshin and Ilyin.

Some of the philosophers who were expelled from the Soviet Union in 1922 had been Marxists for a while. This is true of Frank, Berdyaev and Bulgakov, but the change from Marxism to religiously oriented philosophy was not accompanied by an abandonment of social concern. It was more a question of these thinkers having come to the conclusion that Marxism was inadequate as a philosophy for life and as a basis for social ideals. In his autobiography Berdyaev remarks that his revolutionary and socialist sympathies were formed before his entry into the University and his participation in Marxist circles.[2] These sympathies led him to embrace Marxism, but they did not originate from it, and his passion for the regeneration of mankind did not disappear with his abandonment of Marxism. Again, Bulgakov maintained that it was precisely his search for an adequate basis for social ideals which brought him to religion. In other words, Bulgakov came to the conclusion that Marxism lacked any real ethics (as distinct from a theory about the relativity of ethical beliefs), and reflection on ethics brought him back to religious faith. True, he eventually became a professional theologian, but he did not become indifferent to social justice.

Whereas Berdyaev and Bulgakov turned back to Orthodox Christianity, Frank was a Jew. Arrested in 1899 for his Marxist-inspired activities, he went for a while to Germany, where he became disillusioned with Marxism. Coming to Christianity by way of Kantianism, he entered the Russian Orthodox Church in 1912. In the case of neither Berdyaev nor Frank, however, did the transition from Marxism to Christianity involve either an abandonment of freedom of thought in favour of subservience to ecclesiastical dogmatism or an exchange of one form of dogmatism for another. For one thing, although they once adhered to Marxism, they were to all intents and purposes revisionists from the start. For another, they did not regard adherence to Christian faith as demanding all abandonment of freedom to speculate in interpreting human life and reality in general. Berdyaev said of himself that he spoke

1 In 1947 the University of Cambridge conferred on Berdyaev the honorary degree of doctor of divinity. Referring to this honour, he remarked that he regarded himself as a 'religious philosopher' and not as a theologian. *Dream and Reality*, p. 325.
2 *Ibid.*, p. 115.

'with the voice of free religious thought',[1] and that though he stood nearer to Orthodoxy than to Catholicism or Protestantism, he was not 'a typical "orthodox" of any kind'.[2] As for Bulgakov, his Solovyev-inspired speculative doctrine of Sophia led to his being attacked by the Moscow patriarchate and also by some emigré ecclesiastical groups.

Lapshin, who was a Neo-Kantian, believed that metaphysics as a science was impossible. To a good many Western readers, however, the more well-known Russian philosophers in exile probably tend to give the impression of pursuing metaphysical speculation in which appeal is made to intuitive knowledge rather than to closely reasoned argument. To put the matter bluntly, they may seem to make assertions about what is the case without giving any convincing reasons for believing that reality actually is what they claim it to be.

It is understandable that writers such as Berdyaev, Frank, Karsavin and Lossky should make an impression of this sort, not only on those who are positivistically inclined and mistrust metaphysics in any case, but also on those whose ideas of what philosophy should be have been derived from the analytic tradition. Berdyaev said that his vocation was 'to proclaim not a doctrine but a vision', and that he worked 'by inspiration'.[3] This autobiographical statement is unlikely to encourage the reader who has been taught to lay great emphasis on argumentation to regard Berdyaev as a 'philosopher'. He may even be inclined to conclude that the Russian thinker was more akin to a poet. Is it not significant that the circle which represented the pre-revolutionary cultural renaissance in Russia and which contributed to the periodical *Problems of Life* (or *Questions of Life*) included such literary figures as Andrey Bely, the symbolist poet, Alexander Blok and Vyacheslav Ivanov?

We must remember, however, that the twentieth-century Russian religious thinkers adhered to a line of thought going back to, for example, Kireevsky and continued by Solovyev, which was consciously opposed to Western 'rationalism'. The representatives of this line of thought did not deny that logical argument has a role to play. What they maintained was that for an integral grasp of reality intuitive knowledge was also required. Whether or not we agree, the Russian religious thinkers were aware what they were doing. They did not accept the idea of philosophy which gives rise to the sort of impression mentioned above. Whatever our evaluation of their writings may be, we should be careful to avoid the presupposition that they were trying, but failing, to

1 *Dream and Reality*, p. 177.
2 *Ibid.*
3 *Ibid.*, p. 289.

exemplify a concept of philosophy which they consciously rejected. Incidentally, when Berdyaev, for example, rejects rationalism, he is not thinking simply of atheist philosophers. He includes Thomism.

In any case it would be an exaggeration to claim that the Russian religious thinkers never argue, never give reasons, but simply state. Frank certainly argued. So did Lossky. One may or may not find the arguments convincing, but it is not true to say that argument is entirely lacking. Even Berdyaev – who admitted that he had 'little, if any, capacity' for 'analytical and discursive reasoning'[1] – uses argument of some kind, even if it bears little resemblance to the formal structure employed by Spinoza in his *Ethics*. The case of Shestov is different. For he was largely concerned with calling in question the competence of the theoretical reason. As Berdyaev remarks, however, Shestov used philosophy to attack philosophy.[2]

Since it is impossible to treat adequately in one chapter all the Russian exiled philosophers, the present writer proposes to confine his attention to some of the lines of thought of a few selected thinkers. Readers who desire a more extensive treatment can consult, for example, the histories of Russian philosophy by V. V. Zenkovsky and N. O. Lossky. Zenkovsky was a professor at the Orthodox Theological Institute at Paris (he was ordained a priest in 1942), while Lossky, after teaching in Czechoslovakia, went to America as a professor at the Russian Theological Academy in New York. As both men were philosophers in exile, it is natural that they should dwell at length on Russian thought as it developed outside the Soviet Union.

In his history Lossky expresses the hope that his account of this thought will arouse 'a sympathetic interest in Christianity in the minds of highly cultured people who have grown indifferent to religion'.[3] To what extent this hope has been fulfilled, the present writer is unable to say. A good many readers have, however, found the Russian writers both refreshing and stimulating. Among the writers, this applies especially to Berdyaev, who has doubtless been the most widely read. As for the reader, provided that he or she is not so much under the influence of a concept of philosophy which is alien to the Russian religious thinkers that the relevant literature is a source of constant irritation, the writings of the Russians may well tend to awaken a greater respect for a religious vision of the world and of human life. What to one mind may be either nonsensical or airy speculation may seem enlightening and stimulating to another mind. A lot depends on one's predispositions and expectations.

1 *Ibid.*, p. 88.
2 *Ibid.*
3 *History of Russian Philosophy*, p. 408.

2. In an article entitled 'the ethics of nihilism' Semyon Frank maintained that the Russian intelligentsia did not recognize or explicitly rejected 'absolute (objective) values'.[1] For example, the pursuit of 'theoretical, scientific truth', of knowledge for the sake of knowledge, and a 'disinterested striving for an adequate intellectual representation of the world' had no place in the mentality of the intelligentsia.[2] Again, in the sphere of aesthetics the intelligentsia, instead of recognizing beauty as an objective value, adopted the utilitarian views expounded by Chernyshevsky and Pisarev. As for religion, it was sometimes claimed that, in spite of appearances, the members of the intelligentsia were deeply religious. One's assessment of this claim, Frank remarked, depends on the meaning one gives to the word 'religion'. If religiosity and fanaticism are regarded as the same thing, 'the Russian intelligentsia is religious in the highest degree'.[3] For Frank, however, religion involved belief in an ultimate reality in which being and value are fused, are one, a belief which the intelligentsia conspicuously lacked. We can say that his subsequent philosophizing was a sustained attempt to justify and commend a religious vision of the world and human life, a vision centering around the idea of a total-unity or all-unity. In defending this idea of an all-embracing unity Frank stood, of course, close to Solovyev. But he was also considerably influenced, as was Karsavin, by the writings of the fifteenth-century western religious thinker Nicholas of Cusa (1401–64). Among other sources of inspiration was the Neoplatonist Plotinus.

Frank's approach to the idea of an ultimate unity in his early work *The Object of Knowledge* can be described in the following way. Through sense-perception we are acquainted with a multiplicity of determinate objects, distinct from one another. We conceive these objects as being of different kinds and as subject to the basic logical principles of identity, contradiction and excluded middle. A given object, a dog for example, is itself and not something else. To generalize, A is A and excludes or is opposed to *non-A*. As, however, we cannot conceive A as A, as a determinate self-identical object, without distinguishing it from *non-A*, there is a correlation between the two. Indeed, all determinate objects are interrelated in this way. This correlation, Frank argues, presupposes as its ground a unity which transcends the opposition between A and

1 *Filosofiya i Zhizn (Philosophy and Life)*, p. 226 (St Petersburg, 1910). This work is a collection of articles written between 1903 and 1909. By 'nihilism' Frank understood the rejection of the concept of objective and absolute values. The article mentioned is dated 1909.
  2 *Ibid.*, p. 223.
  3 *Ibid.*, p. 224.

non-A. This is a 'metalogical unity',[1] in the sense that it transcends all oppositions or contradictions. In the language of Nicholas of Cusa, it is the *coincidentia oppositorum*, the unity or identity of all opposites.

This line of thought was not, of course, a novelty. The British idealist Edward Caird (1835–1908) had argued that the distinction, inseparable from a correlation, between subject and object presupposed and pointed to an underlying and grounding unity. When Frank, however, refers to the self in the context of the idea of an ultimate unity, he tends to emphasize personal encounter, the encounter between persons, more than the subject-object relation as such. True, he argues against Hume's phenomenalistic analysis of the self. It is all very well for Hume to maintain that introspection reveals no 'I', apart from successive psychical phenomena. He forgets that if there were no 'I', the search for an 'I' would not be possible.[2] Frank certainly does not deny that the self performs the function of epistemological subject. But if we look at his work *The Unfathomable*,[3] we find him arguing that the self becomes an 'I' as related to a 'Thou', that in experiences such as those of loving the I and the Thou interpenetrate, become one, and that such interpenetration presupposes and is made possible by a unity at a deeper level. This line of thought reminds one more of thinkers such as Gabriel Marcel than of those who have emphasized the subject-object relation to such an extent that it is difficult to see how solipsism can be consistently avoided. But when he is treating to the subject-object relation in an epistemological sense, Frank is inclined to stress the idea of interpenetration, of subject and object becoming one.

The 'metalogical unity', the ultimate all-embracing reality, obviously does not belong to the empirical world of determinate things. Though presupposed by them, it is not one of them and cannot, therefore, be found among them. It transcends them. Further, it transcends conceptual thought, inasmuch as it is unique and thus cannot be grasped by universal or abstract concepts. It can be approached only through the process of negation and is known only indirectly through what Nicholas of Cusa called *docta ignorantia* (learned ignorance). The world of the 'fathomable' is the world of objects, the world which is graspable in concepts and to which the basic principles of logic are applicable. The all-embracing unity, however, the ultimate reality, is not and cannot be

---

1 *Predmet Znaniya (The Object of Knowledge)*, p. 237 (St Petersburg, 1915). There is a French translation, *La Connaissance et l'Être* (Paris, 1937).
2 See *Reality and Man*, translated by Natalie Duddington, p. 12 (London, 1965). The Russian original *Realnost i Chelovek* was published posthumously at Paris in 1956.
3 *Nepostizhimoye* (Paris, 1939).

an object. For by trying to objectify it, one sets it over against oneself, as something which one can contemplate. And that which is set against oneself is not the all-embracing unity. As therefore the ultimate reality is not and cannot be an object of knowledge, it is the unfathomable. It is the unity of being or existence and truth, and it can be experienced. But as this experience is not an experience of an object but a lived experience in which experiencer and experienced are one, it is inexpressible.

This is more or less the theory expounded in *The Unfathomable*. But Frank could hardly fail to be aware of the objections to which the fact that he had written a book on the unfathomable could give rise. He laid himself open to the retort that he had succeeded in saying a good deal about the inexpressible, and that this would not be possible if we were really 'ignorant' of the nature of reality. In *Reality and Man* he insisted, therefore, that the experience in question is not completely inexpressible, in a sense which would compel us to remain silent or dumb. 'The field of consciousness or experience is wider than that of thought,'[1] and the existence and nature of poetry show that 'the purpose of words is not limited to their function of designating concepts; words are also the instrument of spiritually mastering and imparting meaning to experience in its actual, super-logical nature'.[2] A poet can use language to suggest the actual experience of loving, though this actual experience is not identifiable with thought about love. In this sense the poet can express the experience of love. Analogously, language can be used to express or suggest the experience of the One, even though the One transcends logical analysis and conceptual thought. This function of language is not confined to poetry, and Frank defines philosophy, somewhat paradoxically, as '*the rational transcendence of the limitations of rational thought*'.[3]

It is hardly necessary to say that this conception of philosophy would be unacceptable not only in most university departments of philosophy in English-speaking countries but also among the officially recognized philosophers of Frank's homeland. The reply can, of course, be made that as Frank accepted neither Western 'rationalism' nor Marxism–Leninism, this state of affairs is only to be expected, and that it does not prove that Frank's position is untenable. Though, however, it is true that the unfashionability of a position does not prove that it is intellectually untenable, it is obviously arguable that Frank tries to have things both ways, to assert that there is a metalogical reality which cannot be

1 *Reality and Man*, p. 37.
2 *Ibid.*, p. 42.
3 *Ibid.*, p. 44.

conceptualized and at the same time to think and reason about it. Rather, however, than pursuing this theme, let us turn our attention to the religious aspect of Frank's theory. The ultimate unity is called by him 'God'. How does he understand this term?

In the first place Frank subjects what might be described as 'pictorial theism' to severe criticism. 'The prevalent type of religious thought tends to conceive God as a reality existing outside us, as an *object* the existence of which has to be intellectually established'.[1] In this line of thought God is objectified as an object 'out there', not as in the world but as beyond it. Reality consists of the world and of the supramundane God. Any attempt to prove God's existence by starting with empirical entities and then arguing that there must also be a God (as First Mover or First Cause or divine Architect, for example) implies this view of reality. But it is obvious that it is a view or picture which Frank cannot accept, given his theory of total-unity. If God is objectified as 'out there', he cannot be the all-embracing unity. For we then have myself, the objectifier, on the one hand and God on the other. Reality, for Frank, is one. It is not divided into two 'halves', God and the world.

The atheist argues that 'in our direct experience of objective reality we do not encounter any such object as God and that all that we know about the world gives us no sufficient grounds, to say the least of it, for inferring the existence of God, which is therefore an unjustified hypothesis'.[2] As Frank rejects the conception of God as an object among objects, he naturally endorses the first part of the atheist's statement. For anyone who equates the world of objects with reality in general, atheism is the natural position. As for the second part of the atheist's statement, Frank agrees with this too. God cannot be found by a process of dispassionate rational thought or argument, not if he transcends the logical sphere and conceptualization. At the same time Frank is not prepared to accept the atheist's conclusion, namely that faith in God is unjustified. God can be sought and found only through an inner experience, by which we come into direct contact with reality itself, with God that is to say, an experience in which reality reveals itself. This experience is *sui generis*, 'completely independent of any other knowledge'.[3] Given this experience, we can then try to use language to suggest or express its content.

If God is conceived as the Absolute, the total-unity, the question arises whether Frank should not be described as a pantheist. He obviously does not identify God with what he calls 'the world of fact', the empirical

1 *Ibid.*, p. 92.
2 *Ibid.*, p. 93.
3 *Ibid.*, p. 95.

world. As he rightly remarks (following Schopenhauer), if pantheism is understood as the doctrine that 'God' is a label for the empirical world, pantheism is equivalent to atheism. But if Frank conceives God as a 'metalogical unity' which comprises all reality within itself, how, it may well be asked, can he avoid pantheism, supposing that he wishes to do so? For it seems that there is only one reality, namely God. Frank, like Solovyev, can be seen as trying to think the concept of God philosophically, overcoming 'pictorial theism'. But does not this path lead to pantheism?

What Frank has to say about creation (in *The Unfathomable*) seems extremely obscure. He rejects both the idea of creation out of nothing[1] and that of emanation, if, that is to say, these theories are understood literally. At the same time he tells his readers that the world is a theophany, an expression of God, having its real basis and its ideal ground in God. So he certainly makes a distinction between God and the world, though he also maintains that they are inseparable. As for the self, it must not be confused with God; nor must it be conceived as divided from God. One could hardly claim that what Frank says is immediately clear. But it is open to him to reply that as God is a 'metalogical' unity, transcending conceptualization, a 'clear' account of the relation between God and the world is possible. Negations are possible. Apart, however, from negation, language can be used only to suggest what cannot be properly grasped by rational thought.

This is the line which Frank takes when treating of the problem of evil. He does indeed follow the Protestant mystic Jakob Boehme and the German philosopher Schelling in suggesting that the ultimate ground of the possibility of evil must be found in God himself. But in the end evil is inexplicable. The so-called 'problem of evil is rationally insoluble, and to attempt a theodicy is waste of time. Man's task is to overcome evil, to banish it, not to explain it'.[2] The immediate root of evil lies in man's alienation from God, in the act by which he makes himself the centre of the universe, substituting himself for God, deifying himself, as in Dostoevsky's idea of the Man-god. Although it is clear that, for Frank, man's separation of himself from his true centre is a 'fall' and lies at the root of all moral evil, the question arises how, given the theory of total-unity, this fall is possible. And it is this question which Frank regards as unanswerable by us. True, he asserts that the ultimate basis of evil must lie in God himself, as everything is in God, the total-unity. At the same time we are told that though this basis is in God, it is not God himself.

---

1 Lossky aptly remarks that Frank did not properly understand the idea of creation 'out of nothing'. See his *History of Russian Philosophy*, pp. 282–3.
2 *Nepostizhimoye*, p. 300.

Frank has in mind Boehme's theory of the *Ungrund*, the incomprehensible Abyss, which is neither good nor evil, and Schelling's idea of the unconscious, irrational will in the divine being which logically (not temporally) precedes God's positing of himself as a rational loving will. But such theories can hardly be said to explain evil. It would be a case of 'explaining' what is clearly present, namely evil, by deriving it from what is obscure. Indeed, Schelling, while postulating a cosmic Fall, said explicitly that it could not be explained.[1] It could not be deduced. Frank adopts a similar line of thought. As for his practical conclusion, that the human being's task is to try to overcome evil and banish it, rather than to explain it, most people would agree with the programme of trying to overcome the evil in the world. But it is obviously possible to argue that if evil is inexplicable within one framework of thought, we should inquire whether it can be explained within another framework of thought. Frank, however, is confident that the existence of God as total-unity is so evident that no objections are sufficient to refute it.

A good many Christian theologians would doubtless react to Frank's ideas by starting to talk about the God of the philosophers and the God of religion. Frank, they would be inclined to argue, constructs a theory of the all-inclusive Absolute, which he proceeds to call 'God', though the Absolute of the metaphysicians bears little resemblance to the God of the Bible. The Absolute lies beyond good and evil; human moral distinctions are inapplicable to it, as was seen, for example, by the Taoists in China and by Spinoza and F. H. Bradley in the West. But the God of the Bible is certainly not indifferent to good and evil. Further, the God of the Bible is personal, whereas the Absolute is impersonal or, if preferred, suprapersonal. To be sure, Frank was a devout Orthodox Christian, and he would claim to be saying what 'God' must mean. He would not allow that he had substituted a metaphysical construct for the God of religion. The fact remains, however, that his thought moved in the direction of this substitution, even if he did not recognize that this was the case. Much the same can be said of Solovyev before him.

Without undertaking to discuss here the general theme of the alleged dichotomy between the God of the philosophers and the God of religion or, rather, the God of the Bible, we can, none the less draw attention to two points which are relevant to an understanding of Frank's mind. First, though God as the Absolute is suprapersonal, in his relationship to the human being he is a loving 'Thou'. The Deity turns towards us, as it were, the aspect under which it is personal. This idea may well remind us of the

1 *Works*, edited by Manfred Schröter, IV, p. 32 (Munich, 1927–8).

Indian philosopher Śaṁkara's conception of Brahman, the suprapersonal Absolute, as appearing as the personal God to the devout soul. Secondly, Frank finds room for the concept of revelation. There is the primary and basic revelation by which God reveals himself in mystical experience, an experience which philosophy interprets. And there is the positive Christian revelation, communicated through God as the 'Thou' entering history at the Incarnation. Indeed, God is accessible 'only through *revelation* in the general and literal senses of this term',[1] through inner experience, that is to say, and through positive Christian revelation. It may be difficult to harmonize these ideas with the concept of total-unity, but at any rate they show that Frank did not wish to eliminate the representation of God as a loving Father who has revealed himself in and through Christ. It is nonetheless arguable that he could retain the 'God of the Bible' only at the cost of inconsistency with his metaphysics.

In 1930 Frank published a book entitled *The Spiritual Foundations of Society*. As one would expect he sees the ideal goal of social development as the fullest possible realization of the divine life in society. This means unity, harmony, but it also involves freedom. Service of God and working for the communal good must be free.[2] Though, however, the life of society should exemplify the concept of *sobornost*, of a unity in which freedom is respected, and though a society cannot endure unless there is an inner unity, which is expressed in the concept of 'we', it is also true that social unity tends to be broken up by conflicts, struggle, division between members and groups. Hence besides inner unity an external organization is also required, which can exercise coercion. This is the outer aspect of society. According to Frank, the best institution for combining organic unity with externally organizing social will which has been found up to date is constitutional monarchy. Frank was undoubtedly influenced by Hegel, though he sometimes uses Hegelian language in senses which were his own rather than Hegel's.

I have mentioned the influence of the thought of Nicholas of Cusa both on Frank and on Karsavin.[3] The latter developed the idea of the Absolute, of creation as a theophany, and of the return to the Absolute or God in

1 *Reality and Man*, p. 94.

2 According to Solovyev, freedom of will was found only in the choice of evil, a choice which is irrational. Frank reversed this thesis. By nature the human being strives after what is good, and this spontaneous striving is free. As for evil, we are drawn to it involuntarily. If we choose evil, we are mastered by it. On this theory it is difficult to see how anyone can be accounted personally responsible for choosing what is evil.

3 After having been expelled from the Soviet Union Karsavin occupied professorial chairs in Lithuania. The result was that one fine day in 1939 he found himself back in the Soviet Union. He died in a labour camp in 1952.

his own way. But it is Frank who must serve as the representative of the concept of total-unity among the Russian philosophers in exile. Karsavin, however, did pay special attention to philosophy of history, identifying the history of mankind with preparation for the Incarnation and with the development of the Church. He wrote from the point of view of Orthodox Christianity, and he saw religiousness as the essential feature of the Russian people. To make this idea plausible, he had to interpret militant atheism as a form of religion. It is also worth mentioning that in spite of his theory of total-unity Karsavin laid great emphasis on the value of personality, a subject on which he published a work in 1929. He tried to steer a middle course between theism and pantheism or, rather, to transcend the opposition between them. This enterprise, though understandable (if theism is understood 'pictorially'), is obviously not easy to fulfil. Karsavin asserted the doctrine of creation out of nothing, but he interpreted this as meaning that the divine reality bestows content on 'nothing', the content being a theophany. God creates, but what he creates is not a positive reality distinct from himself. There cannot be anything 'outside' God.

3. In his *History of Russian Philosophy* N. O. Lossky[1] criticized Frank and Karsavin for what he regarded as the pantheist tendencies in their thought, for their ideas about creation, for their interpretations of freedom, and for their inability to account for evil without making God ultimately responsible for it. He himself tried to develop a system of theistic metaphysics, believing that this was required for an adequate intellectual Christian interpretation of the world and of human life.[2] In doing this he was influenced by philosophers such as Leibniz and Bergson, though this does not mean that he agreed with all that they said about the themes which influenced his thought.

As Lossky gives a systematic synopsis of his own philosophical theories in his *History of Russian Philosophy*,[3] any treatment of the matter by the present writer may seem superfluous. For who is better qualified than Lossky to summarize his philosophy? A selective sketch of Russian philosophical thought outside the Soviet Union would, however, be even more inadequate if the thought of Lossky were entirely omitted. He was

1 Nikolai Onufrievich Lossky (1870–1965) should not be confused with his son Vladimir Nikolaevich Lossky (1903–58). Both left the Soviet Union in 1922, and both were religious thinkers, though the father, a prolific writer, is much bettern known. References to 'Lossky' in this section are always to the father, N. O. Lossky.

2 I say 'intellectual interpretation' to avoid the impression of implying that Lossky imagined that one could not be a good Christian without studying metaphysics.

3 Pp. 251–66.

one of the more important philosophers in exile, and mention of his theories helps to correct any impression that Solovyev's concept of total-unity governed the minds of all the twentieth-century Russian religious thinkers. It is true that the concept was present in Lossky's thought in the sense that he tried to present a unified conception of reality, but he was at pains to avoid the pantheistic tendency which was a feature of the phil-osophies of Frank and Karsavin. Something should therefore be said about his line of thought. But no attempt will be made to cover their whole range in summarizing form.

In 1906 Lossky published a work entitled *Obosnovaniye Intuitivizma* (*The Foundation* – or *Basis* – *of Intuitivism*),[1] and he is commonly described as 'intuitivist'. The description can be misleading. For it may suggest the idea of someone who relies on hunches, dignified by the name 'intuitions', and who disdains argument. In point of fact Lossky's intuiti-vism is a carefully reasoned position. He attacks the causal theory of perception, understood as meaning that what we know directly are the effects of the causal action of objects on our organs of sense, and not external objects in themselves. This theory gives rise to familiar episte-mological problems. In opposition to it Lossky claims that we are directly aware of external objects in themselves, even if this knowledge is partial or fragmentary. The object, according to Lossky, enters con-sciousness, is immanent in it. Obviously, he does not mean that a tree, for example, abandons its spatial location to enter a human mind. What he means is that when I focus my attention on the tree, it becomes the direct object of my awareness and is in this sense immanent in consciousness. The epistemological relation between subject and object is not a causal relation. That is to say, as far as the epistemological relation is con-cerned, the tree does not cause my perception of it, as empiricism maintains. Nor do I, as subject, act causally as the tree. The relation is one of 'coordination', not of subordination of effect to cause. Of course, Lossky does not deny that there are causal relations. His thesis is simply that the epistemological relation is not one of them. Established by attention, this relation can be described as 'immediate apprehension (contemplation or intuition)'.[2] Evidently, intuition in this sense has nothing to do with hunches.

Reference has just been made to external objects, such as a tree. But it is not simply a question of external objects. I can have, for example,

1 This book has been translated into English by Natalie A. Duddington as *The Intuitive Basis of Knowledge* (London, 1919).
2 From Lossky's paper 'Intuitionalism', printed in the *Proceedings of the Aristotelian Society*, New Series, XIV (1914), p. 131.

immediate awareness or intuitive apprehension of a desire in myself (of myself desiring). Further, intuition, according to Lossky, is not confined to objects, whether external or internal, which exist here and now. For example, when I recall a past event, I have an immediate apprehension of the event as past. And in anticipating a future event, I am conscious of it as a future event.

Some objects of intuition or immediate apprehension belong both to the spatial and to the temporal spheres. A tree, for example, exists in space, and it also becomes, changes, in time. There are other objects which are not spatially located but which are none the less temporal, such as a mental state. Further, there can also be objects of consciousness which do not belong to spatio-temporal reality at all, mathematical truths for example. These 'eternal objects', taken together, form the sphere of 'ideal being', as distinct from the sphere of 'real being'. In other words, Lossky accepts the Platonic theory of the realm of ideas. These objects are apprehended by intellectual intuition.

For Lossky, there is yet another form of intuition, namely mystical intuition of the Absolute, which is metalogical and not accessible either to sensory intuition (sense-perception) or to intellectual intuition in the sense mentioned above, namely immediate apprehension of objects belonging to the sphere of ideal being. As we are considering at the moment an epistemological theory, it would perhaps be better to say that if there is an Absolute (this question being left to metaphysics), it can be the object of intuitive apprehension, inasmuch as intuition is not confined to sensory intuition. But Lossky is, of course, convinced that reflection on mysticism shows that there have been cases of immediate awareness of the Absolute.

Though criticism of causal theories of perception and defence of the idea of immediate apprehension of an object as a relation of coordination pertain to the theory of knowledge, it is evident that Lossky regards his intuitivism as opening the door to metaphysics. If, for example, we were to accept the theory that knowledge is confined to knowledge of impressions made on our organs of sense by external objects, the range of our knowledge would be confined to these impressions or sense-data or, at best, to indirect knowledge of the material world. Intuitivism, however, broadens the field. We can be aware, for instance, of 'ideal being'. Thus in the introduction or preface to *The World as an Organic Whole*[1] Lossky states explicitly that 'the theory of knowledge worked out in my

1 *The World as an Organic Whole*, translated by Natalie A. Duddington (Oxford, 1928), includes some additions to and modifications of the Russian text, made by Lossky.

books *The Intuitive Basis of Knowledge*, the *Handbuch der Logik* and elsewhere, aims at vindicating the validity of metaphysics. Moreover, the intuitional theory renders possible the combination of the most diverse metaphysical doctrines concerning realms of being and aspects of the world that profoundly differ from one another'.[1] Whereas empiricist and Kantian theories of knowledge tend, in their different ways, to bar the door to metaphysics, intuitivism opens it wide.

One of Lossky's main approaches to metaphysics is through a theory of judgment. Consider a simple statement such as 'the grass is green'. The greenness is obviously not an entity existing independently of the subject; it is, for Lossky at any rate, an objective quality of the object. It can be described as an 'aspect'. Before we can predicate greenness of grass, we have first to single out this aspect by mental analysis, which, together with intuitive apprehension, is an element of knowledge. This act of analysis presupposes a complex whole. According to Lossky, the whole is prior to its parts, not constructed out of them. We can designate points in a line, but a line does not consist of juxtaposed points. If it is objected, for example, that a given atom is certainly different from any other atom, Lossky's reply is that neither can exist apart from the system of atoms.

This line of thought is applied to the world, conceived as an organic whole. 'Every element of the world – be it an atom, or a soul, or an event such as movement – (is) an *aspect* of the world discoverable by means of analysis and existing, not independently, but only on the basis of a world-whole, only within a universal system'.[2] This concept of the world is obviously opposed to any idea of it as a collection or aggregate of different entities. The world is not the result of adding up, so to speak, all individual entities. The individual entities develop within the whole, which is prior.

The question naturally arises whether there is any sufficient reason for going beyond the world. If one wishes to use the term Absolute, is not the world itself the Absolute, the supreme whole or totality? To answer this question, Lossky has recourse to the idea of the world as a system. His contention is that 'wherever there is a system, there must be something beyond system'.[3] Whether the idea of the world as a system is consistent with conceiving it as a whole which is prior to its parts, seems to me disputable. But however this may be, Lossky's

1 *The World as an Organic Whole*, p. VI. The *Handbuch der Logik* to which Lossky refers is a German translation of a work on logic which appeared in 1922.
2 *Ibid*., p. 18.
3 *Ibid*., p. 63.

argument is that a system contains plurality, and that plurality must ultimately have its source in 'a Principle which does not contain any plurality in itself'.[1] This Principle is the Absolute, which transcends all plurality. It is the source of the world, but the world is not part of it, nor an emanation from its substance. But 'in speaking about the Absolute as such we can only characterize it by negative definitions'.[2] 'Even the term One, as Plotinus pointed out, can be applied to it in the negative sense only, i.e. as indicating that it contains no plurality'.[3]

In spite of his emphasis on the Absolute's transcendence of the world, it may seem that Lossky's thought is moving in the same direction as that of Frank. After all, he asserts the priority of the whole to its parts, and in *The World as an Organic Whole* he refers appreciatively to Frank's ideas, especially to his book *The Object of Knowledge*[4]. But he endorses Frank's ideas only in so far as they are similar to his own. In any case, we have so far made no mention of the personalist element in Lossky's thought, a subject to which we must now turn.

4. We have noted that the subject of consciousness is capable of contemplating past events and of anticipating the future. According to Lossky, this capacity manifests the supratemporal character of the subject. As such, it belongs to the sphere of ideal being, though it is not, of course, an abstract idea. The subject, however, is capable of activity in time. Discriminating, for example, is a temporal activity. Emotions come and go in time. And actions are performed in time. Such activities manifest the nature of the subject as a 'substantival agent'.[5]

There is a plurality of such agents, agents which Lossky likens to the monads of Leibniz, though he rejects the German philosopher's idea of the monads as 'windowless'. As a system, the world is one organic whole, but it also possesses an aspect of 'unresolved fragmentariness',[6] which shows itself in the plurality of substances or substantival agents. Inasmuch as they are distinct from one another, they can enter into opposition and conflict, but they are nonetheless all interconnected, interrelated, and individual human beings are capable of working together for a common purpose, as they do in various forms of social union.

If we consider simply the idea of a plurality of substantival agents, it

1 *Ibid.*
2 *Ibid.*, p. 65.
3 *Ibid.*
4 *Ibid.*, p. 65, note 1 and p. 66.
5 *Ibid.*, p. 45 and elsewhere.
6 *Ibid.*, p. 53.

does not seem to be incompatible with the idea of the world as a system. For system does not necessarily exclude internal heterogeneity; it may comprise relatively independent elements. But in so far as there is conflict between these elements, the system seems to be impaired. It is true that Lossky regards the whole as prior and as generating its members, rather than the other way round. But this does not appear to affect the issue. If there is conflict between the members, the world is certainly not a perfect organic whole or a well-ordered system. However, it is clear that the concept of the world as one single substance is balanced by the concept of a plurality of substantival agents which, though interrelated in the system, are nonetheless relatively autonomous. All substantival agents are potentially persons, capable of personality, and actual persons are free.[1] The goal of history is the 'kingdom of the spirit', in which whole and part are in perfect accord, each member existing for the whole, while the whole exists for every member. Thus the goal would be a society of persons, united with God and with one another, individuality neither being obliterated nor giving rise to conflict or enmity.

We have seen that Lossky asserts the existence of an Absolute, which transcends the world and can be approached only by 'the negative way'. It does not follow, however, that the Absolute is nothing, a mere blank. For example, 'the Absolute is not personal, but it is not therefore impersonal – it is super-personal'[2]. But when Lossky talks in this way, in accordance with the Neoplatonist tradition, he is keeping within what he regards as the limits of metaphysics. As he says in his own summary of his thought, 'the conception of the Supreme Principle is purely philosophical'[3]. In religious experience, Lossky maintains, the Absolute reveals itself as the living personal God and as the supreme value, goodness, truth, beauty in one. Further, revelation discloses to us God as the Trinity of Persons and Christ as the God-man. Given this enriched conception of the ultimate reality, the vocation of the human being is seen to be return to God, not by absorption but through participation in the life of the God-man, and the goal of history appears as realization of the kingdom of God.

There does not seem to be any good ground for disputing Lossky's claim that his vision of reality is theistic. God is the transcendent creator.

---

1 Lossky distinguishes between formal and material freedom. Formal freedom is the power of an agent to refrain from doing A and to do something else instead. All human agents possess freedom in this sense, and they cannot lose it. Material freedom is the degree of creative power enjoyed by an agent, and one can have less or more creative power.

2 *Ibid.*, p. 85.

3 *History of Russian Philosophy*, p. 257.

Even the sphere of ideal being is created, though not temporally, in a sense, that is to say, which would imply that there was a time when there was no sphere of ideal being. Again, though, according to Lossky, the world as a system or organic whole presupposes a world spirit, identified with Sophia, Sophia is said to be a creature. Further, the return of persons to God, who will be all in all, is not understood by Lossky as involving the disappearance of individuality. The union of persons with God and with one another is envisaged as a union *of* persons, not as a vanishing of plurality.

Lossky's hierarchic conception of reality, a conception which can be associated with the Neoplatonist tradition, does not, of course, exclude the idea of development, of change. Together with Leibniz, he envisages the possibility of a substantival agent or monad evolving from the stage of being an electron or an atom to the status of a person. This process of development he calls 'reincarnation'. So he says of himself that 'Lossky champions the doctrine of reincarnation as worked out by Leibniz under the name of metamorphosis'.[1] At each stage the body or material aspect of the monad is in a sense the monad's own creation; it manifests or expresses the monad. In the realized kingdom of God the risen body is said to consist solely of qualities which manifest the spiritual qualities of the person. Further, as the members of the kingdom of God are united with each other and with the whole body, each will have a 'cosmic' body, in the sense that the whole world serves as the agent's body.

Obviously, some of these ideas are likely to seem odd, even fantastic, not only to those who reject Lossky's general religious view of reality but also to those who sympathize with or share it. For example, though the idea of emergent evolution is familiar enough, the notion that an entity such as an electron is potentially a person and in the process of metamorphosis or 'reincarnation' can become actually a person would probably seem eccentric to many people, whether or not they believe in God. True, Leibniz maintained that monads which were previously purely sensitive souls can be 'elevated to the rank of reason and to the prerogative of spirits'.[2] But appeal to Leibniz does not necessarily make a theory less odd. However, some of those ideas of Lossky which may seem silly at first hearing are not quite as silly as they may sound. To claim that the human substantival agent creates its body certainly may well seem odd. But Lossky does not mean that the soul creates its body out of nothing. What he means is that the material elements are constituted as a human

1 *Ibid.*, p. 264.
2 *Monadology*, p. 82.

body through the agency of the dominant monad, to use Leibnizian language, or, as Aristotle might put it, through the organizing activity of the entelechy, the soul as actualizing the body's potentialities. Without this organizing activity the material elements are not a human body. Whether one accepts this view or rejects it, the thesis is at any rate arguable and not simply absurd.

However all this may be, the main point is that, with the help of Leibniz, Lossky tries to correct the tendency to pantheism which he finds in thinkers such as Frank. Personality has for him intrinsic value, though it is only in the kingdom of God that the person fully realizes his or her individuality in an organic union with other persons. Every individual agent is called to make his or her unique contribution to the common cause, realization of the kingdom of God. It is true that, for Lossky, the world and all that is in it depend on God and that all substances are interrelated. In this sense the concept of total-unity certainly has a place in his thought. Apart from God, who was under no necessity to create, no being is completely self-contained and independent. But Lossky is careful not to push the idea of unity to the extent of depriving created agents of freedom and creative power. Further, his philosophical world-view needs, he maintains, to be enriched by the truths derived from reflection on mystical experience and from divine revelation in and through Christ.

Chapter 14

Philosophers in Exile (2)

1. Both Frank and Lossky presented world-views, general interpretations of reality. In these interpretations discussion of the human being, from epistemological, ontological, ethical and social points of view, played an important and prominent role, and Lossky, as we have seen, tried to counteract any tendency to monism by laying stress on the concept of the human person as a 'substantival agent,' analogous to Leibniz's idea of the monad, though not, as with Leibniz, a 'windowless' monad. At the same time, with both men, especially with Frank, emphasis was placed on the ultimate reality from which all plurality proceeds. With Berdyaev, however, emphasis was placed first and foremost on the human person, especially on the human person as free. 'I have put Freedom, rather than Being, at the basis of my philosophy.'[1] 'The problem of freedom is at the centre of all my writings.'[2] If existentialism is taken to mean 'emphasis on the subject as against the object, on the will as against the intellect, on the concrete and individual as against the general and universal'[3], Berdyaev was prepared to call himself an existentialist. But, as he rightly notes, those writers who have commonly been described as existentialists have in fact tended to lay stress on the concept of Being. Sartre developed an ontology, and Heidegger insisted that he was primarily concerned with the problem of the meaning of Being. Thus when Berdyaev asserted that he rejected ontology and with it a long tradition from Parmenides to Solovyev, he was also dissociating himself, up to a point, from some of those to whom the label 'existentialist' has often been attached.[4] He was claiming, in effect, to be more genuinely an existentialist than they.

Berdyaev is doubtless the most widely translated and read of the

1 *Dream and Reality*, p. 46.
2 *Ibid.*, p. 100.
3 *Ibid.*, p. 102.
4 Heidegger repudiated the label 'existentialist'. Jaspers came to do so too, as did Marcel.

Russian philosophers in exile. This is understandable. His philosophy is anthropocentric; he seeks for the meaning of life; his approach to philosophical problems is through their significance and relevance for the human being; he does not concern himself with problems which interest only the professional philosophers; and he writes as a man who is deeply committed to the cause of freedom, not simply in the political sense but also in the sense that he is sharply opposed to any attempt to impose a system of ideas or beliefs, whether of a secular or religious nature, on people's minds. In so far as Marxists sought human emancipation, he was at one with them; but when he came to see Marxism as leading to the sort of society of which Dostoevsky had written in the Legend of the Grand Inquisitor, he ceased to frequent Marxist circles. On turning to religion, however, he diagnosed an analogous attitude among the representatives of orthodoxy. In other words, he championed the freedom of the human person against the pressure of society, whatever the society might be. But although he spoke of himself as having been a rebel all his life,[1] any reader of his work must see that he was not content with negation. 'The meaning of life lies in a return to the mystery of the spirit in which God is born in man and man is born in God'.[2] He did not put his faith in any social utopia, to be attained in this world, but he had a passionate desire for the spiritual regeneration of mankind.

Though Berdyaev's writings have certainly attracted a good deal of attention, the author himself admitted that he found difficulty in giving adequate and precise expression to his ideas. Referring to his book *The Meaning of the Creative Act* (1916) he says that in it 'my thoughts and the normal course of philosophical argument seemed to dissolve into vision'.[3] He was indeed referring to a particular work, an early one; but he also said, speaking generally, that when his critics accused him of being a creator of myths or a 'prophet' who would do well to show a little more precision in the tumultuous sea of his arbitrary assertions and intuitions, 'I can only repeat what I have said on other occasions, namely, that my vocation is to proclaim not a doctrine but a vision; that I work and desire to work by inspiration, fully conscious of being open to all the criticisms systematic philosophers, historians and scholars are likely to make, and, in fact, have made'.[4] This is a frank statement. Again, Berdyaev frankly admitted that he had little capacity for 'the exercise of

1 *Dream and Reality*, p. 54.
2 *Ibid.*, p. 302.
3 *Ibid.*, p. 210.
4 *Ibid.*, p. 289. Berdyaev goes on to ask, 'is not Nietzsche open to the same kind of criticism?' He felt an affinity with Nietzsche, in spite of the differences between their lines of thought.

analytical and discursive reasoning',[1] and he referred to 'the paradoxical and even contradictory character of my thought'.[2] As for his 'arbitrary assertions', he insisted that they were not intended as dogmatic assertions but that they expressed his problems.

The foregoing should not be understood as equivalent to a suggestion that Berdyaev's writings should be left unread. Literature has been enriched by 'visionaries'; their writings can be inspiring and stimulating; and we would be poorer without them. As, however, Berdyaev himself admitted that he experienced difficulty in expressing what he wanted to say, that he was never satisfied with what he had written, and that misunderstandings of his thought not only could arise but had arisen, it can hardly be called carping criticism if one draws attention to features of his thought which he explicitly recognized.

Berdyaev tells us that he rejects ontology, considered as a science of Being, as it is 'a disastrous philosophy of nothing at all, except certain figments of the human brain'.[3] Further, the doctrine of the primacy of Being implies determinism and is irreconcilable with recognition of human freedom. A natural reaction is to claim that these statements are exaggerations. It might be urged, for example, that while some philosophies which assert the primacy of Being eliminate freedom (Spinoza's philosophy, for instance), others do not. But Berdyaev is not saying that while some ontologies produce only figments of the human brain, others do not, and that while some metaphysical systems which assert the primacy of Being eliminate freedom, others preserve it. He speaks, and doubtless intends to speak, quite generally. He even makes the surprising assertion that St Thomas Aquinas 'completely rejected freedom, for which his scholasticism has no place whatever'.[4] Thomists are obviously likely to object. But whether such objections are valid or not, we have first to try to ascertain how Berdyaev understands his generalizations.

It becomes easier to understand Berdyaev's rejection of ontology if we bear in mind his statement that 'my true master in philosophy was Kant'.[5] He did not claim to be a Kantian, but he accepted Kant's contention that the categories by the aid of which we objectify the phenomenal world do not apply to 'things in themselves'. The ontologist, as Berdyaev sees him, believes that reality is rational in the sense that it exemplifies his categories and conforms to his model of a rational system, that ontology

1 *Ibid.*, p. 88.
2 *Ibid.*, p. 101.
3 *Ibid.*, pp. 98–9.
4 *Freedom and the Spirit*, translated by O. F. Clarke, p. 129 (London, 1935).
5 *Dream and Reality*, p. 93.

reveals the essence and structure of reality in itself. Metaphysics conceived the human subject's abstract ideas as constituting the essence of reality. 'Abstractions and the hypostatizing of abstractions created both spiritual and materialistic metaphysical systems.'[1] Referring to a conversation which he had with Plekhanov in 1904, Berdyaev relates that he tried to persuade the father of Russian Marxism that rationalism, particularly materialistic rationalism, was based 'on the dogmatic presupposition concerning the rational nature of Being in general, and of material Being in particular'[2]. According to Berdyaev, 'the rational world with its laws, its determinations and causal connections' was 'a figment of rationalistic human consciousness'.[3] Plekhanov, needless to say, was not persuaded. Indeed, according to Berdyaev, he did not understand what was meant. However this may be, Berdyaev was obviously proposing a substantially Kantian point of view. The categories of the human reason apply to the phenomenal world; but it is a mistake to suppose that they are applicable to 'things in themselves', in the sense that they reveal the nature of reality in itself. Science has its own limited sphere of validity, but the claim of ontology to be a science of Being as such, in itself, is bogus. Obviously, if we wished to challenge Berdyaev's thesis, it would be necessary to discuss basic epistemological themes.

It is hardly necessary to say that Kant's claim that the categories of the human reason are inapplicable to God in any literal sense is congenial to Berdyaev. To conceive God as, for example, a changeless substance or a first (supreme) cause is to adopt a naturalistic attitude. That is to say, God is conceived in terms of the concepts which we employ in talking about the world of nature. But as God is life, his nature is not expressible 'in terms of categories of thought which were framed to deal with nature'.[4] Even to talk about God as a 'supernatural' reality is to think naturalistically, as it expresses an objectification of God 'out there', beyond reason. To conceive God in such terms is to invite an atheist reaction. The appropriate approach to God is through 'spiritual life', through mystical experience, a transcending 'the antithesis between subject and object and the substantialist conception of them'.[5] Such experience yields knowledge, but this knowledge can be expressed only in the form of symbols, which serve to direct us on the way of spiritual

1 *Freedom and the Spirit*, p. 1.
2 *Dream and Reality*, p. 98.
3 *Ibid.*
4 *Freedom and the Spirit*, p. 23.
5 *Ibid.*, p. 55.

life, to see the infinite in the finite, but which should not be taken as fixed or static concepts revealing the essence of the divine reality. 'Knowledge of the divine is a dynamic process which finds no completion within the fixed and static categories of ontology'[1].

Though Berdyaev emphasizes the basic role of mystical experience in knowledge of God, he does not reject the idea of revelation. But he sees it as expressing itself in myths. 'Christianity is mythological through and through, as all religion is'.[2] For example, the union of God and man in Christ 'is not susceptible of rational explanation'[3], but the truth can be expressed in mythological terms. Moreover, it does not follow that a religious truth cannot receive adequate symbolic expression, though there can be degrees of penetration into the spiritual significance of any religious doctrine. It is not a question of changing basic Christian beliefs such as that in the Trinity but rather of understanding that the formulations of the beliefs express mystery, that which transcends rationalization. The Christian dogmas express spiritual life. It is theology, according to Berdyaev, which has given them 'a rationalist character'.[4]

It may have occurred to the reader that, though Berdyaev claims that concepts such as those of substance and cause are inapplicable to God, inasmuch as they are derived from the objectified world of nature and represent naturalistic thinking, he himself speaks of God as life, a concept itself derived from reflection on natural phenomena. Berdyaev, however, makes a sharp distinction between nature on the one hand and spirit on the other. And he would doubtless reply that the concept of life, as applied to God, is based on the life of the spirit. It is in spiritual life or experience that God is known.

We have seen that Berdyaev rejects not only ontology as a science of being but also the primacy of Being, its priority to freedom. At first sight this may seem absurd. For how can anything be free unless it is or exists? We have, however, to understand that Berdyaev uses the term 'Being' in several senses. Sometimes he has in mind the abstract concept of Being as such, devoid of any characteristic whatsoever. He is obviously referring to this abstract concept, when he says that 'Being is a product of thought',[5] and that 'Being does not exist'[6]; he is not talking about beings in the sense of existing things. Sometimes, however, he uses the term

---

1 *Ibid.*, p. 65.
2 *Dream and Reality*, p. 181.
3 *Ibid.*
4 *Freedom and the Spirit*, p. 75.
5 *Towards a New Epoch*, translated from the French by O. F. Clarke, p. 96 (London, 1949). This book is a collection of articles by Berdyaev.
6 *Ibid.*, p. 97.

'Being' to mean primarily nature or the objectified world. This world is the sphere of causal determinism, and, as he puts it, freedom cannot be derived from nature. If we deny the sphere of spirit, which is the sphere of freedom, and recognize only the objectified world of nature, belief in freedom cannot be retained. In this sense freedom 'cannot be derived from being, for it would then be determined'[1]. Perhaps we might express the matter in terms of the philosophy of Kant by saying that if the phenomenal world is conceived as being the only reality, as true Being, there is then no room for freedom. It is the subject which is free, and if it is conceived as part of the objectified world or as its product, it cannot be conceived as free.

Berdyaev also seems to give a third meaning to the word 'Being', for he allows that we can speak of 'true and original Being, which precedes the process of rationalization and is not to be known conceptually'.[2] But as far as the denial of the primacy of Being in relation to freedom is concerned, it is Being in the second sense mentioned above, Being as signifying the objectified world, which is the relevant concept.

When Berdyaev makes a distinction between spirit and nature, he is not opposing soul to body or to the material world in general. In his view, 'soul' is conceived as a substance or at any rate as a substantial principle in the human being, so that the concept falls under that of the objectified world of nature. Soul and body are distinguished, but they are distinguished as realities within the one objectified world. Spirit, however, is life. 'Spirit and the natural world are utterly unlike one another.'[3] Spirit is not an objective reality. But neither can it be described as subjective, in the sense in which subjectivity is opposed to objectivity. Such concepts do not apply, as spirit is altogether different from the world in which these concepts have application.

It is not surprising that Berdyaev was accused of asserting a dualist theory, of splitting reality into two heterogeneous elements. After all, he himself refers explicitly to a dualism between the spirit and the world[4] and even asserts that 'this world is ruled not by God but by the Prince of the World'.[5] Yet Berdyaev describes the accusation that he is a dualist as the fruit of misunderstanding[6] and asserts that 'Manichean dualism is alien to my philosophy'.[7] That is to say, he does not postulate an

1 *Towards a New Epoch*, p. 98.
2 *Dream and Reality*, pp. 96–7.
3 *Freedom and the Spirit*, p. 9.
4 See, for example, *Towards a New Epoch*, p. 11.
5 *Dream and Reality*, p. 299.
6 *Ibid.*, p. 102.
7 *Towards a New Epoch*, p. 11, note 1.

ontological dualism, between two disparate spheres of Being. Dualism of this sort presupposes the reality of both spirit and matter. But 'I do not believe in the autonomous reality of matter'.[1] The objectified world which, in ontological dualism would be set over against the world of spirit, is mind-dependent. 'The objectification of the world takes place through our agency and for our sakes, and this is the fall of the world, this is its loss of freedom'.[2] Berdyaev's 'dualism' is akin, as he notes, to Kant's distinction between the noumenal and phenomenal spheres. As for the phenomenal world being the domain of the prince of darkness or the devil, the following quotation may throw light on Berdyaev's meaning: 'The law which governs this empirical world is that of a desperate struggle for existence and domination between individuals, peoples, tribes, nations, classes, empires. Men are possessed by the devil of the will to power and it drags them down to destruction'[3]. The realm of the spirit, the realm of freedom and love, is in opposition to this 'fallen' world.

We have seen that, according to Berdyaev, freedom cannot be derived from the world of nature, inasmuch as this is the realm of necessity or determinism. It cannot, so we are told, emerge from this world by way of evolution. Whence, then, is it derived? What is its origin? Berdyaev sometimes speaks of freedom as uncaused, groundless. To describe freedom as uncreated or uncaused, however, is said to be 'tantamount to the recognition of an irreducible mystery'.[4] Berdyaev introduces the concept, derived mainly from the mystical writer Jakob Boehme, of the *Ungrund*, the mysterious abyss or void which 'lies at the heart of the whole life of the universe'.[5] Speaking of evil, Berdyaev asserts that the possibility of evil (not its actuality) is latent in the *Ungrund*, which is not a positive being but pure possibility or potentiality. Presumably freedom too is latent in the void or abyss. Speaking against Sartre, however, Berdyaev remarks that 'if one does not derive liberty from nature, one must admit that it presupposes the existence of a spiritual principle in man'.[6] Elsewhere he asserts that 'the origin of man's freedom is in God, man's freedom having the same source as his life'.[7]

It may well be a mistake to spend time trying to reconcile with one another those statements of Berdyaev which seem to conflict. He himself

1 *Ibid.*
2 *The Beginning and the End*, translated by R. M. French, p. 56 (London, 1952).
3 *Towards a New Epoch*, p. 6.
4 *Dream and Reality*, p. 178.
5 *Freedom and Spirit*, p. 165.
6 *Towards a New Epoch*, p. 99.
7 *Freedom and Spirit*, p. 136.

frankly admitted that he was not a systematic writer. But perhaps the statements which we have quoted are not as inconsistent as may at first sight appear. For Berdyaev, freedom as a creative force certainly presupposes a spiritual principle in man, and man was created by God in his own image. In this sense the origin of man's freedom is in God. But the divine life itself is said to presuppose the dark abyss or *Ungrund*, not in the sense that the *Ungrund* existed in a temporal sense before God but in the sense in which the German philosopher Schelling conceived the divine life as rising eternally out of a dark foundation or abyss devoid of all characteristics and ungraspable by the reason. Theosophical ideas of this kind, inspired by such writers as the mystic Boehme and the philosopher Schelling, may seem fantastic. But the point is that the statement that freedom has its origin in God, the free creator of man in his own image, and the claim that freedom has its root in an 'irrational' principle, the *Ungrund*, are not necessarily irreconcilable.

However this may be, let us leave such obscure matters and turn to Berdyaev's idea of the nature of human freedom. He distinguishes between two kinds of freedom. In the first place there is what he describes as 'formal' freedom or initial freedom. This is what is commonly called freedom of the will, the ability to choose one course of action rather than another, to turn to the left or to turn to the right. In the second place there is freedom as a creative force, freedom of the spirit. Each kind of freedom may degenerate, turning, as it were, into its opposite. Exercise of 'formal' freedom can take the form of choosing evil; it can plunge the human being into egoism, self-assertion to the exclusion or at the expense of others. The individual then becomes a slave to the lower elements in his nature, the slave of sin, as St Paul would put it. Formal freedom can thus lead to anarchy, each individual seeking only his or her supposed interests. As for freedom as a creative force, this can lead to the creation of a society, in the name of universal welfare or happiness, in which freedom is extinguished. 'The second kind of liberty is dogged by the temptation of the Grand Inquisitor, who may belong either to the extreme "right" or to the extreme "left".'[1] Obviously, it is not necessary that either kind of freedom should be employed in the ways mentioned. Otherwise freedom would not be freedom. But, Berdyaev insists, if degeneration of freedom is to be avoided, the grace of Christ is required, grace which illuminates but does not coerce. 'Only the Christian revelation, the religion of the God-man, can reconcile the two kinds of freedom'[2], in adherence to God

1 *Ibid.*, p. 133.
2 *Ibid.*, p. 135.

as truth and goodness and in a creativity which expresses and promotes spiritual freedom.

When exalting freedom, Berdyaev makes it clear that he is not referring simply to what philosophers call 'free will'. This is not excluded, of course; it is 'initial freedom'; but freedom, as he uses the term, is something more. What is this something more? One answer is obviously freedom in the second sense mentioned above, freedom as a creative force. This is manifested, for example, in artistic creation. With Berdyaev, however, freedom is conceived as 'the inner dynamic of the spirit',[1] the principle of spiritual life; it tends to be identified with spirit. 'Spirit is freedom unconstrained by the outward and the objective, where what is deep and inward determines all.'[2] Freedom, we might say, is spirit as self-determining. This does not mean determination by given physiological or psychological factors in a human being, with the consequence that freedom can be explained, rationally derived. It is not the result of any factors save the spirit itself, and it cannot be grasped by the categories of the discursive reason.

2. If it is said that such talk is obscure, mysterious, Berdyaev's reply is that freedom is in fact a mystery. But the conclusions which he draws from his idea of freedom are often clear enough. For example, the free spirit resists the pressures not only of objectified nature but also of society. It does not, for example, accept in a passive manner the ethical code or moral convictions taught by society. It does not follow that it must embrace different convictions. The point is that whatever moral ideals and convictions it accepts, whether the same as or different from those inculcated by the social environment, will be those which correspond to its own lived experience of the moral good. 'The Christian conscience is compelled to recognize that the spirit is independent of society and that the individual conscience in all its depth does not depend on any social collectivity whatsoever.'[3] This independence of the collectivity, of society, involves, to take but one example, rejection of society's right to 'interfere' in the erotic relations between men and women, to decide what is moral and what is not. On this Berdyaev expresses agreement with Chernyshevsky, who 'is profoundly right and shows true humanity in advocating the freedom of the bonds uniting man and woman'.[4]

1 *Ibid.*, p. 121.
2 *Ibid.*, p. 117.
3 *Towards a New Epoch*, p. 34.
4 *Dream and Reality*, p. 73.

It is not a question only of morals. Berdyaev applies his line of thought to the acceptance of truth. 'I can accept truth only through, and in, freedom'.[1] This statement stands in need of some interpretation. What Berdyaev excludes by it is acceptance of a belief as true as a result of coercion, of social pressure. In life we often accept statements as true, because they are made by people whom we sincerely believe to possess a knowledge which we do not possess. Most of us are conscious that we know little, if anything, about astronomy, and we accept the testimony of the community of astronomers. We may, of course, accept what they say provisionally, being aware that astronomical hypotheses are subject to revision. But at any rate we are convinced that astronomers know more about astronomy than we do, and we do not prefer some uninformed hunch of our own to their better informed judgment. This is not a case of coercion. It is a matter of common sense. But suppose that a state or a party or a religious body tries to coerce me into accepting something as true, when, left to myself, I do not believe that it is true. For Berdyaev, the free spirit will resist. He himself, for example, rejected the doctrine of eternal torment in hell, as he considered it quite incompatible with belief in the love of God.[2] If Orthodoxy speaks otherwise, this simply shows that Orthodoxy has scant regard for truth. Berdyaev claims freedom of thought, 'but my thought is deeply rooted in an initial act of faith'.[3]

A point emphasized by Berdyaev is that, whatever human societies, secular or ecclesiastical, may have done or do, God does not coerce anybody. He seeks a freely given allegiance. Christ, as represented in Dostoevsky's Legend of the Grand Inquisitor, refused the temptation to exercise coercion of any kind; he sought a free response of love, not submission to power. Berdyaev was wholeheartedly on the side of Christ, not on that of the Inquisitor. The Inquisitor may have been justified in maintaining that the majority of people experienced freedom as a burden and preferred bread and security to freedom[4]. But, for Berdyaev, freedom was beyond price and not something to be bartered away or surrendered.

It is the free, spiritual subject which has personality or is a person. Sociologists, Berdyaev tells us, maintain that the human person is formed

1 *Dream and Reality*, p. 47.
2 Rejection of the doctrine of eternal torment in hell was not uncommon among the Russian religious speculative thinkers. They thought in terms of the return of all things to God, of St Paul's statement that finally God would be all in all (1 *Cor.*, XV, 28).
3 *Dream and Reality*, p. 185.
4 'Bread' stands, of course, for material welfare. The Inquisitor was not advocating what would ordinarily be described as oppression or ill-treatment. He maintained that most people would willingly sacrifice freedom of thought, for example, in return for security, material welfare and being told what to believe and what were the proper standards of behaviour.

by society, by social relations. But 'that which is spiritually most significant in man certainly does not come from social influences, not from his social environment; it comes from within, not from without'.[1] The pressure or influence of society tends to mould human beings to a pattern, or to patterns, whereas each person is unique. The entry of a person into the world signifies a break in continuity, in the sense that personality is not derivable from antecedents but is 'unique and unrepeatable'.[2] The person, however, should not be conceived as a 'windowless monad', an individual cut off from society, though the social relationship appropriate to persons as such is not that of 'the one' (Heidegger's *Das Man*) but that of the 'we', the social relationship exemplified in a true community, one in which the uniqueness of each person is recognized and respected and at the same time enriches the community. In other words, a society of persons would exemplify the Russian ideal of *sobornost*.

The person, however, according to Berdyaev, cannot find fulfilment simply in society but is oriented to the infinite, the divine. Personality is a religious category. That is to say, the human being is a person only as related to God.[3] Indeed, there cannot be a genuine society of persons, unless this religious dimension is recognized, unless it is understood that the human being is more than a member of society. A true humanism requires faith in God and in the human being's orientation to God. Only in this way can the value of the person be fully recognized. A society of persons obviously allows for the free development of the personality of each, as personality is not something given at the start in a completed form but has to be developed through the exercise of creative freedom. This development includes that of spiritual life, of life in God.

Given Berdyaev's views about freedom, personality and creativity, it is hardly necessary to say that he was a strong opponent of all forms of totalitarianism, whether that of German National Socialism or that of Communism. To treat the human person as having value only as a cell in the social organism was abhorrent to him. 'The State preserves functional significance, but it is essential to affirm that the State is the servant of man and not a value of a higher order'.[4] Human beings are called to realize themselves in society, not as isolated units, cut off from their fellows. But to regard them as existing simply for society is to deny the value of the free person.

1 *The Divine and the Human*, translated by R. M. French, p. 135 (London, 1949).
2 *Slavery and Freedom*, translated by R. M. French, p. 21 (London, 1943).
3 *Towards a New Epoch*, p. 23.
4 *Ibid.*, p. 11.

Although Berdyaev was a foe of totalitarianism in any form, and a critic of the Soviet system in particular, his attitude to the Russian Revolution, and to the doctrines and aims of the Communist Party, was nuanced. His insistence on freedom and on human emancipation prevented him from adopting a purely negative attitude to the Revolution. He had no desire for restoration of the previous political system, and he had scant sympathy with the 'Whites'. Further, he accepted Marx's idea of capitalism as exploiting human beings. He was no more a defender of bourgeois capitalism than of Tsarist autocracy. He felt ill at ease with the Russian emigrés who longed, as he saw it, for the clock to be put back, and some of them regarded him as not much better than a Bolshevik. But he was obviously not a Marxist. He rejected materialism, and his philosophical anthropology was clearly different from that of the Marxists. He did not believe that the human being could be regenerated by changes in social structures or by social pressure, still less by coercion. Nor had he any sympathy with the policy, which developed under Stalin, of making artists and poets conform to the demands of the Party on pain of being silenced or 'liquidated'. Religious persecution and coercive pressure in the cultural sphere were for him intolerable attacks on the dignity and freedom of the person. He sympathized, of course, with the ideal of creating a truly human society in which each member would be able to develop himself or herself freely, though he did not believe either that man was destined simply for a materialistic terrestrial paradise or that the development of a terrestrial paradise of any form was inevitable, determined by laws of history. But while he sympathized with Marx's ideal of a truly human society (even if his conception of such a society differed in important respects from that of Marx), he condemned the Communist Party for treating actual human beings, existing here and now, as means to the attainment of a goal in the far distant future. This attitude was incompatible with his personalism. In brief, it was ethical considerations and his belief in the value of personality which led him into his early association with Marxists, and it was the same factors which led him out of the Marxist fold. In his judgment, the Communists were successors of the Grand Inquisitor. They offered people 'bread' at the expense of freedom. But capitalism he saw as being as much a representative of materialism as was Communism, even though it was the latter which openly proclaimed materialism. 'If I opposed Communism, I did so solely on account of the freedom of the spirit, not because I desired to preserve this or that social order. I opposed Communism precisely because I believed in the freedom and ultimate independence of the human person *vis-à-vis* all social and particular orders'.[1] The worship of the collective was for Berdyaev a form of idolatry.

In Berdyaev's writings subsequent to the revolution and his expulsion from the Soviet Union we can indeed find a good many unequivocal condemnations of 'socialism', unencumbered by qualifications. For example, we are told that though socialism is inspired by the ideals of middle-class culture and draws its ideas from the materialism proclaimed by bourgeois prophets, it has given something new to the world, namely 'the phenomenon of an inhuman collectivism, a new Leviathan'.[2] In this collectivism, 'all spiritual culture is wiped out: such a monster has not yet a new human soul, for it has got no human soul at all'.[3] Given such passages, we may receive the impression that when Berdyaev qualifies his forthright condemnation, he is simply expressing his love for his native land and his disgust with the attitude of some of the emigrés. Thus he speaks of the 'sinister and unseemly emigré psychology'[4] of those Russians in Paris who hoped for a German victory over the Soviet Union in the second world war. But though Berdyaev certainly loved his country, it was not simply patriotism which led him to dislike the way in which some fellow exiles were unable to see any good point at all in Marxism. He believed that Marx was animated by a genuine hatred of capitalist exploitation and that he genuinely hoped for the eventual realization of a truly human universal human society, in which human emancipation of all forms of alienation would have been achieved. Indeed, the universalism of Marx was one of the features which attracted him in the first instance to Marxism, and which he contrasted with what he regarded as the provincial mentality of the Populists. Though a patriot, Berdyaev was never a chauvinist. He was concerned with humanity, not simply with Russia. At the same time he conceived the original idealism of Marxism as having been perverted and pretty well extinguished not simply by the excesses of individuals such as Stalin but by Marxism itself, by its materialism and by its subordination of persons to the collective. In other words, the element of genuine idealism could not survive in the framework of the ideology. Communism offered the people 'bread', but at the expense of freedom, the spiritual life and creativity. What it added to bourgeois materialism was the new form of slavery foreseen by Dostoevsky. Referring to the two decades before the revolution, Berdyaev remarked that 'the section of the Marxists who had

1 *Dream and Reality*, p. 241.
2 *The End of Our Time*, translated by Donald Attwater, p. 195 (London, 1933).
3 *Ibid.*
4 *Dream and Reality*, p. 317.

reached a higher degree of culture went over to idealism, and in the end to Christianity'.[1] As Berdyaev was one of them, this may seem to be an arrogant statement. But it seems to be substantially true.

In view of Berdyaev's criticism of existing forms of society, it is natural to ask whether he was content simply with adverse criticism or whether he recommended the creation of some other form of society to take the place of existing societies. It is necessary to understand, however, that what he desired first and foremost was the inner spiritual regeneration of mankind. The old theocratic State was, in his judgment, only outwardly theocratic, in form, in external trappings, but not in substance. Rule by God meant in effect rule by an anointed king or by the Pope. Rule from above, in the name of God, led to a reaction in the name of liberty and so first to democracy, then to socialism. And rule of man by himself led to his self-destruction, to the rejection of spiritual values and the curtailment, if not extinction, of freedom. A return to the past, however, is neither desirable nor possible. There is need for the exercise of human creativity. But without inner spiritual regeneration nothing of real value can be created. 'We must begin to make our Christianity effectively real by a return to the life of the spirit.'[2] The sphere of economics must be subordinated to spiritual values, and politics must be confined to its proper limits. The goal is the kingdom of God, a true theocracy (as constrasted with the old theocracies), but 'the only way to true theocracy, the kingdom of God, is to work for its effective realization, that is, for the achievement of a deeper spiritual life, for the enlightening and transfiguration of man and the world.'[3] We can no longer seriously believe in the saving power of any social-political system as such. Christianity should, indeed, transform society, but any such transformation must proceed from within outwards.

3. History, according to Berdyaev, receives meaning when it is seen as a movement towards a final goal, the kingdom of God, a goal which will be attained. Obviously, Berdyaev did not claim that unless history is seen in this way, it is unintelligible in the sense that we can discern no intelligible connections and patterns, and that historiography is either impossible or no more than fiction. 'There is a rhythm in history, as there is in nature, a measured succession of ages and periods, alternation of diverse types of culture, ebb and flow, rise and fall.'[4] The historian's reconstruction of the

---

1 *The Russian Idea*, translated by R. M. French, p. 222 (London, 1947).
2 *The End of Our Time*, pp. 192–3.
3 *Ibid.*, p. 199.
4 *Ibid.*, p. 69.

past is presupposed. The question is whether history, as presented by historians, has a meaning. For Berdyaev, this is the case only if history is a movement towards a final goal. If historical development took the form of recurrent cycles and could be symbolized by a circle or set of circles, it would be without meaning. History would also be meaningless if it were an endless progress towards a goal which would never be attained. Further, if history is conceived as a movement towards a goal which will be attained only by the generation alive at the time, this conception of history was regarded by Berdyaev as morally unacceptable. For in this case 'nothing but death and the grave' would await 'the vast majority of mankind'.[1] Earlier generations would be simply means to the attainment of full development of personality by a generation yet unborn.

It does not follow that Berdyaev regarded the movement of history as determined throughout. 'The determinism of nature cannot be transferred to history.'[2] What may be described as 'fate' does play a role in history, but there is also human freedom to take into account. What follows is that 'history has a meaning solely because it will come to an end'.[3] That is to say, the meaning of history 'lies beyond the confines of history'.[4] Full realization of the kingdom of God is the goal of the movement of history, but it cannot be attained within the movement itself. If, therefore, the goal is to be attained, history, historical time, must come to an end. Moreover, full realization of the kingdom of God must be conceived as involving the resurrection of the dead. Otherwise earlier generations would be means or instruments to the happiness of a future generation, an idea which would be incompatible with Berdyaev's emphasis on the value of the human person as the image of God[5].

Berdyaev was obviously inspired by Christian eschatology, but he interpreted it in his own way, and it is by no means always easy to make out precisely how his statements should be understood. We are told, for example, that while we should not conceive the end of the world as an event in historical time (symbolized by a line stretching out indefinitely),

---

1 *The Meaning of History*, translated by George Reavey, p. 189 (London, 1936).
2 *The Beginning and the End*, p. 209.
3 *Ibid.*
4 *Ibid.*
5 In emphasizing belief in the resurrection of the dead Berdyaev, like Solovyev before him, was influenced not only by Christian faith but also by the thought of the Russian thinker Nikolai Fyodorovich Fyodorov (1828–1903). To be sure, he did not share Fyodorov's eccentric ideas about the potentialities of physical science for restoring all the departed to life. But he was impressed by Fyodorov's sense of human solidarity and his passionate conviction that human existence and history would be deprived of meaning, if death were final.

neither should we conceive it as an event wholly beyond history. It should be conceived as taking place in existential time, which is 'best symbolized not by the circle nor by the line but by the point'.[1] Existential time is 'inward time . . . the time of the world of subjectivity'.[2] Taking place in existential time means 'moving out from the realm of objectification into the spiritual pattern of things'.[3]

The natural interpretation of such statements, at any rate if taken alone, is in terms of Christ's saying, 'you cannot tell by observation when the kingdom of God comes. There will be no saying, "Look, here it is!" or "there it is!"; for in fact the kingdom of God is within you'.[4] Obviously, Berdyaev does not intend to imply that the coming of the kingdom of God is simply a future event, in which those living here and now cannot participate. 'The kingdom of God is not merely a matter of expectation, it is being founded, its creation is beginning already here and now upon earth'[5]. What Berdyaev calls existential time, 'inward time', in a sense overlaps with historical time. 'That which we project into the sphere of the eternal, and call the end, is the existential experience of contact with the noumenal.'[6] The second coming of Christ and the full realization of the kingdom of God can be conceived as the spiritual regeneration of all mankind.

It would, however, be a mistake to suppose that Berdyaev envisaged human beings as continuing to live, 'after' the end of history, with the same social structures which exist now. For example, the state could hardly exist in the transfigured world, if 'the image of the State will be shown in the final end to be the image of the beast which issues out of the abyss'.[7] It is not a question of improving the actual but of a transformation. 'The kingdom of God is not actually realized in the conditions of our world. What is needed for its realization is not changes *in* this world, but a change *of* this world'.[8] We must beware of interpreting Berdyaev as having in mind endless progress in historical time. After all, he believed in the resurrection of the dead, and he spoke of 'a new man and a new cosmos'.[9]

1 *Slavery and Freedom*, translated by R. M. French, p. 260 (London, 1943). The circle was, for Berdyaev, the appropriate symbol for 'cosmic time'. He recognized three kinds of time, cosmic, historical and existential.
    2 *Ibid.*
    3 *The Beginning and the End*, p. 206.
    4 *Luke*, XVII, 20–1.
    5 *The Beginning and the End*, p. 222.
    6 *Ibid.*, p. 232.
    7 *Ibid.*, p. 221. Berdyaev was in sympathy with Nietzsche's attack on the State in *Thus Spake Zarathustra*.
    8 *The Divine and the Human*, p. 181.
    9 *Ibid.*, p. 200.

Though Berdyaev looked forward to the full realization of the king-dom of God as the goal of history, a meta-historical goal, he had scant sympathy with any policy of passively awaiting a divine intervention, bringing history to an end. 'It is not only God who makes all things new, it is man too'[1]. Indeed, Berdyaev saw what is called the second coming of Christ 'as dependent on the creative act of man'.[2] 'The future coming of Christ presupposes that the way has been prepared for it by man.'[3] The fact of the matter is, according to Berdyaev, that God acts through human beings. God 'acts only in freedom, only through the freedom of man'.[4] Again, 'the outpouring of the Spirit which changes the world, is the activity of the spirit in man himself'.[5] Realization of the goal of history is the result of divine-human creative activity.

Traditional eschatology conceives God as ringing down the curtain on history and making all things new. It conceives Christ as descending in glory from heaven to judge the living and the dead. Berdyaev regards such pictures as symbols. When, however, he tries to tell us what the symbols express, he gives rise to a problem. Let us suppose that instead of Christ coming unexpectedly, like a thief in the night, 'when man does that to which he is called, then only will the second coming of Christ take place'.[6] If human beings are free, as Berdyaev insists that they are, it follows that they may not do that to which they are called. In that case the second coming of Christ would presumably not take place. But Berdyaev seems to be confident that the goal of history will be realized, though not by evolution within historical time. This is doubtless a matter of faith. It involves, however, not simply faith in God but faith that human beings will freely prepare the way for the kingdom of God. At any rate this seems to the present writer to be the case.

Though Berdyaev lays emphasis on the end of history and on reali-zation of the kingdom of God, this is not, of course, all that he has to say about history. For example, following in the footsteps of Slavophile thinkers and of Leontyev, he makes a distinction between culture and civilization. 'Culture, having lost its soul, becomes civilization. Spiritual matters are discounted, quantity displaces quality.'[7] Civilization is exemplified in bourgeois capitalism, which is said to deprive man's economic life of any spiritual foundation. Socialism aims at developing

1 *Ibid.*, p. 202.
2 *Dream and Reality*, p. 297.
3 *The Beginning and the End*, p. 252.
4 *Slavery and Freedom*, p. 262.
5 *Ibid.*, p. 265.
6 *Ibid.*, p. 268.
7 *The Meaning of History*, p. 216.

civilization further, without, however, infusing into it any new spirit. In other words, there are forces at work which strive to extinguish spiritual values, to stifle in man any awareness of his relationship to God, and to concentrate man's attention and desires on purely terrestrial interests. Those forces can be represented by the symbolic figure of Antichrist, and they are engaged in conflict with the movement of the Spirit to prepare the way for the kingdom of God. We are living in the age of darkness, so to speak. In his prophetic capacity Berdyaev foresees the eventual triumph of light, of good over evil.

Berdyaev regarded himself as, and indeed was, a Christian philosopher. He did not, however, conceive a Christian philosopher as being under an obligation to conform his philosophical thought to the requirements of Orthodox, Catholic or Protestant theology, as the case might be. He made a distinction between revelation and theology, the latter being a socialized reaction to or interpretation of revelation, 'even if the fact be concealed'.[1] As theology has a social character and as 'the problems posed and resolved by philosophy are invariably the same as those propounded by theology',[2] it is understandable if theologians are suspicious of or even actively hostile to philosophy. But freedom of thought is essential for the philosopher. The Christian philosopher will try to 'acquire the mind of Christ'[3] his spiritual communion with the divine being both the source of intuitions and a check on arbitrary claims to intuitive knowledge. But, though faithful to revelation, he will not allow his thought to be shackled by theologians' interpretations of revelation in the name of a pressure-exerting society. As for discursive thought, Berdyaev regarded this as an instrument of intuition, and he explicitly rejected any notion that he conceived his philosophical ideas as deduced from self-evidently or necessarily true propositions. In his view, it was creative thinking.

By representing philosophy as creative thought, Berdyaev meant that it is not, or ought not to be, simply a passive mirroring or reflection of the actual, of being. In his early work *The Meaning of Creativity* he claimed that philosophy should be oriented to the transfiguration of the actual. As this work was published in 1916, before the revolution and not so many years after Berdyaev's break with Marxism (for which, as he admitted, he retained a weak spot), it is reasonable to see the influence of

1 *Truth and Revelation*, translated by R. M. French, p. 129 (London, 1953).
2 *Solitude and Society*, translated by George Reavey, p. 4 (London, 1938). This statement can hardly be taken absolutely literally. But Berdyaev looked on philosophy as 'concerned primarily with man's inner life' (*Ibid.*, p. 69).
3 *The Destiny of Man*, translated by Natalie Duddington, p. 7 (London, 1937).

Marx's famous statement that philosophers should not be content simply with understanding the world, but that what was needed was to change the world. But Berdyaev did not abandon emphasis on the prophetic role of the philosopher. To be sure, he desired the advent of the kingdom of God, not that of the kingdom of Man to the exclusion of God. He was convinced, however, that philosophy could contribute to the task of changing the word, of transfiguring it, by stimulating a change of consciousness in human beings, a transvaluation of values.[1]

It is hardly necessary to say that Berdyaev's idea of philosophy is not acceptable to all philosophers, nor, for the matter of that, to all theologians, even if for somewhat different reasons. Many people, however, have found his thought fresh and stimulating. His shortcomings as a philosopher did not bother them much, if at all, as they were more concerned with the prophetic message. To some at any rate Berdyaev's interpretation of Christian faith seemed to make Christianity more credible and more relevant. He was very much a Russian, a Russian aristocrat, but his attack on all forms of totalitarianism, his never-tiring defence of freedom, his emphasis on the primacy of spiritual values, his anthropocentric approach to problems, his personalism, his search for meaning in human life and history, aroused widespread interest, as is shown by the many translations of his writings. It was not a question of his admirers becoming 'Berdyaevians'. This would have been difficult in the case of a thinker who was no system-builder. But a good many non-Russians found that his writings opened from them fresh horizons of thought.

4. We have seen that a prominent feature of religiously oriented philosophical thought in Russia was criticism of 'western rationalism'. It was not a question of refusing to admit that reasoning has any role to play in human life. It was a question of rejecting the claim that in regard to the acquisition of knowledge reason is omnicompetent and of maintaining that other factors can be and are involved, especially intuition. In the field of religious knowledge faith in God was based on religious experience, not on proofs such as were offered by St Thomas Aquinas. A point to notice is that this position was not simply asserted. Reasons were offered for accepting it. For example, according to Solovyev existence is known by immediate experience. Discursive thought discerns relations between ideas or concepts, but it cannot establish existence. To know that something exists verification is required, which, in the case of knowledge of

1 The phrase was obviously borrowed from Nietzsche.

God, is mystical experience. Again, Berdyaev argued that any attempt to prove the existence of God in the way in which Aquinas tried to prove it involved objectification of God as a reality 'out there'. In general, he saw rationalization as objectification, in the sense that symbols were objectified by reason as realities. In his view, traditional theology was far from free from this tendency to mistake symbols for what was symbolized. It was 'rationalistic'. In fact, in spite of his admiration for Solovyev,[1] Berdyaev regarded the development of Solovyev's metaphysics as infected with rationalization.

Though thinkers such as Kireevsky, Solovyev and Berdyaev laid stress on the limitations of reason, it would be misleading to describe them as 'irrationalists'. It would be more appropriate to describe them as 'anti-rationalists', if by rationalism we mean belief in the omnicompetence of reason in regard to knowledge of reality. The term 'irrationalist', however, has been commonly applied to the emigré Russian philosopher Leon Shestov. For example, Professor George L. Kline has described Shestov as 'a thoroughgoing irrationalist',[2] adding that this is not to say that Shestov was an anti-rationalist, inasmuch as the Russian was not weak in logic. Obviously, whether a given descriptive epithet is appropriate or not, depends on the meaning which one gives to the epithet. If rationalism is understood as involving the claim that all reality is in principle knowable by the human reason and that it conforms to all the requirements of logical thought, Shestov can certainly be described as an anti-rationalist. At the same time, if a man who denies that the principle of non-contradiction is universally and necessarily applicable and who believes that important truths can best be expressed by paradox is thought to merit the label 'irrationalist', Shestov can be so labelled. If, however, we regard 'irrationalism' as a form or sign of madness, we should bear in mind the fact that rationalism itself was, for Shestov, a form of madness.

Leon Shestov (1866–1936) was a Russian Jew, his real name being Lev Isakovich Schwarzman. He studied law at the University of Moscow, though he did not become a practising lawyer. After the Revolution, in 1919, he emigrated to Berlin and then settled in Paris. He did not occupy any regular academic post. Referring to his first meeting with Shestov,

1 Berdyaev saw in Solovyev a prophetic thinker, and he thought highly of, for example, the way in which Solovyev rose above both religious sectarianism and chauvinistic nationalism. He was well aware of the importance of Solovyev in the renaissance of religious thought in Russia. As one might expect, however, he detected in Solovyev's metaphysics a tendency to monism which was at variance with his (Berdyaev's) emphasis on freedom.
2 *Russian Philosophy*, III, p. 223.

Berdyaev remarks about his friend, 'I regarded him then and regard him now as one of the most remarkable men I was ever privileged to meet'.[1] Shestov has often been described as an existentialist, and justifiably; but his existentialism was developed independently of those who are generally called existentialists. It was only in his later years that he came to know and to value highly the writings of Kierkegaard. He was, however, influenced by Dostoevsky and Nietzsche. Shestov was an intensely personal thinker, in the sense that his thought was a sustained struggle with problems which were of great importance to him personally. He did not bother about topics simply because it was or might be thought proper for a philosopher to say something about them. Indeed, philosophy was for him essentially a never-ending struggle. When accused of repeating himself, of returning time and again to the same themes, he was unrepentant.

In 1897 G. M. Brandes, the Danish literary historian and critic, published a large volume on Shakespeare. The following year saw the publication of Shestov's first book, *Shakespeare and his Critic Brandes*. Shakespeare, as Shestov saw him, had an intense interest in and understanding of life as it is actually lived. 'The poet felt that one cannot live without reconciling oneself with life'.[2] Shakespeare was, of course, well aware of the tragic elements in life, but in his tragedies he showed us that 'beneath the horrors which are visible to us there is hidden an invisible development of the human soul, that all seek what is best, even when they perform evil deeds, and that all the accusations which people heap upon life proceed only from our inability to understand the tasks of fate'. This reconciled Shakespeare with human tragedy, and it made him the greatest of poets. Brandes, however, 'does not see all this'.[3] Life, with all its tragedy, is self-justifying. There is a kind of immanent ethics in it. Shakespeare portrayed performers of what we conceive as evil deeds, but he did not judge.

At the beginning of his book Shestov maintained that western rationalist philosophy had distorted life. The rationalist metaphysicians recognized only those elements which could be fitted into their mental constructions, their systems, relegating the rest to the sphere of the contingent and the unimportant. For them, from Aristotle onwards, to live was to think. Shakespeare, however, saw life as a whole, and he was well aware that life cannot be simply equated with thought.

Even if the present writer were competent to make judgments about

1 *Dream and Reality*, p. 125.
2 *Shekspir i evo kritik Brandes*, p. 283 (St Petersburg, 1898).
3 *Ibid.*, pp. 283–4.

the issues between Shestov and Brandes in regard to the interpretation of Shakespeare, it would be inappropriate to discuss these issues here. The point which we wish to make is that though Shestov abandoned what has been described as the vague moral optimism of his first book, his attack on rationalist philosophy was to become intensified. In his first book he argued that by trying to fit reality into the framework of the rational and the reasonable, philosophy became progressively more destructive. First it got rid of God. 'Having finished with God, it got to work on morality'[1] and then turned its attention to man. In the name of science positivism (Shestov took Hippolyte Taine as its representative) has tried to reduce psychology to physiology and has eliminated human freedom, conceiving human actions as the effects of determining causes. Shestov never became tired of attacking rationalist philosophy and scientism (rather than science itself).

The book on Shakespeare was followed, in 1900, by *Good in the Teaching of Count Tolstoy and Nietzsche*, a work in which he attacked the tendency, characteristic of Tolstoy among others, to conceive God and the Good as equivalent terms. Shestov was not arguing that God is bad, evil. He was maintaining that Nietzsche's phrase 'beyond good and evil' applies to God, the God of the Bible that is to say. If God is conceived as the Good, religion is reduced to ethics and eventually God disappears. God is above pity, above good, above evil.

Shestov's interest in Nietzsche is shown not only by the title of the book just mentioned but also by that of its successor, *Dostoevsky and Nietzsche: the Philosophy of Tragedy* (1903). In the German thinker he saw a man who did not avert his eyes from the dark and tragic aspects of life or attempt to represent human history as a rational teleological process, in the manner of Hegel. Nietzsche saw life as it is and affirmed it. Shestov also admired Nietzsche for the way in which the latter boldly questioned propositions which most people either took for granted or regarded as self-evidently true. For Nietzsche, even the basic principles of logic were 'fictions', pragmatically useful but not laws of being. Nietzsche did not believe that the world in itself conformed to the demands of the human reason, and he had no use for the rationalist philosophers, of whom the greatest was Hegel. As for Nietzsche's proclamation of the death of God, what won Shestov's approval was the importance which Nietzsche attached to God's demise. In an essay which originally appeared in 1917 in the journal *Problems of Philosophy and Psychology* Shestov referred to philosophers who sacrificed

1 *Ibid.*, p. 12.

God in a spirit of indifference, and he then remarked that 'the only exception to this general rule in modern times is Nietzsche'.[1] For Nietzsche, the so-called death of God was a world-shaking event, with implications of great significance. Further, Nietzsche expressed his position frankly and clearly, whereas Hegel, in Shestov's opinion, while talking a lot about God and the absolute religion (Christianity), expounded a masked atheism.[2]

In Dostoevsky Shestov saw a writer who refused to gloss over evil, to represent the world and human life as rational, to exalt the universal at the expense of the particular, to eliminate human freedom. Though not a philosopher in the traditional sense, Dostoevsky was an existential thinker. Later on, Shestov was to write about him in conjunction with Kierkegaard, as in *Kierkegaard and Existential Philosophy* (1939). Indeed, for Shestov, Kierkegaard was 'the spiritual double of Dostoevsky'.[3]

After writing the above-mentioned books Shestov tended, like Nietzsche, to adopt an aphoristic style, though his later writings also include some fairly lengthy continuous treatments of themes. He also wrote articles. Among his books *The Apotheosis of Groundlessness: An Essay in Undogmatic Thought* appeared in 1905[4], *The Power of the Keys (Potestas Clavium)* in 1923[5], *In Job's Balances* in 1929,[6] *Kierkegaard and Existential Philosophy* in 1939,[7] and *Athens and Jerusalem* in 1951.[8] There are also two collections of essays, *Beginnings and Ends* (1908) and *Speculation and Revelation* (1964). Any attempt to summarize briefly some main features of Shestov's thought, however, can hardly convey the flavour, so to speak, of Shestov's writing. In his sustained attack on rationalism and scientism he discusses a large number of philosophers,

---

1 The article in question, 'A Thousand and One Nights', was reprinted by way of a preface to *Potestas Clavium* (1923). There is an English translation (entitled *Potestas Clavium*), with an introduction, by Bernard Martin (Athens, Ohio, 1968). The sentence quoted appears on p. 17.

2 Hegel's conception of God has been the subject of much discussion and controversy. Here we are concerned simply with Shestov's views.

3 *Athens and Jerusalem*, translated, with an introduction, by Bernard Martin, p. 371 (Athens, Ohio, 1966).

4 There is an English translation of the Russian original by S. S. Koteliansky under the title *All Things are Possible* (London, 1920). The work consists of aphorisms.

5 See note 1 on this page.

6 There is an English translation of the Russian original under the title *In Job's Balances* by Camilla Coventry and C. A. Macartney (London, 1932).

7 There is an English translation by E. Hewitt under the title *Kierkegaard and the Existential Philosophy* (Athens, Ohio, 1969).

8 See note 3 on this page.

from the Greeks up to Husserl.[1] And though some of his judgments may be unacceptable to a good many readers or even provoke them to indignation or exasperation, what he says is generally both perceptive and stimulating, even when one disagrees or would wish to qualify what he says. It is, however, impossible to follow him into all his discussions.

According to Shestov, 'the best, that is the only comprehensive, definition of philosophy is to be found in Plotinus. To the question "what is philosophy?" he answers: τὸ τιμιώτατον, that is what is most important'.[2] Modern philosophy, we are told, having made herself the handmaid of science, is indifferent to our judgments of value about what is important or precious in life.[3] It is not concerned, for example, with beauty. Yet it is out of reflection on what is most important and precious to us in life that true philosophy frames its questions or problems. Moreover, if we accept the definition of Plotinus, the barriers between philosophy on the one hand and religion and art on the other are lifted. For religion and art too are concerned with what is most worthwhile.

The objection can obviously be raised that different people have different ideas of what is most important or worthwhile, and that Shestov is obviously thinking in terms of his own personal evaluations. This objection might not worry Shestov. For he did not look on philosophy as 'impersonal' thought. But he has more to say about the world of science and about philosophy as the handmaid of science. He is quite prepared to admit that 'if you wish to have a solidly established science, you must place it under the protection of the idea of necessity'.[4] In the streets of life there is 'no electric light, no gas, not even a kerosene lamp-bracket'.[5] To obtain light in the darkness, to enable us to predict, the human mind has postulated necessary causal relations; it has constructed a world governed by natural laws. And positivist philosophy, turning itself into the handmaid of science, eliminates human freedom, considered as an exception to the operation of natural law and determining causality.

---

1 Shestov was personally acquainted with Husserl and considered him a major philosopher of the time. This did not prevent him from attacking Husserl's emphasis on the need for philosophy to be scientific. He looked on the German thinker as the very embodiment of rationalism. Perhaps surprisingly (it certainly surprised Shestov), in one of their discussions Husserl urged Shestov to read Kierkegaard, whose writings were previously unknown territory for him. The article 'Memories of an Eminent Philosopher (Edmund Husserl)' which Shestov finished shortly before his death, is printed in an English translation in *Philosophy and Phenomenological Research* for 1962 (vol. 22, pp. 449–71). A somewhat abridged version is reproduced in *Russian Philosophy*, III, pp. 248–76.
2 *In Job's Balances*, pp. 31–2 (Part I, 7).
3 *Ibid.*, p. 160 (Part II, 16).
4 *Athens and Jerusalem*, p. 82.
5 *All Things are Possible*, p. 15 (Part I, 1).

What is, or should be, precious to the human being is thus rejected in the name of science. But though natural science certainly has a pragmatic use, its world of necessity, of determinism, is nonetheless a mental construction. It is to the credit of David Hume that he showed that necessity is not to be found in the world but that it is a subjective contribution. The theory of evolution has undermined the old thesis that like produces like, and that effects must always resemble their causes. As far as possibility goes, anything might follow from anything.

In maintaining that the world is not governed by necessity, that necessity is not really a feature of reality in itself, Shestov is not simply following in the footsteps of Hume, who was concerned with epistemological problems, with the scope and limitations of human knowledge. He was motivated by religious considerations. In a world governed by determining causality, in which every event is in principle predictable, God, if he is acknowledged at all, is pushed to the periphery. There is no place for divine interventions. Once, however, the world of science is seen as a mental construction, though a useful one for certain purposes, the field for divine intervention becomes open. The God of the Bible, bound by no laws of nature, can return into the centre of the picture. And human freedom can be reasserted. (Obviously, Shestov's rejection of the reign of necessity is not confined to natural science. He also rejects, for example, the idea of historical development as an inevitable, law-determined process.)

It is not simply a matter of natural laws and of the world of science. Shestov, like Nietzsche, extends his questioning to principles of logic and to the presuppositions of rationalist philosophy. The principle of identity, for example, symbolized by $A=A$, is a postulate which 'has a purely empirical origin',[1] and, Shestov argues, the theory of evolution shows that one can think otherwise than in accordance with this principle. Again, though from Aristotle onwards the principle of non-contradiction has been regarded as universally valid, as a law of thought and also as a law of being, it is simply a postulate of the human reason. It is, indeed, unsettling to be told that the principles of logic are not eternal truths. But 'the business of philosophy is to teach man to live in uncertainty . . . The business of philosophy is not to reassure people but to upset them'.[2] Nietzsche might have said the same.

Rationalist philosophy has tried to subject reality to the principles of logic and to imprison it, so to speak, in the house built by reason. For

1 *Ibid.*, p. 128 (Part I, 121).
2 *Ibid.*, p. 24 (Part I, 11).

example, 'Husserl stops at nothing to make of philosophy the science of absolute truths'[1]; he speaks of the 'limitless character of objective reason'.[2] This emphasis on reason, from Aristotle onwards, has meant that philosophers have concerned themselves with the universal and the recurrent, rather than with the particular and unique, though 'individual phenomena mean much more to us than the constantly recurrent'.[3] In general, rationalism re-echoes the famous statement of Protagoras that man is the measure of all things. But what is our justification for believing that the statement is true? Needless to say, the rationalist philosophers regard 'irrationalists' as insane. But their rationalism is really the expression of desire, of will. 'The root of all our philosophies lies, not in our objective observations, but in the demands of our own heart, in the subjective moral *will*'[4]. We 'find' reality rational because we want it to be rational. Belief in the rationality of human existence is the 'child of our desires'.[5]

Shestov subjected to attack not only rationalist metaphysics but also autonomous ethics, based on the claim that there are eternal moral principles which even God, if there is a God, must respect and, indeed, obey. He was thus in sympathy with William of Occam's revolt against the subordination of God to an eternal moral law, and also with Nietzsche's denial of any absolute and universal moral law. Philosophy of history also came under attack. People seek for the meaning of history and they find it. But why must history have a meaning? Speculative philosophers of history have 'found' a meaning in history, because they wanted to find one, to subject history to reason, to make it a rational comprehensible process, an advance to whatever goal they desired. But they could do so only by falsifying history. 'Hegel's philosophy of history is a crude and noxious falsification of life.'[6] As for Husserl, in his attack on historicism he 'does not wish to listen to the teachings of history; it is history, on the contrary, that must accept his teaching'.[7]

If we were to pay attention simply to Shestov's criticism of scientism and of rationalist philosophy, we might receive the impression that he is doing his best to spread scepticism, ethical relativism and the idea that human life and history are devoid of meaning. What he is actually doing, however, is to present his readers with an option between rationalism or

1 *Potestas Clavium*, p. 345.
2 *Ibid.*, p. 353. Shestov refers to Husserl's *Logische Untersuchungen*, II, 90.
3 *All Things are Possible*, p. 228 (Part II, 44).
4 *Ibid.*, p. 126 (Part I, 108).
5 *Ibid.*, p. 97.
6 *In Job's Balances*, p. 244 (Part II, 52).
7 *Potestas Clavium*, p. 345.

the worship of science (positivism) on the one had and faith in the God of the Bible on the other. 'Athens *or* Jerusalem, religion *or* philosophy.'[1] When Shestov rejects the idea of eternal truths, the thesis which he wishes to assert is that 'the Bible sees in the eternal truths that are independent of the Creator only a lie, a suggestion, an enchantment'.[2] When he maintains that the principle of non-contradiction is not an absolute, universally true proposition, he is making room for the thesis that God transcends the principles and rules of logic. Following in the footsteps of the medieval theologian St Peter Damian, Shestov maintains that God could bring it about that what has happened did not happen. For example, God could bring it about that Socrates did not drink poison or that Julius Caesar did not cross the Rubicon, thus undoing history, so to speak.[3] Again, when he attacks the theory that there are eternal moral principles or laws, which even God must respect, he is thinking in a manner similar to Kierkegaard's line of thought when he argued that in telling Abraham to sacrifice his son Isaac God was 'suspending the ethical'. The general idea is that God's omnipotence knows no limits set by the human reason.

It should be understood that what Shestov opposes to rationalism is Kierkegaard's leap of faith, the result of an option. 'Religious philosophy is a turning away from knowledge and a surmounting by faith, in a boundless tension of all its forces, of the false fear of the unlimited will of the Creator . . .'[4] Shestov does not claim that the existence of God can be proved. Referring to Dostoevsky, he remarks, with approval of what he takes to be the novelist's view, that 'one cannot demonstrate God. One cannot seek him in history. God is "caprice" incarnate, who rejects all guarantees. He is outside history, like all that people hold to be τὸ τιμιώτατον, of supreme value'[5].

Shestov does, indeed, use phrases such as 'religious philosophy' (as above) or 'biblical philosophy'. For example, he refers to 'the fundamental opposition of biblical philosophy to speculative philosophy'.[6] He also asserts that 'the Judaeo-Christian philosophy can accept neither the

1 *Athens and Jerusalem*, p. 47. The second dichotomy would be better expressed as 'philosophy *or* religion', to correspond with 'Athens *or* Jerusalem'.
2 *Ibid*., p. 351.
3 This thesis must obviously be distinguished from the claim that God could have prevented Julius Caesar from crossing the Rubicon. Shestov is presupposing that Julius Caesar did cross the Rubicon. He then claims that God, in his omnipotence, could abolish this event, cause it not to have happened.
4 *Athens and Jerusalem*, p. 70.
5 *In Job's Balances*, p. 82 (Part I, 14).
6 *Athens and Jerusalem*, p. 59.

fundamental problems nor the principle nor the technique of thought of rational philosophy'.[1] Though, however, he doubtless hoped that he would be able to develop this 'Judaeo-Christian philosophy', a philosophy based on faith, and though he indicated some of the beliefs and attitudes which it would exclude, he did not in fact develop it positively. Some would obviously claim that no such development was possible. If religion and philosophy are really opposed, there cannot be a 'religious philosophy'. Shestov might have replied that there cannot be a truly religious rationalist philosophy, but that there can be a religious philosophy in the sense of wisdom. In point of fact, however, the point to which Shestov's lines of thought converge, is an option between reason and faith, between the God of the philosophers (or no God) on the one hand and the God of the Bible on the other, the God of the Bible being known by faith rather than by speculative philosophy.

The Russian thinker's endorsement of the Kierkegaardian Either-Or attitude finds expression in various ways. For example, at the end of a long article on the thought of Solovyev he remarks that 'in the last days of his life Solovyev turned away from speculative truth (*istina*) and the speculative good, as though he had learned that not by thought but in the thunder is eternal and final truth (*pravda*) attained'.[2] Again, in an essay on the thought of his friend Berdyaev, in which he criticized Berdyaev for trying to combine gnosis with existential philosophy, Shestov expressed his confidence that, if Berdyaev ever succeeded in bringing the two elements into confrontation, he would not hesitate to choose existentialism (which, for Shestov, meant Kierkegaardian existentialism). Another example of Shestov's Either-Or attitude is provided by his essay 'On the philosophy of the Middle Ages', occasioned by publication of Étienne Gilson's *Spirit of Medieval Philosophy*. Shestov saw some medieval thinkers (not all) as succumbing to the temptation of trying to 'transform faith into knowledge'[3] or to ground revealed truth on rational argument[4]. As for Gilson's own idea of Christian philosophy, Shestov thought that it was an attempt to combine two incompatible elements, on the one hand the contention that there is a Judaeo-Christian philosophy with its source in biblical revelation, and on the other hand the claims that every philosophy must be based on evidence leading to demonstrable truths.

Shestov's final word is really a spiritual message. 'God is higher than

1 *Athens and Jerusalem*, p. 372.
2 *Umozrenie i otkrovenie* (*Speculation and Revelation*), p. 91 (Paris, 1964).
3 *Ibid.*, p. 282.
4 *Ibid.*, p. 297.

ethics and higher than our reason. He takes on himself our sins and wipes out the terrors of life.'[1] Again, 'freedom comes to man not from knowledge but from faith, which puts an end to our fears'.[2]

1 *Ibid.*, p. 259.
2 *Ibid.*, p. 295.

Epilogue

The later chapters of this volume have been devoted to two main currents of thought, Marxism in Russia, before and after 1917, and the renaissance of religiously oriented philosophy with Solovyev and his successors. Each movement had, of course, its proximate background. The spread of Marxism in the decades immediately preceding the revolution presupposed the failure of liberalism to achieve its ends,[1] the increasingly revolutionary aspect of the thought of the Russian intelligentsia, and developments in the economic life of the country which made Marxist theory seem more relevant to actual conditions in Russia than it had previously appeared to be. Besides, though Populism was by no means dead at the time of the Revolution (it lived on in the form of Socialist Revolutionary ideas), the superiority of the theoretical content of Marxism to that of the Populist ideology was shown by the way in which Populist thinkers borrowed elements from Marxism. To say this is not, however, to imply that Marxist philosophy was destined by its intrinsic quality to become the official ideology of post-Revolution Russia. The triumph of the Bolshevik Party was made possible by the conditions created by the World War and effected by Lenin's resoluteness in making use of an opportunity for action, and the triumph of the Bolshevik Party eventually involved the elevation of Marxism to the status of official ideology.

The renaissance of religiously oriented philosophy can be seen as one manifestation of a wider reaction against the positivism and materialism which had been conspicuous features of Russian intellectual life, at any rate among the members of the radical intelligentsia, from the middle of the nineteenth century.[2] This reaction expressed itself also in literature, for

1 The 1905 revolution led to liberal concessions, but the monarch did not respect his own enactments when he believed that they threatened the stability of the régime. As for the liberal Provisional Government of 1917, it was short-lived and a failure.
2 The phrase 'positivism and materialism' should not be taken as implying that positivism entails what can be described as metaphysical materialism, the theory that there is an underlying ultimate reality called 'matter'.

example with the symbolist poets such as Vyacheslav Ivanov (1866–1949), Andrey Bely (1880–1934) and Alexander Blok (1880–1921). Perhaps we can speak of a reaction against 'flatness' in favour of 'depth'. But it was not only positivism and materialism which formed the background for the revival of religious philosophy. There was also the lack of creative, developing thought among the official representatives of the Russian Orthodox Church. The Church preserved the formulated dogmas but frowned on anything new.[1] As we saw, Solovyev emphasized the need for giving to the religious consciousness a more adequate intellectual expression. Berdyaev later insisted on 'free philosophical speculation',[2] as distinct from what he described as the socialized collective expression of religious truth by the Church, and maintained that philosophy could not renounce 'its right to consider and, if possible, to resolve the essential problems of religion which theology claims as its monopoly'.[3] Further, in the social-political sphere, according to Berdyaev, the Russian Orthodox Church still thought in terms of an obsolete social organization, as though 'not only the proletarian revolution but even the bourgeois revolution had never happened'.[4] It would be an exaggeration to talk about a reaction against the Church. Solovyev and most of his successors were members of the Church. It was a question of reacting against what they believed to be a static and ossified theology and against the Russian Church's failure to come to grips with social problems and to promote the realization of social justice. It can, of course, be objected that if Solovyev and his successors were concerned with infusing life into the theology of the Russian Orthodox Church, they should be regarded as lay theologians, and that in point of fact they tended to confuse Christian theology and philosophical thought.[5] But what they had primarily in mind was obviously the development of a comprehensive Christian world-view which would

1 We have had occasion to mention the fact that the Theological Academies had on their staffs some notable scholars. These included V. L. Nesmelov (1863–1920), and M. N. Tareev (1866–1934), both theologians, and V. Bolotov (1859–1900), a Church historian. It remains true, however, that the official Church, while concerned with maintaining the Christian faith in its purity, did not encourage original speculative thought.
2 *Solitude and Society*, p. 6.
3 *Ibid.*, p. 8.
4 *Christianity and Class War*, translated by Donald Attwater, p. 113 (London, 1933).
5 It should be remembered that the Orthodox Church laid great emphasis on the patristic writings, especially of the Greek Fathers. With St Gregory of Nyssa, for example, we find a Christian world-view, combining what (in terms of the distinction formulated in western medieval thought) would be described as theological and philosophical themes. Kireevsky and Khomyakov held that belief or faith and reason were both required if religious truth was to be attained.

be meaningful to contemporaries and able to confront secularized
thought on an intellectual level. The point being made here is simply that
it was failure on the part of the Russian Orthodox Church (as represented by the hierarchy and the official theologians) to encourage creative thought and to apply Christian principles to contemporary
problems which formed part of the background of the renaissance of
religiously oriented philosophy. Solovyev and his successors believed
that they were meeting a real need, created not only by the spread of
positivism and materialism but also by what seemed to them the conspicuous failure of the Church to provide any intellectually satisfactory
alternative. They were concerned with promoting genuine thought
within the community of believers, and over-emphasis on what may be,
from an outsider's point of view, a tendency to confuse theology and
philosophy diverts attention from this basic point.

If we include in our field of vision a longer stretch of Russian history,
we may be inclined to see in the Russian Marxists successors to the
so-called Westernizers and to regard the renaissance of religiously oriented philosophy as a fulfilment of the desires of early Slavophiles such as
Kireevsky and Khomyakov. As Marxism was a philosophy of western
origin, imported into Russia, it is natural to look on its increasing
acceptance by members of the radical intelligentsia as an expression of
the policy of learning from the West. And it is also natural to see Solovyev
and his successors as fulfilling the demands of the early Slavophiles for a
philosophy which would be free from western rationalism and in harmony with the religious traditions of Russia.

This line of thought is doubtless valid up to a point. At the same time
the situation is a good deal more complex than is allowed for by any
simple assertion of links between the programme of Westernization and
acceptance of Marxism on the one hand and between early Slavophile
thought and the renaissance of religiously oriented philosophy on the
other. The growing influence of Marxism from the final decade of the
nineteenth century can obviously be seen as involving, or presupposing,
repudiation both of the autocratic régime and of Russia's religious
tradition in favour of western socialist theory and western secular
thought. Marxism, however, was to become an instrument in the hands
of a Party which gave fresh life, in a new form, to the authoritarianism of
the old régime. The original Westernizers wanted different things, but
none of them desired the replacement of one authoritarian régime by
another. Further, though Marxism is a universalist theory, to which
nationalism is alien, in the sense that it is something to be transcended, in
the Soviet Union we have seen the steady growth of nationalism, coupled

with anti-western ideas. To be sure, it can be argued that it is not the West as such which is regarded as an enemy but rather capitalist and imperialist régimes, and that what we may tend to regard as nationalism is really a conviction of the superiority of socialism and a realization that Russia, or the Soviet Union, has the historical mission of enlightening mankind. But it is just here that we can discern a link between Slavophilism and the present-day Russian outlook. The Slavophiles believed that by following her own historical path Russia would blaze a trail for all mankind. Slavophilism, as we have seen, tended to degenerate into a Panslavism which accepted the role of the autocracy in realizing Panslavist ideals. The Panslavists have their successors today. The idea of the greatness of Russia and of her historic mission, an idea which was alien to the mind of Marx, but which provides a link with Slavophilism, has tended to predominate over the universalist elements in Marxism, though these are not, of course, explicitly rejected. When Berdyaev asserted that Russian Communism 'proclaimed light from the East which is destined to enlighten the bourgeois darkness of the West'[1] and that 'Communism is a Russian phenomenon in spite of its Marxist ideology',[2] he may have exaggerated, but he was not simply talking nonsense. We can add that what is called neo-Stalinism is not exclusively an expression of a desire to control, dominate, repress and dragoon; it is also the expression of a desire that Russia, while making use of western science and technology, should avoid contamination by western 'degenerate' attitudes and pursue her own path. Obviously, Slavophile emphasis on Russian Orthodoxy has no place in the official ideology of the Communist Party.[3] But Slavophile emphasis on Russia and her historic mission is very much alive.

Needless to say, developments in Russia after the Revolution do not affect the undeniable fact that it was a philosophy of western origin which came to constitute the official ideology of the country. But it seems that adherence to this philosophy is no longer sufficient (if it ever was) to serve as an effectively uniting factor. Hence the attempt to fill the void by a nationalist spirit which ill accords with Marxism but which provides a link with the Slavophilism of pre-revolutionary Russia. It is certainly

1 *The Russian Idea*, p. 250.
2 *Ibid.*
3 This statement is obviously true, but it seems that there are at any rate some Russians in the Soviet Union who hope for an alliance or collaboration between the régime and the Orthodox Church. I refer to people who have no hankering after western democracy but who believe that Russia can best be herself and renew her genuine spirit through a convergence between an authoritarian socialist régime and the traditional religion of the country. For some documentation see *The Russian New Right: Right-Wing Ideologies in The Contemporary USSR*, by Alexander Yanov (Berkeley, California, 1978).

arguable that the true spiritual descendants of Westernizers such as Belinsky and Herzen are neither the Party ideologists nor the nationalistically minded neo-Stalinists or 'Rightists' but people such as the scientist A. D. Sakharov, who looks, perhaps too optimistically, for a gradual and peaceful convergence between Russia and the West.

There are obvious links between the renaissance of religiously oriented philosophy and the thought of such Slavophiles such as Kireevsky and Khomyakov. For one thing, we can discern a continued desire to develop a Christian philosophy or world-view. There is the common conviction that Russia should not identify herself with the progressive secularization of western thought, that she should preserve her religious tradition and her sense of community (*sobornost*), and that for her to do this successfully an appropriate framework of thought must be developed, one which is meaningful for the reflective mind and which can point the way to the solution of contemporary moral and social problems. For another thing, we find with Solovyev and his successors a more systematic development of theories or ideas already present in the thought of their predecessors. The concept of integral knowledge is an example. At the same time there was a progressive transcending of what one might perhaps describe as the more parochial elements of Slavophile thought. Though Kireevsky and Khomyakov would obviously claim to be concerned with the attainment of universal truth (what is true for all), they tended to speak as though this truth, in the area of Christian philosophy at any rate, could be attained only on the basis of Orthodox faith. Solovyev, though a Russian, a member of the Orthodox Church and a thinker who owed a great deal to the traditions of eastern Christianity, rose above the rather narrow prejudices of the early Slavophiles. The idea of synthesis and development of the concept of total-unity came to the fore. He was more of a systematic philosopher than his predecessors, and less of a polemicist on behalf of Slavdom in general, or Russia in particular. His twentieth-century successors were, of course, deeply concerned with the fate and future of their country. How could they not be? But the historical situation was very different from what it had been in the first half of the nineteenth century. The Slavophiles saw the enemy as located in the West and as infiltrating into Russia through members of the small educated élite, whereas for the twentieth-century Russian philosophers in exile the enemy was enthroned in Russia itself and was working outwards. As it was a question of a secular ideology which claimed to be the one scientific truth and the one reliable guide to human happiness, what was at stake was not simply the soul of Russia, so to speak, but the human soul as such. What was needed to counter a universalist

secular ideology was a universalist Christian world-view and interpretation of human life and history, without any element of Slavophile
antiquarianism. It can be objected that Berdyaev, for example, was a
thoroughly Russian thinker, constantly referring to Russian history, Russian writers and the Russian mind. This is true. But it is also true that he
spoke to and about the human being as such. So had Dostoevsky before
him. Perhaps we can sum up by saying that the philosophical elements
in Slavophile thought developed in such a way as to adapt themselves
to different historical circumstances.

   The concept of 'Christian philosophy' is not clear. Some would maintain that there can be both Christian theology and philosophical thought,
but that there is not and cannot be 'Christian philosophy', even though
some philosophical theories are easier than others to harmonize with
Christian beliefs. Others would maintain that there can perfectly well be
a general Christian world-view in which philosophizing is involved. We
cannot pursue this general theme here. It may, however, be as well to
warn the reader that a statement by a Russian religious philosopher to
the effect that genuine philosophy presupposes faith or revelation is not
necessarily to be understood in a sense which would force us to conclude
that the self-styled philosopher was really a Christian theologian dressed
in lay clothes. The word 'faith' may be used to mean not assent to a set of
propositions formulated by the Church but rather an intuitive apprehension of oneness or of spiritual reality. As for revelation, Berdyaev
describes it as 'a primary phenomenon, or relationship with God'.[1]
According to him, this primary phenomenon contains 'no cognitive
element'.[2] It stands in need of interpretation. The Church gives it a social,
collective interpretation which becomes authoritative, static, ossified.
Hence the need for 'free philosophical speculation'.[3] Obviously, this sort
of idea would not be acceptable to everyone. One could approach and
criticize it from different angles. But to say that religious philosophy
presupposes revelation in the sense of some kind of spiritual experience is
clearly not equivalent to saying that philosophy should be based on
acceptance of certain doctrines as formulated by the Church.[4]

   Some of the Russian thinkers in exile had been adherents of Marxism

1 *Solitude and Society*, p. 13.
2 *Ibid.*, p. 5.
3 *Ibid.*, p. 6.
4 By quoting Berdyaev one lays oneself open to the comment that one is taking an
exception as the rule. But even when a Russian religious philosopher quite clearly
maintained that genuine religious philosophy presupposed Christian faith, he was
thinking primarily of sharing in the faith-attitude of the community, of participation in a
common life of Christian faith, rather than of accepting all ecclesiastical pronouncements
in an unquestioning manner.

for a while, attracted not so much by the philosophy of dialectical
materialism as by the crusading revolutionary zeal and social idealism of
the Russian Social Democrats. The future religious philosophers fre-
quented Marxist circles mainly because Marxism proclaimed the advent
of a better world not only for Russians but also for mankind in general,
providing an impressive theory of history to support their claims. If
people such as Frank, Berdyaev and Bulgakov soon turned away from
Marxism, it was largely because they were unable to find in it any firm
ethical basis for its own ideals, because it excluded any religious dimension from human life, and because it seemed (to Berdyaev in particular)
to subordinate truth to expediency, to alleged class-interest. Having
turned away from Marxism, they proceeded to develop their own lines of
thought. But, apart from a very brief period, they had to do so as exiles
from their country, and they died abroad. The Soviet authorities saw to it
that the philosophers in exile had little, if any opportunity of influencing
intellectual circles in the Soviet Union, and that they could not occupy a
position analogous to that which Herzen had occupied for a time, when
it was said that he ran a 'second government' from London. It is natural
therefore to ask whether the Russian religious philosophers, now dead,
have anything to say to citizens of the Soviet Union today, or whether
their thought has become irrelevant for anyone brought up and educated
in modern Russia. Obviously, such questions cannot be answered except
in a highly conjectural manner. But it is natural to raise them.

It hardly needs saying that there are plenty of people in the Soviet
Union who are concerned with obtaining tangible benefits in this world
and who bother little, if at all, with the so-called 'ultimate questions'.
They may have no real interest in the ideology, but it does not follow that
this lack of interest is compensated for by a hankering after a religious
faith or an 'idealist' philosophy. Nor, for the matter of that, does indifference towards the ideology entail a desire for revolution. There are
doubtless many Soviet citizens who would be quite content with what
has been described as 'goulash Communism'. The 'Rightists' are, of
course, well aware of this situation. They see the rapid spread of what is
to them a western, bourgeois spirit; and they look to nationalism, to an
updated form of Slavophilism, to fill the void created by the decay of the
spirit of the 1917 revolution. There are also, however, minds which are
open to religious ideas, and which look to religion to fill the void. Some
find what they are looking for in the Orthodox Church or in adherence to
some other religious group, such as the Baptists. But available evidence
suggests that there are also educated Soviet citizens who look for a
non-materialist line of thought which can provide a basis for spiritual

and moral values and give to life a religious dimension, a line of thought, that is to say, which provides an intellectual alternative to dialectical materialism.[1] There used at any rate to be talk about the new 'Soviet man', who would presumably have left religion and religiously oriented philosophical thought far behind. But Russians are human beings, not robots, and we know that together with an increasing indifference to the ideology there has been an increasing interest in religion. Some interest in religion is only to be expected in view of the increasing sense of continuity between the old Russia and the new and of a growing historical sense. But I am talking about a personal or existential interest rather than about an historical or antiquarian interest. Further, in a country in which higher education has undergone a notable development, one would expect to find a number of people who are attracted to religion but who are not satisfied with simple faith and piety. Such people look for an intellectually viable alternative to a discredited ideology.

Even if, however, it is assumed that the situation is substantially as described above, it does not necessarily follow that the felt need can be met by the philosophical theories of the Russian religious thinkers who now belong to the past. I dare say that some of their lines of thought are capable of exercising an intellectual stimulus, of providing points of departure for reflection. Perhaps this is most true of Berdyaev, inasmuch as he did not present any take-it-or-leave-it system but pursued a variety of lines of thought relating to the human being and to history. But it seems to me unlikely (though I may, of course, be wrong) that the rather abstruse metaphysics of Solovyev or Frank would have much attraction for minds educated in the Soviet Union. In my opinion, any real revival of religiously oriented philosophy or of what the Marxists would describe as 'idealist' philosophy would have to emerge within the Soviet Union itself, rather than through importation of theories of deceased Russian exiles or even through resuscitation of the philosophy of Solovyev, which, though impressive, presupposes a certain historical context. Just as Solovyev's successors were influenced by him in varying degrees but thought for themselves, so the leaders of any revival of 'idealist' philosophy in the Soviet Union would have to follow their own paths, though this would not exclude meditation on and learning from their predecessors.

---

1 Some years ago a non-Russian who had studied for six years at Moscow told me about a professor in a higher institute who developed an interest in religious and philosophical problems and discussed them with a circle of friends at his apartment. The foreign student helped the professor in obtaining some recent relevant literature. When the authorities learned of the professor's private activity, he was relieved of his post.

Obviously, there can be no open revival of religiously oriented philosophy in the Soviet Union without genuine freedom of expression. At present the Soviet authorities are not disposed to grant such freedom. True, there is a certain measure of freedom. Philosophers are expected to contribute to the building of Communism by developing Marxism-Leninism and applying its principles to current problems, and this cannot be done without some independent thought. Then there are the 'neutral' areas, such as mathematical logic. But to encourage Marxist philosophers to think for themselves, while remaining Marxists, and to permit intensive study of formal logic or of the philosophy of language are not the same thing as to allow open defence of positions which are incompatible with basic Marxist theses.[1] It may be said that it is idle to imagine that there could be real freedom of expression as long as the Communist Party occupies its present dominant position in the state. This may well be the case. But absence of competition is detrimental to Marxism itself. If Marxist philosophers had to defend basic positions and principles against freely expressed radical criticism, this might infuse some life into their thought. With real freedom, however, revisionist tendencies would very quickly show themselves, tendencies which up to now have been held in check. One can understand the authorities' exercise of watchfulness and close control, especially in view of the doctrine of the unity of theory and practice. Scientists, of course, can pay lip service to the ideology and get on with their work. But if a person's work is precisely philosophical thought, the shackles are heavier and more painful.

All this should not be understood as implying that, in the author's opinion, religiously oriented philosophy would soon occupy the centre of the stage, if there were genuine freedom of expression in the Soviet Union. Marxism would doubtless have other competitors too. It is highly probable, however, that moral philosophy would develop, giving abstract expression to the awareness of problems relating to values, moral standards and obligation which has been exemplified in concrete ways in a good deal of Russian literature since the death of Stalin.[2] Further, it is reasonable to expect that as an interest in religion has already manifested itself (to an extent which it is obviously difficult to

1 The Orthodox Church and other religious bodies obviously maintain doctrines which conflict with basic Marxist theses. But the influence of the Church is confined as much as possible by the régime to the walls of the functioning churches. When a Moscow priest started to draw attention and arouse interest by his sermons or talks on problems of the day, steps were taken to ensure his removal to some obscure locality (though not, I believe, to prison or labour camp).

2 See, for example, *Soviet Russian Literature since Stalin*, by Deming Brown (Cambridge, London, New York and Melbourne, 1978).

determine), this interest should find expression in attempts to give to the religious consciousness an appropriate intellectual framework or world-view. Whether one does or does not desire such developments clearly depends on one's own beliefs about the human being and about reality. In any case the growth of philosophical pluralism would demand considerable changes in the Soviet Union. Marxists such as Roy Medvedev seem to think that such changes could take place without the monopoly of power by the Communist Party being destroyed. This seems doubtful. Alexander Solzhenitsyn has called upon the Soviet leaders to abandon the ideology. If, however, the ideology were abandoned, it would then be difficult to see how the Party could make out a plausible case in support of its claim to exercise authoritarian rule over the Soviet Union. Challenges to Marxism-Leninism would doubtless involve explicit or implicit challenges to monopolization of power by the Party. It is understandable that the Party tries to maintain the dominant position of the ideology, even if cynical attitudes to it are on the increase. But this is likely to become progressively more difficult, and the present writer at any rate hopes that it will be possible for liberalizing changes to occur without the Russian people having to experience any further catastrophic events.

Emphasis has been laid in this Epilogue on the deleterious effect produced by imposition of an official ideology. It should not be concluded, however, that restrictions on freedom of expression necessarily produces uniformity of thought. In his book *History's Carnival*[1] Leonid Plyushch draws attention to the variety of ideas held by Soviet philosophers and to the use of 'Aesopian language' to conceal this fact from those who are not perceptive and who are misled by a few quotations from Marx, Engels or Lenin. The author relates that among official philosophers he met some who were 'Sartreans or theosophists', though it was logical positivists whom he encountered most frequently.[2] When the author expounded his Marxist views to one prominent philosopher, the latter remarked 'how strange that some young people are still Marxists'.[3] Given this state of affairs, the prophecy that if there were real freedom of expression a variety of non-Marxist lines of thought would at once show themselves, is obviously not simply an example of wishful thinking by a bourgeois historian of philosophy. It is easy to be misled. For instance, if a Soviet philosopher expounds and attacks Wittgenstein, one would do well to examine whether, in the course of what he has to say, he does not perhaps accept aspects of Wittgenstein's thought in a

1 Paris, 1977; English translation, London, 1979.
2 *Ibid.*, p. 92.
3 *Ibid.*

way which betrays a basic sympathy with the philosopher who is supposedly under attack from a Marxist point of view. Things are not always what they seem to be at first sight.

As for the relation between theory and practice, dissatisfaction with purely academic or ivory-tower philosophizing is understandable. But the ways in which philosophy can be relevant to social and political issues need to be carefully considered and worked out. If philosophy is transformed into an ideology, the basic ideas of which are treated as being, in effect, immune to radical criticism, the philosophical spirit is lost sight of. For understandable reasons this has tended to occur both in pre-Revolutionary and post-Revolutionary Russian thought. At the same time thinking directed to revolutionary change (unless it is a case of foreign bourgeois societies) is, for obvious reasons, no longer acceptable in the Soviet Union. Those who appeal to Marx against the régime and its ways are more obnoxious to the authorities than any of the classical western philosophers who have been laid to rest in their graves and whose ideas can be made the subject-matter of learned works and posthumous criticism.

Bibliography

Bibliography

General Works

Anderson, T. *Russian Political Thought*. Ithaca, New York, 1967.

Avrich, P. *The Russian Anarchists*. Princeton, N.J., 1967.

Berdyaev, N. *The Russian Idea*. Translated by R. W. French. London, 1947.

Billington, J. H. *The Icon and the Axe. An Interpretive History of Russian Culture*. New York, 1966.

Carr, E. H. *A History of Soviet Russia*. 14 vols. London, 1950–78.

Edwards, J. W. *Russian Thinkers and Europe*. Ann Arbor, Mich., 1953.

Florinsky, M. T. *Russia: A History and An Interpretation*. New York, 1953.

Harcave, S. *Years of the Golden Cockerel. The Last Romanov Tsars*, 1814–1917. London, 1968.

Hare, R. *Pioneers of Russian Social Thought*. London, 1951.

Hellie, R. *Slavery in Russia*, 1450–1725, Chicago and London, 1982.

Hosking, G. *A History of the Soviet Union*. London, 1985.

Karamzin, N. M. *Karamzin's Memoir on Ancient and Modern Russia. A Translation and Analysis*. Edited by R. Pipes. Cambridge, Mass., 1959.

Kliuchevski, V. O. *A History of Russia*. Translated by C. J. Hogarth. 5 vols. London, 1911–1931.

Kochan, L., and Abraham, R. *The Making of Modern Russia*. Harmondsworth. Second edition, 1983.

Lossky, N. O. *History of Russian Philosophy*. New York and London, 1951.

Masaryk, T. G. *The Spirit of Russia. Studies in History, Literature and Philosophy*. Translated by E. and C. Paul. London and New York, 1955 (1913).

Miliukov, P. N. *Outlines of Russian Culture*. New York, 1962. (Abridged English version of the Russian original.)

Mirsky, D. *A History of Russian Literatur*. New York, 1958.

Pares, Sir B. *A History of Russia*. London, 1982. (Revised edition.)

Pipes, R. *Russia under the old Regime*. London and New York, 1974.

—, (editor). *The Russian Intelligentsia*. New York, 1961.

Pokrovsky, M. N. *History of Russia from the Earliest Times to the Rise of Commercial Capitalism*. 2 vols. New York, 1931.

Riasanovsky, N. V. *A History of Russia*. New York and Oxford, 1984 (4th edition).

Robinson, G. T. *Rural Russia under the Old Regime*. New York, 1961.

Schapiro, L. *Rationalism and Nationalism in Russian Nineteenth-Century Political Thought*. New Haven, Conn., and London, 1967.

Shpet, G. *Ocherk razvitia filosofii v Rossii* (Outline of the Development of Philosophy in Russia). Petrograd, 1922.

Shukman, H. (General Editor) *Longman History of Russia*. 7 vols. London and New York, 1981– (four volumes so far published).

Sumner, B. H. *Survey of Russian History*. London, 1947 (2nd. edition).

Szamuely, T. *The Russian Tradition*. London, 1976.

Thaden, C. *Conservative Nationalism in Nineteenth-Century Russia*. Seattle, Wash., 1964.

Ulam, A. *In the Name of the People. Prophets and Conspirators in Pre-revolutionary Russia*. New York, 1977.

——, *Russia's Failed Revolutions. From the Decembrists to the Dissidents*. London, 1981.

Utechin, S. V. *Russian Political Thought. A Concise History*. London and New York 1964.

Vernadsky, G. *A Source Book for Russian History from Early Times to 1917*. New Haven and London, 1972.

Vucinich, A. *Science in Russian Culture. A History to 1860*. Stanford, Cal., 1963.

Walicki, A. *A History of Russian Thought from the Enlightenment to Marxism*. Translated by H. Andrews-Rusiecka. Oxford and Stanford, Cal., 1979.

Wittfogel, K. A. *Oriental Despotism. A Comparative Study of Total Power*. New Haven, Conn., and London, 1976 (first edition 1957). (Though this is a general work on 'oriental despotism', it includes a discussion of the Russian autocracy.)

Zenkovsky, V. V. *A History of Russian Philosophy*. Translated by G. L. Kline. 2 vols. London and New York, 1953.

Zernov, N. *The Russians and Their Church*. London, 1978 (3rd edition).

For a very useful selection of texts from Russian philosophers, translated into English and accompanied by introductions and bibliographies see: *Russian Philosophy*, edited by J. M. Edie, J. P. Scanlan and M.-B. Zeldin, with the collaboration of G. L. Kline. 3 vols. Chicago, 1964.

There are articles on a number of Russian philosophers in the two following works:

> *The Encyclopedia of Philosophy*. Edited by P. Edwards. 8 vols. New York and London, 1967.
> *Great Soviet Encyclopedia, translated from the third Russian edition*. London and New York. 1973–81.

Reference is made in the present work to *Istoria filosofii i CCCR*, (History of Philosophy in the USSR). Edited by M. A. Dinnika and Others. 5 vols. Moscow, 1957–65. (Mention of the USSR in the title does not mean that the history is confined to the period after 1917.)

Chapter 1

Texts

Catherine II (the Great). *Documents of Catherine the Great*. Edited by W. F. Reddaway. Cambridge, 1931 (reissued 1971).

Fennell, J. L. I. (editor). *The Correspondence between Prince A. M. Kurbsky and Tsar Ivan IV of Russia*, 1564–79. Cambridge, 1955 (reprinted 1963).

Herberstein, S. von *Description of Moscow and Muscovy, 1577*. Edited by B. Picard and translated by J. B. C. Grundy. London, 1969.

Radischev, A. N. *A Journey from St. Petersburg to Moscow*. Translated by L. Wiener and edited by R. P. Thaler. Cambridge, Mass., 1958.

Skovoroda, G. S. *Works in Two Volumes*. Kiev, 1961. (Russian and Latin text, but introduction, commentaries and notes in Ukrainian.)

Vernadsky, G. (translator). *Medieval Russian Laws*. New York, 1947.

Studies

Chadwick, N. K. *The Beginnings of Russian History*. Cambridge, 1946.

Clardy, J. V. *The Philosophical Ideas of A. Radischev*. New York, 1964.

De Jonge, A. *Fire and Water. A Life of Peter the Great*. London, 1979.

De Madariaga, I. *Russia in the Age of Catherine the Great*. London, 1981.

Evgeniev, B. *Alexander Radischev*. London, 1946.

Fennell, J. L. I. *Ivan the Great of Moscow*. London, 1961.

——, *The Emergence of Moscow, 1304–1359*. Berkeley and los Angeles, 1968.

Kennan, E. L., Jr. *The Kurbskii – Groznyi Apocrypha*. Cambridge, Mass., 1971.

Lamb, H. *The March of Muscovy: Ivan the Terrible and the Growth of the Russian Empire, 1400–1648*. Garden City, New York, 1948.

Longworth, P. *Alexis: Tsar of All the Russias*. London, 1984.

McConnel, A. *A Russian Philosopher, Alexander Radischev*. The Hague, 1964.

Meyendorff, J. *Byzantium and the Rise of Russia. A Study of Byzantine–Russian Relations in the Fourteenth Century*. Cambridge, 1980.

Paszhiewicz, H. *The Origin of Russia*. London, 1954.

——, *The Making of the Russian Nation*. London, 1963.

Raeff, M. *Peter the Great, Reformer or Revolutionary?* Boston, 1972 (revised edition of 1963 book).

——, Catherine the Great, A Profile. London, 1972.

Riasanovsky, N. V. *The Image of Peter the Great in Russian History and Thought*. New York and Oxford, 1985.

Sumner, B. H. *Peter the Great and the Emergence of Russia*. London, 1950.

Vernadsky, G. *Kievan Russia*. New Haven, Conn., 1948.

——, *The Mongols and Russia*. New Haven, Conn., 1953.

——, *The Origins of Russia*. Oxford, 1959.

Yanov, A. *The Origins of Autocracy. Ivan the Terrible in Russian History*. Translated by S. Dunn. Berkeley, Los Angeles and London, 1981.

Zetlin, M. *The Decembrists*. Translated by G. Panin. New York, 1958.

Chapter 2

Texts

Chaadaev, P. *Sochineniya i Pis'ma* (Works and Letters). Edited by M. Gerschenzon. 2 vols. Moscow, 1914.

——, *The Major Works of Peter Chaadayev*. Translation and Commentary by R. T. McNally, with an introduction by R. Pipes. Notre Dame, Ind., and London, 1969.

——, *Philosophical Letters and Apology of a Madman*. Translated and introduced by M.-B. Zeldin. Knoxville, Tenn., 1969.

Studies

Gerschenzon, M. *P. I. Chaadaev: Zhizn i Myshlenie* (Life and Thought). St Petersburg, 1908.

McNally, R. T. *Chaadayev and His Friends*. Tallahassee, Flo., 1971.

Mentioned

Copleston, F. C. *A History of Philosophy: Vol. IX, Maine de Biran to Sartre*. London, 1975.

Lammenais, H. F. R. de, *Essai sur l'indifférence en matière de religion*. 4 vols. Paris, 1817–24.

Spinoza, B. *Ethics*.

Chapter 3

Texts

Aksakov, K. S. *Polnoe sobranie sochinenii* (Complete Collected Works). 3 vols. Moscow, 1861–80.

Aksakov, S. *Years of Childhood*. London, 1916.

——, *The Autobiography of a Russian Schoolboy*. London, 1917.

——, *A Russian Gentleman*. London, 1923.
(All three translated by J. J. Duff.)

Khomyakov, A. S. *Polnoe sobranie sochinenii* (Complete Collected Works). 8 vols. Moscow, 1911. (4th edition.)

Kireevsky, I. V. *Polnoe sobranie sochinenii* (Complete Collected Works). 2 vols. Moscow, 1911.

Samarin, Y. *Sochinenya* (Works). Moscow, 1877.

Studies

Bolshakoff, S. *The Doctrine of the Unity of the Church in the Works of Khomyakov and Moehler*. London, 1946.

Christoff, P. *An Introduction to Nineteenth-Century Russian Slavophilism. A Study in Ideas*. Vol. I, A. S. Khomyakov, The Hague, 1961; vol. 2, I. V. Kireevskij, The Hague, 1972.

Gleason, A. *European and Muscovite: Ivan Kireevsky and the Origins of Slavophilism*. Cambridge, Mass., 1972.

Lukashevich, S. *Ivan Aksakov (1823–1886). A study in Russian Thought and Politics*. Cambridge, Mass., 1965.

Müller, E. *Russischer Intellekt in Europäischer Krise. Ivan S. Kireevskij (1806–1856)*. Cologne, 1966.

Riasanovsky, N. V. *Russia and the West in the Teaching of the Slavophiles*. Cambridge, Mass., 1952.

Walicki, A. *The Slavophile Controversy. History of a Conservative Utopia in Nineteenth-Century Russian Thought*. Translated by H. Andrews-Rusiecka. Oxford, 1975.

Mentioned

Copleston, F. C. *A History of Philosophy: Vol. IV, Descartes to Leibniz.* London, 1958.

Deutsch, E. *On Truth. An Ontological Theory.* Honolulu, 1979.

Hofstadter, A. *Truth and Art.* New York, 1965.

Pascal, B. *Pensées.* Edited by L. Brunschvicg. Paris, 1914, 1934.

Studies of Panslavism. See bibliography to chapter 8.

Chapter 4

Texts

Bakunin, M. *Sobranie sochinenii i pisem* (Collected Works and Letters). 4 vols. Moscow, 1934–36. (There are also German and French editions of Bakunin's writings. But as yet there is no complete edition.)

——, *Selected Writings.* Edited by A. Lehning. Translated by S. Cox and O. Stevens. London, 1973.

——, *Marxism, Freedom and the State.* Translated by K. J. Kenafick. London, 1950.

——, *The Political Philosophy of Bakunin.* Edited by G. P. Maximoff. Glencoe, Ill., 1953. (Excerpts from Bakunin's writings, translated and systematically arranged under topics.)

Belinsky, V. G. *Polnoe sobranie sochinenii* (Complete Collected Works). 13 vols. Moscow, 1953–59.

——, *Selected Philosophical Works.* Moscow, 1948.

Herzen, A. I. *Sobranie sochinenii* (Collected Works). 30 vols. Moscow, 1954–66.

——, *My Past and Thoughts.* Translated by C. Garnett, revised by H. Higgens. 4 vols. London, 1968.

——, *Selected Philosophical Works.* Translated by L. Navrozov. Moscow, 1956.

Kropotkin, P. *Ethics: Origin and Development.* Translated by L. S. Friedland and J. R. Piroshnikoff. New York, 1924.

——, *Memoirs of a Revolutionist.* Introduction and notes by N. Walter. New York, 1971.

Studies

Berlin, Sir I. *Russian Thinkers.* London, 1979. (Includes essays dealing with Bakunin, Belinsky and Herzen.)

Bowman, H. E. *Vissarion Belinsky, 1811–1848*. Cambridge, Mass., 1954.

Brown, E. J. *Stankevich and His Moscow Circle*. Stanford, Cal., 1966.

Carr, E. J. *Michael Bakunin*. London, 1937.

Joll, J. *The Anarchists*. London, 1964.

Lampert, E. *Studies in Rebellion*. London, 1957. (On Bakunin, Belinsky and Herzen.)

Malia, M. *Alexander Herzen and the Birth of the Russian Intelligentsia*. Cambridge, Mass., 1961.

Miller, M. A. *Kropotkin*. Chicago, 1976.

Raeff, M. *The Decembrist Movement*. Englewood Cliffs, N. J., 1966.

——, *Michael Speransky: Statesman of Imperial Russia*. The Hague, 1969 (2nd edition).

Riasanovsky, N. V. *Nicholas I and Official Nationality in Russia, 1825–1855*. Berkeley, Cal., 1959.

Terras, V. *Belinskij and Russian Literary Criticism. The Heritage of Organic Aesthetics*. Madison, Wisc., 1974.

Woodcock, G. *Anarchism. A History of Libertarian Ideas and Movements*. New York, 1962.

Woodcock, G. and Avakumovic, I. *The Anarchist Prince*. London, 1950. (On Kropotkin.)

Zetlin, M. *The Decembrists*. Translated by G. Panin. New York, 1958.

Mentioned

Feuerbach, L. *The Essence of Christianity*. Translated by G. Eliot. New York, 1957.

Hegel, G. W. F. *Werke*. Edited by H. G. Glockner. Vol. 7, Stuttgart, 1928.

Marx, K. and Engels, F. *The Communist Manifesto* (1848). Edited by H. J. Laski, London, 1948. Many other editions.

Chapter 5

Texts

Chernyshevsky, N. G. *Polnoe sobranie sochinenii* (Completed Collected Works). 16 vols. Moscow, 1939–53.

——, *Selected Philosophical Essays*. Moscow, 1953.

——, *What Is To Be Done? Tales about New People*. Translated by B. R. Tucker, revised and abridged by L. B. Turkevich. New York, 1961.

Dobrolyubov, N. A. *Sobranie sochinenii* (Collected Works). Edited by B. H. Bursov. 9 vols. Moscow, 1961–64.

——, *Selected Philosophical Essays*. Translated by J. Fineberg. Moscow, 1956.

Pisarev, D. *Sochinenya* (Works). 6 vols. St Petersburg, 1894–97.

——, *Selected Philosophical, Social and Political Essays*. Moscow, 1958.

For S. Nechaev's 'Revolutionary Catechism' see *The Catechism of the Revolutionist*. London, 1971.

Studies

Lampert, E. *Sons against Fathers. Studies in Russian Radicalism and Revolution*. Oxford, 1965. (On Chernyshevsky, Dobrolyubov and Pisarev.)

Pereira, N. G. *The Thought and Teaching of N. G. Černyševskii*. The Hague, 1975.

Randall, F. B. *N. G. Chernyshevskii*. New York, 1967.

Woehrlin, W. F. *Chernyshevskii: The Man and the Journalist*. Cambridge, Mass., 1971.

Mentioned

Pomyalovsky, N. G. *Seminary Sketches*. Translated, with an introduction and notes, by A. Kuhn. Ithaca, New York, and London, 1973.

Turgenev, I. S. *Polnoe sobranie sochinenii i pisem* (Complete Collected Works and Letters). Edited by M. P. Alekseev. 28 vols. Leningrad and Moscow, 1960–68.

——, *Fathers and Sons*. Translated by C. J. Hogarth. London, 1921 and reprints. And other editions.

Chapter 6

Texts

Lavrov, P. *Sobranie sochinenii* (Collected Works). 11 vols. Petrograd, 1917–20.

——, *Historical Letters*. Translated with an introduction and notes by J. P. Scanlon. Berkeley and Los Angeles, 1967.

Mikhailovsky, N. K. *Polnoe sobranie sochinenii*. (Complete Collected Works). 10 vols. St Petersburg, 1906–1914.

Tkachev, P. N. *Izbrannye sochineniya na sotsialno-politicheskie temi* (Selected Writings on Social-Political Themes). Edited by B.-P. Kozmin. 4 vols. Moscow, 1932.

Studies

Billington, J. H. *Mikhailovsky and Russian Populism*. Oxford, 1958.

Gleason, A. *Young Russia. The Genesis of Russian Radicalism in the 1860's.* New York, 1980.

Hardy, D. *Peter Tkachev. The Critic as Jacobin.* Seattle, Wash., 1977.

Hecker, J. F. *Russian Sociology. A Contribution to the History of Sociological Thought and Theory.* New York, 1915 (revised edition 1934).

Pomper, P. *Peter Lavrov and the Russian Revolutionary Movement.* Chicago, 1972.

Seth, R. *The Russian Terrorists: The Story of the Narodniki.* London, 1966. (Narodniki = Populists.)

Tikhomirov, L. *Russia, Political and Social.* Translated by E. Aveling. London, 1888.

Venturi, F. *Roots of Revolution. A History of the Populist and Socialist Movements in Nineteenth-Century Russia.* Translated by F. Haskell. London and New York, 1960.

Walicki, A. *The Controversy over Capitalism. Studies in the Social Philosophy of the Russian Populists.* Oxford, 1969.

Wortman, R. *The Crisis of Russian Populism.* London, 1967.

Chapter 7

Texts

Dostoevsky, F. M. *Polnoe sobranie sochinenii* (Complete Collected Works). 30 vols. Leningrad, 1972–81.

——, *Pisma* (Letters). 4 vols. Moscow and Leningrad, 1928–59.

——, *Dostoevsky's Occasional Writings.* Selected, translated and introduced by D. Magarshack. New York, 1963.

——, *The Diary of a Writer.* Translated and annotated by B. Brasol. 2 vols. New York, 1949.

——, *Notes from Underground.* Edited by R. R. Durgy, translated by S. Shiskoff. New York, 1969.

Translations of the famous novels are easily available, for example in Penguin Classics.

Studies

Berdyaev, N. *Dostoevsky. An Interpretation.* Translated by D. Attwater. London, 1934.

Frank, J. *Dostoevsky. The Seeds of Revolt, 1821–1849.* Princeton, N.J., and London, 1977.

——, *The Years of Ordeal, 1850–1859.* London, 1983.

Gibbon, A. B. *The Religion of Dostoevsky*. London, 1973.

Jones, M. V. *Dostoevsky. The Novel of Discord*. London, 1976.

Ivanov, V. *Freedom and the Tragic Life: A Study in Dostoevsky*. Translated by N. Cameron. New York, 1957.

Mochulsky, K. V. *Dostoevsky: His Life and Work*. Translated, with an introduction, by M. A. Minihan. Princeton, N.J., 1967.

Mentioned

Bradley, F. H. *The Principles of Logic*. 2 vols. London, 1922 (2nd edition).

Marcel, G. *Philosophy of Existence*. Translated by M. Harari. London, 1948.

Chapter 8

Texts

Danilevsky, N. *Rossia i Evropa* (Russia and Europe). St Petersburg, 1888 (2nd edition).

Leontyev, K. N. *Sobranie sochinenii* (Collected Works). 9 vols. Moscow, 1912–1914.

Rozanov, V. V. *O Ponimanii* (On the Understanding). Moscow, 1886.

——, *Dostoevsky and the Legend of the Grand Inquisitor*. Translated (from the Russian original of 1894) by S. E. Roberts. Ithaca, New York, 1972.

——, *Religya i Kultura (Religion and Culture)*. St Petersburg, 1899.

——, *Okolo tserkovnykh sten* (Near the Walls of the Church) St Petersburg, 1906.

——, *Solitaria*. Translated (from the Russian original of 1912) by S. S. Koteliansky. London, 1927.

——, *Izbrannoye* (Selections). Edited by G. Ivask. New York, 1956.

Tolstoy, L. N. *Polnoe sobranie sochinenii* (Complete Collected Works). 91 vols. Moscow, 1928–64.

——, *Works*. Translated by L. Wiener. 24 vols. Boston and London, 1904–1905.

——, *Works*. Translated by L. and A. Maude. 21 vols. Oxford, 1928–1937.

Roberts, S. E. (editor). *Essays in Russian Literature. The Conservative View: Leontiev, Rozanov, Shestov*. Athens, Ohio, 1968.

Studies

Berdyaev, N. *K. N. Leontiev*. Translated by G. Reavey. London, 1949.

Berlin, Sir I. *The Hedgehog and the Fox. An Essay on Tolstoy's View of*

History. London and New York, 1953. Reprinted in *Russian Thinkers*.

Craufurd, A. H. *The Religion and Ethics of Tolstoy*. London, 1912.

Garrod, H. W. *Tolstoy's Theory of Art*. London, 1935.

Kritko, D. *A Philosophic Study of Tolstoy*. New York, 1927.

Lukashevich, S. *Konstantin Leontiev (1831–1891): A Study in Russian 'Heroic Vitalism'*. New York, 1967.

McMaster, R. E. *Danilevsky: A Russian Totalitarian Philosopher*. Cambridge, Mass., 1967.

Redpath, T. *Tolstoy*. London, 1960.

Chapter 9

Texts

Solovyev, V. S. *Sobranie sochinenii* (Collected Works). 10 vols. Brussels, 1966. (Photographic edition of St Petersburg 1911–14 edition.)

——, *Lectures on Godmanhood*. Edited, with an introduction, by P. P. Zouboff. London and Dublin, 1948.

——, *The Justification of the Good: An Essay in Moral Philosophy*. Translated by N. A. Duddington. London and New York, 1918.

——, *The Meaning of Love*. Translated by J. Marshall. London. 1945; New York, 1947.

——, *Three Conversations concerning War, Progress and the End of History, including a Short Story of the Antichrist*. Translated by A. Bakshy. London, 1915.

——, *Russia and the Universal Church*. Translated by H. Rees. London, 1948.

——, *A Solovyev Anthology*. Arranged by S. L. Frank, translated by N. A. Duddington. London and New York, 1950.

The selections in *Russian Philosophy, vol. 3*, include passages from *Theoretical Philosophy*.

Studies

D'Harbigny, M. *Vladimir Solovyev, A Russian Newman*. Translated by A. M. Buchanan. London, 1918.

Lopatin, L. M. *The Philosophy of Vladimir Solovyev*. Translated by A. Bakshy. Aberdeen, 1916. (Offprinted from *Mind*, 1916).

Munzer, E. *Solovyev, Prophet of Russian-Western Unity*. London and New York, 1956.

Mayne, E. *The Christian Philosophy of Vladimir Solovyev*. Richmond Hill, 1958. (A lecture.)

Zernov, N. *Three Russian: Khomyakov, Dostoevsky, Solovyev*. London, 1944.

Chapters 10–12

Texts

Akimov, V. *Vladimir Akimov on the Dilemmas of Russian Marxism, 1895–1903*. Edited and introduced by J. Frankel. Cambridge, 1969.

Bogdanov, A. A. *Empiriomonizm: Stati po Filosofii* (Empiriomonism: Articles on Philosophy). Moscow, 1904–1906.

——, *Filosotiya Zhivovo Opyta* (A Philosophy of Living Experience). St Petersburg, 1912.

Bukharin, N. *Historical Materialism: A System of Sociology*. Translated from the third Russian edition. London, 1926.

and Others. *Marxism and Modern Thought*. Translated by R. Fox. London, 1935.

Deborin, A. M. *Vvedenie v Filosofiyu Dialekticheskovo Materializma* (Introduction to the Philosophy of Dialectical Materialism). Petrograd, 1916; Moscow, 1922.

——, *Marx i Hegel* (Marx and Hegel). Moscow, 1924.

——, *Filosofia i Marksizm* (Philosophy and Marxism). Moscow, 1926.

——, *Dailektika i Estestvoznanie* (Dialectics and Natural Science). Moscow and Leningrad, 1930.

——, *Lenin kak Myslitel* (Lenin as a Thinker). Moscow, 1929 (3rd edition).

——, *Filosofia i Politika* (Philosophy and Politics). Moscow, 1961.

Lenin (V. I. Ulyanov) *Sobranie sochinenii* (Collected Works). 40 vols. Moscow, 1941–1962 (4th edition).

——, *Polnoe sobranie sochinenii* (Complete Collected Works). 55 vols. Moscow, 1959–65 (5th edition).

——, *Collected Works* (English translation of 4th edition). 47 vols. (2 vols. of indices). London, 1960–1980.

——, *Selected Works*. 3 vols. Moscow, 1963–64.

——, *The Development of Capitalism in Russia*. (English translation.) Moscow, 1956.

——, *Materialism and Empirio-Criticism. Critical Comments on a Reactionary Philosophy*. Translated by A. Fineberg. New York, 1927

(reprint 1930); Moscow, 1947 and 1951; London, 1948 and 1972.
——, *Filosofskie tetradi* (Philosophical Notebooks). Leningrad, 1947.
——, *The State and Revolution.* Moscow, 1972.
Plekhanov, G. V. *Sochinenya* (Works). Edited by D. Ryazanov. 24 vols. Moscow and Leningrad, 1923–27. (3rd edition.)
——, *Literaturnoe Nasledie G. V. Plekhanova* (The Literary Heritage of G. V. Plekhanov). 8 vols. Moscow, 1934–1940. English translation by A. Rothstein, London, 1947.
——, *Selected Philosophical Works.* (English translation of *Izbrannye filosofskie proizvedeniya.* Moscow.) 5 vols. London, 1974–1981.
——, *Anarchism and Socialism.* Translated by E. M. Aveling. London, 1895.
——, *In Defence of Materialism. The Development of the Monist View of History.* Translated by A. Rothstein. London, 1947. (Also as *The Development of the Monist View of History.* Moscow, 1956 and 1972.
——, *Essays in the History of Materialism.* Translated by R. Fox. London, 1934; New York, 1967.
——, *Fundamental Problems of Marxism.* Translated by E. and C. Paul, Moscow, 1974.
——, *The Role of the Individual in History.* London, 1940 (Reprint 1950).
——, *The Materialist Conception of History.* New York, 1964.
——, *Unaddressed Letters. Art and Social Life.* Translated by A. Fineberg. Moscow, 1957.
——, *History of Russian Social Thought.* New York, 1967.
Stalin (J. V. Dzhugashvili) *Sochinenya* (Works). 16 vols. Moscow, 1946–67. (Certain volumes were published abroad.)
——, *Selected Works.* 3 vols. Moscow, 1963–64.
——, *Selected Writings.* Westport, Conn., 1970.
——, *Leninism* (English translation of *Problems of Leninism*). London, 1940.
——, *Dialectical and Historical Materialism.* New York, 1940s, Calcutta, 1941 and 1943.
——, *Concerning Marxism in Linguistics.* London, 1950.

Mentioned
Alexandrov, G. P. *Istoria zapadno-evropeskoi filosofii.* Moscow, 1946. (A History of Western European Philosophy. New York, 1949.)
Arkhangelsky, L. M. *Kategorii marksistkoi etiki* (Categories of Marxist Ethics). Moscow, 1963.

Narsky, I. S. *Zapadno-Evropyeskaya Filosofia XVII Veka* (Western European Philosophy of the Seventeenth Century). Moscow, 1974. *XVIII Veka* (of the Eighteenth Century), Moscow, 1973. *XIX Veka* (of the Nineteenth Century), Moscow, 1976.

Cornforth, M. *Communism and Philosophy. Contemporary Dogmas and Revisions of Marxism.* London, 1980.

Shishkin, A. P. *Osnovy marksistkoi etiki* (Foundations of Marxist Ethics). Moscow, 1961).

Tavents, P. B. *Voprosy logiki* (Problems of Logic). Moscow, 1955.

Tugarinov, V. P. *O cennostyakh zizni i kulturi* (On the Values of Life and Culture). Moscow, 1963.

——, *Teorya cennostey v marksizme* (The Theory of Values in Marxism). Leningrad, 1960.

——, *Lichnost i Obschestvo.* (The Person and Society). Moscow. 1965.

Uemov, A. I. *Vesci, svoystva i otnosheniya* (Things, Properties and Relations). Moscow, 1965.

Zinoviev, A. A. *Philosophical Problems of Many-valued Logic.* Revised edition, edited and translated by G. Küng and D. D. Comey. Dordrecht, Holland, 1963.

——, *Foundations of the Logical Theory of Scientific Knowledge.* Revised and enlarged English edition, Dordrecht, 1973.

Studies

Alexandrovna, A. *A History of Soviet Literature, 1917–1962, or from Gorky to Evtushenko.* New York, 1963.

Anderson, T. *Masters of Russian Marxism.* New York, 1963.

Antonov-Ovseyenko, A. *The Time of Stalin. Portrait of a Tyranny.* Translated by G. Saunders, with an introduction by S. F. Cohen. New York, 1981.

Baron, S. H. *Plekhanov: The Father of Russian Marxism.* Stanford, Cal., 1963.

Berdyaev, N. *The Origin of Russian Communism.* Translated by R. M. French. London, 1937.

Besançon A. *The Intellectual Origins of Leninism.* Translated by Sarah Matthews. Oxford, 1980.

Blakeley, T. J. *Soviet Philosophy.* Dordrecht, Holland, 1964.

Bochenski, J. M. *Soviet Dialectical Materialism.* Translated by N. Sollohub from the 3rd German edition. Dordrecht, Holland, 1963.

Brown, Deming *Soviet Russian Literature since Stalin.* Cambridge, London, New York and Melbourne, 1978.

Callinicos, A. *Marxism and Philosophy.* Oxford, 1983.

Cohen, S. F. *Bukharin and the Bolshevik Revolution.* London, 1980.

De George, R. T. *Patterns of Soviet Thought.* Ann Arbor, Mich., 1966.

Fischer, G. *Russian Liberalism from Gentry to Intelligentsia.* Cambridge, Mass., 1958.

Haimson, L. H. *The Russian Marxists and the Origins of Bolshevism.* Cambridge, Mass., 1955.

Harcave, S. *First Blood: The Russian Revolution of 1905.* London and New York, 1964.

Joravsky, D. *The Lysenko Affair,* Cambridge, Mass., 1970.

Keep, J. L. H. *The Rise of Social Democracy in Russia.* Oxford, 1963.

Kindersley, R. H. *The First Russian Revisionists. A Study of 'Legal Marxism' in Russia.* Oxford, 1962.

Kochan, L. *Russia in Revolution, 1890–1918.* London, 1967, and reprints.

Kolakowski, L. *Main Currents of Marxism: Its Origin, Growth and Dissolution.* 3 vols. Oxford, 1978.

Laszlo, E. (compiler and editor). *Philosophy in the Soviet Union. A Survey of the Mid-Sixties.* Dordrecht, 1967.

Marcuse, H. *Soviet Marxism: A Critical Analysis.* New York, 1958.

Medvedev, R. *The October Revolution.* Translated by G. Saunders. London, 1979.

Medvedev, Z. A. *The Rise and Fall of T. D. Lysenko,* New York, 1971.

Mendel, A. P. *Dilemmas of Progress in Tsarist Russia: Legal Marxism and Legal Populism.* Cambridge, Mass., 1961.

Miliukov, P. *Russia and Its Crisis.* Foreword by D. W. Treadgold. London, 1962. (Based on lectures given at Chicago in 1903 and at Boston in 1904).

Pipes, R. *Struve, Liberal on the left, 1870–1905.* Cambridge, Mass., 1970.

Plamenatz, J. *German Marxism and Russian Communism. London, 1954.*

Plyushch, L. *History's Carnival. A Dissident's Autobiography.* Translated by M. Carynnyk. London, 1979.

Pobedonostsev, K. P. *Reflections of a Russian Statesman.* Translated by R. C. Long. Ann Arbor, Mich., 1965. (Original 1898).

Sakharov, A. D. *Progress, Coexistence and Intellectual Freedom,* with introduction, afterword and notes by Harrison E. Salisbury. New York, 1968.

Schapiro, L. *The Origin of the Communist Autocracy.* London, 1956.

——, *The Communist Party of the Soviet Union.* London, 1960.

Schatz, Marshall S. *Soviet Dissent in Historical Perspective.* Cambridge and London, 1980.

Somerville, J. *Soviet Philosophy: A Study of Theory and Practice*. New York, 1946.

Thomson, Boris *The Premature Revolution. Russian Literature and Society, 1917–1946*. London, 1972.

Tokes, R. L. (editor). *Dissent in the USSR. Politics, Ideology and People*. Baltimore and London, 1976.

Ulam, A. *The Unfinished Revolution. An Essay on the Sources of Influence of Marxism and Communism*. New York, 1960.

——, *Stalin: The Man and His Era*. London, 1974.

Von Laue, T. H. *Sergei Witte and the Industrialization of Russia*. New York, 1963.

Vucinich, A. *Empire of Knowledge. The Academy of Sciences of the USSR, 1917–1970*. Berkeley, Los Angeles and London, 1984.

Wetter, G. A. *Dialectical Materialism. A Historical and Systematic Survey of Philosophy in the Soviet Union*. Translated from the 4th German edition by P. Heath. London and New York, 1958.

Yanov, A. *The Russian New Right. Right-Wing Ideologies in the Contemporary USSR*. Berkeley, Cal., 1978.

Chapters 13–14

Texts

Berdyaev, N. (English translations only).

——, *The End of Our Time*. Translated by D. Attwater. London, 1933.

——, *Christianity and Class War*. Translated by D. Attwater. London, 1933.

——, *Dostoevsky: An Interpretation*. Translated by D. Attwater. London, 1934.

——, *Freedom and the Spirit*. Translated by O. F. Clarke. London, 1935.

——, *The Meaning of History*. Translated by G. Reavey. London, 1936.

——, *The Origin of Russian Communism*. Translated by R. M. French. London, 1937.

——, *The Destiny of Man*. Translated by N. A. Duddington. London, 1937.

——, *Solitude and Society*. Translated by G. Reavey. London, 1938.

——, *Slavery and Freedom*. Translated by R. M. French. London, 1943.

——, *The Russian Idea*. Translated by R. M. French. London, 1947.

——, *Towards a New Epoch*. Translated by O. F. Clarke. London, 1949.

——, *The Divine and the Human*. Translated by R. M. French. London, 1949.

——, *Dream and Reality. An Essay in Autobiography.* Translated by K. Lampert. London, 1950.

——, *The Beginning and the End.* Translated by R. M. French. London, 1952.

——, *Truth and Revelation.* Translated by R. M. French. London, 1957.

Frank, S. L. *Filosofya i Zhizn* (Philosophy and Life). St Petersburg, 1910.

——, *Predmet znaniya* (The Object of Knowledge). St Petersburg, 1915.

——, *Nepostizhimoye* (The Unfathomable). Paris, 1939.

——, *Reality and Man.* Translated by N. A. Duddington. London, 1965. (Russian original, *Realnost i Chelovek*, Paris, 1956.)

Lossky, N. O. *The Intuitive Basis of Knowledge.* Translated by N. A. Duddington. London, 1919. (Russian original, St Petersburg, 1906.)

——, *The World as an Organic Whole.* Translated by N. A. Duddington. Oxford, 1928. (Russian original, Moscow, 1917.)

——, *Freedom of Will.* Translated by N. A. Duddington, London, 1932. (Russian original, Paris, 1927.)

——, *Value and Existence.* Translated by S. S. Vinokooroff. London, 1935. (Russian original, Paris, 1931.)

——, *History of Russian Philosophy.* London and New York, 1951.

Shestov, L. *Shekspir i evo kritik Brandes* (Shakespeare and His Critic Brandes). St Petersburg, 1898.

——, *Dobro v uchenii Tolstovo i Nitshe* (Good in the Teaching of Tolstoy and Nietzsche). St Petersburg, 1900.

——, *Dostoyevski i Nitshe: Filosofia tragedii.* (Dostoevsky and Nietzsche. The Philosophy of Tragedy). St Petersburg, 1903.

——, *All Things are Possible.* Translated by S. S. Koteliansky. London, 1920. (Russian original, St Petersburg, 1905.)

——, *Potestas Clavium.* Translated by B. Martin. Athens, Ohio, 1968. (Russian original, Paris, 1923.)

——, *In Job's Balances.* Translated by A. Coventry and C. A. Macartney. London, 1932. (Russian original, Paris, 1929.)

——, *Kierkegaard and the Existential Philosophy.* Translated by E. Hewitt. Athens, Ohio, 1969. (Russian original, Paris, 1939.)

——, *Athens and Jerusalem.* Translated, with an introduction, by B. Martin. Athens, Ohio, 1966. (Russian original, Paris, 1951).

——, *Umozrenie i otkrovenie* (Speculation and Revelation). Paris, 1964.

Studies

Bulgakov, S. N. *The Orthodox Church.* Translated by E. Cram. London, 1935.

Clarke, O. F. *Introduction to Berdyaev.* London, 1950.

Fletcher, W. C. *The Russian Orthodox Church Underground, 1917–1970*. London, New York and Toronto, 1971.

Kohanski, A. S. *Lossky's Theory of Knowledge*. Nashville, Tenn., 1936.

Seaver, G. *Nicolas Berdyaev*. London, 1950.

Spinka, M. *N. Berdyaev, Captive of Freedom*. Philadelphia, 1950.

Zernov, N. *The Russian Religious Renaissance of the Twentieth Century*. London, 1963.

And see the histories of Russian philosophy by Lossky and Zenkovsky (General Works above).

Mentioned

Gilson, E. *The Spirit of Medieval Philosophy*. Translated by A. H. C. Downes. London, 1950 (reprint).

Index

Principal references to a particular philosopher or theme are given in bold type. A small *n* indicates that the reference is to a note, but when there is already a reference to the relevant page, no separate mention of footnotes is made. The index does not include references to the bibliography.

A HISTORY OF PHILOSOPHY
by Frederick Copleston

This nine-volume work, by the former Professor of the History of Philosophy in the University of London, is one of the most remarkable single-handed scholarly enterprises of recent times. *The Listener* said that 'for breadth of learning and understanding, for lucidity and economy of exposition, for elegance of language, his *History* has no rival in modern English literature'; the *New Statesman* spoke of it as a 'monumental history . . . learned, lucid, patient and comprehensive', and *The Times Literary Supplement* said: 'We can only applaud at the end of each act and look forward to applauding again at the final curtain.'

Although *Philosophy in Russia* is not formally part of Professor Copleston's *A History of Philosophy*, for its subject-matter and the breadth of scale of treatment, it can reasonably be regarded as a companion volume to the series.

VOLUME I: GREECE AND ROME: 'A triumph of objectivity' – *Church Times*.

ISBN 0 85532 181 4

VOLUME II: AUGUSTINE TO SCOTUS: 'Firmness, clarity and such obvious knowledge as commands the reader's respect' – *The Scotsman*.

ISBN 0 85532 182 2

VOLUME III: OCKHAM TO SUAREZ: 'Displays his now familiar combination of erudition and sympathy' – *The Times Literary Supplement*.

ISBN 0 85532 183 0

VOLUME IV: DESCARTES TO LEIBNIZ: 'Lucidity, objectivity, ability to disengage the fundamental principles and issues of a particular philosophy render (it) a classic' – *The Tablet*.

ISBN 0 85532 184 9

VOLUME V: HOBBES TO HUME: 'The same tenor pervades the writing and thinking, judicious, masterly, lucid, interesting' – *The Scotsman*.

ISBN 0 85532 185 7

VOLUME VI: WOLFF TO KANT: 'The same thoroughness, the same dispassionate objectivity and the same lucidity of exposition' – *The Times Literary Supplement*.

ISBN 0 85532 186 5

VOLUME VII: FICHTE TO NIETZSCHE: 'The author's whole oeuvre constitutes a descriptive account of European philosophy as comprehensive as any one man's pen could be expected to supply. He is surely without a rival in his chosen field' – *The Times Educational Supplement*.

ISBN 0 85532 187 3

VOLUME VIII: BENTHAM TO RUSSELL: 'Immensely erudite, lucid in analysis, and almost incredibly dispassionate' – *The Month*.

ISBN 0 85532 188 1

VOLUME IX: MAINE DE BIRAN TO SARTRE: 'To write a history of philosophy single-handed is a mammoth undertaking. To write it with the lucidity, scholarship and comprehensive dispassionate discernment displayed by Professor Copleston is to produce a triumph of learning that defies description' – *The Expository Times*.

ISBN 0 85532 341 8

COMPLETE SET OF NINE VOLUMES ISBN 0 85532 438 4
Each Volume 224mm × 150mm hb

Other books by Frederick Copleston

ON THE HISTORY OF PHILOSOPHY

The problems of the subject-matter and methodology of the history of philosophy, and the question of objectivity and modern-day perspective.

172 pages   216mm × 138mm
ISBN 0 85532 371 X hb

THOMAS AQUINAS

Professor Copleston explains Aquinas' ideas so they they can be understood by anyone not previously acquainted with mediaeval thought.

272 pages   216mm × 138mm
ISBN 0 85532 369 8 hb

ARTHUR SCHOPENHAUER
Philosopher of Pessimism

One of the best introductions in any language to Schopenhauer's life and thought; his peculiar combination of classicism and romanticism, and his notions of life as dream and tragedy.

248 pages   216mm × 138mm
ISBN 0 85532 254 X hb

FRIEDRICH NIETZSCHE
Philosopher of Culture

The second edition of Copleston's first book, which received considerable praise on publication; it contains a second preface and three new essays on aspects of Nietzsche.

288 pages   216mm × 138mm
ISBN 0 85532 352 6 hb

RELIGION AND THE ONE
Philosophies East and West

The author describes, with characteristic learning and lucidity, the approach of different philosophies, east and west, to the question of divine reality, with special reference to the metaphysics of the One which expresses this movement of man's mind towards an ultimate goal.

288 pages   216mm × 138mm
ISBN 0 85532 514 3 hb

CONTEMPORARY PHILOSOPHY

The revised edition of Copleston's studies of logical positivism and existentialism.

240 pages   216mm × 138mm
ISBN 0 85532 436 8 hb

PHILOSOPHERS AND PHILOSOPHIES

Professor Copleston examines fourteen important philosophical topics including the key concepts of philosophers such as Hegel, Aquinas, Spinoza and Sartre.

192 pages   216mm × 138mm
ISBN 0 85532 370 1 hb

Books of general Christian interest as well as books on theology, scripture, spirituality and mysticism are available from the publishers Burns and Oates and Search Press Limited. A catalogue will be sent free on request.

Burns and Oates
Search Press Limited
Wellwood, North Farm Road, Tunbridge Wells, Kent TN2 3DR
Tel. (0892) 44037/8